Cognition

THIRD EDITION

John G. Benjafield

OXFORD
UNIVERSITY PRESS

OXFORD

UNIVERSITY PRESS

70 Wynford Drive, Don Mills, Ontario M3C 1J9
www.oup.com/ca

Oxford University Press is a department of the University of Oxford.
It furthers the University's objective of excellence in research, scholarship,
and education by publishing worldwide in

Oxford New York
Auckland Cape Town Dar es Salaam Hong Kong Karachi
Kuala Lumpur Madrid Melbourne Mexico City Nairobi
New Delhi Shanghai Taipei Toronto

With offices in
Argentina Austria Brazil Chile Czech Republic France Greece
Guatemala Hungary Italy Japan Poland Portugal Singapore
South Korea Switzerland Thailand Turkey Ukraine Vietnam

Oxford is a trade mark of Oxford University Press
in the UK and in certain other countries

Published in Canada
by Oxford University Press

Library and Archives Canada Cataloguing in Publication Data
Benjafield, John G
Cognition / John G. Benjafield. — 3rd ed.

Includes bibliographical references and index.
ISBN-13: 978-0-19-542286-3
ISBN: 10: 0-19-542286-4

1. Cognition—Textbooks. 2. Cognitive psychology—Textbooks.
I. Title.

BF311.B4525 2006   153   C2006-901370-5

Cover Image: Lynn James/Photonica/Getty Images
Cover Design: Andrea Katwaroo

1 2 3 4 –10 09 08 07
This book is printed on permanent (acid-free) paper ∞.
Printed in Canada

Contents

Preface to the Third Edition

Research in cognition has been especially fruitful since the second edition of *Cognition* was published in 1997. I have tried to incorporate as much of this new material as I can while still preserving what continues to be relevant from the second edition. While I have not kept an exact count of the number of new citations, it is easily over 500. I have also pruned from each chapter those parts that are not currently active research areas. Taken as a whole, the new research in cognitive psychology demonstrates its continuing relevance to the psychology curriculum.

While important changes have been made to each chapter, some of these changes are more notable than others. Chapter 1 now contains a preliminary discussion of the localization of function controversy and its role in cognition. Chapter 2 (Basic Approaches to Cognition) provides an overview of the relationships between information theory, information-processing, connectionism, cognitive neuroscience, and ecological validity. Chapter 3 (Attention) includes material on task-switching, inattentional blindness, the attentional blink, and déjà vu. Chapter 4 (Memory Traces and Memory Schemas) now includes a discussion of phantom limbs as an illustration of schema theory as well as the role of the hippocampus in the consolidation and reconsolidation of memory traces. A box in Chapter 5 (Memory Systems) considers the evolution of memory systems in terms of natural selection, exaptation, and the Baldwin effect, and the chapter considers the contributions of Tulving as well as what aging and, in particular, Alzheimer's have taught us about memory systems. Chapter 6 (Imagery) explores synaesthesia in much more depth. Embodied cognition and folk biology are two topics added to Chapter 7 (Concepts). Figuring prominently in Chapter 8 (Language) are recent developments in Chomskyan theory as well as in the linguistic relativity controversy. Chapter 9 (Problem-Solving) combines research on the psychology and neuropsychology of insight and reviews research on problem-solving in science. Chapter 10 (Reasoning) discusses dual process theories of reasoning, which also are important in Chapter 11 (Judgement and Choice). The latter chapter provides discussions of the perception of streakiness and its role in the 'hot hand' belief, as well as in ecological rationality. Intelligence and Creativity (Chapter 12) reviews possible explanations of the Flynn effect. Both Chapters 13 (Personal Cognition) and 14 (Applied Cognitive Psychology) are examples of topics that should be included in cognition texts, but are not always. They contain a number of prominent research areas that are of special interest to students, such as autobiographical memory and successful learning strategies.

The 14 chapters in this book each cover different aspects of cognition. The first 11 chapters form a sequence, in that the material covered in each chapter is to some extent dependent on that which has preceded it, and anticipates topics that are to follow. It would be possible to teach them in a different order, should the instructor desire to do so. For example, in a previous edition of this book, Chapter 7 (Concepts) followed the chapter on attention (Chapter 3) to indicate the range of the discipline. Chapter 6 (Imagery) is also quite movable, as is Chapter 8 (Language). However, some sequences seem to me to be invariant. For example, Chapter 11 (Judgement and Choice) should follow the chapters on problem-solving and reasoning, and harks back to those topics. Two of the last three chapters should be considered only after the previous 11. Chapter 12 (Intelligence and Creativity) draws heavily on what has gone before, as does Chapter 13 (Personal Cognition). The last chapter, on applied psychology, stands on its own reasonably well and has even been used as an introductory chapter by some instructors to convey to students that cognitive psychology has much to say about the 'real world'.

In addition to the foregoing, the following specific changes have been made for the new edition.

1. Web links are included where appropriate. I have tried to make these links to sites that have a good chance of survival. I have also included some links to relevant demonstrations and activities on the Web.
2. There are places in each chapter that engage the reader directly. These interactions range from a request for a simple response or opinion to more elaborate demonstrations and activities.
3. The boxes included in most chapters develop in more depth important issues.

At the end of each chapter are the following pedagogically useful sections.

- *Key concepts.* These are printed in bold throughout the chapter, then collected and listed with definitions at the end.
- *Questions for study and discussion.* These should help the reader prepare for evaluation and also facilitate group discussion.
- *Further reading.* Students are encouraged to read further, and reasons are given for specific readings.
- *Links to other chapters.* Listed here are the key concepts in the chapter that also are discussed in other chapters.

■ Acknowledgements

I am extremely grateful to David Stover, whose interest in this project made it possible. My developmental editors, Lisa Proctor and Lisa Meschino, have provided me with expert guidance. Laurna and Richard Tallman did a fine job of editing the manuscript.

Finally, I must belatedly thank Ken Proctor, whose encouragement more than 15 years ago awoke my interest in writing textbooks. This has proven to be a very enjoyable activity. Without Ken's encouragement, I might never have begun.

Chapter 1

Introduction

■ What Is Cognition?

Because this is a book about cognition, it would be nice to start with a precise definition of cognition. However, this is not at all easy to do. As you will see, cognition has meant different things to different people at different times. In order to explore the field of cognition, we first need some kind of map of the territory. One approach is to examine the ways in which the word 'cognition' has been used. This approach was successfully taken by Natsoulas (1978) when he explored the concept of consciousness. Natsoulas pointed out that scientific psychology develops out of the concerns of everyday life. Our psychological concepts originate in ordinary language. Of course, scientific psychology refines the common-sense concepts we find expressed in ordinary language. However, to get a feeling for the range of possible topics that cognitive psychology might cover, it makes sense to examine the set of concepts that typically are associated with cognition in everyday discourse. Natsoulas used *The Oxford English Dictionary* as a guide to the various meanings of consciousness, and we will also use that dictionary to give us an outline of the meaning of *cognition* and allied concepts.

The Oxford English Dictionary lists several meanings of *cognition*, including the action or faculty of knowing. This definition underscores two things worth emphasizing. First, cognition is the *action* of knowing. The study of cognition is the study of processes: the ways in which we become acquainted with things. Second, cognition can be seen as a faculty. As we shall see, it has been common to divide the mind into faculties that represent the different mental activities of which we are capable.

Some of the other concepts cognition is associated with in the dictionary include *awareness, comprehension, intelligence, intuition, personal acquaintance, recognition, skill,* and *understanding*. It might be useful to list these concepts together with other concepts that have similar meanings. After all, a large part of learning any subject is acquiring the special vocabulary that the subject employs. G.A. Miller (1986), one of the founders of cognitive psychology, observed that a good way of increasing a person's vocabulary with respect to a particular subject is to provide information about the relations between the words that are characteristic of that area. Table 1.1 lists a set of concepts linked with *cognition*. Along with them are other concepts that *The Oxford English Dictionary* lists as having a similar meaning, as well as the chapter in which these concepts are considered.

You can see that an enormous range of phenomena are described by these words. All of these are concepts we deal with in this book. Let us quickly go through each set of words, and examine one or two of the questions and issues to which consideration of these concepts gives rise. Our goal now is not to give precise definitions of these concepts, but only to begin to get a nodding acquaintance with them. Later on we more precisely define them, as well as many others.

- *Awareness.* The role that awareness plays in cognition is an issue that arises for us at several points in this text. Some basic questions are: Do we have to attend consciously to information in order to acquire it? Can unattended information influence subsequent cognitive processes?

Table 1.1 Cognitive Concepts

Concept	Associated Concepts	Chapter
Awareness	Consciousness	Attention (3), Concepts (7), Imagery and Cognitive Maps (6), Personal Cognition (13)
Intelligence	Quickness of Understanding	Intelligence and Creativity (12)
	Information	Basic Approaches to Cognition (2)
	Sagacity	Problem-Solving (9)
Intuition	Immediate Insight	Problem-Solving (9), Intelligence and Creativity (12)
Personal Acquaintance	Social Knowledge	Personal Cognition (13)
Recognition	Categorizing	Concepts (7), Applied Cognitive Psychology (14)
	Reviewing and Revising	Memory Traces and Memory Schemas (4), Applied Cognitive Psychology (14)
Skill	Reasoning	Reasoning (10)
	Practical Knowledge	Intelligence and Creativity (12), Applied Cognitive Psychology (14)
	Expertise	Intelligence and Creativity (12)
Understanding	Judgement, Decision-Making	Judgement and Choice (11)
	Comprehension	Language (8), Memory Systems (5)

- *Intelligence.* Intelligence is one of the most complex concepts in all of psychology. Is intelligence best measured by how quickly someone can process information, or is there more to it than that? What about sagacity, which is the ability to think wisely? Sometimes the wise answer is not the first one that comes to mind.
- *Intuition.* Occasionally, we have sudden flashes of insight that yield the answers to problems in an apparently effortless way. However, might not insight be the outcome of prior work, rather than something that just happens?
- *Personal acquaintance.* Many of our cognitive processes have a very personal side to them. Are the cognitive processes we use to understand other people similar to the ones we use to understand impersonal events? How do our emotions influence our cognition, and vice versa?
- *Recognition.* The process of recognition is as fundamental a cognitive process as can be. It literally means 'to know again'. When we recognize something, we categorize it as something we have experienced before. How do we decide which events go together, or belong to the same class? Another very old sense of the word 'recognition' is 'reviewing and revising'. We will see that memory is often a very active process in which our recollection of previous experiences is continuously being reviewed and revised.
- *Skill.* Skill is another word that has come frequently to be used with respect to topics in cognitive psychology. Skill often means applying a reasoned approach to solving a problem. Skill can manifest itself in a variety of ways, but is perhaps best understood when observed in the application of practical knowledge in a real-world situation. What about expertise? How does a person become an expert in areas as diverse as chess and movies?
- *Understanding.* The concept of understanding is basic to cognition, and has many facets. The ability to make good decisions, reasonable judgements, comprehend what is going on around us—these and many other processes are parts of the way that we understand our situation.

■ Cognition as a Faculty

Many psychologists have believed that mental activities can be classified into three faculties, and what follows is largely based on Hilgard's (1980) account of this **faculty psychology**. The three faculties can be called *cognition*, *emotion*, and *volition*. Less formal names for them are *knowing*, *feeling*, and *choosing*. During the eighteenth century, faculty psychologists originally believed that the mind imposed its own structure on experience. This is to say that the mind organizes experience according to its own rules and, therefore, mental life is determined by the intrinsic nature of the mind itself. For the faculty psychologist, the meaning of events is something people create. They also believe that people reorganize events to make them consistent with their own structure. In any situation, people have certain thoughts, certain feelings, and make certain choices. The particular thoughts, feelings, and choices will differ in different situations, but people will still have experiences corresponding to those three classes of mental events. From the viewpoint of most faculty psychologists, this is because the mind is innately constructed to think, feel, and make choices.

One of the people whose work led to faculty psychology was the German philosopher Immanuel Kant (1781/1929), who lived between 1724 and 1804 (Hatfield, 1992, 1998; Mischel, 1967). Kant made much of the fact that people tend to organize their experiences in terms of causes and effects. That is, cause-and-effect relationships are not given in the world, but are categories people impose on the world. As an example, several years ago there was a power blackout throughout the eastern United States and Canada. According to one story, the blackout occurred just as a small boy was walking home from school. In fact, the lights went off just as he kicked a telephone pole. Although it was just a coincidence that he kicked the pole precisely at the moment when all the lights went off, he nevertheless felt very guilty for causing the blackout. Although this story may be apocryphal, it still illustrates Kant's point: people do tend to interpret events close together in space and time as causing one another, whether they really do or not. A faculty psychologist would say that causality is a way in which we think about events, and is not something given by the events themselves.

The general theme of faculty psychology is that the structure of experience is due to the structure of the mind rather than due to the world impressing itself on the mind. Thus, we are prepared to require that all experiences have certain characteristics. There are certain activities the mind performs on all mental contents, and these activities are: knowing, feeling, and choosing. Faculty psychology was very influential in the eighteenth and nineteenth centuries. Much of faculty psychology consisted of trying to map out the various parts of the faculties. Cognition is the faculty concerned with activities such as memory, imagination, judgement, and reason. Emotion is the faculty that evaluates events in terms of the pleasure or the pain to which they give rise. Volition is the faculty responsible for choices. Choices can be rational, or they can be the outcome of irrational processes.

It is easy to see that, in practice, these three mental activities must influence one another. In order to make a decision, for example, an individual may very well draw on cognitive and emotional faculties. Decisions may be based on a reasoned evaluation of the alternatives, or on the way the individual feels about the alternatives, or on a mixture of both. Although this book is about cognition, we also consider the ways that cognitive processes interact with other processes that have traditionally been seen as belonging to the psychology of emotion and decision-making.

Although psychologists seldom use the word *faculty* any longer, they still occasionally theorize about the mind in a way that is reminiscent of faculty psychology. This is particularly true when psychologists argue that the mind is composed of specific parts, or **modules**, each of which is responsible for particular cognitive operations. For example, Fodor (1983) called his very influential book *The modularity of mind: An essay in faculty psychology*. There have been differences of opinion concerning the extent to which the mind is modular, as well as considerable debate about the number and kind of mental modules that may exist (e.g., Pinker, 1997; Sperber, 2002). However, once one begins to speculate about how many different cognitive functions there may be, it is but a short step to wonder which parts of the brain might be responsible for them. Perhaps the brain should be 'seen as a mosaic of organs specialized to deal with, for example, language, number, music, and color' (Marshall & Fink, 2003, p. 53).

■ The Brain as the Organ of the Mind

As has been often observed (e.g., Krech, 1962; Fodor, 1983), the attempt to discover which parts of the brain are specialized for which tasks goes back at least to Franz Joseph Gall (1758–1828) and his student J.G. Spurzheim (1776–1832). Gall and Spurzheim promoted **phrenology**. You have probably seen phrenological charts like the one in Figure 1.1. They purport to represent the locations in the brain of various psychological functions. Although Gall and Spurzheim's charts are not taken seriously any longer, their underlying premises still deserve consideration.

> Their argument reduced to three basic principles: (1) The brain is the sole organ of the mind. (2) Basic character and intellectual traits are innately determined. (3) Since there are differences in character and intellectual traits among individuals as well as differences in various intellectual capacities within a single individual, there must exist differentially developed areas in the brain, responsible for these differences! Where there is variation in *function* there must be variation in the controlling *structures*. (Krech, 1962, p. 33)

Gall and Spurzheim's method for locating functions in the brain was highly speculative. They believed that the more highly developed a function, the larger it would

Figure 1.1 A Phrenological Chart.

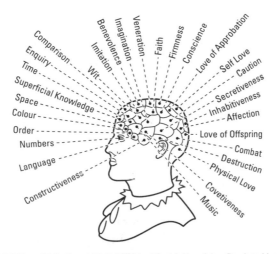

be. Furthermore, the larger a function, the more it would manifest itself as a protrusion on the skull. Thus, one could divine a person's strengths and weaknesses by examining the shape of the skull. Phrenology had a powerful impact on nineteenth-century cultural practices, and many paying customers relied on the phrenologist's advice (Sokal, 2001). In spite of the now obvious weakness of their method, the underlying hypothesis that specific functions are localized in specific parts of the brain has guided much subsequent research (e.g., Gardner, 1983; Sarter, Berntson, & Cacioppo, 1996).

Not everyone has taken a strong **localization of function** position, meaning that there is a strict one-to-one correspondence between specific cognitive functions and specific parts of the brain. A landmark in the history of the localization of function controversy was the work of Shepherd Ivory Franz (1874–1933). Franz was an expert in the technique of ablation, whereby parts of the cortex of an animal are destroyed and the results observed. If functions were localized in the cortex, then the effect of ablation of cortical tissue should depend on the area destroyed. However, on the basis of his observations, Franz (1912) concluded that 'mental processes are not due to the independent activities of individual parts of the brain, but to the activities of the brain as a whole' and that 'it would appear best and most scientific that we should not adhere to any of the phrenological systems' (p. 328).

Franz and his student Karl Lashley (1890–1958) studied the effects of ablation of the frontal lobes in rats. Their technique was to make 'small holes in the animal's skull rather than opening up the skull, and determine by later histology precisely where the lesions had occurred' (Bruce, 1986, p. 38), thus determining the effect of such lesions on the retention of a simple learned maze habit. Their results persuaded them that as long as sufficient tissue remained after the operation, then the location of the tissue was irrelevant.

Lashley subsequently published what became a classic in the area of localization of function, called *Brain mechanisms and intelligence* (1929). This research developed further the procedures he had learned from Franz. Lashley lesioned the cortex of rats in different places and to different degrees. He reasoned that 'if there were reflex paths transversing the cortex . . . then surgery would destroy them' (Weidman, 1994, p. 166). Lashley (1929, p. 74) observed the ability of rats to learn or remember such tasks as finding their ways through mazes of different levels of difficulty, and found that performance in simple mazes was not greatly affected by brain damage. Rather, performance declined as the difficulty of the task increased and/or the amount of brain damage increased. Lashley (1930/1978) summarized the implications of his results as follows.

> Small lesions either produce no symptoms or very transient ones, so that it is clear that the mechanisms for habits are not closely grouped within small areas. When larger areas are involved, there are usually amnesias for many activities . . . . After injuries to the brain, the rate of formation of some habits is directly proportional to the extent of the injury and independent of the position within any part of the cortex. (p. 271)

There was no evidence for specialized connections developed as a result of learning in the brain. Rather, neither learning nor memory is 'dependent upon the properties of individual cells'; instead, they are functions of 'the total mass of tissue' (Lashley, 1930/1978, p. 271). These results came to be formulated as the **law of mass action** (learning and memory depend on the total mass of brain tissue remaining) and the **law of equipotentiality** (even though some areas of the cortex may become specialized for certain tasks, within limits any part of an area can do the job of any other part of that area). Lashley (1930, p. 271) used the metaphor of an electric sign as a model to explain his findings. The 'functional organization plays over' cortical cells 'just as the pattern of letters plays over the bank of lamps in an electric sign.' A single bank of bulbs in an electronic sign can be used to display any number of messages, and similarly the cortex can be organized in any number of ways depending on circumstances.

Just from the two cases of Gall and Lashley you can see a very great range of possible positions with respect to localization of function. In subsequent chapters we will see how cognitive psychologists use many sophisticated techniques to try to sort things out.

Metacognition and Cognitive Psychology

Metacognition is the name for the knowledge that people have about the way that cognitive processes work. The study of cognitive psychology can be seen as a process of developing our metacognition (Rebok, 1987). We all begin in pretty much the same place, with our common-sense understanding of cognition, and the goal of studying cognitive psychology is to develop this understanding further. Sometimes this means changing our beliefs, or giving them up altogether. Often it means accepting some uncertainty concerning what we should believe about cognition. Cognitive psychology is not in a finished state. It is very much an actively developing area of inquiry. There are usually not definite answers, but a series of alternative hypotheses about the way that the mind works. In the next chapter, we will review some of the better-known approaches to the field to get a better idea of the 'lay of the land'.

The biggest problem for a beginning student of cognitive psychology may be to get over the feeling that thinking about thinking is an impossibly abstract activity that can be mastered by only a few select initiates. In fact, you probably already have a pretty elaborate way of thinking about thinking. As you work through this book, you should relate the concepts and hypotheses you find to the concepts and hypotheses you already have. Of course, this means that you will need to work out what it is that you presently believe. You may occasionally discover that you can generate hypotheses about the way that cognition works that seem to you to be interesting alternatives to the ones that cognitive psychologists have already developed. When that happens, then you are becoming a cognitive psychologist yourself. Try to think up ways of testing the hypotheses that you come up with. As many psychologists have observed (e.g., Kuhn, 1989), formulating and testing hypotheses about how the mind works are some of the ways that personal beliefs can develop into scientific knowledge.

■ The Range of Cognitive Psychology

Cognitive psychology provides an important tool for the analysis of problems of all kinds. One of the things you will notice in this book are concrete, practical examples of the application of cognitive psychology. In fact, the last chapter is devoted entirely to this topic. The book also discusses the study of social and emotional aspects of cognition. These topics have been influenced greatly by cognitive psychology, but are not always included in cognition texts. Now that cognitive psychology has developed, students can access some of the areas to which cognitive psychology is being applied. Cognitive psychology is now integral to most other forms of psychology, and you should become aware of at least some of the ways it has been extended to other areas in psychology and applied to real-world problems.

■ Questions for Study and Discussion

1. Discuss the origins of cognitive psychology, paying particular attention to faculty psychology and its relation to phrenology.

2. Which alternative strikes you as more plausible, the strong localization of function position or Lashley's arguments against it?

■ Key Concepts

What follows here and near the end of each chapter is a list of some of the most influential ideas in the area we have just reviewed, which have appeared in boldface in the chapter. Some concepts are quite general and not associated with any particular psychologist. However, in other cases, the name of a psychologist is paired with the concept, or concepts, with which he or she is identified. If any of the names or concepts seem unfamiliar, reread the appropriate section of the chapter. You should be able to define each concept and discuss research that is relevant to it.

Categories of cause and effect (Kant) Individuals impose categories, such as cause and effect, on their experience.

Faculty psychology The theory that the mind can be divided into different types of mental activities, usually called cognition (knowing), emotion (feeling), and volition (choosing).

Localization of function The attempt to discover correspondences between specific cognitive functions and specific parts of the brain.

Mass action and equipotentiality (Lashley) Learning and memory depend on the total mass of brain tissue remaining, and even though some areas of the cortex may become specialized for certain tasks, within limits any part of an area can do the job of any other part of that area.

Metacognition The knowledge that people have about the way that cognitive processes work.

Modules The belief that the mind is composed of specific parts, or modules, each of which is responsible for particular cognitive operations.

Phrenology (Gall) The more highly developed a psychological function, the larger its proportion of the brain will be. Furthermore, the larger a function, the more it would manifest itself as a protrusion on the skull.

■ Links to Other Chapters

Modules
Chapter 3 (domain-specific modules)
Chapter5 (teaching domain-specific
knowledge)
Chapter 7 (folk biology)
Chapter 8 (language acquisition device,
communication, and comprehension)
Chapter 10 (social contract theory)
Chapter 11 (training in statistical reasoning)
Chapter 12 (evolution of 'g')
Chapter 14 (design of the user interface)
Localization of function
Chapter 2 (methods in cognitive
neuroscience)

Phrenology (Gall)
Chapter 12 (Gardner and the theory of
multiple intelligences)
Lashley
Chapter 2 (priming)
Chapter 8 (structure and development of
language)
Metacognition
Chapter 4 (elaboration and distinctiveness)
Chapter 9 (feeling of knowing)
Chapter 14 (illusions of competence)

■ Further Reading

A history of early developments in cognitive psychology is in Chapter 14 of Benjafield, J. (2005). *A history of psychology*. Toronto: Oxford University Press. A particularly well-informed analysis of the development of cognitive psychology is Mandler, G. (2002). Origins of the cognitive (r)evolution. *Journal of the History of the Behavioral Sciences, 38*, 339–353.

A useful analysis of how the history of the study of the brain has implications for current investigations is provided in Zimmer, C. (2004). A distant mirror for the brain. *Science, 303*, 43–44.

Analyses of *folk psychology*, or people's beliefs about how the mind works, are Rips, L.J., & Conrad, F.G. (1989). Folk psychology of mental activities. *Psychological Review, 96*, 187–207, and Fellbaum, C., & Miller, G.A. (1990). Folk psychology or semantic entailment? *Psychological Review, 97*, 565–570. Additional elaboration on folk psychology can be found in D'Andrade, R. (1987). A folk model of the mind. In D. Holland & N. Quinn (Eds.), *Cultural models in language and thought* (pp. 112–148). Cambridge: Cambridge University Press, and Vendler, Z. (1972). *Res cogitans: An essay in rational psychology*. Ithaca, NY: Cornell University Press. A classic critique of folk psychology is Stich, S. (1983). *From folk psychology to cognitive science: The case against belief*. Cambridge, Mass.: MIT Press. A more appreciative survey of the pervasiveness and variability of folk psychology is Lillard, A. (1998). Ethnopsychologies: Cultural variations in theories of mind. *Psychological Bulletin, 123*, 3–32

We review the large literature on metacognition at various places in this book. A paper that will get you started is by one of the psychologists most responsible for introducing this notion: Flavell, J. (1979). Metacognition and cognitive monitoring. *American Psychologist, 34*, 906–911. A more recent perspective is Sternberg, R.J. (1998). Metacognition, abilities, and developing expertise. *Instructional Science, 26*, 127–140.

Chapter 2

Basic Approaches to Cognition

■ The Concept of Information

Over the last several decades, computer science has had an enormous impact on a great many academic disciplines, including psychology. A computer can be seen as an information-processing system. The interesting question is: To what extent can people also be seen as information-processing systems? That is one of the central issues we will explore in this section.

A revolutionary way of conceiving of information was initiated by theorists such as Shannon and Weaver (1949). Intuitively, 'information is something that occurs when some person or machine tells us something we didn't know before' (Garner, 1962, p. 2). Information theorists went beyond this rough definition and proposed to measure the amount of information transmitted when an event occurs. An event can be any one of a number of possible occurrences, such as a coin coming up heads or tails. The basic idea was that 'any communicative act provides information only insofar as it reduces a condition of ignorance or uncertainty about the state of things under consideration' (Garner, 1962, p. 3). Thus, **information** is the opposite of uncertainty. Consider tossing a coin, for example. Before tossing the coin, we are uncertain about which alternative (heads or tails) will occur. After tossing the coin, our uncertainty is eliminated. Any event that reduces or eliminates uncertainty provides us with information.

Some situations contain more uncertainty than others. In the case of coin tossing, there are only two possible outcomes—heads or tails. In other situations, such as rolling a single die, there are six possible outcomes—the numbers 1 to 6. There is more prior uncertainty in the latter case than in the former, and consequently rolling a die provides more information than does tossing a coin. It is possible to quantify the amount of information provided by the occurrence of an event in terms of **bits**. 'Bit' is short for 'binary digit'. Imagine a situation, such as flipping an unbiased coin, in which we are uncertain about which of two equally likely events will occur. When one of the two events occurs, then we get one bit of information. Every time the number of equally likely alternatives doubles, then the number of bits goes up by one. A popular illustration of this relationship is a guessing game in which one person thinks of a number and another person tries to guess it (Garner, 1962, p. 5). The number of bits corresponds to the number of questions you would need to ask in order to guess the right answer. For example, if I am thinking of a number between 1 and 8, you need three questions to find it. The correct strategy is to reduce the number of possibilities by half with each question. First, ask if it is above 4. If the answer is 'yes', then ask if it is above 6. If the answer is 'yes' again, then ask if it is above 7. If the answer is 'yes', then the number is 8, if it is 'no', then the number is 7, and so on.

George A. Miller (1953) was one of the first psychologists to use information theory in his research. A famous example of his work in this area was his paper 'The magical number seven: plus or minus two' (Miller, 1956), where he considered experiments in which an experimental participant was regarded as a 'communication channel', and the experimenter was interested in how much information can be accurately transmitted through this channel. This amount is called **channel capacity**. For example, a participant might be asked to estimate the magnitude of a stimulus dimension. The dimension might be anything from sounds of different pitch or loudness, to tastes of different saltiness. In experiments like these, participants could discriminate between about seven different magnitudes, giving a channel capacity of about 2.5 bits of information. A similar result occurred in investigations of the number of items we can be aware of at one time. Miller's review of the literature suggests that we can hold about 7 items in mind at one time. He called this the **span of immediate memory** (Miller, 1956, p. 34), and observed that the amount of information we can retain in this way is quite limited.

This kind of research led to several important lines of investigation we will explore in later chapters. For example, is the amount of information that people can process fixed, or does it vary with the kind of task, the kind of person, and the amount of training the person has had? Are human information-processing resources limited, or can people learn to acquire an unlimited amount of information?

It is important to note that the quantitative definition of information given above has not been the most common concept of 'information' in cognitive psychology. Communication engineers can happily work with the quantitative definition of information, but in psychological experiments the meaning of the information presented to participants must also be taken into account (Luce, 2003, p. 185). In practice, 'the word information has been almost seamlessly transformed into the concept of "information processing models" in which information theory per se plays no role. The idea of the mind being an information-processing network with capacity limitations has stayed with us, but in far more complex ways than information theory. Much theorizing in cognitive psychology is of this type, now being more or less well augmented by brain imaging techniques' (Luce, 2003, p. 186). In what follows we will expand on Luce's statement.

■ Models of Information-Processing Stages

Primary and Secondary Memory

Cognitive psychologists working within the information-processing approach have suggested several models of the relations between different cognitive processes. Let us begin with a simple model that captures a fundamental distinction. Consider Figure 2.1, which is from an early but still important paper by Waugh and Norman (1965). The flow of information is indicated by the arrows. Upon being stimulated, we may have an experience called a primary memory, a concept derived from William James (1890/1983), who is perhaps the most influential of all American psychologists. **Primary memory** consists of the 'immediately present moment' (James, 1890/1983, p. 608), and is thus also often termed **immediate memory**. The arrow labelled 'rehearsal' conveys the fact that primary memories tend to be quickly forgotten unless they are repeated, as one might repeat a telephone number to oneself upon looking it up. While primary memory belongs to the present, **secondary memory** belongs to the past.

> An object which is recollected, in the proper sense of that term, is one which has been absent from consciousness, and now revives anew. It is brought back, recalled, fished up, so to speak, from a reservoir in which, with countless other objects, it lay buried and lost from view. But an object of primary memory is not thus brought back; it never was lost; its date was never cut off in consciousness from that of the immediately present moment. (James, 1890/1983, p. 608)

> Memory proper, or secondary memory as it might be styled, is the knowledge of a former state of mind after it has already once dropped from consciousness; or rather *it is the knowledge of an event, or fact,* of which meantime we have not been thinking, *with the additional consciousness that we have thought or experienced it before.* (James, 1890/1983, p. 610)

Waugh and Norman (1965) noted that James's distinction between primary and secondary memory was based on introspective evidence. Such evidence is seldom treated as definitive in cognitive psychology. However, the subjective reports of participants are often used in conjunction with more objective evidence, such as that provided by well-designed experiments (Jack & Shallice, 2001). Experimental evidence for the

Figure 2.1 Waugh and Norman's Model of Information Processing.

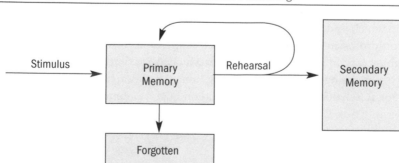

From Waugh, N.C., & Norman, D.A. (1965). Primary memory. *Psychological Review, 72,* pp. 89–104. Copyright 1965 by the American Psychological Association. Reprinted by permission.

primary/secondary memory distinction came from an analysis of the **Brown-Peterson task** (J. Brown, 1958; Peterson & Peterson, 1959). This has been one of the most widely used types of task in memory research. In the typical Brown-Peterson experimental paradigm, participants are given a set of items, and then a number. Participants immediately begin counting backward by threes from the number. Thus, the participant might hear the letters B, Q, R and the number 107. The participant would then count backward like this: 104, 101, 98, and so on. After a specific interval, such as 6, 9, 12, 15, or 18 seconds, participants are asked to recall the items (in this case, the letters B, Q, R). The filled interval of counting backward presumably prevents any kind of rehearsal of the letters and interferes with their continuous presence in primary memory. An unfilled interval, on the other hand, would allow participants to rehearse the items and maintain them in primary memory. Waugh and Norman's analysis showed that participants' ability to recall letters declined as the number of interfering items increased.

Waugh and Norman (1965) pointed out that primary memory makes it possible for us to immediately and accurately recall our most recent experiences. For example, we are able 'to recall verbatim the most recent few words in a sentence [we are] hearing or speaking' (p. 102), provided nothing else interferes with it. Although we take primary memory for granted, it is nonetheless of great importance to us.

The Modal Model

A number of proposed information-processing models are much more complex than that of Waugh and Norman. One such model became so widely accepted as to be called 'the modal model' (Gardner, 1985, p. 122). This model, created by Atkinson and Shiffrin (1968, 1971; Shiffrin & Atkinson, 1969), is given in Figure 2.2. It describes the flow of information from the time the person first begins processing a stimulus. Information is initially held in the **sensory register**. The potential importance of the sensory register emerged as a result of the work of Sperling (1960). Sperling investigated the effects of briefly exposing a stimulus to a participant.

You can best understand how the sensory register works by looking at the block of letters in Figure 2.3. Suppose you present a participant with those letters on a screen for a brief interval, such as 50 milliseconds. Then turn the stimulus off for 50 milliseconds. The participant then hears a high, medium, or low tone. A high tone means that the participant should try to report the top row, a medium tone the middle row, and a low tone the bottom row. It turns out that the participant can still read off the correct row, even if it is no longer being presented. This means that a copy of the visual stimulus, in a form similar to a visual image, persists even after the stimulus has ceased. A visual **icon** (Neisser, 1967) briefly outlasts the stimulus itself.

Sperling's experiment was very influential, partly because it implied that one could analyze cognition as a sequence of information-processing stages. Thus, after the stimulus was stored briefly in the sensory register, it could be processed further. In the Shiffrin and Atkinson model, the next stage of processing occurs in the **short-term store**, which is similar to what Waugh and Norman called primary memory. Information can be retained indefinitely in the short-term store by means of

Figure 2.2 The Modal Model.

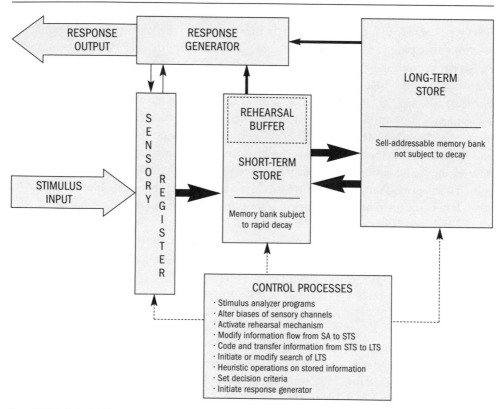

From Shiffrin, R.M., & Atkinson, R.C. (1969). Storage and retrieval processes in long-term memory. *Psychological Review,* 76, pp. 179–193. Copyright 1969 by the American Psychological Association. Reprinted by permission.

rehearsal. Moreover, the short-term store 'provides a working memory in which manipulations of information may take place on a temporary basis' (Shiffrin & Atkinson, 1969, p. 180). The concept of a **working memory** that can be used not only as a temporary store but also to manipulate information has proved to be a very useful and durable idea (Baddeley, 2001).

Some or all of the contents of the short-term store may be transferred to the **long-term store**, 'which is assumed to be a permanent repository of information' although 'factors such as traumatic brain damage, lesions, and deterioration with extreme age must lead to memory loss' (Shiffrin & Atkinson, 1969, p. 180). Notice that in addition to the three stores, control processes regulate the flow of information in the system. 'Control processes govern informational flow, rehearsal, memory search, output of responses, and so forth' (p. 180).

In discussing their model, Shiffrin and Atkinson (1969) explicitly compared it to a computer program. Indeed, there is a very close relationship between information-processing models and computer programs. In an influential book, Neisser (1967) argued that the analogy between cognition and a computer program is very powerful:

Figure 2.3 Stimulus Letters for Sperling's Experiment.

TDR

SRN

FZR

From Sperling, G. (1960). The information available in brief visual presentations. *Psychological Monographs: General and Applied, 74*, no. 11, pp. 1–29. Reprinted with the permission of the author.

The task of a psychologist trying to understand human cognition is analogous to that of a [person] trying to discover how a computer has been programmed . . . if the program seems to store and reuse information, [the person] would like to know by what 'routines' or 'procedures' this is done. . . . A program is . . . a series of instructions for dealing with symbols: 'If the input has certain characteristics . . . then carry out certain procedures . . . otherwise other procedures . . . combine the results in various ways . . . store and retrieve various items . . . etc.' The cognitive psychologist would like to give a similar account of the way information is processed by people. (pp. 6–8)

One facet of the information-processing approach to cognition is the study of the ways in which we are programmed, so to speak. To some extent, the cognitive psychologist studies mental 'software'. Cognitive psychologists also study the 'hardware' of cognition, as we shall see when we consider the brain. However, the first step in constructing an information-processing model is to provide a precise, step-by-step analysis of the flow of information. A good example of such an analysis is a study of children's arithmetic by Groen and Parkman (1972). Although done many years ago, this study has held up well and is still cited favourably (e.g., Lucangeli, Trassoldi, Bendotti, Bonanomi, & Siegel, 2003; Mayer, 2004).

Groen and Parkman (1972) studied first-grade children who had not yet been taught arithmetic. Thus, they are unlikely to be able to recall the answers to simple arithmetic problems from long-term memory but will have to work them out. Each child was shown 55 problems of the form '$m + n=?$' where m and n are numbers the sum of which is 9 or less. The child was presented with a row of buttons labelled with possible answers and was to press the button corresponding to the right one. The experimenters measured the time taken from presentation of the problem to pressing the correct button.

Now examine Figure 2.4. The part labelled 'A' is a flow chart representing one way in which children could solve the problems. First they could select the smallest number and keep it in working memory ('set the counter to the smallest number'). They could then follow a routine of adding 1's as many times as required by the size of the larger number. Once they have done so, then they exit the routine with the sum. Thus if the problem was '5 + 3 = ?', they would begin by setting the counter to 3. They would then add 1 a total of 5 times, giving them 8.

Figure 2.4 Flow Chart Modelling the Process of Adding Two Numbers by Children.

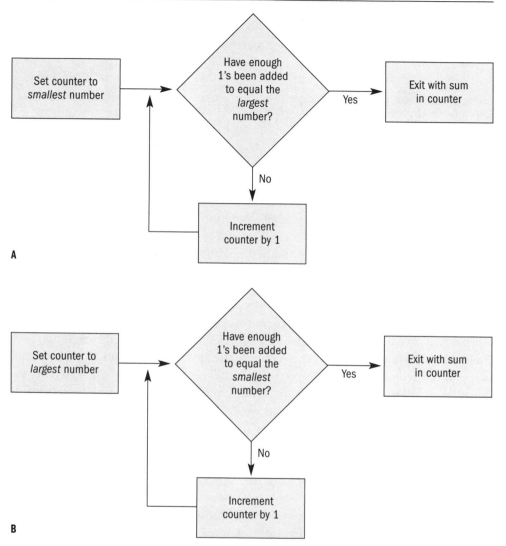

Adapted from Groen, G.J., & Parkman, J.M. (1972). A chronometric analysis of simple addition. *Psychological Review, 79*, pp. 329–343.

Now examine the flow chart labelled 'B'. Here the child sets the counter to the largest number, rather than the smallest, and adds 1 as many times as required by the size of the smaller number. Thus, if the problem was '5 + 3 = ?', then they would begin by setting the counter to 5, and adding 1 a total of 3 times, giving them 8.

Both models make very specific predictions concerning the latency, or amount of time taken to reach the answer. If children use the procedure described in A, then the latency should increase with the size of the larger number, and the size of the smaller number will not matter. Thus adding 1 + 5 should take the same time as adding 4 + 5 because each problem requires adding 1 a total of 5 times. However, the data are not consistent with this model, but rather with the model given in B. It turns out that latency varies with the size of the smaller number, as it should if the child is adding 1's as required by the size of the smaller number. Adding 1 + 5 means adding 1 only once, but adding 4 + 5 means adding 1 a total of 4 times.

The Groen and Parkman (1972) work illustrates information-processing approaches nicely because it is an explicit, step-by step account of how young children do arithmetic problems. The model is precise enough to enable the experimenter to distinguish between different alternative possibilities. A more general point is that the use of latency as a dependent variable is quite common in cognitive psychology, the assumption being that the more steps a process requires, the longer it will take. This use of time as a measure of cognitive processes is called **mental chronometry** (Posner, 1986).

Groen and Parkman (1972) studied a process that was simple enough that it could be tested by means of a simple experiment. However, many models of cognitive processes are much more complex than this and cannot be evaluated quite so directly. Computer models have been very useful resources for cognitive psychologists in their attempts to understand complex cognition.

Computer Simulation

People often discuss the question 'Can computers really think?' This is a deep question, and perhaps undecidable. Turing (1950) proposed that we not try to settle this question through endless discussion, but pay more attention to a concrete situation that illustrates the problem underlying the question. The concrete situation he considered is called the **imitation game** or **Turing's test**.

Turing described a game involving three people: a man and a woman, who are in one room, and an interrogator who is in another room. The interrogator is linked to the others by means of a computer terminal. Thus, the interrogator is able to ask questions of the man (let us call him Frank) and/or the woman (let us call her Annette), and they are able to reply using the computer interface. The object of the game is for the interrogator to be able to distinguish between the replies of the man and the replies of the woman.

You might think that this would be a trivial task for the interrogator, because the only question that needs to be asked of either respondent is 'Are you Frank or Annette?' However, just like ordinary people, the players of this game can lie. Thus, this game is not as easy as it appears to be at first. Now suppose that we make a change. In place of one of the people, we install a computer. Suppose, for example, we remove the man, and replace him with a computer we also name 'Frank'. The computer has been programmed to answer questions in the same way that Frank would. The interrogator's job is still to distinguish between Frank and Annette, but now one of the respondents is a computer, while the other is a person. Suppose that the interrogator could not reliably tell which was which. Then, according to Turing, we would have programmed the computer so that it could successfully play the imitation game.

The computer would have passed Turing's test, and the computer program would be an adequate model of the psychological processes involved when one person answers another person's questions.

By no means has everyone been persuaded that Turing's test is the right way to evaluate a psychological model. Over the years, a lot of ink has been spilled over the question of whether or not a computer program can ever be a realistic model of psychological processes (French, 2000). However, regardless of how we feel about this question, an enormous amount of work has been undertaken by psychologists who use some version of Turing's test as a methodological tool for evaluating a psychological theory. Notice that the computer itself does not constitute the psychological model; rather, the computer *program* actually is the model. Herbert Simon (1916–2001), together with his associate Alan Newell (1927–1992), was at the forefront of computer simulation for many years, and Simon won a Nobel Prize in part for this work. (You can read Simon's own account of his life and work at the Nobel Prize site: http://nobelprize.org/economics/laureates/1978/simon-autobio.html).

> Computers, then, could be general symbol systems, capable of processing symbols of any kind-numerical or not. This insight, which dawned on me only gradually, led Al [Newell] and me even more gradually to the idea that the computer could provide the formalism we were seeking—that we could use the computer to simulate all sorts of information processes and use computer languages as formal descriptions of those processes. (Simon, 1991, p. 201)

The fruit of Simon and Newell's discussions was a series of computer simulations of human thinking. Among the first simulations they produced was a chess-playing program (Newell, Shaw, & Simon, 1958; Newell & Simon, 1972). The programs they wrote were among the first examples of **artificial intelligence**, in that their output mimics the intelligent behaviour of people.

> One test of our knowledge of thinking is that we have created expert systems that can and do perform a substantial number of human tasks at a professional level: diagnosing illnesses, designing electric motors and transformers, judging credit risks and many others. . . . Not all of these expert systems behave in a humanoid manner—some of them (e.g., the grandmaster-level chess-playing program *Deep Thought*) take advantage of computer speed and memory capacity that we humans simply do not possess. But others (e.g., the chess playing program MATER), staying within severe limits on speed of processing, on short-term memory capacity, and on the time required to transfer knowledge to long-term memory, have been shown to behave very similarly, on almost a second-by-second basis, to humans performing the same tasks. (Simon, 1995, p. 507)

Computer simulation has been a very powerful force in cognitive psychology. We examine its influence at several points in this book.

■ Connectionist Models

It is not intuitively obvious how the information-processing flow-chart models we have considered so far could also be models of how the brain works. Even Herbert Simon acknowledged that 'explanation of cognitive processes at the information processing (symbolic) level is largely independent of explanation at the physiological (neurological) level that shows how processes are implemented' (Simon, 1992, p. 153). The approach called **connectionism** is an alternative to the more traditional information-processing approaches we have considered thus far (Schneider, 1987), and is intended to capture fundamental cognitive processes as they might be instantiated in the brain. The brain is made up of an enormous number of interconnected neurons, and these neurons can be seen as the elementary units of the brain. A model of the way these neurons form networks of connections might be a very useful way of understanding cognitive processes. Connectionist networks are models of **neural networks** as they might exist in the brain.

The two basic connectionist ideas are that information can be broken down into elementary units (neurons), and that there are connections between these units. These connections can have different strengths, and a neural network learns by modifying the strength of connections between elements so that the proper output occurs to a particular input. Assumptions are made about the way in which connections between neurons are formed and strengthened. One of these assumptions is the **Hebb rule**, named after the Canadian D.O. Hebb, one of the founders of neuropsychology. The Hebb rule states that 'when an axon of cell A is near enough to excite a cell B and repeatedly or persistently takes part in firing it, some growth process or metabolic change takes place in one or both cells such that A's efficiency, as one of the cells firing B, is increased' (Hebb, 1949, p. 62). This 'idea that a connection between two neurons takes place only if both neurons are firing at about the same time' has greatly influenced subsequent theorizing (Milner, 2003, p. 5).

Another assumption of connectionist models is that many connections can be active at the same time. This is an example of **parallel processing** as opposed to **serial processing**, which is restricted to only one connection operating at a time. Thus, another name for connectionist models is that they are **parallel distributed processing** models (McClelland & Rumelhart, 1986a, 1988). Let us see how these concepts work by examining a simple example.

A Simple Connectionist Network

Jones and Hoskins (1987) have illustrated some aspects of the way in which connectionist networks operate by means of the story of Little Red Riding Hood. Little Red Riding Hood must learn how to respond appropriately to three different inputs: Grandma, the Woodcutter, and the Wolf. Each of these three characters can be described as having three features, or **input units**. Grandma is kindly and wrinkled and has big eyes. The Woodcutter is handsome and kindly and has big ears. The Wolf has big ears, big eyes, and big teeth. Specific behaviours, or **output units**, are appropriate to the three characters. Little Red Riding Hood should approach, kiss on the cheek, and offer food to Grandma; approach, flirt with, and offer food to the Woodcutter; and scream, look for the Woodcutter, and run away from the Wolf.

Figure 2.5 shows a network of connections between these input and output units. How does this network get established? At first, the connections between input and output units have no particular value. On each trial (each time Little Red Riding Hood encounters a character) the connections are modified according to whether or not the output pattern matches a state of affairs that is predetermined to be desirable. This process can get quite complicated mathematically, but basically it involves feedback from each trial modifying the nature and strength of the various connections.

The connections develop different strengths as a result of experience. Thus, after being exposed to the inputs a number of times, some connections become stronger (more positive). Other connections may become weaker, or even negative. A negative connection between two units would be inhibitory. That is, a negative connection would tend to prevent the output unit from being active if the input unit is active. This is represented in the figure by solid lines for positive connections, and dotted lines for negative connections. Figure 2.5 is a trained network, one that has emerged in Little Red Riding Hood as a result of her experience.

Figure 2.5 A Simple Connectionist Network.

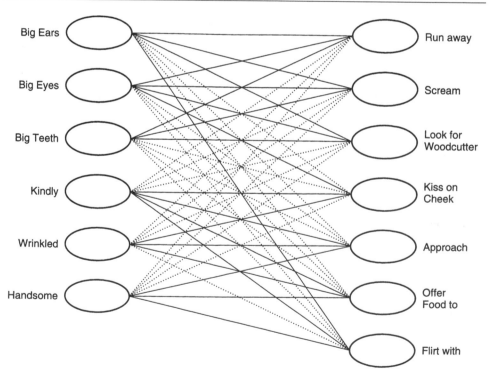

From Jones, W.P., & Hoskins, J. (October 1987). Back propagation: A generalized delta learning rule. *Byte Magazine*, pp. 155–162. Copyright 1987 by McGraw-Hill, Inc. Reprinted by permission.

The figure we have been discussing has only one layer of connections, and it can be shown mathematically that such a system is not capable of representing very complicated situations (Minsky & Papert, 1969). A better way of representing connections is to make use of **hidden units**, as in Figure 2.6. Suppose we have three hidden units that initially are connected to all input and all output units. The strength of the connections is arbitrarily determined at first. The figure represents the state of a system after it has been trained. Once again, the solid lines represent positive connections and the dotted lines indicate negative connections. As a result of a number of trials, the hidden units develop appropriate connections between input and output units. They come to represent our concepts of the three creatures that Little Red Riding Hood encounters, and 'it is often the case that hidden units . . . will come to represent useful abstractions of the outside world' (Jones & Hoskins, 1987, p. 160).

A big difference between connectionism and older information-processing approaches is that knowledge is embodied in the connections that make up the network rather than in a series of information-processing stages. Connectionist models are quite good at simulating many cognitive processes, and we examine some of these models in succeeding chapters.

In order to get a deeper understanding of how connectionist models actually work, you would do well to consult Michael R. Dawson's (2005) book. The book provides a framework allowing you to make use of the programs at Dawson's site at www.bcp.psych.ualberta.ca/%7emike/Software/James/index.html. There you can download programs that will enable you to explore connectionist networks, from very simple ones to rather more complex ones.

■ Cognitive Neuroscience

Cognitive neuroscience draws on several disciplines, including biology, linguistics, philosophy, and psychology, in an attempt to provide an integrated understanding of the mind and the brain (Gold & Stoljar, 1999). We will begin by examining some classic attempts to provide such an integration.

The Relation between Mind and Brain

We noted in Chapter 1 that the brain is often seen as the 'organ of the mind'. However, specifying the exact relation between mind and brain is far from easy, and debate on this issue is very much alive and ongoing (e.g., Noë & Thompson, 2004). Some of the more traditional attempts to formulate an answer to the mind/brain relation include **interactionism**, **epiphenomenalism**, **parallelism**, and **isomorphism**. In what follows, it is important to distinguish between 'consciousness' and 'mind'. Consciousness is the narrower concept, often taken to mean what we are aware of at any point in time. Mind is the broader concept. It includes consciousness, but also

Figure 2.6 A Connectionist Network with Hidden Units.

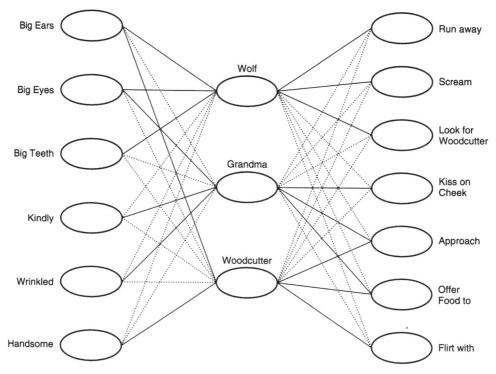

From Jones, W.P., & Hoskins, J. (October 1987). Back propagation: A generalized delta learning rule. *Byte Magazine*, pp. 155–162. Copyright 1987 by McGraw-Hill, Inc. Reprinted by permission.

includes processes that may take place outside of our awareness. Both of these concepts are the focus of intense research activity, and consequently have no meaning that is universally agreed upon.

Interactionism is linked with Descartes (1596–1650), who maintained that mind and brain were separate substances that interacted with and influenced each other. Descartes even postulated a site in the centre of the brain—the pineal gland—at which this interaction was supposed to take place (Finger, 1994, p. 26). Ingenious though it was, Descartes's specific solution to the mind/brain problem was not widely adopted by subsequent investigators (Finger, 2000, p. 80). However, there are recent examples of eminent psychologists who have adopted interactionist positions. One such example is Nobel Prize winner Roger Sperry, whose work is discussed below.

Epiphenomenalism maintains that the mind is simply a by-product of brain processes and has no causal role in determining behaviour. T.H. Huxley (1825–1895) illustrated epiphenomenalism by means of the following analogy. Consciousness is to the brain as the steam from a steam whistle is to a coal-powered locomotive. Just as you would not discover much about the locomotive by studying the steam from the whistle, so you would not discover much about the brain by examining what goes on in the mind. Many twentieth-century psychologists adopted positions similar to epiphenomenalism, believing that consciousness was irrelevant to an understanding of behaviour (e.g., Skinner, 1989).

Parallelism found its purest expression in the work of G.T. Fechner (1801–1887), whose studies of the relationships between events in the external world and the mind and brain have not lost any of their relevance (Dehaene, 2003; Link, 1994; Murray, 1993). For the parallelist, mind and brain are two aspects of the same reality. For all events in the mind there will be corresponding events in the brain. Notice that if mental events are correlated with brain events then one might learn something of value about the brain by studying mental events. Having persons introspect while at the same time recording events in their brains might provide insight into the meaning of those brain events (Jack & Roepstorff, 2002).

Isomorphism can be traced to Gestalt psychologists such as Wolfgang Köhler (1887–1967). 'Gestalt' means form or configuration. Gestalt psychologists argued that consciousness does not consist simply of one event after another but tends to be organized into a coherent whole. Some still maintain that this is a fundamental property of consciousness (e.g., Searle, 2000, p. 9). The doctrine of isomorphism holds that an experience and its corresponding brain process share the same pattern (e.g., Lehar, 2003). The difference between parallelism and isomorphism is that the latter requires more than a simple point-for-point correspondence between mental events and brain events. Rather, 'psychological facts and the underlying events in the brain resemble each other in all their structural characteristics' (Köhler, 1969, p. 64). Figure 2.7 is an example often used to convey this hypothesis. It is called a Necker cube, named after Louis Albert Necker (1832/1964), who was the first to remark on its psychologically interesting properties. When you focus on the cube face labelled ABCD, then that face seems to be in the foreground. However, the figure can reverse itself, with the face labelled EFGH coming to the foreground. This is an important example because the 'external stimulus is constant but . . . the internal subjective experience varies' (Searle,

Figure 2.7 A Necker Cube.

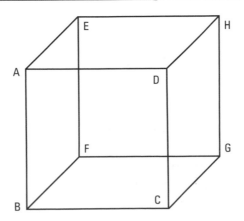

2000, p. 15). For each subjective experience the parts of the cube are organized differently. When the cube switches from one organization to the other, there must also be a corresponding change in the structure of the underlying brain process. Köhler's idea was that such alterations were produced as a result of prolonged inspection of a figure. The cortical representation of the figure becomes fatigued, or only weakly capable of supporting electrical fields, and so another part of the cortex then begins to represent the figure. As the cortical representation changes, so too does one's perception of it. Although Köhler's specific hypothesis was discredited, the relation between such 'Gestalt switches' and the underlying brain organization still remains the focus of considerable research interest (e.g., Kornmeier & Bach, 2004; Long & Toppino, 2004; Parker, Krug, & Cumming, 2003; Toppino, 2003).

There are numerous more recent alternatives to and variations of the preceding formulations (e.g., Baars, 2002), and we will consider some of them as we go along. However, we should not expect solutions to come easily to such a long-standing and difficult problem. The following quotation from the brilliant neuroanatomist Larry Swanson (2003) helps us appreciate what we are up against.

> Gram for gram, the brain is the far and away the most complex object we know of in the universe, and we simply haven't figured out its basic plan yet—despite its supreme importance and a great deal of effort. There is nothing equivalent to the periodic table of the elements, relativity, or the theory of evolution for organizing and explaining a large (but still woefully incomplete and often contradictory) body of information about brain structure and function. No Mendeleyev, Einstein, or Darwin has succeeded in grasping and articulating the general principles of its architecture; no one has presented a coherent theory or model of its functional organization. (p. 2)

Given the magnitude of the challenge, it is fortunate indeed that we do not need to decide the mind/brain issue in order to discover extremely interesting and suggestive correlations between psychological functions and brain activity. In what follows we will outline some of the ways in which the study of the brain can facilitate the inquiries of cognitive psychologists.

■ Methods in Cognitive Neuroscience

The Study of Brain Injuries

Brain injuries can be natural experiments that provide evidence for the localization of one or more functions. It may be possible to relate the symptoms displayed by brain-injured patients to parts of the brain that have been damaged. The study of cases of brain injury is seldom neat and tidy, and it is difficult for such studies to yield definitive evidence concerning localization of function. However, they are certainly more informative than the phrenological studies that we considered in the first chapter.

A classic study of the consequences of brain injury is Paul Broca's (1824–1880) investigation of the loss of the ability to express ideas by means of speech. The plight of the sort of people Broca studied is that they often know what it is they want to say, but they are unable to do so. While ordinary people are often dissatisfied with their ability to put their thoughts into speech, imagine how frustrating it would be to lose this ability more or less entirely. This disability is often called **Broca's aphasia**. Broca (1861/1966) described a patient who fit this pattern of being unable to speak, but still apparently able to understand what was said to him. An autopsy showed severe damage to the part of the left hemisphere labelled B in Figure 2.8, which has since become known as **Broca's area**. These results were subsequently replicated by Broca himself, as well as by others.

There is another class of patients who are able to speak, but unable to comprehend what is said to them. In extreme cases, these patients may ramble incoherently, their words bearing no obvious relation to thought. Karl Wernicke (1848–1905) studied 10 such cases and found that the lesions apparently responsible for their symptoms were located in the left hemisphere in the area labelled W in Figure 2.8. This area became known as **Wernicke's area**, and the corresponding disorder as **Wernicke's aphasia**.

Although Broca and Wernicke made lasting contributions to the problem of localization of function, discoveries such as theirs cannot be interpreted in any straightforward way. It is tempting to believe that Broca's area is responsible for speech production and Wernicke's area for speech comprehension, but such a simple

Figure 2.8 Broca's (B) and Wernicke's (W) areas.

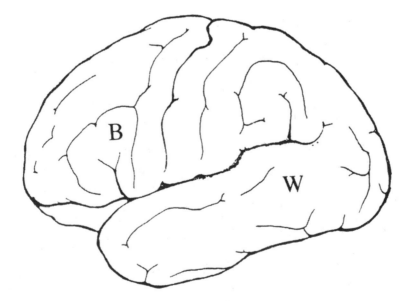

Adapted from Trevarthen, C. (1987). Brian development. In R.L. Gregory (Ed.), *The Oxford companion to the mind*. Oxford: Oxford University Press.

conclusion is untenable. For one thing, the aphasias are not particularly well defined and 'we now appreciate that clinical aphasic syndromes are comprised of variable clusters of symptoms' (Poeppel & Hickock, 2004, p. 4). It is difficult to see how such ill-defined phenomena could be regulated by a precisely located part of the brain. More importantly, the exact location of, for example, Wernicke's area is difficult to determine on the basis of anatomy alone (Cacioppo et al., 2003, p. 654). Even more importantly, 'modern work has identified areas outside of the classical regions that are implicated in language processing' (Poeppel & Hickock, 2004, p. 5). Although Broca's and Wernicke's areas combine to form 'an image with iconic status in neuroscience, [that] forms the basis of a neurolinguistic model that has informed research for almost 150 years and constitutes the canonical model of brain and language taught across disciplines' (Poeppel & Hickock, 2004, p. 1), they cannot bear the full weight of explanation. The general lesson to be learned from studies of the relation between the loss of psychological functions and brain damage is that such studies can be a very suggestive source of evidence, but are seldom definitive or complete (Marshall & Fink, 2003).

Surgical Intervention

We saw in Chapter 1 how Lashley used the method of ablation to investigate localization of function. Roger Sperry (1913–1994) also used surgical techniques, but in a more precise manner. Sperry received the Nobel Prize in 1981, in part for his work on **interhemispheric transfer**. (You can read more about Sperry's life and work at the Nobel Prize website http://nobelprize.org/medicine/articles/sperry/). As shown in Figure 2.9, this work initially involved severing the optical chiasm in cats with the result that information coming from the right eye was projected only onto the visual areas of the right hemisphere, and information from the left eye projected only onto the visual areas of the left hemisphere. Sperry also severed the corpus callosum, which 'plays the dominant role in interhemispheric interaction' (Hoptman & Davidson, 1994, p. 2). When the corpus callosum is severed, then information transfer between the hemispheres is disrupted. Under these conditions, each hemisphere appeared to be 'a separate mental domain operating with complete disregard—indeed with a complete lack of awareness—of what went on in the other. The **split brain** animal behaved . . . as if it had two entirely separate brains' (Sperry, 1964, p. 43).

Sperry's work broadened considerably when he was able to study humans whose corpus callosum had been severed by neurosurgeons in the hope of alleviating epilepsy. In a series of clever experiments, Sperry and his associates claimed to have shown not only that 'the two hemispheres of the brain had unique capabilities' but also that 'the combination of both hemispheres working together produced a unified state of consciousness that amounted to more than the simple additive effects of the two hemispheres alone' (Puente, 1995, p. 941). Sperry's work led to an avalanche of research attempting to discover the 'unique capabilities' of each hemisphere. As we have already seen, the work of Broca and Wernicke suggested that the left hemisphere was typically associated with linguistic functions. Split-brain research seemed to many to lead to the more general conclusion that the left hemisphere managed 'analytic' (e.g., verbal,

Figure 2.9 Effect of Sectioning Crossed Fibres in Optic Chiasm.

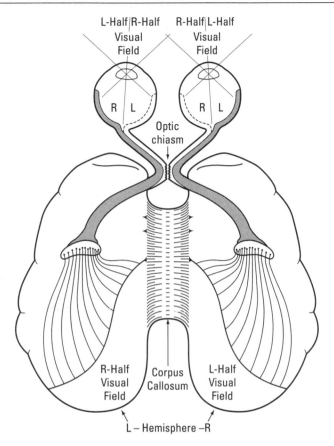

From Sperry, R.W. (June 1961). Cerebral organization and behaviour. *Science, 133*, p. 1750. Copyright 1961 by the American Association for the Advancement of Science. Reprinted by permission of the author's estate.

rational) tasks and the right hemisphere 'holistic' (e.g., non-verbal, intuitive) tasks (e.g., Jaynes, 1976, pp. 100–125; Martindale, 1981, pp. 286–287). However, it subsequently became clear that there was no simple division of labour between the two hemispheres in an intact brain (e.g., Gardner, 1982, pp. 278–285; Hoptman & Davidson, 1994). Indeed, 'because of their complexity, the actual organization of intracerebral connections may well lie beyond the limits of human comprehension' (Swanson, 2003, p. 166). While the split brain is a fascinating object of study, it is difficult to see how one can make very general conclusions on the basis of such an atypical set of cases.

In the final phase of his career, Sperry's attention turned to issues of the greatest generality, such as the nature of consciousness (Erdmann & Stover, 1991/2000; Stover & Erdmann, 2000). Sperry argued that consciousness was an **emergent property** of the brain, meaning that it is not reducible to or predictable from other features of the brain. Once consciousness emerges, then, it can have an influence on lower-level functions, a process that may be termed **emergent causation** (Erdmann & Stover, 1991/2000, p. 50).

Sperry (1987, p. 165) recognized a 'mutual interaction between neural and mental events' such that 'the brain physiology determines the mental events' but is in turn 'governed by the higher subjective properties of the enveloping mental events.' The mind was seen as **supervenient**, meaning that mental states may 'exert downward control over their constituent neuronal events—at the same time that they are being determined by them' (Sperry, 1988, p. 609). Although Sperry's speculations on the mind/brain relation were greeted with skepticism by his colleagues, they nonetheless were an important part of the discussion that led to a more open consideration of the problem of consciousness.

Event-Related Potentials

The brain emits electrical signals that can be recorded by means of electrodes placed on the scalp. Suppose you record the electrical signals that occur after the onset of a stimulus, such as the presentation of a word. The resultant pattern of electrical activity is called an **event-related potential (ERP)** and can be represented by waveforms like those shown in Figure 2.10. A single trial is usually not enough to provide unambiguous information, but when the electrical responses to a stimulus are averaged over a great many trials, interesting patterns may emerge. One such pattern is shown in Figure 2.10, which characterizes the results of studies reviewed by Rugg (1995). In these studies, the experimental paradigm consists of initially presenting to participants a series of

Figure 2.10 Differences in Neural Activity for Remembered versus Forgotten Items.

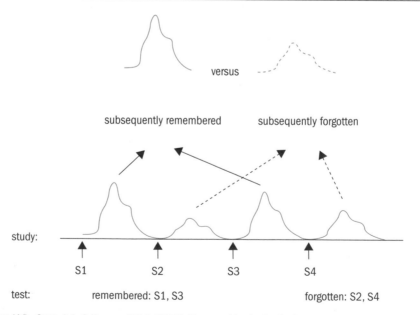

From Rugg, M.D., Otten, L.J., & Henson, R.N.A. (2003). The neural basis of episodic memory: Evidence from functional neuroimaging. In A. Parker, A. Derrington, & C. Blakemore (Eds.), *The physiology of cognitive processes*, figure 10.1 (pp. 211–233). By permission of Oxford University Press.

items (such as words, labelled S1, S2, S3, S4 in Figure 2.10) and recording the event-related potential arising from each item. Note the waveforms arising after each of the items in Figure 2.10. Subsequently, the participants are asked to recall the items. The experimenter then sorts the items into those that were recalled and those that were not, and looks for differences in the event-related potentials for each class of item. Figure 2.10 suggests that the waveform for items that will be remembered is different from that for items that will be forgotten. So far so good—it looks as if the event-related potential can predict the subsequent recall of items. However, it is not easy to interpret event-related potentials in terms of the underlying cognitive process they represent. In this case, perhaps the different waveforms simply represent the fact that the participants pay attention to some items and ignore others (Rugg, Otten, & Henson, 2003, p. 213), or perhaps they represent more complex processes. In general, while event-related potentials can provide suggestive information, they need to be supplemented by other techniques in order to provide a more complete picture of brain processes.

Positron Emission Tomography

One assumption underlying **positron emission tomography (PET)** is that when a specific psychological function is engaged, then only those parts of the brain responsible for that function will also be engaged (Papanicolaou, 1998, p. 23). If a participant is given a specific cognitive task, the parts of the brain responsible for that task will 'work harder' than when the participant is not performing that task. When a part of the brain is active in this way, it will use up oxygen at a faster rate than when it is inactive. This will in turn require an increased blood flow to that area in order to replenish it with oxygen. PET takes advantage of this chain of events. The participant in a PET study is first given a radioactive substance that mingles with the blood and thus circulates to the brain. This procedure allows the detection of the flow of blood to particular areas of the brain. This information enables the construction of images that show which parts of the brain are particularly active in relation to the performance of different tasks.

One problem with PET methodology is that there are obvious limits on the amount of radiation to which a participant may be exposed, and therefore limits on how much information can be obtained from each participant. Although extremely popular until the mid-1990s, PET has given way to functional magnetic resonance imaging as a method of choice (Rugg, 2002, p. 59).

Functional Magnetic Resonance Imagery

One advantage of **functional magnetic resonance imaging (fMRI)** is that it does not depend on a radioactive signal. Moreover, data can be acquired more rapidly using fMRI than is possible using PET (Rugg, 1999, p. 22). The fMRI technique involves placing the participant's head inside a very large magnetic field. This causes atoms in the brain to become aligned with the magnetic field (Papanicolaou, 1998, p. 49). Changes in the flow of oxygenated blood can be picked up as alterations in the magnetic field. This information can in turn be used to construct an image of cortical activity. The following is an example of an fMRI study that bears on Broca's and Wernicke's areas.

In an experiment conducted by Bavalier et al. (1997), participants engaged in sentence reading and the viewing of consonant strings. Sentence reading 'has been acknowledged to invoke many different aspects of language processing', while 'the presentation of consonant strings is believed to activate only basic visual recognition routines. . . . The comparison of these two conditions should reveal brain areas concerned with . . . language processing' (Bavalier et al., 1997, p. 667). The results revealed wide individual differences in the pattern of activation shown by each of the eight participants. Examination of the pattern of activation that best characterized the entire group of participants did show that Broca's and Werrnicke's areas were more activated by the sentence-reading task than by the viewing of consonant strings. However, other areas were also consistently activated by sentence reading compared with consonant viewing. Bavelier et al. (2003, p. 678) concluded that language is not simply localized 'in a few cortically well-circumscribed areas'.

It is tempting to wish for a technique that constituted a 'magic bullet' that would precisely reveal the unique cortical locations for all psychological functions. If brain-imaging techniques were such a 'magic bullet', then they would be 'no more than a modern and extraordinarily expensive version of 19th century phrenology' (Raichle, 2003, p. 3959). However, the view of the brain that seems to be emerging is not at all phrenological. Marshall and Fink (2003) observed that 'there are suggestions from recent work that functional localization is not such a fixed property of brain regions as either lesion studies or early neuroimaging work might have suggested' (p. 56). They illustrate this point with respect to Broca's area. Neuroimaging studies have found that it plays 'a role in natural language syntactic processing (Caplan, Alpert, Waters, & Olivieri, 2000; Heim, Opitz, & Freiderichi, 2003), in processing musical syntax (Maess, Ko'lsch, Gunter, & Friederichi (2001), in the perception of rhythmic motion (Schubotz & von Cramon, 2001), in imaging movement trajectories (Binkofski, et al., 2000)', and so on. Marshall and Fink conclude that 'it is difficult to see how a single common function (localized in Broca's area) could underlie such a disparate collection of effects' (p. 56), and suggest that, at least to some extent, the interaction of different areas of the brain determines their function on a particular occasion. This point is reinforced by Cabeza and Nyberg (2003, p. 241), who observed that 'the vast majority of functional neuroimaging studies have investigated a single cognitive function. Yet, with the accumulation of functional neuroimaging data, it has become obvious that . . . the neural correlates of cognitive functions overlap considerably, with most brain regions being involved in a variety of cognitive functions.' Marshall and Fink (2003, p. 56) anticipate the development of 'new methods of measuring the functional integration of different brain regions' that will improve our current models of the brain.

One final comment on the methods and problems of cognitive neuropsychology is in order. We have been considering various methods for localizing cognitive processes in the brain. Most of the time we act as if we know what those cognitive processes are, and that the task is to find their brain correlates. However, if we reflect on it honestly, we must admit that if we had to make a list of basic cognitive processes we would not be able to do so in a way that met universal assent (Fodor, 2000; Marshall & Fink, 2003,

p. 54; Uttal, 2001). One of the most important goals of this text is to present current per-spectives on cognitive processes. We should expect that our understanding of the nature of cognitive processes and their relation to the brain will never be fixed once and for all. It is in the nature of science that our theories are always provisional and constantly evolving.

■ Ecological Validity

In standard information-processing models such as that in Figure 2.2, there is a lot of detail concerning the 'internal processing' required to make a stimulus meaningful. However, such models may not say very much about the information available in the stimulus itself. Other psychologists, such as J.J. Gibson (1904–1979), took more of an interest in the richness of the information provided by the environment in which people ordinarily find themselves. Gibson (1950, 1966) argued that the stimuli used by information-processing psychologists in their experiments were often impover-ished relative to the information available in the real world. Gibson argued for the creation of an **ecological approach** to perception that would describe environmental stimulation at the appropriate level. 'The environment consists of *opportunities* for perception, of *available* information, of potential stimuli. Not all opportunities are grasped, not all information is registered, not all stimuli excite receptors. But what the environment *affords* an individual in the way of discrimination is enormous, and this should be our first consideration' (Gibson, 1966, p. 23). Gibson described a num-ber of *stimulus gradients* that provided information about the environment. A gradi-ent is an 'increase or decrease of something along a given dimension' (Gibson, 1950, p. 73). Simple examples of stimulus gradients are given in Figure 2.11. It is easy to see the gradient on the left as a receding pathway and the converging lines on the right as a hallway. By looking around you, you can probably observe similar gradients,

Figure 2.11 Stimulus Gradients that Give Rise to the Perception of Depth.

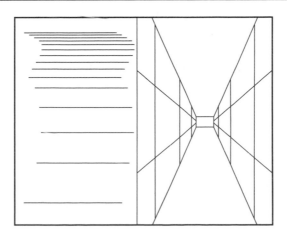

such as the changing distances between floorboards or the changing texture of a rug as it recedes from you (cf. Gibson, 1966, pp. 254–255). Gibson (1950, pp. 88–89) argued that these kinds of information are readily available in the environment, especially as we move around in it. The perceiver often does not need to add anything to the information available in the world.

Gibson also believed that the meaning of objects and events can be perceived by means of what he called **affordances**, by which he meant 'simply what things furnish, for good or ill' (Gibson, 1966, p. 285). Thus, stairs afford climbing, food affords eating, ice affords skating, and so on. Of course, one has to learn the affordances of objects, but affordances are still tied to the properties of objects. Gibson's is a theory, then, of **information pickup**, in which learning means becoming progressively more attuned to what the environment affords us.

Many psychologists expanded on Gibson's ecological approach, arguing that the study of cognition needed to become more **ecologically valid**. The concept of ecological validity was originally introduced by Egon Brunswik (1903–1955) (1956) to refer to the extent to which the information available to a perceiver is truly representative of the environment. Others have used 'ecological validity' in a broader sense to mean that cognitive psychologists should 'get out of the laboratory and study how individuals actually behave in the real world' (Kingstone, Smilek, Ristic, Friesen, & Eastwood, 2003, p. 179). An oft-cited example of an ecologically valid study is Bahrick's (1984) study of long-term retention of Spanish learned as a second language. Instead of studying what participants learn in a laboratory, Bahrick studied what ordinary people had learned in school.

The relative virtues of laboratory-based and ecological approaches to cognitive research have been hotly debated (e.g., Anderson & Bushman, 1997; Chayter & Scmitter-Edgecomb, 2003; Loftus, 1991; Neisser, 1978; Schmuckler, 2001). Whatever the merits of the case, many cognitive psychologists wish to do ecologically valid research, either in the 'real world' or by designing experiments that are more realistic than many of those done in the past. In order to guide those who wish to conduct ecologically valid research, Neisser (1976, p. 21) proposed a cyclical model of cognition. Rather than accept Gibson's view that the perceiver may simply pick up information available in the environment, Neisser suggested that the perceiver possesses a **schema** that represents what the person is likely to find in the environment. This schema directs the person's exploration of the environment. As the environment is explored, the person encounters information that is expected as well as information that is unexpected. The latter kind of information is capable of modifying the schema so as to increase the accuracy with which it represents the environment. Thus, the **perceptual cycle** begins with the schema directing exploration of the environment, which brings the person into contact with information, which in turn can correct the schema, and so on.

To see how this 'perceptual cycle' might work, consider Figures 2.12a and 2.12b. Halper (1997) noticed that the balconies of a building in Manhattan appear to tilt

Figure 2.12 Balconies on *The Future*, a Building in New York City.

From Halper, F. (1997). The illusion of *The Future*. *Perception, 26*, pp. 1321–1322. Reprinted with permission of the author.

upward. Obviously, it would be absurd to build balconies like that, so what is going on here? In terms of the perceptual cycle, we might describe this process as follows. Our schema is our cognitive model of the environment, constructed over time through our interactions with that environment. Our schema provides us with rather general expectations of what we are likely to find in the environment, although we need not be aware of the assumptions we make about what we will find. One of our expectations is that balconies will be square or rectangular (i.e., bounded by right angles). We automatically impose this expectation on the buildings in Figures 2.12a and 2.12b. As a consequence we perceive the orientation of the balconies of the building in the foreground as tilting upward, as they would have to be if they were rectangular. As we explore this building from a different angle, our expectations may even lead us to see the balconies as tilting downward, as in Figure 2.12c! However, by continuing to explore the situation, we can come to an understanding of the true state of affairs. In fact, 'the balconies are parallelograms vertically perpendicular to the face of the building' (Halper, 1997, p. 1322), as can be discerned in Figure 2.12d. Our schema for buildings has become modified and now includes the possibility that balconies can have other than right angles. In general, the perceptual cycle allows us to become increasingly sophisticated in our dealings with the environment.

■ What Comes Next?

We have identified several different approaches to the study of cognition. These approaches have been applied to the various cognitive processes that we will now go on to examine. Sometimes a theory or a method is used to guide research on a particular problem, such as memory, attention, or problem-solving. Such research is relatively theory-driven. Thus, we will see all of the approaches we have considered in action in the following chapters. However, research is not always directed by a general theory of cognition.

Sometimes research on a cognitive process such as memory, attention, or problem-solving is guided by an interest in the area itself, rather than in seeing whether or not a theory is right. Such research is relatively data-driven; it is concerned only with understanding how a particular cognitive process works.

Obviously, theory and data should match up in the end. However, we are not yet at a point in the study of cognition where one theory matches up with all the data. Rather, there are several theories, and lots of data, and these do not always coincide. I wish the study of cognition was simpler than it is, but you should get a picture of cognition that is reasonably accurate, even if not very tidy.

In what follows, we will adopt an eclectic approach, with no particular bias in favour of one or another orientation. All orientations will be discussed as complementary approaches to cognition, and we will try to understand the strong and weak aspects of each.

■ Questions for Study and Discussion

1. Outline the flow of information in Atkinson and Shiffrin's *modal model*. Briefly criticize these models from either a connectionist or an ecological viewpoint.
2. Review the approaches to the mind/ brain issue given in your text (including Sperry). Which of these approaches (if any) do you prefer? If you do not prefer any of them, what is your alternative?
3. Briefly describe Gibson's approach, and show how Neisser adapted it in his concept of the *perceptual cycle*. In your review, give at least one example of an affordance that is not given in your text.

■ Key Concepts

Affordances The possible functions or uses of stimuli in the real world.

Artificial intelligence Programs that mimic the intelligent behaviour of people.

Bit Short for binary digit—an event that occurs in a situation with two equally likely outcomes provides one bit of information.

Broca's aphasia A deficit in the ability to produce speech as a result of damage to **Broca's area** in the left hemisphere.

Brown-Peterson task An experimental paradigm in which subjects are given a set of items and then a number. Subjects immediately begin counting backward by 3's from the number. After a specific interval, subjects are asked to recall the original items.

Channel capacity The maximum amount of information that can be transmitted by an information-processing device.

Connectionism The theory that cognitive processes are regulated by complex systems consisting of a large number of interconnected elements.

Ecological approach Forms of psychological inquiry that reflect conditions in the real world.

Ecologically valid Studies that generalize to conditions in the real world.

Emergent causation In Sperry's sense, once the mind emerges from the brain, it then has the power to effect other processes.

Emergent property In Sperry's sense, mind comes about as a result of brain processes, but is not itself a component of the brain. This means that the mind is not reducible to or predictable from other features of the brain

Epiphenomenalism Mind is a superfluous by-product of bodily functioning.

Event-related potential Recordings of electrical signals from the brain that occur after the onset of a stimulus.

Functional magnetic resonance imaging (fMRI) A non-radioactive, magnetic procedure for detecting the flow of oxygenated blood to various parts of the brain.

Hebb rule A connection between two neurons takes place only if both neurons are firing at about the same time.

Hidden units A layer of units that mediates between **input units** and **output units**.

Icon The initial, brief representation of the information contained in a visual stimulus.

Information An event provides information to the extent it reduces prior uncertainty.

Information pickup The process whereby we perceive information directly.

Interactionism Mind and brain are separate substances that interact with and influence each other.

Interhemispheric transfer Communication between the hemispheres enabled in large part by the corpus callosum.

Isomorphism Mental events and neural events share the same structure.

Long-term store Relatively permanent, enduring memories.

Mental chronometry Measuring how long different cognitive processes take.

Neural networks A system of connections between elements that models connections between neurons in the nervous system.

Parallel distributed processing Another name for connectionist models that allow parallel processing.

Parallelism Mind and brain are two aspects of the same reality and flow in parallel.

Parallel processing and serial processing In connectionist systems, it is assumed that many connections may be active at the same time, unlike **serial processing** in which only one activity may take place at any one time.

Perceptual cycle The process whereby our schema not only guides exploration of the world, but is also shaped by what it finds there.

Positron emission tomography The participant is first given a radioactive substance that mingles with the blood and thus circulates to the brain. This procedure allows the detection of the flow of blood to particular areas of the brain.

Primary memory (William James) Consists of what we are aware of in the 'immediately present moment' and is thus also often termed **immediate memory**.

Schema Our expectations concerning what we are likely to find as we explore the world.

Secondary memory (William James) The knowledge of a former state of mind after it has already once been absent from awareness for some period of time.

Sensory register Where information is very briefly stored in forms like the **icon**.

Short-term store The contents of awareness at any one time; sometimes also called **working memory**.

Span of immediate memory The number of items we can hold in mind at the same time.

Split brain A condition created by severing the corpus callosum.

Supervenient In Sperry's sense, mental states may influence neuronal events while being influenced by them.

Turing's test or **imitation game** A procedure designed to determine whether or not the output of a computer can be distinguished from that of a person.

Wernicke's aphasia A deficit in the ability to comprehend speech as a result of damage to **Wernicke's area** in the left hemisphere.

■ Links to Other Chapters

Primary memory
Chapter 3 (pattern recognition)
Chapter 4 (levels of processing)
Icon
Chapter 6 (synaesthesia)
Mental chronometry
Chapter 5 (semantic memory)
Artificial intelligence
Chapter 9 (artificial intelligence approaches to problem-solving)
Connectionism
Chapter 3 (pattern recognition)
Chapter 5 (connectionist models of memory)
Broca's area
Chapter 8 (evolution of language)
Left and right hemispheres
Chapter 6 (mental rotation)
Event-related potential (ERP)
Chapter 6 (mental rotation)
Chapter 9 (insight)
Chapter 11 (negativity bias)
Positron emission tomography (PET)
Chapter 3 (Stroop task)
Functional magnetic resonance imaging (fMRI)
Chapter 3 (preattentive processes, Stroop task)

Chapter 4 (levels of processing)
Chapter 6 (dual coding)
Chapter 11 (perception of streaks)
Chapter 12 (expertise)

Ecological approach and ecological validity
Chapter 3 (implicit perception and inattentional blindness)
Chapter 4 (ecological approaches to memory)
Chapter 5 (involuntary semantic memories)
Chapter 6 (criticisms of classical concept research)
Chapter 9 (in vivo/in vitro methods)
Chapter 11 (ecological rationality)
Chapter 12 (practical intelligence)
Chapter 14 (ecologically valid approaches)
Affordances
Chapter 7 (prototypicality)
Chapter 14 (affordances)
Schema
Chapter 3 (task switching)
Chapter 4 (schema theories, Bartlett, body schema, phantom limbs, scripts)
Perceptual cycle
Chapter 3 (attention capture and inattentional blindness)
Chapter 6 (images as anticipations)

■ Further Reading

For excellent histories of the emergence of cognitive psychology, see the following: Baars, B.J. (1986). *The cognitive revolution in psychology*. New York: Guilford Press; Gardner, H. (1985). *The mind's new science*. New York: Basic Books; and Hilgard, E.R. (1987). *Psychology in America: An historical survey*. New York: Harcourt Brace Jovanovich.

A famous critical discussion of computer simulation may be found in Searle, J.R. (1980). Minds, brains, and programs. *Behavioral and Brain Sciences, 3*, 417–424. A very readable account of some of his views is Searle, J.R. (1999, April 8). I married a computer. *New York Review of Books*, pp. 34–38. A sophisticated analysis of many of the issues surrounding computer simulation is by Green, C.D. (1996). Fodor, functions, physics, and fantasyland: Is AI a Mickey Mouse discipline? *Journal of Experimental and Theoretical Artificial Intelligence, 8*, 95–106.

A basic introduction to neural networks is Hinton, G.E. (1992, September). How neural networks learn from experience. *Scientific American, 267*, 144–151. Another introduction to connectionism that also shows some of its broader implications is Smith, E.R. (1996). What do connectionism and social psychology have to offer each other? *Journal of Personality and Social Psychology, 79*, 893–912. An influential book by a connectionist enthusiast is Churchland, P.M. (1996). *The engine of reason, the seat of the soul*. Chichester: Wiley. Rock, I., & Palmer, S. (1990, December). The legacy of Gestalt psychology. *Scientific American, 263*, 84–90, provides a suggestive review of the contributions of Gestalt psychology that shows its similarity to some aspects of connectionism.

The following are overviews of the mind/brain issue by four eminent scientists and one philosopher: Crick, F., & Koch, C. (2003). A framework for consciousness. *Nature Neuroscience, 6*, 119–126; Edelman, G.M. (2004). *Wider than the sky: The phenomenal gift of consciousness*. New Haven: Yale University Press; LeDoux, J. (2002). *Synaptic self: How our brains become who we are*. New York: Penguin; and Chalmers, D.J. (1996). *The conscious mind: In search of a fundamental theory*. New York: Oxford University Press.

Not everyone is enthusiastic about the achievements of cognitive neuroscience. A well-argued and well-informed critique is Bennett, M.R., & Hacker, P.M.S. (2003). *Philosophical foundations of neuroscience*. Oxford: Blackwell. They argue, in a way that is reminiscent of Wittgenstein (1953, p. 232e), that in cognitive neuroscience 'problem and method pass one another by.' An oversimplified paraphrase of that point is that neuroscience is not addressing the problems it thinks it is addressing. If you want to understand Bennett and Hacker's line of argument, you would do well to become acquainted with Wittgenstein first. However, understanding Wittgenstein's approach is itself no mean achievement.

For a basic introduction to event-related potentials, see Begleiter, H. (1977). *Evoked brain potentials and behavior*. New York: Plenum. N.K. Logothetis is one of the most highly respected workers in the field of fMRI. The following paper is demanding but worth the effort. Logothetis, N.K. (2003). The neural basis of the blood-oxygen-level-dependent functional magnetic resonance imaging signal. In A. Parker, A. Derrington, & C. Blakemore (Eds.), *The physiology of cognitive processes* (pp. 62–116). Oxford: Oxford University Press.

A set of papers presented in appreciation of Neisser's contribution to ecologically valid studies is by Winograd, E., Fivush, R., & Hirst, W. (Eds.). (1999). *Ecological approaches to cognition*. Mahwah, NJ: Erlbaum.

Chapter 3

The Varieties
of Attention

■ James's Description of Attention

At the turn of the twentieth century, Harvard's William James was the leading American psychologist (Cattell, 1903). James's great textbook, *Principles of psychology* (1890/1983) contains a chapter on attention that many psychologists are still fond of citing (e.g., Johnston & Dark, 1986; LaBerge, 1990; Fernandez-Duque & Johnson, 2002). Here is one of James's (1890/1983) most famous passages concerning attention.

> Everyone knows what attention is. It is the taking possession by the mind, in clear and vivid form, of one out of what seem several simultaneously possible objects or trains of thought. . . . It implies withdrawal from some things in order to deal effectively with others, and is a condition which has a real opposite in the confused, dazed, scatterbrained state which . . . is called distraction (pp. 381–382).

At the turn of the twenty-first century, not everyone was as confident as James had been concerning the definition of attention. Harold Pashler (1998), an eminent contemporary cognitive psychologist, went so far as to say that 'No one knows what attention is, and . . . there may even not be an "it" there to be known about (although of course there might be)' (p.1).

Pashler's statement exemplifies the sophistication that cognitive psychologists now have as a result of over 100 years of studying cognitive processes. We no longer think that just because there is one word (e.g., 'attention') that there must be one process to which the word corresponds. 'Attention' refers to a variety of possible processes and methods for studying them. Even James acknowledged this when he called a section of his chapter 'The Varieties of Attention'. Some of the varieties we will address in this chapter include: selecting what to attend to; not attending to what we could attend to; involuntary attention; attempting to attend to more than one thing at a time; switching our attention between tasks; and the possibility of perceiving without attention or awareness.

■ Preattentive Processes

Anne Treisman has been an influential student of attention for many years. We will begin by considering her work on **feature integration theory (FIT)** (Treisman, 1986; Treisman & Gelade, 1980; Treisman & Gormican, 1988). Her approach is based on the assumption that before we can attend to objects in the world we must extract the features that make up these objects. The process of feature extraction is said to operate outside of awareness, and so is called **preattentive processing**. The preattentive processes extract features such as the colour and orientation of events in the external world.

In order to identify the basic features that we extract, Treisman relied on a clever series of demonstrations. If a feature **pops out** of a display, then that feature is a good candidate for being a basic property out of which we construct perceived objects. For example, in Figure 3.1 the boundary between the tilted T's and the upright T's *pops out* at you. However, you may not notice the boundary between the T's and L's until it is pointed out to you. This suggests that a property such as the orientation of a line is extracted preattentively. Treisman argued that individual features are extracted independent of one another. Subsequently, they are combined to form the world we experience and to which we can attend (Treisman, 1996).

It has been suggested by some that the concept of preattentive processing may have outlived its usefulness (e.g., De Lillo, Kawahara, Zuvic, & Visser, 2001), and it is true that Treisman's FIT theory is far from being universally accepted (Quinlan, 2003). Others have pointed out that, however we explain it, the existence of preattentive processing is almost a logical necessity. We only pay attention to some of the things to which we could potentially attend. The process that ends up providing us with objects to which we then attend is necessarily 'preattentive'. 'Preattentive processing may represent a fast but relatively high-level abstraction of the visual scene. On the basis of that abstraction, attention selects specific objects for further processing' (Wolfe, 2003, p. 71).

Treisman used the metaphor of attention as being a kind of spotlight on certain aspects of the experienced world. As the spotlight moves, different parts of the visual

Figure 3.1 How Many Boundaries Are There?

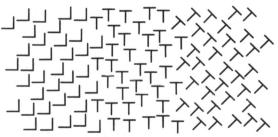

From Beck, J. (1966). Effect of orientation and shape similarity on perceptual grouping. *Perception and Psychophysics*, *1*, pp. 300–301. Copyright Psychonomic Society, Inc. Reprinted by permission.

field are 'highlighted' (i.e., attended to). The spotlight metaphor can be grounded in neuroscience (Shipp, 2004). For example, 'objects close or adjacent to each other in the world activate brain areas close to or adjacent to each other in the visual cortex' (Fernandez-Duque & Johnson, 2002, p. 155).

The spotlight metaphor suggests that shifting attention from the centre to the periphery of the visual field, or vice versa, should yield corresponding shifts of activation in the visual cortex. In a functional magnetic resonance imaging (fMRI) study, Brefczynski and DeYoe (1999) asked participants to fixate a spot on a screen. Participants were also asked to simultaneously monitor targets as they appeared in different locations on the screen. Activation of different areas of the visual cortex was recorded as participants shifted their attention to different locations on the screen. The location of the attended targets on the screen had a high correlation to the corresponding locations in the visual cortex. It is as if the 'searchlight' of attention picked out targets that were then represented in the analogous areas of the visual cortex. However, this is only a small part of the story of the relation between attention and brain processes (Pessoa, Kastner, & Ungerleider, 2003), about which we will have more to say as we go along.

■ Pattern Recognition

The phrase **pattern recognition** was adopted from computer science, where it was invented to refer to a computer's ability to identify configurations such as the account numbers on bank cheques. In an analogous manner, people are also able to identify many of the configurations with which they are presented. You are able to recognize the words in this sentence as words and not just meaningless squiggles. To take another example, when we are confronted with a small cylindrical object with a handle, then we can recognize it as a *coffee cup*. Currently, machines outperform humans in 'highly constrained' situations such as 'ensuring alignment of printed labels on medicine bottles', but humans outperform machines in 'real world tasks' such as face recognition (Sinha, 2002).

Recognizing a configuration involves the relationship between perception and memory. This process is sketched in Figure 3.2. Suppose you are shown the letter *a* on one occasion. We can imagine a sequence of events whereby you *perceive* the letter *a*, and then a memory trace of the letter is formed. The phrase **memory trace** simply refers to the trace of our experience that is left in memory (Rock & Ceraso, 1964). (We will have more to say about memory traces below, and will explore them in detail in the next chapter.) In order to *recognize* the letter *a*, should it appear on another occasion, my perception of *a* must somehow make contact with the memory trace of *a*. The process whereby a perception makes contact with a memory trace is called the **Höffding function**, named after a nineteenth-century Danish psychologist (Neisser, 1967, p. 50).

Several theories have been advanced to explain the process of pattern recognition. Traditionally, two theories, **feature detection** and **template matching**, have been the subject of the most research.

Figure 3.2 The Höffding Function.

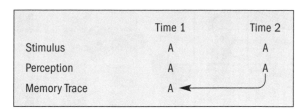

	Time 1	Time 2
Stimulus	A	A
Perception	A	A
Memory Trace	A	

Feature Detection

One approach to pattern recognition had its origin in the **feature detection theory** of Selfridge (1959; Neisser, 1967, p. 71). A simple version of his pattern recognition model was called **pandemonium**. This model consists of three levels and has a whimsical quality. At the bottom level are the data, or image, in which a pattern of features is represented. These features might be things like size, colour, shape, and so on. The next level consists of so-called *cognitive demons*. These are like little elves who examine the pattern of attributes in the image. Each demon is ready to detect a particular pattern. Thus, there might be a demon for detecting apples, one for detecting oranges, one for detecting baseballs, and so on. If a cognitive demon thinks that it detects the pattern it is ready for, then it shouts. The more similar that the pattern in the image is to the one the demon is looking for, then the louder the demon shouts. All the demons may be shouting at the same time with different levels of intensity, depending on their similarity to the data in the image. These shouts create a real ruckus, and thus the model is called pandemonium. Sitting on top of this hullabaloo is the decision demon, which selects the cognitive demon that is shouting loudest. This choice constitutes the pattern that is recognized.

Of course, in practice the process would be much more complicated than this. However, the basic ideas of Selfridge's model, and others like it, have been very influential. The notions that objects and events are made up of features, and that in identifying them we pay attention to clusters of features, have been embedded in many theories of pattern recognition.

Now examine Figure 3.3. All of those strings of letters are somewhat ambiguous. How we interpret each letter depends on the interpretation of all the other letters, a point that was made by Selfridge (1959). This observation, and others like it, has formed the basis for connectionist approaches to pattern recognition. Connectionist approaches, which you should recall from Chapter 2, make use of parallel distributed processing (PDP). PDP models 'assume that information processing takes place through the interactions of a large number of simple processing elements called units, each sending excitatory and inhibitory signals to other units' (McClelland, Rumelhart, & Hinton, 1986).

Figure 3.3 Examples of Ambiguous Letter Strings.

From Rumelhart, D.E., & McClelland, J.L. (Eds.). (1986). *Parallel distributed processing: Explorations in the microstructure of cognition: Vol. 1.* Cambridge, Mass.: MIT Press, p. 8. Copyright 1986 by the Massachusetts Institute of Technology. Reprinted by permission.

PDP models are attempts to specify the microstructure of cognition. That is, they are interested in working out detailed models on a highly specific level of the way in which processes like pattern recognition work (McClelland & Rumelhart, 1986a, 1986b; Rumelhart & McClelland, 1986). For example, Figure 3.4 shows a part of McClelland and Rumelhart's (1981) model of context effects in letter perception. This model is designed to explain the sort of phenomena illustrated in Figure 3.3. Notice that all the units in the model are very richly interconnected.

At the bottom of the model are units that correspond to basic features of letters. A unit is activated by being present in the letter being perceived. Suppose you are shown a four-letter word, like *trap*. The first unit, which is a horizontal line at the top of a letter, is consistent with the hypothesis that the first letter is a *t*. This hypothesis is also consistent with the possibility that the word is *trap*, but it is inconsistent with the possibility that the word is *able*. Thus, if the first letter is taken as a *t*, then that will facilitate the hypothesis that the word is *trap*, but inhibit the hypothesis that the word is *able*. The hypothesis that the word is *trap* will in turn facilitate the perception of the second letter as being *r*, but inhibit the perception that the second letter is *b*. Excitatory and inhibitory connections between units determine what you end up seeing. Thus, when you look at

Figure 3.4 McClelland and Rumelhart's Pattern Recognition Model.

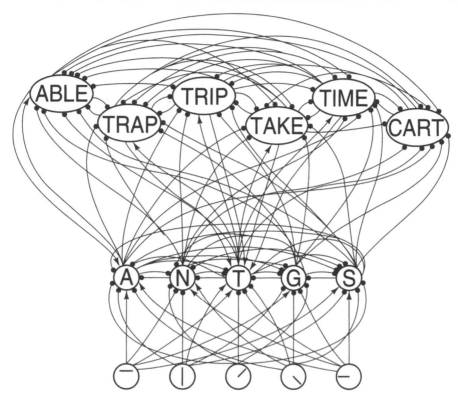

From McClelland, J.L., & Rumelhart, D.E. (1981). An interactive activation model of context effects in letter perception: Part I. An account of basic findings. *Psychological Review, 88*, p. 380. Copyright 1981 by the American Psychological Association. Reprinted by permission.

one of the degraded words in Figure 3.3, you see a particular set of letters even though one or more of them are ambiguous. This occurs because all the connections between units in the word recognition system influence one another to produce a stable pattern.

Pelli, Farell, and Moore (2003) have provided data that bear on the feature detection stage of models such as Selfridge's and McClelland and Rumelhart's. Pelli et al. investigated the effect of the contrast between the letters in a word and the background on which they are printed. For example, a grey letter printed on a grey background would be unreadable, a grey letter printed on a white background would be readable, and a black letter on a white background would be more readable still. In their terms, black letters on a white background will have more **contrast energy** than will grey letters on the same background. Pelli et al. reported a study in which they varied both contrast energy and word length (number of letters in a word). Participants were shown common English words varying in length between 2 and 16 letters. Each word was shown on a screen for 200 milliseconds. The participants were then presented with a list of 26 words of the same length as the word previously shown and asked to pick out the word they had just seen. All told, the participants were exposed to 26 words for each word length between 2 and 16 letters. Within each set of 26 words, contrast energy was varied. This allowed the experimenters to determine how much contrast energy was required for each word length. The result was that the contrast energy required for a participant to identify a word was very highly related to word length. The more letters in a word, the greater the contrast energy required.

Pelli et al. argue that their results show that letters are crucial features that the visual system attempts to detect during the process of word recognition. Remember that the participant is shown a word for only 200 milliseconds. The longer the word, the more letters the participant must detect per unit of time. For high contrast-energy words, the signal presented by each letter is strong enough to enable detection even for such a brief presentation. However, if the contrast energy of individual letters is too low, identifying a large number of letters in a short time period becomes too difficult, and the process of word recognition grinds to a halt. Letters that have low contrast energy are weak signals that the visual system may 'squelch'. **Squelching** refers to the tendency of the visual system to block further processing of features unless they are clearly present. The visual system tends not to 'guess' but to rigorously detect features. In doing so, it 'achieves reliability at the expense of efficiency. . . . The human visual system has a vast number of feature detectors, each of which can raise a false alarm, mistaking noise for signal. Squelching blocks the intrusion of countless false features that would besiege us if weak features were not suppressed' (Pelli, Farell, & Moore, 2003, p. 754).

Although the detection of individual features is obviously important, the effect of context on pattern recognition is also important. A good example of the importance of context in word recognition is the **word superiority effect** (Reicher, 1969). It is easier to identify a letter (e.g., P) if it appears in a word (e.g., WARP) rather than by itself. This effect may occur because after 'years of fast reading' we are able to 'more efficiently map strings of tentatively identified letters to real words' (Pelli, Farell, & Moore, 2003, p. 755). A similar explanation may account for the **jumbled word effect** (Grainger & Whitney, 2004). People are able to read 'How does the huamn mnid raed wrods?' as an English sentence, rather than reject it as a nonsense string of letters.

The effect of context extends well beyond word recognition, as the examples given by Bar (2004) demonstrate.

> [S]eeing a steering wheel inside a car sets expectations about where the radio, ashtray and mirrors might be. . . . Recognizing someone's hand, for instance, significantly limits the possible interpretations of the object on that person's wrist to either a watch or a bracelet; it is not likely to be a chair or an elephant. This *a priori* knowledge allows the visual system to sensitize the corresponding visual representations of a watch and a bracelet so that it is easier to recognize the surrounding objects when we attend to them. (p. 617)

Although 'we know very little about how the brain arranges and retains such contextually associated information' (Bar, 2004, p. 618), some important conclusions can be drawn from our discussion so far. On the one hand, stimulus-driven, bottom-up processes, such as feature detection, provide the data for pattern recognition. On the other hand, top-down processes are expectations about what we are likely to find in the current context. Neither the data alone nor our expectations alone determine the outcome. Pattern recognition, like '[m]ost human behavior would seem to lie in between these two extremes reflecting the joint impact of high-level goals (so-called **top-down influences**) and recent stimuli (so-called **bottom-up influences**)' (Pashler, Johnston, & Ruthruff, 2001, p. 630).

Template Matching

According to *The Oxford English Dictionary*, the word *template* originally meant a 'gauge or a guide to be used in bringing a piece of work to its desired shape'. Such a guide might have edges corresponding to the outline of the finished product. For example, if you were painting letters, you might make a cut-out, or stencil, of the letters you wanted to paint. The cut-out is a template. It is possible that we store templates in memory that correspond to the standard forms of the configurations we see. The process of template matching would involve comparing the current configuration with the standard or **prototypical** forms that we have in memory. Thus, a letter can take any one of many different forms. Here is the lower-case letter *a* printed in several different fonts, or typefaces:

a   a   a   a   a   ɑ   *a*

Which one strikes you as the most prototypical? Which the least prototypical? Why? According to a **template-matching theory**, we would compare each *a* with the prototypical *a* that we have in memory, and, if the match is good enough, then we would recognize the letter.

Although superficially plausible, template matching is a difficult process to spell out in detail (e.g., Hofstadter, 1982). The prototypical pattern must differ somewhat from the particular patterns we perceive, just as each of the *a*'s given above differs from the others. As Uhr (1966, pp. 372ff.) observed, the problem is to specify the way in which a template can match not only patterns that are identical to it, but also patterns that are *similar* enough to it. It is not easy to spell out the characteristics a pattern must have in order to be similar enough to a template to be considered a match. For this reason template models have often been criticized. However, the hypothesis that we see things as similar to one another because they resemble an underlying prototype is a hypothesis that, in various forms, has been extensively investigated.

One clever approach to the role of prototypes in recognition comes from Hintzman (1986; Hintzman, Curran, & Oppy, 1992), who proposed a **multiple-trace memory model** that accounts for prototype effects in an interesting way. Hintzman's multiple-trace model assumes that traces of each individual experience are recorded in memory. No matter how often a particular kind of event is experienced, a memory trace of the event is recorded every time it is experienced.

Hintzman's approach distinguishes between primary and secondary memory, which we considered in the last chapter. Primary memory refers to what people are experiencing at any point in time, whereas secondary memory refers to all of the memory traces created out of all the experiences that a person has had. Secondary memory can be activated by means of a probe from primary memory. When a probe goes out from primary to secondary memory, then memory traces are activated to the extent that they are similar to the probe. The activated memory traces are said to return an echo to primary memory. The echo is made up of contributions from all the activated memory traces.

Hintzman suggested that one way to think of his use of the term 'echo' is that recognition is a bit like listening to a choir. Rather than one hearing only one voice in response to a probe of memory, a person may hear an entire chorus of voices if many memory traces are similar to the current experience. In such a chorus, the properties of individual memory traces will tend to be lost, and only a general impression of what they all have in common will remain.

Hintzman used his theory to account for the results of classic studies by Posner and his colleagues (Posner, Goldsmith, & Welton, 1967; Posner & Keele, 1968, 1970). In these experiments, participants were shown distortions of prototypical patterns. Examples of the prototypes are shown in Figure 3.5. Distortions of the prototype were formed by randomly moving the dots away from their position in the prototype. Examples of the distortions are shown in Figure 3.6. Participants were shown the distortions but did not actually see the prototypes. Subsequently, participants were required to classify another set of patterns consisting of the prototypes, the original distortions, and some new distortions of the prototypes. The interesting result was that the prototypical patterns were quite well classified, even though they had never been seen before. In another experiment, Posner (1969) showed that sometimes participants falsely recognized the prototype as a pattern they had seen before, even though they had previously only seen distortions of the prototype.

Hintzman explained Posner's findings as follows. The memory traces of the set of distorted patterns produce an echo. The echo contains what the different distortions have in common, and not the peculiarities of each individual distortion. Consequently, the prototype is recognized, even though it has never been seen before. An interesting consequence of this approach is that once an echo has been experienced in primary memory, it can leave a memory trace of itself in secondary memory. In this way, relatively abstract experiences can later be directly remembered, as 'echoes of echoes' (cf. Goldinger, 1998)

Pattern recognition is very basic and plays a role in a wide variety of processes. Thus, you will come across pattern recognition in numerous places in this book. For example, in the next chapter, on memory traces and schemas, as well as in Chapter 7, on concepts, we investigate further the role of *features* and *prototypes*. In Chapter 6, on imagery and cognitive maps, we observe how the process of pattern recognition can be influenced by simply changing the orientation of an object. In Chapter 12, on intelligence, we will discuss expertise in terms of an enhanced ability to recognize patterns.

Figure 3.5 Prototypical Patterns.

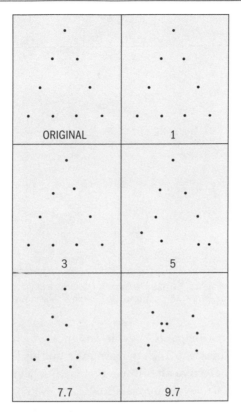

From Posner, M.I., Goldsmith, R., & Welton, K.E. (1967). Perceived distance and the classification of distorted patterns. *Journal of Experimental Psychology, 73*, 28–38. Copyright 1967 by the American Psychological Association. Reprinted by permission.

Even this brief outline is enough to indicate that to discuss an apparently simple process like pattern recognition you need to consider not only how we perceive an event, but also how our memory of previous events relates to our current experiences.

■ Selective Attention

Early research on attention was driven by practical problems experienced by armed forces personnel. One such problem concerned 'those arising in communication centers, where many different streams of speech reached the person at the same time' (Broadbent, 1980, p. 54). The investigation of this problem led to the creation of a task in which the participant was required to 'answer one of two messages which start at the same point in time, but one of which is irrelevant' (Broadbent, 1952/1992, p. 125). The experimental technique Broadbent used is called **dichotic listening**. Participants were exposed to two previously recorded verbal messages presented simultaneously and were required to answer questions posed in only one

Figure 3.6 A Set of Distortions of a Prototype.

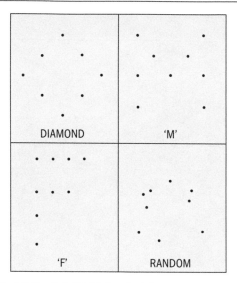

From Posner, M.I., Goldsmith, R., & Welton, K.E. (1967). Perceived distance and the classification of distorted patterns. *Journal of Experimental Psychology, 73,* 28–38. Copyright 1967 by the American Psychological Association. Reprinted with permission.

of the messages. When participants knew in advance which of two different voices contained the required message, then performance on this task was very good. Participants were good at **selective attention**—that is, they were able to select relevant information and ignore irrelevant information.

Broadbent also worked closely with Colin Cherry (1953), who became well known for drawing attention to the **cocktail party phenomenon** and invented a seminal technique for investigating attention (Wood & Cowan, 1995). The cocktail party phenomenon occurs when you are able to attend to one conversation in a crowded room in which many other conversations are going on. Cherry studied the ability to attend to one message while ignoring another by using a **shadowing task**, in which an experimental participant wears headphones and is given two messages, one in each ear. The participant shadows one of the two messages by repeating it as it is heard. Early information-processing theories suggested that people must *filter out* information to which they did not wish to attend (Treisman, 1969). Thus, one of the stages of information processing might be a kind of **filter** that admits some messages but blocks others.

A study by Neisser and Becklen (1975) used a visual analogue of dichotic listening, called **selective looking**. Suppose you take videotapes of two different sequences of events, such as a hand-slapping game and a game involving throwing a basketball. What happens if you show the two videotapes overlapping? This would be like watching two television channels on the same screen. In the Neisser and Becklen study, people were able to attend to either sequence quite easily. They simply saw only the attended sequence and were not distracted by the unattended sequence.

The studies of both dichotic listening and selective looking produced results consistent with what is called the **early selection** view of attention. This view holds that 'attention can effectively prevent early perceptual processing of irrelevant distractors' (Lavie, Hirst, Fockert, & Viding, 2004). On this account, the participant literally does not see or hear the irrelevant information. However, other tasks have produced results that appear to be more consistent with a **late selection** view of attention. Such a view holds that both relevant and irrelevant stimuli are perceived, so that the person must actively ignore the irrelevant stimuli in order to focus on the relevant ones. The Stroop task is often used to illustrate late selection.

The Stroop Task

Consider the following series of colour names: red, green, blue, green, red, yellow, blue, yellow, blue, green. Of course, it is easy to read the names. However, suppose the colour names were printed in colours that are different from their names. For example, suppose the word *red* is printed in *blue*, the word *green* in *yellow*, and so on. This is called a **Stroop task** (Stroop, 1935/1992), after the psychologist who invented it. (There are several demonstrations of the Stroop task on the Internet (e.g., www.apa.org/science/stroop.html). You should try at least one. You will find that naming the colours of the words takes longer than reading the colour words themselves.) As experiences, the difference between reading the colour names and naming the colours is quite striking. When you try to name the colours, it is as if you are constantly being distracted by the tendency to read the names. We could say that the tendency to read the names interferes with the attempt to name the colours. The Stroop task is one of the most useful research tools ever invented. Its continuing popularity is shown by the fact that the number of studies using it has been increasing each year, with the result that it has been employed in thousands of experiments (MacLeod, 1991, 1992; MacLeod & MacDonald, 2000). There are several variants of this task. For example, suppose you show someone a picture of a bird that is labelled 'camel' and ask the person to name the picture. The tendency to say 'camel' interferes with the correct response 'bird' (MacLeod & MacDonald, 2000, p. 384).

A typical Stroop experiment compares performance in an incongruent condition (e.g., the word *red* is printed in green and the participant's task is to name the colour in which the word is printed) with control conditions (e.g., the letters XXX are printed in green and the participant's task is to name the colour in which the letters are printed). It is reliably found that the incongruent condition takes more time than does a control condition.

If a process has been overlearned, then there may be a tendency to execute that process whether or not we wish to do so. Something like that may be going on in a Stroop task. If you have learned how to read, then when you are presented with a list of words, it is hard not to read them. The Stroop situation requires the participant to deliberately inhibit reading the colour words in order to accomplish the goal of naming the colours.

The results of Stroop experiments have often been taken to illustrate the difference between **automatic** and **controlled** processes. Some processes may pick up information more or less automatically. A truly **automatic process** is autonomous; it just runs itself off without the necessity of our paying attention to it. By contrast, with other activities we must pay attention if we are to execute them properly. Such processes are often called **controlled processes** (Shiffrin & Schneider, 1977). Although the distinction between automatic and controlled processes is still widely used (Birnboim, 2003; Schneider & Chein, 2003), you should be aware of the similarity of this distinction to the bottom-up/top-down distinction we introduced in the section on pattern recognition. Indeed, there is a family of constructs that are intended to capture similar distinctions. Thus what are called automatic processes also tend to be called bottom-up, stimulus-driven, and involuntary, while what are called controlled processes also tend to be called top-down, goal-directed, and voluntary (cf. Pashler, Johnston, & Ruthruff, 2001, p. 641). In the Stroop situation, an incongruent condition requires you to keep the goal of naming colours in mind even though you have an involuntary tendency to read the words.

The use of hypnosis is one of the most intriguing ways of investigating the Stroop phenomenon (MacLeod & Sheehan, 2003; Raz et al., 2003). People vary in the extent to which they can be hypnotized. A standard technique used to measure this is the Stanford Hypnotic Susceptibility Scale (Weitzenhoffer & Hilgard, 1962), which is available on the Internet (http://ist-socrates.berkeley.edu/~kihlstrm/PDFfiles/Hypnotizability/SHSSC%20Script.pdf). Participants are given a hypnotic induction procedure and several suggestions, such as being annoyed by a (non-existent) mosquito in the room. Those participants who are highly suggestible are more susceptible to hypnosis than those who are not. Raz and his colleagues gave participants, who were able to read English, the post-hypnotic suggestion that any words they saw would look like those in an unknown foreign language and 'you will not attempt to attribute any meaning to them' (Raz et al., 2003, p. 337). The participant's sole task was to name the colours in which the 'meaningless' letter strings were displayed. Of course, the participants were actually being given a standard Stroop task with English words. The interesting result was that the highly suggestible participants did not show the typical Stroop effect, although the less suggestible participants did.

This result has been replicated by Raz as well as by others (MacLeod & Sheehan, 2003). A possible explanation is that the reading of words is suppressed in the highly suggestible participants, enabling them to easily name the colour in which the word is printed. This would mean that even an apparently automatic process such as word reading can be controlled by means of hypnosis. More generally, it suggests that cognitive processes normally considered to be automatic are nonetheless susceptible to 'top-down influences exerted by suggestion at the neural level' (Raz et al., 2003, p. 343).

Several PET and fMRI studies have been designed to shed light on the brain processes underlying Stroop task performance (MacLeod & MacDonald, 2000, pp. 386–390). These studies compare blood flow to different regions of the brain for performance in an incongruent condition with performance in control conditions. Among the brain regions most often identified in these studies are the **dorsolateral prefrontal cortex (DLPFC)** and the **anterior cingulate cortex (ACC)**. The relative locations of these areas are shown in Figure 3.7. The DLPFC is called *dorso* (short for *dorsal*), meaning it is towards the top rather than the bottom (or *ventral*) part of the cortex. *Lateral* refers to the outside rather than the inside (or *medial*) part of the cortex. *Prefrontal* means it is located at the front of the frontal lobes. So *dorsolateral prefrontal cortex* means towards the top, outside part of the front of the frontal lobes (Harrison, 2001, p. 160). The ACC is called *anterior*, meaning towards the front as opposed to the back (or *posterior*) part of the cortex. *Cingulate* means 'arch-shaped'.

In general, the prefrontal areas are thought to provide 'a top-down bias that favors the selection of task-relevant information. . . . [S]uch a bias is especially important for exerting control when task-irrelevant information can effectively compete with task-relevant information for priority in processing' (Milham, Banich, & Barad, 2004, p. 212). Both the DLPFC and the ACC may be 'activated among some tasks that require processes to resolve among competing responses. We also know that these brain

Figure 3.7 The Dorsolateral Prefrontal Cortex and the Anterior Cingulate Cortex.

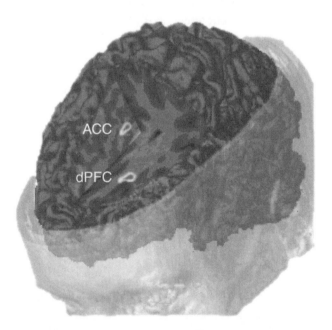

From MacLeod, C.M., & MacDonald, P.A. (2000). Interdimensional interference in the Stroop effect: Uncovering the cognitive and neural anatomy of attention. *Trends in Cognitive Sciences, 4*, 382–391. Copyright 2000. Reprinted by permission of Elsevier.

regions are not necessarily involved in all such tasks, but that other regions may be recruited instead' (Jonides, Badre, Curtis, Thompson-Schill, & Smith, 2002, p. 243).

A great deal of speculation has centred on the role of the ACC. One possibility is that it detects conflicting response tendencies of the sort that the Stroop task elicits. It is also possible that heightened ACC activity is accompanied by the person becoming aware of such conflicts (Mayr, 2004). However, the precise role of the ACC may change depending on the specific task with which the person is dealing (Kéri, Decety, Roland, & Gulyás, 2003, p. 31). The ACC should probably be seen as one part of a network responsible for attentional control, 'communicating with other equally essential components within this network . . . [and having] multiple functions depending on the content and origin of the signals from other components in the attentional network' (Tibbetts, 2001, p. 329).

Attention Capture and Inattentional Blindness

If you are walking down the hall and someone behind you says your name, you are likely to attend to that voice and turn around to see who it is. This is called **attention capture**—the power of some stimuli on some occasions to elicit attention in spite of the fact that we did not intend to pay attention to them. Intuitively, attention capture would appear to be 'ecologically useful . . . [because it enables] attention to be drawn to new objects in the field because these may well represent either an important threat to be avoided (like a predator) or an important opportunity to be sought out (like prey)' (Pashler, Johnston, & Ruthruff, 2001, p.632). It is possible that we are 'tuned' to pick up useful information even when our attention is directed elsewhere.

The flip side of attention capture is **inattentional blindness**, which refers to our failure to attend to events that we might be expected to notice. 'Imagine an experienced pilot attempting to land an airplane on a busy runway. He pays close attention to his display console, carefully watching the airspeed indicator on his windshield to make sure he does not stall, yet he never sees that another airplane is blocking his runway' (Mack, 2003, p. 180)! A great many accidents may be due to inattentional blindness.

Although attention capture and inattentional blindness may appear to be contradictory, they actually admit of a coherent explanation. Let us begin with inattentional blindness. Recall the Neisser and Becklen (1975) experiment on selective looking that we discussed at the beginning of the section on selective attention. Participants were shown two overlapping videos of different sequences of events and could attend to one sequence without being distracted by the other. In a subsequent study using the selective looking paradigm, Simons (2000; Simons & Chabris, 1999) showed participants overlapping teams playing basketball, one team wearing black and the other white shirts. The participants paid attention only to one of the teams, and 73 per cent of them failed to notice a gorilla walk across the screen. Even when the gorilla stopped and pounded its chest, only 50 per cent of the participants noticed it! You can see Simons's demonstrations on-line at http://viscog.beckman.uiuc.edu/djs_lab/demos.html.

A different experimental paradigm was used by Mack and Rock (1998; Mack, 2003) to investigate inattentional blindness. Participants were shown a series of asymmetrical crosses and on each trial were asked to judge which arm of the cross was longer. On the fourth trial the participant was unexpectedly shown a small black square located in one of the quadrants defined by the cross. Thus, the critical fourth trial looked something like Figure 3.8. When participants were asked if they had seen anything other than the cross, many of the participants said they had not. They had been paying attention to the cross, and failed to perceive the unexpected intrusion.

In one variation of their experiment, Mack and Rock (1998) used a happy cartoon face rather than small black squares. The happy faces were detected 85 per cent of the time. Other stimulus categories such as simple circles were detected as little as 15 per cent of the time. This result suggests that faces may be special. Indeed, Lavie and her colleagues (Lavie, Ro, & Russell, 2003; Ro, Russell, & Lavie, 2001) have provided evidence for the hypothesis that faces will attract attention to a greater extent than will other classes of stimuli. In one experiment they used a version of what is called a **flanker task**. Participants had to search for the name of a famous show-business personality (e.g., Michael Jackson) or a famous politician (e.g., Bill Clinton) that was presented on a screen either by itself or in a list of 2-, 4-, or 6-letter strings (e.g., Csiprmy Qhplrt). On the periphery of the screen was a picture of either the person whose name was being sought (congruent condition) or a person from the opposite category (incongruent condition). An example of this task is given in Figure 3.9. Thus, a congruent condition would be to search for Bill Clinton's name while his picture was also being shown, while an incongruent condition would be to search for Michael Jackson's name while Bill Clinton's picture was being shown. Participants were told to ignore the face and to press a key when they had identified the name as either belonging to a celebrity or a politician. Of course, it takes longer to identify the name correctly as the length of the list increases from 1 to 2 to 4 to 6 (i.e., the more alternatives through which the participant must search). Incongruent conditions also take longer than congruent ones, showing that these faces were not ignored but interfered with reaction time. Importantly, the size of this distractor effect was the same at all levels of list length. This contrasts with the results of a parallel study in which participants searched for the names of either musical instruments or fruits while pictures of musical instruments or fruits

Figure 3.8 Asymmetrical Crosses and Inattentional Blindness.

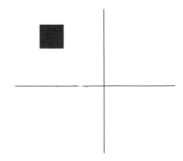

The participant judges the relative line lengths of the cross and may fail to see the black square.

were the distractor items. Here again there was an effect of list length and a congruence effect, with incongruent trials generally taking longer. However, this congruence effect was reduced and eventually disappeared as the list got longer. If we compare the two studies, we see that as task difficulty increases faces are still distractors but musical instruments and fruits are not. One way of putting this is to say that faces are being attended to no matter what else the participant must do. By contrast, the participant 'gives up' on attending to musical instruments when the overall task becomes too difficult. Lavie, Ro, and Russell (2003, p. 510) conclude that 'face processing may be mandatory', meaning that we attend to faces involuntarily even when our goal is to ignore them.

Faces are not the only events that capture our attention. It turns out that representations of the human body do as well. Downing, Bray, Rogers, and Childs (2004) used the same technique as had Mack and Rock, with silhouettes of whole human bodies appearing in quadrants of the cross. These were detected at a much higher rate than were silhouettes of other objects (e.g., telephones, guns, or even human hands).

Downing and his colleagues discussed their findings in relation to the suggestion that there may be **domain-specific modules** in the brain that automatically process faces (e.g., Farah, 1996; Kanwisher, McDermott, & Chun, 1997). The existence of such a module would mean that in the presence of a face you could not help but attend to it. Does the finding that human bodies capture attention mean that there would also be a module specialized for detecting bodies? There may be such 'independent neural systems for a few object types' (Downing et al., 2003, p. B28). However, it need not be the case that such modules are given innately. Rather, it may be that over time we gain expertise in dealing with particular categories of stimuli, such as faces and bodies. Instead of there being innate modules for faces and bodies, certain brain areas may be recruited to process events with which we have a great deal

Figure 3.9 Example of Stimulus Display.

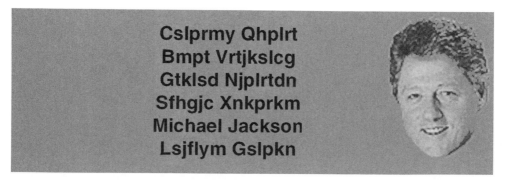

This example is of an incongruent condition with a list of six names. The target name (Michael Jackson) could appear in any of the positions in the list, and the face could be on the left or on the right.
From Lavie, N., Ro, T., & Russell, C. (2003). The role of perceptual load in processing distractor faces. *Psychological Science, 14,* 510–515. Reprinted with permission of Blackwell Publishing.

of experience (Gauthier, Skudlarski, Gore, & Anderson, 2000). This issue is likely to be a focus of research for some time (Gauthier, Curran, Curby, & Collins, 2003; Rhodes, Byatt, Michie, & Puce, 2004).

Just to add to the mix, it has been known for a long time that a person's own name has the power to capture that person's attention (e.g., Moray, 1959). Mack and his colleagues (Mack, Pappas, Silverman, & Gay, 2002), who considered this result in conjunction with other studies of attention capture, have suggested that highly meaningful stimuli are able to capture our attention.

> [A] whimpering infant readily awakens its sleeping mother and no one else. . . . [M]eaning is the primary determinant of selective attention and therefore of the content of perceptual consciousness. We see what interests us, what we are looking for and what we are expecting. (p. 504)

Finally, Horstmann (2002) has placed the discussion of attention capture in the context of the perceptual cycle (Neisser, 1976) that we discussed in Chapter 2. You should recall that this cycle results in our expectancies guiding our exploration of the environment, but that the environment is capable of influencing our experience of it. 'If attentional capture were always conditional on an intention, organisms would perceive only what they intended to see; other events would rarely be recognized, and threats would be frequently overlooked' (Horstmann, 2002, p. 504). Although we often see only what we are looking for, we are also able to rapidly become aware of meaningful events that are unexpected. What examples from your own experience can you think of?

■ Dual Tasks and the Limits of Attention

One obvious question about how we deploy attention concerns its capacity. How many things can we attend to at once? The answer to this question may depend on what sort of things we are trying to do and how skilled we are at doing them. Although it is easy to see how people could perform a voluntary task in conjunction with an automatic task, such as carrying on a conversation while walking, it is harder to imagine people doing two goal-directed things at once. One way of thinking about it is that we can do more than one simple task at a time, but as tasks become more complex, then they begin to interfere with one another. An example often used to make this point involves the task of driving a car (e.g., C.D. Wickens, 1984). If you are a skilled driver and you are driving a route you know well, then your task is relatively simple. Under these conditions, you may also be able to carry on a lively conversation as you drive. However, should something out of the ordinary happen, such as having to drive in heavy traffic in a snowstorm, then driving home may no longer be a simple task. Under these conditions, your conversation may be reduced to a few sighs.

As Hirst (1986; Hirst & Kalmar, 1987) pointed out, the notion that attention is limited might be conceptualized in different ways. It might mean that attention is like a power supply (Kahneman, 1973). From this viewpoint, it is as if a task taps a reservoir of fuel. If you try to do too much, you will just run out of gas. Performance on a task has a limit given by the capacity of the fuel tank that powers attention. For obvious reasons, this kind of model of attention is called a **capacity model**.

Another possibility is that attention has **structural limits**. If two tasks require the same kind of activity, then they may interfere with each other more than if each requires a different kind of activity. For example, one can make a distinction between auditory and visual processes. A person might very well be able to have a visual image of his or her living room and describe it in words at the same time. However, suppose you were asked to imagine the sentence, 'A bird in the hand is worth two in the bush', and then categorize each word in the sentence as either a noun or not a noun by saying yes or no (L.R. Brooks, 1968). Thus, the proper sequence is: no, yes, no, no, yes, no, no, yes, no, no, yes.

This task turns out to be quite hard. Try it yourself for the sentence, 'Wise men make proverbs and fools repeat them.' The problem is that you are trying to do two highly verbal tasks at the same time: imagining a sentence may require you to say it to yourself, and categorizing the words requires you to say yes and no. Saying two things at once is not easy. If you do the same task by tapping with your left hand for a noun and tapping with your right hand for a non-noun, then it is easier. This is because the two tasks are quite different: tapping is a non-verbal process and interferes less with a verbal task. From this viewpoint, interference between tasks is more likely to occur to the extent that they share the same processing resources (e.g., both visual or both verbal) (Kahneman & Treisman, 1984).

Some theories see attention as involving a central processor (e.g., Broadbent, 1984). If attention requires a central processor, then we should be able to pay attention to only one thing at a time. This is because the central processor will be able to handle only one task at a time, and if another task is added, then the central processor will have to switch from one task to another. It is as if there is a **central bottleneck** through which information relevant to only one task at a time can pass (Pashler, 1994). From this viewpoint, doing two things at once will require you to alternate your attention between the two tasks and selectively attend to one task at a time. Another possibility is that people can learn to attend to more than one thing at a time. If people could learn to do this, then they would have succeeded in mastering the skill of **divided attention**. If they were able to successfully divide their attention, then perhaps with practice their attention could improve beyond normal limits.

An influential study of divided attention was conducted by Spelke, Hirst, and Neisser (1976). Few students would attempt trying to read and take lecture notes at the same time. Yet this is essentially what these researchers taught their participants to do. In their first study, they attempted to train two participants, named Diane and John, to read short stories and copy dictated words. They were given comprehension tests of what they had read while taking dictation. Although this dual task was very difficult at first, after about six weeks of practice their comprehension was as good as it had been for reading stories alone. However, at this stage Diane and John were not picking up information about the words being dictated to them. They were then told to try to notice any special characteristics of the dictated words. The word lists were all drawn from a specific category, such as animal names or furniture. The two participants were able to pick up this information even while reading with comprehension. In another experiment with new participants, even when the difficulty of material to be read was increased, comprehension and speed of reading while doing both tasks were equal to performance when reading alone.

In a follow-up study, Hirst, Spelke, Reaves, Caharack, and Neisser (1980) trained two participants, Arlene and Mary, to both read and copy complete sentences. Here are examples of some of the dictated sentences:

The rope broke.
Spot got free.
Father chased him.

The participants were tested to see if they could recognize sentences that had been dictated to them. Here are examples of some of the test sentences:

Father chased him.
Spot chased Father.
Spot's rope broke.

The first of the test sentences should be recognized as one of the originally dictated sentences. The second sentence should not be recognized. The third sentence might be falsely recognized if the participants were paying attention to the dictated sentences. The reason for this is that people will often make inferences on the basis of what they hear (Bransford & Franks, 1971). They will then often falsely recognize these inferences as being sentences they actually heard. This is in fact what happened in the study by Hirst et al. This can be taken as demonstrating that the participants genuinely understood the sentences that they were writing while they were reading. They were not just writing the sentences mechanically. Taking dictation was not being done without paying attention, any more than reading for meaning was being done without paying attention.

Perhaps people can learn to genuinely divide their attention between two tasks, rather than just switch it rapidly back and forth between two tasks. Perhaps so-called 'simultaneous' translators, who can listen to a speaker in one language and very quickly translate that speech into another language, have perfected this skill as well (Hirst, Neisser, & Spelke, 1978, p. 61). However, the studies we have just reviewed do not disprove the hypothesis that participants are switching very rapidly between the two tasks. 'It is quite possible that critical mental operations on the two tasks never proceed at the same time, but [participants] are nonetheless able to smoothly switch back and forth between the two tasks' (Pashler, Johnston, & Ruthruff , 2001, p. 644).

A continuing line of research has been to try to determine if a bottleneck still exists in highly practised tasks. The sort of task typically used in experiments involves mapping a set of stimuli onto a set of responses. For example, one task might present participants with one of three tones—low, middle, or high. The participant would say 'one' for the low, 'two' for the middle, and 'three' for the high tone. This task maps auditory stimuli onto verbal responses. Another task might map visual stimuli onto manual responses. For example, the participant might see a stimulus appear in one of three locations on a computer screen and respond by pressing a key with one of three fingers (index, middle, or ring finger). Suppose we conceptualize tasks like these as consisting of three stages (Hazeltine, Teague, & Ivry, 2002, p. 532). The first stage involves identifying the stimulus, the second is the attentional bottleneck or central processor in which the appropriate response is selected, and the third stage is the execution of the response.

One of the experiments reported by Hazeltine, Teague, and Ivry (2002) used the tasks described in the previous paragraph. Participants were trained on each task separately, after which they were required to execute both tasks simultaneously. That is, the visual and auditory stimuli occurred at the same time, and participants were instructed to execute both tasks as fast as they could. Experimental sessions consisted of several trials of each kind and occurred on consecutive days, where possible. The conclusion was that 'participants were able to achieve levels of performance under dual task conditions that were similar to those obtained under single task conditions' (Hazeltine, Teague, & Ivry, 2002, p. 530). The experimenters found no evidence for a central bottleneck that could not be overcome through practice. They also pointed out that the ability to perform tasks simultaneously without interference may require that the stimulus and response phases of each process be from different modalities (e.g., auditory and visual stimuli, verbal and motor responses).

You might think that that would be the end of the matter, but Ruthruff, Johnston, Van Selst, Whitsell, and Remington (2003) observed that it is still logically possible for a 'latent' bottleneck to exist even for highly practised tasks. This possibility is represented in Figure 3.10. Notice that the 'pre-bottleneck' stages finish at different times. This allows each task to pass through the bottleneck separately. You can see how many logical possibilities there are even in such an apparently simple situation as the dual-task experiment. That is one reason why research in cognition seldom progresses rapidly. It is necessary to examine all the logical possibilities before definitive conclusions can be drawn, and this is a labour-intensive and time-consuming process.

■ Task Switching

The concept of a **set** was reintroduced into psychology after a prolonged absence (Allport, Styles, & Hsieh, 1994). One of the reasons why it had fallen into disuse was that the concept of a set was considered by some to be too vague to be useful (e.g., J.J. Gibson, 1941). However, many others, such as R.S. Woodworth (1869–1962), found sets to be essential for explaining human behaviour. One example of a set is the way that 'an individual often prepares to act before beginning the overt effective action', as when sprinters take their mark on the starting line (Woodworth, 1940, p. 29). Woodworth argued that there are many different kinds of sets. For example, there are preparatory

Figure 3.10 A Latent Bottleneck.

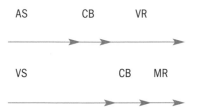

AS = auditory stimulus, VS = visual stimulus, CB = central bottleneck, VR = verbal response, MR = motor response. The processing stages for AS and VS end at different times, allowing each to be processed separately by the central bottleneck.

sets, as illustrated by the sprinters; executive sets that guide the organism through a sequence of responses, as when you drive a car; and goal sets that represent what the person aims to achieve. Woodworth regarded sets as temporary organizations in the brain that act 'by facilitating some responses, while preventing or inhibiting others. . . . While looking eagerly for a lost object you do not notice sounds that at other times would surely attract your attention. Readiness for one act is at the same time unreadiness for other acts' (Woodworth, 1940, p. 33). In the context of the distinctions we have been using throughout this chapter, a set is a top-down process that organizes our action to meet the goals we have.

Task switching is one of the research contexts that have led to the revival of the 'set' concept. The first systematic investigation of this topic is usually attributed to Jersild (1927). Monsell (2003, p. 134) gives a good example of what task switching means, of which the following is a modified version. Suppose you are at your computer, trying to finish an essay. You suddenly get an e-mail from the registrar's office, reminding you that today is the deadline for paying the remainder of your fees. You are annoyed at this interruption, but realize the importance of the registrar's message. You look around for your bank card, find it, and head off to the registrar's office. Along the way, you stop and talk with some friends. You have a series of tasks—writing an essay, reading an e-mail, going to the registrar's office, talking to friends—each of which 'requires an appropriate configuration of mental resources, a procedural "schema". . . or "task-set". . . . We exercise intentional "executive" control to select and implement the task-set, or the combination of task-sets, that are appropriate to our dominant goals . . . , resisting temptations to satisfy other goals' (p. 134).

A basic phenomenon associated with task switching is the **switch cost** (Monsell, 2003, p. 135). This refers to the fact that performance on a task immediately after a switch is worse than typical performance on the same task. To continue with the example from the previous paragraph, when you return from the registrar's office and start working on your essay again, you may not be able to smoothly pick up where you left off. You may need to reconstruct exactly what you were doing before you switched to the task of going to the registrar's office. Sometimes switching back to a task almost feels as if you need to start all over again. This may be due to the time required to reset the cognitive system so that the behaviours appropriate to the current task are engaged once again and behaviours appropriate to the previous task are inhibited (Leung & Monsell, 2003, p. 919).

Usually experiments on this topic require the participant to switch tasks when given a certain cue by the experimenter. For example, the participant may be shown a series of letter number pairs, such as 'H 3' (Yeung & Monsell, 2003, p. 923). Participants are required to perform one of two tasks on each trial. In the 'alphabet arithmetic' task, they must 'add' the number to the letter. In this case the participant would say K, because K is the third letter in the alphabet from H. In the 'perceptual comparison task' the participant must say 'yes' if the letter and the number both contain curved lines or both contain only straight lines. For a pair such as 'H 2' the answer would be 'no' because the letter has only straight lines while the number has curved lines (Yeung & Monsell, 2003, p. 922). When cued to do so, participants must switch from whatever task they are currently doing to the other task. A switch cost is reliably observed under such conditions.

Arrington and Logan (2004) did a clever experiment that shed light on task switching when the participant, rather than the experimenter, controls precisely when the task switch occurs. Such voluntary task switching was enabled by telling the participants that they had to decide which tasks to perform on each trial. The participant's goal was to do each task about half the time and to try to switch randomly between them. Participants were neither to count the number of times they had performed each task nor to alternate between them (Arrington & Logan, 2004, p. 611). The tasks between which the participants had to choose were as follows. On each trial the participant was shown one of the following digits: 1, 2, 3, 4, 5, 7, 8, and 9. The participant could either indicate whether the digit was even or odd or indicate whether the digit was larger or smaller than 5.

Even though task switch was voluntary, there was still a switch cost for each task. The participants performed each task approximately half the time. However, although the participants had been instructed to try to switch randomly, they did not in fact do so. Rather, they tended to produce a series of runs on one task, then switch to a series of runs on the other task, then switch back to a series of runs on the first task, and so on. This suggests that once participants are used to one task they may be reluctant to incur the cost of switching to the other. Notice that these participants were not completely free to choose which task to perform but were constrained to try to perform each task about half the time. It is possible that, in a situation in which we are completely free to choose which task to perform, we may persist with one task until boredom sets in and we are prepared to pay the switch cost. In Chapter 13, on personal cognition, we will consider the important role that boredom plays in directing our attention.

Like other topics we have examined in this chapter, task switching shows the importance of top-down processes in regulating our attention. Indeed, Pashler, Johnston, and Ruthruff (2001) have concluded that one of the 'main themes to emerge from' recent research 'is the idea that the effects of mental set are more pervasive than had been previously thought' (p. 648). It is also true that recent research has reached 'a rather broad consensus that higher level control operations—those operations that implement task sets by selecting, ordering, and chaining lower level task execution processes—are intimately linked to conscious awareness' (Meiran, Hommel, Bibi, & Lev, 2001, p. 10). Task switching requires people to change their set, just the sort of operation that might be expected to be correlated with awareness. Presumably, people are aware of achieving a preparatory set and know when they are ready to perform the next task. Meiran et al., 2001) tested this assumption by asking participants in a task-switching experiment to indicate for each trial when they are ready. Longer preparation times were not related to better performance, suggesting that people are not actually aware of whether or not they are ready.

All of this fits in with earlier work, reviewed by Humphrey (1951/1963, Ch. 2), that people may be aware of the goal they are trying to achieve, but not of the operations that need to be executed to achieve that goal. While we have reviewed many studies suggesting that we often do have control of our attention, we may still wonder about the extent to which we are aware of, and thus in control of, our attentional processes. This leads directly to our next topic.

■ Attention, Awareness, and Unconscious Processes

James (1890/1983, p. 275) made the point that people are not actually aware of all the things in their environment of which they could be aware. There are lots of things going on of which they are seemingly unconscious. James talked about how different travellers visiting the same place will often bring back very different accounts of what they have seen. One way in which James's point is made nowadays is to say that people encode events in different ways. A code is 'a set of rules or operations that transforms items, objects or data from one systematic form into another. . . . Thus, for example, the hearer of a sentence will code the sequence of physical, acoustic events into a meaningful form' (Reber, 1985). The words you hear arrive at your ear as physical, acoustic events. You encode these events as words. Thus, **encoding** refers to the process of transforming information into one or more forms of representation.

How does a person encode information? Obviously, information could be encoded in several different ways. Consider how we might encode a word. In an influential paper, D.D. Wickens (1970) used this example: 'When a person hears the word horse, it is encoded into the broader categories of beasts of burden, four-legged creatures, mammals, warm blooded animals, and finally of animals in general' (p. 1). How does this encoding process happen? Wickens suggested that it was largely automatic. There is just too much richness in the world for us to be aware of all the dimensions along which we are encoding it. Thus, we are able to encode an event without being aware of it. If we were aware of what we were doing, it would be an impossibly complex task. Wickens drew the analogy of a Major League Baseball player who is able to hit a ball or catch it without paying attention to what he is doing. In fact, there is evidence that if a highly skilled performer does try to pay attention to what he or she is doing, then performance declines (Baumeister, 1984; Bielock, 2002; Grey, 2004; Schlenker & Leary, 1982).

Wickens suggested that the process of encoding was not only unconscious but also very fast. Moreover, an event can be encoded along several different dimensions simultaneously. Thus, a word would be encoded in terms of such varied dimensions as its frequency of occurrence, how we feel about it, as well as its physical characteristics, such as its size, shape, and so on. This process is called multi-dimensional encoding.

Perception without Awareness

Wickens's point of view is consistent with the existence of a phenomenon called **subliminal perception** (N.F. Dixon, 1971; Lazarus & McCleary, 1951). Subliminal perception refers to a class of phenomena in which a stimulus has an effect on behaviour even though it has been exposed too rapidly or at too low an intensity for the person to be able to identify the stimulus. For example, suppose that a series of words is presented to a participant for a very brief duration. The stimulus can be exposed for such a short interval that it is below the participant's threshold for reporting the occurrence of an event. Another word for threshold is **limen**, and so a stimulus that is 'below threshold' is called *subliminal*. Even though the participant does not identify the stimulus, the stimulus may still have an effect. Wickens reviewed experiments in which participants can say whether or not the stimulus is a pleasant or unpleasant word, without reporting that they can actually see the word (e.g., Eriksen, Azuma, & Hicks, 1959).

Subliminal perception effects often involve semantics, which is the study of meaning. A word that is similar in meaning to another word is called a semantically related word. Thus, *duck* and *swan* are semantically related, because both refer to water birds (Eagle, Wolitzky, & Klein, 1966). In some early subliminal perception experiments, participants would report seeing a word that is semantically related to the stimulus word and not report seeing the word they were actually shown (Postman, Bruner, & McGinnis, 1948).

Experiments like the ones we have just described were often criticized. For one thing, these experiments appear to have serious methodological problems. How can we be sure that a stimulus presented below threshold was not actually seen? If the stimulus was attended to, however briefly, then the subsequent effects of the stimulus on behaviour are not that surprising. However, novel experimental techniques revived the notion that information is extensively encoded outside of awareness. Among the most influential of these were studies that employed a technique called backward masking.

Backward Masking

Backward masking involves presenting a stimulus, called the target, to the participant and then covering, or masking, the target with another stimulus. The time difference between the first stimulus and the masking stimulus is called the **stimulus onset asynchrony**, or SOA.

In one early experiment (Marcel, Katz, & Smith, 1974), participants were briefly shown a single word that was then masked by a pattern. The participants were asked to report whatever they could. Sometimes participants reported words that they had not been shown but that were semantically related to the stimulus word (e.g., *queen* instead of *king*, or *apple* instead of *orange*). This phenomenon is sometimes called **priming**, by analogy with the activity of priming a pump. The stimulus acts as a *prime* by making a semantically related response more likely.

Other studies done by Marcel used a time difference between the first stimulus and the masking stimulus (SOA), which was apparently too brief to enable detection of the stimulus. In one study, a Stroop-like task was used. After a target word was presented and masked, a colour patch was presented. For example, the target might be the word blue, and the colour patch might be red. Some trials had target words and colours that were congruent (e.g., the target word was red and the colour patch was red), whereas in other trials the target words were incongruent (e.g., the target word was blue and the colour patch was red). In one condition, participants were required to name the colour patch. Even when participants were not able to say anything about the word that occurred before the mask (the target), they still made faster responses to congruent than to incongruent trials. This suggests that the target stimulus had an effect on colour-naming latency in spite of the fact that participants were not aware of it.

Marcel thought that these studies lent support to the following conclusion: 'When an indirect measure of perceptual processing is used, such as associative effects of the undetected word on a subsequent task, all participants show effect of undetected stimuli' (Marcel, 1983a, p. 232). Thus, in order to determine whether or not a stimulus has affected cognitive processes, one could use **indirect measures** of perceptual processes, rather than merely relying on **direct measures** of cognitive processes, such as the participants' verbal report that they have not seen the stimulus. Masking a stimulus so that it is not reported by the participant does not mean that the stimulus has no effect. Perhaps the stimulus continues to be processed and may influence a person's subsequent behaviour.

Objective and Subjective Thresholds

Experiments such as Marcel's are examples of the **dissociation paradigm**. This experimental strategy attempts 'to demonstrate that it is possible to perceive stimuli in the complete absence of any conscious awareness of these stimuli' (Merikle & Reingold, 1998, p. 304). This experimental design is intended to show that **perception without awareness** is a real phenomenon, and, according to Merikle (1992), has the following general form:

> First, a measure of conscious perceptual experience (C) is selected. Second, a measure that is sensitive to unconscious perceptual processes (U) is identified. Third, experimental procedures are initiated to ensure that C exhibits no sensitivity to the critical perceptual information. If U can then be shown to exhibit some sensitivity to the same perceptual information that C is insensitive to, then it is concluded that perception without awareness has been demonstrated. (p. 792)

However, this paradigm still does not eliminate the threshold problem. Merikle and his colleagues (Cheesman and Merikle, 1986; Merikle, Smilek, & Eastwood, 2001) have pointed out the importance of making a distinction between the **objective threshold** and the **subjective threshold**. The objective threshold is the level at which a participant can detect a target stimulus no more often than would be expected by chance. For example, if a participant indicates on each trial whether or not the stimulus has been detected and is correct only half the time, then it seems reasonable to conclude that the participant is only guessing and is not aware of the presence or absence of the stimulus. The participant's performance is the same as that which 'would be obtained by a blind observer' (Erdelyi, 2004, p. 75). The subjective threshold can be determined by degrading 'the stimulus conditions until the quality of the stimulus information is so poor that observers claim not to be able to perceive the stimuli' (Merikle & Daneman, 2000, p. 1296). Thus, the stimulus may be presented so quickly or at such a low intensity that the participant *says* it has not been perceived.

In backward-masking experiments, the objective threshold refers to an SOA at which a participant can only detect the target stimulus at a chance level. The subjective threshold refers to an SOA at which a participant claims not to be able to detect the stimulus. The subjective threshold has been used to make a distinction between conscious and unconscious processes. However, it is far from obvious that one can assume that perception without awareness occurs when participants 'do not believe any useful stimulus information was perceived' (Merikle & Joordens, 1997, p. 111). One problem is that 'it is impossible to demonstrate in a completely convincing fashion' that 'no relevant information was consciously perceived' (Merikle & Joordens, 1997, p. 111). One cannot completely assess the contents of consciousness so as to rule out this possibility (Merikle & Reingold, 1998). Rather than try to make a sharp distinction between conscious and unconscious effects, a better research strategy might be to try to investigate the relative contributions of each (Merikle & Joordens, 1997, p. 112).

One study often cited as an example of just such a strategy was conducted by Debner and Jacoby (1994), who used a **process dissociation procedure**. This technique requires participants *not* to respond with items they have seen previously. If participants are aware of having previously seen an item, then they can exclude it. If, however, they are not aware of having previously seen an item, then there is no reason for them to exclude it. Items were masked and presented for short (50 milliseconds) or long (500 milliseconds) durations. Then a word stem appeared on the screen, consisting of the first three letters of a five-letter word. An example would be *tab– –*, which could be completed with different solutions such as *table*, *tabby*, or *taboo* (Debner & Jacobi, 1994, p. 308). When participants were shown items for a long duration, they were easily able to exclude them. Thus, shown *table* for 500 milliseconds and then shown *tab– –*, participants who were asked to exclude the item they had just seen did not complete the word stem with *table*, but with another word. This shows that participants had perceived the item and were able to control their response on the stem completion task. However, if participants were shown *table* for only a short duration, they were much less likely to exclude it as a solution to the stem completion task. In fact, they were much more likely to complete the stem using the item they had been shown than they would have by chance alone. This suggests that they did not perceive the item, because they were unable to exclude it. It also suggests that the participant's behaviour is being influenced by events of which the participant is unaware. The participant is not in conscious control of his or her own behaviour.

Mindful of the controversies surrounding perception without awareness, Kihlstrom (2004) proposed using the term **implicit perception** for the phenomena we have reviewed in this section. By implicit perception is meant 'the effect on the subject's experience, thought or action of an object in the current stimulus environment in the absence of, or independently of, conscious perception of that event' (Kihlstrom, 2004, p. 94). This definition is intended to link unconscious perception to similar phenomena in other areas of cognition. We will examine some of these in Chapter 5, on memory systems.

The Attentional Blink

Results similar to those we have been discussing have been obtained in investigations into the **attentional blink** (Shapiro, Arnell, & Raymond, 1997). Suppose you present participants with a series of letters in the centre of a screen. The participant's task is to identify them. The attentional blink occurs when two of these stimuli are presented within 550 milliseconds of each other. During that interval, the probability of the second letter being reported is much less than it would be for longer intervals. This is not due to a real eye blink, but it is as if attention 'blinks', and leaves the participant with nothing to report. Nevertheless, the second stimulus can still have a priming effect. Suppose you present *three* targets in a row, with the second and third being semantically related words (e.g., *lawyer*, *judge*). Suppose further that the second word (*lawyer*) is 'blinked'. It turns out that the third word (*judge*) is more likely to be correctly identified than it would be if the second word had been semantically unrelated to it (e.g., *tree*) (Shapiro, Arnell, & Raymond, 1997, pp. 291–292).

Barnard, Scott, Taylor, May, and Knightley (2004) have used the attentional blink to reinforce the connection between attention and meaning. In a clever study, they presented 'lists of 35 words . . . at a rate of 110 ms/item, with one word replacing another with no interstimulus interval. Most words referred to things or events occurring in natural environments (e.g., *island*, *snowstorm*). Participants were instructed to report a single target, a word that referred to a job or profession that people engage in for pay (e.g., *banker*, *shepherd*). On test trials, targets were preceded . . . by a potential distractor word and the semantic relationship between distractor and target was varied' (p. 179). One class of distractor items included words referring to activities for which people are not paid, such as *shopper*, *coward*, and *witness*. Because these distractors are also properties of people, they are semantically related to the target. Another class of distractor was inanimate (e.g., *freezer*, *cupboard*, *wireless*), and thus less closely related to the target. When a semantically related word preceded a target word, there was a greater likelihood of an attentional blink than when an inanimate word preceded the target. That is, people were less likely to report the target when it followed a semantically related word than when it followed an inanimate word.

One important feature of this study is that targets and distractors only differ in terms of their meaning (Barnard et al., 2004, p. 179). The participant is set to attend to *jobs that people do for pay*. The more that an item is meaningfully related to the target, the more it will be attended to. Barnard et al. (2004, p. 185) conceive of this process as involving an initial 'glance' at an item, followed by a closer 'look' if it seems to be a possible target. The more time spent looking at an item, the less likely the next item will receive even a 'glance'. The result will be an attentional blink. This account of the attentional blink harks back to Mack's point that highly meaningful stimuli capture our attention. It also anticipates the notion that much of cognition involves an 'effort after meaning' (Bartlett, 1932), a point we will consider in detail in the next chapter.

Implicit Perception and Inattentional Blindness

Mack and Rock's (1998) series of experiments, which we have already considered at several points in this chapter, is rich with implications for the study of attention. Recall that their basic procedure involved participants being shown a series of asymmetrical crosses and on each trial being asked to judge which arm of the cross was longer. On some trials, the participant was unexpectedly shown an item located in one of the quadrants defined by the cross, as in Figure 3.8. Many participants said that they did not see anything other than the cross. In one variation of this experiment, Mack and Rock presented a word located in one of the quadrants. Their hypothesis was that if a priming effect was observed for a word to which participants were inattentionally blind, then 'it would indicate that the unseen word was registered and encoded below the level of conscious awareness' (p. 176).

Mack and Rock present words like *chart* in one of the quadrants of the cross. Subsequently, participants were asked to complete a word stem, like *cha– –*. Completing the word stem with *chart* is very unlikely by chance, since it is not the most common word that fits. Other more common possibilities include *chair*, *champ*, *chase*, *charm*, etc. However, on trials when participants had been shown a word like *chart* and claimed not to have seen it, they were much more likely to complete the stem with *chart* than were participants who had not been shown that word. These results were evidence 'of the processing, registration and encoding of the unseen and unidentified words presented under conditions of inattention' (Mack & Rock, 1998, p. 179).

Merikle, Smilek, and Eastwood (2001) observed that Mack and Rock's technique for studying attention is more ecologically valid than other techniques that rely on masking or manipulations of the quality of the stimulus. The Mack and Rock paradigm reflects a very common occurrence in which people are:

> in situations where there are many unattended stimuli outside their immediate focus of attention which are not consciously experienced. In these situations, the unattended stimuli could be consciously experienced if the person's focus of attention changed so that it was directed toward the relevant spatial locations. For this

reason, the experimental conditions in studies in which unattended stimuli are presented at spatial locations removed from the current focus of attention more closely resemble the conditions under which visual stimuli are perceived in everyday situations. (p. 121)

Déjà Vu

This is a common experience in which a person has the impression of having previously experienced the situation in which one finds oneself, accompanied by the sense that this may not in fact be the case. **Déjà vu** has been studied by psychologists for at least 100 years. As Brown (2003) observed, it is unfortunate that déjà vu has typically been associated with paranormal and pathological experiences, because this has hindered its investigation as a common experience for 'ordinary' people. In fact, the results of over 41 surveys of the frequency of occurrence of déjà vu suggest that approximately two-thirds of individuals report having had one or more déjà vu experiences (Brown, 2003, p. 397). Are you one of these people? If so, you have lots of company.

There are interesting demographics associated with the experience of déjà vu. For one thing, fewer people over 60 years old report ever having a déjà vu experience than do people in their twenties. As Brown observes, this is an illogical outcome, since people in their sixties were once 20 years old. The explanation seems to be that déjà vu has become a much more acceptable experience to report than it was when people now in their sixties were in their twenties (Brown, 2003, p. 400). There are no reliable gender differences, but there are socio-economic, educational, and travel differences. Those higher on the socio-economic scale, the better-educated, and the well-travelled are more likely to report déjà vu experiences. Such differences may occur because wealthy, well-educated, and worldly people are likely to experience novel situations that may provide the occasion for a déjà vu experience.

Brown reviews several possible explanations of déjà vu. One plausible explanation relies on priming associated with inattentional blindness. Remember that Mack and Rock's studies showed that people often fail to perceive something right in front of them, 'hiding in plain sight' as it were. What they did not see can still register outside of awareness and influence the way they structure their subsequent experience. 'For example, one may enter a room talking on a cell phone while looking directly at a particular stimulus, and moments later this same stimulus is consciously perceived and elicits a déjà vu' (Brown, 2003, p. 407).

Conscious and Unconscious Processes: Summary and Conclusion

Although Marcel's (1983a, 1983b) experiments have been superseded, the conclusions he drew from them are still of value. His studies and the others we have reviewed point to the importance of the distinction between conscious and unconscious mental processes. People are not always aware of perceptual processes. What they are aware of and what they perceive can be two different things. Their conscious experience is not simply a copy of what has been unconsciously processed.

Remember Wickens's point that people encode virtually every aspect of the stimuli that impinge on them, but very little of what is encoded reaches awareness. Rather, people impose a structure on some of what they have encoded. This structure is in the form of one hypothesis—out of many possible hypotheses—about what they might be experiencing. Hypotheses that people reject are inhibited. In general, unconscious processes are unlimited in capacity. However, as we have seen, conscious processes are usually limited to one thing at a time.

Marcel suggested that what ends up as consciousness is a functional way of organizing what we are given. Conscious mental processes have an essential characteristic that was described by Brentano (1874). When people are conscious, they are always conscious of something. Consciousness always has an object. This point is less mysterious than it sounds. At any one time there could be many different things of which people could be conscious, but they end up being conscious only of a limited subset of all those things. Remember James's point about the different travellers. They each organized their conscious experience in terms of what was the most functional for them. Consciousness is not just the end result of perception. It is a deliberate structuring of information so as to yield the most useful organization for us in a particular situation.

■ Questions for Study and Discussion

1. Compare and contrast feature detection and template matching approaches to pattern recognition.
2. Why has the Stroop task been such a popular research tool?
3. Discuss the ways in which inattentional blindness and attention capture reveal complementary aspects of cognition.
4. Can we attend to two things at once? Discuss research relating to this question.
5. Consider some of the difficulties involved in determining whether or not a process is 'unconscious'.

■ Key Concepts

Anterior cingulate cortex (ACC) An area of the brain that may detect conflicting response tendencies of the sort that the Stroop task elicits.

Attentional blink When two stimuli are presented within 550 milliseconds of each other, the probability of the second letter being reported is much less than it would be for longer intervals.

Attention capture The power of some stimuli on some occasions to elicit attention in spite of the fact that we did not intend to pay attention to them.

Backward masking Presenting a stimulus, called the target, to the participant and then covering, or masking, the target with another stimulus.

Bottom-up influences The effect of recent stimuli on attention.

Capacity model The hypothesis that attention is like a power supply that can only support a limited amount of attentional activity.

Central bottleneck The hypothesis that there is only one path through which information relevant to only one task at a time can pass.

Cocktail party phenomenon Attending to one conversation in a crowded room in which many other conversations are going on.

Contrast energy The ease with which a stimulus can be discriminated from the background against which it is displayed.

Controlled versus automatic processes Processes to which we must pay attention in order to execute them properly versus processes than run themselves off without the necessity of our paying attention to them.

Déjà vu The impression of having previously experienced the situation in which one finds oneself, accompanied by the sense that this may not in fact be the case.

Dichotic listening Participants are exposed to two verbal messages presented simultaneously, and are required to answer questions posed in only one of the messages.

Direct versus indirect measures Participants' verbal report that they have seen a stimulus versus the effects of an undetected stimulus on a subsequent task.

Dissociation paradigm An experimental strategy that attempts to demonstrate that it is possible to perceive stimuli in the complete absence of any conscious awareness of these stimuli.

Divided attention The ability to attend to more than one thing at a time.

Domain-specific modules The hypothesis that parts of the brain may be specialized for particular tasks, such as recognizing faces.

Dorsolateral prefrontal cortex (DLPFC) An area of the brain that may exert a top-down bias that favours the selection of task-relevant information.

Early selection The hypothesis that attention prevents early perceptual processing of distractors.

Encoding The process of transforming information into one or more forms of representation.

Feature detection The hypothesis that we detect patterns on the basis of their properties, or features.

Feature integration theory (Treisman) Before we can attend to objects in the world we must extract the features that make up these objects.

Filter The hypothesis that one of the stages of information processing might be a filter that admits some messages but blocks others.

Flanker task Participants may be influenced by an irrelevant stimulus beside the target.

Höffding function The process whereby an experience makes contact with a memory trace, resulting in recognition.

Implicit perception The effect on a person's experience, thought, or action of an object in the current stimulus environment in the absence of, or independent of, conscious perception of that event.

Inattentional blindness Our failure to attend to events that we might be expected to notice.

Jumbled word effect The ability to raed sentences in spite of the fcat that there are mixed-up ltteers in the middle of smoe of the wrods.

Late selection The hypothesis that both relevant and irrelevant stimuli are perceived, so that the person must actively ignore the irrelevant stimuli in order to focus on the relevant ones.

Limen Another term for threshold.

Memory trace The trace that an experience leaves behind in memory.

Multiple-trace memory model (Hintzman) Traces of each individual experience are recorded in memory. No matter how often a particular kind of event is experienced, a memory trace of the event is recorded each time.

Objective and subjective threshold The point at which a participant can detect a stimulus at a chance level versus the point at which a participant says she or he is unaware of a stimulus.

Pandemonium (Selfridge) A model of pattern recognition consisting of three levels: data, cognitive demons, and decision demons.

Pattern recognition The ability to recognize an event as an instance of a particular category of event.

Perception without awareness A stimulus that has an effect even though it is below the participant's subjective threshold.

Pop-out effects Features of objects, such as orientation, that may be extracted preattentively.

Preattentive processes The process of feature extraction that operates outside of awareness.

Priming The tendency for some initial stimuli to make subsequent responses more likely.

Process dissociation procedure An experimental technique that requires participants *not* to respond with items they have observed previously.

Prototypical The degree to which an event is representative of a pattern or category.

Selective attention Attending to relevant information and ignoring irrelevant information.

Selective looking A visual analogue of dichotic listening in which one is exposed to two sequences of events simultaneously, but attends only to one.

Set Temporary, top-down organizations that facilitate some responses, while inhibiting others, in order to achieve the person's goals.

Shadowing task Being exposed to two mes-sages simultaneously while repeating one of them.

Squelching The tendency of the nervous system to inhibit the processing of unclear features.

Stimulus onset asynchrony (SOA) The time difference between the first stimulus and a masking stimulus.

Stroop task A list of colour names each of which is printed in a colour other than its name.

Structural limits The hypothesis that attentional tasks interfere with one another to the extent that they share similar activities.

Subliminal perception Cases in which a stimulus has an effect on behaviour even though it has been exposed too rapidly or at too low an intensity for the person to be able to identify the stimulus.

Switch cost The finding that performance declines immediately upon people switching tasks.

Task switching People must change their set from working on one task to working on another. Usually studied in situations in which the switch is involuntary.

Template matching The hypothesis that the process of pattern recognition takes place through the use of templates or prototypes.

Top-down influences The effect of high-level goals on attention.

Word superiority effect It is easier to identify a letter (e.g., D) if it appears in a word (e.g., WORD) rather than by itself.

■ Links to Other Chapters

■ Further Reading

People can discriminate between human and computer voices very early in the process of attention according to Lattner, S., Maess, B., Wang, Y., Schauer, M., Alter, K., & Friederici, A.D. (2003). Dissociation of human and computer voices in the brain: Evidence for a pre-attentive gestalt-like perception. *Human Brain Mapping, 20,* 13–21.

An intriguing demonstration that the spotlight of attention may not always be unitary is Müller, M.M., Malinoski, P., Gruber, T., & Hillyard, S.A. (2003). Sustained division of the attentional spotlight. *Nature, 424,* 309–312.

A connectionist model of Stroop performance is given by Cohen, J.D., Dunbar, K., & McClelland, J.L. (1990). On the control of automatic processes: A parallel distributed processing account of the Stroop effect. *Psychological Review, 97,* 332–361.

Attention is sometimes characterized as a limited resource, as discussed in Norman, D.A., & Bobrow, D.G. (1975). On data limited and resource limited processes. *Cognitive Psychology, 7,* 44–64. However, it is not an easy matter to specify precisely what kind of resource attention is, as is shown by Allport, D.A. (1980). Attention and performance. In G. Claxton (Ed.), *New directions in cognitive psychology* (pp. 26–64). London: Routledge & Kegan Paul.

More on inattentional blindness may be found in Most, S.B., Simons, D.J., Scholl, B.J., Jimenez, R., Clifford, E., & Chabris, C.F. (2001). How not to be seen: The contribution of similarity and selective ignoring to sustained inattentional blindness. *Psychological Science, 12,* 9–17.

Some preliminary findings in the neuropsychology of task switching are reviewed by Gurd, J.M., Weiss, P.H., Amunts, K., & Fink, G.R. (2003). Within-task switching in the verbal domain. *NeuroImage, 20,* S50–S57.

So-called subliminal perception potentially has great commercial value, as is observed in Kihlstrom, J.F. (1987). The cognitive unconscious. *Science, 237,* 1335–1552. One way of exploiting the commercial value of subliminal perception is through so-called subliminal self-help audiotapes. Greenwald, A.G., Spangenberg, E.R., Pratkanis, A.R., & Eskanazi, J. (1991). Double-blind tests of subliminal self-help audiotapes. *Psychological Science, 2,* 119–122, outlines a clever study to determine what effects such audiotapes actually have. They found that the tape label (e.g., improves memory) led participants to believe they had improved, but these beliefs were not reflected in participants' actual performance. Studies such as theirs do suggest that one should be skeptical about the claims of the manufacturers of such aids. Also see Moore, T.E. (1995). Subliminal self-help audiotapes: An empirical test of auditory consequences. *Canadian Journal of Behavioural Science, 27,* 9–20.

Chapter 4

Memory Traces and Memory Schemas

■ Schema Theories of Memory

We have already made use of the schema concept in previous chapters. In what follows, we will explore the schema concept in more detail than we have thus far. Probably no idea is more important in cognitive psychology generally and in theories of memory in particular. We will begin this chapter with a discussion of some of the ways in which the schema concept has been used.

In the last chapter, we noted that one way that experience can have an effect on memory is by leaving behind a trace of itself. Memory traces are often conceived of as replicas of previous experiences. Paul (1967) noted that the typical conception of the memory trace views memory as being similar to a recording device. Suppose that memory was like a machine for making and storing faithful copies of events, such as a video recorder. Such a device would not only make a copy of events, but it would also preserve the copy for an indefinitely long period of time. The tape could be played back, and the previously recorded event re-experienced in a form quite similar to the original experience. The number of times the event could be played back is, in principle, unlimited. However, each replay would be the same as the previous replay. Over long periods of time, there may be some decay in the quality of the recording due to age and wear and tear on the machine, but you could still recover a great deal of information about the original event for a very long time. This model of memory works as long as it is true that recall of previous experiences is accurate.

Both Paul and Erdelyi (1985) have drawn attention to Freud's (1925/1961) analogy of the **mystic writing pad**, which may be a good way of beginning to think about how memory traces become organized into memory schemas. Far from being a mysterious entity, the mystic writing pad was a common children's toy in which a layer of black wax underlies a sheet of waxed paper which in turn underlies a sheet of clear plastic (celluloid). When you write on the plastic, you can see what you have written, because it is engraved in the wax. When you lift the plastic, what you have written disappears.

The plastic layer is like our perception of an event. Our perceptions are transitory—we pass from one experience to the next. Memories are similar to what remains on the wax tablet after we lift the plastic. From this viewpoint, memories are aftereffects of perception, but they tend to run into one another. Thus, if you examine the black wax layer after you have used the pad for a long time, you will see numerous lines all overlapping as in Figure 4.1. How could you tell what had originally been written? The only way would be by making inferences. Thus, I could imagine that the word *pear* had been written by following some of the lines, and inferring that the remainder of the word pear was covered up. If memory is like this, then recall would seldom be a literal re-experiencing of the past. Rather, it would be a reconstruction (Neisser, 1967) of the past, and extremely prone to error.

The mystic writing pad analogy is not perfect. It is unlikely that memory has the truly haphazard structure of a wax tablet. We will see that schemas may, in fact, be quite well organized. However, the analogy helps to clarify the distinction between memory traces and memory schemas. The pure concept of memory traces is that they are laid down in memory as distinct, permanent copies of previous experiences. If memory is entirely based on the recall of memory traces, then remembering would be a re-experiencing of the past. This notion is what Neisser (1967) called the **reappearance hypothesis**: 'it implies that the same "memory" . . . can disappear and reappear over and over again' (p. 282). By contrast, if memory is schematic then it does not use "stored copies of finished mental events" but relies instead on "fragments . . . used to support a new construction' (p. 286). Another analogy Neisser used was that when we remember something, we are like a paleontologist trying to reconstruct a dinosaur from a few remaining bone fragments. There are many possible outcomes. We try to do the best we can given rather limited information. What we end up with relies on a lot of guesswork, and may not bear a very close resemblance to the original.

Obviously, one of the more interesting questions concerns the extent to which memory involves the recall of memory traces that are faithful renditions of the past. One source of evidence for pure trace memory might be the presence of very vivid, accurate memories for particular events.

Figure 4.1 The Mystic Writing Pad.

From Erdelyi, M.H. (1985). *Psychoanalysis: Freud's cognitive psychology*. San Francisco: Freeman, p. 119. Copyright 1985 by Matthew Hugh Erdelyi. Used with permission.

Flashbulb Memories

Do we have any memories that are especially clear and distinct? Some psychologists have argued for such a class of memories. These are our recollections of particularly important events. For example, a great many people who were of school age or older when President Kennedy was assassinated claimed to be able to remember vividly the circumstances under which they learned of the assassination. Such memories were first investigated by R. Brown and Kulik (1977).

Brown and Kulik asked 80 Harvard undergraduates to try to recall the circumstances under which they heard of the death of President Kennedy. This study took place in the mid-1970s, and Kennedy's assassination took place in 1963. The participants wrote a free recall account of what they remembered. Participants also estimated how consequential they felt that event was, and how frequently they had talked about it. Participants followed a similar procedure for the assassinations or attempted assassinations of some other prominent figures, such as Martin Luther King Jr.

The results were that almost every participant had what appeared to be vivid, detailed memories of the Kennedy assassination, and often of the others. Their reports typically contained information in the following five categories: (a) the place in which they were when they learned of the assassination; (b) what they were doing when they were interrupted by the news of the assassination; (c) the person who was their informant; (d) affect—how they felt at the time; (e) the aftermath—what they did immediately after learning the news. An additional finding was that the more consequential the event was rated, then the more often it had been rehearsed (i.e., discussed with others).

Brown and Kulik called such vivid, detailed accounts **flashbulb memories**. They proposed a specific theory of the mechanism that produces such memories. This theory is called the **Now Print theory**, and is adapted from the work of Livingston (1967). Now Print theory proposes that information is processed in the following sequence, which is given diagrammatically in Figure 4.2.

First, an event is tested for 'surprisingness'. If the event is completely ordinary, then we may pay no attention to it at all. If, however, the event is quite extraordinary, like assassinations were in the early 1960s, then we will tend to pay very close attention to it. Brown and Kulik allowed for the additional possibility that an event could be sufficiently traumatic for us not to process it at all, leading to a total amnesia for the event. The second stage is to test the event for consequentiality. If we regard the event as both surprising and important, then the third stage is the formation of a flashbulb memory. Flashbulb memories will vary in vividness and completeness depending on how surprising and consequential they are. The fourth stage is rehearsal. We tend to think about our flashbulb memories more than we might think about other memories, and we are also likely to create verbal accounts of them. These rehearsals produce the fifth stage, which is the flashbulb account of our memories we tell to other people.

The focus of Now Print theory is on the third stage, the production of the memory. It is as if we can preserve flashbulb kinds of experience in the same way that a photocopier makes a copy of a page. When you copy something, you press the Print button on the machine and the machine makes a faithful reproduction of everything on the

Figure 4.2 Brown and Kulik's Model of Flashbulb Memories.

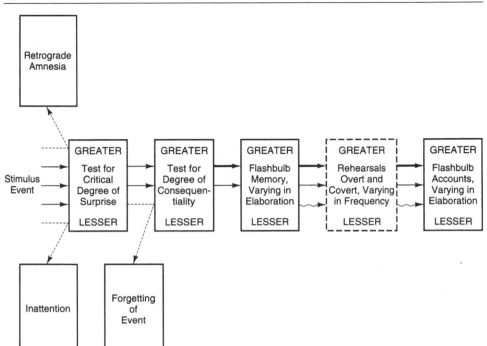

From Brown, R., & Kulik, J. (1977). Flashbulb memories. *Cognition, 5*, pp. 73–99. Copyright 1977 by Elsevier Science Publishers. Reprinted by permission.

page. Perhaps something similar happens when we encounter an event that is sufficiently surprising and emotionally significant. Perhaps there is a mechanism for laying down in memory an enduring record of an experience, including the context in which the experience occurred. Flashbulb memories would be an example of highly detailed memory traces for certain kinds of events.

Brown and Kulik speculated that such a Now Print mechanism might be a very primitive form of memory, which would have been useful when there were no records of events in books or in any other medium. In prehistoric times, for example, it would have been useful to have what amounts to a photographic record in memory of surprising and significant events. This form of memory becomes less useful as other kinds of records evolve, and people can keep track of events by means of external memory aids like books. As memory evolves, it becomes less and less concrete and specific, and more and more abstract and general. That is, the evolution of memory would be away from memory traces and towards memory schemas.

Is There a Flashbulb Memory Mechanism?

Brown and Kulik's work elicited a great deal of attention. A number of historically important events have subsequently been investigated as possible sources of 'flashbulbs'.

These included memory for the *Challenger* space shuttle explosion on 28 January 1986 (Bohannon, 1988; Bohannon & Symons, 1992; McCloskey, Wible, & Cohen, 1988). McCloskey and his co-workers collected questionnaire data from 45 people three days after the shuttle disaster. Approximately nine months later, 27 of these participants filled in a follow-up questionnaire. In addition, 31 people who had not filled in the first questionnaire completed the second questionnaire. The questionnaires included four questions about the *Challenger* explosion: Where were you when you first learned of the explosion? What were you doing when you first learned of the explosion? Did you see the event at the time it was actually happening, or did you learn about it later? What were your first thoughts upon hearing the news?

All participants remembered something about the circumstances in which they had heard about the disaster. However, comparison of the immediate and the nine-month questionnaire data showed that there had been quite a bit of information loss over the interval, and that the two accounts were not always consistent. Thus, the nine-month accounts were more general (less specific) than the immediate accounts. For example, someone might have named the person who told them about the explosion in the immediate account, but only referred to 'a friend' in the nine-month account. Twenty accounts became more general, but only seven became more specific. Seven participants gave inconsistent accounts. For example, they might have said that they were at their desks when they heard about it, and then nine months later say that they were walking out the office door.

It is important to note, however, that none of the nine-month responses was wildly inconsistent with the earlier descriptions. Rather, the inconsistencies were 'the same sort of reconstructive errors that seem to occur frequently for "ordinary" memories. That is, for flashbulb memories, inaccuracies may be introduced when information that cannot be retrieved from memory is filled in through inference or guesswork' (McCloskey et al., 1988, p. 175).

McCloskey et al. concluded that flashbulb memories are not necessarily more accurate than normal memories, and that a special flashbulb mechanism need not be postulated in order to account for them. Rather, so-called flashbulb memories are the consequences of the same factors that influence ordinary memories. To buttress this point, McCloskey et al. cited Neisser, who pointed out the relevance for flashbulb memories of the parallel between remembering something and telling a story. Memory often has a narrative structure:

> All of us have a rough narrative conception of public affairs: Time runs on, events unfold, and occasionally there are 'historic moments'. History has to have such moments, because otherwise it wouldn't be much of a story. The death of a prominent person—or the resignation of a president—is a good place to end a chapter or to highlight a theme . . . in addition to the narrative of public events that we all keep to some extent, everyone elaborates another and more detailed story as well: his own. Our lives are laid out behind us in a richly structured way, full of landmarks and stages and critical moments . . . . My suggestion is that we remember

the details of a flashbulb occasion because those details are the links between our own histories and 'History'.

. . .

[Flashbulb memories] are places where we line up our own lives with the course of history and say 'I was there.' (Neisser, 1982a, p. 47)

Weaver (1993) took advantage of a chance occurrence to investigate similarities and differences between flashbulb and ordinary memories. The first part of the study took place on Wednesday 16 January 1991. Participants 'were told that the next time they saw a roommate (or friend if they lived alone) they should do their best to remember all the circumstances surrounding that event' (p. 40). By chance, President George H.W. Bush signalled the beginning of the first war in Iraq by ordering the bombing of Baghdad to begin that very evening. Weaver (1991) realized that this presented him with a natural experiment, and on 18 January 1991 he asked his participants to fill out questionnaires dealing with their memories of both the meeting with their roommate/friend and the bombing of Iraq. Follow-up questionnaires were done in April 1991 and in January 1992. Comparing the April and January memories with the original ones, Weaver found that both events were recalled with approximately equal accuracy, and tended to be less accurate as time passed. However, participants were much more confident about their memory for the Iraq bombing than they were about their memory for the meeting with their roommate/friend. Weaver, like Neisser (1982), suggested that the confidence we have in flashbulb memories comes from our realization that we have witnessed a historically important event, and wish to preserve in our memory a sense of having participated in it. However, our actual memory of historically important events may be only as accurate as our memory for other events.

A number of investigations have explored flashbulb memories for the 11 September 2001 destruction of the twin towers of the World Trade Center in New York City (e.g., Greenberg, 2004; Neisser, 2003). Talarico and Rubin (2003) did perhaps the best designed of all studies of the 'flashbulb' phenomenon. On 12 September 2001, they tested 54 Duke University students using an open-ended questionnaire similar to Brown and Kulik's to get descriptions not only of the momentous events of the previous day, but also of an ordinary event, such as a party, that each participant had recently experienced. Talarico and Rubin added other tests designed to measure additional aspects of the flashbulb phenomenon, such as the intensity of the emotion felt when the events were recalled. They then divided the 54 participants into three groups of 18 each and re-tested each group once. The first group was tested one week later, the second was tested six weeks later, and the third was tested 32 weeks later. The major variable of interest was the consistency of the account given at the three different intervals. For example, if a participant said on 12 September that 'Fred' was with him when the event was initially experienced, and then subsequently said that 'Alice' was with him, but not 'Fred', then that response was scored as inconsistent. Each participant's recall was given a consistency score in terms of the number of details consistently recalled, as well as an inconsistency score. Figure 4.3 shows the change in consistency and inconsistency scores as a function of time. Notice that both flashbulb and everyday memories show a decline in consistency and an increase in inconsistency. Although the flashbulb memories had more emotion associated with them, in terms of their actual content they are certainly no more accurate than 'ordinary' memories. However, participants erroneously believed that their flashbulb memories were more accurate than their 'ordinary' memories. A flashbulb event 'reliably enhances memory characteristics such as vividness and confidence', but people should not put that much faith 'in the accuracy of their flashbulb memories' (Talarico & Rubin, 2003, p. 460).

■ Are Memory Traces Permanent?

The results of flashbulb memory experiments have led many to question whether memory traces persist unchanged over time. The theory of memory traces has been

Figure 4.3 Properties of Flashbulb Memories.

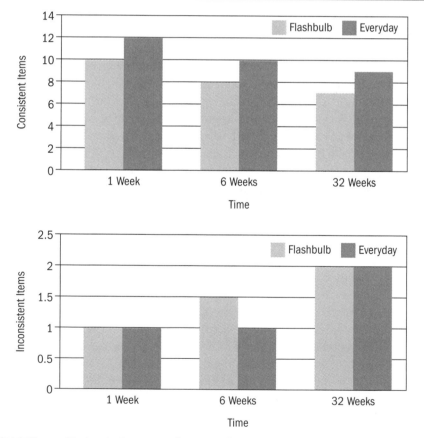

Notice that the Y-axes of the two graphs are not to the same scale.
Data from Talarico, J.M., & Rubin, D.C. (2003). Confidence, not consistency, characterizes flashbulb memories. *Psychological Science, 14*, 455–461.

undergoing considerable modification (Dudai, 2004; Nader, 2003; Wixted, 2004a). The classic approach to memory traces is called **consolidation theory** (Woodworth, 1938, p. 51). The basic idea is that memory traces of an event are not fully formed immediately after that event, but take some time to become complete. This process of consolidation can be disrupted by events that occur after the to-be-remembered event, a phenomenon called **retroactive interference**. Woodworth's (1938, p. 227) review of the classic literature (e.g., Jenkins & Dallenbach, 1924) concluded that 'rest immediately after learning . . . allows for full consolidation of the traces, while strenuous mental work just at this time . . . leaves the traces weak.' This conclusion is echoed in the current literature. For example, Wixted (2004a, p. 247) said that 'even if the intervening study material is not related to the original learning in any obvious way, the new learning draws on a limited pool of resources that may have otherwise been available to consolidate the original learning. As a result, memory for the original material suffers.'

It is known that the **hippocampus** is a crucial site for the consolidation of memory traces, converting immediate memories into long-term memories. In evolutionary terms, the hippocampus is a relatively 'old' part of the brain. Its name comes from the Greek for 'sea horse', the shape of which it resembles. 'If the hippocampal formation is damaged before the consolidation process is complete, recently formed memories that are still undergoing the consolidation process will be impaired' (Wixted, 2004a, p.242). It is likely that retroactive interference occurs because 'ordinary mental exertion and memory formation' detract from an ongoing process of [hippocampal] consolidation' (Wixted, 2004a, p. 264).

It was long believed that once the consolidation process was complete, then it was also permanent and fixed. However, it now appears likely that when the stored trace is re-activated, it becomes labile (i.e., changeable) (Dudai, 2004; Nader, 2003). Thus, the recall of a previous experience places it in working memory, where it comes into contact with other experiences. For example, the context in which you recall a flashbulb experience may be quite different from the original context in which you experienced it. This provides an opportunity for the memory trace to be revised, although the *extent* to which traces are susceptible to revision is controversial. In any case, the revised trace would then undergo **reconsolidation** in the hippocampus (Nader, 2003, p. 66). Of course, there is nothing to prevent a cycle whereby a memory trace is reactivated and reconsolidated indefinitely. There is thus no reason to believe that a memory trace is necessarily a faithful rendition of the original experience.

Nader (2003, p. 70) reviewed the memory reconsolidation literature, and his conclusion is extremely important. 'There can be no doubt at this point that memories are fundamentally dynamic processes, as first explicitly demonstrated by Bartlett (1932). They are not snapshots of events that are passively read out but, rather, are constructive in nature and always changing (Tulving & Thomson, 1973; Loftus & Yuille, 1984; Schacter, 1999).' In reaching this conclusion, Nader cites Bartlett (1932), whose book *Remembering* has profoundly influenced cognitive psychology. It is to an examination of that work that we now turn.

■ Bartlett's Remembering

The schema concept was made a central part of the psychology of memory by the work of Bartlett (1932; Roediger, 1997; Thompson, 1997; Weiskrantz, 2000; Zangwill, 1972). Bartlett's best-known experimental techniques were the method of **repeated reproduction** and the method of **serial reproduction**. In the former a participant would read the material, and then attempt to reproduce it 15 minutes later, and at longer subsequent intervals. In the latter, one participant, A, is given something to remember. A writes down what he or she can recall. A's version is given to the next participant, B, who reads it and tries to recall it. B's version is in turn given to C, and so on. Thus, each participant is trying to recall the previous participant's version of the original to-be-remembered material. In one study, the first participant was given a North American folktale to recall. Both methods yielded similar results, but the most dramatic results came from the method of serial reproduction. The story to be reproduced was as follows.

The War of the Ghosts

One night two young men from Egulac went down to the river to hunt seals, and while they were there it became foggy and calm. Then they heard war-cries, and they thought: 'Maybe this is a war party.' They escaped to the shore and hid behind a log. Now canoes came up, and they heard the noise of paddles and saw one canoe coming up to them. There were five men in the canoe, and they said:

'What do you think? We wish to take you along. We are going up the river to make war on the people.'

One of the young men said: 'I have no arrows.'

'Arrows are in the canoe', they said.

'I will not go along. I might get killed. My relatives do not know where I have gone. But you', he said, turning to the other, 'may go with them.'

So one of the men went, but the other returned home.

And the warriors went on up the river to a town on the other side of Kalama. The people came down to the water, and they began to fight, and many were killed. But presently the young man heard one of the warriors say: 'Quick, let us go home: that Indian has been hit.' Now he thought: 'Oh, they are ghosts.' He did not feel sick, but he said he had been shot.

So the canoes went back to Egulac, and the young man went ashore to his house and made a fire. And he told everybody and said: 'Behold I accompanied the ghosts, and we went to fight. Many of our fellows were killed, and many of those who attacked us were killed. They said I was hit, and I did not feel sick.'

He told it all, and then became quiet. When the sun rose he fell down. Something black came out of his mouth. His face became contorted. The people jumped up and cried.

He was dead. (Bartlett, 1932, p. 65)

At this point you should not read any further, but wait 15 minutes and then attempt to reproduce the story.

As you can imagine, as the reproductions progressed, they became increasingly less like the original. Using the method of serial reproduction, by the tenth person the story had become the following:

The War of the Ghosts (2)

Two Indians were out fishing for seals in the Bay of Manpapan, when along came five other Indians in a war canoe. They were going fighting.

'Come with us', said the five to the two, 'and fight.'

'I cannot come', was the answer of the one, 'for I have an old mother at home who is dependent upon me.' The other also said he could not come, because he had no arms. 'That is no difficulty', the others replied, 'for we have plenty in the canoe with us'; so he got into the canoe and went with them.

In a fight soon afterwards this Indian received a mortal wound. Finding that his hour was come, he cried out that he was about to die. 'Nonsense', said one of the others, 'you will not die.' But he did. (Bartlett, 1932, p. 124)

Bartlett believed that such a series of reproductions shows what happens to memory over time. Obviously, there are several omissions from the original, so that the story is simplified. Notice that, in spite of the title, there is no longer any mention of ghosts by reproduction 10. People tended to select some material to remember and to omit other material. These omissions reflect a process of **rationalization**. The person attempts to make the story as coherent and sensible as possible, from his or her viewpoint. Material that does not fit in tends to drop out of the narrative. Recall the death of the Indian in the original version: 'When the sun rose he fell down. Something black came out of his mouth. His face became contorted.' Over successive reproductions this changed into a 'black thing' that 'rushed from his mouth', to 'his soul fled black from his mouth', to 'his spirit fled', and finally, by version 10, these details are missing altogether. The mysterious blackness becomes conventionalized as a soul and then is dropped altogether. Bartlett noted that unfamiliar material was transformed over time into more and more familiar content.

Bergman and Roediger (1997) have replicated Bartlett's results using the method of repeated reproduction and testing of participants 15 minutes, one week, and six months after the initial exposure to the story. (Does your reproduction show the sort of changes we have just discussed? Given that it was just 15 minutes after initially reading the story, the changes might not be so dramatic. Try to recall the story again next week.)

On the basis of his experiments, Bartlett concluded:

Remembering is not the re-excitation of innumerable fixed, lifeless and fragmentary traces. It is imaginative reconstruction, or construction, built out of the relation of our attitude towards a whole active mass of organized past reactions or experience, and to a little outstanding detail which commonly appears in image or in language form. (p. 213)

This 'active mass of organized past reactions' is what Bartlett meant by a **schema**. As such, a schema is an organized setting that guides our behaviour, a standard that can be adjusted to fit changing circumstances.

Bartlett used as an example the ability to make the proper stroke in a ball game such as tennis. You must adjust your posture and bodily movements to fit the current situation. You do not simply repeat a stroke you have made before, because the ball is not likely to be exactly the same place twice, and neither are you. A schema is a flexible organization, and that is what makes it useful. If our memory was just a set of traces, then it would be far less useful because it would be too rigid. A schema is a more abstract and general setting within which memory traces have meaning.

It is important to note that Bartlett never denied the existence of memory traces (Ost & Costall, 2002). The case of Professor Aitken (Hunter, 1977) is a very good example of the way in which memory traces and memory schemas can work together. This case is discussed in Box 4.1.

Phantom Limbs and the Body Schema

Bartlett (1958, p. 146) began using the schema concept as a result of his work with the great neurologist Sir Henry Head. Head wanted to understand how people could generally have a very good sense of their posture and be able to alter their posture so as to successfully move around in the world. Thus, without thinking about it, we 'know' where our arms, legs, and the rest of our body parts are positioned at any time and smoothly co-ordinate them when we walk, sit down, turn around, and so on. Head proposed the word 'schema' to mean the 'standard against which all subsequent changes of posture are measured before they enter consciousness. . . . By means of perpetual alterations in position we are constantly building up a postural model of ourselves which constantly changes. Every new posture of movement is recorded on this plastic schema, and the activity of the cortex brings every fresh group of sensations evoked by altered posture into relation with it' (Bartlett, 1932, pp. 199–200). Head was talking about our **body schema**, which is also sometimes called our **body image**.

The way that the body schema works is well illustrated by the phenomenon of **phantom limbs**. A phantom limb occurs when a body part, such as an arm or leg, is suddenly missing through amputation or other means. The person still experiences the missing body part as 'being there' even though he knows perfectly well that it is missing (Simmel, 1956). 'Many patients awake from an anaesthetic after an amputation feeling certain that the operation has not been performed. They feel the lost limb so vividly that only when they reach out to touch it, or peer beneath the bed sheets to see it, do they realize that it has been cut off' (Katz, 1993, p. 336). The phantom limb is a vivid but false memory. The phantom develops immediately after amputation in approximately 75 per cent of patients and by eight days post-operatively the incidence is 85 per cent (Katz, 1993; Ramachandran & Hirstein, 1998). There is often

Box 4.1 An Exceptional Memory

Professor A.G. Aitken was a 'brilliant mathematician . . . and an accomplished violinist' whose phenomenal memory was studied for decades by psychologists (Hunter, 1977). Often people with an extraordinary memory are said to have a correspondingly poor ability to think abstractly, but that was not the case with Aitken. In fact, it was precisely because of his ability to rapidly schematize information that his memory was so prodigious. According to Hunter (1977, p. 157) what Bartlett called **effort after meaning** describes the process whereby Aitken was able to take even the most mundane sequence of events and weave them into an 'unusually rich densely structured gestalt of properties' that still preserved the uniqueness of each event. Typically, material was remembered as an unintended consequence of his attempts to make things meaningful. He never wanted to 'memorize' anything merely by rote.

Aitken felt that the most important thing was to relax and become absorbed in the material to be learned. Once you allow yourself to become interested in it, then you will begin to comprehend it in deeper and deeper ways. The more deeply you comprehend something, the better you will remember it. (This is a theme that will recur towards the end of this chapter when we discuss the levels of processing approach to memory.) Aitken observed that 'the thing to do is to learn by heart, not because one has to, but because one loves the thing and is interested in it' (Hunter, 1977, p. 158).

Because he was interested in his own mental processes, Aitken agreed to be a participant in a variety of experiments. In 1933, Aitken was asked to memorize 25 unrelated words. Twenty-seven years later (1960) he attempted to recall them, and could do so. However, Aitken did not recall even this 'meaningless' list of words by rote. Rather, he proceeded by inference to reconstruct the list. Aitken's memory operated in a schematic way even for a list of words. In the chapter on imagery we will examine some very different techniques for memorizing large amounts of material.

More typical of Aitken's memory was his knowledge of music. He believed that musical memory could be both rich and precise because music has so many different aspects. These included 'a metre and a rhythm, a tune, . . . the harmony, the instrumental colour, a particular emotion, . . . a meaning, . . . perhaps a human interest in the composer' (Hunter, 1977, p. 157). All of these combined to provide a framework within which the act of recall could take place. You should be reminded of Aitken's musical memory when, towards the end of this chapter, we review the ways in which actors learn their lines.

intense pain associated with the phantom limb, and 'more than 70 per cent of amputees continue to experience phantom limb pain of considerable intensity as long as 25 years after amputation' (Katz, 1993, p. 336).

Phantom limbs occur as a consequence of the way the body schema represents the parts of our bodies and their relationships. If the loss of a body part, such as a finger, occurs slowly, as in people who have leprosy, then there is much less likelihood that the person will experience a phantom (Simmel, 1956; Ramachandran & Hirstein, 1998, p. 1625). Perhaps the schema is better able to adjust when the change is gradual. However, just as people have difficulty adjusting to any sudden loss, it is the abrupt loss of a limb that creates the most difficulty. Nevertheless, the schema does change even in response to such devastating incidents. To see how the schema

Figure 4.4 The Penfield 'Homunculus'.

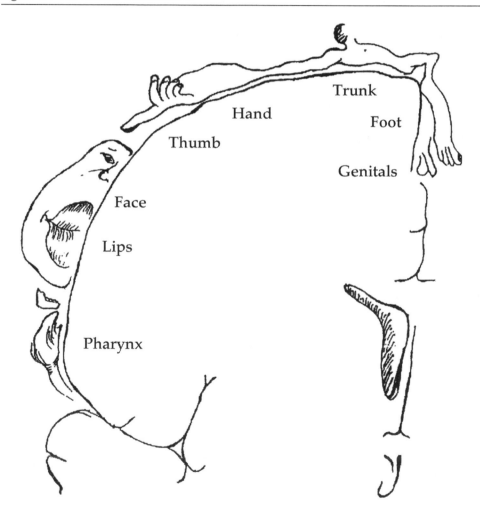

Reproduced from Ramachandran V.S., & Hirstein, W. (1998). The perception of phantom limbs. *Brain, 121*, 1603–30. Reprinted by permission of Oxford University Press and the authors.

changes, we must first examine the way in which the body is represented in intact people. Examine Figure 4.4, which is known as the **Penfield homunculus** after the neuroscientist who uncovered it. It is a map of the parts of the sensory cortex that represent the various parts of the body. The area of each body part in the map is proportional to the area of the cortex that represents it. Notice that the hands are represented in an area that is adjacent to the face.

Ramachandran (2004, p. 10; Ramachandran, 1993; Ramachandran, Rodgers-Ramachandran, & Cobb, 1995) discusses a case of a man who had his arm amputated above the left elbow. He developed a phantom limb. Amazingly, when stimulated with a Q-tip on the surface of his face he felt as if parts of his missing hand were being stimulated. There have been several reports of cases similar to this one. Why does this happen? Recall that the face is next to the hand in the Penfield homunculus.

> When an arm is amputated, no signals are received by the part of the brain's cortex corresponding to the hand. It becomes hungry for sensory input and the sensory input from the facial skin now invades the adjacent vacated territory corresponding to the missing hand. (Ramachandran, 2004, p. 13)

Brain-imaging techniques have supported this hypothesis, showing that for the sort of patient just described 'input from the face and upper arm could now activate the hand area' of the homunculus (Ramachandran & Hirstein, 1998, p. 1616). The body schema is not fixed, but shows considerable **plasticity** (i.e., flexibility). This flexibility is well illustrated by a clever technique used to ameliorate phantom pain. Sometimes a patient feels as if the phantom hand is clenching, with the fingernails painfully digging into the skin. If the person could unclench the phantom hand, perhaps the pain would go away. Now look at Figure 4.5. This apparatus allows the person to see the mirror image of his existing hand in a way that creates the illusion that the missing hand has returned. If the person unclenches his real hand then he also experiences his phantom hand as unclenching and the pain goes away in many patients (Jackson & Simpson, 2004). Nothing could better demonstrate the extent to which the body schema, and schemas generally, are organized and reorganized in extremely dynamic ways (Ramachandran & Hirstein, 1998, p. 1622).

You can experience an analog of a phantom limb by setting up a variant of the procedure in Figure 4.5. You will need a plastic hand or a glove. Put your left hand in your lap, and your right hand flat on a table. Your right hand must be hidden from your view by some sort of screen (e.g., a pile of books). Then put the fake hand on the table in front of you, similar to the set-up in Figure 4.5. Have a confederate 'repeatedly tap and stroke your concealed right hand in a random sequence. Tap, tap, tap, stroke, stroke, tap, stroke, stroke. At the same time, while you watch, he must also tap and stroke the visible dummy in perfect synchrony' (Ramachandran & Rogers-Ramachandran, 2005). After a while, you will feel as if *you* are being touched on the dummy hand.

Figure 4.5 The Phantom Limb Mirror Box.

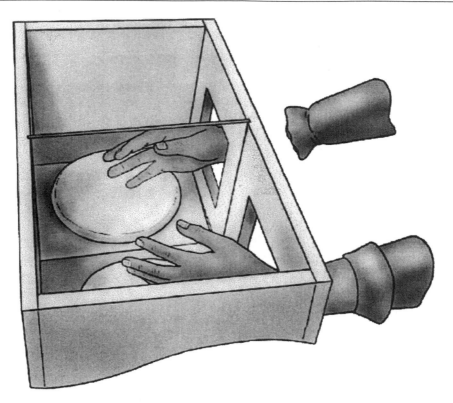

■ Research Based on Schema Theory

Over the years, reviews of schema theory approaches to memory noted that many studies of memory have employed the schema concept in the same rather general way as did Bartlett. These reviews (e.g., Alba & Hasher, 1983, p. 204; Koriat, Goldsmith, & Pansky, 2000, pp. 494–495) suggested that most schema theories assume that memory is best described in terms of the following four processes: **selection; abstraction; interpretation; integration**. The schema selects information consistent with our interests at the time. We then convert the information we have selected into a more abstract form. Thus, we extract the gist, or meaning, of something rather than try to preserve the exact event itself. We then interpret the information in terms of other information in memory. Finally, we integrate the information in such a way to make it consistent with the schema. Koriat, Goldsmith, and Pansky (2000) add a fifth process, reconstruction, whereby the act of recall blends both general knowledge and individual experiences in order to 'imaginatively reconstruct' the past.

Thus, when you are finished with this chapter, it is unlikely that you will remember every word. You probably will have selected some information, and not other information, on the basis of your interests and concerns at the time of reading. If someone asks you what the chapter is about, you will be more likely to be able to give them the gist, or a selective abstract of it, rather than a literal recall of it. Over time, you may realize that you not only interpreted the material in this chapter, but you also integrated it with other things that you know. For example, it may occur to you that the notion that the schema is selective is similar to the point we considered in the last chapter about attention being selective. Moreover, the processes we are now discussing may reflect the way in which information is encoded, a process we also considered in Chapter 3. Of course, these connections may seem to you to be somewhat vague (i.e., schematic), and you may need to reread those sections in order to fully remember these earlier concepts. Finally, years from now you may have to reconstruct this chapter from only fragmentary clues. It may not be easy to figure out precisely when you read it, or who was in your class at the time, or how many questions were on the test from this chapter, or what grades you got on them, and so on.

Let us now review representative studies illustrative of schematic memory.

Selection

Anderson and Pichert (1978) showed that we select information both as we receive it and as we recall it. Participants read a narrative about two boys playing hooky from school. The narrative can be summarized as follows:

> They go to the home of one of the boys because his mother is never there on Thursdays. The family is well-to-do. They have a fine old home, set back from the road, with attractive grounds. Since it is old it has some defects—a leaky roof, a damp and musty basement. Because the family has considerable wealth, they have a lot of valuable possessions—10-speed bikes, a colour TV set, a rare coin collection.

Some participants were asked to read the story from the point of view of a burglar. Other participants were asked to read the story from the point of view of a prospective homebuyer. They then tried to remember the story. Typically, participants remembered more information that was relevant to the perspective they had taken when they read the story. If you take the perspective of a homebuyer, then a leaky roof is more relevant than a 10-speed bike. However, if you take a burglar's perspective, then a 10-speed bike is definitely more interesting. The fact that people tended to recall more information that was consistent with their original perspective could mean that they selected that information as they read the story. However, suppose you ask half of the participants in each condition to switch their perspective after they have recalled the story once. That is, if participants had been taking a burglar's perspective, then have them take a homebuyer's perspective, and vice versa. Now participants are able to recall information that they had not been able to remember when they first tried to recall the story. Once you imagine yourself to be a homebuyer instead of a burglar, then you can remember things about the house that you did not remember when you were thinking of yourself as a burglar. For example, this is a comment made by one participant:

> Well, a funny thing happened. When he gave me the homebuyer perspective, I remembered the end of the story, you know, about the leak in the roof. The first time through I knew there was an ending, but I couldn't remember what it was. But it just popped into my mind when I thought about the story from the home-buyer perspective. (R.C. Anderson & Pichert, 1978, p. 10)

This is interesting because it suggests that people do in fact acquire information that is irrelevant to the perspective from which they encode the story. The perspective from which people read the story may not make them reject other information. Rather, the Anderson and Pichert study suggests that the process of selection can occur when people try to remember what they have read. At that point, they are more likely to remember information that is relevant to the point of view they are taking at the time of recall.

The Anderson and Pichert study implies that the active schema may not determine all the information that an individual ends up being able to remember. We may be able to remember more than we think we can by changing our perspective on what we have learned. the schema 'not only organizes material at the time of encounter (encoding) but also reorganizes previously encountered material into new structures and new retrievals' (Mandler, 2002, p. 336).

Abstraction

Do people abstract the meaning of what they experience and remember only the gist rather than the particulars? A study by Sachs (1967) is often cited in support of the notion that people remember the meaning of a sentence they hear, but forget the actual wording (Cofer, 1973; Altmann, 2001). What Sachs did was ask participants to listen to a tape-recorded story about the discovery of the telescope. The following sentence (the original sentence) occurred either near the beginning, in the middle, or at the end of the story: 'He sent a letter about it to Galileo, the great Italian scientist.'

After participants heard the story, they were given another sentence (the test sentence) and asked if it was identical to the one they had heard in the story. Sometimes the test sentence was, in fact, identical. Sometimes the meaning was the same, but the wording was different: 'A letter about it was sent to Galileo, the great Italian scientist.' On other occasions the meaning was actually changed: 'Galileo, the great Italian scientist, sent him a letter about it.'

The results were that memory for the original sentence was quite good if the original sentence had come at the end of the story. This means that participants could remember the wording of the original sentence if the interval between the time they heard the original sentence and the time they heard the test sentence was not very long. However, if the original sentence came earlier in the story, then memory for it was not so good. People were no longer always able to correctly identify the form of the sentence. However, they were usually able to correctly detect changes in meaning between the original and the test sentence. Sachs's results have often been taken as supporting 'Bartlett's finding that an "impression" is preserved but that "style" is lost' (Cofer, 1973, p. 538). Still, it is important to note that participants in the Sachs study sometimes did remember the form of the sentence, and so style may not always be lost.

Bartlett's original findings concerning memory for prose have been replicated in a striking way by Vicente and Brewer (1993). They showed that even scientists tend to remember only the gist of scientific literature and lose important details. Johnston (2001) makes the similar and highly relevant point that Bartlett's own work has been remembered in remarkably different ways by psychologists depending upon their own theoretical orientation. 'It is fitting that the reproduction of Bartlett's own work within the psychological literature confirms his thesis about the constructive nature of human remembering and thinking' (p. 362). These facts have important consequences for readers of textbooks, which are written by scholars who are familiar with the literature, but who may be prone to the same errors in recall as anyone else. Vicente and Brewer (1993) cite a paper by Cole (1939, p. 516), who observed that Bartlett's research 'might well cause the student of psychology to do some reflecting, since the very textbook which he reads is a reproduction often many times removed from that source (human behavior) to which it professedly refers.'

Interpretation

It is possible that people may interpret information they are given by making inferences and then remembering the inferences as part of the original information. If you are told at one time that a person is in one place (New York, for example), and at another time that the same person is in another place (Toronto, for example), then it will be hard not to infer that the person has moved from one place to the other (Bregman, 1977). You may subsequently even remember that the person moved from New York to Toronto, without ever needing to be explicitly told. The critical question is whether you will realize that you inferred this fact, or whether you will believe, for example, that someone told you.

A good example of the way that inferences can distort our memory comes from an experiment by French and Richards (1993). The experiment derived from a conversation that one of the authors (Christopher C. French—CCF) was once having with the other author's daughter, Lucy Richards. The daughter's

> attention was caught by the Roman numerals upon a clock face in the room. The conversation then proceeded something like this:
>
> Lucy: On the clock, why does 'V' come after 'IIII'?
>
> CCF (without looking at the clock): It doesn't say 'IIII'. It says 'IV' for four.
>
> Lucy: It doesn't. Look.
>
> CCF (looking at clock): Incredible! You'd think clock-makers of all people would know Roman numerals! But this is how it should be. (Shows his wristwatch.) Would you believe it, they've got it wrong here as well! (p. 250)

In fact, as French and Richards then went on to discover, clock faces typically have IIII rather than IV. Thus, many people will have seen clock faces with IIII, but still tend to *remember* them as having 'IV' because that is the more familiar form of the Roman numeral IV in common use and, therefore, what they would infer as being used also on a clock face. French and Richards (1993) allowed participants to look at a clock face for one minute, after which they were asked to draw it. Most participants incorrectly drew a clock face with 'IV'. Even when participants were told before seeing the clock face that they would be asked to draw it from memory, the majority incorrectly drew a clock face with 'IV'. This is powerful evidence that our inferences can override the evidence of our senses and actually change what we believe we saw. The issue of how well we are able to discriminate actual memories from things we have inferred or imagined (Johnson, 1985) is discussed in the next section.

Integration

Alba and Hasher called integration 'the set piece of schema theories' (1983, p. 216). There has been a lot of evidence presented suggesting that the meaning we abstract from an event is put together with the rest of our knowledge to form a coherent, consistent whole, or 'Gestalt'. The experiment usually cited in this connection was conducted by Bransford and Franks (1971, 1972). Look at the sentences in Table 4.1.

Table 4.1 Acquisition and Recognition Sentences

ACQUISITION SENTENCES: READ EACH SENTENCE, COUNT TO FIVE, ANSWER THE QUESTION, GO ON TO THE NEXT SENTENCE.

The girl broke the window on the porch. Broke what?

The tree in the front yard shaded the man who was smoking his pipe. Where?

The hill was steep. What was?

The cat, running from the barking dog, jumped on the table. From what?

The tree was tall. Was what?

The old car climbed the hill. What did?

The cat running from the dog jumped on the table. Where?

The girl who lives next door broke the window on the porch. Lives where?

The car pulled the trailer. Did what?

The scared cat was running from the barking dog. What was?

The girl lives next door. Who does?

The tree shaded the man who was smoking his pipe. What did?

The scared cat jumped on the table. What did?

The girl who lives next door broke the large window. Broke what?

The man was smoking his pipe. Who was?

The old car climbed the steep hill. The what?

The large window was on the porch. Where?

The tall tree was in the front yard. What was?

The car pulling the trailer climbed the steep hill. Did what?

The cat jumped on the table. Where?

The tall tree in the front yard shaded the man. Did what?

The car pulling the trailer climbed the hill. Which car?

The dog was barking. Was what?

The window was large. What was?

STOP—COVER THE PRECEDING SENTENCES. NOW READ EACH SENTENCE BELOW AND DECIDE IF IT IS A SENTENCE FROM THE LIST GIVEN ABOVE.

Test set. . . . How many are new?

The car climbed the hill.   (old___, new___)

The girl who lives next door broke the window.   (old___, new___)

The old man who was smoking his pipe climbed the steep hill.   (old___, new___)

The tree was in the front yard.   (old___, new___)

The scared cat, running from the barking dog, jumped on the table.   (old___, new___)

The window was on the porch.   (old___, new___)

The barking dog jumped on the old car in the front yard.   (old___, new___)

The tree in the front yard shaded the man.   (old___, new___)

The cat was running from the dog.   (old___, new___)

The old car pulled the trailer.   (old___, new___)

The tall tree in the front yard shaded the old car.   (old___, new___)

The tall tree shaded the man who was smoking his pipe.   (old___, new___)

The scared cat was running from the dog.   (old___, new___)

The old car, pulling the trailer, climbed the hill.   (old___, new___)

The girl who lives next door broke the large window on the porch.   (old___, new___)

The tall tree shaded the man.   (old___, new___)

The cat was running from the barking dog.   (old___, new___)

The car was old.   (old___, new___)

The girl broke the large window.   (old___, new___)

The scared cat ran from the barking dog that jumped on the table.   (old___, new___)

The scared cat, running from the dog, jumped on the table.   (old___, new___)

The old car pulling the trailer climbed the steep hill.   (old___, new___)

The girl broke the large window on the porch.   (old___, new___)

The scared cat which broke the window on the porch climbed the tree.   (old___, new___)

The tree shaded the man.   (old___, new___)

The car climbed the steep hill.   (old___, new___)

The girl broke the window.   (old___, new___)

The man who lives next door broke the large window on the porch.   (old___, new___)

The tall tree in the front yard shaded the man who was smoking his pipe.   (old___, new___)

The cat was scared.   (old___, new___)

The reader who has never participated in such an experiment is invited to read each acquisition sentence, one at a time, count to five, answer the question, then go on to the next sentence, repeat the routine, etc. The reader should then take the recognition test. The best way to understand the experiment is to take it (Jenkins, 1974, p. 790).

If you compare the test sentences with the acquisition sentences, then you will discover that none of them is the same as any other. Yet people typically believe that at least some of them are the same, and, certainly, it is hard to deny that the test sentences are at least somewhat familiar. From a schema theory viewpoint, the feeling of familiarity is generated because we have abstracted and integrated the ideas that underlie the acquisition set of sentences. Consider the test sentence 'The tall tree in the front yard shaded the man who was smoking his pipe.' It expresses the following simple ideas: The tree was tall; the tree was in the front yard; the tree shaded the man; the man was smoking his pipe. Perhaps what people do is abstract these simple ideas from the acquisition sentences and then integrate them into a coherent representation. Then, any sentence that is consistent with this idea set will tend to be recognized as one that they have seen before. In fact, Bransford and Franks presented evidence that the more simple ideas contained in a test sentence, the more likely it will be misrecognized as an old sentence.

Should this kind of misrecognition be taken as evidence that we forget the particulars of our experience? Not necessarily. Even Bransford and Franks realized that people were able to remember some information about individual sentences, and other investigators have concluded that integrating individual idea units does not always occur (Moeser, 1982).

Eyewitness Testimony

Loftus and Palmer (1974) did a classic study of eyewitness testimony. Participants were shown a film depicting a traffic accident. Some participants were asked, 'About how fast were the cars going when they hit each other?' Other participants were asked the same question, but with the words *smashed, collided, bumped*, and *contacted* in the place of 'hit'. The results are given in Figure 4.6. Notice that the estimate of the cars' speed is a function of the intensity of the verb in the question asked. If cars 'smash', then they are reported as going faster than if they come in 'contact'.

In another experiment, participants were also shown a film of a collision, and then asked either 'How fast were the cars going when they hit each other?' or 'How fast were the cars going when they smashed into each other?' One week later, participants were asked some questions about the accident they had seen on film the week before. One of the questions was 'Did you see any broken glass?' More of the participants who had earlier been asked if the cars 'had smashed into each other' reported that they had seen broken glass than did the participants who had been asked if the cars 'had hit each other'. Loftus and Palmer (1974) interpreted these results as follows:

We would like to propose that two kinds of information go into one's memory for some complex occurrence. The first is information gleaned during the perception

Figure 4.6 Results of Loftus and Palmer's Experiment.

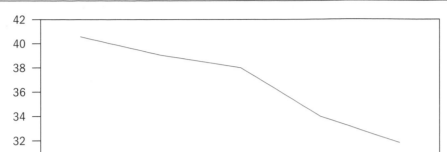

of the original event; the second is external information supplied after the fact. Over time, information from these two sources may be integrated in such a way that we are unable to tell from which source some specific detail is recalled. All we have is one 'memory'. (p. 588)

In several subsequent publications, Loftus and others have provided a great deal of evidence that misleading post-event information often becomes integrated with the original information (e.g., Cole & Loftus, 1979; Loftus, 1992, 2003; Loftus & Loftus, 1980). This has been termed the **misinformation effect** (Loftus, 2004, p. 868; Loftus & Hoffman, 1989). Loftus (2004, p. 145) observed that recent research strongly suggests that more can be changed than 'a detail in memory for a previously experienced event'. Indeed, it appears that one can 'plant an entirely false memory into the mind'.

False Memories

Notice that a key aspect of Loftus and Palmer's original argument was that people sometimes cannot tell from which source the misleading post-event information comes. It actually comes from a source other than the event itself, but people may be unable to recover this fact. People may sometimes not be very good at discriminating between memory for real events and memory for imagined events (Johnson, Hashtroudi, & Lindsay, 1993; Johnson & Raye, 1981; Lindsay, 1993). If they imagine an event in a particularly vivid way, they may later have the illusion that the event actually happened. The process whereby people fail to monitor the source of their memories was investigated by D.S. Lindsay and Johnson (1989).

Lindsay and Johnson's experiment is typical of studies of source monitoring. Participants were shown a picture of an office. The office contained four people and a variety of objects (e.g., coffee cup, pencil holder). After seeing the picture some participants also read a text describing the office. Sometimes the text contained misleading descriptions (e.g., 'There is a filing cabinet behind the women on the right', when there was no filing cabinet). Participants were tested in two different ways. One test simply asked participants to read a list of items and indicate whether or not each item (e.g., filing cabinet) occurred in the picture. This is called the recognition test. Another test asked participants to indicate whether or not each item was in the picture, in the text, or in both. This last test is called the source-monitoring test.

The results of the recognition test showed evidence of suggestibility, as had been found in similar experiments of this type. That is, participants attributed suggested items to the picture when they had in fact only occurred in the text. However, the source-monitoring test resulted in fewer errors of this sort. Lindsay and Johnson argued that these data suggest that the mistakes people make when they try to recall an event are often due to faulty source monitoring. In general, the framework within which Johnson and others have investigated this and similar phenomena is called the **source monitoring framework** (e.g., Johnson & Raye, 1998; Lindsay & Johnson, 2000; Mitchell & Johnson, 2000).

A particularly effective demonstration of the implantation of false memories was conducted by Lindsay, Hagen, Read, Wade, and Garry (2004). It was based on the assumption that viewing photographs from one's childhood could facilitate vividly imagined autobiographical events. Even if these events were false they might still be recalled as actually having happened. Participants in the study were undergraduate students whose parents had supplied a class photo from Grade 1 or Grade 2. The parents had also provided the researchers with descriptions of true episodes from each participant's primary school experience in Grades 3–5. The participants were presented with both the true episodes and a false episode. The false episode described 'putting Slime, a brightly colored gelatinous compound manufactured by Mattel as a toy on the teacher's desk' in either Grades 1 or 2 (p. 150). Approximately half the participants were given a photograph of their Grade 1 or 2 class and all were given a written description of the 'Slime' event. The participants were encouraged to try to remember the earliest of the episodes, namely the false one. A week later the participants were asked if they had remembered the 'Slime' event. Amazingly, two-thirds of the participants who had been given the photograph 'remembered' the 'Slime' event, compared with 23 per cent who had not been given the photograph.

It is of interest that the no-photograph condition still elicited a number of false memories. It is of greater interest that the photograph stimulated still more false memories. As the authors observe, it is a common practice for psychotherapists to suggest that patients ruminate about their past while they observe photographs of their childhood, in order to recover lost childhood memories. The implication of this study is that such rumination may lead to false memories.

Lindsay et al. (2004) note that their results may be understood within the framework of source monitoring theory. The no-photo condition was not as conducive to imagining what might have occurred long ago. Looking at a photograph of one's childhood, however, encourages imagining what might have been. Such active imagination may lead to the confusion of what might have been with what actually happened.

■ Evaluation of Schema Theory

We have examined those aspects of memory that are often explained using a general schema theory. The last word on this topic should belong to Elizabeth Loftus (2004, p. 147), who has done more than anyone else to expose the vagaries of memory.

> A half century ago, Frederic C. Bartlett . . . posited that remembering is 'imaginative reconstruction, or construction', and 'it is thus hardly ever exact' (Bartlett, 1932, p. 213). His insights link up directly with contemporary research on memory distortion, although even he might have been surprised to find out just how inexact memory can be. . . . Bartlett died in 1969, just missing the beginning of a vast effort to investigate the memory processes that he so intelligently foreshadowed, and that show unequivocally how humans are the authors or creators of their own memories. They can also be the authors or creators of someone else's memory.

■ Scripts

We have seen how the schema concept has been used to explain a great deal. Some other approaches are quite a bit like schema theory, but are sufficiently distinctive to merit their own treatment. The concept of a script, for example, can be used to do much the same work as the schema concept.

The use of the **script** idea in memory research can be traced to the work of Schank and Abelson (1975, 1977; Schank, 1982a, 1982b). Schank and Abelson originally defined a script as a 'structure that describes an appropriate sequence of events in a particular context' or 'a predetermined stereotyped sequence of actions that defines a well-known situation' (Schank, 1982a, p. 170).

> A script is a kind of play that we can engage in where our lines are prepared by a kind of general societal agreement, where we anticipate the lines of our partner in their likely place in the play and react accordingly. We play our role the same way each time and hope that our partners do their bit. The more they do what we expect, the less we have to think up what to do. We can keep reading our lines and expect that our partners will do the same. Knowledge of a situation means knowing the script.' (Schank, 1991, p. 83)

Originally, Schank and Abelson's attention was focused on particular scripts, such as going to a restaurant. If people are asked to describe what typically happens when you go to a restaurant, there will usually be a sequence of events that will be common to their stories. For example, you expect to order food, to eat food, to pay the bill, and so on. Although the particulars of stories will vary, there will still be quite a bit of generality across situations and people (Bower, Black, & Turner, 1979).

Berntsen and Rubin (2004) have drawn attention to the importance of **life scripts**. These are 'culturally shared expectations as to the order and timing of life events in a prototypical life course' (p. 427). Life scripts are more abstract than Schank and Abelson's scripts. Rather than being concerned with prototypical situations (e.g., *going to a restaurant*), life scripts are concerned with the age norms that each society uses to 'structure expectations and regulate behavior' (p. 429). Life scripts are prescriptive and not descriptive. That is, they do not describe an individual's life precisely, but rather prescribe what the sequence of important events in an individual's life should be. Life scripts contain events that the culture prescribes as important, such as marriage. They do not contain events that are biologically rather than culturally cued, such as menopause. Life scripts are not abstracted from personal experiences, as is a *restaurant* script, but are 'handed down from older generations, from stories, and from observations of the behavior of other, typically older, people within the same culture' (p. 429).

In one of their experiments, Berntsen and Rubin (2004, p. 435) asked Danish undergraduate students to imagine a 'quite ordinary infant' and list the seven most important events that are likely to take place in that person's life. The participants also estimated the age at which these events would occur. The 10 most commonly listed events and their predicted ages are given in Figure 4.7. While particular cultures may have different ages associated with each event, the sequence of events may be quite general for many European as well as English-speaking countries. Research into life scripts in other cultures would be a useful undertaking. If you are from a non-European and/or non-English speaking country, how do you think your life script might differ from the illustration?

Notice that the curve flattens out between roughly ages 15 to 30. This is because there are relatively more culturally prescribed events during this interval than during others (Berntsen & Rubin, 2004, p. 438). We will return to this phenomenon and its relation to autobiographical memory in Chapter 13 on Personal Cognition. For now, however, we will simply note that in Berntsen & Rubin's study the order in which participants listed life script events was correlated with the age at which they were expected to occur. That is, events predicted to come early in life were listed before events predicted to come later in life. The life script does indeed provide a serial order in which events are supposed to occur. As we shall see in more detail in Chapter 13:

> events that fit into the life script are more easily recalled than events that do not. Life scripts are likely to also influence encoding and retention by endowing events that match the life script with an importance and consequentiality that is socially agreed upon and by providing a shared background for rehearsing such events in social settings. (Berntsen & Rubin, 2004, p. 440)

■ Levels of Processing

Think back to the information-processing tradition, which was reviewed in Chapter 2. Craik (1980) noted that early information-processing models were more concerned with the *structure* of cognition than with the *process* of cognition. That is, early information-processing approaches were preoccupied with the different components of the cognitive system. As we have already seen, these components were identified by labels such as

Figure 4.7 Relation between Life Script Events and Predicted Age of Occurrence in Berntsen and Rubin's (2004) Experiment.

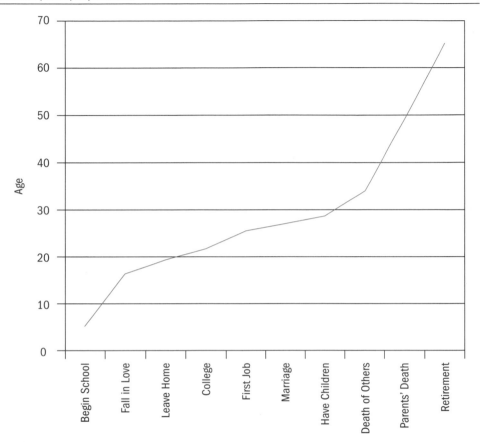

primary storage and secondary storage (Waugh & Norman, 1965) or short-term memory and long-term memory (Atkinson & Shiffrin, 1971). In order to remind you of the sort of information-processing model Craik criticized, look again at the diagram depicting the Waugh and Norman model given in Figure 2.1. This model draws our attention to the structure of memory by dividing it into primary and secondary components.

Craik criticized models such as Waugh and Norman's because they do not tell us very much about the processes that determine what will be remembered. The capacity of structures like primary memory is highly variable, depending on the process the person uses to deal with information. One example Craik used to make this point is that the capacity of primary memory is about four or five items, if the person is asked to retain unrelated items, such as a random order of digits. However, as Craik pointed out, the capacity of primary memory is much higher if the to-be-remembered items are related to one another. Thus, if I ask you to remember 10 words, and the words form a sentence such as 'The lazy brown dog ran over the energetic green turtle', then it is no problem. This kind of result suggests that a more fruitful approach to the study of memory would be to focus on the *process* of remembering, rather than on the nature of the structures that might underlie memory. Primary memory, as Lockhart and Craik (1990) conceived of it, is a 'processing activity and not a structure'; it is not located in any one place, but is a way of 'paying attention to different types of information' (p. 105).

Craik and Lockhart (1972) presented an approach to memory research that did indeed focus on the processes that influence memory. This approach begins by distinguishing between shallow and deep ways of processing an event. For example, consider the word 'TRAIN'. A relatively shallow way of processing that word is to observe that it is printed in capital letters. This is shallow because it deals only with the physical characteristics of the word. A deeper way of processing the word would be to observe that the word refers to a form of transportation. Now you are processing the word in terms of its meaning. The more meaning you extract from an event, the more deeply you are processing it. Thus, **depth of processing** is a continuum that is related to the way in which you analyze an event. This continuum ranges from an analysis of an event purely in terms of its physical characteristics to grasping an event in terms of its relationship to other things that you know. These relationships are illustrated in the diagram below.

Depth of Processing

Shallow ←————————————→ Deep

Physical ←————————————→ Meaning
Properties

According to Craik and Lockhart, cognition is a system designed for perception and understanding. The more deeply we process an event, the more we will have comprehended it. The more important an event is to us, the more we will try to comprehend it. Comprehension requires that we process an event as deeply as possible. The greater the depth of processing, the more we will be able to remember. This is because, from Craik and Lockhart's viewpoint, memory is the record of the operations carried out when we process an event. If we process the event in a relatively shallow way, then we will not remember much about it. If, however, we process an event more deeply, then we will remember relatively more about it.

Elaboration and Distinctiveness

As Lockhart and Craik (1990; Craik, 2002) observed, the concepts of elaboration and distinctiveness provide a more precise version of the vaguer notion of 'depth of processing'. **Elaboration** refers to 'the amount of extra processing one does that results in additional, related or redundant' material (Reder, 1980, p. 7). **Distinctiveness** refers to how precisely an item is encoded. For example, encoding the word 'cabbage' as referring to a 'food' is a less distinctive encoding than is encoding the word 'cabbage' as referring to a 'vegetable' (Frase & Kamman, 1974).

There is evidence that the more distinctively an item is elaborated, the better it will be remembered. For example, Stein et al. (1982) studied the different kinds of elaborations made by academically successful students and by less academically successful students. In one of their experiments, students were given statements expressing apparently arbitrary actions, such as 'The hungry man got into his car.' In this statement, the fact that the man is hungry seems to bear no obvious relationship to the fact that he got into his car. Participants had to write continuations for the sentences they were given. An academically successful student was likely to write a precise elaboration such as 'The hungry man got into his car to go to the restaurant.' This elaboration is precise because it adds material directly related to the fact that the man is hungry. Less academically successful students tended to produce elaborations such as 'The hungry man got into his car and drove away.' This is a less precise elaboration because it doesn't explain why the man got into his car. It turned out that the academically successful students also were able to recall more statements than were the less academically successful students.

The authors concluded that the less academically successful students did not spontaneously elaborate material to be learned in a precise way. They pointed out that it is possible that academically successful students have a better understanding of the importance of elaborating information in a meaningful way. Knowing what strategies to employ in order to facilitate cognitive processes is another example of metacognition. Training students how to make use of elaboration may be an important way of improving their performance. In Chapter 6, on imagery, we will review additional work on the role of distinctiveness in facilitating memory.

The importance of elaboration in memory has been further demonstrated in a series of studies of the way professional actors learn their lines. Noice (1991, 1992, 1993) showed that professional actors do not memorize scripts by rote. In one study, Noice (1991) compared the way that professional actors and novices learned a six-page scene. She found that the professionals made many more elaborations of the to-be-learned material. These elaborations included considering the perspective of the character and asking questions concerning such factors as the character's motivations. In another study, Noice (1992) had professional actors describe their strategies for learning a part. These actors denied using rote memory, but stressed the importance of 'finding reasons why [a] character says each line and performs each action'. Therefore, when it is said that an actor 'creates a character, it is literally true. The author supplies the words but the actor ferrets out the meaning' (Noice, 1992, p. 425). A by-product of actors' relentless search for meaning is that they end up having memorized the part, without doing so by rote. This should remind you of Aitken's musical memory, which we discussed in Box 4.1.

Levels of Processing and Aging

Craik (2002) has suggested that the distinction between **general** and **specific levels of representation** may be a useful way of thinking about levels of processing, particularly in order to account for some of the more prominent changes in memory performance associated with aging. Among these changes is a loss of the ability to remember people's names, even the names of people who are close acquaintances. Another change is a tendency to tell stories more than once to the same audience. Craik argues that names are relatively superficial details about a person, and not a crucial part of a deep under-standing of someone's character. Similarly, remembering the occasion on which one had previously told a story is a detail that pales in comparison to the importance of the story itself. With advancing age, the specific details of events may be forgotten but their deeper meaning may still be retained.

Levels of Processing and the Brain

Roediger, Gallo, and Geraci (2002) observed that one of the implications of the levels of processing approach is that there is no particular place in the brain where memories are stored. Rather, the same parts of the brain used to comprehend an event will be activated when the event is recalled. They describe an MRI study done by Wheeler, Petersen, and Buckner (2002) in which participants were shown a word (e.g., dog) and either a compatible sound (e.g., barking) or a picture (e.g., of a dog). Subsequently, par-ticipants were shown the word and asked to recall what went with it. When recall was successful, the predicted area of the brain was activated. Thus, if the person had heard a dog barking, then at recall the auditory cortex was more activated, while if the person had been shown a picture, then the visual cortex was more activated. The conclusion is that 'the type of processing during test recruits the same brain regions as engaged dur-ing study' (Roediger, Gallo, & Geraci, 2002, p. 328). Evidence supporting a similar con-clusion is reported by Nyberg (2002).

Evaluation of the Levels of Processing Approach

The levels of processing approach has had an enduring influence on memory research. This influence was reviewed by Lockhart and Craik (1990) and in a set of papers look-ing back over 30 years of levels of processing research (Clifford, 2004). A persistent crit-icism has been that the concept of levels of processing is too vague (Baddeley. 1978). Although there is general agreement on what constitutes deep as opposed to shallow processing, there is still no objective measure of depth (Craik, 2002, p. 308). At its most superficial, levels of processing research has simply extended Bartlett's point that the effort after meaning is a crucial determinant of what is remembered (Craik, 2002, p. 312). However, as Lockhart and Craik (1990, Craik, 2002) pointed out, the levels of processing framework has generated and is still generating important research. Its heuristic value is undeniable.

■ The General Principles and the Ecological Approaches to Memory

Much of the memory research from the past several decades has been rooted in labo-ratory experiments designed to uncover general principles regulating memory. Bruce (1985) called this the tradition of **general principles** memory research. The tradition of general principles memory research goes back at least to Ebbinghaus (1885/1964), whose work has been enormously influential (Gorfein & Hoffman, 1987; Slamecka, 1985). He pioneered the use of **nonsense syllables**, which consist of a consonant followed by a vowel followed by a consonant, such as PIB or WOL. In one of his experiments, he read and re-read lists of 13 nonsense syllables each until he could recite each list perfectly twice from memory. After various intervals, he then determined how long it took him to relearn a list. Naturally, the longer the time since the original learning, the longer it took to relearn a list. From these experiments, he was able to estimate how much had been forgotten after different periods of time. In general, forgetting was greatest immediately after learning, followed by a more gradual decline. Ebbinghaus's results were replicated by other experimenters, and can be summarized in the famous **forgetting curve**, an example of which is shown in Figure 4.8.

One general principle that has fared very well over time is **Jost's law of forgetting**, which was first published in 1897. This law states that of two memory traces of equal strength, the younger trace will decay faster than the older trace (Wixted, 2004b). Another way of putting it is to say that the rate at which forgetting occurs will become slower over time. Figure 4.8 illustrates this nicely. Notice that more than 70 per cent of the material is lost in the first two days, but that there is only a very slow decline in the subsequent four days. Of course the specific amount of forgetting that takes place during a particular interval will depend on a lot of factors, such as the kind of material learned. However, the general phenomenon of a slower rate of forgetting with the passage of time is extremely robust.

A likely explanation of Jost's law comes from the process of consolidation, which we considered earlier in this chapter. We noted then that over time memories tend to become more resistant to interference from more recently acquired information. This suggests that 'as a result of the process of consolidation . . . forgetting functions would be expected to exhibit an ever-decreasing rate of decay and Jost's law of forgetting would follow naturally' (Wixted, 2004b, p. 877). Another implication of Jost's law is **Ribot's law of retrograde amnesia**. This law holds that older memories are less likely to be lost as a result of brain damage than are newer memories. Ribot's law illustrates a very general tendency that R. Brown (1958, p. 297) called the **law of progressions and pathologies**. This is a 'last in, first out' principle that refers to the possibility that the

Figure 4.8 The Ebbinghaus Forgetting Curve.

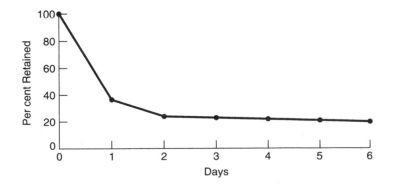

last system to emerge is the first to show the effects of degeneration. Whether this is a truly general law or not, we will have occasion to refer to it when we discuss the effects of age on memory.

Are the General Principles and Ecological Approaches Compatible?

The **general principles** approach can be contrasted with the **ecological approach** to the study of memory (Loftus, 1991). People who take the ecological approach to the study of memory have often been highly critical of the general principles approach. In part, the argument is that general principles research does not come to grips with understanding the complexity of memory as it occurs in everyday life (Neisser, 1978b, 1982b). An ecological approach to the study of memory would examine memory in natural settings (Neisser, 1985). This would be a difficult enterprise because it requires the exploration of the way memory functions as you find it in complex real-world situations (Hirst & Levine, 1985).

The ecological approach to memory was criticized precisely because it appears not to lead to 'generalizable principles' of memory (Banaji & Crowder, 1989, p. 1192). Adherents of the ecological approach (e.g., Neisser, 1991) then replied that the kind of field studies done by those with an ecological orientation are an important part of other sciences, such as biology, and should also be a central part of the scientific study of memory as well.

Neisser (1997) sounded a conciliatory note in this dispute. He drew on Koriat and Goldsmith (1996) in order to recast the issue as being between those who investigate how memory is stored (e.g., Ebbinghaus) and those who investigate how memory is used (e.g., Bartlett). 'Memories are not so much retrieved as they are constructed, usually with a specific goal in mind' (Neisser, 1997, p. 1697). If the goal changes, then the memory that is reconstructed may change, too. It is useful here to recall the Anderson and Pichert study in which what was remembered depended on the perspective taken (burglar or homebuyer) during the act of recall.

Neisser described those who study how memory is used as ecologically oriented because they are concerned with how memory operates in the real world. However, he notes that the general principles approach will provide us with an understanding of 'the neural systems that preserve information in the brain', and that both approaches are necessary 'if we are ever to understand the exquisitely human activity of remembering in an adequate way' (Neisser, 1997, p. 170).

Bahrick and the Permastore

Studies of flashbulb memories, which we reviewed earlier in the chapter, are often cited as models of ecologically valid research. Also singled out in this regard are Bahrick's (1984, 2000; Bahrick & Hall, 1991) studies of long-term memory material learned in school. Bahrick's studies are good ones to contrast with Ebbinghaus's studies of memory. Writing in 1984, Bahrick pointed out that while there had been many laboratory studies of learning, there were few studies of the fate of what we learn in school. Most of us spend years in school, supposedly learning a wide variety of things, and it is important to study how long we remember what we learn. Neisser (1978b, p. 5) had noted that higher education 'depends heavily on the assumption that students remember something valuable from their educational experience. One might expect psychologists to leap at the opportunity to study a critical memory problem so close to hand, but they never do.' However, thanks in large part to Bahrick's work, we now know much more about what we remember from our educational experiences.

Bahrick (2000, p. 347) observed that since the 1980s there had gradually emerged a consensus 'that important questions about memory should not be ignored just because they are not amenable to laboratory exploration.' Although there are serious methodological problems involved in studying long-term retention of school learning, researchers simply must do the best they can under the constraints of real world environments. In studying learning in school, the investigator needs to know such things as how well something was originally learned, and how often it has been rehearsed in the interval. This kind of information is hard to come by, and its acquisition is very time-consuming. Bahrick (1984) attempted to overcome these problems in a naturalistic study of Spanish learned in school.

Bahrick enrolled 773 participants in his study, which made it a very large study, indeed. Some of these participants were current students of Spanish at the high school or college level. Some other participants had taken Spanish from 1 to 50 years earlier. All participants were classified in terms of the level of Spanish instruction they had attained by considering the number and level of high school and college Spanish courses they had taken.

Participants gave autobiographical information concerning such things as their grades in Spanish courses and how often they had been able to use Spanish since they had last studied it. Participants also took a comprehensive test of their knowledge of Spanish, which included measures of reading comprehension, vocabulary, grammar, and knowledge of idioms and word order. In the reading comprehension test participants were asked to read a passage in Spanish and then had to answer questions about it. The vocabulary test, in part, required participants to write the English meaning of a Spanish word, and vice versa. Grammar items required the participants to write the proper form of a verb to use with a sentence. Knowledge of idioms was tapped by asking participants to identify the English meaning of Spanish idioms such as *desde luego* (immediately) and knowledge of Spanish word order was measured by giving participants a random sequence of Spanish words to reorder to make a proper sentence.

The first thing to note is that the absolute level of performance varied with the amount of Spanish studied and the grade level obtained. The more Spanish a participant had studied and the higher one's grades, then the better was the knowledge of the participant later on. There was little evidence of rehearsal of Spanish after one stopped taking courses. However, the most striking result was that the majority of the measures of knowledge of Spanish showed the same pattern. For the first three to six years after someone stopped studying Spanish, there was a continuous loss of knowledge.

However, after that period, there was a period of roughly 25 years during which there was no further loss of knowledge. The general shape of the curve describing the amount of knowledge at different times is given in Figure 4.9. Of course, the absolute level of knowledge will vary with the amount of and quality of prior learning, but the shape of the curve tends to be similar for everyone.

Bahrick argued for the existence of a relatively permanent state of memory that he called a **permastore**. It is important to realize that by 'permastore' Bahrick does not mean a particular place where memories are stored, but a state of relative permanence. Most studies of memory do not examine memory for long enough periods to discover that some kinds of memory may stop decaying after a certain point. Such memory is in permastore, and Bahrick gave examples such as knowledge of the rules of arithmetic and motor skills such as bicycle-riding or piano-playing (Neisser, 1967). Because Bahrick's study found so little evidence of rehearsal after learning had stopped, it appears that rehearsing material after it is learned does not affect the transfer of information to permastore. Whether or not material ends up in permastore appears to be determined at the time the material is learned, but the precise mechanism for transferring information to permastore is unclear.

In a reassuring illustration of the complementarity of the general principles and ecological approaches, Wixted (2004b) has observed that Jost's law fits the forgetting curve in Figure 4.9 quite well. After reanalyzing some of Bahrick's data, Wixted concluded that even after very long periods, forgetting is still occurring but at an extremely slow rate. In fact the rate of decline is so slow as to not be of any practical significance. Thus Bahrick's permastore concept is for all practical purposes correct.

Figure 4.9 The Rate at which Knowledge of Spanish is Lost.

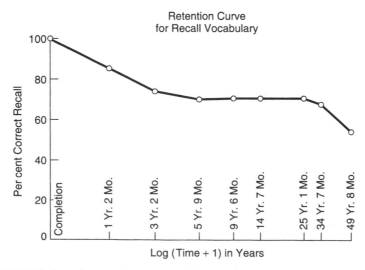

From Bahrick, H.P. (1984). Semantic memory in permastore: Fifty years of memory for Spanish learned in school. *Journal of Experimental Psychology: General, 113*, pp. 1–31. Copyright 1984 by the American Psychological Association. Reprinted by permission.

Additional Demonstrations of Long-Term Memory Due to Education

Bahrick and Hall (1991) also studied long-term retention for mathematics, in which they enrolled 1, 726 participants. They sampled items from standardized tests of algebra and geometry from high school mathematics courses taught from 1937 to 1986. Participants varied in terms of the amount of mathematical training from no algebra or geometry courses, to having had university-level training. They ranged in age from 19 to 84.

It turned out that long-term retention of knowledge from one's first algebra or geometry course is influenced most by the amount of subsequent exposure to or practice with algebra. 'When exposure to mathematics is extended over several years, performance levels remain stable for half a century without the further benefit of practice. . . . [People] who took three or more college-level math courses, with the highest of these above calculus, show' virtually no loss of high school algebra knowledge during 50 years, even if there has been no measurable rehearsal in the interim (Bahrick & Hall, 1991, p. 24). Whether a student gets A's or C's matters less than how many courses are taken. There were similar findings for geometry knowledge. One interesting feature of these results is that subsequent learning reinforces and consolidates prior learning.

Practical Implications of Long-Term Memory Research

Bahrick (2000; Bahrick & Hall, 1991) argued that his work has the following implications. Retention is 'relatively unaffected by individual differences variables pertaining to aptitude and achievement and . . . much more influenced by . . . variables pertaining to the curriculum and schedule of instruction. Changes that increase the duration of acquisition or exposure and require maintenance and relearning of content during an extended period extend the life span of knowledge' (Bahrick & Hall, 1991, p. 32). '[A] variety of curricular interventions could produce such changes', among which are: longer courses, 'while keeping the number of instructional hours constant; cumulative re-examinations at the end of a program of several years; and . . . capstone review courses at the end of programs' (Bahrick & Hall, 1991, p. 32).

Bahrick's studies suggest that how well someone does in a subject is far from being the only thing that determines how much a student will remember in the long run. Rather, the data suggest that students who may not be getting outstanding grades, but who are prepared to take several courses in a discipline, will forget less of the material they were exposed to even after several years have gone by. In order to prevent long-term forgetting of information learned in school, it appears to be very important to spread courses in a subject over several years, with lots of repetition of central concepts, rather than to take a concentrated, short course of study. It appears to be entirely possible for students to learn at least some aspects of a subject and never forget them. They would be permanently stored in memory, and recallable when required. (You might like to have a look at one of your old examinations. You may be surprised at how much you can still remember from your previous courses.) In fact, Conway, Cohen, and Stanhope (1991) have shown that students in a cognitive psychology course may retain general factual knowledge from the course for at least 12 years.

■ Questions for Study and Discussion

1. Discuss the differences between memory traces and memory schemas. How might they be related?
2. What are flashbulb memories? Discuss alternative explanations of their nature. Do you have any memories that fall into this category? Is there any way for you to check on their accuracy?
3. Discuss research relevant to the general form of schema theory as outlined by Alba and Hasher as well as Koriat, Goldsmith, and Pansky.
4. Review work on eyewitness testimony and false memories. How does misinformation acceptance work?
5. Summarize the strengths and weaknesses of Craik and Lockhart's 'levels of processing' framework.

■ Key Concepts

Abstraction The hypothesis that people tend to remember only the gist, rather than the particulars, of what they experience.

Body schema or **body image** One's schematic representation of one's body.

Consolidation theory The theory that memory traces of an event are not fully formed immediately after that event, but take some time to become complete.

Curve of forgetting Ebbinghaus's finding that forgetting was greatest immediately after learning, followed by a more gradual decline.

Depth of processing (Craik and Lockhart) A continuum that ranges from an analysis of an event purely in terms of its physical characteristics to understanding an event in terms of its relationship to other things that you know.

Elaboration and distinctiveness Elaboration refers to processing that goes beyond the original information, while distinctiveness refers to how precisely an item is encoded.

Flashbulb memories Vivid, detailed memories of significant events.

General and specific levels of representation As people age there is a tendency to forget details but to still remember deeper meanings.

General principles versus ecological memory research Two contrasting approaches to the study of memory. The former emphasizes laboratory investigations in the search for general principles. The latter emphasizes real-world investigations in the search for practical applications.

Hippocampus A site in the brain crucial for the consolidation of memory traces.

Integration The hypothesis that after we abstract the meaning of an event, that meaning is put together with the rest of our knowledge to form a coherent, consistent whole.

Interpretation The hypothesis that people interpret information by making inferences, and then remember the inferences as part of the original information.

Jost's law Of two memory traces of equal strength, the younger trace will decay faster than the older trace.

Law of progressions and pathologies A 'last in, first out' principle referring to the possibility that the last system to emerge is the first to show the effects of degeneration.

Life scripts Culturally shared expectations as to the order and timing of life events in a prototypical life course.

Method of repeated reproduction (Bartlett) One participant is given multiple opportunities to recall something over time.

Method of serial reproduction (Bartlett) One participant, A, is given something to remember. A writes down what he or she can recall. A's version is given to the next participant, B, who reads it and tries to recall it. B's version is in turn given to C, and so on.

Misinformation effect (Loftus) The hypothesis that misleading post-event information can become integrated with memory for the original event.

Mystic writing pad (Freud) A model of memory based on a children's toy that allows new messages to be written on one level, while old messages accumulate on another level.

Nonsense syllables Nonsense words formed by a consonant followed by as vowel followed by a consonant.

Now Print theory The theory that there is a specific process, similar to xerography, that lays down in memory copies of especially significant experiences.

Penfield homunculus A map of the parts of the sensory cortex that represent the various parts of the body.

Permastore (Bahrick) The hypothesis that there can be a relatively permanent state of memory over very long periods of time.

Phantom limbs After a sudden loss of a body part, the experience that it is still there.

Plasticity Our schemas are not fixed, but show considerable flexibility.

Rationalization (Bartlett) The attempt to make memory as coherent and sensible as possible.

Reappearance hypothesis The hypothesis that memory is a re-experiencing of the past.

Reconsolidation The hypothetical process whereby a memory trace is revised and undergoes consolidation again.

Retroactive interference Suppose you experience one thing (A) and then experience something else (B). Retroactive interference refers to a decline in your recall of A as a result of your experiencing B.

Ribot's law of retrograde amnesia Older memories are less likely to be lost as a result of brain damage than are newer memories.

Schema (Bartlett) An active mass of organized past reactions that provides a setting that guides our behaviour.

Scripts Expectations concerning the actions and events that are appropriate in a particular situation.

Selection The hypothesis that people select information both as they receive it and as they recall it.

Source monitoring framework A theory of the process whereby people may fail to distinguish between a real and an imagined event.

■ Links to Other Chapters

Consolidation theory
   Chapter 9 (insight and the brain)
Hippocampus
   Chapter 6 (cognitive maps and the hippocampus)
   Chapter 9 (insight and the brain)
   Chapter 12 (expertise)
Bartlett
   Chapter 14 (human error)

Plasticity
   Chapter 12 (neural plasticity and g)
Scripts
   Chapter 13 (autobiographical memory)
Depth of processing
   Chapter 9 (literacy)
Distinctiveness
   Chapter 6 (imagery and distinctiveness)
   Chapter 13 (autobiographical memory)

■ Further Reading

A useful collection of papers dealing with so-called 'flashbulb memories' is Winograd, T., & Neisser, U. (1992). *Affect and accuracy in recall*. New York: Cambridge University Press.

For a thorough and occasionally surprising application of schema theory to just about everything, see Arbib, M.A., & Hesse, M.B. (1986). *The construction of reality*. Cambridge: Cambridge University Press.

Bartlett emphasized the social nature of remembering, and this is brought out in a study by Weldon, M.S., & Bellinger, K.D. (1997). Collective memory: Collaborative and individual processes in remembering. *Journal of Experimental Psychology: Learning, Memory, and Cognition, 23,* 1160–1175.

Wells, G.L., & Olson, E.A. (2003). Eyewitness testimony. *Annual Review of Psychology, 54,* 277–295, is a fascinating review of the factors that influence the eyewitness identification of suspects in contexts such as police lineups. Tuckey, M.R., & Brewer, N. (2003). The influence of schemas, stimulus ambiguity, and interview schedule on eyewitness memory over time. *Journal of Experimental Psychology: General, 9,* 101–118, shows how important it is to interview witnesses as close to the time of the crime as possible.

There has been a great deal of additional work with the script concept. If you are interested in deepening your knowledge of this topic, you should read Mandler, J.M. (1984). *Stories, scripts and scenes*. Hillsdale, NJ: Erlbaum; and Mandler, J.M., & Murphy, C.M. (1983). Subjective judgements of script structure. *Journal of Experimental Psychology: Learning, Memory, and Cognition, 9,* 534–543. See also Thorndyke, P.W. (1984). Applications of schema theory in cognitive research. In J.R. Anderson & S.M. Kosslyn (Eds.), *Tutorials in learning and memory* (pp. 167–191). San Francisco: Freeman.

For more on forgetting curves, see Rubin, D.C., & Wenzel, A.E. (1996). One hundred years of forgetting: A quantitative description of retention. *Psychological Review, 103,* 734–760.

Noice, T., & Noice, H. (2002) Very long-term recall and recognition of well-learned material. *Applied Cognitive Psychology, 16,* 259–272, examines very long-term memory on the part of professional actors and reaches conclusions similar to those of Bahrick.

Ecological approaches to memory are well illustrated by the work of Herrmann, D.J., & Neisser, U. (1979). An inventory of everyday memory experiences. In M.M. Gruneberg & P.E. Morris (Eds.), *Applied problems in memory*. London: Academic Press. In the same edited volume, see also Hunter, I.M.L. (1979). Memory in everyday life. Perhaps the tour de force on ecological approaches to memory is Rubin, D.C. (1995). *Memory in oral tradition: The cognitive psychology of epic, ballads, and counting out rhymes*. New York: Oxford University Press.

Chapter 5

Memory Systems

■ Tulving and the Theory of Memory Systems

By now you will have realized that there are different ways of thinking about how memory works. Each approach highlights different aspects of memory. The intention of memory theorists, like other scientists, is to carve nature at her joints (Ghiselin, 1981; Gould, 1985). Because memory is extremely complex, there are many possible ways of carving it up and we must be careful not to 'hack off parts like a clumsy butcher' (Plato, *Phaedo*, 265). One very influential way of carving up memory is due to Endel Tulving (www.rotman-baycrest.on.ca/content/people/profiles/tulving.html), who has explored in depth the issue of how many and what kinds of memory systems there are.

Encoding Specificity

Tulving's early experimental work concerned the way in which the principle of **encoding specificity** regulates memory (e.g., Tulving & Thomson, 1973). This principle states that a cue is more likely to lead to the recall of an item if the cue was initially encoded along with that item. 'Thus, a critical condition for effective retrieval is the extent to which the processing that occurs during retrieval reinstates the processing that took place during encoding' (Koriat, 2000, p. 337). A good example of this principle is that 'if the word BRIDGE is encoded as an engineering structure' then the cue *a card game* will not be as likely to lead to the recall of BRIDGE as would the cue words *girder* or *span* (Brown & Craik, 2000, p. 99).

As the preceding example demonstrates, items can be stored in different ways. The word 'BRIDGE' can be understood, or encoded, as either an engineering structure or as a card game. In Tulving and Thomson's (1973) now-classic experiments, they exploited this fact. Participants learned a list of 24 pairs of words. The pairs of words were only weakly associated, and one of the words was printed in lower case, with the other in upper case. For example, *plant* might be paired with BUG. BUG is very unlikely to be among first things you think of when you think of *plant*, showing that plant is weakly associated with BUG. The same is true for *ground* and COLD. The first word of each pair is called the *weak cue word*, and the second word of each pair is called the *target word*.

After learning a list of such weakly associated pairs, participants were given a series of tasks. In one task, they were shown a list of 24 words, each of which was strongly associated with one member of the original list of 24 target words. For example, *insect* is strongly associated with BUG, and *hot* is strongly associated with COLD. These new, strongly associated words can be called *strong cue words*. Participants were asked to free associate to the entire set of strong cue words they had been given, by writing up to six words that came to mind for each of the strong cue words. On average, participants generated about 18 of the original 24 target words in this way. Participants were then asked to examine the list of words they had generated. The question was: How many of the words they had generated would they be able to recognize as target words? If they were able to recognize all the target words they had generated, they would have recognized about 18 words on average. However, they were only able to recognize about four of the words they had generated. Notice that this means that the participants were able to generate target words without being able to recognize them as being target words.

Finally, participants were given the original 24 weak cue words and asked to recall the target words. At this point, participants were able to recall about 15 of the target words. There are several interesting points to be made about these results.

The most important thing to realize is that participants were generating words in response to the strong cues that were the same as the words that they learned in response to the weak cues. However, participants were often not able to recognize the words they were generating. Thus, 'conditions can be created in which information about a word event is available in . . . memory . . . in a form sufficient for the production of the appropriate response and yet a literal copy of the word is not recognized' (Tulving & Thomson, 1973). This phenomenon is called recognition failure of recallable words, and has been extensively investigated (e.g., Tulving & Wiseman, 1975).

Tulving argued that the ability to remember an item depends on how the item was encoded at input. The nature of the encoding will influence the memory trace for the item. In the Tulving and Thomson experiments, participants learned the target words in the context of the weak cues. This way of encoding the target words meant that the weak cues were a more effective retrieval cue than were strong cues. The strong cues were not a part of the memories formed when the participant learned the original list of word pairs. Only the weak cues were a part of the memories formed at that time. The strong cues are associated with the target words because those relationships are part of one's general knowledge about words. Because general knowledge is not very helpful in remembering specifically what was learned in the experiment, one might conclude that these are examples of two different kinds of memory.

Episodic and Semantic Memory

Experiments such as the one just described led Tulving (1972) to propose a distinction between episodic and semantic memory. **Episodic memory** refers to the 'storage and retrieval of temporally dated, spatially located, and personally experienced events or episodes', whereas **semantic memory** refers to the 'storage and utilization of knowledge about words and concepts, their properties and interrelations' (Tulving & Thomson, 1973, p. 354). Examples of episodic memories given by Tulving (1972) included the following:

> I remember seeing a flash of light a short while ago, followed by a loud sound a few seconds later.
>
> Last year, while on my summer vacation, I met a retired sea captain who knew more jokes than any other person I have ever met.
>
> I remember that I have an appointment with a student at 9:30 tomorrow morning. (p. 386)

Tulving proposed that an event could be stored purely as an episodic memory, that is, as an autobiographical event. By contrast, consider the following examples of semantic memories, which are also taken from Tulving (1972):

> I remember that the chemical formula for common table salt is NaCl.
>
> I know that the name of the month that follows June is July. (p. 387)

Tulving (1972) observed that such examples are unlike episodic memories because they are not 'personally experienced unique episodes' (p. 387). Rather, they constitute general knowledge as opposed to personally experienced events.

Neuropsychological Evidence for the Independence of Episodic and Semantic Memory

Studies of brain-injured persons have provided compelling evidence for the distinction between episodic and semantic memory. A good example is a study by Klein, Loftus, and Kihlstrom (1996) concerning self-knowledge of an amnesic patient. These authors discovered a case of someone, identified as WJ, who suffered retrograde amnesia following a closed head injury. Retrograde amnesia is the inability to recall events prior to the injury. As a result, her episodic memory was impaired. The issue this case addresses is whether episodic memory is necessary in order to have a sense of personal identity. 'Is it possible for someone who cannot recall any personal experiences—and therefore cannot know how he or she behaved—to know what he or she is like?' (Klein, Loftus, & Kihlstrom, 1996, p. 250).

How would semantic personal knowledge and episodic personal knowledge differ? Semantic personal knowledge 'might include the facts that the person is kind, outgoing or lazy. . . . Episodic personal knowledge, by contrast, consists of memories of specific events involving the self [and] could include memories of instances in which one was kind, outgoing or lazy' for example (Klein, Loftus, & Kihlstrom, 1996, pp. 250–251). If semantic personal memory and episodic personal memory were truly independent of one another, then damage to one system should not affect the other system.

WJ was 18 years old, a female undergraduate who fell and as a result sustained a concussion. When she was initially tested about five days after the injury, WJ had no episodic memories for the preceding six–seven months. However, WJ's general knowledge was good. She knew which classes she was enrolled in, although she could not remember attending a single one. She also knew names of teachers and friends, but could not recall any personal experiences involving them. In the case of closed head injuries, retrograde amnesia is usually temporary and the patient recovers within a few weeks. By three weeks after the event, WJ's memory for events prior to the incident had returned to normal.

A technique invented by Crovitz and Schiffman (1974) was used to evaluate WJ's episodic memory during the period in which she was amnesic. WJ was given a list of 24 words, each of which was a picturable noun such as 'oven'. The task was to recall a personal event in relation to each word from any time in the past, and then date the memory in terms of when it occurred. Thus, one could recall putting bread in the *oven* this morning. When tested five days after her injury, WJ produced a very different pattern of results compared with that of a control group of three undergraduate women of approximately her age. Figure 5.1 shows that the control participants had a **recency bias** in that they tended to recall experiences from the previous 12 months. By contrast, WJ showed a **primacy bias** in that she tended to recall experiences that were in the rel-

Figure 5.1 Percentage of Personal Memories for Different Time Periods.

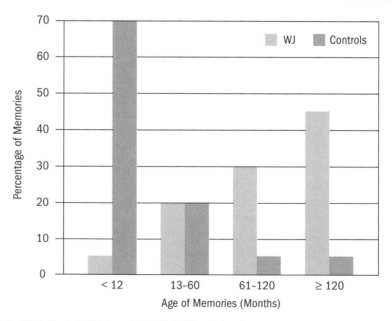

Data from Klein, S.B., Loftus, J., & Kihlstrom, J.F. (1996). Self-knowledge of an amnesic patient: Toward a neuropsychology of personality and social psychology. *Journal of Experimental Psychology: General, 125*, p. 255.

atively distant past. However, when WJ recovered four weeks later, her pattern of episodic memory was similar to that of the control participants.

While still amnesic, WJ was asked to rate herself in terms of 80 personality traits in order to test her semantic personal memory. For example, she judged the extent to which she was *agreeable* or *dominant* and so on. She repeated this exercise after her amnesia had lifted. There was strong agreement between her ratings on these two occasions. The consistency of her ratings was similar to that for control participants. While amnesic, WJ also rated herself as if she was in high school. These ratings were different from her current self-rating, indicating that she was aware that she had changed while at college. 'WJ knew something about what she had been like at college, which was different from what she was like in high school; but she knew this despite the fact that she could not recall anything from her time in college' (Klein, Loftus, & Kihlstrom, 1996, p. 256). These results are consistent with the hypothesis that episodic and semantic memory are represented separately, and that one can have access to semantic knowledge without having access to episodic memory.

Tulving (1985, 2002) reported on another well-known case of amnesia that has been studied for many years and that also supports the dissociation between episodic and semantic memory. This individual was born in 1951 and suffered a closed head injury when he was 30 as a result of a motorcycle accident. He received 'extensive brain lesions in multiple cortical and subcortical brain regions' (Tulving, 2002, p. 130) and never recovered his episodic memory. However, his other intellectual skills remained intact. For example, he is able to outline a standard restaurant script of the sort we considered in the previous chapter—evidence that semantic memory is still functioning. However, neither can he recall individual events from his past, nor can he imagine what he might do in the future. Tulving (1985) gave a fragment of an interview he (ET) conducted with this patient, then called NN:

> ET: Let's try the question again about the future. What will you be doing tomorrow?
>
> (There is a 15-second pause)
>
> NN: smiles faintly, and says, 'I don't know.'
>
> ET: Do you remember the question?
>
> NN: About what I'll be doing tomorrow?
>
> ET: Yes. How would you describe your state of mind when you try to think about it?
>
> (A 5-second pause)
>
> NN: A blank I guess. (p. 4)

NN described his blank state of mind as 'like being asleep', or as like 'being in a room with nothing there and having a guy tell you to go find a chair, and there's nothing there.' Another description he uses is 'It's like swimming in the middle of a lake. There's nothing there to hold you up or do anything with' (Tulving, 1985, p. 4). Thus, while NN has retained his semantic memory systems, he has an episodic memory system that is drastically impaired.

In subsequent publications, Tulving referred to this patient as KC, and a picture of him is in Tulving's 2002 article on episodic memory (Tulving, 2002a, p. 13). We will consider cases like his in more detail in the section on memory disorders later in the chapter.

■ The Development of the Theory of Memory Systems

For more than 30 years a great deal of work has been stimulated by Tulving's distinction between episodic and semantic memory. Over such a long period of time, there will inevitably be changes in any theory as it responds to new research. Tulving himself has published a series of changes to his basic theory (e.g., Tulving, 1983, 1984, 1985, 1986, 2000, 2001a, 2001b, 2002a, 2002b). In addition to episodic and semantic memory, it has been suggested that there may be as many as five memory systems (Schacter & Tulving, 1994; Schacter, Wagner, & Buckner, 2000). The five systems are episodic memory, semantic memory, procedural memory, perceptual representation system, and working memory.

■ Procedural Memory

Procedural memory (J.R. Anderson, 1976) underlies skilled performances. One way of thinking about the distinction between procedural memory and other forms of memory is in terms of the distinction between **tacit** and **explicit knowledge**. Polanyi (1958) pointed out that 'the aim of a skilled performance is achieved by the observance of a set of rules which are not known as such to the person following them' (p. 49). Here is a passage from Polanyi (1958) that is often used to make this point:

> From my interrogations of physicists, engineers and bicycle manufacturers, I have come to the conclusion that the principle by which the cyclist keeps his balance is not generally known. The rule observed by the cyclist is this. When he starts falling to the right he turns the handlebars to the right, so that the course of the bicycle is deflected along a curve towards the right. This results in a centrifugal force pushing the cyclist to the left and offsets the gravitational force dragging him down to the right. This maneuver presently throws the cyclist out of balance to the left, which he counteracts by turning the handle bars to the left; and so he continues to keep himself in balance by winding along a series of appropriate curvatures. . . . But does this tell us exactly how to ride a bicycle? No. . . . Rules of art can be useful, but they do not determine the practice of an art; they are maxims, which can serve as a guide to an art only if they can be integrated into the practical knowledge of the art. They cannot replace this knowledge. (p. 49)

The knowledge we use to ride a bicycle is procedural knowledge. Procedural knowledge is a form of tacit knowledge. It is knowledge we have without necessarily being aware of what it is that we know. I can ride a bicycle even if I am not able to tell you how I do it. When Polanyi describes the principles that regulate bicycle-riding, he is converting this tacit knowledge into explicit knowledge. When we are able to describe what we know, then we rely on semantic memory. Semantic memory contains our explicit knowledge about things like how to ride a bicycle. Procedural memory is what we actually use to ride the bicycle. Sometimes we are able to do something without being able to say very much about it. Finally, episodic memory would contain particular experiences of riding bicycles, such as 'Remember that time we spent all day bicycling between Campbellford and Belleville, and it rained all the time, and we ran out of food . . . .'

Procedural memory was the first memory system to be added to the theory after the initial distinction between episodic and semantic memory. Tulving's (1985) view of the relation between these three memory systems is given in Table 5.1. In evolutionary terms, episodic memory was seen as the most recent and procedural memory the oldest of the three systems. The evolutionary mechanisms leading to different memory systems are considered in Box 5.1.

■ Episodic Memory and Autonoetic Consciousness

Tulving (1985) suggested that each of the three systems is associated with a different kind of consciousness. These three types of consciousness are also given in Table 5.1. **Anoetic** means 'non-knowing'. To say that procedural memory is anoetic means that when we use this type of memory we are aware of only our immediate situation. Procedural memory does not go beyond itself; it involves responding to only the here and now. When I am riding a bicycle, I am concerned with responding appropriately to a particular bicycle (the one I am on) in a particular situation (the one I am in) at a particular time (now). **Noetic** means 'knowing'. Thus, semantic memory is noetic because when we use it we are aware not only of our immediate surroundings, but also of things that may be absent. Thus, if I remember that Polanyi wrote about the sort of skill bicycle-riding requires, then my memory would be accompanied by noetic consciousness. Autonoetic means 'self-knowing'. Episodic memory is **autonoetic** because it involves remembering personal experiences.

Table 5.1 The Relation between Memory Systems and Consciousness

Memory System	Consciousness
Episodic	Autonoetic
Semantic	Noetic
Procedural	Anoetic

From Tulving, E. (1985). Memory and consciousness. *Canadian Psychology, 26,* pp. 1–12. Copyright 1985 by the Canadian Psychology Association. Reprinted by permission.

Box 5.1 The Evolution of Memory Systems

There is more than one way in which memory systems could have come to have the properties they have today. The first way is through the process of natural selection (Heyes, 2003; Klein, Cosmides, Tooby, & Chance, 2002; Pinker, 1997). *Natural selection* is a process of random variation and selective retention of those variations that further the organism's adaptive capabilities. These variations are *blind*, in the sense that they occur by chance and without any foresight on the part of the organism as to their adaptive consequences. Those variations that happen to be adaptive tend to be *retained*, in that they further the organism's opportunity 'to survive, to reproduce, and to transmit their attributes to the next generation' (Mayr, 1991). Perhaps each of our memory systems has evolved because it solves a particular adaptive problem. The separation of episodic and semantic memory systems may make sense when seen in this light.

> We humans place two very different demands on our memory system at the same time. We have to remember individual episodes of who did what to whom, when, where, and why, and that requires stamping each episode with a date, a time and a serial number. But we must also extract generic knowledge about how people work and how the world works. [Perhaps] nature gave us one memory system for each requirement . . . . (Pinker, 1997, p. 124)

Natural selection may not be the whole story, however. As we saw in the last chapter, there is abundant evidence that memory can be notoriously inaccurate, a fact that must be squared with the hypothesis that memory systems have evolved as solutions to adaptive problems. One possibility is that the deficiencies of memory 'are by-products of otherwise adaptive features of memory' (Schacter, 1999, p. 197). Rather than being adaptations, such features of memory may best be characterized as *exaptations* (Gould & Vrba, 1982). 'An exaptation is a pre-existing trait (i.e., one that has already evolved)' that produces an effect that 'was not designed for it by selection' (Andrews, Gangestad, & Matthews, 2002, p. 491). While exaptations may be beneficial, they need not be. Thus, phenomena such as source memory errors may be the consequence of a memory system 'that does not routinely preserve all the details required to specify the exact source of an experience' (Schacter, 1999, p. 198). The negative features of memory systems may be likened to *spandrels*, which are necessary consequences of the way in which something is constructed (Gould & Lewontin, 1979). 'Spandrel' is an architectural term referring to the space between two adjacent arches. This space occurs of necessity, but may be put to use as a surface to be painted. By analogy, there may be features of our memory systems that occur of necessity and which may have either fortunate or unfortunate consequences (Schacter & Dodson,

2001, p. 1391). They are 'side consequences of a generally adaptive architecture that sometimes gets us into trouble' (Schacter, 1999, p. 198).

Tulving (2002a, p. 7) maintained that 'at some point in human evolution, possibly rather recently, episodic memory emerged as an "embellishment" of the semantic memory system.' Tulving also suggested that the process whereby episodic memory and autonoetic consciousness emerged may be an instance of the *Baldwin effect*, named after the developmental psychologist James Mark Baldwin (1861–1934). Baldwin attempted to solve the problem of explaining how individual adaptive variations could be transmitted to successive generations. This is a problem with which Darwin himself had struggled. For a while, Darwin had considered Lamarckism, which is the hypothesis of the inheritance of acquired characteristics. The classic Lamarckian example is the giraffe's long neck, supposedly acquired as a result of subsequent generations' attempts to reach the tops of trees for food. Lamarckism was discredited in favour of the process of natural selection. Although Baldwin did not support Lamarckian interpretations, he did believe that 'the gains of earlier generations' could be transmitted 'from one generation to another' (Baldwin, 1897, p. 204). The phrase 'Baldwin effect' refers to processes whereby changes that occur during an individual's lifetime can influence subsequent evolution in a non-Lamarckian way (Suzuki & Arita, 2004). The possibility that a Baldwin effect has played a role in the evolution of cognitive processes has been endorsed by some well-known theorists (e.g., Dennett, 1991, 1995, 2003).

How might the Baldwin effect work? One possibility is that a skill acquired by one or a few organisms during their lifetimes proves to be of real benefit. They in turn teach the skill to others and to the next generation. If the skill solves a 'significant, pressing adaptive problem', then it will quickly 'spread through the population' (Depew, 2003, p. 25). The next step is for natural selection to reinforce any tendency for individuals to manifest this skill. Eventually what was an acquired skill becomes an innate tendency. At the simplest level, the Baldwin effect refers to the possibility that 'through evolution, unlearned can replace learned behaviour' (Shettleworth, 2004, p. 105).

The factors we have considered here may play a role not only in the evolution of memory systems but also in the evolution of other cognitive processes such as concepts, language, reasoning, judgement, choice, intelligence, and creativity. We will have an opportunity to explore the evolution of these processes as we go along.

Tulving (2001, 2002a, 2002b) has been especially interested in episodic memory and autonoetic consciousness. Normal adults are able to see themselves as having a past and a future, as well as a present. Their individual experiences are located in time, and they are able to engage in 'mental time travel' (Tulving, 2002a, p. 2). Although remembering a personal past is a crucial aspect of episodic memory, so is the ability to project oneself into the future and imagine what one might find there. This ability makes a number of useful activities possible, such as setting goals and planning future actions (Atance & O'Neill, 2001).

Frontal lobe damage can diminish autonoetic consciousness. One of the largest sources of evidence for this relationship comes from the now-abandoned medical practice of **prefrontal leucotomy**. This was a surgical procedure invented by Moniz (1954/1968; Freeman & Watts, 1950/1968) whereby the connections between the prefrontal lobes and other parts of the brain were severed. One goal of this procedure was to calm patients who ruminated excessively about themselves and their problems. Among the effects of this form of psychosurgery were listlessness and apathy. 'Frontal leucotomies change patients so that they are no longer interested in the sorts of past, present, and future problems that were so absorbing and incapacitating before the operations' (Wheeler, 2000, p. 602). It is easy to conclude that autonoetic awareness is dependent on healthy frontal lobe functioning.

Tulving (2002b) has argued that autonoetic consciousness is not only uniquely human, but has also played a crucial role in the evolution of human culture and civilization. He has called our sense of subjective time **chronesthesia**, and regards it as a cognitive capacity as important in its own way as are the abilities to see and hear. 'The development of civilization and culture was, and its continuation is, critically dependent on human beings' awareness of their own and their progeny's *continued existence* in time that includes not only the past and the present but also the future' (Tulving, 2002b, p. 321). Given this capacity, people can contemplate changing the environment to better suit them, rather than simply adapting to it. The consequence is the emergence of our human culture that has altered the environment in a variety of ways. Autonoesis and chronesthesia depend on the prefrontal lobes, as we have seen. 'The conclusion follows that the human prefrontal cortex, undoubtedly in collaboration with other areas of the brain, is directly responsible for the cultured world as it exists today' (Tulving, 2002b, p. 321).

Of course, the emergence of chronesthesia does not mean that human evolution has come to an end. The course of human history has provided numerous examples of behaviours that are less than optimal even during the period when people have been autonoetic (Dupré, 1987). For example, it is a commonplace to observe that our impact on the environment may have negative consequences for the future survival of the species. The activities that chronesthesia makes possible include the exploitation of resources (such as oil) in anticipation of future benefits (such as ease of transportation). This exploitation may have unintended consequences such as environmental pollution, and thus may well have maladaptive consequences for us in the long run. Although Tulving does not make this inference, it seems reasonable to conclude that the human ability to anticipate the consequences of our actions must continue to evolve if it is to meet the needs of our future environment.

Not everyone agrees that autonoesis is a uniquely human achievement. For example, it has been argued that 'episodic-like' memory can be observed in scrub jays (Clayton & Dickinson, 1998). These birds stored both larvae (which they value highly as food but spoils quickly) and peanuts (which they value less highly as food, but remains edible for a long time) in different locations. When the birds were allowed to retrieve stored food, the food they retrieved depended on how long the interval was between storage and retrieval. If the interval was short, then they retrieved the larvae, but if the interval was long then they retrieved the peanuts. This was taken as evidence that the birds remember particular episodes and locate these episodes in time. Thus, they might remember that the larvae were stored too long ago for them to still be edible, and choose to locate and eat the peanuts instead. However, the counter-argument is that these results do not show mental time travel in the sense of being able to anticipate the future, they only show that the birds know something about the past (Suddendorf & Busby, 2003). What they know may not be experienced subjectively as anything resembling a human episodic memory. 'It could be that episodic memory represents a sharp discontinuity in evolution, and humans are unique in possessing it' (Hampton & Schwartz, 2004, p. 195).

Episodic Memory and Development

Tulving (1985) argued that children acquire episodic memory relatively late compared with other kinds of memory. In this connection, Tulving cited the work of authors as diverse as K. Nelson and Gruendel (1981) and Neisser (1978a), who suggested that very young children do not experience anything that adults would call episodic memory. The hypothesis is that episodic memory develops out of semantic memory (Kinsbourne & Wood, 1975). Although small children are prodigious learners, their learning might largely involve the acquisition of general knowledge, rather than the accumulation of individual experience.

Perner (2000, p. 301) suggested that episodic memory does not emerge until roughly four to six years of age. It is then that children are able to discriminate between things they have known for a long time and things they have learned recently. In a similar vein, children at four can discriminate between events they have observed and events they have been told about, which younger children can seldom do. Wheeler, Stuss, and Tulving (1997, p. 345) conclude that 'the self-knowledge necessary for episodic remembering is not reached until around age 4 or later.'

The Distinction between Remembering and Knowing

A central distinction made by Tulving (1985) is that between remembering and knowing. He wanted to reserve the term *remembering* for autonoetic experiences (i.e., episodic memory). Tulving (1985) noted that 'even when a person does not remember an event, she may know something about it' (p. 6). Thus, while I may not remember the experience of eating a specific meal in a particular restaurant on a specific occasion, I may still know that I ate a meal in that restaurant at that time. The feeling of knowing in the absence of episodic memory has been called the **butcher-on-the-bus phenomenon** (Yovel & Paller, 2004). Suppose an acquaintance, such as your butcher, appears in an unexpected place, such as in the same bus on which you are riding. You might feel that you know the person, while 'at the same time not being able to remember the circumstances of any previous meeting or anything else about the person' (Yovel & Paller, 2004, p. 789).

The distinction Tulving made has also been made in various forms by other memory researchers (e.g., Gardiner, 2001; Gardiner & Richardson-Klavehn, 2000; Squire, 2004). It has stimulated quite a bit of ingenious research. A good example is research on implicit memory.

Implicit Memory

There are many situations in which a person remembers something without being aware of doing so (e.g., Jacoby & Dallas, 1981; Jacoby & Witherspoon, 1982). 'It is possible to distinguish the effects of memory for prior episodes or experiences on a person's current behavior from the person's awareness that he or she is remembering events of the past' (Eich, 1984, p. 105). Schacter (1987, 1992) proposed that the phrase **implicit memory** be used as a label for such phenomena. Implicit memory occurs when 'information that was encoded during a particular episode is subsequently expressed without conscious or deliberate recollection' (Schacter, 1987, p. 501). Implicit memory is often demonstrated by means of priming studies similar to those of Marcel, which we discussed in Chapter 3 on attention.

A demonstration of the practical consequences of participating in priming experiments is Jacoby and Hollingshead's (1990) study in which participants read incorrectly spelled words. This experience subsequently increased the likelihood of students unintentionally making those spelling mistakes themselves. As Jacoby and Hollingshead observe, this kind of research may be unethical, because it leads to a degradation of the participant's performance in an important area (spelling), without participants necessarily being aware of this occurrence. The research also shows that 'reading student essays may be hazardous to one's spelling accuracy' (Jacoby & Hollingshead, 1990, p. 345), if those essays contain spelling errors! An unintended consequence of this research was described by Jacoby and Hollingshead (1990), who noted that:

> dramatic results were produced by Ann Hollingshead, a research technician in our laboratory and the second author of this paper. In the course of collecting the data for the experiments reported here, she read the incorrectly spelled words a large number of times. As a result of this extended experience with those incorrect spellings, she reports having lost confidence in her spelling accuracy. She can no longer judge spelling accuracy on the basis of a word 'looking right.' The word might look right because it was one of our incorrectly spelled words. (p. 356)

Implicit memory has also been studied using a fame judgement task (Jacoby & Kelley, 1992; Kelley & Jacoby, 2000). Participants read a list of non-famous names (e.g., *Sebastian Weisdorf*). As the names appear on a computer screen, the participant reads them either with full attention (i.e., no distractions) or divided attention. The divided attention condition consisted of an additional task such as listening to a series of numbers and pressing a key if there are three odd numbers in a row. Then names from the first trial (old non-famous names) are mixed with new non-famous names and the participant judges them as famous or not. Participants are also told that all the names on first list were non-famous. Consequently, if a participant recognized a name as coming from the first list, then the participant also knew it was non-famous. Now examine Figure 5.2, in which the vertical axis is the percentage of non-famous names judged to be famous. The higher the number, the more non-famous names judged to be famous. Under conditions of full attention people tend to recognize names if they are from the first list, and so say that fewer names from the first list are judged to be famous. However, under conditions of divided attention, the person has implicit memories of the old names without explicitly recognizing them as being from the first list. Therefore, the divided attention participant is more likely to categorize names from the first list as famous because these names seem familiar. It's as if they say to themselves, 'Oh, I've heard that name before, but I don't remember where—it must be famous.' Thus does *Sebastien Weisdorf* become famous.

Studies of fragmented words are another way of showing unconscious influences in memory (Jacoby, 1998; Jacoby & Kelley, 1992; Toth, 2000). Such studies are similar to studies we reviewed in the chapter on attention (e.g., Debner & Jacoby, 1994) that use the **method of opposition** (Curran, 2001). This method pits conscious (explicit) and unconscious (implicit) tendencies against one another, and works as follows. Suppose participants are shown words, such as *motel*, under conditions of either full or divided attention. They are then given word stems (e.g., *mot– –*). Half the participants in each of the full or divided attention conditions are asked to complete the word stems using a word from the list previously seen, or, if they could not remember one, to complete the stem with the first word they think of. The other half is asked to complete the word stems by *not* using a word from the list previously seen. So if *motel* was on previous list, they should not complete the stem with mot*el*,

Figure 5.2 Fame Judgement Task (full versus divided attention).

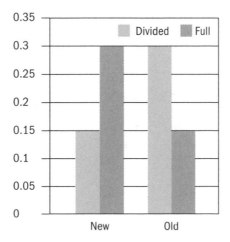

but with another word, like mo*tor*. The first instruction is the *inclusion* condition, while the second instruction is the *exclusion* condition.

Now examine Figure 5.3. The vertical axis is the percentage of stems completed with words from the first list. Under full attention, participants perform well in either the inclusion or the exclusion condition. When told to include words from the first list, participants complete the word stems with words from the first list 61 per cent of the time. When told to exclude words from the first list, the number of stem completions using words from the first list drops to 36 per cent. This difference indicates that these participants have a degree of conscious control over the process of stem completion. However, in the divided attention condition, there is no difference between the inclusion and exclusion task. These participants complete the stems with words from the first list equally often, whether they are trying to do so or trying not to do so. Therefore, these participants do not demonstrate any conscious control over their behaviour in these tasks.

Conscious control is reflected by the difference between performance when one is trying to do something, and performance when one is trying *not* to do it (Jacoby & Kelley, 1992, p. 177). A good analogy to the memory experiments we have been reviewing might be the various real-world attempts we make *not* to do something. For example, when we diet we try not to eat as much, or when we attempt to quit smoking we try not to smoke. If there is a difference between our behaviour when we are trying *not* to do something and our 'ordinary' behaviour, then we are demonstrating that we can consciously control that behaviour. However, if our behaviour when we are trying *not* to do something is the same as it always has been, then we are demonstrating that we are unable to consciously control that behaviour.

Figure 5.3 Inclusion versus Exclusion Task (full versus divided attention).

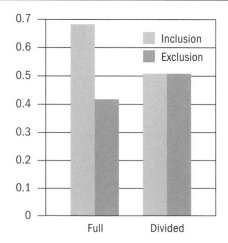

Data from Jacoby, L.L., & Kelley, C.M. (1994). A process-dissociation framework for investigating unconscious influences: Freudian slips, projective tests, subliminal perception, and signal detection theory. *Current Directions in Psychological Science, 1*, p. 177.

■ Perceptual Representation System

The results of experiments on implicit memory are consistent with the notion that there is a memory system called the **perceptual representation system** (Hayman & Tulving, 1989; Tulving & Schacter, 1990; Schacter, Wagner, & Buckner, 2000). This system would be responsible for priming effects. The important distinction is between 'systems concerned with explicit recollection of past events' as opposed to 'primed identification of previously encountered objects' (p. 247). The perceptual representation system contains very specific representations of previously encountered events. If shown a word fragment such as (M–S–OU–I), the word that completes it (*MISSOURI*) is not in the PRS system, only the fragment itself. The episodic memory system and the PRS system would be driven by different processes. The episodic memory system operates with a deeper understanding of information, whereas the PRS system deals with information on a more superficial level. Amnesics have an impaired episodic memory system, but their PRS system may be relatively intact. Precisely how the PRS system relates to other memory systems, such as semantic memory, is still unclear. As Berry and Dienes (1991) observed, there may be similarities between the processes responsible for implicit memory and those underlying implicit learning, a topic we will consider in Chapter 7 on concepts.

■ Semantic Memory

As we have already seen, semantic memory refers to our general knowledge. Tulving (1972) compared semantic memory to a mental thesaurus, containing words, concepts, and their relations. A good example of semantic memory is the attempt to remember someone's name. Sometimes, and it happens often enough, you cannot quite come up with it. James (1890) described this **tip-of-the-tongue phenomenon** like this:

> Suppose we try to remember a forgotten name. The state of our knowledge is peculiar. There is a gap therein; but no mere gap. It is a gap that is intensely active. A sort of wraith of the name is in it, beckoning us in a given direction, making us at moments tingle with the sense of our closeness, and then letting us sink back without the longed for term. If the wrong names are proposed to us, this singularly definite gap acts immediately so as to negate them. They do not fit into its mold. And the gap of one word does not feel like the gap of another, all empty of content as both might seem necessarily to be when described as gaps. When I try vainly to recall the name of Spalding, my consciousness is far removed from what it is when I vainly try to recall the name of Bowles. (p. 251)

The Tip-of-the-Tongue Phenomenon

R. Brown and McNeill (1966) conducted a famous study in which they gathered data on the properties of tip-of-the-tongue phenomena (TOT). First, they observed this state when it occurred in themselves. For example, one of them was trying to remember the name of the street on which a relative lived. He kept coming up with names like *Congress*, *Corinth*, and *Concord*. When he looked up the street name, it turned out to be *Cornish*. This example illustrates several properties of the TOT state that Brown and McNeill subsequently found in an experiment.

In their experiment, Brown and McNeill gave participants the definitions of 49 low-frequency words, such as *apse, nepotism, cloaca, ambergris*, and *sampan*. When a definition elicited a TOT state, participants were often able to identify some aspects of the sought-after, or target, word such as its first letter and the number of syllables. Participants were often also able to make judgements about words that came to mind while they searched for the target word. Sometimes participants knew that incorrect guesses were similar in sound or meaning to the target. For example, while searching for *sampan*, some participants knew that *Siam* and *sarong* had a similar sound, and that *barge* and *houseboat* had a similar meaning. Thus, participants had access to quite a bit of information about a word before they were actually able to recall it. *Generic recall* is the term Brown and McNeill used for this ability to recall parts and attributes of a word without explicitly recalling the word itself.

There have been several different experimental techniques used to elicit the TOT state. If you want to experience it yourself, try naming the Seven Dwarfs (Meyer & Hilterbrand, 1984). A.S. Brown (1991) described a study exploring the relation between TOTS and stress. He surveyed 79 undergraduate psychology majors, 75 per cent of whom said that TOTS occurred more often under stress (e.g., exams). Studies of the frequency with which TOTS occur find that generally they happen to adults about once a week. There also appears to be a tendency for the TOT state to occur more frequently in older than in younger participants.

Several studies have replicated Brown and McNeill's finding that when people are experiencing a TOT, then they are also likely to recall words which are similar in either sound or in meaning. Participants also appear to be able to guess the first letter of the desired word with a high degree of accuracy (e.g., Rubin, 1975). Participants may also have awareness of the last letter, but to a lesser extent than the first (A.S. Brown, 1991, p. 212). One of the most intriguing aspects of the TOT phenomenon is the oft-reported experience of recalling the desired term only after one has stopped trying to recall it. Norman and Bobrow (1976) described this process as follows:

> 1 hour and 39 minutes after the start of the recall attempt, the word came without hesitation. There was no doubt that it was correct. For the hours prior to the solution, there was no recollection of thought on the topic. (p. 116)

Burke, McKay, Worthley, and Wade (1991) had young (mean age = 19), mid-age (mean age = 39), and older (mean age = 71) participants keep four-week diaries concerning their TOTS. It turned out that 95 per cent of the 686 TOTS recorded had eventually been recalled at the end of the four-week period. Participants kept track of how their TOTS were resolved: by a memory search strategy; by consulting a book or another person; or by having the word involuntarily come to mind ('pop up'). Pop-ups were the most frequent for all ages, but most frequent for older participants, for whom 61 per cent of the TOT resolutions were pop-ups.

Burke et al. (1991) also presented data showing that the TOT state takes longer to resolve if there are persistent alternates, which are 'incorrect words that come repeatedly to mind' (p. 542). This effect may be due to the activation of alternate items that interfere with the recall of the desired word. Burke et al. (1991; Rastle & Burke, 1996) believe that TOTs occur predominantly with words that have not been used very often or not very recently, with the result that the link between a word's meaning and its pronunciation may have atrophied due to disuse. Consequently, other words that have a similar sound and/or meaning may be elicited along with the correct word. For example, consider *charity* and *chastity*. These words sound alike and can have similar meanings (both are sometimes considered to be virtues), but are not used very often. Thus they may interfere with one another, causing a TOT state. Burke et al. (1991) also reported the interesting result that the names of famous people are particularly likely to lead to TOTs in older people. It is possible that this effect comes about because older people learned these names longer ago than did younger people. As a result, the names may be fresher in the memory of younger people and less prone to interference.

Brown and McNeill suggested that memory for words and their definitions (what is usually thought of as a central part of semantic memory) is organized like a dictionary. However, Brown and McNeill realized that the structure of a real dictionary was unlikely to be the same as the structure of mental dictionaries. Subsequently, a great deal of work has gone into trying to determine how the mental dictionary is organized and how people go about searching through it to find the information they require.

Quillian's Teachable Language Comprehender

The first generation of semantic memory models began with the work of Quillian (1969), who wanted to create a computer program that would understand natural language. His program was called the **teachable language comprehender**, or TLC for short. Such a program must contain information about concepts and their relations to one another. Because it contained this information, TLC was not only a computer program but also a model of semantic memory.

Quillian's model represented semantic memory as having the structure of a network. Figure 5.4 presents a portion of a semantic network. The network consists of three types of elements: units, properties, and pointers. Units are usually sets of objects, and they are the nodes of the network. They are typically labelled by nouns, such as *fish* or *shark*. Properties are often described by adjectives or verbs, such as *yellow* or *sing*. Pointers specify the relations between different units, and between units and properties. They can be described by such verbs as *is*, *has*, or *can*. Thus, in Figure 5.4, the following sort of information is represented by the network: *A canary is a bird*; *A canary can sing*; *A bird is an animal*; *A bird has wings*.

From the point of view of a model like Quillian's, semantic memory involves searching through the network for the information you are seeking. A basic type of search would be to verify a sentence as either true or false. Suppose you were asked whether or not it is true that *A robin is a bird*. Then you would search the paths of the network to see if such a relationship exists. Because the information corresponding to *A robin is a bird* is in fact in the network, you would conclude that the statement is true. By contrast, because presumably you could not find information corresponding to a statement like *A robin is a machine*, you would say that such a statement is false. As we shall see, however, the actual mechanism for rejecting false statements is complex.

One assumption that Collins and Quillian (1972) made was that searching through a semantic network takes time. Although this seems like an obvious assumption, it is nevertheless essential. It is essential because measuring how long it takes to conduct searches through semantic networks is a basic way of getting data about their structure. You should recall from our discussion in Chapter 2 that such an approach to the study of psychological structures is called *mental chronometry* (e.g., Posner, 1986). The experimenter gives participants different tasks that, on theoretical grounds, should take different times to complete. Measuring how long it takes the participant to complete various tasks is a way of testing the theory. For example, one implication of the semantic memory model in Figure 5.4 is that it will take longer to verify sentences specifying relationships that are far apart in the network than it would to verify sentences specifying relationships that are close together in the network.

Collins and Quillian (1972) discussed several experiments bearing on this hypothesis. When they did these experiments they made the additional assumption that the times required to complete each step of the search are additive. Suppose

Figure 5.4 A Portion of a Semantic Network.

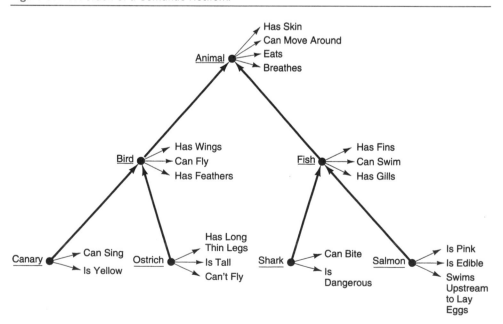

From Collins, A.M., & Quillian, M.R. (1969). Retrieval time from semantic memory. *Journal of Verbal Learning and Verbal Behavior, 8*, pp. 240–248. Copyright 1969 by Academic Press. Reprinted by permission.

you travel along one path and then travel along another path. The total time it takes to travel along both paths equals the time it takes to travel along the first path plus the time it takes to travel along the other path.

Now examine the paths leading from *Canary* in Figure 5.4. *Canary* is directly connected to *can sing*, but there are two pointers between *Canary* and *can fly*. Thus, it should take longer to verify the sentence *A canary can fly* than it does to verify the sentence *A canary can sing*. A similar prediction would be made about the difference between the sentences *A canary is a bird* and *A canary is an animal*. The former requires one step; the latter requires two steps. Collins and Quillian (1972) presented data that were more or less consistent with predictions from their model.

Subsequent research uncovered several difficulties with the Quillian model and others like it (Chang, 1986; Johnson-Laird, Herrmann, & Chafin, 1984). One problem the model has is that it does not specify very clearly the procedure used to tell if a sentence is false. A suggestion made by Collins and Quillian (1972) was called the *conditional stopping hypothesis*. Consider a false sentence like *A polar bear has hands*. According to the conditional stopping hypothesis, people conduct a search for paths connecting *polar bear* and *hands*. The search can be terminated if it arrives at a contradiction. A contradiction can occur if, for example, the property specified by the sentence and the property specified in memory are inconsistent. Thus, you could find a path leading from *polar bear* to *paws*. The information in memory that *A polar bear has paws* contradicts the information contained by the sentence *A polar bear has hands*. However, it is not clear what happens if no paths can be found leading to a contradiction.

In spite of difficulties with the Collins and Quillian (1972) model, the experimental procedure of asking participants to search their semantic memories for the answers to questions has been extremely productive. A good example of such experiments is the **Moses illusion** (Erickson & Matson, 1981; Reder & Kusbit, 1991). The Moses illusion refers to the fact that people will respond to the question *How many animals of each kind did Moses take on the Ark?* by saying *Two*. Of course, Moses did not take any animals on the Ark. It was Noah who did.

The Moses illusion is a very robust phenomenon, and can be demonstrated with other questions, as the following examples, from Reder and Kusbit (1991), demonstrate. If asked *What country was Margaret Thatcher president of?* people will answer *England*, even though Margaret Thatcher was prime minister, and not president. When asked *Who found the glass slipper left at the ball by Snow White?* people will answer *The Prince*, even though it was Cinderella, not Snow White, who lost her glass slipper. Finally, when asked *What superhero does Clark Kent become when he changes in a toll booth?* people will answer *Superman*, even though Clark Kent actually changes in a phone booth, not a toll booth.

People typically fail to notice the mistake in the question and answer it anyway. Why do people not notice the error in the question? Why do they appear to respond instead to a 'corrected' version of the question? Shafto and MacKay (2000) have suggested that the Moses illusion occurs for two main reasons. One reason is that both the correct term (*Noah*) and the lure (*Moses*) are semantically related (i.e., have some shared meaning). Thus, both *Moses* and *Noah* are Old Testament male figures who saved people from adversity. The other reason is that *Moses* and *Noah* are phonologically related (i.e., have a similar sound). Thus, both share the same initial vowel sound. However, people are less likely to answer the question *How many animals did Abraham take on the Ark?* by saying *Two* (Erickson & Mattson, 1981). The reason is that, while *Abraham and Noah* are semantically related (e.g., both are Old Testament male figures), they are not as phonologically related (e.g., they do not share the same first vowel and do not have the same number of syllables). Thus, participants are less likely to confuse *Abraham* and *Noah* than they are to confuse *Moses* and *Noah*.

Spreading Activation

An important notion to emerge from the study of semantic memory is the concept of **spreading activation** (J.R. Anderson, 1984). Spreading activation was proposed by Quillian (1969) and elaborated by Collins and Loftus (1975). The idea is that when you search a semantic network, you activate the paths where the search takes place. This activation spreads from the node at which the search begins. 'The spread of activation constantly expands, first to all the nodes linked to the first node, then to all the nodes linked to each of these nodes, and so on' (Collins & Loftus, 1975, p. 408). The more active a node is, the more easily its information can be processed. For example, information from active nodes can be retrieved more quickly. Let us examine how the idea of spreading activation can be used to understand how priming works.

Several experiments on priming have been done within the framework of the study of semantic memory. Some of the best known of these were reviewed by Meyer and Schvaneveldt (1976). One experiment on word recognition followed the procedure outlined in Figure 5.5. Participants looked at a screen with two dots, one above the other. Then a string of letters appeared at the top dot. Sometimes the letter string was an English word such as *wine* and sometimes it was a non-word such as *plame*. The participant's task was to decide whether or not the letter string was a word, and to respond yes if it was a word and no if it was a non-word. The time it took to make this response was recorded. Then another string of letters appeared at the bottom dot. Participants also had to decide if this second string of letters was a word.

Sometimes the first letter string was a word semantically related to the second letter string. For example, suppose that the first word was *bus* and the second word *truck*; or suppose that the first word was *sunset* and the second word *sunrise*. These are pairs of words that one might expect to be close together in a semantic network. By contrast, if the first word was *sunset* and the second word was *truck*, then this pair would be semantically unrelated. You would not expect these two words to be close together in a semantic network.

One of the results of this study was that the time it took to correctly recognize the second word was partly determined by the nature of the first word. If the first word was semantically related to the second word, then the time it took to recognize the second word was less than if the first word was semantically unrelated to the second word. That is, if the first word was semantically related to the second word (e.g., *sun-*

Figure 5.5 Meyer, Schvaneveldt, and Ruddy's Priming Procedure.

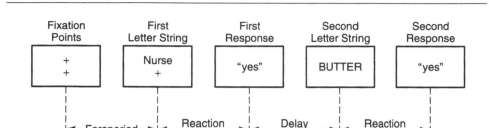

From Meyer, D.E., Schvaneveldt, R.W., & Ruddy, M.G. (1975). Loci of contextual effects on visual recognition. In P.M.A. Rabbitt & S. Dornic (Eds.), *Attention and performance V* (p. 100). London: Academic Press. Copyright 1975 by Academic Press. Reprinted by permission of Elsevier.

set-sunrise), then the first word primed recognition of the second word. This priming effect did not occur if the two words were semantically unrelated (e.g., *sunset-truck*).

One way of understanding this result is in terms of the spreading activation theory outlined above. Consider the fragment of a semantic network in Figure 5.6. In this diagram, the greater the distance between any two concepts, the less they are related to one another. Thus, *cherries* and *apples* are directly connected, but the connection between *street* and *flowers* is through several paths. The closer together concepts are, the more easily will activation spread from one concept to another. If *clouds* is activated, it will in turn activate, or prime, *sunrises* and *sunsets* more than it will prime *vehicle*.

Now let us consider Meyer and Schvaneveldt's results in relation to Figure 5.6. Suppose that *bus* and *truck* and *sunset* and *sunrise* are connected in a semantic network in the way depicted in that figure. When the word *bus* is seen, activation quickly spreads to the *truck* node. The nodes for *sunrise* and *sunset* are much further away in the network and so will be less activated. Consequently, *truck* will be primed by *bus* much more so than by either *sunset* or *sunrise*. Conversely, if the participant sees *sunset* first, then *sunrise* will be primed much more than either *bus* or *truck*. In this way, semantic network models can explain the effects of priming.

The precise mechanisms governing spreading activation still need to be worked out (Bodner & Masson, 2003; Chwilla & Kolk, 2002; McRae & Boisvert, 1998). However, the concept of spreading activation has proven to be quite durable (McNamara, 1992), and continues to be a useful explanatory tool for studies of semantic memory. A good example of this is a study by Kvavilashvili and Mandler (2004) of **involuntary semantic memories.**

Involuntary Semantic Memories

An involuntary semantic memory occurs whenever a semantic memory (e.g., a tune) pops into your mind without any episodic context. Thus, you do not recall any

Figure 5.6 Fragment of a Semantic Network.

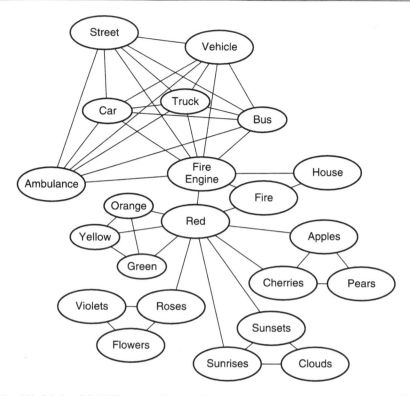

From Collins, A.M., & Loftus, E.F. (1975). A spreading-activation theory of semantic processing. *Psychological Review, 82,* pp. 407–428. Copyright 1975 by the American Psychological Association. Reprinted by permission.

autobiographical information concerning the semantic memory; it just pops up by itself and appears to be irrelevant to what you are currently thinking about. Kvavilashvili and Mandler (2004) call this **mind popping**.

Kvavilashvili and Mandler (2004) reported on diary and questionnaire studies designed to probe the mind-popping phenomenon. Kvavilashvili kept two diaries of her semantic mind pops for 19 and 18 weeks when she was 35 and 37 years old, respectively. She logged a total of 428 memories, which tended to be either words (e.g., *rummage*) or images (e.g., *a view of a road and a small church in Cardiff*). She had no episodic information accompanying these involuntary semantic memories. Most of the mind pops occurred while she was engaged in routine activities not requiring a lot of attention, and at first appeared unrelated to the current activity. However, Kvavilashvili was often able to retrospectively find cues that had triggered the memories without her awareness. For example, one pop-up was *Itchy and Scratchy*, the names of characters from *The Simpsons* television show. Kvavilashvili noticed she was scratching her back when the pop-up occurred. Examples like this suggest that involuntary semantic memories are primed by events of which we typically are unaware. These events need not have occurred recently, but may have occurred weeks or months ago. Priming effects may be much more long-lasting than had previously been thought.

Kvavilashvili and Mandler also created a Mind Popping Questionnaire (MPQ) consisting of four questions. Undergraduate student participants first indicated whether they had ever experienced involuntary semantic memories. They then indicated how frequently they experienced them on a scale ranging from *only a few times* to *three or more times a day*. The participant's third task was to select from a list of common popsups (e.g., melodies, visual images) those they had experienced. Finally participants gave examples of their mind pops. You should try answering these questions yourself, or even keep a diary of mind pops.

The results of the MPQ extended the findings of the diary study. Eighty-four per cent of participants reported experiencing mind pops, on average about two to four times a week. Melodies were the most frequent, followed by visual images, proper names (e.g., of a *person*, *town*, or *street*), and then words. Pop-ups usually occurred during routine everyday activities (e.g., *driving*, *cleaning*) and participants were unaware of their source.

Kvavilashvili and Mandler (2004) conclude that:

> the occurrence of involuntary semantic memories in everyday life is indicative of priming in a novel, spontaneous, and often long-term mode . . . . [A]utomatic and unconscious processes of activation and spreading activation . . . operate outside the laboratory in people's everyday life. . . . Given that priming can produce activation over relatively long periods (see Roediger & McDermott, 1993), we thus wander through the world with a spreading web of activation going on in our representational mind. (pp. 78–80)

Kvavilashvili and Mandler's (2004) study shows how their ecologically valid research complements and extends laboratory work. We will return to the way in which ongoing activations can affect the way we think in the chapters on problem-solving and on creativity.

The Fan Effect

The concept of spreading activation has been incorporated into J.R. Anderson's studies of the so-called *fan effect* (Anderson, 1983, 1984; Anderson, Bothell, & Douglass, 2004; Anderson & Bower, 1973; Anderson & Reder, 1999; Sohn, Anderson, Reder, & Goode, 2004). The fan effect works like this. Imagine that you are a participant in a fact-retrieval experiment. First, you learn a set of propositions. These are statements about people and their locations. Here is a sample of four such statements, taken from Anderson, Bothell, and Douglass (2004, p. 225).

1. The doctor is in the bank. (1-1)
2. The fireman is in the park. (1-2)
3. The hippie is in the church. (2-1)
4. The hippie is in the park. (2-2)

The numbers in parentheses after each statement refer to the number of facts with which each subject or predicate is associated across all four statements. Thus, the *doctor* is only in one place, the *bank*, and the *bank* is only associated with one person, the *doctor*. However, the *hippie* has two associations, being in both the *church* and the *park*. The *park* has two associations as well: the *hippie* and the *fireman* are both there. The fireman has one association, being in the *park*. The number of associations each person or place has is called its *fan*.

Suppose a participant learned a set of 26 statements similar to the ones given above. As a result the participant would acquire a **propositional network** of which Figure 5.7 would represent a part. The network specifies the relations between a set of concepts. The circles are relationships, which in this case are all *is in* (e.g., the *hippie* is in the *park*). Participants are then given a set of statements containing both propositions that were learned and propositions not seen before that contain novel relations between people and places (e.g., *The hippie is in the bank*). The participants' task is to say which statements were studied before (targets) and which ones were not (foils). The experimenter measures the time it takes for each participant to make each decision.

The results are that the more facts you know about a person or a location, the longer it takes to make a decision about whether or not you have seen a statement about that person or location before. For example, if two facts have been learned about the *hippie* and one fact has been learned about the *doctor*, then it takes longer to determine whether or not you have seen a statement about the *hippie* than it does to make the same kind of decision for statements about the *doctor*.

The **fan effect** refers to the sort of results we have just described. In general, the more a person knows about a particular concept, the longer it takes to recognize specific information about it. J.R. Anderson (1984) related the fan effect to spreading activation in a propositional network. The basic idea is that 'as more facts are associated with a concept, the weaker the strength of associations from the concepts to these facts become and less activation is spread to these facts' (Anderson & Reder, 1999, p. 191). Look at Figure 5.7 again. There are more facts about the *hippie* than about the *doctor* or about the *fireman*. The node for *hippie* is activated by seeing a statement about the *hippie*. Then activation will begin to spread throughout that part of the network associated with *hippie*. There is only so much activation to go around. Activating a network is a bit like filling up glasses of water from a single pitcher. The more glasses there are, the less you can put in each one. Consequently, the part of the network associated with *hippie* will be activated less than it would be if there were fewer facts associated with it. By contrast, the part of the network associated with *doctor* will be activated relatively more because there are fewer facts associated with it. The speed with which a response is made is determined by the level of activation. Since *hippie* facts are activated at a lower level, they are responded to more slowly.

There are several different aspects of the meaning of a concept, of which one is the number of associations it has to other concepts (Deese, 1965; Noble, 1952). An interesting implication of the fan effect is that the more meaningful the material, the more time

Figure 5.7 A Fragment of a Propositional Network.

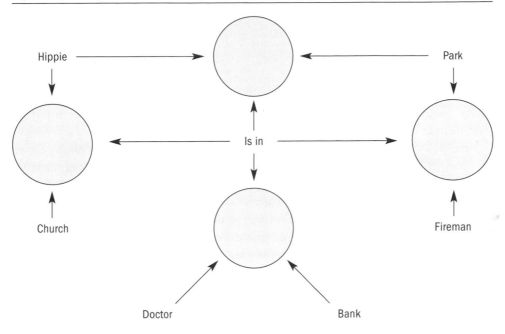

it takes to think it through. This is a topic we will return to in the chapters on language and on creativity.

■ Working Memory

The concept of **working memory** has been at the centre of Alan Baddeley's (1986, 1989, 2000a, 2001, 2002a, 2002b; Baddeley & Hitch, 1974; N. Morris & Jones, 1990; Parkin & Hunkin, 2001) influential research program. Working memory 'involves the temporary storage and manipulation of information that is assumed to be necessary for a wide range of complex cognitive activities' (Baddeley, 2003a, p. 189). Working memory pulls all the other memory systems together. Figure 5.8 illustrates the working memory model. The **central executive** co-ordinates information that may be represented in subsystems such as the **phonological loop**, **visuo-spatial sketchpad**, and the **episodic buffer**. One can roughly distinguish between the phonological loop and the visuo-spatial sketchpad in terms of the former using language and the latter using imagery. Both the phonological loop and the visuo-spatial sketchpad hold information only temporarily and have a limited capacity. Both can interact with long-term memory, the phonological loop drawing on linguistically encoded knowledge, and the visuo-spatial sketchpad drawing on non-verbal general knowledge. The episodic buffer is used to move information both to and from episodic long-term memory. Like the other components, the episodic buffer also represents information temporarily and has a limited capacity (Baddeley, 2000b, p. 421). Its most important function is to organize information 'from the phonological and visuo-spatial subsystems of [working memory] with information from [long-term memory]' (Baddeley, 2001, p. 1349). The central executive selects and integrates information from across the subsystems. As such, the central executive is intimately associated with consciousness, constituting a workspace within which solutions are formulated (Baars, 2002). Finally, notice the distinction in Figure 5.8 between **fluid systems** and **crystallized systems**. This difference is between cognitive processes that manipulate information but are 'themselves unchanged by learning' and 'cognitive systems capable of accumulating long-term knowledge' (Baddeley, 2000b, p. 421).

Baddeley (1989, p. 36) illustrated how some of the components of working memory interact by means of the following simple example, which has also been used by Shepard (1966) and by Neisser (1970). Suppose you are asked to remember the number of windows in your house or in your apartment. Most people will form a mental image of their house, and perhaps imagine walking around it. This information is provided by the visuo-spatial sketchpad. As you imagine walking around the house, you can count the windows as you go. The counting is done by the articulatory loop. The central executive co-ordinates the entire process.

Baddeley (2003b) suggested that the phonological loop evolved as an aid in the acquisition of language. Sounds can be represented and rehearsed by means of the phonological loop, facilitating the learning of words. Once learned, speech becomes a powerful tool for influencing not only the behaviour of others, but also one's own behaviour. Sub-vocal speech can be used to articulate one's plans and is an important aspect of self-control. This is a topic we will explore at length in Chapter 8 on language. Baddeley (2003b) also suggested that the visuo-spatial sketchpad evolved in order to facilitate the representation of things and their relations. As such it aids in tasks as diverse as planning a route in the environment (e.g., getting home from a novel location) or figuring out how to put the parts of something together (e.g., assembling furniture components). Processes like these will be explored in the chapters on imagery, problem-solving, reasoning, and creativity.

Working Memory and the Brain

Baddeley (2002a) observed that working memory is a complex system and 'unlikely to map in a simple way onto an anatomical structure such as the frontal lobes. However, it is clear that the frontal lobes play an important role in integrating information from many other areas of the brain, and are crucially involved in its manipulation for purposes such as learning, comprehension, and reasoning. . . . [T]hese are precisely the roles attributed to working memory' (p. 258).

One frontal area has been singled out as having a particularly important role in working memory. We discussed the dorsolateral prefrontal cortex (DLPFC) when we reviewed Stroop research in Chapter 3 on attention. We noted then that it was believed to play a role in selecting between alternative response tendencies. This is, of course, an important function of working memory, in particular of the central executive. Curtis and D'Esposito (2003) have suggested that DLPFC should be seen as

Figure 5.8 Working Memory Model.

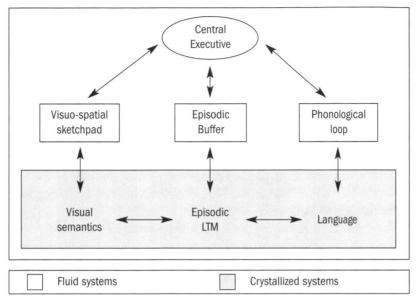

From Baddeley, A. (2003). Fractionating the central executive. In Stuss, D.T., & Knight, R.T. (Eds.), *Principles of frontal lobe function* (pp. 246–260).New York: Oxford University Press.

an integral part of working memory, acting to monitor and control alternative courses of action.

■ Connectionist Models of Memory

When connectionist models were introduced in Chapter 2, we noted that they were designed to represent neural networks as they might exist in the brain. McClelland (2000, p. 583) observed that from a connectionist viewpoint individual items are not 'stored in memory', but rather that a pattern of activity constitutes a memory. In a connectionist framework, copies of particular experiences are not stored as memory traces. Rather, there are neuron-like units that are connected to other neuron-like units. These units represent each of the properties of an experience. McClelland et al. (1986) pointed out that some experiences will have the same properties, and so the unit for a particular property will tend to be connected with several different experiences. Anytime a property is activated, it also tends to activate all the units to which it is connected. Thus, the system needs to **inhibit** some connections as well as **excite** other connections between units in order to accurately recall previous experiences.

McClelland (1981) and McClelland et al. (1986, pp. 27ff.) have presented a demonstration of how a simple connectionist system might work. Figure 5.9 gives a list of individuals and some of their properties, such as their names, the name of the gang they belong to, and their age, education, marital status, and occupation. Some of the units that would be required to represent these individuals in memory are given in Figure 5.10. In the centre of the diagram are units for each of the persons listed in Figure 5.9. These individual units are connected to the appropriate property units. For convenience, the property units are represented as being grouped within different 'clouds', and units within a particular cloud inhibit each other. Thus, an individual cannot be called both *Lance* and *Art* at the same time.

Imagine that you have met all these individuals at one time or another. Imagine also that you find yourself in a conversation in which people are talking about the individual whose name is *Art*. When you try to remember what *Art* is like, what happens? Initially, when you hear the name *Art*, the name unit for *Art* will be activated. This name unit is connected to the individual unit for *Art*. The individual unit for *Art* is connected to all the property units that *Art* possesses. Activation of all of these property units corresponds to remembering *Art*. This model can be seen as an extension of the spreading activation models we considered earlier.

Of course, the act of remembering is not always so straightforward. If you hear a person talking about someone who is single, you will not be able to identify the person without more information. Several individual units are connected to the property of being single. However, information about a combination of properties might serve to specify the individual more or less completely. Thus, if you also hear that the person is a *bookie* and went to *college* as well as being *single*, then both those connections will tend to activate the unit for *Sam* more than other units. Activating the *Sam* unit will also activate the property units associated with *Sam*, and make you think that the person being talked about is a member of the *Jets*.

In this kind of memory model, information about individual experiences is derived from the state of the entire system at a particular time. The pattern of excitation and inhibition in the system as a whole determines what you will remember.

■ Aging and Memory Disorders

Memory and Aging

It is a part of folk wisdom to say that memory declines with age. However, it is not memory in general that declines. While some forms of memory are relatively unscathed by advancing years, episodic memory in particular shows a strong effect of age (Craik & Grady, 2002, p. 529). A good illustration of this is a study by Mitchell (1989) that explored differences in the way that *episodic* and *semantic* memories decline with age. Remembering that *I put salt on my food at lunch yesterday* is an episodic memory; remembering that *the formula for salt is NaCl* is a semantic memory. Mitchell tested the memories of a group of young people (19–32 years old) and a group of older people (63–80 years old). The young people clearly outperformed the old ones on the episodic memory tasks, but did not do so on the semantic memory tasks. Thus, while old people may sometimes have trouble recollecting recent personal experiences, they may yet have a lot of general knowledge that they can continue to communicate.

Figure 5.9 Some Properties of Gang Members.

The Jets and the Sharks					
Name	Gang	Age	Edu.	Mar.	Occupation
Art	Jets	40s	J.H.	Sing.	Pusher
Al	Jets	30s	J.H.	Mar.	Burglar
Sam	Jets	20s	COL.	Sing.	Bookie
Clyde	Jets	40s	J.H.	Sing.	Bookie
Mike	Jets	30s	J.H.	Sing.	Bookie
Jim	Jets	20s	J.H.	Div.	Burglar
Greg	Jets	20s	H.S.	Mar.	Pusher
John	Jets	20s	J.H.	Mar.	Burglar
Doug	Jets	30s	H.S.	Sing.	Bookie
Lance	Jets	20s	J.H.	Mar.	Burglar
George	Jets	20s	J.H.	Div.	Burglar
Pete	Jets	20s	H.S.	Sing.	Bookie
Fred	Jets	20s	H.S.	Sing.	Pusher
Gene	Jets	20s	COL.	Sing.	Pusher
Ralph	Jets	30s	J.H.	Sing.	Pusher
Phil	Sharks	30s	COL.	Mar.	Pusher
Ike	Sharks	30s	J.H.	Sing.	Bookie
Nick	Sharks	30s	H.S.	Sing.	Pusher
Don	Sharks	30s	COL.	Mar.	Burglar
Ned	Sharks	30s	COL.	Mar.	Bookie
Karl	Sharks	40s	H.S.	Mar.	Bookie
Ken	Sharks	20s	H.S.	Sing.	Burglar
Earl	Sharks	40s	H.S.	Mar.	Burglar
Rick	Sharks	30s	H.S.	Div.	Burglar
Ol	Sharks	30s	COL.	Mar.	Pusher
Neal	Sharks	30s	H.S.	Sing.	Bookie
Dave	Sharks	30s	H.S.	Div.	Pusher

From McClelland, J.L. (1981). Retrieving general and specific knowledge from stored knowledge of specifics, from Proceedings of the Third Annual Conference of the Cognitive Science Society, Berkeley, Calif., p. 27. Copyright 1981 by J.L. McClelland. Reprinted by permission.

As we observed in the last chapter, in the section on levels of processing and aging, one of the more frustrating aspects of getting older is the deterioration in the ability to recognize people and/or recall their names. In one study by Schweich, van der Linden, Bredart, Bruey, Nelles, and Schils (1992), three groups of participants kept diaries of the occasions on which they had experienced such difficulties. Group 1 contained young university students (19–25 years old) who reported no previous difficulties in recognizing faces; Group 2 contained young university students (19–25 years old) who claimed to often be embarrassed by their inability to recognize faces; and Group 3 consisted of older

Figure 5.10 A Connectionist Model of the Information in Figure 5.9.

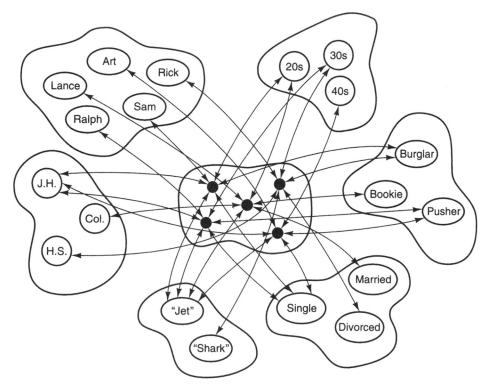

From McClelland, J.L. (1981). Retrieving general and specific knowledge from stored knowledge of specifics, from Proceedings of the Third Annual Conference of the Cognitive Science Society, Berkeley, Calif., p. 28. Copyright by J.L. McClelland. Reprinted by permission.

(54–73 years old) people also attending university. Over a one-month period, Group 2 reported the greatest incidence of difficulties, and the other groups did not differ. However, the types of difficulties reported were different across the groups. Group 2 had the greatest difficulty with recognizing faces. The difficulties of those in Group 3 centred on being able to come up with someone's name. Being unable to consciously retrieve a name, given the face, is a failure that is similar to the inability to directly remember the episodic associations described in the previous paragraph. However, in the diary study, most of the older people were able to recall wanted names given enough time to do so.

Naveh-Benjamin (2000; Naveh-Benjamin, Hussain, Guez, & Bar-on, 2003) has shown how the difficulty older people have in remembering names and faces may have the same source as the more general difficulty they have with episodic memory. Naveh-Benjamin has proposed an **associative deficit hypothesis**: older adults have a 'deficiency in creating and retrieving links between single units of information' (Naveh-Benjamin, Guez, Kilb, & Reedy, 2004, p. 541). In one experiment, the ability to recall face-name associations was examined for both a younger group (mean age of about 21) and an older group (mean age of about 72) of participants. Each participant saw 40 pairs of names and faces presented for three seconds per pair. Participants were told to try to learn not only faces and names, but also their pairings. Participants then received a name recognition test, a face recognition test, and a face-name association test. In the first test, participants were shown a name they had seen in the first part of the experiment, paired with one they had not seen. They were asked to name the one they had seen before. They were shown 16 such pairs in all. The face recognition test was the same, except the pairs were faces. In the face-name association test, participants were shown eight names they had seen before, each one paired with two faces, one of which they had seen previously and one they had not. They were also shown eight faces they had seen before paired with two names, one of which they had seen previously and one they had not. The task was to correctly identify the correct name or the correct face.

In general, the older participants were less able to correctly identify names or faces when they were presented by themselves. However, this difference was quite small. The big difference associated with age was correctly identifying the name that went with a face, or the face that went with a name. In this task the older participants were considerably less able than the younger participants. Thus, it is not so much that the older participants do not recognize names or faces as it is that they cannot bind them together as successfully. Older adults have trouble in situations requiring the 'merging of different aspects of an episode into a cohesive unit' (Naveh-Benjamin, Guez, Kilb, & Reedy, 2004, p. 541). As a result, recalling previous episodes will be difficult because the parts of a previous experience have not been bound together to form a coherent whole.

While older people may have difficulty consciously recalling recently experienced events, Howard, Fry, and Brune (1991, Experiment 2) found that they can still demonstrate knowledge of those events when tested more subtly. Younger (18–24 years) and older (62–75 years) people were asked to learn new associations. They were shown pairs of words (e.g., *queen-stairs*, *author-project*) and asked to make up a sentence containing them. When participants, given the first member of a pair, are asked to recall the second member, then younger participants tended to do better than older ones. However, on a more indirect test of memory, older participants did as well as younger participants. The indirect test was a word fragment completion task similar to those reviewed earlier in the section on implicit memory. Participants were shown the first word of a pair plus a fragment of the second. Sometimes the word-fragment pairs corresponded to pairs shown in the first phase of the experiment (e.g., *queen-sta——*, *author-pro——*) but sometimes the pairs were mixed up (e.g., *queen-pro——*, *author-sta——*). Participants were asked to complete the stem with the first word that came to mind. Notice that there are several words that could come to mind, such as *star*. However, if the pair-stem combination corresponded to one they had seen before (e.g., *queen-sta——*), then both younger and older participants tended to choose the word originally shown (*stairs*), an effect that is not present if the word fragment pair was not previously seen (e.g., *queen-pro——*). This demonstrates that the older participants had implicitly learned new associations, even though they may not have realized that they had done so. Howard, Fry, and Brune concluded that you *can* teach old dogs new tricks. They warned, however, that such learning depends on older people being given as much time as they want to learn something. Self-pacing appears to be very important.

In a review of studies such as that of Howard, Fry, and Brune (1991), Mitchell and Bruss (2003) confirmed that older adults seem to be able to form implicit memories as easily as do younger people. Older people show priming effects as readily as do younger people. Implicit memory appears to be stable across age.

Thus, memory deficits in older people tend not to be general (Rabbitt, 1990). Not only may there be great individual differences in the rate at which memory declines, but the memory deficit displayed may be determined by the particular context in which it is tested. Rabbitt (1990, p. 230) suggested that repeated testing may lead to improvements in the elderly that eliminate age differences altogether.

The Amnesic Syndrome

Both Schacter (1987) and Baddeley (1987a) pointed out the relevance of **Korsakoff's syndrome** for the study of memory. This is a form of amnesia that occurs in some chronic alcoholics. In Korsakoff's syndrome there is atrophy of brain tissue due to malnutrition, particularly thiamine deficiency (Brokate, Hildebrandt, Eling, Fuchtner, Runge, & Timm, 2003). Edouard Claparède (1873–1940) was a pioneer in the investigation of this syndrome (Kihlstrom, 1995). Here is Claparède's (1911/1951) famous description of a 47-year-old Korsakoff's patient.

> Her old memories remained intact. She could correctly name the capitals of Europe, make mental calculations, and so on. But she did not know where she was, though she had been at the asylum five years. She did not recognize the doctors whom she saw every day, nor her nurse who had been with her for six months. When the latter asked the patient whether she knew her, the patient said: 'No Madame, with whom have I the honor of speaking?' She forgot from one minute to the next what she was told, or the events that took place. She did not know what year, month, and day it was, though she was being told constantly. (p. 68)

Schacter (1987) also reviewed research on the so-called *amnesic syndrome*. This is a disorder produced by brain lesions, and includes patients with Korsakoff's syndrome, as well as Tulving's NN, who was described previously in this chapter. Amnesic patients may be able to operate normally in many areas, but be unable to remember events that have occurred since the beginning of their affliction. Talland (1968) described this kind of patient:

> If time has come to a stop for the amnesic patient it is because he remembers virtually none of the events that he has witnessed since the onset of his illness. The days go by and none seems to be different from the others. Staff members and fellow patients re-appear looking no more familiar than complete strangers. A

story gives as much satisfaction on the tenth as it did on the first reading, its novelty never seems to wear off. If the patient recognizes a new figure in his environment, his doctor for example, as someone familiar, he may easily confuse him with another figure encountered in the same environment or name him correctly but as diffidently as if it were a wild guess. In the literature there are several accounts of the medical examination that had to be interrupted for a few minutes, in which the patient greeted the doctor on his return as someone he had not met for a long time. (p. 123)

Warrington and Weiskrantz (1982) referred to such patients as having a **disconnection syndrome**, because the patients may be able to acquire new information and yet not be aware of the fact that learning has taken place. It is as if there are at least two memory systems (Tulving, 1985) that normally interact but that have become disconnected in amnesics. This interpretation is reinforced by studies using the *famous name paradigm* we considered earlier. Squire and McKee (1992) showed lists of names to both amnesics and normals. Some of the names were of famous people (e.g., *Olga Korbut*) while others were not (e.g., *Emia Lekovic*). After seeing the names, all participants were shown another set of famous and non-famous names, some of which were from the previous list and some of which had not been shown to participants before. Participants were asked to rate these names as famous or non-famous. Both normals and amnesics tended to rate a name as famous if it had appeared on the first list, even if it was not really famous. Thus, simply being exposed to a name tends to influence participants' judgements. However, while normals were usually able to recognize a name as one that had appeared on the first list, amnesics were much less able to do so. Thus, amnesics could judge a non-famous name as famous because they had just seen it on the previous list, and yet not know that they had just seen it.

Amnesics show the effects of implicit memory. Warrington and Weiskrantz (1982) reviewed several studies that combine to strongly suggest that tasks in which amnesic patients do poorly are those requiring explicit memory, whereas they do much better on those requiring implicit memory. Graf and Schacter (1985) were able to further demonstrate this in a word fragment completion experiment using both normal and amnesic participants. Participants were presented with pairs of words. Some of the pairs were related by existing associations (e.g., *buttoned shirt*), whereas others were not (e.g., *window shirt*). In one part of the experiment, participants were required to make up a sentence that related each of the words 'in a meaningful manner'. Thus, given the word pair *ripe/apple*, a participant might generate the sentence, 'He ate the ripe apple.' Participants were then allowed to study each pair of words once.

Each participant was given a word completion test and a cued recall test. The word fragment completion test was a test of implicit memory, whereas the cued recall test was a test of explicit memory. In the implicit test, participants would be shown the first member of a word pair and the first three letters of the second member of the pair, called a word fragment. The participant had to complete the word.

The interesting question is: Will participants complete the fragment with the same word as they were shown initially? Both amnesics and normals tended to do so. However, on the cued recall test, in which participants had to recall the second member of a word pair given the first member, the performance of amnesics was much worse than that of normals.

Amnesics and normals show similar performance on an implicit memory task, in spite of the fact that amnesics' performance on an explicit memory task is far below normal performance (Levy, Stark, & Squire, 2004). Amnesics may be able to form associations, and thus learn new material (Schacter & Graf, 1986; Kihlstrom, Schacter, Cork, Hurt, & Behr, 1990). However, this learning would not be available to them in an explicit form. It would only be available implicitly. Korsakoff himself (1899, pp. 512, 518, as cited by Schacter, 1987, p. 503) had described this phenomenon in the following terms:

> Although the patient was not aware that he preserved traces of impressions that he received, those traces however probably existed and had an influence in one way or another on the course of ideas, at least in unconscious intellectual activity.
>
> We notice that a whole series of traces which could in no way be restored to consciousness, neither actively or passively, continue to exist in unconscious life, continue to direct the course of ideas of the patient, suggesting to him some or other inferences and decisions. That seems to me to be one of the most interesting peculiarities of the disturbance about which we are speaking.

Alzheimer's Disease

Alzheimer's disease is one of the most feared of memory disorders. In an American survey conducted in 2002, 95 per cent of those polled said that Alzheimer's was a 'serious problem facing the whole nation' and that 64 per cent of people between 35 and 49 years of age were afraid of getting the disease (Halpern, 2002, p. 16). 'Four million Americans already have the disease, a number that is expected to grow to fourteen million by midcentury' (Halpern, 2002, p. 16). Similar rates are likely in other industrialized countries (DiCarlo et al., 2002).

The diagnosis of Alzheimer's disease has become much better differentiated since the first recorded case seen by Alois Alzheimer in 1907. The disease is progressive, beginning with a deterioration of episodic memory. A decline in the ability to retain recently acquired information is characteristic of the early stages (Hodges, 2000, p. 443). Jacoby (1999) gives a good example illustrating how frustrating Alzheimer's can be for caregivers. He describes someone who was diagnosed with Alzheimer's and who was taken to visit a nursing home prior to going to live there. The Alzheimer's sufferer was introduced to the customs of the nursing home, one of which was that there was no tipping in the dining room. This fact was repeated several times. When the visit was drawing to a close, the prospective resident was asked if she had any questions. At that point she wanted to know if she should tip in the dining room. '[R]epeated asking of questions is one of the most striking and frustrating symptoms of memory impairment resulting from Alzheimer's disease' (Jacoby, 1999, p. 3).

It is not necessarily the case that someone with an inability to learn new material will go on to develop Alzheimer's. 'It is also necessary to follow such patients for years in order to determine that they do indeed have' Alzheimer's (Hodges, 2000, p. 445). The ultimate diagnosis of Alzheimer's occurs after death when the brain can be examined. There is a characteristic pattern of tangled neurons, as well as plaque deposits, but it is unclear whether this form of degeneration is a cause or an outcome of Alzheimer's disease (Hodges, 2000, p. 443).

As the disease progresses, Alzheimer's patients will show impaired semantic memory (Glosser & Friedman, 1991; Hodges, 2000, p. 445). For example, Hodges, Salmon, and Butters (1992) gave a group of Alzheimer's patients a battery of semantic memory tests, including naming as many exemplars of a category (e.g., *animals*) as possible; naming drawings of objects; and generating definitions of words (e.g., *alligator*) that could be understood by 'someone from a different country who has never seen or heard of such a thing' (p. 305). On all tests the Alzheimer's patients performed more poorly than normal controls. Moreover, performance on one test was correlated with performance on other tests, such that, for example, failure to name a drawing of an object (e.g., an alligator) went with an inability to generate a definition of the name (e.g., *alligator*). This suggests that Alzheimer's disease does not involve the inability to retrieve existing knowledge so much as the deterioration of knowledge that once existed. Hodges, Salmon, and Butters (1992, p. 312) observe that the definitions given by the Alzheimer's patients were particularly instructive. They included very general, non-specific characteristics (defining a *land animal* as *four-legged*), as well as inappropriate intrusions (defining a *rhinoceros* in terms appropriate for *elephants*).

Salmon, Butters, and Chan (1999), in a review of a large number of studies, concluded that the evidence supported the hypothesis of semantic memory deterioration in Alzheimer's patients:

> The normal organization of semantic memory is disrupted by this loss of semantic knowledge and the semantic network appears to deteriorate as the disease progresses. Although the neuroanatomical basis of the deterioration of semantic memory in patients with [Alzheimer's] is currently unknown, it is likely that it results from synapse loss, neuron loss, and other neurodegenerative changes in the association cortices that presumably store semantic representations. (p. 115)

The Retraining of Memory

The rehabilitation of memory has usually been based on intuitively plausible procedures, rather than treatments based on adequate theories of memory disorders. B.A. Wilson and her colleagues (Kapur, Glisky, & Wilson, 2002; Wilson, 2002; Wilson & Moffat, 1984; Wilson & Patterson, 1990) have tried to identify treatment approaches that have a history of working and/or are grounded in a sound theoretical basis.

Environmental Adaptations

One can try to minimize the number of situations requiring memory. Written timetables, located so that the patient cannot miss them, can serve to guide the patient from activity to activity. Simply posting signs in rooms that tell patients where they are can be valuable (Giles & Clark-Wilson, 1988). In general, one should design the environment so that it elicits the desired behaviour. This is a sound strategy even for people without memory disorders, and is a topic we shall return to in Chapter 14 on applied cognitive psychology.

External Memory Aids

Prospective memory requires someone to remember to do something at some future time. Older people in general, as well as those with memory disorders specifically, may not only forget when to do something, but they may also forget whether or not they have previously performed the required action. For example, someone may not only forget to take medication on time, but also forget when one has actually taken it, and so take it again (Einstein, McDaniel, Smith, & Shaw, 1998). An electronic diary that sounds an alarm when the patient is supposed to perform a task and keeps track of the patient's behaviour may get around this problem to some extent (Harris, 1984). One potentially useful device is the Palm Pilot and other similar electronic organizers. These can act as 'prosthetic memories' with 'a built in camera, handwriting recognition system and diary' (Abraham, 2004). The patient can take pictures of people as an aid to future recognition. These devices can also be programmed with a week's 'to do' list and prompt the user to 'remember' on each occasion. Of course, the patient must be taught how to use the device. This is a painstaking and lengthy procedure, because most patients must rely on implicit rather than explicit memory. Sheer repetition makes a difference, and it is important for the teacher to help the patient avoid making errors. **Errorless learning** is widely believed to maximize the patient's ability to use whatever memory resources he or she still has. The patient only does what should be done and never learns to do something incorrectly (Wilson, 2002, p. 667).

Teaching Domain-Specific Knowledge

Learning in amnesics is unlikely to generalize to contexts very different from the one in which the original learning took place. Indeed, there is no evidence that attempting to restore 'general memory ability' through practice actually accomplishes anything for the patient (Kapur, Glisky, & Wilson, 2002, p. 772). A more realistic goal is to attempt to teach amnesics a specific skill that might be useful to them. To this end, Glisky and Schacter (1989) reported on a procedure called the **method of vanishing cues**. Amnesic participants learned the meaning of computer commands by being presented with definitions of the commands and fragments of their names (e.g., S——— for the command SAVE). Additional letters were presented until the participant guessed the word. Then letters were progressively removed until the patient was able to give the name of the command upon being presented with its definition. Glisky and Schacter report that this technique allowed amnesic patients to successfully perform basic microcomputer operations. It is important that the to-be-learned material be concrete and specific and that the person not be required to generalize very far from the original learning context.

■ Questions for Study and Discussion

1. Outline Tulving's approach to memory, emphasizing the distinctions between different memory systems.
2. How might different memory systems have evolved? Rank the following in importance: natural selection, exaptation, the Baldwin effect. Give reasons for your ranking.
3. Discuss the role of spreading activation in semantic memory. Illustrate your answer by means of relevant experiments.
4. What do older people, people with the amnesic syndrome, and people with Alzheimer's disease tell us about the nature of memory? What kind of treatments might be effective with such persons? Why might these treatments be effective?

■ Key Concepts

Anoetic, noetic, and autonoetic (Tulving) Three levels of consciousness corresponding to procedural, semantic, and episodic memory systems.

Associative deficit hypothesis Older adults have a deficiency in creating and retrieving links between single units of information.

Butcher-on-the-bus phenomenon A feeling of knowing a person without being able to remember the circumstances of any previous meeting or anything else about the person.

Central executive The function of the brain that co-ordinates information that may be represented in the subsystems of working memory.

Chronesthesia (Tulving) Our subjective sense of time.

Crystallized systems Cognitive systems that accumulate long-term knowledge.

Disconnection syndrome Amnesic patients may be able to acquire new information and yet not be aware of the fact that learning has taken place.

Episodic buffer The ability to move information both to and from episodic and long-term memory.

Episodic memory (Tulving) The memory system concerned with personally experienced events.

Errorless learning The patient in a learning situation is allowed only to perform the task correctly to prevent any opportunity of learning to do something incorrectly.

Evolution of memory Ways in which memory systems possibly evolved include natural selection, exaptation, and the Baldwin effect.

Excitatory and inhibitory connections A neural network is made up of connections that either enhance or diminish the associations between units.

Explicit knowledge Knowing that something is the case.

Fan effect The more a person knows about a particular concept, the longer it takes to recognize specific information about it.

Fluid systems Cognitive processes that manipulate information.

Implicit memory Memory without episodic awareness—the expression of previous experience without conscious recollection of the prior episode.

Involuntary semantic memory and mind popping Whenever a semantic memory pops into your mind without any episodic context.

Korsakoff's syndrome A form of amnesia typically due to chronic alcoholism combined with thiamine deficiency.

Method of opposition Pitting conscious (explicit) and unconscious (implicit) tendencies against one another.

Method of vanishing cues Amnesic participants learned the meaning of computer commands by being presented with definitions of the commands and fragments of their names (e.g., S—— for the command SAVE). Additional letters were presented until the participant guessed the word. Then letters were progressively removed until the patient was able to give the name of the command upon being presented with its definition.

Moses illusion People will respond to questions such as *How many animals of each kind did Moses take on the Ark?* by saying *Two*.

Perceptual representation system The memory system containing very specific representations of events that is hypothesized to be responsible for priming effects.

Phonological loop and visuo-spatial sketchpad Temporary stores of linguistic and nonverbal information, respectively.

Prefrontal leucotomy A surgical procedure whereby the connections between the prefrontal lobes and other parts of the brain are severed.

Principle of encoding specificity (Tulving) How an item is retrieved from memory depends on how it was stored in memory.

Procedural memory The memory system concerned with knowing how to do things.

Propositional network A network that specifies the relations between a set of concepts.

Prospective memory The intention to remember to do something at some future time.

Recency bias vs primacy bias A tendency to recall experiences from the recent past vs a tendency to recall experiences that were in the relatively distant past.

Semantic memory (Tulving) The memory system concerned with knowledge of words, concepts, and their relationships.

Spreading activation Searching a semantic network activates paths spreading from the node at which the search begins.

Tacit knowledge Knowing how to do something without necessarily knowing how you do it.

Teachable language comprehender A computer program that is a model of semantic memory.

Tip-of-the-tongue phenomenon Knowing that you know something without quite being able to recall it.

Working memory The temporary storage and manipulation of information that is necessary for a wide range of cognitive activities.

■ Links to Other Chapters

■ Further Reading

Additional angles on memory systems are provided by the following: Gaffan, D. (2003). Against memory systems. In A. Parker, A. Derrington, & C. Blakemore (Eds.), *The physiology of cognitive processes* (pp. 234–251). Oxford: Oxford University Press; Moscovitch, M. (2000). Theories of memory and consciousness. In E. Tulving & F.I.M. Craik (Eds.), *The Oxford handbook of memory* (pp. 609–625). New York: Oxford University Press; Roediger, H.L. (1990). Implicit memory: Retention without remembering. *American Psychologist, 45,* 1043–1056; Roediger, H.L., & Blaxton, T.A. (1987). Retrieval modes produce dissociations in memory for surface information. In D. Gorfein & R.R. Hoffman (Eds.), *Memory and cognitive processes: The Ebbinghaus centennial conference* (pp. 349–377). Hillsdale, NJ: Erlbaum.

A theoretical context for and a survey of chronesthetic experiences is presented in D'Argembeau, A., & Van der Linden, M. (2003). Phenomenal characteristics associated with projecting oneself back into the past and forward into the future: Influence of valence and temporal distance. *Consciousness and Cognition, 13,* 844–858.

Evidence from functional neuroimaging studies illustrating the variety of areas in the brain involved in semantic memory is discussed in Maguire, E.A., & Frith, C.D. (2004). The brain network associated with acquiring semantic knowledge. *NeuroImage, 22,* 171–178; and Thompson-Schill, S.L. (2003). Neuroimaging studies of semantic memory: Inferring 'how' from 'where'. *Neuropsychologia, 41,* 280–292.

Tulving and his colleagues have presented a model suggesting that the left prefrontal cortex is more involved than the right prefrontal cortex in acquiring episodic memories, but that the reverse is true for recalling episodic memories. See Nyberg, L., Cabeza, R., & Tulving, E. (1996). PET studies of encoding and retrieval: The HERA model. *Psychonomic Bulletin and Review, 3,* 135–148; Habib, R., Nyberg, L., & Tulving, E. (2003). Hemispheric asymmetries of memory: The HERA model revisited. *Trends in Cognitive Sciences, 7,* 241–244. A critique of this model is presented by Owen, A. (2003). HERA today, gone tomorrow? *Trends in Cognitive Sciences, 7,* 383–384.

It is difficult for 'normals' to imagine what the state of mind of amnesics might be. A good analogy to the kind of learning demonstrated by amnesics may be the kind of learning that takes place while a normal person is unconscious. For example, Kihlstrom, J.F., Schacter, D., Cork, R., Hurt, C., & Behr, S. (1990). Implicit and explicit memory following surgical anaesthesia. *Psychological Science, 1,* 303–306, investigated memory for events that occur while a (non-amnesic) patient is anaesthetized. They pointed out that following surgical anaesthesia, patients are typically not able to recall any of the events that took place while they were unconscious. However, there is also some information suggesting that events that took place during surgery can affect patients' subsequent behaviour, although this result is controversial.

A thorough review that supplements our discussion of the rehabilitation of cognitive deficits is Park, N.W., & Ingles, J.L. (2001). Effectiveness of attention rehabilitation after an acquired brain injury: A meta-analysis. *Neuropsychology, 15,* 199–210.

Chapter 6

Imagery

It is not easy to say precisely what images are. The similarity between images and pictures has often been noted, and, in fact, in *The Oxford English Dictionary* the verb *to picture* has as one of its meanings 'To form a mental image of, to imagine.' Although a mental image can be defined as a 'picture in the head', a number of qualifications must be added to this simple definition (Reber, 1985). This chapter is about those qualifications. We will examine the ways in which images arise, how they operate, and how they influence other psychological processes.

■ Memory and Imagery

Paivio's Dual-Coding Theory

Images seem to be a very subjective phenomenon, and for a while during the twentieth century many psychologists believed that they were too subjective to be studied scientifically. However, interest in imagery began to re-emerge during the 1960s. This renewal of interest was to an important extent due to the research program initiated by Alan Paivio (1971, 1986, 1991; Paivio & Begg, 1981). In Paivio's theory, imagery is defined as the ease with which something elicits a mental image, where the term mental image refers to experiences such as 'a mental picture, or sound' (e.g., Toglia & Battig, 1978, p. 4).

Paivio's (1971, 1986, 1991) approach is called **dual-coding theory**. This theory postulates the existence of verbal and non-verbal systems that are alternative ways of representing events (Johnson, Paivio, & Clark, 1996, p. 115). For example, an event can be described in words using the verbal system, or it can be imagined using the non-verbal system. Thus, information can be represented in either system, using the code that is peculiar to that system.

The relationships between the two systems are outlined in Figure 6.1. If you follow the diagram from the top down, you see that incoming information can be either verbal or non-verbal. After being picked up by the sensory systems, information can be represented in either the verbal or the non-verbal system. The units that comprise the verbal system are called **logogens**, a term borrowed from Morton (1969). A logogen contains the information underlying our use of a word. The units that make up the non-verbal system are called **imagens**, which contain information that generates mental images. Imagens 'correspond to natural objects, holistic parts of objects, and natural groupings of objects' (Paivio, 1986, p. 60). Imagens operate synchronously: the parts that they contain are simultaneously available for inspection. This means that a variety of related mental images can be generated from imagens. For example, you can imagine a group of people, one person from the group, the face of that person, the nose on the face of that person, and so on. By contrast with imagens, logogens operate sequentially. For example, when you listen to a sentence, the words are not present all at once, but come one after the other.

Information in one system can give rise to a process in the other system. Paivio (1986, p. 62) used the example of describing your dining-room table. If you are somewhere other than your dining room, then you can still probably experience a mental image of the table. What you then describe is that image. This means that the two systems have interconnections, and these are also presented in Figure 6.1, as referential connections. A verbal description of something can elicit an image of what is being described, and an image can in turn elicit a description of what is being imagined.

Figure 6.1 Faivio's Dual-Coding Theory.

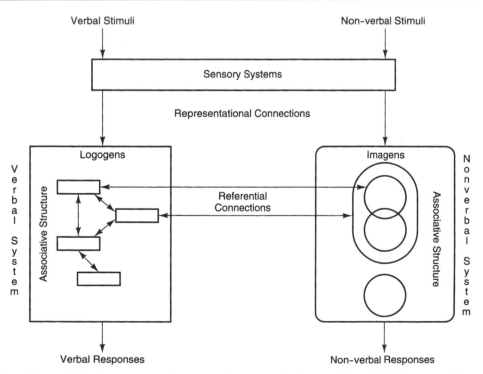

Paivio's (1971) theory holds that words easily eliciting a mental image will also tend to be concrete (such as *table*), whereas words not easily eliciting a mental image will tend to be abstract (e.g., *purpose*). **Concreteness** is defined as the degree to which a word refers to 'concrete objects, persons, places, or things that can be heard, felt, smelled or tasted' (e.g., Toglia & Battig, 1978). Thus, by this definition, concreteness measures the degree to which a word refers to something that can be experienced by the senses. The notion that ideas have their origin in concrete sensory experience has a long tradition in the history of Western thought (see, e.g., R. Brown, 1968; J.M. Clark & Paivio, 1989).

The measurement of imagery and concreteness begins by giving participants the definitions of imagery and concreteness outlined above. Keeping these definitions in mind, participants rate imagery and concreteness on seven-point scales anchored either with 'low imagery' and 'high imagery' or with 'low concreteness' and 'high concreteness'. Imagery and concreteness are usually found to be very highly correlated (e.g., Paivio, Yuille, & Madigan, 1968). This has led Paivio (e.g., Paivio & Begg, 1981) to argue that imagery and concreteness measure two aspects of the same process because our experience of concrete events is necessarily saturated with images.

Notice that one of the implications of the foregoing is that such concepts as *pain* and *love* are not concrete. Although this seems puzzling at first, remember that concreteness is used to refer to objects, persons, and places. Pain and love can certainly be caused by concrete things, but they are not themselves concrete events. Thus, there are some words, such as *pain* and *love*, which are not concrete but still elicit vivid mental imagery. These words often refer to emotions (Benjafield, 1987; Paivio, 1971, p. 83; Yuille, 1968). Thus, in addition to external sources of imagery, there are also internal, emotional sources of imagery. This is a point we return to later on when we discuss the effects of imagery on memory.

Research Related to Dual-Coding Theory

One of Paivio's earliest studies (Paivio, 1965) was concerned with the role of imagery in learning. This study employed a paired-associate learning task. Four groups of participants each learned 16 pairs of words.

Each group learned a different kind of stimulus-response pair. One group learned pairs in which both words were concrete (e.g., *coffee/pencil*); for the second group, the first member of each pair was concrete and the second abstract (e.g., *string/idea*); for the third group, the first member was abstract and the second concrete (e.g., *virtue/chair*); whereas for the fourth group, both words were abstract (e.g., *event/theory*). The first learning trial occurred when participants heard the list of words, after which they were given the first (stimulus) word of each pair and asked to write down the second word. After four such trials, examination of the total number of correct responses revealed clear differences between the groups. These data are presented graphically in Figure 6.2.

Notice that learning is best when both words are concrete and worst when both words are abstract. Notice also that the biggest difference between recall for concrete

Figure 6.2 The Relation between Concreteness and Learning.

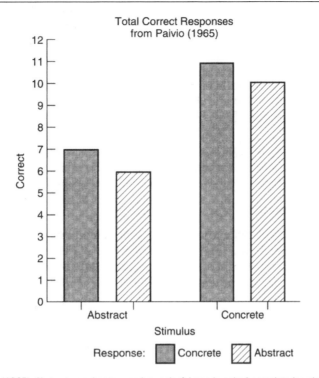

Data from Paivio, A. (1965). Abstractness, imagery and meaningfulness in paired-associate learning. *Journal of Verbal Learning and Verbal Behavior, 4*, 32–38.

and abstract items is between concrete and abstract stimuli. If the stimulus is concrete, then it leads to much better recall of the response than if the stimulus is abstract. Paivio also had participants rate the image-ability of each word, and found that the concrete words were higher in imagery than the abstract ones. This sort of result has been replicated many times (Marschark, Richman, Yuille, & Hunt, 1987; Paivio, 1983; Paivio, Khan, & Begg, 2000; Paivio, Walsh, & Bons, 1994).

Within dual-coding theory (Paivio, 1969, 1971), results such as those shown in Figure 6.2 are accounted for as follows. A concrete word can be coded by either the verbal or non-verbal system, whereas an abstract word will tend to be coded only by the verbal system because it will tend not to elicit much of an image. It will generally be relatively easy to recall a concrete word because it is available in both codes in memory. By contrast, abstract words will only be coded verbally. Concrete words have an advantage because of the presence of both codes.

Stimulus concreteness is particularly important because of the way that pairs of words may be learned. Suppose you are given the stimulus-response pair *coffee/pencil* to learn. You might imagine a coffee cup with a pencil in it. Thus, both words may give rise to a single image, and this imaginal code may be stored in memory. When the stimulus word *coffee* is later presented by itself, 'its image arousing value would be particularly important, for the stimulus member must serve as a cue that reinstitutes the compound image from which the response component can be retrieved' (Paivio, 1969, p. 244). Abstract words would be less effective cues because they are not imaginally coded.

Paivio's dual-coding theory has been applied to various phenomena. For example, in addition to the findings on the relation between memory and imagery that we have already reviewed, dual-coding theory has been extended to the investigation of figurative language, such as metaphor (Katz, Paivio, Marschark, & Clark, 1988). Finally, the theory has also been used as a framework for understanding literacy (Sadoski & Paivio, 2001; Whitehead, 2003).

Dual-Coding Theory and the Brain

We noted in Chapter 2 that, for many researchers, split-brain research seemed to imply that the left hemisphere managed 'analytic' (e.g., verbal, rational) tasks and the right hemisphere 'holistic' (e.g., non-verbal, intuitive) tasks. Consistent with this viewpoint, Paivio (1991) argued that the verbal and non-verbal systems are each:

> dependent on different parts of the brain. The **left hemisphere** of most people controls speech and is more efficient than the **right hemisphere** at processing verbal material in such tasks as perceptual recognition, episodic memory, and comprehension. The right hemisphere has the advantage in such nonverbal tasks as face identification and discrimination, recognition of nonverbal sounds, and memory for faces and spatial patterns. The generalization holds for different sensory modalities, justifying the conclusions that the distinction is a verbal/nonverbal symbolic one that cuts across sensory modalities. (p. 272)

The hypothesis that imagery is predominantly a right hemisphere activity and verbal representation a left hemisphere activity has been challenged by fMRI work done by Fiebach and Friederici (2003). A clear implication of dual-coding theory is that concrete words will elicit greater activity in the right hemisphere than will abstract words. After a review of the relevant neuroimaging research, Fiebach and Friederici (2003, p. 66) concluded that the cumulative evidence 'does not fully support the assumption of a specific right-hemispheric involvement during the processing of concrete relative to abstract words.'

Fiebach and Friederici (2003) conducted an fMRI study of their own in which participants were shown concrete words (e.g., *bike, church, basket*), abstract words (e.g., *norm, feature, status*), and pseudo words, which are words in which one or two letters have been randomly replaced. The participants were given a **lexical decision task** in which they had to indicate by a manual response whether each stimulus was a word or not. This task allows the experimenter to compare the functional brain images that are elicited by abstract and concrete words even though the participant makes the same response to both abstract and concrete words (i.e., both are words). This means that participants did not intentionally process abstract and concrete words differently, and thus any differences in brain activation were solely due to the different properties of abstract and concrete words. The results showed that abstract and concrete words elicited different patterns of activity in the left hemisphere, but that concrete words did not elicit heightened activity in the right hemisphere. Fiebach and Friederici (2003, p. 68) concluded that the hypothesis that concrete words yield greater left hemisphere activation than abstract words was not supported. Commenting on these results, Scott (2004) suggested that linking imagery strongly with the right hemisphere is one example among many of 'simplistic right brain/left brain attributions of cognitive functions, which in reality are supported by rather more complex bilateral systems' (p. 152).

Imagery and Mnemonics

Yates's *The Art of Memory* (1966) is a history of **mnemonic techniques**. A mnemonic technique is a procedure used to aid memory. Yates showed that imagery has been used as a mnemonic technique since ancient times. Yates described a second-century document called the *Ad Herennium*, which gave instructions that would enable a student to remember accurately a great many items in order to be able, for example, to recite a long speech from memory. The technique to be learned, usually called the **method of loci**, basically had two parts: places (loci) and images. The person learned the loci first, which were usually places in a building, perhaps a deserted temple. Loci were chosen so as to be as dissimilar as possible, a fair distance apart, and were learned and overlearned until the student could go in either direction from any particular locus. Once the student had learned the loci, he or she had an accurate cognitive map of a building. Having built his cognitive map, the student now invented images to stand for the material he or she wanted to remember. One image was formed for each thing to be remembered. Each image was placed in a particular locus, and the images were to be as distinctive as possible, even **bizarre**. For example, if you wanted to remember someone whose name was *Gorden* then you might form an image of a garden and then 'choose a prominent feature of the person's face and link the image of the name to it. Thus if Gorden has a large nose, an image could be formed of a garden growing over his nose' (P.E. Morris, Jones, & Hampson, 1978, p. 335). Such an image could then be placed in a locus. Memory then consisted of mentally strolling through the loci, collecting the images stored there. Yates reported that great feats of memory were accomplished using this technique, including being able to recite 2,000 names in the order in which they were given, after hearing the list only once.

Yates's account of ancient mnemonic techniques stimulated quite a bit of contemporary research. Are these old procedures really effective? There is some reason to believe that they are. Not only are similar procedures promoted by professional teachers of mnemonic techniques (e.g., Lorayne & Lucas, 1976), but psychologists have shown that aspects of them really do aid memory. An important account of the psychological principles behind mnemonics was given by Bower (1970a, 1970b). He pointed out that a central part of this mnemonic technique was the process of relating images to particular locations. The example Bower used was of a homeowner going shopping. The homeowner can form images of various locations around the house, such as the living room, the bedroom, and so on. In order to remember items on the shopping list, the homeowner needs to form vivid images of the items, such as milk and bread, and then relate those images to specific locations. Thus, imagining someone milking a cow in the living room would do for milk, and imagining a loaf of bread tucked in bed would do for the bread. While shopping, the homeowner knows what items to buy by imagining each place and recalling the images located there.

Items interrelated to form units are more easily remembered than are items not so unified (Asch, 1969). The effectiveness of imagery may be partly due to its ability to organize disparate items into meaningful units. However, a mental image does not only organize information; it may also make that information distinctive (Begg, 1982). We have already observed, in our discussion of levels of processing in the chapter on memory traces and memory schemas, that **distinctiveness** is an important aid to memory. The relation between imagery and distinctiveness has been the subject of some interesting research, to which we now turn.

Imagery and Distinctiveness

Yates (1966) noted that the author of the *Ad Herennium* recommended images that are 'active, [with] exceptional beauty or singular ugliness', 'ornamented "with crowns or purple cloaks"', disfigured by 'introducing one stained with blood or soiled with mud or smeared with red paint' (p. 10). The possibility that memory is facilitated by such bizarre images has been extensively investigated. Initially, experiments did not demonstrate an effect of bizarreness (e.g., Nappe & Wollen, 1973). However, subsequent research showed that bizarreness can have an effect under certain circumstances (e.g., D. Anderson & Buyer, 1994; O'Brien & Wolford, 1982; Richman, 1994).

The specific conditions under which bizarreness has an effect have been explored in some detail (e.g., Einstein & McDaniel, 1987; Einstein, McDaniel, & Lackey, 1989; McDaniel, DeLosh, & Merritt, 2000; McDaniel, Einstein, DeLosh, May, & Brady, 1995). One of the more reliable findings has been that people remember bizarre items better when they occur along with common items. Thus, if participants are given a list of sentences to learn, some of which are bizarre (e.g., *the maid licked ammonia off the table*) and the others common (e.g., *the maid spilled ammonia on the table*), then the bizarre items are remembered better. However, if participants are given a list consisting solely of bizarre items, then recall is generally no better than that for a list composed entirely of common items.

The finding that bizarre items are memorable when they occur together with common items is reminiscent of a long-standing phenomenon called the **von Restorff effect** (von Restorff, 1933; Hunt, 1995), which holds that if one item in a set is different from the others then it will be more likely to be recalled. It is important to realize that 'being different' is a relative and not an absolute property (Hunt & Lamb, 2001). In a list of bizarre and common items, the bizarre items are distinctive in relation to the common items. This distinctiveness makes them memorable in a way that they are not in a list composed entirely of bizarre items. In a list composed entirely of bizarre items, none of them are distinctive.

Humour and Distinctiveness

Schmidt (2002; Schmidt & Williams, 2001) has observed that an effect similar to that of bizarreness is found with humorous items. In his experiments, humorous items consisted of cartoons created by a well-known cartoonist. A set of literal items was created by eliminating incongruous information in the cartoons, rendering them humourless. A final set of weird cartoons consisted of adding irrelevant elements to the original cartoons. In one study, participants were shown a set of cartoons and then unexpectedly asked to provide a brief description of each cartoon. Participants provided more accurate descriptions of humorous cartoons than literal or weird cartoons when they had been shown a mixed list containing all three cartoon types. However, if participants are given a list consisting solely of humorous items, then their cartoon descriptions were generally no better than those for a list composed entirely of literal or weird items. This outcome parallels the one described above for bizarre items, with humorous items being more memorable only when contrasted with non-humorous items. However, humorous items are apparently more memorable than weird items, raising the possibility that the effect of bizarreness may be due at least in part to the fact that bizarre items often strike people as funny. Humour by itself may be a strong aid to memory, especially in situations in which humorous material is contrasted with neutral material (Schmidt, 2002, p. 135).

The Downside of Distinctiveness

E. Winograd and Soloway (1986) noted that people often believe that they can remember things better if they make the to-be-remembered material distinctive. One of the ways in which people act on this belief is by storing things in special places. If they have something valuable to store, and they want to make sure that they remember where it is squirrelled away, then they often will carefully put it in a peculiar location. The problem with this strategy is that when you go to recover the item you stored in a special place, you cannot remember where you put it. Winograd and Soloway (1986) pointed out that, at first, the special-places strategy looks suspiciously like the method of loci that Yates (1966) described. However, there are important differences between the two.

Winograd and Soloway (1986) began with the observation that a special place to store an item is an unlikely place in which to find it. That is sometimes why special places are used. People wish to make sure that no one else, especially not a burglar, will find the item. Winograd and Soloway (1986, p. 371) commented that this is presumably why so many people store valuables, such as cash, in unlikely places, such as the freezer.

In one of Winograd and Soloway's experiments, participants were given sentences describing the locations of objects, such as 'The milk is in the refrigerator' or 'The tickets are in the freezer.' Some participants rated these sentences for likelihood: how likely it was that somebody would store the object in that location. Some other participants also rated these sentences for memorability: how memorable it would be to store the item in that location. A final set of participants were told to imagine putting each item in the location described, and then rate each location for memorability. All groups were administered a recall test in which the experimenter gave the participant the name of the item and asked the participant to recall its location. Thus, the participant would be asked questions like 'Where is the milk?' and 'Where are the tickets?'

Winograd and Soloway compared recall for items of different levels of likelihood and memorability. It turned out that items rated low in likelihood were remembered less well than items rated high in likelihood, regardless of the level of rated memorability. To put this result a slightly different way, no matter how memorable we think that a location will be, we will in fact remember it less well if it is an unlikely location than we will if it is a likely location. So the next time you decide to store your spare credit card in the medicine cabinet, perhaps you should think again.

Winograd and Soloway agreed with Begg's (1982) suggestion that distinctiveness is an effective memory aid for remembering individual items, but is not as useful for remembering the association between items. Consider why this difference is so important when you store an item in an unlikely place. When you want to retrieve the item, you know what the item is and you want to remember where you stored it. You need to come up with the association between the object and the location. The stored object is not an effective retrieval cue for remembering the location, and the distinctiveness of the location is irrelevant to the process of remembering.

Notice how the process of trying to remember an object stored in a special place is different from the method of loci. When you use the method of loci, you first learn a set of places, and then store objects in them by forming an imaginary relationship between the two. When you try to remember something, you first recall the locus and then the object stored there. The process of recall goes from place to object. By contrast, there is usually no imaginary relationship created when you store objects in special places, and the process of recall goes from object to location, rather than from location to object.

Brown, Bracken, Zoccoli, and Douglas (2004, p. 650) have observed that the **special places strategy** is similar to a strategy that people often use when creating passwords. People try to create passwords that they can easily remember, but that others will be unable to discover. As we have just seen, it is very difficult to satisfy these two requirements simultaneously. Brown et al. (2004, p. 650) suggest using easily remembered (and therefore easily discovered) passwords in most situations not requiring security, and only creating distinctive passwords when necessary. You should test yourself on a new password for a few times over the next several days. Finally, you should keep a written record of your passwords in a secure, but not special, location.

Putting things in special places or creating unique passwords involves relying on distinctiveness alone to be a sufficient aid to recall. Winograd and Soloway (1986) suggested that this is an example of a mistaken belief that we have about the way memory works. **Metamemory** is the name for our beliefs about how memory works. When we squirrel things away in unusual locations, we are exhibiting a failure of metamemory. It is obviously very important to have accurate beliefs about how memory operates, and we will discuss this topic further in Chapter 14.

■ Synaesthesia and Eidetic Imagery

One of the most intriguing psychological states is **synaesthesia**, which refers to the power of the stimulus appropriate to one sense (e.g., a sound) to arouse an experience appropriate to another sense (e.g., a colour). Here is a report of an extreme synaesthetic experience from a participant under the influence of mescaline (Werner, 1948/1961). 'I think that I hear noises and see faces, and yet everything is one and the same. I cannot tell whether I am seeing or hearing. I feel, I taste, and smell the sound. It's all one. I, myself, am the tone' (p. 92). People who routinely have such experiences in everyday life are called *synaesthetes*, and the most common experience that they report is **chromaesthesia**, or *coloured hearing* (Harrison, 2001, p. 182). This is the experience of colour in response to an auditory stimulus. For example, a synaesthete may experience a colour when hearing someone's name. The cue that elicits a synaesthetic experience is called an **inducer**, and the synaesthetic response itself is called the **concurrent** (Grossenbacher & Lovelace, 2001)

As many as one in 200 people may be synaesthetes (Ramachandran, 2004, p. 19). Synaesthesia appears to run in families and occurs more often in women than in men (Bailey & Johnson, 1997). Perhaps the most famous synaesthete was the novelist Vladimir Nabokov, who routinely experienced coloured hearing, as did his wife and his mother (Harrison, 2001, p. 131).

Cytowic (2002) described several cases of synaesthetes who believed that synaesthesia improved their memory. Smilek, Dixon, Cudahy, and Merikle (2002) provided evidence that this may indeed be the case. They reported on a synaesthete, called C, who is possessed of an extraordinary memory. For example, when asked to remember four lists of nine digits each, she could recall them all, and after an interval of two months could recall all but two of the digits. In C's case, each digit is the inducer of a particular colour. For C, each digit always induces the same colour. Thus, the number 2 printed in black always induces the colour *red*, which is projected onto the number. Smilek et al. (2002) compared C's digit memory with that of a control group of non-synaesthetes. Each participant was asked to memorize three displays of 50 numbers each. The first display had numbers printed in black. The second display had numbers printed in colours that were different from C's concurrents. For example, 2 induces *red* in C, but was printed in *purple*. This is called the *incongruent display*. The third display was composed of numbers printed in C's concurrents (e.g., 2 was printed in *red*). This is called the *congruent display*. C outperformed all other participants in the first, black-digit display. However, the incongruent display caused C's performance to plummet from 66 per cent correct in the first display to only 4 per cent correct in the second. By contrast, the performance of other participants was similar on both displays. C found the incongruent display discombobulating, saying that she 'had never had this happen' to her before, and that she had 'all these numbers swirling around' in her head. It seems reasonable to think that the colour of each digit in the incongruent display interfered with the colour she projected onto each digit. This interpretation is particularly likely since the congruent display did not adversely affect her performance. Although C typically remembered digits extremely well, her memory for other kinds of material was similar to that of control participants. Thus, it seems reasonable to conclude that synaesthesia is an aid to memory in C's case, and perhaps in other synaesthetes as well.

Theories of Synaesthesia

A traditional explanation of synaesthesia is that it reveals the underlying unity of the senses (e.g., Werner, 1948/1961, p. 93). The idea is that our five senses evolved out of one primordial sense, and that synaesthetic phenomena reflect this common origin. A more recent version of this theory was advanced by Maurer (1997), who suggested that 'the newborn's senses are not well differentiated but are instead intermingled in a synaesthetic confusion' (p. 227). This lack of differentiation could be due to inborn connections between different areas of the infant's brain, such as between 'the visual and auditory areas of the immature cortex' (Kennedy, Batardiere, Dehay, & Barone, 1997, p. 253). These are called *transient connections*, because, over time, they are pruned, much as surplus branches may be pruned from a tree. This pruning allows the senses to become differentiated from each other. This pruning process is called **apoptosis**, a form of programmed cell death. Perhaps adult synaesthesia occurs when this pruning process fails to run its course, and what were supposed to be transient connections end up being permanent. It has been suggested that, in the case of synaesthetes, 'the "pruning" gene is defective', resulting 'in cross-activation between areas of the brain' (Ramachandran, 2004, p. 68).

Failure to weed out inter-sensory connections cannot be the whole story, however. It turns out that synaesthetic responses can be elicited by concepts as well as percepts. Thinking about the number 7 is different from seeing the number 7 printed on a page. If simply thinking of a number can induce the same synaesthetic response as perceiving the number, then cross-activation between sensory areas cannot be all there is to synaesthesia. Dixon, Smilek, Cudahy, & Merikle (2000), in another study of C, had her perform the following task. After being shown two numbers (e.g., 5 + 2), she was shown a colour and asked to name it. It turned out that if the colour shown was incongruent with the sum of the two numbers then C took longer to name the colour than if the colour shown was congruent with that sum. For example, suppose C was shown 5 + 2. For C, 7 is the inducer for *yellow*. Thus, C could then name the colour *yellow* faster than she could name the colour *red*. However, 2 is the inducer for *red*. Thus, when shown 1+1, then C could name the colour *red* faster than she could name the colour *yellow*. Incongruent colours interfered with C's ability to name the concurrent induced by the sum of the two numbers. Notice that this sum was not shown to C, but was calculated by her. Consequently, this experiment is evidence that synaesthesia can be elicited by a concept, such as the sum of two numbers, and does not have to be elicited by an external sensory stimulus. This suggests that synaesthesia need not simply be the result of connections between sensory systems, but can also be the outcome of a conceptual process.

Ward and Simner (2003) have further explored linguistic and conceptual factors in synaesthesia. They reported on a man, named JIW, who is a lifelong synaesthete. In his case, the sounds of specific words induce particular tastes. For example, the word *Chicago* induces an *avocado* taste. Notice that *Chicago* sounds a bit like *avocado*, and some of the inducer words have this relationship to the taste concurrents. Thus, *Virginia* induces *vinegar* and *Barbara* induces *rhubarb*. Some other word-taste links involve the meaning of the word. For example, *bar* induces *milk chocolate*. In general, the tastes that JIW experiences can be traced back to foods he had as a child. More recently acquired tastes, such as *coffee*, are not often induced. The links between foods and their tastes are obviously acquired, not inborn. These links may properly be said to belong to semantic memory. These results 'suggest a strong role for language and conceptual factors in the development of this type of synaesthesia' (Ward & Simner, 2003, p. 254). In at least some cases, the experiences of synaesthetes may be 'entirely mediated by neural connections that exist in normal adult human brains' (Grossenbacher & Lovelace, 2001, p. 40).

Strong and Weak Synaesthesia

Martino and Marks (2001) have distinguished between *strong* and *weak* forms of synaesthesia. Strong forms of synaesthesia are the 'classic' instances, involving an inducer in one sensory modality (e.g., a sound) and a concurrent image in another sensory modality (e.g., a colour). Martino and Marks give the example of Carol, who experiences colour (e.g., orange) in response to pain (e.g., as a result of a leg injury). The people we have discussed in the preceding section are **strong synaesthetes**.

Even people who are not strong synaesthetes may still show similar **cross-modal effects**. L.E. Marks (1982) observed that most people will judge *sneezes* to be brighter than *coughs*, and *sunlight* to be louder than *moonlight*. These, and other similar phenomena, demonstrate that visual and auditory sensations share certain qualities for most people. For example, brightness and loudness seem to go together. Most of us are **weak synaesthetes** in that we can appreciate these cross-modal associations, without having strong synaesthetic experiences. Martino and Marks (2001) suggested that these synaesthetic associations 'develop over childhood from experience with percepts and language' (p. 64).

Synaesthesia can influence the way in which we label our experiences. McManus (1983) showed that some colour words are used more frequently than other colour words in such diverse contexts as English and Chinese poetry, modern English novels, and popular literature. The colour words used most frequently are those that emerged earliest in the language (such as *black*). A word such as *black* has great synaesthetic power; it can be used to describe a wide variety of experiences, while labels such as *pink* have emerged later in the history of the language and have a more restricted range of synaesthetic meanings.

The fact that one sense can represent information from another sense facilitates the use of figurative language, such as metaphor. Consider this line from Keats's 'Isabella': 'Taste the music of that pale vision.' By uniting three senses (taste, audition, and vision), the line becomes especially memorable (Pollio, Barlow, Fine, & Pollio, 1977, p. 60; Ullmann, 1957). We will discuss some additional properties of colour words in Chapter 8 on language.

Eidetic Imagery

At this point you should recall our earlier discussion of the icon in Chapter 2. The icon is a snapshot of the information contained in a visual stimulus. This information persists briefly, even though the stimulus itself is no longer present. The icon's occurrence seems to depend on the eye's being stationary, a situation that seldom happens naturally (Haber, 1983). However, it is useful to compare the icon with a related phenomenon, **eidetic imagery**. Like iconic imagery, eidetic images persist even after a stimulus, such as a picture, is removed. Unlike the icon, which decays rapidly, eidetic images may persist for a minute or more. Eidetic imagery is similar to synaesthesia, in that both are examples of **cognitive dedifferentiation** (Glicksohn, Steinbach, & Elimalac-Malmilyan, 1999). By this is meant that processes that typically function independently are fused instead. 'For example, synaesthesia entails the dedifferentiation of sense modalities, while eidetic imagery entails the dedifferentiation of imagery and perception' (Cytowic, 2002, p. 109). An eidetic image is a fusion of imagery and perception, such that the image is experienced as a percept.

Here are some of the features of eidetic images, as given by Haber (1979).

- The eidetic experience is not the same as having a vivid mental image: the image is located 'out there' and not inside the person's head.
- The image can be scanned and its parts described.
- Descriptions of an eidetic image are quicker and more assured than are reports from memory.
- Eidetic imagery is much more common in children than in adults.

Here is an excerpt from an 11-year-old child's description of her eidetic image of a picture she had been shown for 30 seconds (Haber, 1979). The picture depicted a feast, and contained many people, objects, and actions.

> Experimenter: Tell me what you see.
>
> Participant: Up above it looks like stairs coming down and then there's a bench and a boy, then a girl and a couple of boys sitting on it, and then there's a very long table it looks like more plates without anything on them than food. There's a lady serving behind the table and then by the doorway it looks like children just gushing in and there's a clock by that—up in the left hand corner there's a china cabinet and a big hefty woman is putting dishes in there. (p. 587)

This is only approximately one-quarter of the child's complete description of her image. In spite of the detail, it appears that eidetic image descriptions are generally no more accurate than are ordinary memories collected from non-eidetic viewers of the same scene. Thus, eidetic images are not *photographic* images, since they are not literal copies of the scene.

Jaynes (1979) made the intriguing suggestion that paleolithic cave paintings, such as those in France and Spain, are 'tracings of eidetic images' (p. 606). Cro-Magnon artists may have had eidetic images of emotionally significant objects, such as animals, and then drawn these images on cave walls. Jaynes bases this hypothesis on facts such as: each cave picture appears to have been done all at once, and is not the result of repeated attempts at representation; and multiple drawings are superimposed, as if an image had been projected onto the cave surface, covering up what had been there before. Jaynes believes that describing an eidetic image may cause it to fade, and that Cro-Magnon eidetic images may have lasted longer than contemporary, laboratory-generated images because they were images of events that were significant to the viewer and did not have to be put in words.

An excellent test for persons who claim to have a photographic memory for pages in a text is to ask them to recall a page from the last word to the first. If they are actually 'looking' at an image of the page, then they should be able to read it backwards as well as forwards. Typically, however, it is impossible to do this; recall is much better in the forward direction (Neisser, 1967). However, Strohmeyer (1970/1982) reported the case of a woman, Elizabeth, an accomplished artist, who was, in fact, able to form an image of a printed page and then write out the lines from the last to the first. Elizabeth's eidetic imagery abilities were truly astounding. For example, you are probably familiar with stereograms—two pictures of a scene, one for each eye, that combine to form a three-dimensional representation of the scene. Elizabeth would look at one picture with one eye and form an eidetic image of it. She then would look at the second picture with the other eye and project an eidetic image of the first picture onto the second. The result was an image in depth. If you have an old stereoscope around the house, you might like to try this, although eidetic imagery abilities like Elizabeth's are quite rare.

Vividness of Visual Imagery

Eidetic imagery seems to be an extraordinary form of imagery (Neisser, 1979), but it may only be an extreme form of an ability that is present in everyone (Paivio, 1986, p. 119). In the case of ordinary visual memory images, there are important individual differences in their occurrence (Harshman & Paivio, 1987). One of the ways in which people vary is in terms of their **vividness of visual imagery**, and one way of measuring this is the Vividness of Visual Imagery Questionnaire or vviq (D.F. Marks, 1972, 1999). Vividness is defined in terms of 'clarity and liveliness' as well as similarity to an actual percept (D.F. Marks, 1999, p. 570). A clear and lively image is one in which its various aspects (e.g., colour and form) are bright and well-defined. The current version of the vviq (D.F. Marks, 1999, p. 583) asks participants to imagine a series of people and scenes such as 'a relative or friend'. Participants then rate the vividness of parts of the resulting image (e.g., the colours of a friend's clothes) on a scale ranging from 'perfectly clear and as vivid as normal vision' to 'No image at all.' On the basis of these ratings, participants receive a vviq score.

The vviq has been used in a large number of studies, and McKelvie (1995) reviewed over 250 of them. One of the obvious questions is whether people who score high on the vviq can learn and remember items better than low scorers. The answer is that vividness of visual imagery does not appear to be a good predictor of superior performance on memory tasks. Baddeley and Andrade (2000) noted that the relation between vivid imagery and memory is complex. Participants examined pictures taken from a book of British and European birds after having judged their prior knowledge of birds as either 'poor', 'moderate', or 'good'. Participants were also given the names of each bird as it was presented. Then they were given the names again in the same order as they were originally presented. Participants were asked to form an image of each bird as they heard its name and to rate the vividness of their image on a scale ranging from 0 (no image at all) to 10 (image as clear and vivid as normal vision). Those who rated their prior knowledge of birds as either 'moderate' or 'good' had higher vividness ratings than those who rated their prior knowledge as 'poor'. Baddeley and Andrade speculate that vividness of visual imagery is proportional to how familiar you are with a topic. However, vividness is not an index of the accuracy of memory, only of its richness. One can have very vivid imagery associated with events that are untrue (Gonsalves, Reber, Gitelman, Parrish, & Paller, 2004).

■ Mental Rotation

Thus far we have considered mental images in their role as mental pictures. Such a view of images is quite limited because it presents images as relatively static pictures in an individual's mind that are at least a bit like pictures on a wall. However, unlike pictures of objects on a wall, one can imagine objects that move.

One of the canonical demonstrations of the dynamic nature of mental images was by Shepard and Metzler (1971). In their experiment, participants were presented with 1,600 pairs of line drawings like those in Figure 6.3. Half the pairs were drawings of the same object (as in Figures 6.3a and 6.3b), and half were drawings of different objects (as in Figure 6.3c). The pairs of drawings of the same object varied in the angular rotation that would be required in order to bring the two objects into alignment. The angular rotation required varied from 0° to 180° through 20° intervals. Some of the correct pairs required an angular rotation in the picture plane (as in Figure 6.3a), whereas others required an angular rotation in depth (Figure 6.3b).

For each pair, the participant had to make a decision about whether or not the drawings depicted the same object or a different object. If the decision was that they were the same, then the participant pulled a lever with his or her right hand, whereas if the decision was that they were different, then the participant pulled a lever with his or her left hand. Shepard and Metzler (1971) also measured the amount of time it took to make each decision.

The most interesting data concerned the relationship between angular rotation and reaction time for correct responses to drawings of the same object. This relationship is shown in Figure 6.4. For both picture-plane and depth pairs, the relationship between the two variables is almost perfect. The greater the angular rotation required, the longer it takes the participant to make a decision. Shepard and Metzler (1971) concluded that participants determine whether or not the drawings depict the same object by means of a process called **mental rotation**. Perhaps participants imagine the rotation of one of the pairs to determine if it matches the other member of the pair. The greater the angular rotation required, the longer it would take to imagine the rotation of one of the pairs until it comes into alignment with the other. On the basis of Shepard and Metzler's (1971) data, it appears that the speed of mental rotation in this task was 60° per second.

There have been several subsequent demonstrations of the accuracy with which people can imagine the rotation of objects (Shepard, 1978; Shepard & Cooper, 1982). Shepard (e.g., 1984) has compared the process of imagining an object to the process of perceiving an object, and has noted that the two processes seem to be quite similar. 'What we imagine, as much as what we perceive, are external objects; although in imagining, these objects may be absent or even nonexistent' (Shepard, 1984, p. 420). As we shall see, considerable research has examined the apparent similarity between the processes of imagining and perceiving.

Is Mental Rotation a Right Hemisphere Process?

When we considered Paivio's theory, we concluded that imagery was not confined to the right hemisphere. However, mental rotation is a more dynamic process than the static images of the sort elicited by concrete words. Mental rotation is a non-linguistic process, and, for that reason, may show a tendency to be localized in the right hemisphere. However, the existing evidence is not decisive (Corballis, 1997). In an event-related potentials (ERP) study, Milivojevic, Johnson, Hamm, and Corballis (2003) further

Figure 6.3 Which Pairs Are Drawing the Same Object?

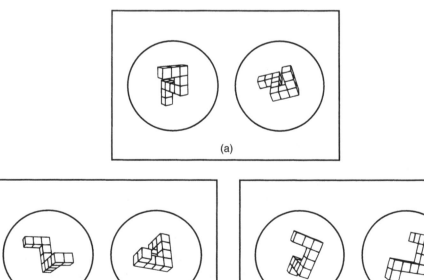

(a)

(b)

(c)

From Shepard, R.N., & Metzler, J. (1971). Mental rotation of three-dimensional objects. *Science, 171*, pp. 701–703. Copyright 1971 by the American Association for the Advancement of Science. Reprinted by permission.

Figure 6.4 Time Taken to Mentally Rotate an Object as a Function of Angular Rotation.

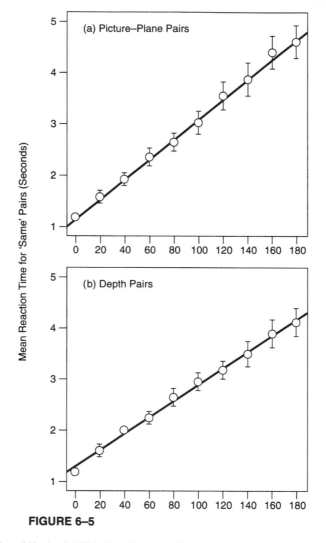

FIGURE 6–5

From Shepard, R.N., and Metzler, J. (1971). Mental rotation of three-dimensional objects. *Science, 171*, pp. 701–703. Copyright 1971 by the American Association for the Advancement of Science. Reprinted by permission.

investigated the lateralization of mental rotation. They had participants perform two different tasks. One was a simple letter rotation task, in which letters were presented in normal or mirror reversed orientation at varying degrees of tilt. For example, participants might see the letter R like this:

The participants' task was to say whether or not the letter was normal or mirror reversed. What would you conclude about the letter above? How did you do it? The second task involved more complex folding tasks like this.

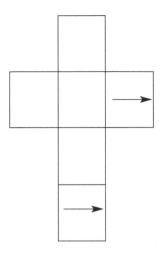

The participant was to say whether or not the arrowheads would be aligned if the squares were folded to make a box. Again, what would you conclude? How did you do it? The first task required one mental transformation, while the second required a series of transformations. The second task took longer than the first, reflecting its greater difficulty. The ERP analysis showed that the mental rotation task tended to be carried out in the right hemisphere. However, the mental folding task was not lateralized, and both hemispheres were equally involved. Milivojevic et al. (2003, p. 1359) concluded that 'the right hemisphere may be preferentially engaged when the task is simple' but 'the left hemisphere is also engaged as the task becomes more complex.'

Scanning Mental Images

In a series of experiments Kosslyn and his co-workers explored the imagery/perception relationship (e.g., Kosslyn, 1980, 1983; Denis & Kosslyn, 1999). In one such study (Kosslyn, Ball, & Reiser, 1978), participants were asked to memorize a map of an island that contained seven different locations, such as a tree, a beach, a hut, and so on. Some of the distances between the various locations were longer than others. For example, the distance from the hut to the beach was longer than the distance from the hut to the tree. The time it would take you to scan from one location to another on the real map would depend on the real distance. The greater the real distance, the longer it would take you. For example, it would take you longer to scan from the hut to the beach than from the hut to the tree.

What about the participant's memory image of the map? Does it take longer to scan between parts of the memory image that are far apart than between the parts that are close together? To answer this question, Kosslyn and his colleagues asked participants to imagine one of the locations on their memory image of the map. Then they were to imagine 'a little black speck zipping in the shortest straight line' (Kosslyn et al., 1978, p. 52) from that location to another location. Sometimes they were asked to scan to locations that were not on the map. For example, they might imagine the hut and then be asked to scan from the hut to the beach (which is on the map) or from the hut to a location that is not on the map. If they could find the location, they pressed one button, and if they could not find it they pressed another button. The results showed that, for places actually on the map, the farther apart were the two objects, the longer it took to scan between them. This was interpreted by Kosslyn and his co-workers to mean that **objective distances** are preserved in our mental images of perceived scenes.

Rinck and Denis (2004) have shown that objective distance is not the only feature that determines how long it takes to scan from one part of a mental image to another. Another important variable is **categorical distance**, which refers to 'the number of units that are traversed during mental scanning, for instance, landmarks on an island map, rooms in a building, or counties in a state' (Rinck & Denis, 2004, p. 1212). To investigate the relative influences of objective and categorical distances, participants were given a map of a museum floor to memorize. The floor was divided into different rooms of different sizes, and each room contained paintings by different well-known artists (e.g., van Gogh, Leonardo da Vinci). (At this point, in order to visualize the task, imagine the floor plan of your own dwelling, and imagine paintings by different artists in each room. Now imagine walking across a room from one painting to another. This would be an objective distance. Now imagine walking from a painting in one room to another painting in another room. This would involve not only an objective distance but also a categorical distance. This is the sort of task given to participants in this experiment.) Both the objective distance travelled as well as the categorical distance determined the amount of time taken to travel mentally between one painting and another. This result suggests that images may be structured hierarchically, with objective distances being nested within categorical differences. We will return to this possibility in our discussion of cognitive maps, below.

Images as Anticipations

Podgorny and Shepard (1978) did an experiment using grids like those in Figure 6.5. The participant's task was to imagine a letter superimposed on a grid, such as the letter F in Figure 6.5a. Try it yourself. Imagine the F superimposed on the grid in Figure 6.5b. If you were a participant in this experiment, then a dot probe would appear in one of the squares in the grid, as in Figure 6.5c. Your task would be to decide, as quickly as possible, whether or not the dot was in a square covered by your imaginary

Figure 6.5 Grid Used in the Podgorny and Shepard Experiment.

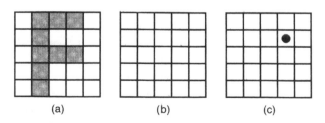

(a)   (b)   (c)

From Shepard, R.N. (1978). The mental image. *American Psychologist, 33*, pp. 125–137. Copyright 1978 by the American Psychological Association. Reprinted by permission.

F. It turns out that this is a task that people can do both rapidly and accurately. In fact, performance on this particular task with imaginary letters is strikingly like performance when letters are actually present in the grid.

Farah (1989) used a similar task to demonstrate the role of **images as anticipations**. Participants imagined a letter superimposed on a grid, as in the Podgorny and Shepard experiment. However, the probe stimulus, an asterisk (*), was presented only for a very brief interval, and the participants had to detect its occurrence. The asterisk could fall in a square covered by a participant's image, or in a square not covered by the participant's image. Probes were more often detected in the former case than in the latter case.

Farah also reported evidence suggesting that imagery lowers the participant's criterion for detecting a stimulus. It is not so much that participants are more sensitive to stimuli falling within the imaged region as it is that they are better prepared to pick up stimuli falling within the area of a projected image. Farah characterized this process in terms used by Ryle (1949) and Neisser (1976). Neisser (1976, p. 130) defined an image as a readiness to perceive something.

To understand what is meant by a readiness to perceive something, remember the perceptual cycle we discussed in Chapter 2. At any point in time, we anticipate picking up certain kinds of information, and not others. When we anticipate something, the perceptual cycle is ready to pick up the information, but it is not there yet. These anticipations are mental images (Neisser, 1978a). For example, if I imagine what is inside my desk drawer, I am anticipating what I would see if I opened the drawer. We pick up information that we anticipate more readily than information that is unanticipated. In Farah's experiment, when participants project an image onto the grid, they are anticipating seeing something in the squares covered by the image. Participants are prepared to pick up a target that occurs in those squares.

Farah did another experiment that elaborates on the anticipatory nature of images. Participants were shown a pattern of shaded squares that could be seen as either an H or a T, as in Figure 6.6. They were told to attend to one letter or the other. Try this yourself. You can see the configuration in Figure 6.6 as an H by attending only to those squares in the grid that make up an H, or you can see the configuration as a T by attending only to those squares that make up T. Attending to one pattern or the other facilitates the pick up of probes in that area, just as projecting an image does. That projecting an image onto an area gives similar results as attending to that area suggests that imagery is an active process that prepares you for perceiving information, and not just a passive representation of information.

Brockmole, Wang, and Irwin (2002) conducted a detailed investigation of the conditions under which images and percepts may be combined. They presented participants with a 4 x 4 grid in which several squares were filled with a dot. That grid disappeared and was replaced by another grid with dots in several other squares. One square only was not filled with a dot on either occasion, and the participant's task was to identify that square. Performance on this task was best when the interval between the first and second grid was about 1,300 milliseconds. It is likely that participants require about that long to form an image of the first grid. The percept of the second

Figure 6.6 Grids used in Farah's Experiment.

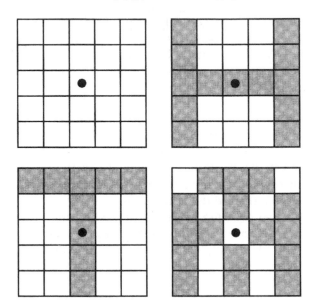

From Farah, M. (1989). Mechanisms of imagery-perception interaction. *Journal of Experimental Psychology: Human Perception and Performance, 15*, pp. 203–211. Copyright 1989 by the American Psychological Association. Reprinted by permission.

grid can then be integrated with the image of the first grid to yield a representation that combines both grids and allows the participant to identify the empty square. This integration of images and percepts shows that perception and imagery must share many of the same mechanisms (Kosslyn, Ganis, & Thompson, 2001). Box 6.1 explores how we construct real pictures out of what we see and imagine.

Images and Ambiguous Figures

Farah's H or T figure is an example of an ambiguous figure. Some very interesting properties of images can be explored further through the use of drawings like these, other examples of which are in Figure 6.9. They are ambiguous figures in that they may be seen as representing either one thing or another (Shepard, 1978, p. 129). The drawing on the left can be seen as either a duck or a rabbit, and the drawing on the right may be seen as a chef or a dog. An interesting question is whether ambiguous figures can be imagined as ambiguous. If imagining something is a bit like perceiving it, then it might be possible to shift from seeing one thing in an imaginary ambiguous figure to seeing something else. That is, perhaps I could imagine Figure 6.9a as a duck, and then imagine it as a rabbit, and then back again to imagining it as a duck, and so on.

In a clever study, Chambers and Reisberg (1985) investigated this possibility. Participants were introduced to ambiguous figures by being shown examples of them, and the experimenter made sure that each participant could see them reverse from one view to another. Then participants were shown a slide of the duck/rabbit in Figure 6.9a

Box 6.1 Mental Images and Real Pictures

As we said at the beginning of this chapter, when people imagine a scene, the experience is a bit like looking at a picture. That is partly why it is so tempting to define images as mental pictures. Pinker and Finke (1980) compared the properties of images with the properties of actual pictures. Although images seem to be accurate representations of a scene as it appears from a particular viewpoint, the pictures people actually make of scenes do not always have this property. Look at the drawing at the left in Figure 6.7. There is no way that such a scene could actually be seen. The picture appears to us to be a distorted representation of an actual scene, because there is more in the picture than you could possibly see from one vantage point. The drawing at the right in Figure 6.7 more accurately represents what would actually be seen from a single vantage point. Nevertheless, many people make drawings that are more like the left drawing than the right one in Figure 6.7. How can we explain the apparent discrepancy between the accurate images we have and the inaccurate drawings so many of us make?

Figure 6.7 Viewpoint.

Left: Drawing done without a single viewpoint. Right: Drawing of the top scene from a single viewpoint. From Arnheim, R. (1974). *Art and visual perception: A psychology of the creative eye.* Berkeley: University of California Press, Figures 86 and 87. Copyright 1974 by the Regents of the University of California. Reprinted by permission.

There are at least three possible explanations for this discrepancy, according to Pinker and Finke. One is that even if you can accurately imagine how something will look, you may not be able to draw your image. It is not always easy to translate what is in your image into a sequence of arm movements that would put the right lines on the page. Another possibility is that you do not try to draw your image, but try instead to make a drawing of the object as you know it really is. This is a critical

(continued)

drawing error, as art historians have frequently observed (e.g., Edgerton, 1975). When you draw something the way you think it should be, then the result is a distorted representation of something that does not look at all like what you actually see. This point is illustrated in Figure 6.8. What the artist represents on the *picture plane* is a *projection* of the surface of an object. The result is that objects depicted in a picture appear to lie behind the picture plane. The picture plane is like a window through which you are looking at objects in the distance. The eye can only be at one place when the picture is constructed. That position is called the *station point* (Sedgwick, 1980, p. 40). The station point gives the spectator a *point of view*. Notice that a circle will appear as an ellipse on the picture plane when viewed from a particular station point. Changing the station point changes what will be represented in the picture, just as moving in relation to a window changes what you see through it. 'As we approach a window we see more of the scene; as we move to the left, a portion of the scene on the left side becomes hidden by the window frame while more is revealed on the right, etc.' (Sedgwick, 1980, p. 41). An artist using classical rules of perspective eliminates the third source of error mentioned by Pinker and Finke, which is attempting to draw parts of the scene from different vantage points, so that there is no consistent point of view.

Figure 6.8 The Picture Plane.

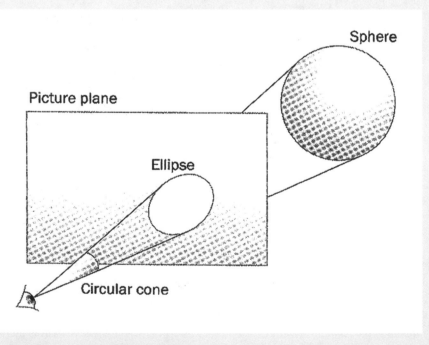

From Gregory, R.L. (Ed.). (2004). *The Oxford companion to the mind* (2nd ed.). Oxford: Oxford University Press, p. 722.

Figure 6.9 The Duck/Rabbit and Chef/Dog Stimuli.

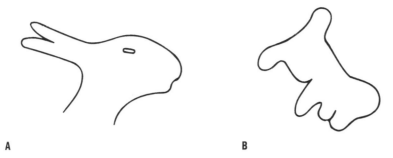

A   B

From Chambers, D., and Reisberg, D. (1985). Can mental images be ambiguous? *Journal of Experimental Psychology: Human Perception and Performance, 11,* pp. 317–328. Copyright 1985 by the American Psychological Association. Reprinted by permission.

and asked to form a 'mental picture of the slide so that they would be able to draw it later' (Chambers & Reisberg, 1985, p. 320). They were then shown the chef/dog picture in Figure 6.9b and told that they could see two different things in the picture by looking at different parts of the figure. (Try this yourself. If you look at the lower right you tend to see a dog, but if you look at the upper left you tend to see a chef.) Participants were asked to try to reverse their mental image of the duck/rabbit slide in the same way. None of the participants could do so. However, they all could draw the duck/rabbit figure from memory.

Chambers and Reisberg (1985) argued that these and similar results from other studies suggest that mental images are not ambiguous. Rather, a mental image appears to be only one thing. If Chambers and Reisberg are right, then this would be one of the ways in which images are not like perceptions. However, Finke, Pinker, and Farah (1989) have questioned the generality of Chambers and Reisberg's results. They used a procedure whereby participants constructed images in stages. Here is an example of this process. First, participants would imagine the first figure (e.g., 'Imagine a capital letter H.'). Then they were asked to imagine a capital letter X on top of the H. Follow these instructions yourself, and then inspect your image and see if there are familiar forms that you can see in your image. Participants often reported geometric shapes and letters such as M and N. This result is important because it means that more can be found in a mental image than whatever went into its construction (Shepard, 1978a). In the process of constructing an image, new properties may emerge. These are often referred to as **emergent properties** (e.g., Finke, 1996; Pinker & Finke, 1980).

Other researchers (e.g., Brandimonte & Gerbino, 1993; Hyman & Neisser, 1991; Peterson, Kihlstrom, Rose, & Glisky, 1992) have also found that images often can be reinterpreted. An insightful study by Mast and Kosslyn (2002; Lyddy, 2002) shows how mental rotation can lead to a new interpretation of an image. They constructed the configuration shown in Figure 6.10 that can be seen as a young woman when upright and an older woman when rotated 180 degrees. Participants were first shown

Figure 6.10 A Reversible Figure.

Young Woman

Old Woman

From Mast, F.W., and Kosslyn, S.M. (2002). Visual mental images can be ambiguous: Insights from individual differences in spatial transformation abilities. *Cognition, 86,* pp. 57-70. Copyright 2002. Reprinted by permission of Elsevier.

the figure in one of the two orientations and memorized it so it could be drawn from memory. Participants were not told that the figure was reversible. They then imagined the figure rotated to different angles. Several participants discovered the alternate figure when their image had been rotated 180 degrees. The conclusion is that 'at least some people can detect a previously unrecognized interpretation' of a mental image (Mast & Kosslyn, 2002, p. 69).

It has often been argued that imagery is an **analog form of representation** (e.g., Shepard, 1978, p. 135). An analog embodies the essential relationships of the thing it represents. Spence (1973) gave the following example of an analog device. A carpenter who is building a picket fence wants to keep the distance between the pickets equal. The best procedure for accomplishing this is to cut a stick as long as the desired distance between the pickets. Then, put up the first picket and use the stick to place the next picket. By following this procedure, you can make sure the distances between pickets are constant. The stick is an analog of the distance. Similarly, mental images may be analogs of situations in the external world, and useful not only for capturing essential relationships about things in the external world, but also for discovering new relationships.

■ Egocentric Perspective Transformations

As Franklin and Tversky (1991) observed, reading a story produces a lot of mental imagery. To make their point, they quote the following passage from Ernest Hemingway's 1927 story, 'The Snows of Kilimanjaro':

> Out of the window of the hospital you could see a field with tumble weed coming out of the snow, and a bare clay butte . . . . From the other window, if the bed was turned, you could see the town, with a little smoke above it, and the Dawson mountains looking like real mountains with the winter snow on them.

Did you experience any mental imagery while reading that passage? Did you imagine yourself located in the narrative? Could you locate the objects described relative to yourself?

Consider the relation of this kind of mental imagery to the Shepard and Metzler mental rotation task we considered earlier in this chapter. In that task, the participant sees something and then performs imaginary operations on it. When people read stories, they typically construct an imaginary representation of the environment the text describes. In such a representation, some things are in front of you, some behind, some above, some below, some to the right, some to the left. Does it matter where things are located? For example, could you imagine something behind you as quickly as something ahead of you? Such tasks require **egocentric perspective transformations**, in which your point of view changes. Rather than your being an object rotated in space, as in the Shepard and Metzler task, you must imagine yourself moving, while the objects in the environment remain still (Zacks, Mires, Tversky, & Hazeltine, 2000).

In one of their experiments, Franklin and Tversky (1991) had participants read different narratives. Here is a fragment of one of the stories.

> You are . . . at the opera. . . . you are standing next to the railing of a . . . balcony, overlooking the first floor. Directly behind you, at your eye level is . . . a lamp . . . mounted on a nearby wall beyond the balcony, you see a large bronze plaque . . . sitting on a shelf directly to your right is a beautiful bouquet of flowers . . . (p. 65)

The story goes on quite a bit further, but you get the idea. If you had been a participant in this experiment, you would have then answered questions about the locations of the objects described. For example, was the lamp ahead of you, behind you, above you, below you, to your right, or to your left? Then you would have been asked to imagine yourself turned to face a different direction (e.g., 90 degrees to your left), and to answer the same questions.

All participants reported that they relied on mental imagery to recall the scene. Moreover, some questions are easier to answer than others. You can locate something quickly if it is above or below you. It also takes less time to locate something ahead of you than it does to locate something behind you, perhaps because you have to imagine yourself turning around. However, locating something that is to the right or left of you is a relatively slow process. These results may be due to the fact that normally we imagine ourselves as being upright in a **spatial framework** that has one vertical (*above-below*) and two horizontal dimensions (*ahead-behind* and *left-right*) (Tversky, 2003). With respect to our bodies, *above-below* and *ahead-behind* are asymmetrical: Our head is different from our feet, and our front is different from our back! However, our bodies are bilaterally symmetric: the left half of our body is the mirror image of the right half. Thus, the two asymmetric dimensions are easily distinguished, but the symmetric dimension (*right-left*) is not. This symmetry may explain why we sometimes have so much difficulty remembering our right from our left (Bryant, Tversky, & Franklin, 1992; Franklin & Tversky, 1990, p. 74).

■ Controversy Concerning the Nature of Mental Imagery

Although an enormous amount of research has been done on imagery, some have felt that this work has overestimated the importance of mental imagery. Beginning with Pylyshyn (1973) there have been persistent criticisms of imagery research (e.g., Anderson, 1978). At the centre of this long-standing controversy is the issue of how knowledge is represented. In the last chapter, we reviewed models of memory, such as J.R. Anderson's (1983), which hold that knowledge about the world is stored in memory in the form of propositions. Suppose we accept that argument just to see where it leads. If our **knowledge is propositional**, then what role do images have in cognition?

One possibility is that images are *epiphenomenal*. You should recall from our discussion of the mind/brain issue in Chapter 2 that an epiphenomenon is a by-product, or symptom, of something else. An example of an epiphenomenon is the smoke that comes from a steam locomotive. The smoke is a by-product of the locomotive's operation, and itself serves no function. Similarly imagery may serve no function. Images might be merely decorative, like pictures on the wall of your room, and not essential aspects of the mind's functioning.

Pylyshyn (2002, 2003a, 2003b) argued that it is a mistake to believe that images are 'two-dimensional moving pictures' on 'the surface of your visual cortex' (Pylyshyn, 2003a, p. 114), which we scan in order to extract information. Rather, you imagine something by 'considering what it would look like if you saw it' (p. 114). Being able to imagine how objects look from other viewpoints is dependent on a process of inference and is susceptible to error. A similar argument was made by Rock, Wheeler, and Tudor (1989). They presented evidence that mental rotation is only accurate in highly practised tasks. When the task requires the rotation of unfamiliar objects, such as twisted wire shapes, then inaccuracy is the norm. This may be because people find it harder to make the correct inferences concerning what an unfamiliar object will look like when it is rotated. Deciding how things will look from different perspectives requires thinking, and can be difficult in unfamiliar situations.

Naturally enough, those who are particularly intrigued by imagery find such criticisms unwarranted. They point out that imagery is interesting in its own right, regardless of its function (e.g., Kosslyn, 1980, p. 21; Kosslyn, Ganis, & Thompson, 2003; Kosslyn, Thomas, & Ganis, 2002, p. 201). Indeed, there is evidence that scores on the Vividness of Visual Imagery Scale relate to the degree to which people regard vividness of visual imagery as being worth investigating (Reisberg, Pearson, & Kosslyn, 2003). The more vivid ones imagery, the more interested in imagery one is likely to be. The debate over the nature and function of imagery is sure to continue.

■ Cognitive Maps and Mental Models

Basic Properties of Cognitive Maps

It was Tolman (1948) who put **cognitive maps** on the map, so to speak. Tolman believed that information from the environment was 'worked over and elaborated . . . into a tentative, cognitive-like map of the environment. And it is this tentative map, indicating routes and paths and environmental relationships' (p. 193), that determines our behaviour. Tolman thought that broad and comprehensive cognitive maps were more useful than narrow, strip maps. Narrow, overspecialized cognitive maps only contain information about one or a few routes through the environment. They may facilitate adaptation to specific environments, but do not transfer very well to new circumstances. For Tolman, a cognitive map was more useful if it gave its user a big picture of the environment and could be employed in a variety of situations.

The partial nature of our cognitive maps means that we are capable of making several interesting errors. For example, which of the following statements are true?

- Madrid (Spain) is farther north than Washington (District of Columbia).
- Seattle (USA) is farther north than Montreal (Canada).
- The Pacific entrance of the Panama Canal is east of the Atlantic entrance.

In fact, *all* of these statements are true (Stevens & Coupe, 1978, p. 423). The reason why they may seem to be false can be seen by comparing the statements above with the following.

- Spain is farther north than the District of Columbia.
- The USA is farther north than Canada.
- The Pacific Ocean is east of the Atlantic Ocean.

All of the preceding statements are untrue. Thus, large geographic units (such as countries, states, counties, etc.) can, in general, have one relationship to one another, while some of their members (e.g., cities) can bear the opposite relationship to one another. Because people have simplified cognitive maps, they tend to assume that *all* members of a large geographic unit have the same relationship to *all* members of other large geographic units. Some people will totally reject the statement about the Atlantic and Pacific entrances of the Panama Canal until they have verified it for themselves on a map. Our cognitive maps are partly convenient fictions, designed to represent reality in a way that strikes us as useful but that may not be very accurate.

To illustrate this last point, draw your cognitive map of your campus. Then get some classmates to do the same. Pay attention to the various *landmarks* (e.g., important buildings), *paths* (e.g., roads), and *boundaries* (e.g., streams) that people use in their drawings (Lynch, 1960). You may be surprised at how different these maps are. Try to explain how these differences have arisen. For example, does it matter how long someone has been at your campus?

Cognitive Maps and the Hippocampus

Cognitive maps have been linked with hippocampal activity at least since the classic work of O'Keefe and Nadel (1978; Nadel & Hardt, 2004). Among the most direct sources of evidence for hippocampal involvement comes from studies relating the relative size of the hippocampus to the amount of knowledge required to successfully navigate in a complex environment. A particularly dramatic example of this relationship is the knowledge London taxi drivers have. Before being licensed, they are required to learn the routes that connect thousands of places in London, a procedure that takes two years on average. London taxi drivers have a highly complex, detailed cognitive map of the city. Maguire, Gadian, Johnsrude, Good, Ashburner, Frackowiak, and Frith (2000) compared MRI brain scans of licensed London taxi drivers with those of non-taxi drivers. The posterior part of the hippocampus of taxi drivers was enlarged relative to the control participants. Moreover, this increase varied with years of experience as a taxi driver. Thus, it is not that people who have an enlarged hippocampus are able to become taxi drivers, but the other way around. In order to store the immense cognitive map necessary for the task, the posterior part of the hippocampus of taxi drivers becomes enlarged.

Egocentric Frames of Reference

When people find their way through the environment there are at least two ways in which they can proceed. One way is to use a cognitive map of the environment in the same way as one would use a real map. When one navigates using a real map one locates one's position on the map, then figures out how to go on from there. This appears to be what London taxi drivers do. A second possibility is to use an **egocentric frame of reference** (McNamara, Rump, & Werner, 2003). Using an egocentric frame of reference involves taking the sort of egocentric perspective that was discussed above. People imagine themselves at the centre of the action, and use information available from their current perspective to orient themselves.

Some aspects of egocentric frames of reference can be illustrated by means of the following example. Draw the following situation, which is taken from Hutchins (1983,

p. 209): 'Go at dawn to a high place and point directly to the centre of the rising sun. That defines a line. Return to that same high place at noon and point again to the centre of the sun. That defines a second line.' If you are anything like me, your drawing looks like Figure 6.11. Notice that this drawing defines the position of the sun relative to your position on the earth. The drawing appears to suggest that you stay still while the sun moves overhead. Of course, we both know better. However, it is natural to represent the situation that way. It corresponds to the situation from our egocentric perspective and allows us to think about it easily.

Wang and Spelke (2000, 2002) suggest that people often use egocentric frames of reference when they navigate. This process does not require an enduring cognitive map that is consulted as you travel. Rather, it involves the creation of a temporary representation that is continuously updated. Other animals and insects appear to also use egocentric forms of navigation. One example of such a process is **path integration**, a process whereby one's position in relation to an important location (e.g., home) is continuously updated as one moves through the environment. For example, 'desert ants forage by traveling on new and apparently random routes and then return home on a direct path once food is found' (Wang & Spelke, 2002, p. 376). Similarly, people can, in principle, explore a novel environment (e.g., a city you are visiting as a tourist) while keeping track of where they are in relation to some important landmark (e.g., your hotel).

Cognitive Maps as Mental Models

The term **mental model** refers to representations of situations that enable us to understand and reason about them (Gentner, 2002, p. 9683). People have mental models for a very wide range of situations, and use them to describe, explain, and predict events (Rouse & Morris, 1986). For example, people often have mental models of the way in which machines, such as vacuum cleaners, work. DiSessa (1983) asked participants to 'think of a vacuum cleaner whose nozzle you hold in your hand. If you put your hand over the nozzle, will the pitch of the sound you hear from the motor go up or down?' (p. 23). Ordinary people come up with different answers

Figure 6.11 Is this the Relation between the Sun and an Observer at Dawn and at Noon?

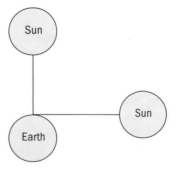

to this question. Some people think that the pitch will go down, and the speed of the motor will be reduced. This is because their mental model of the way a vacuum cleaner works suggests to them that placing a hand over the nozzle will interfere with the working of the motor and make it harder for the motor to run. Other people correctly say that the motor speed and the pitch will go up. The explanation they give is that, because the motor is being interfered with, it must put out more effort to overcome the resistance.

Notice that the vacuum cleaner models are quite anthropomorphic. They attribute human characteristics to the machine. The machine is represented as responding to interference by working harder, for example. Mental models are often like this. They are 'unscientific' and even 'superstitious' (D.A. Norman, 1983, p. 8). However, they may still be useful for representing the world. One of their functions is that they permit the user of a mental model to make analogies between different domains (Gentner, 1983). Here is an example of one person's mental model of how electricity works:

> Question: When you plug in a lamp and it lights up, how does it happen?

> Answer: . . . basically there is a pool of electricity that plug-in buys for you . . . the electricity goes into the cord for the appliance, for the lamp and flows up to— flows—I think of it as flowing because of the negative to positive images I have, and also because . . . a cord is a narrow contained entity like a river. (Gentner & Gentner, 1983, p. 99)

The virtue of such mental models is that they provide the person with a way of representing and making inferences about the behaviour of things in a wide range of contexts. Of course, a person's mental models do not always lead him or her to make the correct inference about what will happen in a particular situation. The mental model in Figure 6.11 is based on an erroneous assumption, for example. Mental models can be a source of error as well as insight. We will explore mental models further in the chapter on reasoning.

■ Questions for Study and Discussion

1. Review Paivio's dual-coding theory, paying attention to relevant experimental and neuropsychological evidence.

2. When it comes to memory, is distinctiveness always a good thing? Have you ever used the special places strategy? Did you ever find what you hid there?

3. Are images like pictures? Discuss their similarities and differences.

4. What do synaesthesia and eidetic imagery have in common? How is each process related to ordinary imagery?

5. Discuss the similarities and differences between mental rotation, mental scanning, and egocentric perspectives.

6. Compare and contrast cognitive maps and egocentric frames of reference.

■ Key Concepts

Analog form of representation The hypothesis that a mental image embodies the essential relationships of the thing it represents.

Apoptosis Programmed pruning of neurons.

Bizarre imagery The hypothesis that bizarre images facilitate recall.

Categorical distance The number of units traversed during mental scanning, for instance, landmarks on an island map, rooms in a building, or counties in a state.

Chromaesthesia Coloured hearing.

Cognitive dedifferentiation Processes that typically function independently are fused instead.

Cognitive map (Tolman) Information from the environment is 'worked over and elaborated . . . into a tentative, cognitive-like map . . . indicating routes and paths and environmental relationships.'

Concreteness The degree to which a word refers to 'concrete objects, persons, places, or things that can be heard, felt, smelled, or tasted'.

Cross-modal effects The ability to appreciate that the sensations of one modality can be similar to those in another modality.

Distinctiveness The hypothesis that the more distinctive the item, the easier it is to recall.

Dual-coding theory (Paivio) The theory that verbal and non-verbal systems are alternative ways of representing events.

Egocentric frame of reference People use information available from their current perspective to orient themselves.

Egocentric perspective transformations You imagine yourself moving, while the objects in the environment remain still.

Eidetic imagery Images projected onto the external world that persist for a minute or more even after a stimulus, such as a picture, is removed.

Emergent properties New properties that emerge when a mental image is constructed.

Imagens (Paivio) The units containing information that generates mental images that make up the non-verbal system.

Images as anticipations The hypothesis that an image is a readiness to perceive something.

Inducers and concurrents The cue that elicits a synaesthetic experience is called an *inducer*, and the synaesthetic response itself is called the *concurrent*.

Left and right hemispheres The theory that 'the *left hemisphere* of most people controls speech and is more efficient than the *right hemisphere* at processing verbal material in such tasks as perceptual recognition, episodic memory, and comprehension. The right hemisphere has the advantage in such non-verbal tasks as face identification and discrimination, recognition of non-verbal sounds, and memory for faces and spatial patterns.'

Lexical decision task Participants must indicate whether each stimulus is a word or not.

Logogens (Paivio) The units containing the information underlying our use of a word that comprise the verbal system.

Mental models Representations of situations that enable us to understand and reason about them.

Mental rotation (Shepard) The ability to imagine an object in motion and view it from different perspectives.

Metamemory The name for our beliefs about how memory works.

Method of loci A mnemonic technique based on places and images.

Mnemonic techniques Procedures used to aid memory.

Objective distances The true distances between objects in the real world are preserved in our mental images.

Path integration One's position in relation to an important location is continuously updated as one moves through the environment.

Propositional form of representation The hypothesis that knowledge about the world is stored in memory in the form of propositions.

Spatial framework An imaginary space with one vertical (*above-below*) and two horizontal dimensions (*ahead-behind* and *left-right*).

Special places strategy People try to put items in places that they can easily remember, but that others will be unable to discover.

Strong synaesthetes People who are susceptible to an inducer in one sensory modality (e.g., a sound) producing a concurrent image in another sensory modality (e.g., a colour).

Synaesthesia The power of the stimulus appropriate to one sense (e.g., a sound) to arouse an experience appropriate to another sense (e.g., a colour).

Vividness of visual imagery The degree to which images are clear, lively, and resemble an actual percept.

Von Restorff effect If one item in a set is different from the others then it will be more likely to be recalled.

Weak synaesthetes People who can appreciate cross-modal associations, without having strong synaesthetic experiences.

■ Links to Other Chapters

Distinctiveness
  Chapter 4 (levels of processing)
  Chapter 13 (autobiographical memory)
Vividness of visual imagery
  Chapter 7 (perceptual symbol systems)
Emergent properties (new properties that emerge when a mental image is constructed)

Chapter 2 (Sperry)
Chapter 10 (mental models)
Analog form of representation
  Chapter 10 (analogical transfer)
Mental model
  Chapter 10 (mental models and deductive reasoning)

■ Further Reading

The Paivio, Yuille, and Madigan word norms are among the most widely used in psycholinguistic research. An update of them has been published by J.M. Clark and A. Paivio in 'Extensions of the Paivio, Yuille, & Madigan (1968) norms' (2004). This update appeared in *Behavior Research Methods Instruments and Computers*, a special Web-based archive of norms, stimuli, and data, which can be accessed at www.psychonomic.org/brm.htm.

Mental scanning for the auditory imagery that we have for familiar songs was investigated by Halpern, A.R. (1988). Mental scanning in auditory imagery for songs. *Journal of Experimental Psychology: Learning, Memory, and Cognition, 14,* 434–443. As she pointed out, an auditory image has different locations just like a visual image. Imagined songs have a beginning, middle, and end just like songs you really hear. Try imagining the song *Happy Birthday to You*. When you imagine it, you find yourself starting at the beginning ('Happy birthday to you, Happy birthday to you . . .') before you get to the next line ('Happy birthday, dear . . .'), and then comes the last line ('Happy birthday to you'). Auditory imagery is extended in time just as visual imagery is extended in space. This point is developed further in Cupchik, G.C., Philips, K., & Hill, D.S. (2001). Shared processes in spatial rotation and musical permutation. *Brain and Cognition, 46,* 373–382.

Another fascinating history of mnemonic techniques is Carruthers, M. (1990). *The book of memory: A study of memory in medieval culture.* New York: Cambridge University Press.

The ways in which the development of literacy has changed our strategies for remembering is explored in Eskritt, M., Lee, K., & Donald, M. (2001). The influence of symbolic literacy on memory: Testing Plato's hypothesis. *Canadian Journal of Experimental Psychology, 55*, 39–41.

Under certain circumstances, our ability to recall things we have learned can actually improve as we attempt to recall them on successive occasions. This phenomenon is called *hypermnesia*: 'improvements in net recall levels associated with increasing retention intervals'. See Payne, D.G. (1987). Hypermnesia and reminiscence in recall: A historical and empirical review. *Psychological Bulletin, 101*, 5–27. M.H. Erdelyi was primarily responsible for rekindling interest in a phenomenon discovered many years ago (Ballard, 1913). Erdelyi argued that imagery leads to better recall initially and to hypermnesia subsequently. See, e.g., Erdelyi, M.H., & Becker, J. (1974). Hypermnesia for pictures: Incremental memory for pictures but not for words in multiple recall trials. *Cognitive Psychology, 6*, 159–171; Erdelyi, M.H., & Kleinbard, J. (1978). Has Ebbinghaus decayed with time? The growth of recall (hypermnesia) over days. *Journal of Experimental Psychology: Human Learning and Memory, 4*, 275–289. However, the role of imagery in hypermnesia has been called into question. See, e.g., Mulligan, N.W. (2002). The emergent generation effect and hypermnesia: Influences of semantic and nonsemantic generation tasks. *Journal of Experimental Psychology: Learning, Memory, and Cognition, 28*, 541–554.

Mental imagery as an aid to creativity is explored by Shepard, R.N. (1978). The externalization of mental images and the act of creation. In B.S. Randhawa & W.E. Coffman (Eds.), *Visual learning, thinking and communication* (pp. 133–187). New York: Academic Press; Shepard, R.N. (1990). *Mind sights*. New York: Freeman.

A fascinating study of the ways in which blind people represent space is in Kennedy, J.M. (1993). *Drawing & the blind: Pictures to touch*. New Haven: Yale University Press.

Chapter 7

Concepts

■ The Classical Approach

What Are Concepts?

An important milestone in the study of cognition was the publication of Bruner, Goodnow, and Austin's *A study of thinking* in 1956. That book described a series of experiments concerned with the way in which people acquire concepts. All people make use of concepts. They seldom see events as entirely unique. Rather, they are likely to see an event as belonging to a particular category. Whenever people see something as belonging to a particular category, they are seeing that event as an instance of a particular concept. Thus, the object you are now reading is not unlike other objects with which you are familiar. It is an **instance** of the concept *book*. It has a number of attributes in common with other instances of the concept *book*. You classify something as a book if it has *attributes* like pages, print, a cover, and so on. Each attribute can take on a number of *values*. Thus, print can be large or small, the cover can be hardcover or softcover.

The work of Bruner et al. was concerned with the relations between attributes and concepts. Clearly, attributes could define a concept in several possible ways. Some concepts are simply conjunctions of attributes. Other concepts are more complex. A *disjunctive concept* is one in which one set of attributes or another set of attributes defines class membership. Thus, someone can be a Canadian citizen either by being born in Canada or by becoming a naturalized citizen. Another example used by Bruner et al. is that of a strike in baseball. Either the batter swings and misses or the umpire calls a strike. Yet another type of concept is **relational**. Here the relation between attributes determines the class into which an event will fall. For example, consider the concept of marriage, which is a relationship between two people (Holloway, 1978).

Bruner et al.'s *A study of thinking* stimulated a large number of experiments concerned with how people attain concepts using information about the attributes that define membership in a category. The original experiments done by Bruner et al. made use of the cards shown in Figure 7.1. Suppose each card is either an instance of a particular concept, or it is not. If it is an instance of a particular concept, then it is a *positive instance*. Thus, a simple *conjunctive concept* might be *black* and *square*. Any card with these two attributes would be a positive instance. This means that all cards in column 6 in Figure 7.1 are positive instances. If a card does not contain the right attributes, then it is a *negative instance*. Thus, the top, leftmost card is a negative instance. In this example, attributes such as the number of figures on a card are irrelevant.

To understand why something is a positive instance of a simple, conjunctive concept like the one in the preceding example, you need to know which attributes are criterial for membership in the concept and which ones are not. You might try to figure this out by noting which attributes recur in positive instances. If an attribute is present in all positive instances, then you might conclude that it is a **criterial attribute**—its presence is necessary for something to be a member of the concept. All attributes that do not recur in positive instances would be irrelevant.

The process of including recurring attributes and excluding non-recurring ones is the process of *abstraction*. According to *The Oxford English Dictionary*, abstraction originally meant 'to take away from'. When you abstract the recurrent attributes from a set of positive instances you take them away from all the others. The recurrent attributes form a set that defines the concept.

Sometimes the process of abstraction is likened to a *composite photograph* (e.g., Galton, 1883). Imagine that negatives of photographs of all members of your family for several generations were laid on top of one another. Then we could hold the pile of negatives up to the light. The recurrent attributes or features of the individual family members would be darker than non-recurrent features. These recurrent features would stand out more clearly than the non-recurrent ones. In this way we could abstract the recurrent

Figure 7.1 The Bruner Cards.

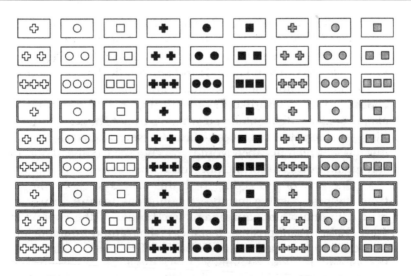

features. This abstract set of features does not belong to any one person. Rather, it defines the concept of what a member of your family looks like. (Incidentally, such composite photographs were actually quite popular in the nineteenth century. It was believed that the composite photograph evoked images of what the typical family member looked like.)

There are some problems with the notion that concepts are like composite photographs, and we consider them in detail later on. For now it is only important that you ask yourself the following questions. Would all members of your family share some attributes? Or would there be some family members who did not have any of the characteristics of the others? What does the idea of *family resemblance* really mean?

Concept Attainment Tasks

In their experiments, Bruner et al. made use of both **selection** and **reception tasks**. Let's look at how this works for a simple, conjunctive concept like one black square. To begin with, the experimenter would give you one of the cards in Figure 7.1 and tell you that it is a positive instance. Suppose it was a card with one black square and one border. Then you might be told to choose any card you like in order to try to find out what the concept is. The experimenter will then tell you whether or not the card you have chosen is a positive or a negative instance. This is a selection task, because you select the instances. Which instance would you choose? What reason would you give for the one you chose?

One way of proceeding with this task is to choose an instance that differs from the first positive instance by only one feature. Thus, you might choose a card with one white square, and one border. If the experimenter told you that your choice was a positive instance, what would you conclude? It must be that the attribute that has changed from the first positive instance is not included in the concept, because when it changes, the instance remains positive. By contrast, if the experimenter told you that your choice was a negative instance, what would you know? Because the card you have chosen differs in only one value of one attribute from the first positive instance, that attribute must be a criterial attribute and black must be in the concept. The colour of the figure is important because, when it changes, an instance changes from being positive to being negative.

Notice that the process we are describing is not a passive one in which the attributes in the concept are automatically abstracted after you have seen enough instances. Rather, you are actively formulating hypotheses and selecting instances to see if your hypotheses are correct. That is, you are using a strategy to try to discover what the concept is. The particular strategy we have been describing is called **conservative focusing** because, when you use it, you focus on only one attribute at a time and select instances that vary only in that attribute.

Bruner and his co-workers found other strategies that people used in this task. They included **focus gambling**, **simultaneous scanning**, and **successive scanning**. When people use focus gambling, they select instances that vary from the first positive instance in more than one attribute. You may get lucky and be able to eliminate a number of hypotheses quickly. Thus, if after being shown a card with one black square with one border, I choose two black squares with two borders and it turns out to be a positive instance, then I know that the number of squares and the number of borders are irrelevant. Simultaneous scanning involves keeping in mind all possible hypotheses and trying to eliminate as many as possible with each instance selection. This places a very great load on memory, because you must always keep in mind which hypotheses could be correct and which have been proven incorrect. Successive scanning is less demanding. The participant formulates a single hypothesis and tests it by selecting instances until the correct hypothesis emerges. Thus, if black square was your hypothesis, you would keep selecting cards consistent with that hypothesis until it was disconfirmed. Then you would formulate another hypothesis and carry on as before.

Reception Strategies

Another way of administering concept problems to people is for the order in which instances are presented to be under the experimenter's control, rather than the participant's. This is called a **reception task**. Under these conditions, many participants in the Bruner et al. study appeared to adopt one of two strategies, **wholist** or **partist**.

If you use a wholist strategy, then you have as your first hypothesis that all attributes in the first positive instance are in the concept. If the next instance confirms your hypothesis, then you retain that hypothesis. If, however, the next positive instance is inconsistent with your hypothesis, then you form a new hypothesis that is consistent with what both the old hypothesis and the current instance have in common.

If you use a partist strategy, then you initially select a part of the first positive instance as your initial hypothesis. Then you maintain that hypothesis until you receive some disconfirming evidence. At that point, you change your hypothesis to make it consistent with all instances you have previously seen. This strategy, in its ideal form, places a heavy load on memory, because you must recall all previous instances if you are to successfully revise your hypothesis.

The Bruner et al. study stimulated a great deal of research. Some of this work was concerned with the logical relations between different types of concepts (e.g., Hunt & Hovland, 1960; Neisser & Weene, 1962). Excellent reviews of this period of concept research exist (e.g., Bourne, 1966; Pikas, 1966). Gradually, however, psychologists began to have doubts about the legitimacy of this kind of research.

Criticisms of Classical Concept Research

Experiments like the ones Bruner et al. did are reminiscent of certain kinds of games. In fact, there is a real similarity between the Bruner task and the popular game Mastermind (Best, 2001; Laughlin, Lange, & Adamopoulos, 1982). In that game, one player creates a code that another player must guess by proposing possible solutions and receiving feedback on how accurate the proposed solution is. Similarly, in the Bruner task, the experimenter is the codemaker and the participant is the codebreaker. The participant tries to read the experimenter's mind and guess the code. The experimenter gives the participant feedback that the participant can use to tell how 'warm' or 'cold' his or her guesses are. If you have never played Mastermind, you can try it at the following website: http://nlvm.usu.edu/en/nav/frames_asid_179_g_3_t_1.html?open=instructions.

When the Bruner task is described like this, it begins to sound rather artificial. By the late 1960s and early 1970s many psychologists began to have serious doubts about this kind of laboratory study of concepts. Are not real-world concepts more complex than the sort of concepts being studied in a Bruner-type task? Recall our discussion of ecological validity in Chapter 2. If you want to study how people actually acquire and use concepts, perhaps there is a better method.

Notice that this sort of criticism can be responded to in at least two ways. One is to continue studying artificial concepts, because you can have more experimental control over their properties, but to try to make the concepts you study resemble real-world concepts in important ways. Another way is to give up studying artificial concepts and concentrate on studying concepts that people actually use.

■ Learning Complex Rules

Consider the diagram in Figure 7.2. It is an example of a *finite state grammar*. Such diagrams are also sometimes called *railroad diagrams*. The reason that they are called railroad diagrams becomes clear if you imagine that each number in the diagram is a railroad station and each arrow is a track that you can follow from one station to another. The tracks go one way, so you can only travel in the direction indicated by the arrow. All journeys begin at 1 and end at 4, 5, or 6. Each track is labelled by a particular letter, and some are even called by the same letter. Notice that some tracks are recursive: they go back to the place where they started. Can you write down all possible track combinations that get you from 1 to 6?

The finite state grammar in Figure 7.2 is really a set of rules for generating strings of letters. It is capable of generating all the strings of letters given in the bottom of Figure 7.2 (and several others as well). They are letter strings that are consistent with this particular grammar. A letter string like VXRT would be inconsistent with this particular grammar.

Suppose you were asked to distinguish between those strings of letters that are consistent with the grammar (positive instances) and those that are inconsistent with the grammar (negative instances). This concept task would require you to know the grammar in order to be able to make the proper distinctions. What would be the best way to go about learning such a grammar?

Reber and his associates (1967; Allen & Reber, 1980; Reber & Allen, 1978; Reber, Allen, & Regan, 1985; Reber & Lewis, 1977) investigated the way in which people acquire knowledge about artificial grammars. Reber's work explored the distinction between **implicit and explicit learning**. Implicit learning can be illustrated by the following procedure. Suppose participants are shown some letter strings like those in Figure 7.2 and told to memorize as many of them as possible. These participants are not told that the letter strings follow a set of rules. This group of participants constitutes the implicit learning condition. Suppose a second group of participants is told that the letter strings do follow a set of rules and that they should try to discover what the rules are. This group constitutes the explicit learning group. Which group do you think will best be able to tell grammatical from non-grammatical letter strings?

Participants can be tested in the following way. They can be shown a set containing both grammatical and ungrammatical strings of letters and asked to say which strings had the same structure as the first set of strings they had seen. It turns out that the implicit learning condition leads to a significant amount of rule learning. Sometimes implicit learning leads to better performance than does the explicit learning condition!

This result is surprising because it means that people who are not trying to learn the rule structure appear to learn it at least as well as people who are trying to learn it. Rather than actively forming and testing hypotheses, the people in the implicit learning group are abstracting the structure of the grammar without realizing it. Perhaps the implicit learning group is acquiring knowledge unconsciously and more efficiently than the explicit learning group.

According to Reber, people who learn implicitly have a vague sense of what is grammatical and what is not grammatical without being able to say explicitly what the grammatical structure really is. The higher the level of performance, the better the participants' ability to say what they have learned. However, their knowledge is largely tacit—they know something without being able to say exactly what it is they know.

Reber's work might tell us something about how people acquire other complex rule systems, such as those underlying natural (as opposed to artificial) languages. For

Figure 7.2 A Finite State Grammar.

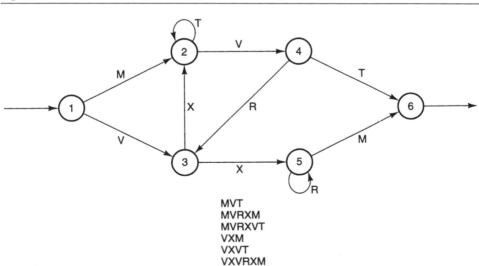

```
MVT
MVRXM
MVRXVT
VXM
VXVT
VXVRXM
```

From Reber, A.S., & Allen, R. (1978). Analogic and abstraction strategies in synthetic grammar learning: A functionalist interpretation. *Cognition, 6*, pp. 189–222. Copyright 1978 by Elsevier Science Publishers. Reprinted by permission.

example, when you first acquired your native tongue, your parents did not give you explicit instruction (e.g., grammar lessons) first, and then expect you to go on to become proficient in generating grammatical sentences. Rather, you were able to learn the structure of your language without knowing what that structure was, simply by listening to the utterances in your environment.

We know that preschool children learn a great deal about the structure of the language because they are able to make more or less grammatical utterances. Preschool children are like participants in Reber's implicit learning condition. Of course, children may innately come equipped with powerful knowledge structures that allow them to acquire complex grammars quickly, and we will consider this possibility in Chapter 8, on language. In any case, it would appear that knowledge of a language is largely tacit. According to Reber, Kassin, Lewis, and Cantor (1980), other forms of knowledge may work this way as well. Perhaps 'complex structures, such as those underlying language, socialization, perception, and sophisticated games are acquired implicitly and unconsciously' (p. 492).

Reber (1989, 1990; Reber, Walkenfeld, & Hernstadt, 1991) argued that his work shows that the **cognitive unconscious** plays an important role in cognition, and has suggested that 'implicit and unconscious cognitive processes appeared early in our evolutionary history; consciousness is a late arriver on the phylogenetic scene' (Reber, 1990, p. 342). An implication of Reber's analysis is that conscious mental processes will be associated with relatively recent forms of cognition. Reber, Walkenfeld, and Hernstadt (1991) argued that what we call 'academic intelligence' is an example of a form of cognition that has evolved relatively recently. Examples of such cognitive abilities are arithmetic and vocabulary scores as measured by standard IQ tests. These tests measure explicit, as opposed to implicit, cognitive abilities. Reber, Walkenfeld, and Hernstadt hypothesized that explicit cognitive abilities would predict performance on a task requiring explicit cognition, but not performance on a task requiring implicit cognition. To test their hypothesis, they gave participants a standard IQ test, as well as tests of implicit and explicit cognition. The implicit task was similar to the finite state grammar task we have already considered. The explicit task required participants to pick which letter was the best completion for a series of letters. An example of such a series is ABCBCDCDE–, where the participant is asked to choose between D and C as the next letter. (You can probably figure out that D is the right answer, but if you have trouble seeing this, ask a friend to help you.) As predicted, the correlation between scores on the IQ test and scores on the explicit task was much higher than the correlation between IQ scores and the implicit task. Moreover, there was only a small correlation between scores on the implicit and explicit tasks.

Reber (1997; Reber, Walkenfeld, & Hernstadt, 1991) concluded that the implicit cognitive system is very old in evolutionary terms and has not changed for a long time. 'Once an adaptive, functional system evolves, and . . . the system is broadly operational in diverse environments, there is no adaptive value in change' (Reber, Walkenfeld, & Hernstadt, 1991, p. 894). By contrast, explicit cognition is newer, and less fixed by evolutionary processes. Consequently, while people differ widely in terms of explicit cognitive abilities, they do not differ very much in terms of implicit cognitive processes. Implicit cognition is a process in which we all share and share alike.

Dulany, Carlson, and Dewey (1984) argued that Reber's interpretation of his results is not justified. In a replication of an implicit learning experiment, they found that participants who had learned a grammar implicitly were actually able to formulate hypotheses about the rules of the grammar. However, these hypotheses were not perfect. Rather, they were imperfect, somewhat personal ways of describing the grammar. The participants were generating novel, conscious rules that were correlated with the actual grammar. Their behaviour might be under the control of these informal but conscious rules and not determined by unconscious processes.

Dulany, Carlson, and Dewey's argument has been refined and extended by others (e.g., Cleeremans, Destrebecqz, & Boyer, 1998). In a series of studies, Shanks and his colleagues (e.g., Kinder, Shanks, Cock, & Timney, 2003; Shanks, 2004; Tunney & Shanks, 2003) have presented additional evidence that implicit learning is accompanied by awareness. In one study, Tunney and Shanks (2003) had participants learn an artificial grammar implicitly, following a procedure similar to the one used by Reber, as discussed above. However, participants not only had to judge a letter string as grammatical or ungrammatical, but also to indicate how confident they were that their judgement was correct. One way in which participants indicated their confidence was by means of a dichotomous rating scale. This dichotomous rating scale simply asked participants to indicate whether they were confident in their judgement or not. If participants are more confident in their correct than in their incorrect judgements, then they must be aware of the basis for their decision. To put it another way, if they are aware of the basis for their decision, then they are confident, but if they are unsure, then they are not confident. If confidence ratings are unrelated to the correctness of a judgement, then that would indicate that participants were unaware of what they had learned. It turned out that dichotomous confidence ratings were related to accuracy of judgement, suggesting that participants do indeed have some conscious awareness of the basis for their decisions.

Our discussion of implicit learning should remind you of our previous discussion of *implicit attention* in Chapter 3, as well as our previous discussion of *implicit memory* in Chapter 5. These three processes raise many of the same issues concerning the boundary between conscious and unconscious processes. As we have seen repeatedly, deciding whether or not a process is conscious or unconscious is an extremely difficult methodological problem that will be with us for some time yet.

■ Wittgenstein's Analysis of Concepts

Up to this point, we have considered concepts that have a definite rule structure. However, how realistic is it to believe that the concepts we use in everyday life are as well defined as those in the Bruner-type experiment? The philosopher Wittgenstein (1953) was interested in this type of question. The way he approached it has been very influential both in philosophy and psychology. Read the following quotation carefully. Wittgenstein is speaking to the question, 'What do all members of a category have in common?' For example, what do all vegetables have in common that makes them all vegetables? Or what do all pieces of furniture have in common that makes them all furniture?

> I am saying that these phenomena have no one thing in common which makes us use the same word for all—but that they are related to one another in many different ways. Consider for example the proceedings we call 'games.' I mean board-games, card-games, ball-games, Olympic games, and so on. What is common to them all? Don't say: 'There must be something common, or they would not be called "games"'—but look and see whether there is anything common to all.—For if you look at them you will not see something that is common to all, but similarities, relationships, and a whole series of them at that. To repeat: don't think, but look!—Look for example at board-games, with their multifarious relationships. Now pass to card games; here you find many correspondences with the first group, but many common features drop out, and others appear. When we pass next to ball-games, much that is common is retained, but much is lost.—Are they all 'amusing'? Compare chess with noughts and crosses [X's and O's]. Or is there always winning and losing, or competition between players? Think of patience. In ball games there is winning and losing; but when a child throws his ball at the wall and catches it again, this feature has disappeared. Look at the parts played by skill and luck; and at the difference between skill in chess and skill in tennis. Think now of games like ring-a-ring-a-roses; here is the element of amusement, but how many other characteristic features have disappeared! And we can go through the many, many other groups of games in the same way; can see how similarities crop up and disappear.
>
> And the result of this examination is: we see a complicated network of similarities overlapping and criss-crossing: sometimes overall similarities, sometimes similarities of detail.
>
> And I can think of no better expression to characterize these similarities than 'family resemblances'; for the various resemblances between members of a family: build, features, color of eyes, gait, temperament, etc. etc. overlap and criss-cross in the same way.—And I shall say: 'games form a family.' (Wittgenstein, 1953, pp. 31–32)

Wittgenstein also compared the members of a category to the individual fibres that make up a thread or a rope. No one fibre runs the entire length of the thread. Rather, the individual fibres overlap with one another: 'And the strength of the thread does not reside in the fact that some one fibre runs through its whole length, but in the overlapping of many fibres. . . . One might say that the concept of games is a concept with blurred edges' (pp. 32, 34).

Several ideas in this passage are worth noting. The most important is that the members of a category may not share common features. Rather, the attributes that category members have may constitute a complicated network of overlapping features. This is a part of what is meant by saying that the members of a category have a **family resemblance** to one another. Individual instances of a concept may shade into one another without any clearly definable boundary to the concept itself. Wittgenstein's example of the game concept illustrates this nicely. Perhaps some activities could not be games, but it is hard to say precisely where the concept of *game* begins and ends.

Wittgenstein's philosophical analysis is open to the criticism that it is based only on his intuitions and may not be true for everyone (Nichols, 2004). Psychologists wanted to extend Wittgenstein's insights by examining the way that ordinary people use concepts. More than anyone else, Eleanor Rosch was responsible for taking this next step.

■ Rosch and Prototypicality

In some of her earliest studies, Rosch (née Heider) (Heider, 1971a, 1971b; Heider & Olivier, 1972) was interested in the structure of colour categories. Colour is a fascinating topic, and we will consider it further in Chapter 8, on language. For now, it is only important to grasp the point that some colours are better examples of a colour category than others. For example, some colours to which English speakers apply the word *red* seem 'redder' than others. That is, some colours are more **prototypical** than others. Colours are not the only categories for which this is true. Some breeds of dog (such as retrievers) are more representative of the meaning of dog than others (such as Pekingese). Notice that, in this respect, natural concepts are unlike the artificial concepts with which we began this chapter. For the Bruner cards, all instances that are black and square are intended to be equally good examples of the concept 'black square'.

Rosch went on to develop a highly influential view of the nature of concepts. In doing so, she formulated two principles that she believed underlay how we use concepts (Rosch, 1978): **cognitive economy** and **perceived world structure**.

Cognitive economy refers to our constant attempts to balance two opposing tendencies. One tendency is to use our categories in such a way as to maximize the amount of information they give us. This could be accomplished by having as many categories as possible. The more categories you have the more distinctions you can make between events. The limit of this tendency would be to have as many categories as there are events in the world. However, if there is a one-to-one correspondence between your categories and events in the world, why have any categories at all?

One of the reasons for having categories is to reduce the amount of information with which we have to deal. Although we want to be able to discriminate between events in the world, we also want to be able to group them together. There is a general tendency for us to try to make our concepts as simple as possible (Feldman, 2003). We can accomplish this by ignoring differences between events and focusing on similarities. That way, many events that are different in some ways but similar in others can be treated as members of the same class. However, this tendency towards simplification has to be balanced against the necessity of differentiation. This tension between simplicity and complexity can create problems, as described in Box 7.1.

Box 7.1 The Downside of Categories

Suppose that at the beginning of the baseball season the Toronto Blue Jays are favoured to win the World Series. However, given that there will also be a number of strong American-based teams with an excellent chance to win, and since Toronto is the only Canadian city with a team in the league, it would also be true that a team from an American city is likely to win the World Series. This apparent contradiction comes about because there are two different levels of category in this example, and the prediction one should make depends on the level you choose. There is the subordinate level of individual teams, and the superordinate level of the countries to which these teams belong. If you are betting on which *team* will win, then Toronto is the best pick. However, if you are betting on which *country* will win, then you should bet that an American team will win. Lagnado and Shanks (2003, p. 158) call examples like this **misaligned hierarchies**, by which they mean that a 'judgment made with respect to one level of hierarchy' (e.g., Toronto will probably win) 'may suggest one conclusion' (e.g., bet on Toronto) 'whereas a . . . judgment made at a different level of hierarchy' (e.g., an American team will probably win) 'may suggest a contrasting conclusion' (e.g., bet on an American team).

Lagnado and Shanks asked participants to make inferences based on a hierarchy similar to that in Figure 7.3. The superordinate categories are types of newspaper, either tabloid or broadsheet (full-size). The subordinate categories are the newspapers themselves. Below each newspaper is the percentage of readers it has. Thus the *Globe* has the most readers (35 per cent) and the *Post* the fewest (5 per cent). The next line gives the party for which the readers of each newspaper tend to vote. Thus, both the *Sun* and the *Star* tend to have readers who vote Liberal. It is important to realize that all tabloid readers tend to vote Liberal. Notice that the hierarchy is misaligned, such that the most popular *kind* of newspaper is a tabloid, but the most popular newspaper is a broadsheet (the *Globe*).

Suppose we ask a participant to predict what newspaper a citizen chosen at random is likely to read. Lagnado and Shanks's results suggest that the participant will tend to choose the *Globe*, because it is the most widely read newspaper. If then asked which party the citizen is likely to vote for, the participant is likely to choose Conservative, because that is the party for which *Globe* readers tend to vote. However, the inferential pattern is likely to change if we first ask the participant to predict which *type* of newspaper a citizen chosen at random is likely to read. Participants will then tend to say 'tabloid', because that is the most frequently occurring type of newspaper. If then asked which party the citizen is likely to vote for, the participant is likely to choose Liberal, because that is the party for which tabloid readers vote.

If the participants' behaviour strikes you as logical, then think again. Remember that the participant is making predictions about a citizen chosen at random. Such a person *may* read the *Globe*, but whether or not that individual actually *does*

Figure 7.3 A Misaligned Hierarchy of Newspapers.

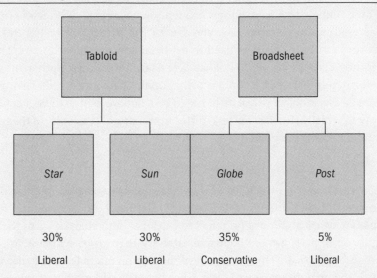

read the *Globe* is unknown. However, participants treat their prediction as being *true*, and then behave as if the randomly chosen voter actually does read the *Globe*. Lagnado and Shanks call this the **commitment heuristic**. A *heuristic* is a strategy that often works, but does not guarantee the right solution. By committing themselves to the *Globe*, the participants are simplifying their task. If it is *true* that the citizen reads the *Globe*, then it is also true that he or she will tend to vote *Conservative*. Lagnado and Shanks (2003, p. 173) conclude that people:

> do not just *consider* the most probable category, but *commit* in some way to its truth. We believe that this generalizes to many real world situations. Faced with uncertain information about multiple categories, people adopt a short-cut strategy that focuses on just the most probable pathway, and neglects the less probable alternatives. This can empower their inferential capabilities, but will sometimes lead to error.

The title of this box is taken from an article by Murphy (2003), who drew out some of the implications of the Lagnado and Shanks study. He suggested that we may habitually use the commitment heuristic because we often need to make decisions rapidly. Suppose you are speeding and see a car behind you in the distance on the highway. You think that it may be a police car, but you are not sure. If you decide that it *is* a police car and slow down, then you may avoid the ticket that you would have received if you had waited until the situation clarified itself. Although the commitment heuristic may lead us into error in some situations, it may be of value in others. 'One does not overuse a heuristic that is useless; one overuses one that has proved invaluable in the past' (Murphy, 2003, p. 514).

Perceived world structure refers to the fact that particular combinations of the attributes of objects in the world tend to occur more frequently than do other combinations. Thus, animals that have wings also tend to be animals with feathers. Animals with wings tend not to be animals covered with fur. Rosch contrasted this example with the sort of attribute relations used in artificial concept experiments. The Bruner cards in Figure 7.1, for example, do not have correlated attributes. Rather, the attributes of colour, form, number, and so on are orthogonal, or uncorrelated. This means, for example, that a black object is just as likely to be a square as it is to be a circle. This is another way in which artificial concepts differ from natural concepts. In the real world, attributes tend to cluster together.

Vertical and Horizontal Dimensions

Rosch suggested that the principles of *cognitive economy* and *perceived world structure* result in concepts being organized in a system that has both vertical and horizontal dimensions. The vertical dimension refers to the level of inclusiveness of the category. For example, *furniture* is a more inclusive category than *chair*, which is in turn more inclusive than *kitchen chair*. Thus, the vertical dimension refers to how general the concept is. The horizontal dimension distinguishes between different concepts at the same level of inclusiveness. For example, *dog* and *cat* are both concepts at roughly the same level of generality.

The Vertical Dimension

It is no accident that, in the example given above of *furniture, chair, kitchen chair*, there are three levels of inclusiveness. This is just what Rosch found in her studies of concepts. The three levels are called **superordinate**, **basic**, and **subordinate**. Examples of concepts occurring at these three levels are shown in Table 7.1. There is considerable evidence in favour of there being three levels. For example, in one experiment, Rosch, Mervis, Gray, Johnson, and Boyes-Braem (1976) asked participants to list all of the attributes for concepts such as those in Table 7.1. Concepts at the basic level had more attributes in common than did those at the superordinate level. In another experiment, participants were asked to describe their body movements when interacting with objects. Objects in superordinate categories showed fewer common movements than did categories at the basic level. Thus, what can you say about actions that go with clothing? Not much, right? But how about pants? You can probably imagine a fairly clear sequence of actions that are specified by pants. Subordinate categories, like Levi's, have common movements, too, but they do not constitute an important difference over basic-level categories. Interestingly, Rosch also showed that children name basic-level categories accurately before they name superordinate categories. Thus, words like *chair* are acquired earlier than words like *furniture*.

All of the foregoing testifies to the importance of basic-level concepts. They are a balance between the very inclusive superordinate concepts and the highly differentiated subordinate concepts. 'Basic objects should generally be the most useful level of classification. Universally, basic object categories should be the basic classifications

Table 7.1 Different Levels of Concept

Superordinate	Basic Level	Subordinates	
Musical Instrument	Guitar	Folk guitar	Classical guitar
	Piano	Grand piano	Upright piano
	Drum	Kettle drum	Bass drum
Fruit	Apple	Delicious apple	Macintosh apple
	Peach	Freestone peach	Cling peach
	Grapes	Concord grapes	Green seedless grapes
Tool	Hammer	Ball-peen hammer	Claw hammer
	Saw	Hack hand saw	Cross-cutting hand saw
	Screwdriver	Phillips screwdriver	Regular screwdriver
Clothing	Pants	Levi's	Double knit pants
	Socks	Knee socks	Ankle socks
	Shirt	Dress shirt	Knit shirt
Furniture	Table	Kitchen table	Dining room table
	Lamp	Floor lamp	Desk lamp
	Chair	Kitchen chair	Living room chair
Vehicle	Car	Sports car	Four-door sedan car
	Bus	City bus	Cross-country bus
	Truck	Pick-up truck	Tractor-trailer truck

From Rosch, E.H., Mervis, C.B., Gray, W.D., Johnson, D.M., & Boyes-Braem, P. (1976). Basic objects in natural categories. *Cognitive Psychology, 8*, pp. 382–439. Copyright 1976 by Academic Press. Reprinted by permission of Elsevier.

made during perception, the first learned and first named by children, and the . . . most necessary in the language of any people' (Rosch, 1978, p. 435).

Rosch had often noted that what was taken as being a basic-level object might depend on the sophistication of the person. Thus, *piano* is a basic-level object for most people. But what about for musicians? Perhaps they show greater differentiation among pianos as instruments, so that what is a basic-level object for a non-musician may be a superordinate-level object for a musician. Palmer, Jones, Hennessy, Unze, and Pick (1989) showed that something like this is in fact the case. Musicians and non-musicians were asked to list all the attributes they could think of for several instruments (e.g., *flute, violin, trumpet, piano, drum*). Musicians tended to give more distinctive descriptions for individual instruments. This suggests that our perception of the properties of individual objects becomes more differentiated with experience.

Recall our discussion of J.J. Gibson's (1977; E.J. Gibson & Spelke, 1983) theory of perception in Chapter 2. Gibson's notion of *affordances* is relevant to the findings of Palmer et al. Objects afford particular actions. For example, a piano affords playing in a particular way that is different from what an organ affords. The more experience you have with a particular class of objects, the more of its affordances you will discover. One consequence of this process is, as Palmer et al. suggest, that the more expertise we have, the more subtle will be the distinctions we make between categories.

The Horizontal Dimension

Within each category level some category members are more prototypical than others. This is the horizontal dimension of category structure. Rosch (1975) asked participants to rate category members according to how good an example of a category they were. The results probably would not surprise you. For example, *chair* is a better example of the category of furniture than is *telephone*. *Car* is a better example of the category of vehicles than is *elevator*. *Gun* is a better example of the category of weapons than are *shoes*. People tend to have similar intuitions about how well an instance fits a particular category.

Rosch and Mervis (1975) showed that the more prototypical category members have more attributes in common than do those category members that are judged atypical. Prototypical members also have the fewest attributes in common with members of other categories. This suggests that prototypical category members are the most representative of their own category and the least representative of other categories. Rosch and Mervis argued that this is what is meant by the phrase *family resemblance*. A category member has a strong family resemblance to the extent that it is a good example of the category to which it belongs and a poor example of any other category.

These findings with respect to the horizontal dimension of category structure can be summarized by saying that concepts have a **graded structure**. A concept is usually said to have a graded structure if some members of the category are better examples of the category than others, and the boundaries of a category are unclear. However, Armstrong, Gleitman, and Gleitman (1983) showed that even some well-defined concepts show prototypicality effects. Consider the concept of *odd number*. It does not have a fuzzy boundary. Something is either an odd number or it is not an odd number. Armstrong et al. asked participants to rate examples of different well-defined categories, such as even-number and odd-number, for prototypicality. It turned out that participants rated some odd and even numbers as better examples of their category than others. *Three* is a better example of odd-numberedness than is *fifty-seven*. Similarly, *four* is a better example of even-numberedness than is *eight-hundred and six*. Thus, a concept can have members that are more prototypical than others, and yet still have a clear definition. This shows that prototype effects are very general and show up even in concepts in which you might not expect them.

■ Embodied Cognition

In an important paper, Glenberg (1997) suggested that concepts should not be seen as disembodied abstract representations. Rather:

> the world is conceptualized (in part) as patterns of possible bodily interactions, that is, how can we move our hands and fingers, our legs and bodies, our eyes and ears, to deal with the world that presents itself? That is, to a particular person, the

meaning of an object, event, or sentence is what that person can do with the object, event or sentence. (p. 3)

We often ignore the fact that the brain/mind is situated in a body, and the 'body requires a mind to make it function' (M. Wilson, 2002, p. 625). Cognition is **embodied**, meaning that its role is to facilitate successful interaction with the environment. Concepts must be understood as a part of the process whereby possible action patterns are determined. At any particular time, the environment affords many different actions. Concepts provide the bridge between our goals, on the one hand, and the environmental possibilities, on the other. For example, suppose I am looking for a vase in which to put a flower. I can select from among the objects in the environment those that meet that goal. A Coke bottle might do, if nothing else is around (Glenberg, 1997, p. 18). In this case, a Coke bottle would become a positive instance of the concept *vase* because it allows me to act in accordance with my current goal. If my goals change, then the meaning of a Coke bottle can change too. It can be a *doorstop* or even a *weapon*. 'The meaning of a Coke bottle (how we interact with it) is not fixed, but infinitely varied depending on the context of use' (Glenberg, 1997, p. 18).

Goal-Derived Categories

If your house caught fire, what would you try to save first? Presumably your list contains items like children, pets, stereo, and so on. The interesting thing about this list is that you may never have thought of it before. Rather, it is possible to construct a category of *things to save from home during a fire* on the spot. Such concepts are called *ad hoc categories* or **goal-derived categories** (Barsalou, 1983, 1987, 1999). Goal-derived categories may have members with no attributes in common, and they may never have been thought of by most people.

Barsalou (1983) showed that goal-derived categories have a graded structure. In one experiment, participants were asked to judge items in terms of how well they exemplified a particular category. For example, consider the concept *ways to escape being killed by the mob*. How well do each of the following fit in that category?

Change your identity and move to the mountains of South America.

Stay where you are presently living in New Jersey.

Barsalou (1983) found substantial agreement between participants concerning good and poor instances of goal-derived categories, suggesting that such categories have a graded structure. What determines how typical an item is in a goal-derived category? Barsalou suggested that the important determinant is how relevant the item is to the goal that the category serves. Thus suppose you construct the category of *things not to eat on a diet*. The attribute 'high in calories' is relevant to this category, but many other properties of foods to which we ordinarily attend are irrelevant.

As Rosch suggested, people may initially prefer to classify an object using basic-level category names. Thus, your first response to a particular piece of furniture may be that it is a *chair*. However, as poverty-stricken aristocrats have occasionally discovered, when you run out of firewood, you can burn a chair to keep you warm, even if it is a priceless antique. As Barsalou (1987) noted, the goal-derived category of *emergency firewood* allows you to cross-classify a chair. The ability to cross-classify an object both in terms of its basic-level name and in terms of other goal-derived categories may be an important aspect of the ability to think creatively. 'Perceiving these new organizations may be necessary to achieving new goals or to approaching old ones in novel ways' (Barsalou, 1987, p. 226).

A study by Ratneshwar, Barsalou, Pechmann, and Moore (2001) showed how changing goals affects the extent to which objects are viewed as similar or different. Consumers often construct categories based on personal goals, such as *healthy lunch substitutes*, a category that might include *sliced melon*, *green salad*, and *tuna sandwich*. These personal goals will also be shaped by particular situational goals. For example, the situational goal of finding *things to eat while driving a car* will probably preclude *green salad*. In Ratneshwar et al.'s study participants were asked to judge the similarity of different pairs of food products (e.g., *apple-orange*). Their judgements were made as a function of different situational goals (e.g., *things to eat as snacks when in a hurry*). Notice that in this example the two foods (*apple-orange*) are similar as healthy foods, but dissimilar in relation to the situational goal of *things to eat as snacks when in a hurry*. In the Ratneshwar et al. study, the judged similarity between foods was reduced (i.e., they were seen as more different) when one was consistent with the situational goal but the other was not. One advertising strategy that this research suggests would be to make situational goals more salient for consumers. Perhaps *soup* could even come to be seen as a *breakfast food* if it is presented as satisfying the goal of *eating a hot and nutritious breakfast* (cf. Ratneshwar et al., 2001, p. 155).

Perceptual Symbol Systems

In the previous section, we saw the enormous flexibility possessed by the conceptual process. Barsalou (2003) argued that 'there are no permanent or complete abstractions of a category in memory. Instead, abstraction is the skill to construct temporary . . . interpretations of a category's members' (p. 1177). This is why it is usually not possible to list all the criterial attributes that define a concept. As we saw when we discussed Wittgenstein, no matter how one defines a concept (e.g., *games*) there will be some members of the category to which that definition does not apply. Once we realize that concepts are usually temporary constructions designed to satisfy a specific goal in a particular situation, then their variability is no longer puzzling.

For Barsalou (1999, 2003) the study of conception involves studying the skills that enable us to construct temporary categories. These skills are rooted in perceptual experience. In the last chapter we observed that imagery and perception shared common mechanisms. Barsalou goes further and suggests that perception and conception also have much in common. Recall our discussion of *selective attention* in Chapter 3, in which we noted that we perceive only a subset of all the information available. What perception delivers to memory are schematic instances of particular categories. For example, on many separate occasions we perceive different *cars*. Over time, these instances become integrated across all of our senses and become a categorical representation. 'For cars, such knowledge includes not only how they look but also how they sound, smell and feel, how to operate them, and emotions they arouse' (Barsalou, Simmons, Barbey, & Wilson, 2003, p. 88).

Thus, the knowledge of a particular category is distributed across all of our senses. This knowledge is called a **simulator** because it enables us to re-enact perceptual experience. The activity of conceptualization involves simulating sensory experiences. When we simulate sensory experiences we do not reconstruct all of our previous perceptions. Rather, the simulation we conduct on a specific occasion is sensitive to the situation in which we find ourselves and our momentary goals. 'On one occasion' we 'might produce a simulation of travelling in a car, whereas on others it might produce simulations of repairing a car, seeing a car park and so forth' (Barsalou, 2003, p. 1180). We have no invariant concept of a *car*, but we construct different versions of *cars* on different occasions, each version focusing on different aspects of *cars*. Not every simulation of a car contains a *seatbelt*, or a *stereo*, or an *airbag*, etc. Simulations represent those properties that are relevant for the task at hand.

Conceptualizing involves **perceptual symbol systems**, meaning that aspects of perceptual memories 'function symbolically, standing for referents in the world and entering into all forms of symbolic activity' (Barsalou, Solomon, & Wu, 1999, p. 210). Studies requiring participants to list the features of category members provide evidence for the perceptual nature of conception. For example, ask yourself what the features of a *watermelon* are. Now ask yourself what the features of a *half watermelon* are. Repeat this exercise for *computer* and *open computer*. If you are like the participants in the study conducted by Barsalou et al. (1999), the simulation of a *watermelon* or a *computer* is different from the simulation of a *half watermelon* or an *open computer*. The former brings to mind external perceptual properties, such as the colour of the surface of the object, while the latter reveals internal perceptual properties such as *seeds* or *wires*. It is likely that the object you imagine changes as its description changes. However, as we saw in the last chapter on imagery, people vary widely in the vividness of their visual imagery. Consequently, Barsalou made the point that we do not need to be aware of the activity of perceptual symbol systems, although we often will be. At bottom, perceptual symbols are brain states. 'Most importantly, the basic definition of perceptual symbols resides at the neural level: unconscious neural representations—not conscious mental images—constitute the core content of perceptual symbols' (Barsalou, 1999, p. 583).

Perceptual Symbol Systems and the Brain

Like other approaches to embodied cognition (Wilson, 2003), the theory of perceptual symbol systems regards conceptualization as a process that connects our perceptions and our actions. As such, the theory of perceptual symbol systems has much in common with other approaches to categorization that are collectively called *sensory-functional theories* (Cree and McRae, 2003, p. 168). Such approaches have their roots in a study by Warrington and Shallice (1984) of **category-specific deficits** due to brain damage. The four patients they studied had been able to recover partially from encephalitis, and were able to correctly identify inanimate objects. For example, one patient defined a *submarine* as a *ship that goes underneath the sea*. However, they were unable to provide satisfactory definitions for living things. Thus, one patient defined *ostrich* simply as *unusual* (Farah & McClelland, 1991, p. 340). To account for this selective impairment, it has been proposed that *living things* are understood primarily in terms of their sensory features, while *inanimate objects* are understood primarily in terms of their function. Thus, for example, a *moose* might have *antlers* as one of its most salient features, while a *knife* might have *used for cutting* as one of its most salient features (Cree & McRae, 2003, p. 199). Sensory-functional theories assume that 'knowledge of a specific category is located near the sensory-motor areas of the brain that process its instances. . . . Consequently, a deficit for living things may arise from damage to brain regions that process sensory information, whereas a deficit for manipulable artefacts may arise from damage to regions that implement functional action' (Simmons & Barsalou, 2003, p. 452). The sensory-functional theory accounts for some cases, but not all. The theory predicts that objects that are equally 'sensory' should all be equally affected by a conceptual deficit. For example, a deficit for *living things* should span all *living things*. However, some patients demonstrate a conceptual deficit for *fruits* and *vegetables* but not for *animals* (Martin & Caramazza, 2003, p. 199; Samson & Pilon, 2003). Findings such as these mean that a simple sensory-functional theory cannot be the whole story, and complementary viewpoints need to be taken into account to provide a fuller account of conceptual deficits (Simmons & Barsalou, 2003, p. 454). We will become acquainted with some of these alternatives in the remainder of the chapter.

■ Idealized Cognitive Models

Lakoff and Johnson's (1980, 1999; Johnson & Lakoff, 2002) work has been a major influence on theories of embodied cognition (Wilson, 2003). However, their work is sufficiently distinctive to merit treatment on its own. Consider the title of one of George Lakoff's (1987) books: *Women, fire and dangerous things*. The title appears to suggest that these three have something in common. Are women fiery and dangerous? There is in fact a language in which women, fire, and dangerous things are placed in the same category. This language is **Dyirbal**, an aboriginal language in Australia. Dyirbal speakers have four words that classify all possible objects and events: *bayi*, *balan*, *balam*, and *bala*. Some of the members of these four categories are given below; they are derived from the work of R.M.W. Dixon (1982) and condensed from Lakoff (1987, p. 92):

> *bayi*: men, most snakes, most fishes, some birds, most insects, the moon, some spears;
>
> *balan*: women, some snakes, some fishes, most birds, dangerous things, anything connected with water or fire;

balam: all edible fruit and the plants that bear them, ferns, honey, cigarettes, wine, cake;

bala: parts of the body, meat, most trees, language.

How in the world did these items in the natural world get to be grouped in this way? What principles govern the development of a natural classification system like that of the Dyirbal speakers? Lakoff stated that the most general principle is the **domain-of-experience principle**: If there is a basic domain of experience associated with A, then it is natural for entities in that domain to be in the same category as A. Let us see how this and other principles work by examining the basic classification system underlying that given above. Lakoff suggested that the basic system is as follows:

bayi: human males

balan: human females

balam: edible plants

bala: everything else

Three distinctions underlie these four categories. One is between *human males* and *human females*. Another distinction is between *people* (categories 1 & 2) and *edible plants* (category 3). The third distinction is between the first three categories and *everything else*. The last category is a miscellaneous category. Anyone who has ever tried to create a filing system knows that a miscellaneous category is always needed!

This basic system is fleshed out in a variety of ways. The domain-of-experience principle allows for links between entities that are related in a particular culture. If men do most of the hunting and fishing, then men and most animals will tend to be in the same category. Two other, more specific, principles are the *myth-and-belief principle* and the *important property principle*. The *myth-and-belief principle* allows things to be placed together with things that are connected by myth or belief. Women are linked by myth to the sun, and thus to fire. So, women and fire are in the same category. The important property principle says that if something has a particularly important property, such as dangerousness, then it may be assigned to a class that is different from the class to which it would ordinarily be assigned. Thus, the stone fish could be in class 1, with most other fishes. But the stone fish is dangerous, and so is in fact placed in class 2. This is probably done in order to make an object stand out as distinctive and especially noteworthy, by giving it an odd classification. One result of the whole process is that women, fire, and dangerous things end up in the same category.

Lakoff pointed out that the Dyirbal conceptual system is not accidental or haphazard. Rather, in spite of its complexity, it is regulated by principles. People have **idealized cognitive models** that they modify to suit the particular circumstances they confront. Thus, the base system of the Dyirbal was continuously altered as it was used to represent the complexity of the real world. Idealized cognitive models do not fit the world precisely, and conceptual systems are always being adjusted to better approximate the conditions in which people find themselves.

While the Dyirbal system may strike you as weird, the way it works is not all that different from how we generate categories in our culture. Consider the concept *mother*. What makes someone a mother? As Lakoff (1987, pp. 80ff.) outlined, there are several ways in which a person might get to be a mother. That is because there are several different models underlying our concept of mother. Among the models Lakoff (1987, p. 74) has suggested are the following:

> *The birth model*: The female who gives birth is the mother.
>
> *The genetic model*: The female who contributes the genetic material is the mother.
>
> *The nurturance model*: The female adult who nurtures and raises a child is the mother.
>
> *The marital model*: The wife of the father is the mother.

Notice that there are also models underlying our other concepts, such as father. For example, there obviously are a genetic model of a father (the male who contributes the genetic material) and a marital model of a father (the husband of the mother). What other models of father can you think of?

By combining these (and other) models in various ways, we can generate a variety of mothers and fathers, such as stepmothers and stepfathers, adoptive mothers and adoptive fathers, natural mothers and natural fathers. Can you think of any other examples? A person will be regarded as a prototypical mother or a protoypical father to the extent that she or he exemplifies all the possible ways of being a mother or a father. There will be many people who do not exemplify one or more of the models of mother or father. The result is that there will be a great many different ways in which people can use concepts like mother and father in particular situations (Komatsu, 1992, p. 518). This can lead to conceptual confusion, as Lakoff (1987, p. 75) pointed out. For example, suppose a couple legally adopts a child. Are they the 'real' parents of the child? If you think carefully about these, and similar, questions you will begin to see how complex the concepts are. Furthermore, if you consider the fact that concepts such as *mother* and *father* are only a tiny part of our conceptual system, then you can begin to appreciate the possibility that our system is as dazzlingly complex as the Dyirbal system.

Concepts as Metaphors

Metaphor occurs when we liken someone or something to someone or something else without meaning it literally. There are many famous literary metaphors, such as Shakespeare's use of *Love is blind* in *The Merchant of Venice*. Lakoff and Johnson (1999, p. 46) argued that metaphor is not solely or even primarily a literary device. Rather, metaphor arises naturally as a result of connections between sensory-motor and other forms of experience. For example, when children pour water into a glass they cannot help but notice the level of liquid rise. Repetitive experiences like this lead to the formation of connections between those areas of the brain responsible for representing quantity and those representing verticality. Eventually *more is up* becomes a **primary metaphor**, meaning that it 'pairs subjective experience and judgment with sensorimotor experience' (Lakoff & Johnson, 1999, p. 49). We can then say things like 'Prices are down' or 'The stock market is too high' without even thinking about where this manner of speaking comes from. Another example given by Lakoff and Johnson (1999, p. 50) is the connection between *friendliness* or *affection* and *warmth*. They suggest that this comes about as a result of the experience of warmth when being held affectionately. They also observe that 'we first acquire the bodily and spatial understanding of concepts and later understand their metaphorical extensions in abstract concepts' (Johnson & Lakoff, 2002, p. 254). This is a point first made by Asch (1955, 1958; Asch & Nerlove, 1960), who described the process whereby words are initially applied to physical events and only subsequently used metaphorically to describe persons. Asch (1955) called terms such as *warm* and *cold* **double function words**. On the one hand, they refer to physical properties, such as temperature, but on the other hand they refer to properties of people. Asch and Nerlove (1960) showed that children first tend to use these words to refer to physical objects, and only later use them psychologically. Thus children may have difficulty answering the question 'Is your teacher warm?' unless they are able to use the word *warm* metaphorically.

Lakoff and Johnson (1999, p. 50) list a number of primary metaphors such as *Bad is Stinky* and *Help is Support*. It would be useful for you to work out the sensorimotor basis for these metaphors, as well as try to come up with some of your own.

Gibbs (1996, 2004), in concert with Lakoff and Johnson, argued forcefully that our concepts are inherently metaphorical. Metaphors are particularly valuable in the construction of temporary concepts of the sort we discussed above. 'The LOVE IS A JOURNEY metaphor might be used to create a particular conceptualization of love in certain situations, while LOVE IS AN OPPONENT might be more appropriate to use forming a concept in other situations' (Gibbs, 1996, p. 314). Gibbs (2004, p. 1196) pointed out that a problem with conceptual metaphor theory is that some metaphors do not appear to be fully grounded in sensorimotor experience. For example, compare *love is a journey* with *more is up*. We have already seen that *more is up* can be grounded in sensorimotor experience. However, the experiential link between *travel* and *love* is not so straightforward. Consequently, it is not always easy to give a plausible explanation of the way in which conceptual metaphors are generated from one or more primary metaphors.

■ Folk Biology

In Chapter 1, we introduced the notion that the mind is composed of specific parts, or *modules*, each of which is responsible for particular cognitive operations. We also noted that there are differences of opinion concerning the extent to which the mind is modular, as well as considerable debate about the number and kind of modules that may exist (e.g., Fodor, 1983; Pinker, 1997; Sperber, 2002). In this section we will explore the concept of modularity further in relation to the possibility that our naive understanding of biology is dependent on a **conceptual module**. A conceptual module is one that is responsible for **domain-specific knowledge**, meaning that it deals exclusively with a particular subject matter (Hirschfeld & Gelman, 1994). Although there is considerable controversy concerning the number of domain-specific modules, a likely candidate for domain specificity is **folk biology** (Medin & Atran, 2004), which refers to the concepts that ordinary people use to understand living things.

Folk biology is often introduced by means of a quotation from Darwin (1859, p. 431) (e.g., Atran, 2005, p. 43):

> From the most remote period in the history of the world organic beings have been found to resemble each other in descending degrees, so that they can be classed into groups under groups. This classification is not arbitrary like the grouping of stars in constellations.

Darwin's idea was that people invariably classify living things hierarchically, and this hypothesis has been borne out in subsequent research, beginning with the work of Berlin, Breedlove, and Raven (1974). All cultures have a **folk taxonomy**, or classification system, that 'is composed of a stable hierarchy of inclusive groups of organisms, or taxa, which are mutually exclusive at each level of the hierarchy' (Atran, 1999, p. 316). These ranks can be compared to those described by Rosch in Table 7.1, in that there is a superordinate level (e.g., *tree*, *bird*), followed by a **generic species** level (e.g., *oak*, *robin*), and then a subordinate level (e.g., *white oak, mountain robin*) (Medin & Atran, 2004, p. 962). The generic species level plays the same role in folk biology as do basic-level concepts in Rosch's classification. However, there are important differences between the two, as we will see below.

Psychological Essentialism

We have seen throughout this chapter that the positive instance of concepts need not have any properties in common. Recall Wittgenstein's (1953, p. 34) comparison of the members of a category to the individual fibres that make up a rope. No one fibre runs the entire length of the rope. Rather, the individual fibres overlap with one another. Remember also our discussion of temporary categories, in which we concluded that concepts are designed to satisfy a specific goal in a particular situation. These facts about concepts are in striking contrast to the beliefs of ordinary folk. For ordinary folk, all the members of any particular biological category share an *essence* (Gil-White, 2001). **Essentialism** 'is the view that certain categories have an underlying reality or true nature that one cannot observe directly but that gives an object its identity, and is responsible for other similarities that category members share' (Gelman, 2004, p. 404). This essence remains the same as a plant or animal develops and reproduces. One does not need to be able to say what this essence is in order to believe in its existence (Medin, 1989). Thus, no matter how different a woman may be today from the infant she once was, folk believe that there is still something essential about her that has remained unchanged.

Psychological essentialism is revealed by experiments of the following kind. Gelman and Welman (1991) asked four-year-old children to judge how animals would behave if they were raised by a different generic species. For example, would an adult rabbit prefer carrots or bananas if it had been raised by monkeys? This experiment seeks to discover whether or not children of this age believe in nature or nurture. Do they believe that there is an essence that defines an animal and determines how it will develop regardless of its nurturing environment? If so, then they will also believe that rabbits prefer carrots even if they are raised by monkeys. The evidence strikingly confirmed that children are psychological essentialists. For example, they believe that cows will still say *moo* even if raised by pigs; that kangaroos will still *hop* even if raised by goats; and that mice will still *run away from cats* even if raised by dogs. In another experiment, Hirschfeld and Gelman (1997) asked children to decide which language someone would speak if they had been switched at birth into a family that spoke a different language from that of their biological parents. For example, if a child has English-speaking parents and the child is switched at birth into a family that speaks Portuguese, will the child speak English or Portuguese when he/she grows up? Five-year-olds prefer the nativist hypothesis that the language one speaks is determined by one's biological and not one's adoptive parents. Children regard language as a potential that expresses itself independently of nurture.

Folk Biology as a Conceptual Module

To say that folk biology is a conceptual module means that we are predisposed to acquire knowledge about living things. This predisposition could have evolved because of the importance of plants and animals to the survival of our ancestors (Sperber & Hirschfeld, 2004). One reason for believing in the existence of such a module is the pervasiveness of essentialism even in the face of contradictory evidence. For example, most anthropologists believe that *race* is a scientifically meaningless concept (Gil-White, 2001). Nevertheless, 'racism—the projection of essences onto social groups—seems to be a cognitively facile and culturally universal tendency' (Medin & Atran, 2004, p. 963). The existence of a conceptual module is suggested not only by the apparent universality of folk biology, but also by how difficult it is for us to think in any other way.

A domain-specific conceptual module requires stimulation in order to function. Folk biology does not emerge fully formed, but is a framework that needs to be filled in by receiving the appropriate input. If the conceptual module is not exposed to a cultural environment rich in plants and animals, then it will not develop as fully as it would otherwise. This means that there will be cultural variation in folk-biological expertise as a function of how much exposure there is to nature. Atran, Medin, and Ross (2004, p. 402) observe that the members of technologically advanced cultures show 'a marked deterioration in common-sense understanding of the living world'. Evidence for a decline in folk-biological knowledge, at least in English-speaking countries, was provided by Wolff, Medin, and Pankratz (1999). They analyzed the relative frequency with which words referring to life forms (e.g., trees) were used during the period from the sixteenth century to the twentieth century. Such information is available in *The Oxford English Dictionary*, which provides illustrative quotations for each word it defines. These quotations are dated (e.g., *The many twinkling leaves of aspen tall*, 1728). The relative frequency of tree terms reached its high point in the nineteenth century but began a precipitous decline in the twentieth century. 'Starting around the period of the Industrial Revolution and ending about now, writing about trees dropped to a level lower than at any other time in the history of modern English' (Wolff et al., 1999, p. 187). The relative decline in the use of tree words is paralleled by a decline in words for other life forms.

Atran, Medin, and Ross (2004) regard the decline in the use of words referring to the living world as a measure of the **devolution of knowledge**. One consequence of this devolution is that for educated members of technologically advanced societies the generic species level (e.g., *oak*, *trout*) is no longer the basic level. Rather, the life-form level (e.g., *tree*, *fish*) is the basic-level category in these societies. The loss of contact with nature is reflected in less specific and detailed concepts of living forms.

Of course, the devolution of folk-biological knowledge is accompanied by an evolution of other forms of knowledge. Technological and scientific concepts come to the fore as other forms of knowledge move into the background (Benjafield, 1987). Indeed, Atran (1999, p. 548) observes that the goals of folk biology and scientific biology are quite different. The former 'evolved to provide a generalized framework for understanding and appropriately responding to important and recurrent features in hominid ancestral environments', while the latter 'has developed to understand an organization of life in which humans play only an incidental role no different from other species.' These different goals inevitably lead to the construction of different concepts. The magnitude of this difference is beautifully illustrated by the following quotation from 'an Honours student at a major American research university' (Atran, Medin, & Ross, 2004, p. 395).

> *Interviewer*: Tell me all the kinds of trees you know.
>
> *Student*: Oak, pine, spruce, cherry . . . (Giggle) evergreen, Christmas tree, is that a kind of tree? . . . God, what's the average here? . . . So what do kids say, big tree, small tree?
>
> *Interviewer*: Tell me some plants.
>
> *Student*: I can't think of plants that aren't trees. I know a lot about angiosperms, gymnosperms, gametophytes, and sporophytes . . . but this is *biology*. It's not really about plants and trees.

Folk Biology and the Brain

We saw earlier that some patients display category-specific deficits due to brain damage in which they are unable to provide satisfactory definitions for living things. Such a deficit need not mean that damage to a folk-biological conceptual module is responsible for such deficits. However, advocates of the position that folk biology is a domain-specific module point to such findings in support of their position (e.g., Medin & Atran, 2004, p. 963). In one such study, Farah and Rabinowitz (2003) reported on a case of a person brain-damaged as a result of meningitis at one day of age. However, Adam (a pseudonym) managed to attend public school and had a normal verbal IQ. At age 16, he was given the task of naming pictures of living and non-living things. He showed 'a relatively selective impairment in knowledge of living things necessary for naming pictures' (p. 404). In another test, he was given a questionnaire consisting of four item types:

(1) Visual knowledge of living things (e.g., Do ducks have long ears?)
(2) Non-visual knowledge of living things (e.g., Are roses given on Valentine's day?)
(3) Visual knowledge of non-living things (e.g., Is a canoe widest in the centre?)
(4) Non-visual knowledge of non-living things (e.g., Were wheelbarrows invented before 1920?)

There were a total of 380 questions. Half of the questions in each category were correctly answered *yes*, the rest *no*. Control participants got roughly 80–90 per cent correct in each category. Adam's performance on the non-living things questions was not different from the controls. However, for both types of living things questions, his performance was only 40–45 per cent. Farah and Rabinowitz concluded that Adam's deficit was specific to knowledge about living things. They also drew out the implications of the fact that Adam's brain damage had been present virtually since he was born. This must mean that 'prior to any experience with living and non-living things we are destined to represent our knowledge of living and non-living things with distinct neural substrates' (p. 408).

■ Questions for Study and Discussion

1. Outline the procedure used by Bruner, Goodnow, and Austin to study concepts. What were their major conclusions? Briefly criticize their approach.
2. Outline the procedure used by Reber and his colleagues to study complex rules. What was his major conclusion? Criticize Reber's work from the viewpoint of Dulaney, Carlson, and Dewey and others.
3. What innovations did Rosch introduce to the study of concepts? Outline the horizontal and vertical dimensions of the system she used to understand concepts.
4. In what sense is cognition 'embodied'?
5. Discuss Lakoff's theory of idealized cognitive models. Illustrate your answer by means of the Dyirbal classification system.
6. Are we as good at folk biology as we used to be? Why or why not?

■ Key Concepts

Category-specific deficits As a result of brain damage, some people may show a selective deficit in knowledge.

Cognitive economy and perceived world structure Two principles that regulate the way we use concepts.

Cognitive unconscious The hypothesis that implicit learning represents an evolutionarily primitive form of unconscious cognition.

Commitment heuristic A strategy that involves believing that something *is* true when it is only *likely* to be true.

Conceptual module A module that is responsible for domain-specific knowledge.

Conservative focusing Concept formation strategy of actively formulating hypotheses and selecting instances to see if your hypotheses are correct by focusing on only one attribute at a time and selecting instances that vary only in that attribute.

Correlated attributes The hypothesis that particular combinations of attributes of objects tend to occur more frequently than do other combinations.

Criterial attribute An attribute that is necessary for something to be an instance of a concept.

Devolution of knowledge A decline in a specific kind of knowledge possessed by members of 'advanced' societies.

Domain-of-experience principle If there is a basic domain of experience associated with A, then it is natural for entities in that domain to be in the same category as A.

Domain-specific knowledge Knowledge that is the result of a module that deals exclusively with a particular subject matter.

Double-function words (Asch) Words like *warm* that refer both to physical and psychological properties.

Dyirbal An aboriginal language in Australia used by Lakoff to illustrate idealized cognitive models.

Embodied cognition The role of cognition is to facilitate successful interaction with the environment.

Essentialism Categories have an underlying reality that gives category members their true identity.

Family resemblance (Wittgenstein) Instances of concepts that possess overlapping features, without any features being common to all.

Focus gambling Concept formation strategy of selecting instances that vary from the first positive instance in more than one attribute.

Folk biology The concepts that ordinary folk use to understand living things.

Folk taxonomy A classification system that is composed of a hierarchy of groups.

Goal-derived categories (Barsalou) Categories invented for a specific purpose on a particular occasion.

Graded structure A concept in which some members of the category are better examples of the category than others and the boundaries of the category are vague.

Idealized cognitive models (Lakoff) Prototypical conceptual structures.

Implicit learning versus explicit learning Learning that takes place unintentionally versus learning that takes place intentionally.

Misaligned hierarchies Judgements made with respect to one level suggest one conclusion but judgements made at another level suggest a contrasting conclusion.

Perceptual symbol systems Aspects of perceptual memories stand for events in the world and enter into all forms of symbolic activity.

Primary metaphors A pairing of subjective experience with sensorimotor experience.

Prototypes Instances of concepts that are regarded as particularly good examples.

Reception task A concept formation task in which the instances presented to the participant are chosen by the experimenter.

Selection task A concept formation task in

which the participant selects instances from those presented by the experimenter.

Simultaneous scanning Concept formation strategy involving keeping in mind all possible hypotheses and trying to eliminate as many as possible with each instance selection.

Successive scanning Concept formation strategy involving formulating a single hypothesis and testing it by selecting instances until the correct hypothesis emerges.

Superordinate, basic level, and subordinate

(Rosch) Levels of inclusiveness of a concept, as in *tree, oak,* and *live oak.*

Tacit knowledge Knowledge people have without being able to say exactly what it is that they know.

Wholist versus partist Concept formation strategies used in reception tasks. The participant chooses to initially consider either that all attributes are members of the concept or that only some attributes are members of the concept.

■ Links to Other Chapters

Implicit learning versus explicit learning
    Chapter 13 (mere exposure and implicit learning)
Tacit knowledge
    Chapter 5 (procedural memory)

Domain-specific knowledge
    Chapter 3 (attention capture)
    Chapter 10 (social contract theory, dual-process theories)

■ Further Reading

Many experimental paradigms other than Reber's have been used to investigate implicit or incidental learning. A good example is Lacroix, G.L., Giguére, G., & Larochelle, S. (2005). The origin of exemplar effects in rule-driven categorization. *Journal of Experimental Psychology: Learning, Memory, and Cognition, 31,* 272–288.

Alternative approaches to the cognitive unconscious are explored by Perruchet, P., & Vinter, A. (2002). The self-organizing consciousness. *Behavioral and Brain Sciences, 25,* 297–388.

Do current events have an effect on what we consider to be a typical exemplar? This question is explored in Novick, L.R. (2003). At the forefront of thought: The effect of media exposure on airplane typicality. *Psychonomic Bulletin & Review, 10,* 971–974.

As we saw in the Little Red Riding Hood example in Chapter 2, connectionist models may contain 'hidden units' that function like concepts (e.g., the wolf, grandma, etc.). Good examples of neural network approaches to classical concept formation problems are Carbonaro, M. (2003). Making a connection between computational modeling and educational research. *Journal of Educational Computing Research, 28,* 63–81; and Dawson, M.R.W., Medler, D.A., McCaughan, D.B., Willson, L., & Carbonaro, M. (2000). Using extra output learning to insert a symbolic theory into a connectionist network. *Minds and Machines, 10,* 171–201.

A clever experiment critical of theories of embodied cognition is Markman, A.B., & Brendl, C.M. (2005). Constraining theories of embodied cognition. *Psychological Science, 16,* 6–10.

Lakoff notes that the Dyirbal classification strikes us as being as strange as the entry from Borges's fictitious *Chinese Emporium of Benevolent Knowledge* in Borges, J. (1966). *Other inquisitions.* New York: Washington Square Press:

On those remote pages it is written that animals are divided into (a) those that belong to the Emperor, (b) embalmed ones, (c) those that are trained, (d) suckling pigs, (e) mermaids, (f) fabulous ones, (g) stray dogs, (h) those that are included in this classification, (i) those that tremble as if they were mad, (j) innumerable ones, (k) those drawn with a very fine camel's hair brush, (1) others, (m) those that have just broken a flower vase, (n) those that resemble flies from a distance. (p. 108)

An evolutionary perspective on modularity is given by Geary, D., & Huffman, K. (2002). Brain and cognitive evolution: Forms of modularity and functions of mind. *Psychological Bulletin,* *128,* 667–698.

Chapter 8

Language

■ The Structure of Language

Not only is Wilhelm Wundt (1832–1920) often credited with founding the first laboratory in psychology, but he is also one of the first to do important work on the psychology of language (Blumenthal, 1970; Carroll, 1953). Wundt's view of the structure of language anticipated many contemporary approaches to language. One of his most interesting discussions concerned the relationship between experience and the words used to describe experience. Let us briefly reconsider the structure of our experience.

As we saw in Chapter 3, we are able to attend to 'one out of what seem several simultaneously possible objects or trains of thought' (James, 1890, p. 403). Our attention is like a spotlight that highlights some aspects of a situation, but leaves others in the background (Treisman, 1986). However, all the aspects of a situation to which we could pay attention are available simultaneously. We can shift our attention from one aspect to another, and consider the relationships between the various parts of a situation.

Wundt (1890/1970; Blumenthal, 1970, p. 17) used **tree diagrams** to describe the relationships between different parts of our overall experience of a situation. For example, suppose you are attending to some music. Your experience contains relationships between parts that you can put into words and could be diagrammed as in Figure 8.1. Thus, the music can be described as the subject of a sentence, and its loudness as the predicate of a sentence, as in 'The music is loud.' The process of speech proceeds from one level at which a number of relationships are simultaneously present, to another level at which these relationships are serially ordered as a succession of words in a sentence (e.g., subject, predicate). The listener can reconstruct the speaker's experience by reversing the process whereby the speaker generated the sentence. Wundt's model of sentence production is similar to more modern notions. In particular they resemble some of Noam Chomsky's earlier formulations. Although Chomsky's linguistic theories have had a profound impact on cognitive psychology, they have undergone many changes over the years. We need first to consider some of his earlier ideas, because they are still part of the way in which many cognitive psychologists think about language. We will then explore some of his more recent approaches.

Figure 8.1 A Tree Diagram of the Relations Between some Parts of an Individual's Experience while Listening to Music.

■ Transformational Grammar

Chomsky is one of the most important figures in the history of linguistics (www. chomsky.info/bios.htm). His ideas have always been hotly debated, and he has never shrunk from controversy. Chomsky has been 'among the ten most-cited writers in all of the humanities (beating out Hegel and Cicero and trailing only Marx, Lenin, Shakespeare, the Bible, Aristotle, Plato, and Freud) and the only living member of the top ten' (Pinker, 1994, p. 23). Chomsky's fame was not immediate. In fact, his doctoral dissertation was regarded as so unusual that he found it difficult to get it published. A condensed version of it was published as *Syntactic structures* (1957). In that book, Chomsky considered the way in which we produce sentences. A sentence is a grammatical utterance, and is recognized as such by a native speaker of the language. Chomsky pointed out that the set of possible sentences in a language is infinite. Our **language** is open-ended and consists of all possible sentences, but our **speech**, which consists of those sentences that are actually spoken, is only a small subset of language (de Saussure, 1916). This is a very important point because it means that there must be a set of rules—a *grammar*—that everyone uses to generate sentences in his or her language. This grammar must be capable of producing all possible sentences in the language. From a finite set of rules, the grammar is in principle able to generate an infinite set of sentences. In order to understand the structure of language, we need to understand the structure of this grammar.

Chomsky made the point that a grammatical utterance need not be a meaningful utterance. His famous example of this is the nonsense sentence 'Colourless green ideas sleep furiously' (Chomsky, 1957, p. 15). Although meaningless, it is still grammatical, at least when compared to the utterance 'Furiously sleep ideas green colourless.' This observation, and others like it, led Chomsky to make a sharp distinction between *grammar* and *semantics*, or the study of meaning. He argued that the processes that made a sentence grammatical were different from the processes that made a sentence meaningful.

Chomsky went on to consider the nature of a grammar for a natural language such as English. He rejected the possibility that a finite state grammar is the sort of grammar that could generate all the sentences in a language. We considered finite state grammars in Chapter 7, when we reviewed Reber's work. You may wish to go over that material again now. For purposes of the present discussion, a critical feature of a finite state grammar is that every word in a sentence is produced in a sequence starting with the first word and ending with the last word. A railroad diagram, which produces several sentences, is given in Figure 8.2. This grammar generates sentences such as *The man comes*, *The old man comes*, *The men come*, and *The old men come*. These are only a very, very few of the possible sentences in English. Can you imagine how vast a railroad diagram would have to be in order to be able to generate 1,000 sentences? 10,000? 100,000? There are a great many more possible sentences than these in English. If we had to learn them all using a finite state grammar, then we would need to listen to several sentences a second for over 100 years before we had learned enough sentences to enable us to speak and understand a significant portion of English (G.A. Miller, Galanter, & Pribram, 1960, p. 147).

Chomsky's (1957, p. 21) objection to finite state grammars was that it is impossible to construct a finite state grammar that will generate all and only the grammatical utterances of a natural language. Finite state grammars are too simple to underlie the complexity of natural languages. As an illustration of this complexity, consider the fact that natural languages contain sentences that are embedded within other sentences. To see what this means, consider this example from Chomsky (1957): *The man who said that S is arriving today* (p. 22). The symbol *S* can stand for an unlimited number of possible sentences that can be inserted at that point in the example. Thus, *The man who said that the bank will renew our mortgage is arriving today* and *The man who said that Roscoe will become a star is arriving today* are just two out of indefinitely many possibilities. A grammar must be able to generate such sentences, and Chomsky believed that it was impossible for finite state grammars to do so.

One of the problems with finite state grammars is that they operate at only one level. In finite state grammars, sentences are generated by a process that moves only from left to right, as it were. The alternative proposed by Chomsky (1957) was a top-down

Figure 8.2 A Finite State Grammar.

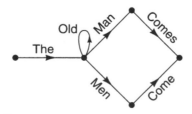

process, which makes use of **phrase structure rules** and grammatical transformations. Phrase structure rules consist of symbols and rewrite rules. Here is a small set of such rules, adapted from Chomsky (1957, p. 26) and J. Greene (1972, p. 35).

1. Sentence (s) → Noun Phrase (NP) + Verb Phrase (VP)
2. NP → Article (*art*) + Noun (N)
3. VP → Verb (V) + NP
4. *Art* → *a, the*
5. N → *car, girl, boy*
6. V → *helps, likes*

These rules describe the way in which symbols, such as s, can be rewritten as other symbols, such as NP and VP. This process of rewriting goes on until it generates actual words, such as *the* and *Tiffany*. These rules allow a number of different sentences to be derived. The derivation of a sentence can be represented using a tree diagram, as in Figure 8.3. Each stage in the process yields a different string (such as NP + VP), and the final sequence of words generated is called a terminal string.

Rewrite rules operate on single symbols, such as NP and VP. Chomsky (1957, p. 44) proposed that there also were **grammatical transformations** operating on entire strings, and converting them to new strings. An example of such a procedure is the *passive transformation*. Consider a sentence with the underlying form:

NP$_1$ + V + NP$_2$.

An example of such a sentence is *Boswell admired Johnson*. The passive transformation, *Johnson was admired by Boswell*, converts the string underlying the terminal string, to produce something like the following (Deese, 1970, p. 26):

Figure 8.3 Derivation of a Sentence using a Tree Diagram.

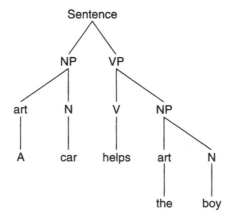

$NP_2 + to\ be + V + by + NP_1.$

That is, this transformation reverses the order of the two noun phrases, and inserts a form of the verb *to be* and the word *by* in their proper places. Instead of *Boswell admired Johnson* we now have *Johnson was admired by Boswell*. The passive transformation is an example of an *optional transformation*. It is not necessary for optional transformations to be applied in order to make a sentence grammatical. Chomsky (1957, p. 45) defined *kernel sentences* as ones that are produced without optional transformations. This suggests that kernel sentences might be easier to understand and remember because they require fewer transformations. Much psychological research was stimulated by this notion (e.g., Mehler, 1963). However, it was difficult to demonstrate that the number of transformations and not such variables as sentence length, determined ease of understanding and recall (J. Greene, 1972, pp. 157ff.). For example, the passive sentence *Johnson was admired by Boswell* has more words than its active counterpart, and may be more difficult to process simply for that reason.

In the end, interest in the concept of kernel sentences declined as Chomsky revised his theory. Chomsky (1965, 1966, 1967, 1968, 1972) went on to introduce several concepts that became very influential. Among the important distinctions Chomsky introduced were those between *competence* and *performance* and between *deep structure* and *surface structure*.

Competence and Performance

Chomsky (e.g., 1967, p. 397) considered what it means to say that a person has a command of a language. On the one hand, it means that the person has internalized a system of rules that relates sound to meaning. This internalized system of rules constitutes a basic linguistic **competence**, which provides the basis on which the person is able to understand and to use the language. This competence is not always reflected in the person's actual use of the language. Linguistic **performance** is not only determined by the person's basic linguistic competence, according to Chomsky, but is also determined by cognitive factors, such as memory and the person's understanding of his or her situation. Thus, although in principle one can generate extremely long sentences, such sentences cannot be easily understood, because they exceed the attentional capacities of listeners. To take another example, the form that utterances take often depends on the age of the speaker. The same thing might not be said in the same way by both an adult and a young child. Thus, although the grammar of a language is a model of linguistic competence, we must except that observations of linguistic performance will not always give us a completely accurate picture of a person's competence.

Chomsky (1967, p. 399) argued that a central problem for psychology is to discover the characteristics of linguistic competence. This would involve specifying the idealized grammar that constitutes this competence. A theory of linguistic performance would specify not only the nature of linguistic competence but also the psychological processes that go into the production of actual sentences.

Deep and Surface Structures

Chomsky believed that linguistic competence had a largely innate internal structure. This innate structure is called *universal grammar*. One aspect of universal grammar is universal syntax, which provides the rules enabling us to transform meaning into words. The meaning is at one level, called the **deep structure**, whereas the words are at another level, called the **surface structure**. The distinction between deep and surface structure allows us to understand a number of interesting linguistic phenomena, including ambiguous sentences.

The reason why ambiguous sentences are interesting is often illustrated by means of sentences like the following (e.g., Bigelow, 1986, p. 379):

1. *Time flies like an arrow.*
2. *Fruit flies like a banana.*

Sentence 1 is usually interpreted to have the sort of meaning illustrated in Figure 8.4a. When we hear this sentence, it makes us think of something like an arrow flying rapidly through the air. Such an interpretation could also be imposed on sentence 2, as illustrated in Figure 8.4b. However, a banana with wings is not the usual meaning we extract from sentence 2. Rather, we are more likely to give sentence 2 the sort of meaning shown in Figure 8.4c. In this context we take flies to be a noun rather than a verb. Of course, such a reading is also possible with sentence 1. We can imagine a creature called a time fly that likes arrows, as shown in Figure 8.4d.

All of this may strike you as more than a bit silly; however, there is a serious point to be made from these light-hearted examples. From Chomsky's viewpoint, the existence of ambiguity in language illustrates why we need to make a distinction between deep and surface structure. The same surface structure can be derived from different deep structures. The two different meanings of sentence 1, for example, are carried by two different deep structures. *Meaning* is not given on the surface of a sentence, but is given by the *deep structure* interpretation of the sentence. When we understand a sentence, we transform a surface structure into a deep structure. When we produce a sentence we go the other way: from a deep structure to the construction of a surface structure.

■ The Innateness Hypothesis

The Poverty of the Stimulus Argument

As we said above, Chomsky believed that linguistic competence was largely innate. Among the reasons for believing in this **innateness hypothesis** was the belief that the speech to which a small child is exposed is an inadequate database from which to abstract the structure of language (e.g., Chomsky, 1972, pp. 13–160). The typical linguistic performance of an adult is too full of errors and too incomplete a sample of language to give a child the data needed to generate a natural language grammar on his or her

Figure 8.4 Flying Arrow, Flying Banana, Fruit Fly, and Time Fly.

own. This is called the **poverty of the stimulus argument** (Chomsky, 1980a, 1980b; Lightfoot, 1982) because it claims that the stimulus for language (which is other people's language) is too deficient to enable children to use it effectively. Children acquire their first language too rapidly for them to start from scratch when they acquire a language. Consequently, children must possess a **language acquisition device**, or LAD (McNeill, 1970). LAD contains principles of **universal grammar**. These are very general principles that apply to any natural language, be it English or Chinese. Among the things that LAD 'knows' are that languages contain such things as noun phrases and verb phrases and that they are arranged in particular ways, such as subject and predicate (McNeill, 1970, p. 71). LAD is a theory of language that children use to discover the structure of the particular language community into which they happen to be raised. LAD must be a very powerful theory because it enables children to quickly make sense out of the language to which they are exposed. Children come equipped with the tools necessary to enable them to rapidly acquire a facility in their first language.

Support for the innateness hypothesis came in part from the findings of a classic study by R. Brown and Hanlon (1970). Pinker (1988) claimed that Brown and Hanlon's findings 'may be one of the most important discoveries in the history of psychology' (p. 104). The reason why Brown and Hanlon's study is so important is that it bears directly on one of the alternatives to the innateness hypothesis. This alternative is usually identified with B.F. Skinner (1957; www.bfskinner.org/bio.asp).

Skinner's approach, and others like it, implied that children must learn a language by receiving informative feedback on their utterances. Perhaps language learning takes place when children are given approval for generating grammatical sentences, and disapproval for making ungrammatical ones (R. Brown & Hanlon, 1970, p. 46). However, Brown and Hanlon found no evidence for such a procedure. Observing the interactions of mothers and their children, Brown and Hanlon found that mothers not only allowed ungrammatical sentences to go uncorrected, but responded to such utterances in the same way as they responded to grammatical utterances. Approval seemed to depend on whether or not the statement the child was trying to make was true, but it did not depend on whether or not the sentence was grammatical. Thus, to a child saying *Mama isn't boy, he a girl* the parent says *That's right*. However, to a child saying *And Walt Disney comes on Tuesday* the parent says *No, he does not* (R. Brown & Hanlon, 1970, p. 49).

One implication of studies such as Brown and Hanlon's is that children do not typically receive information that would tell them when they are making an ungrammatical sentence (Rice, 1989, p. 150). In the absence of such feedback, it is not easy to see how the child could learn to eliminate ungrammatical utterances. From the perspective of the innateness hypothesis, this did not seem like such a big problem. This is because the innateness hypothesis maintains that children come equipped with the kind of knowledge that will allow them to ultimately produce grammatical sentences and avoid ungrammatical ones. However, as we shall see, not everyone accepts the innateness hypothesis. Moreover, even if one accepts some version of the innateness hypothesis, it is still necessary to spell out precisely what it is that must be innate in order for children to acquire language. As we shall now begin to see, this is not at all easy.

Minimalism

As we noted earlier, Chomsky's theory has undergone considerable modification over time (e.g., Chomsky, 1981, 1995, 2005). The current version of the theory is called **minimalism** (Uriagereka, 1998). As the name suggests, the minimalist approach assumes that linguistic competence has only those characteristics that are absolutely necessary, with no added frills. Minimalism operates according to a principle of parsimony (Atran, 2005, p. 58), in that it aims for the simplest possible theory of linguistic competence. The working hypothesis of minimalism is that 'the human language faculty might be a computationally perfect solution to the problem of relating sound to meaning' (Lasnik, 2002, p. 434).

A key hypothesis of the current theory is that the acquisition of a particular language involves **parameter setting** (Piatelli-Palmarini, 1989). Chomsky (1981, 1995) proposed that universal grammar contains a variety of switches, which can be set to one of a number of possible values, or parameters. A parameter is a universal aspect of language that can take on one of a small set of possible values. Here is an example, from Hyams (1986, p. 3). In an English verb phrase the verb always comes before its object, as in 'take the cheese'. A native English speaker would never say 'the cheese take'. However, in a German verb phrase the verb always follows the object. The position of the verb is a parameter set for a specific language. Chomsky (1995) described the process of parameter-setting as follows:

> A plausible assumption today is that the principles of language are fixed and innate, and that variation is restricted . . . . Each language, then, is . . . determined by a choice of values for lexical parameters: with one array of choices, we should be able to deduce Hungarian; with another Yoruba . . . . The conditions of language acquisition make it plain that the process must be largely inner-directed, as in other aspects of growth, which means that all languages must be close to identical, largely fixed by initial state. (p. 17)

As Piatelli-Palmarini (1989) pointed out, the parameter-setting approach implies that children are not instructed to learn a specific language. Children are not given explicit training on the position of verbs in verb phrases, for example. Rather, a language is selected out of the many possible ones that are supported by universal grammar. Through exposure to a particular language, such as English or German, the switches get set to the specific values that characterize that language (Yang, 2004).

Of course, the need for parameter-setting arises because of the variety of languages that children must be prepared to acquire as their native tongue. But why do different languages exist at all? One possibility is that different languages arise for purely historical reasons.

> We find different languages because people move apart and lose touch, or split into factions that hate each other's guts. People always tinker with the way they talk, and as the tinkerings accumulate on different sides of the river, mountain

range, or no-man's land, the original language slowly splits into two. To compare two languages is to behold the histories of two peoples, their migrations, conquests, innovations, and daily struggles *to make themselves understood* (Pinker, 1997, p. 213, italics added).

Thus, it is possible that different languages arose and developed through a series of accidents. However, as the Pinker quote illustrates, most theorists assume that the goal of every speaker, regardless of language, is to be able communicate with others. By contrast, suppose that different languages arose in order to facilitate communication with some people, *but not with others*. That is, 'the language faculty has a **concealing function** as well as a revealing function' (Baker, 2003, p. 351). This would mean that language can usefully be seen as a kind of code. The parameters that are set for one language conceal its meanings from the speakers of another language, and vice versa. Baker points out that the Navajo language was used successfully by the United States as a code in World War II. In general, it would be advantageous for the members of a particular group to be able to pass information to one another, but keep it secret from the members of another group with whom they were at war, or with whom they were competing in some other way. Since war and other forms of human conflict are extremely common, it may be that linguistic parameters evolved precisely in order to keep open the possibility of learning different languages. This example illustrates the extremely broad range of possible evolutionary explanations for the various features that language possesses. Different theories of the psychology of language are intimately associated with specific theories of the evolution of language. It is virtually impossible to disentangle the psychology of language from the story of its evolution. An exploration of some aspects of the way psychologists have dealt with the evolution of language is given in Box 8.1. You should review the material on Broca's area in Chapter 2 before reading Box 8.1.

Is the Stimulus for Language Really Impoverished?

As Pullum and Scholz (2002; Scholz & Pullum, 2002) observed, the poverty of the stimulus argument rests on the premise that the data that a child needs in order to acquire a language from scratch are unavailable. If that is true, then language cannot be acquired solely by means of data-driven learning. However, the poverty of the stimulus argument would be undermined if one could 'identify a set of sentences such that if the learner had access to them, [then] the claim of data driven-learning . . . would be supported' (Pullum & Scholz, 2002, p. 19). Since the Brown and Hanlon (1970) study discussed above, there has been an enormous accumulation of information concerning the kinds of sentences to which children may be exposed (e.g., MacWhinney, 2000). Consequently, investigators now have much richer samples against which to test the poverty of the stimulus argument. By examining large samples of sentences, Pullum and Scholz (2002, pp. 24–26) were able to document the existence of many constructions that had been assumed to either be infrequent or absent from the language to which infants would be exposed. For example, consider how children understand

Box 8.1 The Evolution of Language

Psychologists have speculated endlessly about the evolution of language. At times the speculation is so rampant that it almost seems reasonable to ban discussion of the topic. Indeed, the French Academy of Sciences did exactly that in 1866. Like most prohibitions, it proved ineffective, and we once again have an abundance of theories. However, one theory in particular is currently attracting more attention than any other. It should come as no surprise that this theory is associated with Noam Chomsky.

Recursion and the Evolution of Language
Hauser, Chomsky, and Fitch (2002) made a distinction between broad and narrow conceptions of the faculty of language. In its broad sense, the faculty of language has three parts. There is a sensory-motor system that allows us to both perceive and produce patterns of speech. There is also a conceptual-intentional system that allows us to grasp the meaning of speech. Finally, there is a uniquely human system that mediates between the first two. Let us consider each of these systems in turn.

Sensory-Motor System
Other animals share our ability to perceive and produce speech sounds. For example, vocal imitation occurs in dolphins, parrots, crows, and songbirds. Songbirds are particularly interesting examples. Their acquisition of their songs depends on listening to other birds of the same species. This input must come during a critical period or their songs will not develop properly. This process is similar to human language acquisition. After a certain age people cannot speak a second language and sound completely like a native. This, along with other similarities between human and animal sensory-motor systems, suggests that there is nothing uniquely human about this aspect of language.

Conceptual-Intentional System
The ability of other animals to represent the world and their place in it may not be as rich as that of humans. However, they are still capable of formulating and acting on relatively complex plans. For example, recall our discussion in Chapter 5 of foraging in scrub jays (Clayton & Dickinson, 1998). These birds stored both larvae (which they value highly as food but spoils quickly) and peanuts (which they value less highly as food, but remains edible for a long time) in different locations. When the birds were allowed to retrieve stored food, the food they retrieved depended on how long the interval was between storage and retrieval. If the interval was short, then they retrieved the larvae, but if the interval was long they retrieved the peanuts. 'Individuals often search for food by an optimal strategy, one involving

(continued)

minimal distances, recall of locations searched, and kinds of objects retrieved' (Hauser, Chomsky, & Fitch, 2003, p. 1578). Thus, one would be loath to argue that the conceptual-intentional system was peculiar to humans.

Uniquely Human System

What may be unique to humans is the ability to use symbols recursively. We have already seen an example of **recursion** earlier in this chapter when we considered sentences embedded within other sentences. Recursion is a process that refers to itself. Consider the following examples, adapted from Uriagereka (1999, pp. 3–4).

> $S \rightarrow$ *You are saying that S*
> $S \rightarrow$ *You are saying that you are thinking that S*
> $S \rightarrow$ *You are saying that you are thinking that you are talking to someone that S*

In these examples, *S* calls itself, so that each successive example gets longer and longer. In principle this recursive process could go on indefinitely, but in practice it is limited by what one can keep in working memory.

Morton (1976) gave a witty example of recursion. His article is titled 'On recursive reference'. The body of the paper consists of one sentence: *Further details of this paper may be found in Morton (1976)*. The paper refers to itself. The reader is invited to go back to the beginning and read the paper over again, and then again, and so on. The paper is not only about recursion, but is itself an example of a recursive loop.

Hauser, Chomsky, and Fitch (2002) realized that recursive behaviour may be found in animals someday, but they could find no good examples from existing research. They concluded that recursion may be the uniquely human property of the language faculty. Thus, the narrow conception of the faculty of language is that it consists of the ability to recursively combine symbols. It enables the construction of an infinite number of possible expressions of the conceptual intentional system to be realized as sentences produced by the sensory-motor system (Hauser, Chomsky, & Fitch, 2002, p. 1578). In short, it enables us to translate thought into speech.

Chomsky (2005) describes the evolutionary appearance of this narrow faculty of language as follows:

> The simplest account of the 'Great Leap Forward' in the evolution of humans would be that the brain was rewired, perhaps by some slight mutation . . . . Perhaps . . . the Great Leap Forward was effectively instantaneous, in a single individual, who was instantly endowed with intellectual capacities far superior to those of others, transmitted to offspring and coming to predominate . . . . (p. 12)

From Gesture to Speech

One alternative account of the evolution of language presents much more specific hypotheses about its emergence. Corballis (2003, 2004a, 2004b) weaves together the following facts:

- Other primates do not have speech, but they do have a relatively sophisticated system of gestural communication.
- The area corresponding to Broca's area in monkeys contains **mirror neurons** that not only fire when the animal makes grasping movements, but also fire when the monkey observes other animals making those movements.
- A mutation on a gene called FOXP2 can cause a severe speech disorder. Functional magnetic resonance imagery studies suggest that this disorder may be due to a failure of Broca's area to become an area responsible for speech.
- Around 40,000 years ago, there was a rapid increase in the production of tools, decorations, and cave art.

These facts can be combined to form the following narrative. Like other primates, humans originally communicated by means of gesture. Indeed, people still make meaningful gestures while speaking (McNeill, 1980, 1985a, 1985b, 1989). However, at one time we communicated primarily through gesture supplemented by simple vocalizations bearing little resemblance to modern speech. Broca's area was responsible for gestural communication, enabling us to not only regulate our gestures, but to interpret those of other people as well. A mutation on FOXP2 enabled the recruitment of Broca's area for speech. That is why any further mutation on FOXP2 causes a speech disorder. The emergence of speech took the pressure off gesture as a channel of communication, enabling the hands to become free for other tasks. This in turn enabled the creation of elaborate tools, decorations, and works of art.

Of course, there are other evolutionary narratives (e.g., Pinker & Jackendoff, 2005). All of them are open to question. However, there is no denying that there is a reciprocal influence between the search for the evolutionary origins of language and the psychology of language.

irregular constructions such as plurals in noun-noun compounds. The sentence *I put my books on the book shelf* is fine as an English sentence. However, *I put my books on the books shelf* sounds strange, and we can surmise that children are very unlikely to hear it. Nevertheless, children understand that *a new books shelf* means *a shelf for new books*. They do not think it means *a new shelf of books*. Where does this understanding come from? It has been claimed that the fact that children understand constructions like this is 'another demonstration of knowledge despite "poverty of the input"' (Pinker, 1994,

p. 147). However, the child's knowledge should not be surprising given the number of constructions such as *rules committee, publications catalogue, letters policy, complaints department*, etc., that they will be able to overhear in the speech of adults. Perhaps exposure to these constructions provides all that the child needs in order to use this grammatical form properly.

Pullum and Scholz (2002) render what is called a 'Scottish verdict' on the poverty of the stimulus argument: Not proven. Indeed, Hoff (2004) makes the useful point that it is difficult if not impossible to disprove the poverty of the stimulus argument. No one has given, or perhaps ever can give, a complete account of all the data available to a child that would make language acquisition possible without any innate contribution. Nevertheless, enough evidence has accumulated to suggest that children acquiring language are given much more evidence in support of their efforts than had previously been suspected (MacWhinney, 2004). There is an enormous literature on the topic of language acquisition, but we have space here to consider only two of these sources of evidence. First, it now appears that children do in fact both receive and make use of corrective feedback on their ungrammatical constructions. Second, the complexity of the speech to which the child is exposed is significantly related to the complexity of the speech that the child then produces. We will now briefly examine representative studies illustrating both of these influences.

Adult Reformulations of Child Errors

'Children produce many errors during acquisition, and the issue is how they manage to get rid of them' (Chouinard & Clark, 2003, p. 638). Perhaps **parental reformulations** of a child's erroneous utterances might be particularly informative to the child. For example, consider the following exchange:

> Child: I want butter mine.
>
> Father: OK give it here and I'll put butter on it.
>
> Child: I need butter **on it**. (Chouinard & Clark, 2003, p. 656)

In this example, the child takes up the father's reformulation of his erroneous utterance. The child must realize that both his initial utterance and his father's utterance mean the same thing. However, he also realizes that in order to speak correctly, he must emulate the adult. In general, adult reformulations constitute negative evidence because they inform children when their utterances are erroneous. At the same time, they also provide positive instances of correct speech.

Chouinard and Clark sampled utterances of five children between the ages of two and four years, as well as the parental responses to these utterances, and the child's next utterance. Their data came from a standard archive called The Child Language Data Exchange System (MacWhinney, 2000). The data set they analyzed was quite large, varying from 730 items for one child to 9,187 for another. Chouinard and Clark discovered that reformulations of erroneous utterances occurred between 50 per cent and 70 per cent of the time when the child was about two years old. Moreover, children take up these reformulations as frequently as 50 per cent of the time, as shown by their subsequent repetition of the reformulation. Thus, these interactions provide an occasion for the child to learn how to speak correctly, and they take advantage of it. Reformulations decline as children get older, presumably due to their improved speech.

The Impact of Teachers' Speech

Huttenlocher, Vasilyeva, Cymerman, and Levine (2002, p. 338) note that 'there are substantial variations in the language environments children encounter and . . . these variations may be correlated with differences in development.' For example, children's **syntactic development**—their ability to organize words into grammatical sentences—may be influenced by input from speakers other than parental caregivers. Language development is an ongoing process that does not stop at a specific age. After a certain age, much of the speech that children are exposed to comes from teachers. The complexity of kindergarten and first grade children's syntax develops more in the period between October and April than between April and October (Huttenlocher et al., 2002, p. 343). The latter period includes the summer vacation. A reasonable hypothesis is that exposure to speech at school is the important factor. In order to test this hypothesis, Huttenlocher and her co-workers sampled the speech of different teachers. Huttenlocher et al. recorded preschool teachers' speech during a typical class day. These recordings were analyzed to determine the extent to which individual teachers present children with challenging examples of speech. A particularly important example is the multi-clause sentence (e.g., *The lamp broke because it fell off the table*). Consequently, Huttenlocher et al. calculated the proportion of multi-clause sentences in each teacher's speech, which turned out to vary between 11 per cent and 32 per cent. The children were roughly four years old, and came from three different preschools, which ranged from serving high-income families to serving low-income families. Children were tested by means of a comprehension task that is illustrated in Figure 8.5. Children had to match each sentence with the correct picture. The test included both multi-clause sentences and sentences with varying numbers of noun phrases.

Each class had the same primary teacher throughout the study. Children were tested both at the beginning and the end of the school year. An average comprehension score for each class was calculated for both the first and second tests. Then, the average scores for the first test were subtracted from the average scores on the second test. This gives a measure of how much syntactic growth had taken place *in each class*. This measure was found to be significantly related to the complexity of teacher speech: the more complex the teacher's speech, the greater the syntactic growth in that class. Importantly, 'teacher speech was *not* significantly related to children's skill levels at the start of the school year, but *was* significantly related to growth in children's skill levels over the school year' (Huttenlocher et al., 2002, p. 370).

Figure 8.5 The comprehension task.

The boy is looking for the girl behind a chair, but she is sitting under the table.

The baby is holding the big ball and the small block.

From Huttenlocher, J., Vasilyeva, M., Cymerman, E., & Levine, S. (2002). Language input and child syntax. *Cognitive Psychology, 45*, p. 363. Copyright 2002. Reprinted by permission of Elsevier.

One of the benefits of being exposed to complex speech may be that the child comes to be able to represent more complex ways of thinking of about things. In this context, Huttenlocher et al. (2002, p. 371) cite Vygotsky's (1934/1986) work on the interaction between language and thought. This is a topic we will take up later in the chapter.

Evaluation of Chomskian Theories

If the value of theories is measured by the amount of research they generate, then Chomsky's various theories have been a smashing success. The degree to which they are true or false has still to be determined. However, two complementary trends seem to have been established. The first is that, in comparison with earlier formulations, innate processes are now believed to play less of a role in language acquisition (Pinker & Jackendoff, 2005, p. 204). The second is that the linguistic environment of the child is much richer than had formerly been believed. On balance, language acquisition is increasingly being seen to be dependent on learning.

■ Communication and Comprehension

Obviously, a critical aspect of the psychology of language deals with the way in which listeners comprehend spoken and/or written speech. When you comprehend spoken or written language, then you understand what is meant. The context within which a listener or a reader receives language is extremely important in determining what interpretations the listener will extract from the message. A speaker or a writer must take the audience's context into account.

A useful distinction is between *given* and *new information* (H.H. Clark & E. Clark, 1977, pp. 32, 92). Speakers and listeners are said to enter into a **given, new contract** (H.H. Clark & Haviland, 1977), whereby the speaker agrees to connect new information to what the listener already knows. Thus, for example, a sentence may consist of part that is given, or shared between speaker and listener, and a part that is known to the speaker but new to the listener (Bruner, 1985, p. 31). Suppose that there is a howling winter storm outside, and I say, 'A cold front from Alberta is causing this storm.' I am introducing a new piece of information (*a cold front from Alberta*), and relating it to something my listener and I already know about (*the storm*). Comprehension would be difficult if not impossible if one simply introduced new information without connecting it to things of which the listener already has knowledge.

Sperber and Wilson's (1986/1995; 2002) theory of the way conversation is conducted and comprehended has been very influential. They contrasted two approaches to communication: the **code model** and **inferential model**. The code model derives from information processing theories, such as those we reviewed in Chapter 2. According to this model, the initial stage of communication is a process whereby a speaker's thoughts are encoded in words. When spoken, these words are an acoustic signal that passes through the air and impinges on the listener. The listener must decode the signal to arrive at the thought the speaker originally intended to communicate. Sperber and Wilson pointed out that the code model assumes that both speaker and listener share a great deal of mutual knowledge. Otherwise, the listener would not be able to decode the signal properly and arrive at the correct interpretation. An example used by Sperber and Wilson is of a speaker who says: *Coffee would keep me awake*. This sentence is open to at least two interpretations. One is that the speaker wishes to stay awake, and so wants a cup of coffee, and the other is that the speaker does not wish to stay awake, and so does not want a cup of coffee. Successful interpretation of this sentence depends on the listener sharing the same understanding of the situation. Sperber and Wilson pointed out that a difficulty with the code model is that it is very difficult to spell out the ways in which people could come to have enough mutual knowledge to guarantee successful communication.

The inferential model derives from the work of Grice (1957/1971, 1975), who analyzed communication in terms of *intentions* and *inferences*. A speaker intends to inform a listener, and the listener infers what the speaker intends. Suppose you are sitting in a room with another person. It is the middle of winter, but because you think that the room is stuffy, you open a window. What would you infer if the other person then said, 'Were you raised in a barn?' Would you decode this utterance as a simple request for information, and reply sincerely, 'No, I was raised in a two-bedroom semi-detached house'? Or might you not interpret the utterance as a request that the window be closed, because the speaker is implying that only people raised under primitive conditions would open the window? The meaning of the utterance depends critically on the inferences you make concerning the meaning that the speaker intends. Grice (1957/1971) suggested a person means something by intending an utterance 'to produce some effect in an audience by means of the recognition of this intention' (p. 58). In the example above, when you recognize the speaker's intention, you are likely to close the window or otherwise deal with the fact that the speaker has communicated to you that he or she wants the window closed.

In order to facilitate the process of communication, speakers tend to obey the co-operative principle. According to Grice, there are four kinds of rules or **conversational maxims** that follow from this principle (Paprotte & Sinha, 1987, p. 205). First, speakers attempt to say no more than is necessary (*maxim of quantity*). Second, they try to be truthful (*maxim of quality*). Third, they attempt to be relevant (*maxim of relation*). Fourth, speakers strive to avoid ambiguity and be clear (*maxim of manner*). When we listen to people, we tend to assume that they are following these maxims. On the basis of this assumption, we make inferences, or *implicatures*.

In order to illustrate how the inferential model might work in ordinary conversation, let us return to Sperber and Wilson's example of the person who says, 'Coffee will keep me awake.' Suppose that both speaker and listener are attempting to drive non-stop from Toronto to Miami, and it is the speaker's turn to drive. Because the listener assumes that the speaker is following the **co-operative principle**, and therefore intends to say something concise, truthful, relevant, and unambiguous, the listener can infer that the speaker wants coffee. There is nothing mysterious about this process. It simply involves taking the four maxims about conversation for granted, and making straightforward inferences from them.

For Sperber and Wilson (1986), communication sometimes follows the coding model and sometimes follows the inferential model. People communicate in ways that are blends of coding and inference. Under any circumstance, however, the goal of communication is **relevance**. An utterance is relevant to the extent that it is both true and easy to understand (Van der Henst, Carles, & Sperber, 2002, p. 458). Truthfulness and relevance are not always the same. For example, when asked the time many people will reply with an answer rounded to the nearest five minutes. If your watch says 2:18, you are likely to reply that it is 2:20. In one study, Van der Henst et al. (2002) found that 97 per cent of speakers with analog watches rounded their replies to the nearest five minutes. Perhaps this is because the precise time is usually not relevant, and a rounded time is easier for both speaker and listener to process.

Comprehension may require inferences of the sort Grice proposed, but the inferential process need not be a conscious chain of reasoning. Sperber and Wilson (2002) refer to comprehension as 'intuitive', meaning that it is an 'unreflective process which takes place below the level of consciousness' (p. 9). One possibility is that most people have an implicit theory of how other people's minds work, and they use this theory when they attempt to comprehend what another is saying (Perner, 2000; Sperber & Wilson, 2002, p. 275).

Figurative Language

Insight into the way in which communication works can be gained from the study of **figurative language**, which consists of various figures of speech, such as metaphor and irony (Roberts & Kreuz, 1994). Figurative language may at first seem to be an unusual form of communication. However, in fact, figurative language is commonly used in ordinary discourse (Pollio, Smith, & Pollio, 1990), as we saw in the chapter on concepts. In what follows, we will focus on **irony**, because a great deal of research has been devoted to it. We will see that irony illustrates many facets of communication in everyday life.

Irony

Irony belongs to a family of concepts that includes *satire* and *sarcasm*. A satirical remark holds something up to ridicule. Sarcasm and irony are ways in which satire may be accomplished. Sarcasm is defined by *The Oxford English Dictionary* as a 'sharp, bitter or cutting remark'. The same dictionary defines irony as 'a figure of speech in which the intended meaning is the opposite of that expressed by the words used'. Irony is sometimes considered to be a form of sarcasm, and the two are seen as quite similar by ordinary speakers of the language (Gibbs, 1986).

An ironic statement is intended to communicate the opposite of what it says. Thus, you may say about someone you find particularly cold and unfeeling, 'He is such a warm person.' Given the right context and tone of voice, you can communicate exactly how you feel about the person, even though you are saying the opposite of what you mean. What are the conditions under which a listener perceives the ironic intent of a speaker?

H.H. Clark and Gerrig (1984, p. 121) followed Grice (1978) by arguing that irony involves the use of **pretense**: the speaker is only pretending to mean what he says. They quoted Fowler (1965):

> Irony is a form of utterance that postulates a double audience, consisting of one party that hearing shall hear and shall not understand, and another party that, when more is meant than meets the ear, is aware both of that more and of the outsiders' incomprehension . . . . [It] may be defined as the use of words intended to convey one meaning to the uninitiated . . . and another to the initiated, the delight of it lying in the secret intimacy set up between the latter and the speaker. (pp. 305, 306)

As Clark and Gerrig noted, irony usually involves a particular tone of voice. It is difficult to spell out, but when someone says something like 'What a terrific movie' ironically, there is a way of saying it that is different from the way it would be said if the person really meant it.

Several authors have described (without necessarily accepting) what is sometimes called the *standard theory of irony* (e.g., Gibbs, 1986; Jorgenson, Miller, & Sperber, 1984; Kreuz & Glucksberg, 1989). According to this theory, listeners first take the ironic utterance literally, but realize that the speaker cannot mean it literally. Then the listener reaches the conclusion that the speaker means the opposite of what he or she has just said. Grice's *co-operative principle* could help to explain the way in which the listener arrives at this conclusion (Kreuz & Glucksberg, 1989, p. 374). This principle means that listeners normally expect speakers to be truthful and relevant. The listener realizes that the speaker cannot be both truthful and relevant and literally mean what he or she says. Thus, the listener can infer that the speaker must mean the opposite.

A recurrent issue in the study of irony in particular and figurative language in general is whether or not the listener must understand the literal meaning of an utterance first before then extracting the figurative meaning. Gibbs (1986) presented evidence that people comprehend ironic utterances as quickly as literal ones. Glucksberg (2003) reported that metaphorical utterances (e.g., *My job is a jail*) are also apprehended 'as quickly and as automatically as we apprehend literal meanings'. Results such as these imply that people do not need to extract the literal meaning of an utterance first. This may be particularly true if speakers and listeners share enough common ground (H.H. Clark & Gerrig, 1984, p. 124) to enable the listener to comprehend the ironic utterance more or less directly (Gibbs, 1986, p. 13). However, when figurative language is unexpected, people may take longer to process it. For example, in many cultures people expect men to make more sarcastic utterances than women. Consequently, comprehension of a sarcastic utterance made by a woman is 'delayed as people attempt to integrate' the statement with their expectations (Katz, Blasko, & Kazmerski, 2004, p. 187).

Speech Disfluency

It is very common for speakers to pause at various points while they speak. Such **hesitation pauses** have been extensively researched (e.g., Goldman-Eisler, 1968; Deese, 1984). Stanley Schachter and his colleagues (Schachter, Christenfeld, Ravina, & Bilous, 1991; Schachter, Rauscher, Christenfeld, & Crone, 1994) explored hesitation pauses made by university lecturers. They focused on *pauses* that are filled by *ums, ers, uhs*, and *ahs*. No doubt you will have heard lecturers as well as other speakers uttering such *speech disfluencies*. Schachter and his colleagues counted the number of filled pauses in the speech of 47 lecturers in 10 departments at Columbia University. These measurements were made unobtrusively by a trained observer sitting in the class. The data showed that lecturers in the humanities and social sciences generated more speech disfluencies than did lecturers in the sciences.

Schachter et al. (1991) interpreted the difference in hesitation pauses between the disciplines as being due to a difference in vocabulary between the sciences and the arts. Science lecturers are speaking about a subject matter that is well-defined relative to the arts. As Schachter et al. (1994) observed, there are fewer synonyms for scientific terms than there are for concepts in the humanities and social sciences. 'There are, for example, no synonyms for *molecule*, or *atom* or *ion* . . . . In contrast, consider the alternatives for *love, beauty, group structure, prejudice,* or *style*' (p. 37). This vocabulary difference means that lecturers in the arts have to choose between many more possible words than do lecturers in the sciences. Hesitation pauses represent points at which the lecturers are choosing between the various possibilities afforded by their respective disciplines. Since science lecturers have fewer choices to make, they emit fewer hesitation pauses. Schachter et al. (1994) suggested that the differences they uncovered are not unique to lecturers, but can be found in speech generally. Depending on the topic, the same person may emit many or few speech disfluencies. When talking about a scientific topic, one's speech will be marked by fewer hesitation pauses than when talking about less well-defined topics such as those found in the humanities.

Clark and Fox Tree (2002) suggested that *uh* and *um* should be seen as English words that have specific uses in spontaneous speech. They hypothesized that *uh* is used to signal a short delay in speaking, while *um* is used to signal a longer delay. Clark and Fox Tree examined speech from a variety of sources, ranging from conversations to speech made to answering machines. The results were in line with their predictions. Pauses after *um* were longer than pauses after *uh*. The implication of this finding is that speakers are doing two things at the same time. On the one hand, they are planning what they are going to say. On the other hand, they are monitoring the planning process itself. When they detect an upcoming delay, then they insert *uh* or *um*, depending on how long they think that the delay will be. Of course, this monitoring process may not be fully or even partly conscious. The process can be illustrated by means of the following example (Clark & Fox Tree, 2002, p. 84). It comes from a study in which participants were asked questions that could be answered in one word (Smith & Clark, 1993).

> Questioner: In which sport is the Stanley Cup awarded?
> Participant: (Pauses for 1.4 s) um (Pauses for 1.0 s) hockey.

Pauses after *um* were significantly longer than pauses after *uh*. Moreover, the length of time from the end of the question until the beginning of the answer was longer when *um* was used than when *uh* was used. Participants 'were able to estimate how long it would take them to retrieve the answer even before they had retrieved it' (Clark & Fox Tree, 2002, p. 84).

All of this leads to the conclusion that *uh* and *um* are not merely speech disfluencies. Rather, *uh* and *um* also serve a communicative function. They serve to notify the listener that the speaker has detected either a minor (*uh*) or a major (*um*) problem while attempting to produce the appropriate output.

■ The Social Context of Language

Although L.S. Vygotsky died in the first half of the twentieth century, his ideas have become more influential as time goes by. One reason is that Vygotsky 'provides the still needed provocation to find a way of understanding [the person] as a product of culture as well as a product of nature' (Bruner, 1986, p. 78). A noted Vygotsky scholar (Wertsch, 1985, p. 231) remarked that 'It may strike many as ironic that Vygotsky's ideas should appear so fruitful to people removed from him by time and space . . . . Instead of viewing this as paradoxical, however, it should perhaps be seen as a straightforward example of how human genius can transcend historical, social and cultural barriers.'

Vygotsky's book *Thought and language* was not translated into English until 1962, although a newer translation of this book has since become available (Vygotsky, 1934/1986). Vygotsky (1934/1986, p. 83) was particularly interested in the interaction between thought and speech. Of course, it is possible for thought and speech to function independently of each other. We can think without speaking just as surely as we can speak without thinking! Vygotsky believed, however, that in the second year children begin to think about what they say. Thought and speech begin to influence each other. Children begin to show a marked increase in curiosity about word meanings at about this age (Wertsch, 1985, pp. 99ff.), and vocabulary grows quite rapidly (G.A. Miller, 1986, p. 174).

Vygotsky (1986, p. 226) reanalyzed what Piaget (1923/1948) had called **egocentric speech**. Piaget observed that young children's speech often does not take the listener's viewpoint into account. Egocentric speech declines as the child becomes socialized. In its place emerges social speech. Egocentric speech may be called speech for oneself, whereas social speech may be called speech for others (Werner & Kaplan, 1963, p. 318; Vygotsky, 1986, p. 225). Vygotsky argued that egocentric speech does not disappear, but becomes **inner speech**, and is to be distinguished from external speech.

Inner speech comes to play an important role in regulating thought. The structure and function of inner speech were summarized by Werner and Kaplan (1963, pp. 322ff.) as follows. Because inner speech is silent, it is a rapid medium in which to think. Inner speech is also a condensed form of representation. Vygotsky (1986, pp. 236ff.) observed that inner speech typically makes use of predicates. Because inner speech is speech for oneself, it would be redundant to specify the subject. In this respect, inner speech is similar to the speech that takes place between people who know each other well. Have you ever participated in a three-way conversation in which the other two people know each other intimately, but you are only a minor acquaintance of them both? The people who know each other well can communicate by means of a single word or gesture, whereas you need to spell everything out.

In inner speech, one word can contain a great many meanings. Inner speech conveys the personal meaning of words rather than the conventional meaning. This makes inner speech a very rich medium. Sometimes the richness of inner speech can be observed, especially when speech occurs under unusual conditions. Vygotsky (1986) made this point through a story by Dostoyevsky that told of

> a conversation of drunks that entirely consisted of one unprintable word (*The Diary of a Writer*, for 1873): 'One Sunday night I happened to walk for some fifteen paces next to a group of six drunken young workmen, and I suddenly realized that all thoughts, feelings and even a whole chain of reasoning could be expressed by that one noun, which is moreover extremely short.' (p. 241)

Dostoyevsky then went on to illustrate how the same word can be used to express contempt, doubt, anger, insight, delight, disapproval. (Can you imagine other contexts in which a word can take on many different senses?) In inner speech, all of these senses are available, thus allowing thought to proceed along multiple avenues (Werner & Kaplan, 1963, p. 322).

Inner speech in adults is usually silent, but is occasionally externalized. Goffman (1978) gave several examples of people who emit audible speech that is ostensibly for themselves, but is actually intended for others. People who come in from the cold may say *brr*. How often have you said *brr* when no one else was around? Is not this utterance intended to implicitly communicate your inner state to others? How about saying *oops* when you make a mistake? Do you say *oops* if no one but yourself can hear? Perhaps the most compelling of Goffman's examples is a person who says something like *amazing!* or *incredible!* or *unbelievable!* while reading a newspaper, magazine, or some such in the presence of someone else. Their eyes may never leave the printed page, but they are still attempting to communicate with the other person, although not explicitly. They do not say *I've just read something really interesting that I would like to share with you*. Rather, they attempt to get the other person to pay attention to their inner life without explicitly asking them to do so. Try not responding the next time you are with someone who says something like *Interesting!* while reading in your presence. See what happens.

One function of inner speech that Vygotsky (1986, p. 242) believed to be especially important was the planning of cognitive operations. He compared inner speech to a mental draft. By means of inner speech, one can plan and organize thinking. While engaged in a task, whether it is planning a meal or changing a car tire, inner speech provides direction for the conduct of the operations necessary to complete the task (Benjafield, 1969a; Luria, 1961; Wertsch & Stone, 1985). Switching between tasks is also under the control of inner speech. If participants' inner speech is suppressed by forcing them to repeat the letters *a-b-c*, then their ability to switch between an addition and a subtraction task is impaired (Emerson & Miyake, 2003). Baddeley (2003, p. 199) suggested that one way in which inner speech may be articulated is by means of the phonological loop part of working memory (considered in Chapter 5).

The Zone of Proximal Development

Vygotsky's (1935/1978) concept of the **zone of proximal development** was defined as follows: 'It is the distance between the actual developmental level as determined by independent problem-solving and the level of potential development as determined through problem-solving under adult guidance or in collaboration with more capable peers' (p. 86). The concept of a zone of proximal development draws our attention to the social aspects of cognitive development. 'What is in the zone of proximal development today will be the actual developmental level tomorrow—that is, what a child can do with assistance today she will be able to do herself tomorrow' (Vygotsky, 1978, p. 87). As Berk (1994) observed, there is a close relation between the zone of proximal development and the development of inner speech. 'When a child discusses a challenging task with a mentor, that individual offers spoken directions and strategies. The child incorporates the language of those dialogues into his or her private speech and then uses it to guide independent efforts' (p. 80).

Literacy

Literacy means a great many different things to different people (e.g., Heath, 1986, 1989). Before trying to settle on a definition of literacy, it is useful to consider some work by one of the most important contemporary literacy researchers, David Olson (e.g., Olson, 1977, 1985, 1986, 1996). We will begin our consideration of literacy as Olson and Astington (1986b, p. 8) began theirs, by quoting a famous interview between the Soviet psychologist Luria and an illiterate participant (Luria, 1976, p. 108). Luria was a student of Vygotsky's, and one of the most influential of Russian psychologists.

Luria began by presenting the illiterate participant with a syllogism. The syllogism went like this:

> 'In the Far North, where there is snow, all bears are white. Novaya Zemlya is in the Far North and there is always snow there. What colour are the bears there?'
> The illiterate participant replied, 'There are different sorts of bears.'
> Luria then repeated the syllogism.
> The illiterate participant responded with this: 'I don't know; I've seen a black bear, I've never seen any others . . . . Each locality has its own animals: if it's white, they will be white; if it's yellow, they will be yellow.
> Luria then asked directly, 'But what kind of bears are there in Novaya Zemlya?'
> The illiterate participant said, 'We always speak of what we see; we don't talk about what we haven't seen.'
> Finally, Luria asked, 'But what do my words imply?' and repeated the syllogism.
> The illiterate participant had the last word: 'Well, it's like this: Our tsar isn't like yours, and yours isn't like ours. Your words can be answered only by someone who was there, and if a person wasn't there he can't say anything on the basis of your words.'

The illiterate participant was reluctant to draw any conclusions from what Luria said. As Olson and Astington noted, the illiterate participant wanted to talk about real bears, whereas Luria wanted to talk about hypothetical bears. The illiterate participant did not want to talk about text, where text means either oral or written communication. Luria himself was demonstrating **metalinguistic awareness**, which is the ability to talk about language without worrying about what it refers to (Cazden, 1976; Yaden & Templeton, 1986). Sometimes metalinguistic awareness is described in terms of the ability to make language opaque (Cazden, 1976). When something is opaque, you cannot see through it. Usually the language we read or hear is transparent: we usually do not focus on the words themselves, but rather see through the words to the meaning they convey. Making language opaque means not seeing through the words, but focusing on the language itself.

When we consider language itself, we can begin to talk about that language. Ordinarily we use language to talk about things, but we can also use language to talk about language. When we use language to talk about language, we are using it as a *metalanguage*. Being literate can be taken to mean being able to talk or write about text, as in being able to discuss the text of one of Shakespeare's plays or write an essay about Shakespeare's use of language.

As Olson and Astington (1986b) pointed out, this view of literacy is much broader than simply being able to read and write. **Literacy** means 'being competent to participate in a certain form of discourse, whether one can read and write or not . . . . [Literacy means] competence in talking about talk, about questions, about answers, in a word, competence with a metalanguage' (p. 10). As such, literacy is occasionally thought of as a kind of cognitive steroid, enabling people to think in a way that they could not otherwise.

Literacy makes it possible to make a distinction between the oral or written text and interpretations of that text (Olson, 1986, p. 113). Being literate means being able to discuss different possible interpretations of a variety of texts such as plays, novels, laws, and regulations. As Olson pointed out, such interpretations are seen as subjective. That is, interpretations are regarded as the outcome of mental processes; they are not regarded as objectively given by the text. There is a certain kind of language that is used to describe this kind of mental process. This language includes such words as *interpret* and *infer* (Olson, 1986, p. 120). Such words are a part of the language of literacy: they are used for talking about text (Olson & Astington, 1986b, p. 12).

An implication of the preceding discussion is that when a person becomes literate, his or her language changes. It is likely that a literate person has available a stock of words to use when talking about text. Not surprisingly, the ability to use the language of literacy improves with age, and may not be mastered until the person has had considerable practice with such metalinguistic words (Olson & Astington, 1986a, p. 191).

Just as metalinguistic words emerge relatively late in the development of a person's language, so it turns out that most of the words people use to talk about talking came into the English language relatively late in its history. Olson and Astington (1986a, 1986b) reported that these words, such as *assert*, *contradict*, and *remark*, typically emerged during or after the sixteenth century. Other words, such as *know* and *think*, which are used to describe mental states but which are not used to talk about text, are usually much older. Thus, coinciding with the emergence of literacy is the use of a special language designed to refer to language itself.

The Consequences of Print Exposure

Stanovich and Cunningham (1992) pointed out that literacy is not an all-or-none state of affairs. Even people who are literate differ widely in the degree to which they are exposed to printed materials. It is possible that such variation may be correlated with important cognitive skills such as vocabulary and verbal fluency. To assess the strength of the relationship between print exposure and cognitive skills, Stanovich and Cunningham studied 300 undergraduate students from American state universities. These students were given several tests, including a test of general intelligence, as well as tests of cognitive skills such as vocabulary, verbal fluency, spelling, and history and literature knowledge. In addition, the degree to which the students had been exposed to print was assessed by several measures, including an author recognition test (ART) and a magazine recognition test (MRT). The ART asked students to indicate whether or not they are familiar with a series of book authors, while the MRT did the same for a series of magazines. The results were that scores on the ART and the MRT predicted scores on the cognitive skills measures even after general intelligence had been taken into account.

Stanovich and Cunningham's results suggest that print exposure makes an independent contribution to cognitive skills over and above general intelligence. It is noteworthy that the ART was a particularly powerful predictor of cognitive skills. The ART is an indirect measure of the degree to which a person reads books. 'Relative to magazine reading, exposure to books appears to be more related to positive verbal outcomes . . . . Perhaps there are differences in depth of processing typically associated with different types of reading material, with magazines being more likely to elicit shallow processing' (p. 63).

■ Language, Cognition, and Culture

Linguistic Relativity

In addition to being one of the most influential linguists of the twentieth century, Benjamin Lee Whorf (1956, p. 135) also worked for a fire insurance company. He was responsible for investigating the causes of many fires and explosions. In the course of this work, it became clear to him that fires were often caused by the way people perceived a situation. Moreover, people's perception of that situation was determined by the way that they described it. The words used to label objects shaped the behaviour in relation to those objects. Here is one of Whorf's examples.

People will exercise great caution around a set of containers labelled 'gasoline drums'. Because they know that gasoline is flammable, they will be careful about smoking in the vicinity. However, if the containers are labelled 'empty gasoline drums', then people will be less cautious. This is because the word *empty* not only suggests that there is no gasoline, but also that the containers are inert and not dangerous. In fact, as Whorf pointed out, empty gasoline drums are very dangerous because they contain gasoline vapour and are extremely flammable. However, the way the drums are labelled may make people perceive them as safe when they are not.

Notice the relationship between words and perception that is being brought out by this example. The word *empty* determines that a situation will be perceived as safe. Whorf gave many other examples of this sort, which are intended to show that how we see something is determined by the words we use to describe it. This kind of example shows how a particular language such as English conditions the way we analyze a situation. Suppose we spoke another language, which had a different way of describing the very same situation. Might not the way we perceive that situation be different because the language we used to describe it led to our perceiving it differently? This kind of question led to the formulation of what is often called the **Sapir-Whorf hypothesis**. Sapir was a linguist with whom Whorf studied, and whose ideas influenced Whorf greatly. Whorf began one of his papers by quoting Sapir (1949) on the relationship between language and experience. This quotation nicely gives the flavour of the Sapir-Whorf hypothesis:

> Human beings do not live in the objective world alone, nor alone in the world of social activity as ordinarily understood, but are very much at the mercy of the particular language which has become the medium of expression for their society. It is quite an illusion to imagine that one adjusts to reality essentially without the use of language and that language is merely an incidental means of solving specific problems of communication or reflection. The fact of the matter is that the 'real world' is to a large extent unconsciously built up on the language habits of the group. . . . We see and hear and otherwise experience very largely as we do because the language habits of our community predispose certain choices of interpretation. (p. 162)

The Sapir-Whorf hypothesis is not limited to the influence of the way in which single words shape the way we experience the world. The hypothesis is much more general. Whorf (1956) believed that different languages have different 'grammatical categories, such as plurality, gender, and similar classifications (animate, inanimate, etc.), tenses, voices and other verb forms, classifications of the type of parts of speech' (p. 137), which combine to create a particular system of categories that organizes our experience of the world. Whorf's view leads to **linguistic relativity**: the notion that two languages may be so different from each other as to make their native speakers' experience of the world quite different from each other (e.g., Black, 1962, p. 244). Whorf (1956) put it this way: 'The linguistic relativity principle . . . means, in informal terms, that users of markedly different grammars are . . . not equivalent as observers but must arrive at somewhat different views of the world' (p. 221).

Whorf grouped European languages, such as English, French, and German, together as standard average European (SAE) languages. He contrasted SAE languages with Amerindian languages such as Hopi, which he regarded as having a fundamentally different structure. Here is an example of the sort of basic difference between these languages that Whorf (1956, p. 141) thought was so important. In SAE, we have a pattern of description that follows the formula *form + substance*. We have names for substances such as *water*, *coffee*, and *meat*. These are called mass nouns. In our system, mass nouns denote formless substances. The word *bread*, for example, does not by itself convey anything about the size or shape of the bread. Bread is a substance existing independently of any particular case. Mass nouns refer to unbounded, or limitless, categories. When we describe a particular case using a mass noun, we must also include a description of its limits. Thus, we say *a loaf of bread*, or *a cup of coffee*, or *a glass of water*. We describe a form (e.g., *a glass of*) plus a substance (e.g., *water*). This way of describing things corresponds to the way in which we think about the world. We believe that the world consists of formless substances that are given a specific form on particular occasions. After describing this pattern of thought, which he said is common to speakers of SAE, Whorf went on to claim that Hopi speakers experience the world differently. In Hopi, all nouns refer to particular occurrences: '"water" means one certain mass or quantity of water, not what we call the substance water' (Whorf, 1956, p. 141). The Hopi speaker experiences the world in terms of specific events. This goes along with a different conception of time. Time is not thought of as existing independently of specific occurrences. Rather than having nouns that correspond to our summer and winter, the Hopi talk about specific occasions such as summer now (Whorf, 1956, p. 143).

A famous example of Whorf's is the number of words that the Inuit use for snow. The Inuit, many of whom live in Nunavut, a territory in Canada, used to be called 'Eskimos'. They are now called the Inuit, which means 'the people' in their language, Inuktitut. Whorf claimed that the Inuit have different words for our one word *snow*. This means, Whorf would say, that their perception of snow is more differentiated than ours. This example of the 'Whorfian hypothesis' is very widely believed. In fact, according to a document provided by the Canadian Department of Indian and Northern Affairs (2000), there are at least 14 words for snow in Inuktitut, ranging from *api-giannagaut* (the first snowfall of autumn) to *qiqumaaq* (snow whose surface has frozen after a light spring thaw).

Drawing on research by Martin (1986), Pullum (1991) attempted to debunk the more-words-for-snow hypothesis. He did this in two ways. First, Pullum looked carefully at the words that some researchers have claimed are Inuit words for snow. For example, *igluksaq* is supposed to be *snow for igloo-making*. However, it is actually formed from *iglu* (meaning *house*), and *ksaq* (meaning *material for*). So it means *house-building material*, and 'would probably include plywood, nails, perhaps bricks or roofing tiles' (Pullum, 1991, p. 169). Second, Pullum pointed out that there are many more English words used to refer to snow than are commonly realized. For example, consider *slush, sleet, blizzard, hardpack, powder, flurry, dusting*, and so on. The Inuit may perceive a great many different kinds of snow, but it is probably not because they have more words for it. Pullum suggests that if the Inuit do indeed perceive more different kinds of snow, it is because of their expertise with snow. In this respect, they are like other kinds of specialists. 'Horse breeders have various names for breeds, sizes, and ages of horses; botanists have names for leaf shapes; interior decorators have names for shades of mauve; printers have many different names for different fonts' and so on (Pullum, 1991, p. 165). The names are the result of their expertise and are not what determines their expertise.

In spite of the controversial nature of the Whorfian hypothesis, a milder version of it has nonetheless attracted favourable attention from some psychologists. For example, Hunt and Agnoli (1991) reviewed evidence suggesting that differences between languages may have effects on cognitive processes that are at least as important as the individual differences in cognitive processes found within a particular language community. That is, not only are there differences in cognitive processes between individuals all of whom speak the same language, but there are equally large differences in cognitive processes between people who speak different languages. Among the latter differences are cases in which two different languages 'cause speakers . . . to structure the same experience in different ways' (p. 379). One example of this possibility concerns **polysemy**. A polysemous word has more than one meaning. It turns out that English words are significantly more polysemous than are Italian words. Hunt and Agnoli (1991) point out that the English sentence 'I went out to buy the pot' is ambiguous because we do not 'know whether the speaker spends leisure time in gardening or recreational pharmacology' (p. 382). The corresponding Italian sentence ('Uscii a comperare il vaso') is, however, not ambiguous. Consequently, it is likely that a native English speaker requires more time to disambiguate such a sentence that would a native Italian speaker. On the basis of examples such as this, Hunt and Agnoli conclude that differences between languages can affect performance, even if it is the case that every sentence in any one language can be translated into a sentence in any other language.

Other current lines of investigation are reviving a stronger form of the hypothesis of linguistic relativity (Bloom & Keil, 2001, pp. 356–358). It is to a consideration of these that we now turn.

Colour Words

Another focus for the study of the relationships between language, thought, and culture has been the relation between colour perception and colour naming (Rosch, 1988, pp. 374ff.). On the one hand, colour names provide distinctive categories such as *red* and *green*. On the other hand, the physical stimulus for colour is continuous: different colours, or *hues*, are elicited by different wavelengths of light. The *visible spectrum* refers to those wavelengths of light that we can see. Within the visible spectrum, *blue* is elicited by relatively short wavelengths, whereas *red* is elicited by relatively long wavelengths (Ratliff, 1976, p. 313). Do colour names refer to the same parts of the visible spectrum regardless of culture, so that the same wavelength corresponds to *blue* for everyone? Or do different cultures carve up the visible spectrum differently, so that the wavelength for *blue* in one culture is not the same as the wavelength for *blue* in another? Perhaps what we call *blue* strikes someone from another culture as more *bluish green* because in their colour-naming system a true blue is located differently on the visible spectrum (R. Brown, 1968, p. 238).

A very influential study of the importance of colour names was that of R. Brown and Lenneberg (1956; R. Brown, 1968, pp. 239ff.). They had a group of judges select 24 colours that were representative of the entire range of colours. Of the 24 colours, eight were judged to be ideal examples of *red, green, yellow, blue, orange, purple, brown,* and *pink,* whereas the others were not judged to be as good exemplars of a colour category. This is a distinction between *central* and *peripheral* members of a colour category. Brown and Lenneberg then asked participants, all of whom had English as their native language, to name the 24 different colours. There were several differences between the central and peripheral colours. For example, the central colours were named more rapidly. Moreover, when participants were shown a mixture of colours they had seen earlier and colours to which they had not been exposed, the central colours were recognized as having been seen before. This finding, that colours that can be easily named are also more easily remembered, appeared to be quite reliable (Rosch, 1988, p. 376).

It would be interesting to know whether a culture with different colour names also remembered colours differently. Heider [Eleanor Rosch] and Olivier (1972) studied the Dani, an Indonesian New Guinea people who appeared to have only two colour names. Heider and Olivier reported that memory for colours was similar for both the Dani and American participants. Having a colour name available did not seem to be a prerequisite for being able to remember the colour. Moreover, the Dani appeared to remember central colours better than peripheral ones, just like American participants. These results implied that colours were not arbitrary, but that the structure of colour was similar for everyone. It is possible that central, or focal, colours are more perceptually salient than peripheral colours, and that colour names refer to those aspects of the spectrum that are most readily noticed. Heider and Olivier's work complemented the results of cross-cultural research conducted by Berlin and Kay (1969). They made a remarkable claim that we discuss next.

Berlin and Kay argued that there are 11 **basic colour terms,** and that there appears to be an invariant sequence regulating the emergence of these colour terms in any language. This sequence is diagrammed below, and can be described as follows. Although different languages may have different numbers of colour words, there is a particular order in which colour terms emerge in the history of a given language. If a language has only two colour terms, then those words will be black and white; those with only three colour terms have words for black, white, and red; those with five colour words have black, white, red, green, and yellow; and so on.

Black	Red	Green	Blue	Brown	Purple
White		Yellow			Pink
					Orange
					Grey

This invariance was claimed to arise as a consequence of the nature of the visual system (Kay & McDaniel, 1978; Ratliff, 1976; Rosch, 1988). The model of colour perception that was used to explain the **Berlin-Kay order** derives from Hering (1878/1961). Hering argued that red, green, blue, and yellow were *primary colours*, meaning that they were not experienced as blends of other colours, Hering's theory also attempted to capture the distinction between *achromatic* and *chromatic* colours. Achromatic colours cover the range between black through gray to white. Chromatic colours have hue, and are embodied by colours such as red, green, yellow, and blue. Hering invented the **opponent process theory of colour vision** (Hurvich & Jameson, 1957). Hering imagined that the process of colour vision was based on three pairs of antagonistic processes. The pairs are yellow-blue, red-green, and white-black, the last being responsible for achromatic colours. In the absence of stimulation, all pairs give rise to the experience of grey, which represents a state of balance between opponent processes. Light acts on each pair so as to yield one of its component colours, but inhibit the other. Thus, we cannot experience a 'reddish-green' because red and green form an antagonistic pair. However, one can experience a 'greenish-yellow' or a 'reddish blue', because these colours can both be activated at the same time (Hurvich & Jameson, 1957, p. 400). A Hering type of theory appears to ground the Berlin-Kay order in the visual system. Perhaps black, white, red, green, yellow, and blue refer not only to basic colour terms, but also to basic visual processes. Consequently names for these colours will emerge first. Other colour terms, such as *pink,* are blends of primary visual experiences, and consequently both less salient and less likely to be named.

Unfortunately, the Hering type of theory does not appear to be standing up to the test of time. Without denying that opponent process cells exist, the evidence still does not support the hypothesis for 'exactly two pairs of opponent hues nor three pairs of opponent colours' (Saunders & van Brakel, 1997, p. 178). Moreover, the visual system does not appear to process colour separately from other forms of visual information. 'There is strong evidence that between retina and cortex, processing of wavelength is intricately mixed with luminosity, form, texture, movement response, and other environmental change' (Saunders & van Brakel, 1997, p. 177). Davidoff (2001, p. 382) concluded that 'there is no evidence that neurones respond selectively to any of the four basic colours.' There would not appear to be a strong case for the existence of an isomorphism between the Berlin-Kay series and the physiology of the visual system.

There now appears to be some doubt about the universality of the Berlin-Kay series itself. Recall that, in their studies of the Dani, Heider [Eleanor Rosch] and Olivier (1972) found that having a colour name available did not seem to be a prerequisite for being able to remember the colour. In an attempt to replicate the Heider and Olivier result, Roberson, Davies, and Davidoff (2000) studied the Berinmo, another stone-age tribe from Papua New Guinea. The Berinmo language contains five colour terms:

- Wapa: *white and pale colours; also means European person*
- Kel: *black;* also means *dirty*
- Mehl: *red*
- Wor spans *yellow/orange/brown/khaki*
- Nol spans *green/blue/purple*; also means *live*

Participants were 22 Berinmo speakers and a matched British sample. They all were asked to name 40 different colour chips. They all took a memory task in which they were shown a colour chip for five seconds, then asked to pick it out of an array of 40 colour chips. The results did not replicate Heider and Olivier's findings. Rather, the pattern of Berinmo colour memory was different from that of the English speakers. The pattern of Berinmo colour memory was, however, related to Berinmo colour names. These data do not support the hypothesis that 'the colour space is universally similar and independent of language' (p. 377).

Davidoff, Davies, and Roberson (1999) took advantage of the fact that the Berinmo language does not distinguish between *blue* and *green,* but does make a distinction that is not made in English. Thus, *nol* spans *green/blue/purple* and is categorically different from *wor*, which spans *yellow/orange/brown/khaki*. Participants were shown and then asked to remember a colour for 30 seconds. They were then shown a pair of colours and asked to identify the one they had been shown previously. Suppose the participants are first shown a blue colour and then tested with a blue/green pair. This should be more difficult for the Berinmo than for the English participants, because blue and green are in the same language category for the former but in different categories for the latter. In general, pairs of colours within a category should be more difficult to choose between than pairs of colours from two different categories. This turned out to be true. English participants made relatively more errors when they had to choose between *nol* and *wor* colours, but the Berinmo made relatively more errors when they had to choose between *blue* and *green* colours. What is a qualitative distinction for one culture is a different shade for the other.

In a study that examined the acquisition of colour names in two different languages, Roberson, Davidoff, Davies, and Shapiro (2004) provided more evidence for the linguistic relativity hypothesis. They studied the Himba, 'a semi-nomadic cattle-herding tribe in northern Namibia' (p. 555). The Himba have five basic colour terms:

- Serandu spans *red*, *orange*, and *pink*
- Dumbu spans *beige*, *yellow*, and *light green*
- Zoozu spans all dark colours and *black*
- Vapa spans all light colours and *white*
- Burou spans *green*, *blue*, and *purple*

The acquisition of colour terms was studied for both English and Himba. Beginning at three or four years of age, the children were studied for three years. One finding was that the English children did not necessarily acquire colour words in the Berlin-Kay order. In both languages, there was considerable variability in the order in which colour terms were acquired. As the English and Himba children acquired colour terms, the pattern of their memory for colours changed, and the children began showing superior performance for items that are focal in their language. The conclusion was that colour categories are not the outcome of an innate unfolding of the visual system, but are acquired within a particular culture.

At least as far as colour words are concerned, the evidence is currently tilting towards the linguistic relativity hypothesis. However, Kay and Regier (2003) still maintained that there are 'genuine universal tendencies in colour naming' (p. 9085). They acknowledged that there is considerable variability in colour words between languages. However, based on survey data from over 100 unwritten languages, Kay and Regier conclude that there are 'universally privileged points . . . reflected in the basic colour terms of English' (p. 9089). Only time will tell how this long-standing controversy will play out. One suggestion, made by Regier and Kay (2004, p. 290) is that the 'universalist-relativist' dichotomy has outlived its usefulness, 'and that the field might benefit from its abandonment.' However, precisely what is to replace it remains unclear.

Language and Spatial Frames of Reference

The linguistic relativity hypothesis is certainly alive and well in the study of spatial frames of reference. This topic is related to our discussion of **spatial frames of reference** in the chapter on imagery. The studies reviewed there suggested that we imagine ourselves as being upright in a spatial framework that can be described by such terms as *above-below, ahead-behind*, and *left-right* (Tversky, 2003). However, the *we* in the preceding sentence refers to the speakers of English, who are often the only participants in psychological studies. How about speakers of other languages? It turns out there are at least three spatial frames of reference found in different languages (Levinson, 1996).

The differences between the three can be illustrated by means of Figure 8.6a, which is based on an example from Levinson, Kita, Haun, and Rasch (2002, p. 159). One could say that *the man is at the chair's back*. This illustrates an **intrinsic frame of reference** because it is based on the relations between the objects being described. Another possible description is *the man is to the right of the chair*. This illustrates a **relative frame of reference** because the man is only to the right of the chair *relative to* an observer's position. The relative frame of reference is the one most familiar to speakers of English. Finally, one could say that *the man is to the north of the chair*. This is called an **absolute frame of reference** because the relations between the objects are described in terms of an invariant set of co-ordinates. You might find this last example puzzling, and feel that the man should be described as *east* of the chair. However, that is only because maps are typically drawn with north at the top, and east on the right, *relative to* the observer. In fact, most English speakers are often unaware of the actual direction of *north*. In the figure, the man actually could be north of the chair in an absolute frame of reference.

Now imagine yourself walking around behind the picture, and looking at it from the other side. What you would see is given in Figure 8.6b. Describe the relations between the man and the chair from within each frame of reference. The man is still at the chair's *back* and to the *north* of the chair. However, he is now to the *left* of the chair. Thus, when the spectator moves it affects the orientation of objects within the relative frame of reference, but leaves the other frames of reference unchanged.

Suppose there were languages that described spatial relations in an intrinsic or absolute frame of reference, but not in a relative frame of reference. In fact, there are such languages. For example, Tzeltal, a Mayan language, uses the word *uphill* to mean approximately *south*, and the word *downhill* to mean approximately *north*. In this language you might say the equivalent of *I left my glasses to the north of the telephone* (Majid, Bowerman, Kita, Haun, & Levinson, 2004, p. 109). Does this different way of speaking correspond to a different way of representing space? In a series of clever experiments, Levinson and his colleagues (e.g., Levinson, Kita, Haun, & Rasch, 2002; Pederson, Danziger, Wilkins, Levinson, Kita, & Senft, (1998) have demonstrated the effect of language on spatial representation. One example is given in Figure 8.7. Participants are shown a toy person being moved by the experimenter along the path represented on the viewing table. After a delay of 30 seconds, the participant is then rotated 180° and shown a maze on the testing table. The participant's task was to 'choose the path that the toy person had followed' (Majid, Bowerman, Kita, Haun, & Levinson, 2004, p. 110). If the

Figure 8.6 The man is at the chair's back.

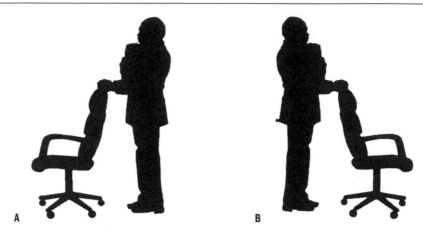

participants spoke Tzeltal, they tended to choose a path based on an absolute frame of reference. However, if the participants were Dutch, then they overwhelmingly chose a path based on a relative frame of reference. Dutch, like English, specializes in a relative linguistic framework. Thus each group's responses were consistent with their habitual frame of reference. The conclusion, based on experiments of this sort, was that the par-

Figure 8.7 The relationship of language and space.

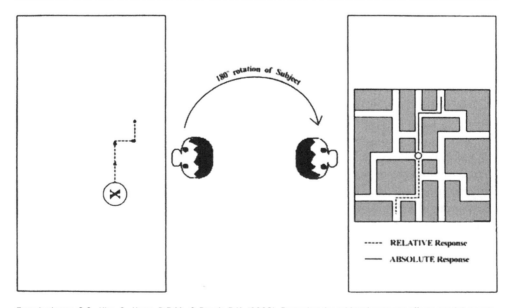

From Levinson, S.C., Kita, S., Haun, D.B.M., & Rasch, B.H. (2002). Returning the tables: Language affects spatial reasoning. *Cognition, 84*, p. 165. Copyright 2002. Reprinted by permission of Elsevier.

ticular language spoken provides speakers with a way of representing space that they must use in order to be able to communicate with others in their linguistic community.

Without endorsing its conclusions, Bloom and Keil (2001, p. 358) considered Levinson's line of research to be 'one of the most promising attempts to explore the relationship between the linguistic difference and cognitive differences'. Some investigators are prepared to conclude that 'Whorf's original idea about how language shapes categories might be right after all' (Yoshida & Smith, 2005). However, there are those who still claim that spatial frames of reference are universal. For example, Gallistel (2002a, 2002b) argued that the brain can represent a number of different spatial frameworks, and that these are available for use quite independently of the language spoken. In a similar vein, Clark (2004) suggested that languages do not obliterate conceptual frameworks that are inconsistent with them. Although different languages highlight certain categories rather than others, one is not fated to think only in the ways that language provides.

We do not yet know the final verdict on the linguistic relativity hypothesis. However, the revival of the linguistic relativity hypothesis is due to 'the kind of cross-cultural work . . . [which] psychologists have traditionally left to linguists and anthropologists . . . . I hope that [these studies] will inspire more cognitive and developmental psychologists to go into the field and pursue these kinds of comparisons, which are the only way to really find out which aspects of perception and cognition are universal and which are culture and language specific' (B. Malt, as quoted in Adelson, 2005, p. 26).

■ Questions for Study and Discussion

1. Outline the development of Chomsky's various approaches to language, including his views of the evolution of language.
2. Review evidence bearing on the innateness hypothesis, paying particular attention to the poverty of the stimulus argument.
3. Discuss the process of communication and comprehension, using figurative language to illustrate the process.
4. Discuss evidence for and against the linguistic relativity hypothesis. Which side of the debate are you on? Why?

■ Key Concepts

Absolute frame of reference Spatial relations are described in terms of an invariant set of co-ordinates.

Basic colour terms (Berlin-Kay order) The hypothesis that there is an invariant sequence regulating the emergence of colour terms in any language.

Code model and inferential model of communication Models of communication based on the information processing and Grice's inferential theory, respectively.

Competence and performance A person may have an internalized system of rules that constitutes a basic linguistic competence, but this competence may not always be reflected in the person's actual use of the language (performance).

Concealing function and revealing function The hypothesis that language is a kind of code. The parameters that are set for one language conceal its meanings from the speakers of another language.

Conversational maxims (relevance theory) Speakers attempt to say no more than is necessary (maxim of quantity); they try to be truthful (maxim of quality); they attempt to be relevant (maxim of relation); and they strive to avoid ambiguity (maxim of manner).

Co-operative principle (Grice) The assumption that the speaker intends to say something concise, truthful, relevant, and unambiguous.

Deep and surface structure The sequence of words that makes up a sentence constitutes a surface structure that is derived from an underlying deep structure.

Definition of literacy (Olson) Competence with a metalanguage.

Egocentric speech (Piaget) Speech that does not take the listener's perspective into account.

Figurative language Various figures of speech, such as metaphor and irony.

Given, new contract A process whereby the speaker agrees to connect new information to what the listener already knows.

Grammatical transformations Rules operating on entire strings of symbols, converting them to new strings.

Hesitation pauses Pauses in speech often characterized by disfluencies, such as *um* or *uh*.

Innateness hypothesis The hypothesis that children innately possess a language acquisition device that comes equipped with principles of universal grammar.

Inner speech (Vygotsky) Speech for oneself that regulates thought.

Intrinsic frame of reference Spatial relations are based solely on the relations between the objects being described.

Language Open-ended verbal communication that consists of all possible sentences.

Language acquisition device (LAD) and universal grammar The hypothesis that children possess a language acquisition device, or LAD, that contains general principles that apply to any natural language (universal grammar).

Minimalism The belief that linguistic competence has only those characteristics that are absolutely necessary.

Mirror neurons Broca's area in monkeys contains neurons that not only fire when the animal makes grasping movements, but also fire when the monkey observes other animals making those movements.

Opponent process theory of colour vision (Hering) The hypothesis that colour vision is based on three pairs of antagonistic processes.

Parameter setting The hypothesis that language acquisition involves a universal grammar that contains a variety of switches, which can be set to one of a number of possible values, or parameters. A parameter is a universal aspect of language that can take on one of a small set of possible values.

Parental reformulations Adult reformulations of children's speech constitute negative evidence because they inform children when their utterances are erroneous. At the same time, they also provide positive instances of correct speech.

Phrase structure rules Rules describing the way in which symbols can be rewritten as other symbols.

Poverty of the stimulus argument The hypothesis that the linguistic environment to which a child is exposed is too deficient to enable the child to acquire language on that basis alone.

Pretense theory of irony When speaking ironically, the speaker is only pretending to say what he or she says.

Recursion A process that refers to itself.

Relative frame of reference Spatial relations are described relative to an observer's viewpoint.

Sapir-Whorf hypothesis The hypothesis that two languages may be so different from each other as to make their native speakers' experience of the world qualitatively different from each other.

Speech Those sentences that are actually spoken; only a small subset of language.

Syntactic development The development of the ability to organize words into grammatical sentences.

Tree diagrams A description of a process that proceeds from one level at which a number of relationships are simultaneously present to other levels at which these relationships are serially ordered.

Zone of proximal development (Vygotsky) 'The distance between the actual developmental level as determined by independent problem-solving and the level of potential development as determined through problem-solving under adult guidance or in collaboration with more capable peers.'

■ Links to Other Chapters

Innateness hypothesis
Chapter 3 (domain-specific modules)
Chapter 5 (evolution of memory systems)
Chapter 7 (implicit and explicit learning)
Chapter 12 (musical intelligence)
Chapter 13 (emotion and memory)
Language acquisition device
Chapter 12 (evolution of *g*)
Recursion
Chapter 10 (paradoxes, reasoning, and recursion)

Relevance theory
Chapter 10 (interpretation of 'some')
Inner speech
Chapter 14 (text messaging)
Zone of proximal development
Chapter 14 (successful versus unsuccessful metacognition)
Frames of reference
Chapter 6 (egocentric frame of reference)

■ Further Reading

D. Bickerton advanced an influential version of the hypothesis that there is a specific innate faculty that contains a model of language. Much of his work is based on fascinating studies of pidgin and creole languages. Pidgin originally referred to Chinese speakers who took English words and rearranged them consistent with Chinese word order, and was a means of communication between Chinese and English speakers at seaports. Thus, pidgin consists of words strung together in a relatively unstructured manner. See Bickerton, D. (1984). The language bioprogram hypothesis. *Behavioral and Brain Sciences, 7,* 173–221; Bickerton, D.J. (1988). A two-stage model of the human language faculty. In S. Straus (Ed.), *Ontogeny, phylogeny and historical development* (pp. 86–105). Norwood, NJ: Ablex; and Bickerton, D. (2000). Resolving discontinuity: A minimalist distinction between human and non-human minds. *American Zoologist, 40,* 862–873.

Judgements of grammaticality often rest on a rather elusive criterion of the intuitions of native speakers of the language. Just how problematic these intuitions can be is spelled out in Carroll, J.M., Bever, T.G., & Pollack, C.R. (1981). The non-uniqueness of linguistic intuitions. *Language, 57,* 368–383.

A study of individual differences in the use of irony is Ivanko, S., Pexman, P.M., & Olineck, K.M. (2004). How sarcastic are you? *Journal of Language and Social Psychology, 23,* 244–271.

An intriguing aspect of literacy is brought out in Eskritt, M., Lee, K., & Donald, M. (2001). The influence of symbolic literacy on memory. *Canadian Journal of Psychology, 55,* 39–50.

More effects of language on categorization are in Sera, M.D., Elieff, C., Forbes, J., Burch, M.C., Rodríguez, W., & Dubois, D.P. (2002). When language affects cognition and when it does not: An analysis of grammatical gender and classification. *Journal of Experimental Psychology: General, 131,* 377–397.

Chapter 9

Problem-Solving

■ Insight Problems and the Gestalt Theory of Thinking

We briefly considered the Gestalt psychologists in Chapter 2. *Gestalt* means form or configuration. Gestalt psychologists argued that consciousness does not consist simply of one event after another but tends to be organized into a coherent whole, or *Gestalt*. As an example, recall Figure 2.7, the Necker cube. This is a reversible cube, in which first one and then another face of the cube is in the foreground. We considered other reversible figures in Chapter 6, on imagery (Figures 6.9 and 6.10). The reversibility of such figures is all-or-none. You can see one or the other organization, but not both. The experience you have when the figure suddenly changes is called a **gestalt switch** (Hanson, 1958; Kuhn, 1970; Searle, 2000; Wright; 1992).

Gestalt switches can also occur in response to verbal material. For example, consider the following, from Koffka (1935, p. 640).

> Swimming under a bridge came two ducks in front of two ducks, two ducks behind two ducks, and two ducks in the middle. How many ducks were there in all?

If you are like most people, your spontaneous answer is *six*, because your representation of the ducks is organized like this.

O O

O O

O O

The description of 'two ducks' makes you think of *pairs* of ducks. However, suppose I told you that the ducks were swimming in a single file. Now you may realize there is another organization that fits the description just as well, and is simpler. The answer is that that there were *four* ducks, organized like this.

O

O

O

O

When you realized that four ducks is a simpler solution to the problem, you may have experienced the sort of gestalt switch that is characteristic of **insight problems**. In an insight problem the participant is typically given all the information needed to solve the problem. The participant does not need to acquire additional information. However, the way the problem is initially represented prevents the participant from seeing the solution. An insight problem may be defined as one that requires 'a re-structuring of the way in which it is represented before [a] solution is possible' (Gilhooly, 2003, p. 478; Weisberg, 1995, p. 161). By no means all problems are insight problems, and we will explore other problem types as we go along. To begin with, however, we will concentrate on insight problems.

The Gestalt theory of insight has been very controversial, but it is still central to current problem-solving research. Before we can evaluate contemporary research on insight, we need to be as clear as we can be about what the Gestalt psychologists meant by the term *insight*. To do this, let us review some examples from the Gestalt psychologists' work on this topic.

Köhler and the Mentality of Apes

Köhler (1925/1956) was marooned on the island of Tenerife during World War I. While there he studied the process of problem-solving in chimpanzees. Köhler described his work as concerned with testing 'the intelligence of the higher apes . . . whether they do not behave with intelligence and insight under conditions which require such behavior' (Köhler, 1925/1956, p. 3). Chimpanzees were useful participants because they could be placed in an experimental situation and required to solve a problem that they may never have faced before. Köhler described the behaviour of one of his chimpanzees, Sultan, who was in a cage with fruit outside beyond his reach. There was a small stick *in* the cage, and a longer stick just *outside* the bars. The longer stick

> cannot be grasped with the hand. But it can be pulled within reach by means of the small stick. Sultan tries to reach the fruit with the smaller of the two sticks. Not succeeding, he tears at a piece of wire that projects from the netting of his cage, but that, too, is in vain. Then he gazes about him; (there are always in the course of these tests some long pauses, during which the animals scrutinize the whole visible area). He suddenly picks up the little stick once more, goes up to the bars directly opposite to the long stick, scratches it towards him with the [small stick],

seizes it, and goes with it to the point opposite to the objective, which he secures. From the moment his eyes fall upon the long stick, his procedure forms one consecutive whole . . . [and] follows, quite suddenly on an interval of hesitation and doubt. (Köhler, 1925/1956, pp. 155–156)

To Köhler, the behavior Sultan displayed was insightful. By *insight*, Köhler meant the ability to understand the way in which the parts of a situation are related to one another. Insight occurred spontaneously and suddenly, and involved a perceptual restructuring of the situation. The animal suddenly saw how to solve the problem. Insightful problem-solving was all-or-none: the animal saw the solution or it did not.

Wertheimer and Productive Thinking

Wertheimer (1959) is often considered to be the founder of Gestalt psychology. His book on problem-solving was called *Productive thinking*. In order to begin to get a handle on what is meant by **productive thinking**, let us consider Wertheimer's (1959, p. 266) *altar window problem*.

The problem goes as follows, and is illustrated in Figure 9.1. Imagine that there is a circular altar window, and that it is to be decorated by surrounding it with gold paint. The area to be painted gold is bounded by two parallel, vertical lines tangent to the circle and equal in length to the diameter of the circle. These lines are joined by semicircles. How much paint is needed? Or what is the area inside the lines but outside the window?

Wertheimer described several attempts to solve this problem. The accounts from some of his adult participants are particularly instructive. They interpreted the problem in terms of what they had learned from similar problems in the past. Some of them felt certain that they could solve such an apparently simple problem. However,

Figure 9.1 The Altar Window Problem.

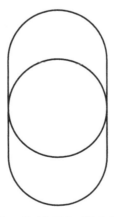

they attempted to apply solution procedures blindly, without any real conception of what the problem required. Thus, it was easy for them to find the area of the window itself because they already knew the formula for finding the area of a circle. Similarly, it was easy to see how the area of the semicircles at the top and the bottom of the figure could be calculated. However, they could not remember any formulas for the area of 'the four funny remainders' (Wertheimer, 1959, p. 267).

Enter a child with no mathematical training. His first reaction to the problem is to say that, of course, he does not know enough to be able to solve it. Humility in the face of problems is always a good way to begin! Then he looks at the figure for a moment and realizes that the top and bottom semicircles fit inside the window. Thus, the area required is simply the area of a square.

The child is capable of seeing the relationships between the parts of the whole figure, and this is all that is required to enable him to see the solution. Too often, as in the case of Wertheimer's educated participants, superficial learning interferes with the ability to see what might be obvious to a more naive person. As the saying goes, a little learning is a dangerous thing.

The altar window example shows why Wertheimer argued that there are two types of thinking. The opposite of productive thinking is **structurally blind** thinking. The latter is the kind of thinking shown by those adult participants who reproduced thinking they had done before in other situations, which was inappropriate for this situation. Instead of thinking reproductively, the child thought productively, by being sensitive to the structural requirements of the particular problem he was asked to solve.

In order to think productively, you need to go beyond just having a little knowledge that you can misapply. From Wertheimer's viewpoint, you need to have a grasp of the general principles that apply in the particular situation in which you find yourself. Here are some insight problems illustrating this process.

Look at Figure 9.2. Suppose that a is 5 inches long and b is $5\frac{1}{2}$ inches long. The problem is to find the area of the square plus the strip (Wertheimer, 1967b, p. 279). The productive approach to a problem such as this is to ask yourself, 'What general truths do I know that might fit situations like this?' In order to discover them, you need to perceptually restructure this situation, and realize that the figure can be decomposed into two triangles of base b and height a. Now you can realize that the general principle you need is the formula for finding the area of a triangle, which is $\frac{1}{2}(a \times b)$. Because there are two triangles, the required area is $(2 \times \frac{1}{2})(a \times b)$, or just $a \times b$. Thus, formulas you have learned in the past can be very useful, but they need to be applied with an understanding of the structural requirements of the situation. That is, they need to be used with insight into the problem's structure.

The tendency to apply previous learning blindly can sometimes lead you to get the right answer without understanding why it is right. Consider the following problem (Wertheimer, 1967b, p. 280). Is this number divisible by nine?

1,000,000,000,000,000,000,000,000,000,000,008

Figure 9.2 Find the Area of the Square Plus the Strip.

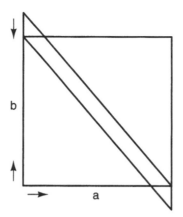

From Wertheimer, M. (1925/1967). The syllogism and productive thinking. In W.D. Ellis (Ed.), *A source book of Gestalt psychology*. New York: Humanities Press, p. 279. Copyright 1967 by Routledge & Kegan Paul. Reprinted by permission.

Suppose you try to solve this by entering the number in a calculator and dividing by nine. It turns out that the answer has no remainder, so you correctly conclude that, yes indeed, the number is divisible by nine. But you do not know why yet. To really have insight into the problem, you need to see that this number can be decomposed into two numbers. Thus:

$$\frac{\begin{array}{r} 999,999,999,999,999,999,999,999,999,999,999 \\ +9 \end{array}}{1,000,000,000,000,000,000,000,000,000,000,008}$$

Because both numbers are divisible by nine, their sum must also be divisible by nine. This insight will hold for any numbers of the same form.

Duncker and Functional Fixedness

Duncker (1945) was particularly interested in the effect that previous experience has on problem-solving. When you have a problem, the easiest way to try to deal with it is to rely on memory. We ask ourselves, 'What did I do in similar situations in the past?' Duncker called this activity **analysis of the situation**, and it involves determining what functions the objects in the situation have and how they can be used to solve the problem. Each object can be seen as potentially performing several different functions. Sometimes we are unable to see that a particular object could perform the function we need to solve a problem. When that happens, we are functionally fixed.

Here is an example of **functional fixedness**, called the coin problem (Simmel, 1953). Suppose you have eight coins and a balance. One of the coins is counterfeit, and therefore lighter than the others. How can you find the counterfeit coin by using the balance only twice? Think about it.

Most people initially think of dividing the coins into two groups of four coins each. One of the groups of four will be lighter and so must contain the counterfeit coin. Then you can take the four coins from that group and weigh them two against two. Of course, one of the groups of two will be lighter. However, you cannot determine which of the two remaining coins is counterfeit, because you have already used the balance twice.

Before we consider how to approach this problem correctly, let us analyze the previous solution attempt. Why do we initially divide the coins into two groups of four? One reason is that we know that eight things can be evenly divided into two groups of four. One of the functions of the number eight is that it can be so divided. The fact that 4 + 4 = 8 is a highly available bit of knowledge for us. Because this property of the number eight is so available, it is the first thing we think of. In fact, when people try to solve this problem, they often keep coming back to the four versus four division. When the obvious way of using materials keeps us from seeing the correct way of using them, then we are functionally fixed.

In Simmel's coin problem, the solution is often very difficult to see. You need to divide the coins in a way that is far from obvious at first. Suppose you divide them into three groups of three, three, and two coins. Then, weigh three versus three. If they balance, then the counterfeit coin must be in the group of two coins. Your second weighing, then, is to take the group of two coins, and weigh one versus one. Alternatively, suppose on your first weighing that one group of three coins is lighter. Then on your second weighing, take any two of the three coins from the lighter group and weigh one against the other. If they balance, then the third (unweighed) coin must be the counterfeit one. If they do not balance, then the lighter one is counterfeit. This procedure is guaranteed to find the solution. However, it is much more complex and unfamiliar than the wrong procedure.

Finding solutions to problems may require you to overcome functional fixedness. It may only be after you have realized that the obvious ways of tackling a problem do not work that you will be open to a reorganization of the problem that will allow you to see the solution. Variables that may determine the presence or absence of functional fixedness are considered later in this chapter.

Maier and the Concept of Direction

N.R.F. Maier was not one of the original Gestalt psychologists, but he adopted many of their ideas in his approach to the study of thinking. He is usually credited with introducing one of the most difficult among insight problems, called the nine-dot problem. This problem is illustrated in Figure 9.3. It requires you to connect all the dots with four straight lines without lifting your pencil from the paper (the solution is given in the second part of the figure). Notice that the solution requires that you draw lines extending outside the square formed by the dots. Many people make the assumption that you can draw lines only within the square, which keeps some people from seeing the solution.

A Gestalt psychologist might say that the problem-solver is fixated by this unnecessary assumption, and once this fixation is overcome, the person can solve the prob-

Figure 9.3 The Nine-dot Problem.

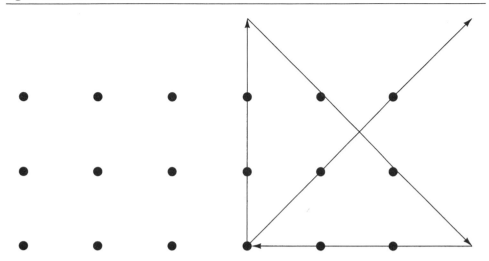

lem. Weisberg and Alba (1981) reasoned that, if participants were told that they could draw lines outside the square area, they should be able to solve the problem more easily than if they were not given such a **hint**. However, even when given the hint many participants still did not solve the problem. 'The Gestalt view holds that once fixation is broken the solution either appears whole in a flash of insight or is produced smoothly as one step leads to another' (Weisberg, 1986, p. 45). Because this is not what happens, Weisberg and Alba concluded that there is no evidence for the Gestalt theory of how problem-solving works.

Weisberg and Alba's conclusion led to a controversy over the nature of insight (e.g., Dominowski, 1981; Ohlsson, 1984). Ellen (1982) tried to show that Weisberg and Alba's account of Gestalt theory was incorrect. To do this he relied on Maier's (1931/1968; 1970) classic explorations of problem-solving in the Gestalt tradition. One of Maier's best-known problems is the two-string problem shown in Figure 9.4. There are two strings hanging from the ceiling. The participant must tie the two strings together, but they are too short for the participant to reach one while holding onto the other. The productive solution is to tie any weight onto one of the strings, set

Figure 9.4 Maier's Two-string Problem.

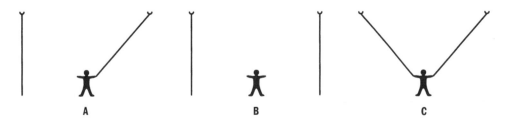

A   B   C

it swinging, go and get the second string, walk over to the middle of the room, and wait for the first string to swing over to you. Then you can tie them together.

If participants did not see the solution spontaneously, Maier gave them a hint. He brushed past one of the strings, setting it swinging. After this hint, several participants solved the problem. For many of them, the solution appeared suddenly, as a whole. However, when the solution appeared suddenly as a whole, participants were unlikely to attribute the solution to the hint that Maier gave them. Maier (1931/1968) interpreted these results in the Gestalt way:

> Changes in meaning and organization are experienced suddenly . . . it is not surprising to find that the very thing which sets off this combination is unexperienced. Before the solution is found there is disharmony. The reasoner cannot quite see the relation of certain things in the room to the solution of the problem. The next experience is of having an idea. The 'transformation' or 'organization' stage is not experienced in reasoning any more than in a reversible perspective. [Just like the reversible figures we considered in the chapter on imagery.] The new organization is suddenly there. It is the dominant experience and covers any factor that just preceded it. (p. 26)

In other words, an insightful experience can mask the hint that gave rise to it.

Maier argued that, in order to be effective, a hint must be consistent with the direction that the person's thinking is taking. A hint cannot be useful unless it responds to a difficulty that the person has already experienced. A hint given out of the blue cannot be seen by the person as relevant to his or her problem. Ellen argued that the hint given by Weisberg and Alba to their participants was irrelevant to the direction of their participants' thought, and so was useless to them. That is why they tended to have no insightful solutions.

Insight is Involuntary

Metcalfe and Wiebe (1987) attempted to clarify the distinction between problems that have insightful solutions and problems that are solved without insight. They pointed out that one of the essential characteristics of an insight problem is that the solution appears suddenly, without warning. In this chapter we have already considered several examples of insight problems with this characteristic. By contrast, problems solved without insight are solved gradually rather than suddenly. In the latter case, the solution process involves a stepwise progression towards the solution. Metcalfe and Wiebe suggested that many arithmetic and algebra problems are in this class. For example, finding the square root of 16 does not require an insightful solution. It requires instead the application of a stepwise solution procedure.

Metcalfe and Wiebe believed that participants should be able to distinguish between these two problem types. As participants solve a non-insight problem, they should be able to tell that they are getting closer to the solution. One way of expressing the feeling participants might have as they approach the solution of a problem is to say that they are 'getting warm'. That is, for non-insight problems participants should have a greater **feeling of warmth** as they get closer and closer to the solution. This is because non-insight problems are solved step by step, and with each step the participant is getting warmer. However, for insight problems there is not a gradual approach to the solution, and so participants should not feel that they are getting warmer until the solution actually appears. Concretely, consider what this means if you ask participants to rate their feelings of warmth as they solve a problem in a four-minute interval. Feeling-of-warmth ratings should gradually get higher as the solution is approached for non-insight problems. However, for insight problems feeling-of-warmth ratings should stay more or less level until the solution is reached, at which time they should rise dramatically. In their experiments, Metcalfe and Wiebe found that this was largely the case.

Metcalfe and Wiebe also examined **feeling-of-knowing** ratings. Before they tried to solve them, participants were asked to rank in order a set of problems from those they thought they would be able to solve to those they thought they might not be able to solve. They then tried to solve the problems. For non-insight problems, participants were able to predict fairly accurately which ones they could solve, and which ones they could not. For insight problems, there was no such predictability. These results are consistent with the hypothesis that participants are aware of the procedures they can

Figure 9.5 Felling-of-warmth Ratings as a Function of Time Spent Solving the Problem.

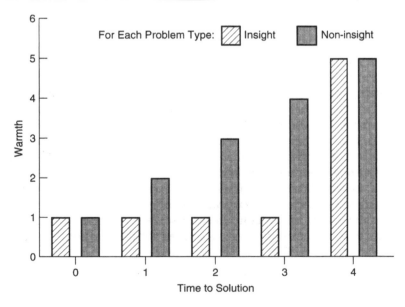

Data from Metcalfe, J., & Wiebe, D. (1987). Intuition in insight and non-insight problem solving. *Memory and Cognition*, *15*, pp. 238–246.

use to solve non-insight problems. They can predict which ones they will be able to solve based on whether or not they possess the relevant knowledge. By contrast, insight problems are solved by the sudden emergence of knowledge of which the participant was not aware before attempting to solve the problem.

Feelings of knowing and feelings of warmth reflect judgements that participants make about their own knowledge. Such judgements are examples of **metacognition**, which refers to what you know about what you know—how accurately you can assess your own cognitive processes. Metcalfe and Wiebe showed that people's metacognitive assessments of their performance on non-insight problems are quite accurate. However, their metacognitive assessments of their performance on insight problems are not accurate, because an insight is not something that can be planned. An insight is something that happens to you, not something that you decide to have.

■ Current Approaches to Insight Problems

Jones (2003) observed that there are two contrasting approaches to the study of insight problems. One approach he called the **progress monitoring theory**, and the other he called the **representational change theory**. Let us look at each of these in turn.

Progress Monitoring Theory

This approach is represented by the work of MacGregor, Ormerod, and Chronicle (2001; Ormerod, MacGregor, & Chronicle, 2002; Chronicle, MacGregor, & Ormerod, 2004). Their central idea is that participants take what seems to them to be the most straightforward route to a solution. However, in an insight problem the most straightforward route invariably leads to failure. Only when the participants realize that they have gone down a blind alley do they then consider alternative possibilities. The participants monitor their progress on a problem, and when they reach an impasse then they are open to an insightful solution.

In one experiment participants were given the nine-dot problem with one correct line already drawn. Look again at Figure 9.3. One group of participants was given the problem with a line connecting three dots horizontally and extending outside the area of the square. Another group of participants group was given the problem with a diagonal line that did not extend outside the area of the square. Since drawing lines outside the square is crucial to the solution, one might think that the horizontal line would be more effective. However, the diagonal line led to the greatest percentage of participants solving the problem.

The reason why the diagonal line is superior is that it leads the participant to reach an impasse more quickly. Participants typically only look ahead one or two moves at a time, and try to connect the most dots possible with each line. Given the diagonal line they can more easily see that if they follow a strategy of connecting the most dots possible with each line, then they will be out of moves before reaching the solution. This realization prompts the participant to consider alternative strategies, eventuating in a solution.

Representational Change Theory

This approach is represented by the work of Knoblich, Ohlsson, Haider, and Rhenius (1999; Knoblich, Ohlsson, & Raney, 2001). Like the Gestalt psychologists, they argued that insight requires a change in the way that the participant represents the problem. Their unique contribution is to hypothesize that there are two processes central to the achieving of representational change. These two processes are **constraint relaxation** and **chunk decomposition**. By constraint relaxation is meant the removal of assumptions that are blocking problem solution. For example, a constraint that may block the solution of the nine-dot problem is the assumption that lines may not go outside of the square area. By chunk decomposition is meant that parts of the problem that are seen as belonging together (chunks) are separated and thought about independently. An example given by Knoblich et al. (1999, p. 1536) is that highly skilled chess players see familiar patterns of chess pieces, but can also decompose these patterns into individual pieces when necessary.

The role of these two processes in insight problems can be illustrated by means of *matchstick arithmetic problems*. These are equations that are composed of Roman numerals which are themselves made up of matchsticks. Here is an example.

$$VI = III+III$$

The equation says that 6 (VI) equals 3 (III) plus 3 (III). Now consider the following:

$$IV = III+III$$

This equation is clearly incorrect, since 4 (IV) does not equal 3 (III) plus 3 (III). However, it can be made correct by moving only one matchstick. Can you tell which one? If not, look again at the first example.

To solve problems like these, people familiar with ordinary arithmetic need to relax constraints that they have learned. For example, in ordinary arithmetic you cannot simply change one number (e.g., 4) into another (e.g., 6). However, as we have just seen, in matchstick arithmetic you *can* change IV into VI by simply moving the matchstick on the left of the V to the right of the V. Another condition for solving matchstick arithmetic problems is that you must be able to decompose chunks. For example, the configuration V is a chunk. Now consider the following equation. What do you need to do to make both sides equal?

$$V = II$$

The V is composed of two matchsticks. If you make them each vertical, then you would have II = II. Alternatively, you could make the right-hand side of the equation into V by tilting the vertical matchsticks obliquely to one another, like this: V = V.

Both constraint relaxation and chunk decomposition promote insight by facilitating the construction of novel representations. In one study, Knoblich, Ohlsson, and

Raney (2001) monitored eye movements as participants solved matchstick arithmetic problems. Presumably eye movements are an index of those parts of the problem about which the participant is thinking. Successful solvers spent more time looking at the parts of the problem that required constraint relaxation and/or chunk decomposition, a result that supports the hypothesis that these processes lead to a change in the way the problem is represented.

The finding that eye movements can successfully predict insightful solutions has been replicated by Grant and Spivey (2003). They made solutions more likely by highlighting those parts of a problem situation to which attention should be paid. Guiding the problem-solver's attention may be a useful way of facilitating solutions. 'Although it may often seem that attention and eye movements are the result of cognitive processing, it may be that sometimes cognitive processing is the result of attention and eye movements' (p. 466).

Jones (2003, p. 1026) noted that both the progress monitoring and the representational change theories are not contradictory. The former theory concerns the processes that produce an impasse that leads the participant to seek an insightful solution. The latter theory provides an account of the processes that provide an insightful solution. Thus, both theories should be seen as complementary.

Insight and the Brain

In the chapter on attention, we discussed evidence that the anterior cingulate cortex (ACC) detects conflicting response tendencies and facilitates the process whereby the person becomes aware of such conflicts. Luo and Niki (2003; Luo, Niki, & Philips, 2004; Mai, Luo, Wu, & Luo, 2004) have found evidence for ACC involvement in the insight process using both functional Magnetic Resonance Imaging and Event-Related Potential techniques. Participants in their studies were given riddles such as *What can move heavy logs but cannot move a small nail?* Most participants cannot come up with the answer, but generate responses they know to be incorrect such as *a crane.* If they could not think of an answer, they were given it. In this case, the answer is *a river.* Participants reported having an *Aha!* experience on learning the answer. Corresponding to these insight experiences was activation in the ACC. The authors suggested that the ACC may be involved in detecting the conflict between the way in which one was thinking and the correct way to solve the problem.

Luo and Niki (2003) also reported hippocampal involvement in the insight process. You should recall that, in the chapter on memory traces and memory schemas, we discussed the importance of the hippocampus for the consolidation of memories. Luo and Niki (2003, p. 321) believe that this function of the hippocampus partly explains its role in insight. 'From an evolutionary perspective, the property of responding to the "insightful" experiences and fixing them in long-term memory can greatly enhance the possibility of an animal's survival . . . . this property of the hippocampus enables the organism to preserve' the sort of information that may facilitate survival at a future date. The relation between the hippocampus and insight is also explored in the studies we will examine next.

Insight and Sleep

When people have a problem and are uncertain of the solution they may say, 'I think I will sleep on it.' Wagner, Gais, Haider, Verleger, and Born (2004) have shown that this may be an excellent strategy. To investigate the relation between sleep and insight, they gave participants a *number reduction task*. This is a demanding task that requires close attention to detail. Participants were given a string of nine numbers. All strings were composed from the numbers 1, 4, and 9. Participants must generate a series of responses using two rules. One rule, called the *same rule*, is that if there is a sequence of two *identical* numbers, then the response is to be one of the numbers. Thus, for the sequence 4 4 the response is 4. The second rule, called the *different rule*, is that for a sequence of two different numbers, then the response is the third number. For example, the sequence 1 4 would be responded to by 9. The response to the first two numbers in a string is then compared with the third number in the string. Thus, if the first two numbers were 4 and 4, for which the response would be 4, then this response (4) would then be compared to the next number in the string. If that next number were 9, then the following response would be 1. How this works can be seen by comparing the given number string with the sequence of responses in the diagram below.

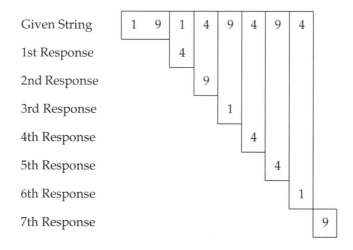

Given String	1	9	1	4	9	4	9	4
1st Response			4					
2nd Response				9				
3rd Response					1			
4th Response						4		
5th Response							4	
6th Response								1
7th Response									9

Comparing 1 and 9, by the second rule, you give 4 as the first response; 4 then compared to 1 requires 9 as the second response, by the same rule; 9 is then compared with 4 so that 1 is the next response, again by the same rule; 1 compared with 9 gives 4, by the same rule. Then 4 compared with 4 gives 4, the first time the first rule is used. You can complete the response sequence for yourself. The participant's task is to find the last number in the response sequence. In this case, the last response is 9, and so that is the answer the problem requires. The participant does not need to provide any other number, only the last one.

Now examine the response sequence for this sequence of numbers: 4 9 1 4 4 1 9. Notice that the last three numbers are the mirror image of the numbers in the second, third, and fourth positions: 4 1 9 is the mirror image of 9 1 4. The second, third, and fourth responses are the mirror image of the last three responses for all the problems the participant is asked to solve. This means that the required response, which is the last one, is always the same as the second response. Consequently the participant has only to generate the second response in order to have the response the problem requires. This is the insightful solution: You do not need to generate seven responses to find the required response; you need only to find the second response.

As you can imagine, few participants achieve an insightful solution, even after solving many problems. Of course, participants solved problems faster with practice. However, once participants gained insight into the problems' structures, their behaviour changed dramatically. They would no longer produce a string of responses, but simply announce the required response immediately after determining the second response. Three groups of participants were given a training period consisting of several number reduction problems, followed by an interval of eight hours, at which point they were tested on additional number reduction problems. One group *slept* during an interval between 11 p.m. and 7 a.m. and then was tested. A second group remained *awake* between 11 p.m. and 7 a.m. and then was tested. The third group remained *awake* between 11 a.m. and 7 p.m. Thus, immediately after training, one group slept for eight hours, another group was awake from 11 p.m. until 7 a.m., and the third group was awake from 11 a.m. until 7 p.m. The interesting result was that 59 per cent of the participants who had slept produced insightful solutions when tested. Across both groups of those who had remained awake, only 22 per cent of participants produced insightful solutions. Sleep promotes insight.

The restructuring process that occurs as a result of sleep may be similar to memory consolidation during sleep, 'resulting in delayed learning without the need for further practice or task engagement' (Stickgold & Walker, 2004, p. 192). Wagner et al. (2004, p. 354) suggested that, partly through interaction with other neural structures, the hippocampus 'not only strengthens memory traces quantitatively, but can also catalyze mental restructuring, thereby setting the stage for the emergence of insight.'

■ Functional Fixedness and the Design of Tools

Although the use of tools is not unique to humans, their use is so common among us that we can justifiably be called 'the ultimate tool users' (Defeyter & German, 2003, p. 134). Most of the tools we use as adults in a technologically advanced society have only one function. For example, lawnmowers, garlic presses, and staplers are usually used solely for the purpose for which they were designed. As we saw in our earlier discussion of Duncker and functional fixedness, we are often unable to think of a use for an object other than its intended function.

In a series of experiments, German and Defeyter (2000; Defeyter & German, 2003) have demonstrated that young children may be less functionally fixed than older children. In one study, five-, six-, and seven-year-olds were divided into two groups at each age level. One group was presented with the *pre-utilization condition*, and the other was presented with the *no-pre-utilization condition*. All participants faced a task in which they had to discover that a box they had been given could be used as something to stand on and not just as a container. In the pre-utilization condition, the box was full of items, demonstrating its conventional function as a container. In the no-pre-utilization condition, the box did not contain any items. The amount of time taken by those children who solved the problem is shown in Figure 9.6. Notice that the five-year-olds are equally fast regardless of the condition of the boxes present. However, the six- and seven-year-olds perform much worse under the pre-utilization condition.

German and Defeyter (2000; Defeyter & German , 2003) account for these and similar results in terms of the development of a tendency to perceive the function of a tool in terms of the use for which it was designed. By age six or thereabouts, children believe that an object's full function is the one for which it was created. For example, when shown boxes that contain things children who are six or older see containment as what the box was designed for, and have difficulty seeing any other use. By contrast, children who are five or younger see the function of an object as being determined by the goal of the *user*, rather than that of the *designer*. If the goal is to find something to stand on, then, to the five-year-old mind, a box will do perfectly well.

Functional fixedness might be acquired solely in technologically advanced countries in which people are exposed to many objects designed for a single purpose. To test this hypothesis, German and Barrett (2005) examined functional fixedness in the Shuar of the Amazon region in Ecuador. These people have been 'exposed only to a small set of manufactured artifacts, and the set of artifacts to which they are exposed tends to be "low tech"' (p. 2). The participants were adolescents and young adults, ranging in age from 12 to 25 years old. One of the tasks they were given was similar to the box problem

Figure 9.6 Effect of Pre-utilization on Functional Fixedness as a Function of Age.

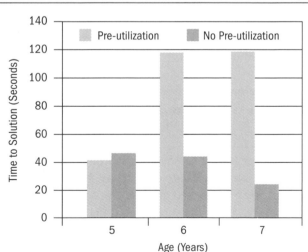

Data from German, T.P., & Defeyter, M.A. (2000). Immunity to functional fixedness in young children. *Psychonomic Bulletin & Review, 7*, p. 710.

described above, with one group of participants in the pre-utilization condition and the other in the non-pre-utilization condition. The Shuar participants showed the same effect of pre-utilization as had the older children in the earlier experiment. That is, it took longer for them to solve the box problem when its function as a container had been shown to them than when this function had not been shown to them. The conclusion was that even in a technologically sparse culture, people will develop the idea that an object's function is that for which it was designed. This leads to the broader conclusion that there may be a universal tendency for people to think about objects 'based on design rather than current use' (German & Barrett, 2005, p. 4). This way of thinking about objects may have evolved because most problems are solved by using objects in the way in which they were designed to be used. It is usually not necessary to think of alternative uses for a lawnmower, for example. Functional fixedness would then come about as a 'costly side effect' of an otherwise efficient system (Defeyter & German, 2003, p. 152).

■ The Flexibility-Rigidity Dimension

The experiments of the Luchinses (1942; Luchins & Luchins, 1950, 1994a, 1994b) are among the most interesting demonstrations of the way in which repeating a particular way of solving a problem can make a person blind to alternative ways of solving the problem. One of the ways the Luchinses showed this was with *water jar problems*. Imagine that you are given three jars, labelled A, B, and C, and a supply of water. Your task is to use the jars to obtain a specific amount of fluid. For example, suppose the three jars had capacities of 21, 127, and 3 litres, respectively. How could you use them to obtain a volume of 100 litres of water? Think about it.

The way to solve this problem involves four steps. First, fill up the 127-litre container. Second, pour out 21 liters into jar A. Third, pour 3 liters into jar C. Fourth, dump out jar C and pour 3 liters into jar C again. You are left with 100 liters in jar B, and the problem is solved. Now consider this problem. Jar A has a capacity of 14 litres, B a capacity of 163 litres, and C a capacity of 25 litres. Your task is to get 99 litres. This problem can be solved in the same way as the first. Fill jar B, subtract jar A, and subtract jar C twice.

In the Luchinses' experiments, participants were given a series of water jar problems just like the two we have considered. All of them could be solved using the same formula: *B minus A minus 2C*. After solving five problems using the same procedure, participants had developed a *rigid set*, or **Einstellung**. As we saw in the chapter on attention, a set facilitates some responses while inhibiting others. In the water jar situation, participants developed a particularly rigid set as shown by their responses to the following problem, which was given next in the series. A, B, and C have capacities of 23, 49, and 3 litres, respectively, and the required amount is 20 litres. Participants typically use the *B minus A minus 2C* formula on this problem, in spite of the fact that a simpler procedure will do. The required amount can be obtained by just filling A and emptying 3 litres out of it into C. So the simpler formula, A minus C, will work, but participants do not see it because of the Einstellung they have developed on the previous trials.

The Luchinses administered this kind of procedure to over 5,000 participants. Einstellung effects were very reliable findings. In one of their experiments (Luchins & Luchins, 1950, experiment 3), with sixth-graders, the effects were quite dramatic. The children were told to work as quickly as possible. After initially solving the problems using the same method throughout, the children were told that there was a simpler method for some of the problems and told to find it. However, under this kind of pressure it was difficult for them to change, and they usually persisted in doing the task in the more complicated way. There was evidence that the children found the demands of the situation quite stressful. Under this kind of pressure to perform quickly, the children were not only unable to be flexible, but also were locked into a rigid way of responding.

Woltz, Gardner, and Bell (2000) used a version of the number reduction task we considered earlier in this chapter in order to test the generality of the Luchinses' findings. Recall that number reduction problems have two rules, a *same* rule and a *different* rule. In the problems used by Woltz et al., the three numbers were always 1, 2, and 3, and the given string was four numbers long (e.g., 3213). Participants were trained on number sequences that required using the same sequence of rules over and over. For example, participants might be required to solve problems in which the rules had to be applied in the sequence *same–different–same* or *different–same–different*. They were then tested on problems that required the use of new rule sequences, such as *same–different– different* or *different–same–same*. Those participants who had the greatest amount of practice during training showed the greatest **negative transfer** when tested with problems requiring a new rule sequence. That is, they kept responding with previously learned rule sequences and their performance dropped as a result. Indeed, for highly practised participants errors increased from 20 per cent during training to 60 per cent during testing. Less practised participants also showed negative transfer, but went from only 20 per cent errors to 35 per cent errors. These results clearly show an Einstellung effect as a result of repetitive practice.

Woltz et al. relate their study to other research into common errors made in everyday life. We will also consider this kind of research in detail in the chapter on applied cognitive psychology. For now it will suffice to note that the Einstellung effect resembles errors we all make when we execute a **strong but wrong** tendency (Reason, 1990). An overlearned response sequence may be executed even when we should do something new. For example, imagine a person, who we will call John, who always takes the bus to and from work. One day, John drove to work instead. There is a good chance that John will execute a strong but wrong sequence and end up taking the bus home, leaving his car in the parking lot. We will examine this and many other kinds of error in Chapter 14.

Flexibility-Rigidity and the Brain

In Chapter 3, on attention, we noted that prefrontal areas of the brain are thought to provide 'a top-down bias that favors the selection of task-relevant information . . . . [S]uch a bias is especially important for exerting control when task-irrelevant information can effectively compete with task-relevant information for priority in processing' (Milham,

Banich, & Barad, 2004, p. 212). Then we discussed the fact that the left dorsolateral pre-frontal cortex (DLPFC) has been singled out as having a particularly important role in selecting between alternative response tendencies. In Chapter 5, on memory systems, we reviewed evidence suggesting that left DLPFC should be seen as an integral part of working memory, acting to monitor and control alternative courses of action.

Colvin, Dunbar, and Grafman (2000) have extended this picture of the role of left DLPFC in a study of water jar problems done with patients with prefrontal lesions. Solu-tions to water jar problems require a counterintuitive move. By counterintuitive is meant that the participant must select a move that appears to take the solver away from, rather than towards, the goal. The solver must inhibit the most obvious move in order to make the counterintuitive move. For example, in the first of the Luchinses' problems discussed above, the most obvious strategy is to find a way to put 100 litres *into* the 127-litre jar. The counterintuitive strategy is to find a way to empty 27 litres *out of* the 127-litre jar.

Both frontal lobe lesion patients and normal controls were given water jar prob-lems. The patients solved fewer problems than the controls, and also made fewer coun-terintuitive moves. When patients were categorized according to the site of their lesions, it was those with damage to the left frontal lobe whose performance was most impaired. It appeared that 'intact left dorsolateral prefrontal cortex function is critical for successful' water jar performance (Colvin et al., 2000, p. 1136). Without it, the per-son is unable to inhibit obvious moves in order to make counterintuitive ones.

Mindlessness

Langer (1989, 2000; Langer & Piper, 1987) proposed conceptualizing the flexibility-rigidity distinction in terms of a dimension of **mindfulness-mindlessness**. People who are showing the influence of Einstellung effects are behaving in a *mindless* way. To behave mindlessly means to act as if a situation has only one possible interpreta-tion. To behave *mindfully* means to actively seek new possibilities. As Langer pointed out, once you have mindfully created a new way of doing something, then that approach may subsequently be engaged in mindlessly. This is what happened to the participants in the Luchinses' experiments. After mindfully discovering the 'B minus A minus 2C' rule, those participants proceeded to mindlessly apply it to sub-sequent problems.

Langer and Piper reasoned that one way of preventing the development of mind-lessness is to encourage people to think about things in a tentative rather than in an absolute way. For example, describing objects in terms that allowed participants to see that objects could have alternative uses might encourage mindfulness, whereas describing them in terms of single uses might not. Langer and Piper did an experi-ment in which participants were shown three objects—a dog's rubber chew toy, a polygraph pen, and a hair dryer attachment. For half the participants, the objects were described unconditionally; that is, an object was defined without qualification as being one thing only, as in, 'This is a dog's chew toy.' For the other half of the partici-pants, the objects were described conditionally; that is, more provisionally, as in, 'This could be a dog's chew toy.' The experimenter then pretended to need an eraser, and asked participants what to do. A mindful response would be to say that the dog's chew toy could be used as an eraser. If the chew toy had been described conditionally, then participants were much more likely to make the mindful response than when the object was described unconditionally.

Responding to new objects and events conditionally appears to be an important aspect of mindfulness. Such conditional understanding allows people to avoid rigid responding. Although unconditional description provides an economical way of categorizing things, it seems to do so at the cost of blinding people to new possibilities.

■ Artificial Intelligence Approaches to Problem-Solving

In Chapter 2, we considered the influence of computer simulation approaches to cognition. At that time, we noted that it might be possible to program a computer so that the way it does things is indistinguishable from the way that a person does things. If so, then the computer program might be a good model of a person's behaviour. Computer simulation approaches to problem-solving have been extremely influential, in large measure because of the work of Nobel Prize winner Herbert Simon. As we shall see, there are computer programs that solve problems in ways that are similar to the intelligent way in which humans solve problems. These programs are examples of **artificial intelligence**. Let us look at some examples and see how computer simulation and artificial intelligence work.

The relation between artificial intelligence approaches and other approaches to problem-solving is well illustrated by Newell's (1983) discussion of the work of George Polya. Polya wrote a famous guide to successful problem-solving called *How to solve it* (Polya, 1945/1957). Polya's book was about heuristic problem-solving methods. A **heuristic** is a useful problem-solving procedure. Heuristics are typically rules of thumb, or shortcuts that allow you to arrive at a solution efficiently. However, heuristics may not always work.

Polya (1945/1957, p. xvi) outlined his heuristic methods as follows. First, you need to understand the problem. Understanding the problem may be facilitated by any of several methods. You need to formulate the problem in a way that allows you to begin thinking about it. This might involve drawing a diagram, for example. Once you think you understand what the problem requires, then you can move on to the next stage, devising a plan. Several methods may be helpful here. You might try to find a similar problem that you know how to solve, and then see if the methods used to solve that problem will also work for the present problem. When you have formulated a plan for attacking the problem, you can go on to step three, carrying out the plan. This is to be done carefully, with attention to detail. Finally, you need to examine the solution obtained. This involves making sure that the result is in fact the one you need, and determining whether or not the methods used to solve this problem can be used to solve other problems.

As Newell (1983, p. 202) observed, Polya's description of problem-solving has much in common with subsequent artificial intelligence techniques. Artificial intelligence requires as clear and precise a formulation of the problem as possible. In order to make a computer program work, we cannot rely on vague hunches and intuitions; we must be able to represent a procedure in an explicit manner. Polya tried to present heuristic methods that were clear, precise, and explicit. It is this kind of heuristic method that people working on artificial intelligence have tried to devise.

In programming heuristic problem-solving methods, artificial intelligence researchers make use of **algorithms**, which consist of unambiguous solution procedures (Dietrich, 1999). Long division is an example of an algorithm. The rules governing long division are unambiguous and a computer can easily be programmed to solve such problems. Algorithms may be divided into two classes: *systematic* and *non-systematic*. 'A systematic algorithm is guaranteed to find the solution if one exists . . . [but] non-systematic algorithms . . . are not guaranteed to find a solution' (Korf, 1999, p. 373). Since Polya's heuristic methods are not guaranteed to find a solution, they are examples of non-systematic algorithms.

A Simple Example of Artificial Intelligence

Computer programs that play games invented by humans are useful examples of artificially intelligent systems. For example, there are excellent programs that play checkers, Scrabble, backgammon, chess, bridge, and solve crossword puzzles (Schaeffer & van den Herik, 2002). A tipping point in the history of artificial intelligence occurred in 1997 when the chess-playing program *Deep Blue* defeated world chess champion Garry Kasparov in a six-game match (Campbell, Hoane, & Hsu, 2002). Interestingly, early research in artificial intelligence centred on creating a chess-playing program (Newell, Shaw, & Simon, 1958; Newell & Simon, 1972, Chap. 11). Chess is a very intricate game, and the programs written to play it are correspondingly complicated. It will be easier for us, and just as useful, if we consider a much simpler game, one that has also been explored by psychologists (e.g., Eisenstadt & Kareev, 1977). The game is called Go-Moku.

Go-Moku is a game played on a lattice, a portion of which is given in Figure 9.7. The game is similar to tic-tac-toe. The goal of the game is to place either five Xs or five Os in a line. One player tries to place five Xs in a line, and the other player tries to place five Os in a line. The situation in Figure 9.7 is such that the person playing Xs is in an unstoppable position. No matter where the person playing Os moves, X will win on the following move. This position is called an *open four*, and you should obviously try to create such a situation. The person playing Os has created another interesting position called an *open three*. If you can create two open threes, then your opponent is in a bad position. If your opponent blocks one open three, then you can turn the other open three into an open four on the next move. Thus, there is one overall goal: make five in a row. There are also different subgoals, such as creating open fours and open threes.

If you were writing a computer program to play Go-Moku against an opponent, what sort of characteristics would your program need to have? The program needs a

Figure 9.7 A Portion of Go-Moku Playing Surface.

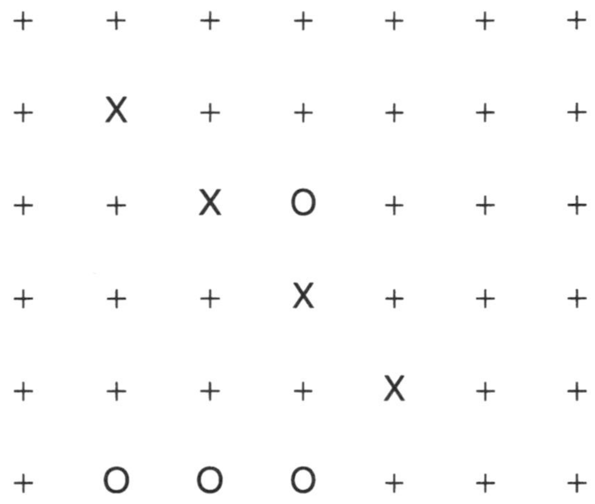

```
+    +    +    +    +    +    +

+    X    +    +    +    +    +

+    +    X    O    +    +    +

+    +    +    X    +    +    +

+    +    +    +    X    +    +

+    O    O    O    +    +    +
```

data structure and an **evaluation function**. The data structure corresponds to what Polya called 'understanding the problem'. It consists of a representation of the playing board, and the possible states of each position on the board, whether X, O, or empty. The evaluation function does all of the things that Polya referred to as 'creating a plan, carrying out the plan and evaluating the plan' (Polya, 1945/1957, p. xvi). Given a particular position on the board, the program works out all possible moves. Each of the possibilities is evaluated. For example, making five in a row has the highest value as a move; making four in a row the next highest, and so on. Defensive moves can also be given a value, with blocking five in a row getting the most points, followed by blocking four in a row, and so on. The move with the highest value is the one that is made.

The Problem Space

In the case of a simple game like Go-Moku, it is possible to have the program evaluate all possible moves at any stage of the game. Thus, a successful computer uses a systematic algorithm: it calculates the best move out of all possible moves. Current Go-Moku programs will win every time, provided they are allowed to go first (Allis, van der Herik, & Huntjens, 1996; Muller, 2001). However, Go-Moku programs typically do not do things that must be done in more complicated games. Go-Moku has a simple **problem space** consisting of the way that the problem is represented, including the goal to be reached and the various ways of transforming the given situation into the solution (Newell & Simon, 1972, p. 59; Keren, 1984). More elaborate games, such as chess, have extremely complicated problem spaces. The problem space cannot simply be analyzed only one move ahead. Good chess players need to be able to anticipate what moves might be made in response to their moves, what moves they might make then, what moves the opponent might make in response, and so on. Thus, the possibilities have to be examined two, three, or more moves ahead. This fact makes it very difficult to have a program that plays chess using a systematic algorithm. This can be made clear by examining **search trees**.

A search tree represents all the possible moves branching out from the initial state of the problem. As Newell, Simon, and Shaw (1962) pointed out, solving a problem is a bit like getting through a maze. In a maze such as the one in Figure 9.8, you must get from the start (S) to the goal (G), and avoid ending up in any of the dead ends. From the starting point you are faced with a series of choices, or branches, in the maze. Finding your way through the maze requires you to make the right move at each choice point. The search tree for a game like chess is enormous. In chess, there are about 30 or 40 legal moves that can be made at any point in the game. Suppose we try to evaluate each alternative in order to see where it would lead. This requires evaluating another 30 or 40 alternatives for each of the first 30 or 40 alternatives. You can begin to see where this will leave us if we wish to anticipate the consequences of a particular move. 'If we undertake to look ahead only 5 moves, with 30 legal alternatives at each step, we must consider 10^{15} positions in order to evaluate a single move' (Newell and Simon, 1972, p. 97). The extremely rapid increase in the number of alternatives that must be considered as you search the problem space for a complex problem is called a *combinatorial explosion*. Such an explosion cannot be effectively managed by a systematic algorithm. 'Even if a computer could examine a million possibilities per second, examining 10^{15} possibilities would take 31.7 years' (Korf, 1999, p. 372). Rather than consider all the alternatives, you need non-systematic methods to find the best route through the problem space. Newell and Simon's (1972; Simon, 1979) General Problem Solver (GPS) became one of the most frequently cited computer programs for accomplishing this kind of heuristic search.

General Problem Solver

In modelling problem-solving, it is often useful to analyze the structure of **toy problems**, which are not real-life problems. Rather, as the name suggests, they are literally

Figure 9.8 A Maze in Which You Must Get From the Start (S) to the Goal (G).

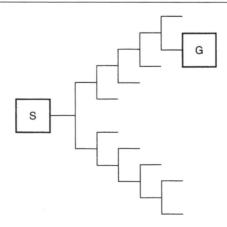

problems you might find in a toy shop. The reasons why it is useful to analyze them are that they have a known structure and that interesting data can be collected from participants as they try to solve them. One of the problems extensively explored by Simon and his co-workers is the *Tower of Hanoi problem* (e.g., Anzai & Simon, 1979; Simon, 1975). This problem is illustrated in Figure 9.9. In one version of the problem, three concentric rings (small, medium, and large) are placed around one of the posts in the figure. The task is to move all the rings from the post labelled A to the post labelled C. The constraints are that only one ring may be moved at a time and no ring may be placed on a ring smaller than itself. Thus, you can move the smallest ring to B, but then you cannot place the medium-sized ring on top of the smallest ring.

Before examining Figure 9.9, which gives you the solution for a three-ring problem, try solving the problem yourself. Although moving all the rings from A to C is the goal of the problem, this goal can be decomposed into a series of subgoals. One subgoal is to move the small and medium rings to post B. This subgoal can be achieved by moving the small disk to C, then the medium disk to B, and finally placing the small disk on top of the medium disk on B. This allows the large disk to be moved to C. The next subgoal is to move the small and medium rings from B to C. First move the small ring to A, then move the medium ring to C, and finally move the small ring to C.

How GPS Solves the Tower of Hanoi Problem

How can such a procedure described in the previous paragraph be programmed on a computer? In GPS this is accomplished by means of **production rules** (Eisenstadt & Simon, 1997; Simon, 2000). A production rule consists of a condition and an action. The

Figure 9.9 Solution for the Three-disk Version of the Tower of Hanoi Problem.

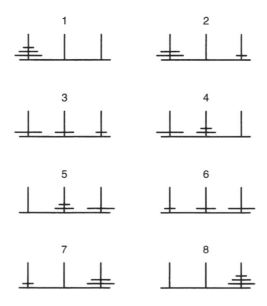

notation that Simon used is C → A, where C stands for a condition and A stands for an action. Thus, an obvious production rule is:

Problem solved → halt

If the condition of solving the problem is met, then the person halts the problem-solving process. How is it determined that the problem is solved? A problem is solved if there is no difference between the state that has been reached and the goal that is being sought. The analysis of differences between the current state and the goal state is an essential part of GPS. At the beginning of the problem-solving process, there is a large difference between the current and the goal states. This is in fact the definition of a problem: being in one state and attempting to reach another state (the goal). **Means-end analysis** is the name for the heuristic procedures GPS uses to reduce differences between current and goal states.

In order for the problem-solving process to progress, **subgoals** may have to be substituted for the original goal. Suppose there is no action that follows from the current condition and would lead directly to the goal. Perhaps there is a subgoal that can be reached directly from the current state. Once that is accomplished, then a part of the difference between the initial state and the goal state has been reduced. Then another subgoal can be formulated, if necessary, and once that is reached, the difference between initial and final states is again reduced. In analyzing a problem GPS creates a **goal stack**. The final goal to be reached is on the bottom of the stack, with the subgoals piled on top of it in the reverse order in which they are to be attained. Thus, the first subgoal to be reached is on the top of the stack, then the next subgoal, and so on.

Notice that the description we have just given is a more general formulation of the specific procedure for solving the Tower of Hanoi problem. Simon (1975) argued that GPS is, as its name implies, a general problem-solving procedure, which can be applied to solve particular problems such as the Tower of Hanoi. The condition-action pairs that would be used to solve the Tower of Hanoi would include rules that recognize when a goal cannot be directly achieved, and then substitute another goal for it, until a legal move is attained. This procedure is applied over and over until the problem is solved.

Thinking Aloud as a Method for Studying Human Problem-Solving

One of the goals of Simon's research program was to write computer programs that mimic the procedures participants actually use when solving problems such as the Tower of Hanoi. In order to find out what procedures people actually use, a technique called **thinking aloud** has often been used (Ericsson & Simon, 1980, 1993; Newell, 1977). Ericsson and Simon referred to the method of thinking aloud as *concurrent verbalization*: the verbalization of information at the time the participant is attending to it. This is to be distinguished from *retrospective verbalization*, in which the participant is asked about cognitive processes that occurred at an earlier point in time. Concurrent verbalization relies on short-term memory, whereas retrospective verbalization relies on long-term memory. When participants think aloud, they put into words a process that normally takes place non-verbally. This provides a description of the participant's solution process. A verbal description so obtained is called a *protocol*. Although there may be omissions in these protocols, they still contain a great deal of useful information.

Here is a typical example of protocol generated by a participant while solving the Tower of Hanoi problem, taken from Anzai and Simon (1979, p. 138). The participant is trying to solve a *five*-disk version of the Tower of Hanoi puzzle. You might find it instructive to try this yourself.

1. I'm not sure, but first I'll take 1 from A and place it on B.
2. And I'll take 2 from A and place it on C.
3. And then, I take 1 from B and place it on C. (The interrogator asks, 'If you can tell me why you placed it there.')
4. Because there was no place else to go, I had to place 1 from B to C.
5. Then, next, I placed 3 from A to B.
6. Well . . . , first I had to place 1 to B, because I had to move all disks to C. I wasn't too sure though.
7. I thought that it would be a problem if I placed 1 on C rather than B.
8. Now I want to place 2 on top of 3, so I'll place 1 on A.
9. Then I'll take 2 from C, and place it from A to B.
10. And I'll take 1 and . . . place it from A to B.
11. So then, 4 will go from A to C.
12. And then . . . , um . . . ; oh . . . , um . . .

As you can see, there is a lot of information in these protocols. In conjunction with observing the actual behaviour of the participant, these protocols can give the experimenter a reasonably complete description of a psychological process. Obviously, the raw protocol needs to be analyzed carefully. Newell (1977) recommended a series of steps in order to clarify the protocol. First, the protocol needs to be divided into phrases, which are descriptions of single acts. Then the experimenter constructs a problem behaviour graph, a concrete description of the way in which the participant moves around in the problem space. This description can be used as the basis for a production system designed to model the participant's behaviour. Generalizing across a number of participants' descriptions begins to provide the kind of system that is eventually embodied in a computer simulation.

Although concurrent verbalization is very widely used, there is evidence suggesting that it may interfere with some aspects of the problem-solving process (Schooler, Ohlsson, & Brooks, 1993). In order to determine the usefulness of thinking aloud protocols, Weisberg and Fleck (2004) performed a detailed analysis of problem-solving protocols. By comparing problem-solving behaviour in both verbalization and non-verbalization conditions, they concluded that 'instructing participants to verbalize did not adversely affect their thought processes' (p. 1003). It is important that the participants 'talk to themselves' rather than talk to the experimenter. This produces a useful record of the problem-solving process without requiring the participant to communicate to anyone other than him/herself. Protocols obtained in this way resemble inner speech, and may capture some aspects of the process whereby speech regulates thought (Benjafield, 1969a).

■ Can Computer Programs Experience Insight?

Michael Wertheimer (1985), the son of Max Wertheimer who wrote *Productive thinking*, criticized computer simulations of problem-solving from a Gestalt perspective. He argued, as have many others, that insight is nowhere to be found in a computer program. 'Missing in such work is the crucial step of *understanding*, that is, grasping both what is crucial in any given problem and why it is crucial. Classical Gestalt analyses of productive thought emphasized precisely this phenomenon of insight' (Wertheimer, 1985, p. 19).

In a reply, Simon (1986, p. 253) argued that there were really two parts to Wertheimer's critique. The first issue is empirical. Can computer programs 'represent, and thereby explain, the rich range of learning and problems solving behaviors with which Gestalt psychology has been centrally concerned'? The second issue concerns whether or not the concepts of Gestalt psychology can be 'sharpened up and made useful to experimental psychology'. Let us deal with each of these issues in turn.

Programming Insight

Kaplan and Simon (1990) showed that even a very difficult insight problem can be analyzed in terms compatible with an artificial intelligence approach. The problem they focused on is the *mutilated checkerboard problem*. This problem is illustrated below. There is a standard 8-by-8 checkerboard, from which two corners have been removed. Participants are asked to imagine placing dominoes on the board. Each domino covers two vertical or two horizontal squares. Dominoes cannot be placed diagonally. There are 62 squares. Can 31 dominoes be placed to cover the 62 squares exactly? If not, why is it not possible for 31 dominoes to cover the 62 squares? Spend a few minutes thinking about this problem.

The way that the typical participant initially represents the problem cannot lead to a solution. Participants can imagine placing tiles on the checkerboard for several hours without reaching a solution. At that point the participant will have reached an impasse. The participant may realize 'a need to look at the problem in a new way' (Simon, 1995, p. 944). A restructuring of the problem's representation can occur if the participant begins to focus on the number of black and white squares. Notice that both the missing squares are white. This means that there are 32 black squares and 30 white ones. Each domino must cover one black and one white square, and there are 31 dominoes. After covering 30 black and 30 white squares with 30 dominoes, there will still be two black squares left over. Remember that a domino must cover one black and one white square. Therefore, no matter where the two black squares are, they cannot be covered by the single remaining domino. It is not possible for 31 dominoes to cover the 62 squares.

The mutilated chessboard problem has all the features of an insight problem. First, the way the problem is initially represented leads the solver nowhere. Consequently, the solver reaches an impasse. This promotes a restructuring in which the solver focuses on previously unattended features of the problem. At that point the solver can insightfully see why the problem cannot be solved.

Simon (1995, pp. 943–944) presented a theory of insight that is intended to explain the process of restructuring. The program begins searching for a problem solution, following a path that will be unsuccessful. There is a *stop rule* that will cause the program to pause when it has been unsuccessful for some period of time. The problem space it has been searching will be abandoned. When the program resumes, it will begin by representing the problem in a new way that involves attending to previously neglected aspects of the problem. This results in the program taking a new direction, which is more likely to be successful.

This theory of insight models the behaviour of human problem-solvers. Someone sympathetic to Gestalt psychology might still say that the program does not capture the richness of the insight experience. This brings us to Simon's second issue: Can the concepts of Gestalt psychology be 'sharpened up and made useful to experimental psychology'? In Simon's theory of insight, the explanatory concepts can all be given a definite meaning. Insofar as *insight* is a scientific concept, it can be modelled just like any other cognitive process. However, as Simon (1986, p. 253) observed, it is still possible to claim that computer simulation of *insight* and *understanding* requires 'twisting these terms out of all semblance to their intended meaning'. From Simon's perspective, anyone who persists in taking this position risks using concepts that are too distant from empirical science to be meaningful. Simon (1986, p. 254) suggested that it may be necessary to abandon the language of Gestalt psychology in order to achieve truly scientific explanations.

◼ Solving Problems in Science

Simon (1981, p. 102) remarked that it was 'reasonable that research on human thinking should begin with relatively contentless tasks' such as the Tower of Hanoi problem.

However, 'research in both cognitive psychology and artificial intelligence has been turning more and more to . . . domains that have substantial, meaningful content . . . .' One of these domains is problem-solving in science. Science has proven to be a fruitful domain in which to study problem-solving. Klahr and Simon (1999, 2001) observed that there are four complementary approaches to the study of problem-solving in science. They are **historical accounts**, **observation of ongoing scientific investigations**, **laboratory studies**, and **computational models**. Let us consider them in turn.

Historical Accounts

Simon (1992, p. 157) recommended the study of the history of science as a source of hypotheses concerning the ways in which knowledge is acquired. However, it was Nersessian (1995) who coined the phrase **cognitive history of science**. This endeavour combines 'case studies of historical scientific practices' with 'scientific investigations of how humans reason, judge, represent, and come to understand' (Nersessian, 1995, p. 195). Thus, case studies of working scientists are informed by the framework provided by cognitive science.

A landmark in cognitive historical studies was Gruber's (1974/1981; Gruber & Wallace, 2001) reconstruction of Darwin's discovery of the theory of evolution. This reconstruction entailed Gruber's studying Darwin's notebooks for 20 years in order to become familiar with the thinking that led to evolutionary theory. Scientists are often meticulous record-keepers, and this is especially so in Darwin's case. Darwin's notebooks trace the development of his ideas over more than 50 years. Gruber observed that Darwin's enterprise illustrated what is called the **Zeigarnik effect**, which is the tendency to persist in finishing incomplete tasks. Although this effect can be detected in a laboratory (Zeigarnik, 1927/1967), its true importance is only revealed when one sees a person working on a problem over many years, or even decades. Many successful scientists are engaged in precisely this sort of lifelong problem-solving. Giving up is not an option for them, and without such persistence complex scientific problems might never be solved.

Another important strand of research in cognitive history is Tweney's (1991, 1999) analysis of the diaries of the nineteenth-century English physicist Michael Faraday. Faraday's 'work revolutionized physics and led directly to both classical field theory and relativity theory' (Williams, 1991, p. 278). Tweney shows how the diaries themselves played an essential role in Faraday's scientific problem-solving. Faraday understood that keeping detailed records of his work was essential because he could not rely on his memory. One reason he could not rely on memory is that he was extraordinarily productive, completing over 30,000 experiments. We have already seen how unreliable memory can be, and Faraday was acutely aware of its failings. Keeping a diary provided Faraday with an external memory aid. However, the diary entries themselves needed to be organized. One way of understanding this necessity is to imagine yourself with an enormous number of files stored on your computer. You will need some indexing system not only to find files, but also to remember what the files contain (Tweney, 1991, p. 303). Faraday used a version of the *method of loci*, which we reviewed in Chapter 6, on imagery, in order to help keep track of diary entries. More importantly, he used paper slips much in the way one might use Post-its now. These slips were reminders of diary entries, and he would arrange and rearrange them, looking for patterns, 'in effect constructing a larger whole from the separate bits and pieces' (Tweney, 1991, p. 305). The larger whole he sought consisted eventually of the scientific laws he discovered. In Faraday's diaries, we can see how important memory is to the process of scientific problem-solving.

The Observation of Ongoing Scientific Investigations/ Laboratory Studies

Dunbar (2000, 2001; Dunbar & Blanchette, 2001; Fugelsang, Stein, Green, & Dunbar, 2004) pioneered what he called the **in vivo/in vitro** method for studying problem-solving in science. *In vivo* means *in the living* and *in vitro* means *in glass*. This distinction comes from biology, where it refers to studies of the living organism (*in vivo*) versus studies in an artificial environment (*in vitro*). In psychology, this distinction corresponds to the distinction between ecologically valid research (*in vivo*) and laboratory research (*in vitro*). In the case of scientific problem-solving, *in vivo* research involves the observation of ongoing scientific investigations, while *in vitro* research involves laboratory studies of scientific problem-solving. 'A key feature of the *in vivo/in vitro* method is that we can investigate a question in a naturalistic situation and then go back to the psychological laboratory and conduct controlled experiments on what has been identified in the naturalistic settings' (Dunbar, 2001, p. 118).

In setting up an *in vivo* study, the investigator needs to find research settings in which successful scientific problem-solving is likely to occur. Dunbar picked the field of molecular biology because it was a very attractive field for ambitious and high-achieving scientists. By interviewing outstanding figures in the field, including a Nobel Prize winner, Dunbar selected a series of laboratories in which important and innovative research had been and was continuing to be done. He eventually ended up with eight laboratories to study (Dunbar, 2000, p. 51). Dunbar found that each laboratory held weekly meetings, attended by the head of the lab, post-doctoral and graduate students, and lab technicians. It was at these meetings that much of the scientific problem-solving took place. Therefore, Dunbar made extensive video- and/or audiotape recordings of these meetings. These tape recordings were part of the data with which Dunbar and his colleagues worked. They also built a molecular genetics laboratory of their own. Using computer models, participants were first taught about molecular genetics and then given tasks such as 'discovering how genes control other genes' (Dunbar, 2000, p. 50). These laboratory studies provide a complementary data set. You can see that the *in vivo/in vitro* method is extremely time-consuming. Several findings emerged from Dunbar's studies, but we have space here to deal with only two of them.

Unexpected Findings
Most people resist accepting information that is inconsistent with their expectations. This is a phenomenon we will deal with at length in the next chapter, on reasoning.

However, you can easily see that ignoring **unexpected findings** would be fatal to successful scientific problem-solving. Although scientists may initially resist information that disconfirms one of their favourite hypotheses, successful problem-solvers attempt to explain surprising results. They set themselves a new goal of trying to explain the unexpected findings, rather than persisting in trying to confirm their original hypotheses. This is an adaptive strategy in science because unexpected results occur very often. Dunbar (2000, p. 52) found that unexpected results occurred 40 to 60 per cent of the time in experiments done across all of the laboratories that were studied. Always being right is not the hallmark of successful scientists. Rather, success is related to the extent the scientific team makes unexpected findings a primary focus of research. Such a focus leads to the reformulation of scientific models, which can themselves be tested in turn.

Distributed Reasoning

While Darwin and other scientists in earlier times may have solved problems largely in isolation, nowadays it is much more common for successful scientific problem-solving to be the outcome of a group effort. The weekly team meetings provided a wealth of information concerning **distributed reasoning**, which is reasoning done by more than one person. Distributed reasoning is particularly effective in changing problem representations. This is because different people reach different conclusions even when all of them are confronted with the same evidence (Dunbar, 2000, p. 55). Consequently, distributed reasoning is a way of avoiding Einstellung effects and of promoting novel lines of investigation instead.

Computational Models

Scientific problem-solving can be studied by creating computer programs that simulate well-known discoveries. These programs can derive scientific laws from the relevant data (Simon, Valdéz-Pérez, & Sleeman, 1997). One example is BACON, a program that incorporates very general heuristics (Langley, Simon, Bradshaw, & Zytkow, 1987). For example, it searches for patterns in the relationship between two variables, such as whether the variables are either increasing together, or whether one increases while the other decreases. BACON is able to 'discover' several well-known scientific laws, including Kepler's third law of planetary motion. This law expresses the relation between the amount of time it takes a planet to orbit the sun and the distance of that planet from the sun. The closer to the sun a planet is, the less time it takes to orbit the sun. Kepler's third law describes this relation precisely, and was originally derived using data that Kepler got from others. Furthermore, Kepler did not make detailed records of the process whereby he discovered the third law. Thus, the heuristics of BACON cannot be compared with a protocol of Kepler's discovery process to see if they are similar. However, Qin and Simon (1990) compared BACON's heuristics with the procedures that students used when confronted with data similar to those used by Kepler. These participants all had experience with physics, calculus, and chemistry. They were told that the experimenters were interested in how scientific laws were discovered. The participants' problem was to 'build a formula describing the relationship between two groups of data' (p. 283). None of the participants realized that Kepler's third law was what they had to discover, but some discovered it nonetheless. There was also a similarity between the heuristics that successful participants used and those used by BACON. This research shows how scientific problem-solving may be entirely data driven, since everything that both BACON and these participants did was determined by the data they were given and not by any theoretical framework.

Klahr and Simon (1999) noted that each approach to scientific problem-solving has its own strengths and weaknesses. For example, studies of historical records are **face valid** in that they are obviously about scientific problem-solving and not something else. Laboratory studies are not obviously face valid, since true scientific problem-solving is not carried out in the short time span of a psychological laboratory experiment. However, these studies can provide rigour and precision through control over variables that are hypothesized to be important determinants of scientific problem-solving. Direct observation of ongoing scientific work is both face valid and may expose new phenomena as well as social factors that other methods may not reveal. Computational modelling is low in face validity, but allows for rigorous testing of models of problem-solving that have been derived from the other methods (Klahr & Simon, 1999, p. 531). No method can replace any other, but all are complementary.

■ Questions for Study and Discussion

1. What is insight? What is responsible for its occurrence? What can be done to facilitate its occurrence?
2. What is functional fixedness? Why does it occur?
3. Outline the basic features of GPS. Use the Tower of Hanoi problem to illustrate your answer.
4. Discuss methods for studying problem-solving in science.

■ Key Concepts

Algorithms Unambiguous solution procedures.

Analysis of the situation Determining what functions the objects in the situation have and how they can be used to solve the problem.

Artificial intelligence Computer programs that solve problems in ways similar to the intelligent ways in which humans solve problems.

BACON A computer program that is able to discover several well-known scientific laws.

Chunk decomposition An aspect of representational change theory: parts of the problem are seen as belonging together; 'chunks' are separated and thought about independently.

Cognitive history of science Case studies of historically important scientific discoveries understood within a framework provided by cognitive science.

Computational models A method for studying problem-solving in science.

Constraint relaxation An aspect of representational change theory: the removal of assumptions that are blocking problem solution.

Distributed reasoning Reasoning done by more than one person.

Einstellung effect (Luchins) Also called a *rigid set*, this is the tendency to respond inflexibly in a problem situation.

Evaluation function A process whereby a plan is created, carried out, and evaluated.

Face valid A method that obviously measures what it is supposed to measure.

Feeling of knowing The feeling a person might have that she/he would be able to solve a particular problem.

Feeling of warmth The feeling people might have as they approach the solution of a problem (i.e., 'getting warm').

Functional fixedness (Duncker) Being unable to see that a particular object could perform the function needed to solve a problem; also, the tendency for people to think about objects based on the function for which they were designed.

Gestalt switch A sudden change in the way information is organized.

Goal stack The final goal to be reached is on the bottom of the stack, with the subgoals piled on top of it in the reverse order in which they are to be attained.

Heuristic A useful problem-solving procedure that may not always guarantee a solution.

Hints A hint must be consistent with the direction that the person's thinking is taking, and cannot be useful unless it responds to a difficulty that the person has already experienced.

Historical accounts A method for studying problem-solving in science.

Insight problem A problem that requires a restructuring of the way in which it is represented before it can be solved.

In vivo/in vitro method (Dunbar) In the case of scientific problem-solving, *in vivo* research involves the observation of ongoing scientific investigations, while *in vitro* research involves laboratory studies of scientific problem-solving.

Laboratory studies A method for studying problem-solving in science.

Means-end analysis The procedures used by General Problem Solver to reduce differences between current and goal states.

Metacognition What you know about what you know—how accurately you can assess your own cognitive processes.

Mindfulness-mindlessness (Langer) Openness to alternative possibilities versus the tendency to act as if a situation has only one possible interpretation.

Negative transfer In the case of Einstellung tasks, this is the tendency to respond with previously learned rule sequences even though they are inappropriate.

Observation of ongoing scientific investigations A method for studying problem-solving in science.

Problem space The way that the problem is represented, including the goal to be reached and the various ways of transforming the given situation into the solution.

Production rules A production rule consists of a condition and an action (C → A).

Productive thinking (Wertheimer) Thinking that occurs as a result of having a grasp of the general principles that apply in the particular situation in which you find yourself.

Progress monitoring theory Participants monitor their progress on a problem, and when they reach an impasse then they are open to an insightful solution.

Representational change theory Insight requires a change in the way that the participant represents the problem.

Search tree A representation of all the possible moves branching out from the initial state of the problem.

Strong but wrong tendency An overlearned response sequence may be executed even when we intend to do something else.

Structurally blind thinking The tendency to reproduce thinking appropriate for other situations, but not for the current situation.

Subgoals A goal derived from the original goal, the solution of which leads to the solution of the problem as a whole.

Thinking aloud Concurrent verbalization: the verbalization of information at the time the participant is attending to it.

Toy problems Problems you might find in a toy shop that are useful for analyzing the problem-solving process.

Unexpected findings Although scientists may initially resist information that disconfirms one of their favourite hypotheses, successful problem-solvers attempt to explain surprising results.

Zeigarnik effect The tendency to persist in finishing incomplete tasks.

◼ Links to Other Chapters

Gestalt switch
Chapter 2 (isomorphism)
Chapter 13 (thinking about persons)
Insight
Chapter 12 (creativity and problem-finding)
Feeling of knowing
Chapter 5 (butcher on the bus phenomenon)
Metacognition
Chapter 4 (elaboration and distinctiveness)
Chapter 14 (illusions of competence)
Heuristic
Chapter 7 (commitment heuristic)

Chapter 11 (heuristics and biases, representativeness, availability, recognition)
Chapter 13 (warm-glow heuristic)
Problem space
Chapter 10 (jumping out of the problem space)
Chapter 11 (the importance of the problem space)
Chapter 12 (creativity and problem-finding)
Distributed reasoning
Chapter 11 (team reasoning)

◼ Further Reading

A simple technique for constructing insight problems that you might like to try yourself was proposed by Gick, M., & Lockhart, R.S. (1995). Cognitive and affective components of insight. In R.J. Sternberg & J.E. Davidson (Eds.), *The nature of insight* (pp. 197–228). Cambridge, Mass.: MIT Press. They noted that the key to a riddle is to get the problem-solver to initially interpret information incorrectly. One way to do this is to select a word that can be interpreted in different ways. For example, the word *lake* can refer to a frozen or unfrozen body of water. Most people interpret the word to refer to an unfrozen body of water. A riddle can be constructed by requiring the problem-solver to come up with the less accessible meaning in order to make sense of what is being described. An example of a riddle solution given by Gick & Lockhart is 'The stone rested on the surface of the lake for three months, after which it sank to the bottom some 10 metres below.' Only when the problem-solver realizes that the lake is initially frozen will the solution to the riddle occur.

Some criticisms of computer simulation approaches to thinking go even further than the Gestalt critique. It has been argued that the activities of computer programs do not really count as thinking. People who express this belief often ally themselves with the German philosopher Heidegger, M. (1968). *What is called thinking?* (J. Glen Gray, Trans.). New York: Harper & Row. The properties of computer programs—that they can represent the chain of inferences leading from one state to another—would not have been the essence of thinking for Heidegger. Computer programs are good simulators of such processes as reasoning and calculating. However, the essence of thinking lies *behind* these processes; it is not reducible to them. Computer programs do not capture the subjective origin of thinking—the concern with the fundamental problem of being alive in the world. Although Heidegger, along with those who identify with him, was often difficult to follow, and even more difficult to paraphrase, he nonetheless still expressed a feeling that many people still have about computers and thought.

It was a commonplace for computer simulation approaches to psychological processes to be criticized for what they appear to leave out. Even some cognitive psychologists suggested that the simulation of emotion by means of a computer program would not be a very meaningful exercise. See, e.g., Neisser, U. (1964). The multiplicity of thought. *British Journal of Psychology, 54,* 1–14. Although Herbert Simon attempted to deal with this problem—see Simon, H.A. (1967). Motivational and emotional controls of cognition. *Psychological Review, 74,* 29–39—most work in this area specialized in cognition, and it is perhaps fair to say that the role of emotion in mental life was neglected. See also Simon, H.A. (1995). The information-processing theory of mind. *American Psychologist, 50,* 507–508.

A wonderful example of cognitive history of science is Netz, R. (1999). *The shaping of deduction in Greek mathematics: A study in cognitive history.* Cambridge: Cambridge University Press.

Chapter 10

Reasoning

■ Syllogistic Reasoning

There has been a veritable explosion of research in reasoning over the last several years, 'turning logic and reasoning into a major field of cognitive psychology' (Evans, 2002, p. 978). One useful definition of **reasoning** is 'a process of thought that yields a conclusion from percepts, thoughts, or assertions' (Johnson-Laird, 1999, p. 110). The 'percepts, thoughts, or assertions' referred to in the definition are called *premises*. Exactly what makes a conclusion follow logically from the premises is not always an easy question to answer because there are different systems of logic (Evans, 2002, p. 985). Aristotelian or syllogistic logic is older than the others, and has been the subject of much psychological research. Thus, syllogistic reasoning is a good place to begin.

A syllogism consists of two premises and a conclusion. Each of the premises specifies a relationship between two categories. Consequently, **syllogistic reasoning** is sometimes called *categorical reasoning*. Each premise in a syllogism can take any of four different forms:

Form	Examples
Universal Affirmative	All A are B.
	All cows are animals.
	All right angles are 90-degree angles.
Universal Negative	No A are B.
	No tomatoes are animals.
	No acute angles are 90-degree angles.
Particular Affirmative	Some A are B.
	Some animals are dangerous.
	Some pigeons are clever.
Particular Negative	Some A are not B.
	Some animals are not cows.
	Some pigeons are not clever.

Let us briefly consider each of these premise forms. The universal affirmative premise can be represented diagrammatically as shown below for the premise 'All A are B.' Notice that this premise might refer to a situation in which 'All A are B, but some B are not A.' This would be the case for a premise such as 'All cows are animals', because some animals are not cows. However, sometimes a universal affirmative premise refers to a situation in which 'All A are B, and all B are A.' This would be true for a statement such as 'All right angles are 90-degree angles' (Chapman & Chapman, 1959, p. 224). This means that a universal affirmative premise may be understood by a person in different ways, even though from a logical point of view all possible ways of understanding a premise are equally important.

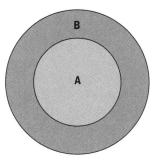

By contrast, the diagrammatic representation for 'No A are B' is completely different. The two circles are separate, meaning that none of the members of one class is a member of the other class. An important property of universal negative premises is that their converse is also true. A premise may be converted by reversing the order of the participant and predicate terms. The converse of 'No A is B' is 'No B is A.' Thus, 'No tomatoes are animals' also means that 'No animals are tomatoes.'

For the particular affirmative case illustrated below, in which 'Some A are B', the diagram shows overlapping circles. Notice that, although 'Some A are B', it may still be true that 'Some A are not B', or that 'Some B are not A.' Thus it is true that 'Some animals are not dangerous' and that 'Some dangerous beings are not animals.' Nevertheless, particular affirmative premises may be converted. If 'Some A are B', then it is also true that 'Some B are A.' To reiterate, it is important to see that people may interpret premises like this in a variety of ways.

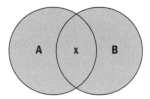

The particular negative case is diagrammed below as overlapping circles, but here we are concerned with the part of the A circle that does not overlap with the B circle. However, 'Some A are not B' is open to a number of specific interpretations. For example, the converse of 'Some A are not B' is 'Some B are not A.' This is an inference that people often accept (Chapman & Chapman, 1959), although it is not necessarily true. It is true that 'Some animals are not cows', but it does not follow that 'Some cows are not animals.' People often also infer that 'Some A are not B' means that 'Some A are B' (Ruby, 1960, p. 195). This interpretation is often what is meant in ordinary language. In the case of 'Some animals are not cows', it turns out that 'Some animals are cows' is also empirically correct. However, consider a statement such as 'Some Saudi Arabians are not ice hockey players.' Perhaps some Saudi Arabians *are* ice hockey players, but we just do not know. However, it is not logically necessary that some Saudi Arabians must be ice hockey players just because some of them are not; it may be the case, also, that all of them are not.

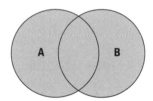

Logicism

At least since Aristotle, many have believed that logical reasoning is an essential part of human nature. **Logicism** is the name for this belief. Logicists point to the **practical syllogism** to illustrate their belief (e.g., Thornton, 1982). We use practical syllogisms when 'the conclusion drawn from the two premises becomes an action' (Henle, 1962/1968, p. 103). Here is an example of a practical syllogism.

> *Premise 1:* It is necessary for me to understand psychology as a whole.
>
> *Premise 2:* The only way to understand psychology as a whole is through the study of cognition.
>
> *Conclusion:* Therefore, it is necessary for me to study cognition.

If you accept the premises, then you will agree that it is necessary for you to study cognition. Some (e.g., Henle, 1962/1968) have argued that the practical syllogism is a common feature of everyday life by using examples such as this: 'People who have a virus should act so as not to infect others. I have a virus. Therefore, I should act so as not to infect others.' Once again, if you accept the premises, then you will act so as not to infect others. For those who believe in the importance of logic in everyday life, the practical syllogism is not just something learned about in a cognition course, but 'the natural mode of functioning of the conscious mind' (Henle, 1962/1968, p. 103). From this perspective, the ability to reason is what most distinguishes human beings from other forms of life.

One problem for logicism is that untrained participants make logical errors when asked to evaluate the validity of syllogistic arguments. This suggests that other processes than logic determine the conclusions participants reach. However, it is also true that the same participants do not always make logical errors. Rather they make logically correct deductions at a level greater than chance (Evans, 2002, p. 992). Consequently, a central concern in reasoning research is to determine the conditions under which participants will reason logically as well as the conditions under which participants reach conclusions in some other way.

The Effect of Content on Syllogistic Reasoning

Consider the following syllogism:

> *All Canadians love snow.*
>
> *All Mounties are Canadians.*
>
> *Therefore, all Mounties love snow.*

You might be prepared to object to this syllogism because you happen to know a Canadian who does not love snow, and so determine the first premise is empirically incorrect. However, when it comes to judging the validity of a syllogism, the truth or falsehood of a premise is irrelevant. The validity of a syllogism depends only on whether or not the conclusion necessarily follows from the premises. However, people often find it difficult to separate the question of the validity of a syllogism from the issue of whether or not the syllogism is consistent with their experience or beliefs. Thus, they may accept the conclusion to an invalid syllogism if they believe that the conclusion is true in the real world (Galotti, 1989, p. 336). However, the really interesting finding is that the effect of the participant's beliefs is greater if the syllogism is invalid (Newstead, Pollard, Evans, & Allen, 1992). To illustrate this point consider the following invalid syllogisms taken from Evans, Handley, & Harper (2001, p. 932).

Premise 1	No addictive things are inexpensive.	No millionaires are hard workers.
Premise 2	Some cigarettes are inexpensive.	Some rich people are hard workers.
Conclusion	Therefore, some addictive things are not cigarettes.	Therefore, some millionaires are not rich people.

Believable but invalid syllogisms like that on the left were accepted as valid by 71 per cent of participants, while unbelievable and invalid syllogisms like that on the right were accepted by only 10 per cent. The difference in acceptance rate is 61 per cent, showing a very large effect of believability for some invalid syllogism types. Now examine the following valid syllogisms, again taken from Evans, Handley, and Harper (2001, p. 932).

Premise 1	No police dogs are vicious.	No nutritional things are inexpensive.
Premise 2	Some highly trained dogs are vicious.	Some vitamin tablets are inexpensive.
Conclusion	Therefore, some highly trained dogs are not police dogs.	Therefore, some vitamin tablets are not nutritional.

Believable and valid syllogisms like the one on the left were accepted as valid by 89 per cent of participants, while unbelievable but valid syllogisms like those on the right were accepted as valid by 56 per cent. The difference in acceptance rate is only 33 per cent, showing a much smaller effect of believability for valid syllogism types. These data are presented graphically in Figure 10.1.

It is natural to focus on the difference between believable and unbelievable invalid syllogisms. What accounts for such a large difference in acceptance rate? One suggestion, made by Evans, Handley, and Harper (2001, p. 955), is that participants in a syllogistic reasoning task initially determine whether or not the conclusion is believable or unbelievable. If it is unbelievable, they then try to find some way of thinking about the premises that renders the conclusion invalid. If, however, the conclusion is believable, they do not try to determine if the syllogism is invalid, but rather try to determine if there is not some way of thinking about the premises that renders the conclusion acceptable. Thus, participants tend to set themselves the goal of discovering a syllogism to be invalid only if the conclusion is unbelievable. Later on in the chapter we will

Figure 10.1 Difference in Acceptance Rate for Four Different Types of Syllogism.

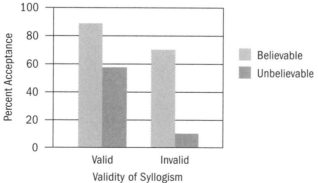

Data from Newstead, S.E., Pollard, P., Evans, J. St B.T., & Allen, J.L. (1992). The source of belief bias effects in syllogistic reasoning. *Cognition, 45,* p. 262.

discuss further the conditions under which people set themselves the goal of discovering whether or not a statement is false.

The Interpretation of 'Some'

The fact that premises often are open to alternative interpretations creates another great difficulty for participants who must judge the validity of syllogisms. In order to judge whether or not a conclusion is valid, the participant must consider only those inferences that are consistent with all possible interpretations of a set of premises. However, people do not always work out *all* the possible interpretations of a set of premises. Consequently, the reasoning that people do depends on the specific way they interpret the premises (Begg, 1987, p. 63; Begg & Harris, 1982; Ceraso & Provitera, 1971). The way participants interpret premises that contain the word *some* provides a good example.

Consider the statement 'Some people are human.' Although it is a meaningful (and empirically true) statement, it violates our feelings about the proper use of the word *some* and may even be offensive. The statement 'Some people are human' seems to imply that 'Some people are not human.' Although that is not one of the logically necessary implications of the statement, it seems to be because we ordinarily interpret the word *some* to mean 'some but not all' (Feeney, Scrafton, Duckworth, & Handley, 2004). Thus, according to our usual understanding of *some*, the statement 'Some people are human' means that '*not all* people are human.' If people use *some* in this way, then they are not using it in the way that is dictated by logic. In logic, *some* means at least one, and *possibly* all (Ruby, 1960, p. 194). A study by Begg (1987) showed how ubiquitous the ordinary, non-logical use of *some* may be.

In Begg's (1987) experiment, participants were given a description of a set of people and their occupations. For example, participants might be told that a group of people consists of 20 artists and 80 writers. Half of each subgroup are men, and the other half are women. Thus, subsets of the group can be described using statements such as:

> *Some men are artists; some men are writers.*
>
> *Some women are artists; some women are writers.*

In one part of the experiment, participants were asked to evaluate certain statements using the word *some* in terms of how misleading they felt them to be. Statements in which *some* referred to a minority of the group of individuals were felt to be less misleading than those that referred to a majority of the group. Thus, statements such as 'Some men are artists' are considered more easily believed and less misleading than statements such as 'Some men are writers' because there are fewer male artists (10) than male writers (40). In other words, for many people the word *some* carries with it the connotation of 'less than the whole amount under consideration'. The same result was found for 'Some women are artists' and 'Some women are writers.' The former kind of statement is seen as more acceptable than the latter kind.

Results such as these are consistent with the view that people typically interpret *some* as meaning *not all*. This fact can be understood within the context of relevance theory, which we discussed in Chapter 8. Speakers are assumed to be saying something relevant to the listener's concerns. Listeners 'follow the path of least effort and stop at the first interpretation that satisfies one's expectation of relevance' (Sperber & Wilson, 1995, pp. 272–273). Someone who eats all of the cookies and then says *I ate some of the cookies* is misleading the listener, who will assume that there is a reason why *some* is used rather than *all*. Since participants in reasoning experiments are like listeners in conversations (Noveck, 2001, p. 166), it is not surprising that they tend to employ the conversational, rather than the strictly logical, meaning of *some*.

Feeney, Scrafton, Duckworth, and Handley (2004) found that by age seven or eight children use *some* in the conversational manner. In other words, these children will tend to judge as false a statement such as *Some giraffes have long necks*. They will tend to make the same judgement of the meaning of *some* when shown a pictorial sequence in which a child eats all of the candies on a table, and then tells her mother that *I ate some of the candies*. In an experiment with adults, Feeney et al. found that it took longer to judge a statement like *Some cats have four legs* to be true than it did to judge such a statement to be false. This suggests that participants are first inclined to make a conversationally correct response. In order to make a logically correct response, they must inhibit their initial response tendency. This result is similar to the result described above for content effects. The initial response people make tends not to be influenced by logical considerations. Nevertheless, people can and do make logically correct inferences. Later on in the chapter we will consider the reasons why some (but not all) people are able to overcome their initial tendencies and put forth the effort necessary to reason logically.

■ Mental Models and Deductive Reasoning

The most influential current theory of syllogistic reasoning is due to Phillip Johnson-Laird (1983, 1988, 2001; Johnson-Laird & Byrne, 1993; Johnson-Laird & Steedman, 1978). According to Johnson-Laird (1988, pp. 277ff.), people construct a mental model of the situation to which a set of premises refers. Once constructed, people can draw conclusions that are consistent with the model. There may be a number of possible **mental models** that can be derived from a set of premises. If a conclusion is consistent with all the mental models that are constructed, then it is accepted.

What does a mental model look like? From Johnson-Laird's viewpoint, the details of the model, such as whether or not it makes use of vivid imagery, are irrelevant. The important thing is how the parts of the model go together. A mental model is a mental structure. Let us see how this might work for a premise such as 'All whales are strong.' We will use the kind of notation employed by Johnson-Laird (1983, Chap. 5; 1988, p. 228). You might first imagine a set of whales, like this:

whale
whale

You might form your model from images of whales, or something else entirely. You can represent them in a variety of ways. You can then add to your mental model the information that *whales are strong*.

```
whale  =  strong
whale  =  strong
          [strong]
```

The purpose of putting brackets around one of the cases of *strong* is to represent the fact that your model may contain cases of strong things that are not whales. If you then think of Moby Dick, a famous fictional whale, you can add him to your model like this:

```
Moby Dick  =  whale  =  strong
              whale  =  strong
                        [strong]
```

Having constructed this model, you are in a position to make an inference. You can now see that Moby Dick is strong, a relationship that may not have occurred to you before you constructed your model.

What makes a syllogism difficult is that there may be a number of alternative mental models. To see why this matters, consider these premises:

No camels are whales.
All whales are endangered animals.

Three mental models can be constructed from these premises. Let us begin with the first model and the first premise, which can be represented like this:

```
camel
camel
  _____

              whales
              whales
              [whales]
```

In Johnson-Laird's notation, the line is a way of representing the fact that camels and whales belong to different sets. 'The two groups are, as it were, fenced off from each other' (Johnson-Laird, 1983, p. 96). The second premise can be incorporated into the model as follows:

```
camel
camel
  _____

   whales  =  endangered animals
   whales  =  endangered animals
   whales  =  endangered animals
              [endangered animals]
```

If the reasoner stops here, having constructed only one model, then the most likely conclusion he or she will draw is that *No camels are endangered animals*. In fact, Johnson-Laird (1988, p. 229) noted this as a very common response when participants are given syllogisms consisting of this particular type of premise pair. However, there is a second mental model that can be constructed from these premises, incorporating the possibility that *camels* might occasionally be *endangered animals*, too.

```
camel
camel = endangered animals
─────────────────────────────────
    whales = endangered animals
    whales = endangered animals
    whales = endangered animals
              [endangered animals]
```

Johnson-Laird reported that some participants draw a conclusion from this kind of model to the effect that *Some camels are not endangered animals*. However, this conclusion also looks risky if you construct the third mental model:

```
    camel = endangered animals
    camel = endangered animals
─────────────────────────────────
    whales = endangered animals
    whales = endangered animals
    whales = endangered animals
              [endangered animals]
```

At this point, you might want to give up without drawing any conclusion from this pair of premises. Johnson-Laird (1983, Table 5.1; 1988, p. 229) reported that in fact no participants in his experiments drew the valid conclusion corresponding to 'Some of the endangered animals are not camels.' Drawing this conclusion requires the inspection of the three models from the bottom up, as it were, to see that this conclusion can be drawn in each case. Johnson-Laird's model seems to fit nicely as an explanation for the sources of difficulty in deductive reasoning. However, it has been challenged by other approaches to deductive reasoning, which we will examine later on.

Relational Reasoning

Over the years the scope of mental models theory has expanded considerably (Johnson-Laird, 2001). A good example of the range of its applicability is **relational reasoning** (Goodwin & Johnson-Laird, 2005). Of particular interest are *transitive relations* (Strawson, 1952, p. 46), which are usually expressed by means of comparative sentences, such as *A is taller than B*. The relation *taller than* is transitive because if *A is taller than B*, and *B is taller than C*, then *A must also be taller than C*. There are a great many transitive relations, such as *wider than* and *deeper than*. Transitive relations typically come in pairs, one of which is the opposite of the other (Clark & Card, 1969;

Harris, 1973). Thus *narrower than* is the opposite of *wider than* and *shallower than* is the opposite of *deeper than*.

A widely investigated form of reasoning is the *linear syllogism*, or **three-term series problem** (Wason & Johnson-Laird, 1972, Ch. 9). These problems consist of two comparative sentences from which a conclusion must be drawn. Suppose you were told that *B is smaller than A* and *B is larger than C*, and then asked *Which is smallest?* In response to such questions, many people construct a mental model consisting of a horizontal or vertical spatial array (DeSoto, London, & Handel, 1965; Johnson-Laird, 1972). A vertical array could be built by first placing B in the array, and then A above it, like this:

A
|
B

Then you could deal with the second premise by putting C below B.

A
|
B
|
C

By inspecting this imaginary array, you can see that C is the smallest. The conclusion is not required in order to construct the array. Rather, the conclusion emerges once the array has been constructed out of the two premises (B < A; B > C).

This example illustrates the fact that mental models are **iconic**, meaning that the relations between the parts of the model correspond to the relations between the parts of the situation it represents (Goodwin & Johnson-Laird, 2005, p. 475). The example also shows that you can get more out of a mental model than you put into it. Goodwin and Johnson-Laird (2005, p. 476) call this the principle of **emergent consequences**. After you construct a mental model, you can see relationships that were not evident before you constructed it.

Another principle is that of **parsimony**, whereby people tend to construct only one mental model if possible, and the simplest one at that. For example, what mental model would you construct given the following premises? *Ann is the blood relative of Chris* and *Chris is the blood relative of Gordon*. If you are like most people, you will construct a mental model something like this:

Ann
|
Chris
|
Gordon

This mental model leads to the conclusion that *Ann is the blood relative of Gordon*. However, treating *blood relative* as a transitive relation leads to an overly simple mental model. It is overly simple because it fails to consider the possibility that Gordon and Ann could be the parents of Chris, and thus not be blood relatives themselves. Participants given linear syllogisms based on such *pseudotransitive relations* drew the logically incorrect conclusion most of the time. However, when encouraged to think about more complicated examples, such as relationships based on marriage, participants can see the error of their thinking. Once again we see the pattern whereby people may at first behave somewhat less than logically, but subsequently can think in a more complex manner.

An Alternative to the Mental Models Approach

The best-known alternative to the mental models approach is based on **natural deduction systems** (Braine, 1978; Gentzen, 1964; Rips, 1983, 1988, 1994). To begin to understand this approach, let us consider a problem from Smullyan (1978, p. 22). The problem is cast in the form of statements made by the inhabitants of an island. Every inhabitant of the island is either a knight or a knave. Knights always tell the truth. Knaves always lie. Suppose you are told the following (Rips, 1989, p. 86):

> We have three inhabitants, A, B, and C, each of whom is a knight or a knave. Two people are said to be of the same type if they both are knights or both are knaves. A and B make the following statements:
>
> A: B is a knave.
>
> B: A and C are of the same type.
>
> What is C?

Knight-knave problems have definite answers. What do you think the answer is? We know that A is either a knight or a knave. Suppose we assume that A is a knight, and is therefore telling the truth. That means that 'B is a knave' is a true statement. Because knaves are liars, B's statement that A and C are of the same type is false. A and C must be of different types. If A is a knight, then C must be a knave. What happens if we begin by assuming that A is a knave, and is therefore lying? That means that 'B is a knave' is a false statement, and that B is a knight. Because knights tell the truth, B's statement that A and C are of the same type must be true. If A is a knave, then C must be a knave as well. Thus, if we begin by assuming that A is a knight, then we conclude that C is a knave, and if we begin by assuming that A is a knave, then we also conclude that C is a knave. C must be a knave.

Knight-knave problems have a solution, but some reasoning problems only look as if they have a solution. We can waste a lot of time trying to solve insoluble problems. This issue is explored in Box 10.1.

Box 10.1 Paradoxes, Reasoning, and Recursion

As we saw in Chapter 8, on language, some processes can refer to themselves. Recall that a process that refers to itself is *recursive*. Recursion can have interesting effects on reasoning. The first thing to see about recursion is that it can sometimes lead to awkward forms of thought. The most famous example of this is the *liar paradox* (P. Hughes & Brecht, 1975). There is a very old story about Epimenides the Cretan, who is supposed to have said, *All Cretans are liars.* Because Epimenides is a Cretan, he is referring to himself when he says that *All Cretans are liars.* Suppose that Epimenides is telling the truth. That means that *All Cretans are liars* is a true statement, and that Epimenides, being a Cretan, is himself a liar. But if Epimenides is a liar, then he cannot be telling the truth. Thus, the assumption that he is telling the truth leads to the conclusion that he is not telling the truth.

What happens if we begin by assuming that Epimenides is lying? That means that his statement that *All Cretans are liars* is a lie. Therefore, Epimenides is being truthful when he says that *All Cretans are liars*, his behaviour itself being an example of the fact. Thus, the assumption that Epimenides is a liar leads to the conclusion that he is being truthful. The general conclusion is that if Epimenides is being truthful, then he lies; and if he is lying, then he is being truthful. As Hughes and Brecht pointed out, this kind of reasoning makes your head swim.

Jumping Out of the Problem Space
Once you start thinking about the liar paradox, you can go around and around in a loop without appearing to get anywhere. Hofstadter (1979) considered this kind of thinking in great detail. One important point he made is that, in order to get out of an unproductive, recursive cycle of thinking, it is necessary to move to another, more inclusive level of thinking. Here is a version of one of Hofstadter's (1979, p. 33) problems that illustrates this point.

> Here are two letters:
>   AB
>
> You can perform several different operations on these letters. For example, you can change the B to BC as follows:
>   AB can be changed to ABC.
>
> You can also double the entire string of letters to the right of A, like this:
>   ABC can be changed to ABCBC. However, you cannot double individual letters to the right of A. Thus, neither ABBC nor ABBCC are consistent with this rule.
>
> If you can manage to generate a string of letters containing BBB, then you can replace BBB with a C, like this:
>   ABBBB can be rewritten as ABC.

Finally, any double C's (i.e., CC) may be dropped entirely, like this:
ABCC can be rewritten as AB.

To summarize, here are the four rules just described:
1.   B can be replaced by BC.
2.   The entire string of letters to the right of A may be doubled.
3.   BBB can be replaced by C.
4.   CC can be dropped entirely.

Now, using these rules, see if you can generate AC from AB. Go ahead and try it.

You may not be able to see that AC cannot be generated from AB if you simply accept the task as given. If you simply generate strings of letters by following the rules, then you will never generate AC. At what point do you decide that AC cannot be produced? There is no limit to the number of strings of letters you could produce, and the search for AC could go on forever. In order to solve the problem, you must see that the number of B's begins at 1, and that no rule will ever generate BBB or any multiple of 3 B's. This means that ABBB, for example, cannot ever be achieved, and so AC cannot either. To use Hofstadter's (1979) phrase, the thinker must *jump out of the system* (p. 37) to see that AC cannot be produced. Rather than reasoning in the system, with the rules as given, and generating endless strings of letters, you must reason outside the system.

The distinction between reasoning inside a problem space and reasoning outside or about a problem space is an important one, and we will return to it when we discuss intelligence. We need to be able to think *about* rules as well as being able to think *using* rules. Most studies of reasoning focus on people's ability to reason inside a problem space, without requiring them to think about the problem itself. It is important to understand how people think about problems and how they are able to tell when a problem is insoluble.

In a classic study, Paige and Simon (1966) gave participants problems like this to solve:

> A board was sawed into two pieces. One piece was two-thirds as long as the whole board, and was exceeded in length by the second piece by 4 feet. How long was the board before it was cut? (p. 89)

One way of approaching this problem is to immediately translate it into equations and try to solve them. Thus, suppose a participant proceeded this way:

> You could let x be equal to the length of the board. One of the pieces is equal to $2/3x$. The other piece is equal to $1/3x$. You know that the second length is 4 feet longer than the first, so the equation you want is $2/3x = 1/3x - 4$. Or is it?

(continued)

Have you seen what has gone wrong here? By taking the problem as given, the participant has arrived at an equation that will yield an impossible answer. If you solve the equation as given, you end up concluding that the board is a negative length—minus 12 feet, in fact. The problem actually refers to a physically impossible situation. If the first piece is two-thirds the length of the entire board, then the second piece cannot be longer than the first. Yet the problem says that the second piece is 4 feet longer than the first. So the problem itself contains a contradiction. In order to see that contradiction, the participant must look at the problem as a whole, rather than immediately begin trying to solve it. Paige and Simon found that some participants who were able to draw a diagram representing the problem were able to see that it contained a contradiction. Rather than immediately trying to solve a problem, the reasoner would do well to first decide if a problem can in fact be solved.

Natural Deduction Systems

Rips (1989) asked undergraduate participants to solve knight-knave problems and to think aloud while they did so. Participants appeared to follow deduction rules, which are part of a *natural deduction system*. A natural deduction system makes use of propositions stored in working memory. Propositions are statements built using connectives such as *if . . . then*, *and*, *or*, and *not*. The system makes use of deduction rules to draw conclusions from these propositions. When one proposition follows from another, the first proposition can be said to *entail* the second. Among the rules belonging to a natural deduction system are the following, where p and q are propositions (Rips, 1989, p. 94):

    1. p AND q entail p, q

This rule means that if you have a proposition of the form p AND q in working memory, then you can derive p and q as separate propositions. Thus, from the proposition 'A is a knight AND B is a knight' you can infer the two propositions 'A is a knight' and 'B is a knight.'

    2. p OR q and NOT p entails q

For example, if you have the propositions 'A is a knight OR B is a knight' and 'A is NOT a knight' in working memory, then you can infer the proposition 'B is a knight.'

    There are other rules that belong to the system, but these are probably enough to give you the general idea. A natural deduction system consists of psychologically basic inference rules. These are 'elementary inference principles' (Rips, 1989, p. 94) that participants rely on to solve reasoning problems. Rips showed that the number of errors and the time taken to solve the knight-knave problem depend on the number of inferences required.

The natural deduction approach to reasoning is different from Johnson-Laird's mental models approach. 'According to the natural deduction model, people carry out deduction tasks by constructing mental proofs. They represent the problem information, make further assumptions, draw inferences, and come to conclusions on the basis of this derivation' (Rips, 1989, p. 107).

Johnson-Laird and Byrne (1990; Johnson-Laird, 1997a, 1997b) proposed a mental models alternative to Rips's theory. However, Rips (1990, 1997) argued that there is no evidence from his data that people construct mental models to solve reasoning puzzles such as knight-knave problems. Gallotti, Baron, and Sabini (1986) studied the solution procedures of participants asked to solve a set of syllogisms and concluded that some participants seemed to take a mental models approach, whereas others used strategies that were more consistent with the sort of rule-following theory suggested by Rips. Nevertheless, it is unlikely that the two approaches can be easily reconciled (e.g., Johnson-Laird, 1997a, 1997b; Rips, 1997).

■ Wason's Puzzles

Syllogisms were not invented for the purpose of psychological research. Research on syllogistic reasoning is an example of an area in which a task familiar to a discipline other than psychology is studied in the hope that it will shed light on psychological processes. Another approach to the study of reasoning is to invent reasoning tasks that directly tap interesting aspects of reasoning. No one was more inventive in the design of psychologically interesting reasoning tasks than Wason (Evans & Johnson-Laird, 2003). His puzzles have been used in hundreds of studies. We will review research springing from three of his inventions: the generative problem, the THOG problem, and the card selection task.

The Generative Problem

According to Wason (1960, 1977a, 1978; Wason & Johnson-Laird, 1972), a generative problem is one in which people do not passively receive information about a problem, but must generate their own information in order to solve it. Wason apparently discovered this problem in a dream, and, as you will see, one of the characteristics of Wason's problems is that they can make your head swim.

Participants in an experiment using Wason's (1966) **generative problem** were told that 'the three numbers 2, 4, 6 conformed to a simple relational rule which the experimenter had in mind, and that their task was to discover the rule by generating sequences of three numbers, the experimenter telling them each time whether the rule held' (p. 139) for the sequence they generated. At each trial, participants would also write down a hypothesis about the rule. When participants felt highly confident that they had discovered the rule, they were allowed to propose it. They were told if they announced the wrong rule, and then they would continue with the task until they discovered the rule.

Participants in such an experiment tend to think that this task is more straightforward than it often turns out to be. For example, one of Wason's (1966, p. 140) participants generated the numbers 8, 10, 12, and was told that this sequence was consistent with the rule that Wason had in mind. At that point, the participant had the hypothesis that two are added to each previous number. Then the participant generated another sequence, 14, 16, 18, and was told that it was also consistent with the rule. The participant generated some other sequences, such as 20, 22, 24, and 1, 3, 5 and then proposed that *The rule is that by starting with any number, two is added each time to form the next number*—but this is not the rule Wason had in mind. The participant went on to propose several other sequences, such as 2, 6, 10, and other rules, such as *The rule is that the difference between two numbers next to each other is the same*. This was not the correct rule, either. Many of Wason's participants went on for quite a while like this and gave up before discovering the rule.

The rule Wason had in mind was *any increasing series of numbers*. Thus, all of the sequences proposed in the preceding paragraph are consistent with this rule (as are 1, 2, 3, or 1, 4, 9, or, for that matter, an infinite number of possible sequences). If you are a participant in this experiment, it is not a very good strategy to propose sequences that are consistent with your hypothesis about the rule. Rather, you should propose a sequence that is *inconsistent* with your hypothesis.

To see why this is so, consider the following example. Suppose you believe that *The rule is that by starting with any number, two is added each time to form the next number*. What will happen if you propose a sequence such as 1, 2, 3, which is inconsistent with your hypothesis? You will be told that it is consistent with the rule that the experimenter has in mind. You can then conclude that your hypothesis is false.

At first, it may not strike you as particularly useful to be able to discover that your hypothesis is false, but that is in fact all you can ever discover with certainty in this task. The appropriate strategy is to attempt to falsify your hypotheses, and thus eliminate incorrect beliefs. In this way, you can arrive at the correct rule by means of what Wason (1966, p. 141) called an **eliminative strategy**.

As influential philosophers of science (e.g., Popper, 1959) have pointed out, and as we saw in Chapter 9 on problem-solving, formulating a hypothesis and then attempting to falsify it is a key aspect of scientific inquiry. From that viewpoint, participants in this task were not behaving very much like scientists. Rather, they persisted in seeking confirmatory evidence for the hypotheses that they had. As we noted in the last chapter, even successful scientists may at first resist evidence that disconfirms a favorite hypothesis. Certainly, Wason's experiments show a strong tendency on the part of ordinary people to engage in what is called a **confirmation bias**. We will explore this inclination in more detail as we go along.

The THOG Problem

Wason (1977b) invented another problem that people often find very difficult to solve. The version of this problem comes from Smyth and Clark (1986, p. 275). Look at the designs on the next page: a *black diamond*, a *white diamond*, a *black circle*, and a *white circle*. Suppose that I have written down on a piece of paper the name of one of the colours (i.e., *black* or *white*) and the name of one of the shapes (i.e., *diamond* or *circle*). If,

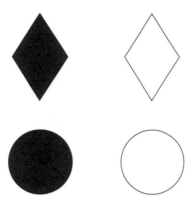

and only if, a design includes either the colour I have written down or the shape I have written down, but not both, then it is a THOG. Now I will tell you that the *black diamond* is a THOG. What can you conclude about each of the remaining three shapes? Are any of them THOGs?

Many people conclude that the *white diamond* and the *black circle* are THOGS, but that the *white circle* is definitely not a THOG (Wason & Brooks, 1979). These are called **intuitive errors** (Wason & Brooks, 1979; Griggs & Newstead, 1983) because participants find these conclusions so easy to reach. In fact, the *white circle* is definitely a THOG, and the *white diamond* and the *black circle* are definitely not THOGs. Do not be dismayed if you cannot see why this is so. As Wason (1978, p. 46) pointed out, many very clever people have difficulty with this problem. In fact, on average, only about 12 per cent of participants solve the THOG problem (Koenig & Griggs, 2004a, p. 558).

Let us see if we can understand why the *white circle* is a THOG. What colour and shape could I have written down? A THOG has one and only one of the properties I wrote down. Because the *black diamond* is a THOG, either I wrote down *black* or I wrote down *diamond*, but not both. Suppose the colour I wrote down was *black*. Then the shape I wrote down must be *circle*. If the colour I wrote down was *black*, then I cannot have written down *diamond*, because then the *black diamond* would have both the names I have written on the paper, and we know that a THOG has only one of the names I have written on the paper. Therefore, if I wrote down *black*, then I must have written down *circle*. Let us continue on and see what it would mean if I wrote down *black* and *circle*. It would mean that the *white circle* was a THOG, because it has one and only one of the properties I wrote down. It would also mean that the *black circle* was not a THOG because it has both of the properties that I wrote down. Moreover, the *white diamond* cannot be a THOG, because it has none of the properties I wrote down.

'All well and good', you might say, 'but how do we know that you wrote down *black* and *circle*? You could have written down something else.' Fair enough. What else could I have written down? We know that the black diamond is a THOG. If I did not write down *black*, then I must have written down *diamond*. Suppose I wrote down *diamond*. Then the colour I wrote down must be *white*. That way, the *black diamond* would be a THOG because it has one and only one of the properties I wrote down. Let us continue on and see what it would mean if I wrote down *white* and *diamond*. It would mean that the *white circle* was a THOG, because it has one and only one of the properties I wrote down. It would also mean that the *black circle* was not a THOG because it has none of the properties that I wrote down. Moreover, the *white diamond* cannot be a THOG, because it has both of the properties I wrote down.

So where are we now? Either I wrote down *white* and *diamond*, or I wrote down *black* and *circle*. If I wrote down *white* and *diamond*, then the *white circle* is a THOG, but the *white diamond* and the *black circle* are not THOGs. If I wrote down *black* and *circle*, then the *white circle* is a THOG, but the *white diamond* and the *black circle* are not THOGs. No matter how you slice it, the conclusion is the same. That is the most important thing about deductive logic: the conclusions are necessary; there is no avoiding them. However, as we have seen, ordinary people often do avoid drawing these necessary conclusions. Why is that?

Two possible explanations of the intuitive errors that people make were proposed by Griggs and Newstead (1983). Remember that a common error is to conclude that the white diamond and the black circle are THOGs because they share one property with the black diamond. Participants could make such an inference if they assumed that the properties of the example of a THOG (*black and diamond*) are also the two properties that constitute the rule for defining a THOG. Although this assumption is based on a misunderstanding of what makes something a THOG, it would explain why participants make intuitive errors. As Wason (1978) has noted, people find it very difficult to separate the properties of a particular THOG from the properties that define THOGness. To put that point more generally, people find it very difficult to separate the properties of a particular object from the properties that define class membership.

The second explanation that Griggs and Newstead suggested is that intuitive errors may be the result of a process that Evans (1982) called **matching bias**. This refers to a process whereby people will see two things as similar to the extent that they share features. If told that the black diamond is a THOG, then participants will think that a figure is a THOG to the extent that it matches the black diamond. Both the white diamond and the black circle have one matching feature with the black diamond, but the white circle has no matches. Griggs and Newstead concluded that both misunderstanding of the problem and matching bias account for the errors that people make in the THOG problem.

Analogical Transfer

When solving the THOG problem, participants must use the rule of exclusive disjunction. The participant must understand that in order to be a THOG something must have one or the other of two properties, but not both. Ever since the work of Bruner, Goodnow, and Austin (1956), which we discussed in the chapter on concepts, it has been known that people find it very difficult to reason with a relationship of exclusive disjunction. Smyth and Clark (1986) wondered whether a more realistic version of the THOG problem would not only be easier to solve, but also facilitate the solution of the original THOG problem.

The process whereby the solution of one problem facilitates the solution of another problem is called **analogical transfer** (Gick & Holyoak, 1983). One real-world example of an exclusive disjunctive relationship is that of *half-sister*. A woman is my half-sister if either my mother or my father is her parent, but not both. Smyth and Clark constructed a half-sister problem that is an analogue of the THOG problem. The problem goes like this: Listed below are the names of four women and their parents. My father and Bill are two different men, and my mother and Sarah are two different women. If Tiffany is my half-sister, which of the others is also my half-sister?

Name	Parent
Tiffany	My father and Sarah
Karen	Bill and Sarah
Louisa	My father and my mother
Kate	Bill and my mother

The correct answers are that Karen and Louisa are definitely not my half-sisters, but Kate definitely is my half-sister. Smyth and Clark gave participants the half-sister problem followed by the THOG problem and found that 14 out of 15 participants solved the half-sister problem, but only two of 15 solved the THOG problem. Participants did not see a relationship between the two problems. This suggests that people can understand a concrete instance of an exclusive disjunction, but have great difficulty reasoning when the rule is stated more abstractly.

Koenig and Griggs (2001, 2004a, 2004b) have reported more success in facilitating analogical transfer. They have done this by attacking the central difficulty that the THOG problem presents to participants. Recall that one source of intuitive errors is that participants tend to assume that the two properties of the *example* of a THOG (*black and diamond*) are also the two properties that constitute the *rule* for defining a THOG. In order to reason correctly, the participant must see that the properties that were *written down* are different from the properties of an *example* of a THOG.

Koenig and Griggs (2001, 2004b) used a version of THOG task designed by O'Brien, Noveck, Davidson, Fusch, Lea, and Freitag (1990). It is called the Blackboard THOG problem, and the following is a version of it (adapted from Koenig & Griggs, 2004b, Appendix B).

Recall the four figures at the beginning of our discussion of the THOG problem. Each figure is either black or white and either diamond or circle. On the left-hand side of a blackboard I have written down one of the colours (either *black* or *white*) and one of the shapes (either *diamond* or *circle*). On the right-hand side of the blackboard I have written down the other colour and the other shape. By writing these down in this way, I have developed the following classification rule.

The rule is: 'A figure will be classified as a THOG if and only if it includes EITHER the colour written down on the left-hand side of the blackboard, OR the shape written down on the left-hand side of the blackboard, BUT NOT BOTH.

I will tell you that the *black diamond* is a THOG.

Given this piece of information about the *black diamond* and the classification rule given above, decide for each of the other figures whether or not it can be classified as a THOG.

This version of the problem allows the participant to construct a mental model containing the principle required to reach the solution. Reaching a solution requires the participant to represent both combinations of properties that could constitute the rule that makes something a THOG. On the one hand they could be *black* or *circle*, but on the other hand they could be *white* or *diamond*. The blackboard format enables just such a representation. In two experiments, Koenig and Griggs (2001) found that participants solved blackboard versions of the problem around 70 per cent of the time, a considerable improvement over the typical rate at which the standard version of the problem is solved. Analogical transfer from the blackboard version of the problem to other versions of the THOG problem was also observed by Koenig and Griggs (2004b), especially when participants had been encouraged to generate hypotheses about what might have been written on the blackboard that resulted in the *black diamond* being called a THOG. In spite of the difficulty of this problem, these studies showed that 'the majority of participants are not only capable of the hypothetico-deductive reasoning required by the THOG task but also that they are capable of transferring this reasoning' (Koenig & Griggs, 2004b, p. 568).

The Selection Task

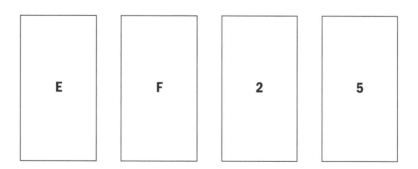

Wason's (1966, p. 145; Wason & Evans, 1975) **selection task** is his most influential invention. It has generated an enormous amount of research. Like Wason's other problems, this problem can appear deceptively simple and lead participants to believe that they know the answer when in fact they are mistaken. If you have not seen this problem before, you might like to try it yourself. If you were a participant in one of Wason's selection task experiments, then you would be shown four cards like the ones above. Every card has a number on one side and a letter on the other side. Suppose the experimenter told you: If a card has a vowel on one side, then it has an even number on the other side. Which cards must you turn over in order to determine whether or not the experimenter is telling the truth?

If you concluded that you need to turn over the E and the 2, or just the E, then you are in good company. Those are the most common types of response to this task. Johnson-Laird and Wason (1970) reported that of 128 participants given the selection task, 59 chose the alternatives corresponding to turning over the E and the 2, and another 42 participants chose just the alternative corresponding to turning over the E. However, these responses are not entirely correct. In order to see why there is another answer, we must explore the logical structure of this task more carefully.

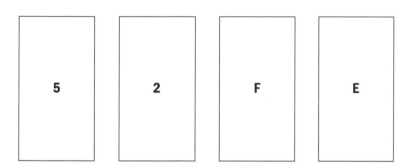

Think again about the rule the experimenter announced: If a card has a vowel on one side, then it has an even number on the other side. Suppose that the backs of the four cards you already have seen were like the ones above. Thus, if you turned over the E, you would find the number 5. Certainly, this discovery falsifies the rule and tells you that the experimenter was not telling the truth. Consequently, it is correct to want to turn over the E, because if you found an odd number, then that would tell you that the rule is false. Now consider what the result for the second card means. Because the F is not a vowel, it does not matter that there is an even number on the other side. No matter what is on the other side of the F, it does not tell you anything about the rule, so you do not need to turn this card over. The result for the third card is irrelevant to the rule, because the rule does not say that having an even number on one side *requires* that there be a vowel on the other. If there was a vowel on the other side it would be consistent with the rule, but having a consonant on the other side does not falsify the rule. You do not need to turn the third card over. The result for the fourth card, however, is particularly informative. If you turn over the 5, you find the letter E on the other side. Notice that this falsifies the rule, because there is a card with a vowel on one side and an odd number on the other. In general, you need to turn over cards displaying odd numbers, because they can falsify the rule.

Wason's selection task illustrates what is called **conditional reasoning**. Conditional reasoning requires the use of conditional statements. Conditional statements have an IF . . . THEN . . . form: IF one condition occurs, THEN another condition occurs. A conditional statement has two parts, the *antecedent* and the *consequent*. The antecedent comes after the word *if*, and the consequent comes after the word *then*. The rule in the selection task is an example of a conditional statement: IF *a card has a vowel on one side,* THEN *it has an even number on the other side.* The antecedent of this rule comes after IF, as in: IF *a card has a vowel on one side.* The consequent comes after the word THEN, as in: THEN *it has an even number on the other side.* In general, we can say that conditional statements have the form IF *p,* THEN *q,* where *p* refers to the antecedent, and *q* refers to the consequent.

Truth tables were invented by Wittgenstein (1921/1974, p. 32) as a way of presenting the various combinations of the constituents of logical statements. In the truth table below are listed the possible truth values for an antecedent (*p*) and a consequent (*q*). The truth value of *p* can be either true (T) or false (F), as can the truth value of *q*. When both *p* and *q* are true, then obviously the conditional statement IF *p* THEN *q* is also true. When *p* is true, but *q* is false, then IF *p* THEN *q* is false. This case corresponds to a card with a vowel on one side, but an odd number on the other. If *p* is false, but *q* is true, then IF *p,* THEN *q* is still true. This case corresponds to a card with a consonant on one side and an even number on the other. As we saw above, such a case does not falsify the rule. To drive this point home, consider a statement such as *If it rains, then the match will be cancelled* (Strawson, 1952, p. 82). The match might be cancelled for a variety of reasons other than rain, and that would not falsify the statement. Finally, if both *p* and *q* are false, then that does not falsify IF *p,* THEN *q.* If it does not rain, and the match is not cancelled, then the rule still stands.

p	Q	If p then q
T	T	T
T	F	F
F	T	T
F	F	T

Initially, the results of experiments using the selection task were taken as evidence in favour of the operation of a confirmation bias. If participants choose a card showing a vowel and a card showing an even number, then they are choosing cards that could confirm the rule. They are not deliberately choosing cards that would disconfirm the rule. Oakhill and Johnson-Laird (1985) argued that actively seeking information that will disconfirm a rule is one of the characteristics of rational thought.

> Rationality depends on the search for counterexamples. If, say, you hold the prejudice that women are bad drivers, and your curiosity is only provoked by cases of bad driving, then you will never be shaken from your bias; if a bad driver turns out to be a woman, your prejudice is confirmed; if a bad driver turns out to be a man your prejudice is not disconfirmed since you don't believe that only women are bad drivers. Unless you somehow are able to grasp the potential relevance of *good* drivers to your belief, then the danger is that you will never be disabused of it, and will never understand the force of counterexamples. (p. 93)

Subsequent research has shown that the selection task is heavily influenced by the content of the cards (Johnson-Laird, 1983, pp. 31ff.). For example, Wason and Shapiro (1971) showed that a more realistic version of the task was much easier to solve. Suppose that the rule is: *Every time I go to Toronto, I travel by plane*. In a task such as this, the majority of participants see that they need to turn over the card with *car* on it. This is because, as you should have guessed by now, if they turn over the card with *car* on it, and it has *Toronto* on the other side, then the rule will have been falsified.

The Selection Task and Domain-Specific Reasoning

Cosmides (1989) pointed out that the evidence is quite weak in favour of the hypothesis that people reason in accordance with the rules of a single logical system. If people did use one logical system when they reason, then their reasoning processes should not be affected by the content of the problem. However, as we have just seen, performance on logical tasks such as Wason's selection task are heavily influenced by content. The inferences people make with a concrete version of the task are different from the inferences they make with an abstract version. Cosmides argued that the evidence is compelling that people do not use the same reasoning processes across different tasks, and consequently there is not a single 'psychologic' that people use when they reason.

Cosmides (1989; Cosmides & Tooby, 1994; Fiddick, Cosmides, & Tooby; 2000) proposed an evolutionary account of human reasoning. 'It is advantageous to reason adaptively, instead of logically, when this allows one to draw conclusions that are likely to be true but cannot be inferred by strict adherence' to formal logic (Cosmides, 1989, p. 193). Natural selection would tend to produce inference procedures for solving 'important and recurrent adaptive problems' (Cosmides, 1989, p. 193). What constitutes adaptive reasoning may differ from one type of problem to another. Consequently, different types of problem may require the use of different, *domain-specific* inference procedures.

One kind of adaptive problem that humans must solve involves 'social exchange—co-operation between two or more individuals for mutual benefit' (Cosmides, 1989, p. 195). People make **social contracts**. They agree to arrangements in which they give something up in order to gain something else. A social contract specifies the relationship between the costs and the benefits of such an arrangement. It would be very important to be able to detect cheaters—individuals who violate social contracts. Such people would attempt to have the benefit without paying the cost (Cosmides, 1989, p. 197). Cosmides hypothesized that inference procedures have evolved that allow us to pay particular attention to such cases.

With this background in mind, consider the inferences required in the Wason selection task. This task can be used to represent a social contract, as shown below. The standard social contract can be stated in the form of the following rule: *If you take the benefit, then you pay the cost*. Obviously, in order to see if the rule is being followed, you would choose the *Cost not paid* and the *Benefit accepted* cards. The other two cards are irrelevant to the detection of cases of rule violation.

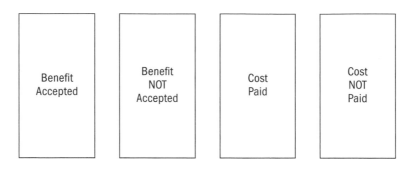

A 'switched' social contract has a different structure. A switched social contract can be stated in this form: *If you pay the cost, then you take the benefit.* How would you detect violations of this rule? If you are to behave logically, then you must choose the *Benefit not accepted* and the *Cost paid* cards shown above. For a switched social contract, the logically correct choices are the two cards that should not be chosen for a standard social contract. Cosmides hypothesized that people will tend to follow a procedure for detecting cheaters, i.e., violations of a social contract. In order to detect cheaters, the person should choose the *Cost not paid* and *Benefit accepted* cards even in the switched social contract version of the problem. Thus, the logically correct and the social contract choices are different for this problem. Cosmides presented evidence that participants given social contract and switched social contract problems make choices that are consistent with social contract theory.

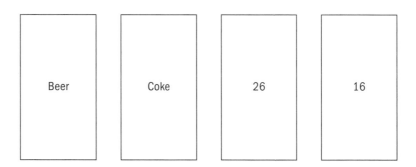

In general, Cosmides argued that in a selection task that has the content of a social contract people will make inferences consistent with social contract theory. However, a selection task that does not have such content does not elicit such inferences. Thus, the abstract version of the Wason selection task does not embody a social contract, and does not elicit the same inferences as does the concrete social contract version shown above, which was invented by Griggs and Cox (1982). In this example, each card has a beverage on one side and an age on the other side. The rule is: *If a person is drinking beer, then he must be over 21 years old.* The benefit, such as it is, is being allowed to drink beer. The cost is waiting until you are 21. In order to detect cheaters, you should turn over the Beer card and the 16 card, and this is in fact what participants do when asked to solve this problem.

Cosmides's results were replicated with similar problems by Gigerenzer and Hug (1992). They have also been replicated in a culture quite remote from Harvard, which is where Cosmides (1989) gathered her original data. Sugiyama, Tooby, and Cosmides (2002) studied the Shiwiar, who are hunter-horticulturalists living in the Ecuadorian Amazon. Sugiyama et al. (2002) hypothesized that a domain-specific reasoning process such as cheater detection would be a cross-cultural universal. This would be because natural selection would have ensured that such a functional process cannot be disrupted by 'cultural or environment variability' (p. 11538). Most tests of the existence of a domain-specific cheater detection module had been conducted in literate, industrialized societies. Consequently, it was important to see if the same sort of reasoning process exists in a very different, much more isolated cultural context. Of course, a selection task about being old enough to drink beer is not an appropriate research tool for the Shiwiar, and so the task was modified to be culturally relevant. The standard social contract was *If you eat an aphrodisiac, then you must be married*. The switched social contract was *If you give me a basket of fish when you return from fishing, then you may use my motorboat*. Given these tasks, the Shiwiar chose the cheater detection response at a rate almost identical to that of Harvard students. Sugiyama et al. (2002, p. 11541) concluded that reasoning governing social contracts is 'a reliably developing, universal feature of the human cognitive architecture, functioning as an evolutionarily stable strategy'.

Cosmides's theory of reasoning holds that there are specialized inference procedures that we use to think about different kinds of problems, although precisely how many inference procedures there may be is an open question. Cosmides argued against the view that people use the same reasoning procedures across all domains. Rather, there may be several different *domain-specific modules* that operate in different ways on problems with different content (Cosmides & Tooby, 1994). We have already seen, in the chapters on attention and concepts, that this modular view has been applied to other aspects of cognition. We will see other examples of this modular approach when we consider theories of intelligence.

■ Dual-Process Theories of Reasoning

As we have seen repeatedly in this chapter, reasoning logically can occur in spite of tendencies to reason in non-logical ways. Some theorists (e.g., Evans, 2003; Sloman, 1996; Stanovich & West, 2000, 2003a) have postulated the existence of two distinct reasoning systems. These **dual-process theories** incorporate many of the distinctions we have made in previous chapters. For example, in Chapter 3 we discussed the distinction between *automatic* processes (also called *bottom-up*, *stimulus-driven*, and *involuntary*) as opposed to *controlled* processes (also called *top-down*, *goal-directed*, and *voluntary*). In studies of reasoning one often finds conclusions drawn more or less automatically, driven by the content of the stimulus materials without much thought on the part of the participant. This sort of process contrasts with the more effortful process of logical reasoning that is under voluntary control. The two processes that underly reasoning have been given different names by different theorists. Evans (2003) and Stanovich and West (2000) called them System 1 and System 2, and that is the convention we will follow.

The distinction between System 1 and System 2 is also similar to the distinction we encountered in Chapter 7 between *implicit* and *explicit learning*. Recall that Reber (1990, 1997) concluded that the implicit cognitive system is very old in evolutionary terms, and has not changed for a long time. 'Once an adaptive, functional system evolves, and . . . the system is broadly operational in diverse environments, there is no adaptive value in change' (Reber, Walkenfeld, & Hernstadt, 1991, p. 894). By contrast, explicit cognition is newer and less fixed by evolutionary processes. Consequently, while people differ widely in terms of explicit cognitive abilities, they do not differ very much in terms of implicit cognitive processes. Implicit cognition is a process in which we all share and share alike.

Stanovich and West (1998) extended Reber's way of thinking by studying individual differences in reasoning. Among other tasks, Stanovich and West gave undergraduate student participants a syllogistic reasoning task and versions of Wason's selection task. The syllogistic reasoning tasks consisted of eight syllogisms, four of which were valid and four invalid. The valid syllogisms had unbelievable conclusions and the invalid ones had believable conclusions. Thus, the tendency for participants to respond to the content of the syllogisms was pitted against the tendency to reason logically. Wason's selection task was represented by five items illustrating five different rules, such as *If Baltimore is on one side of the ticket, then Plane is on the other side*. Participants also provided their scores on the Scholastic Aptitude Test, and took tests of general intelligence and reading comprehension. Scores on these three tests were combined to yield a composite cognitive ability score.

The scores on cognitive ability, scores on the syllogisms task, and scores on the selection task all were positively related. The magnitude of these relationships was statistically significant, but not perfect. Thus, cognitive ability explains some, but not all, of the individual differences in performance on logical reasoning tasks. This conclusion was confirmed by Stanovich and West (1998) in other experiments using different tasks. The imperfect relationship between cognitive ability and logical reasoning means that some participants low in cognitive ability were able to reason logically, and some participants high in cognitive ability managed to reason illogically. However, in general, the higher one's cognitive ability, the better one's logical reasoning performance. This relationship requires an explanation.

Stanovich and West (1998, p. 180) pointed out that one of the most reliable findings in logical reasoning research is that participants' behaviour is contextualized, in the sense that it tends to be influenced by the particular characteristics of the reasoning task. For example, in syllogistic reasoning tasks people are strongly influenced by the believability of the conclusion. Logical reasoning takes place within a particular context, and to be influenced by that context is the **fundamental computational bias** (Stanovich & West, 1998, p. 180). In order to make a de-contextualized response, the participant must ignore the current context. Logical reasoning tasks require the participant to grasp the logical form rather than be driven by the content of the task. High cognitive ability may allow participants to 'flexibly reason so as to override the fundamental computational bias if the situation requires' (Stanovich & West, 1998, p. 181).

Stanovich and West (2000) hypothesized that System 1 is responsible for the fundamental computational bias, while System 2 is responsible for de-contextualized reasoning. System 1 is old in evolutionary terms, and is adapted to environments that existed millennia ago. System 2 evolved much more recently, and can be powerfully influenced by the individual's education. Evans (2003, p. 467) suggested that the emergence of System 2 may be linked to the sudden explosion of cultural artifacts that occurred 40,000–50,000 years ago. In Box 8.1, we discussed the possible association of that period with the evolution of language. Perhaps both language and System-2 reasoning emerged at the same time.

Some of the characteristics imputed to each system by Over (2002, p. 989), Sloman (1996, p. 7), and Stanovich and West (2000, p. 659) are given in Table 10.1. Not all theorists would describe these characteristics in exactly the same terms, but the list in Table 10.1 does give you a sense of the general nature of the distinction. System 1 relies on implicit cognition, which is largely unconscious. Using System 1, the person finds a conclusion compelling without necessarily knowing why. That is because System 1 is an automatic response to a particular situation, and occurs very fast. System 1 is to some extent made up of domain-specific processes, perhaps including the cheater detection module described by Cosmides, and System 1 is pretty much the same in everyone. By contrast, System 2 makes use of explicit rules and is often under conscious control. It considers one thing at a time, and so is comparatively slow. System 2 is relatively domain-general, operating in an abstract and de-contextualized manner. Finally, System 2 plays a greater role in the lives of some people than in those of others. People who excel at System-2 reasoning may have been able to take better advantage of the educational system in order to acquire logical reasoning skills.

Stanovich (2004; Stanovich & West, 2003b) theorized that System 1 and System 2 may have different goals. System 1 is older in evolutionary terms, and is more closely tied to the goal of genetic replication. As Dawkins (1976, 1986) observed, genes are

Table 10.1 Some Characteristics of System 1 and System 2

System 1	System 2
Implicit	Explicit
Automatic	Controlled
Fast	Slow
Mostly domain-specific	Mostly domain-general
Not greatly determined by individual differences	Varies with individual differences in cognitive abilities

selfish. If genes had a viewpoint, it would be that organisms exist in order to provide genes with a method of replicating themselves. System 1 is kept on a 'short leash' (Stanovich, 2004, p. 12) by virtue of being largely, although not entirely, genetically programmed. System 1 exists to serve its genetic master. System 2, by contrast, has a longer leash. It can have the long-term interest of the person as a whole as its goal. Although System 1 and System 2 need not conflict, it is possible for System 2 to override System 1. System 1 may respond automatically to every opportunity to spread the organism's genes around, but System 2 may understand that we are:

> living in a complex technological society in the twenty-first century and that considerations such as spouse, children, job, and societal position dictate that this particular 'go for it!' signal . . . be overridden. Instead, [System 2] has calculated that the individual's entire set of long-term life goals are better served by overriding this [System 1] triggered response tendency even though the latter might result in actions with temporary positive utility. (Stanovich, 2004, p. 63)

This last example may strike you as Freudian, but Stanovich and West (2003a) insisted that the comparison is inappropriate. For one thing, Systems 1 and 2 need not always be in conflict. System 1 should not be seen as 'irrational'. Rather, its aims are more limited than those of System 2, which is flexible enough to be able to acquire the kinds of skills that may be particularly useful in a rapidly changing, post-industrial, knowledge-based society. Abstract System 2 skills that people can use to solve problems and reason in a variety of work environments would appear to be increasingly valuable (Trachtenberg, Streumer, & van Zolingen, 2002).

■ Questions for Study and Discussion

1. Discuss possible sources of difficulty in syllogistic reasoning, paying particular attention to content bias and the meaning of *some*.

2. Do you use practical syllogisms without noticing that you do? If not, how do you decide what to do?

3. Outline Johnson-Laird's mental models approach to syllogistic reasoning. Compare it to natural deduction theory.

4. What does work done with Wason's puzzles suggest about what makes a reasoning problem difficult?

5. Aristotle claimed that people were rational animals. To what extent do you think that is true? Under what conditions might people be the most rational? Can animals other than humans be rational?

6. Could we get along without System-2 reasoning? Isn't System-2 reasoning really superfluous? In fact, why do we need to reason at all? As long as we stay in touch with our feelings we'll be OK, right?

■ Key Concepts

Analogical transfer The process whereby the solution of one problem facilitates the solution of another problem.

Confirmation bias The tendency to seek confirmatory evidence for a hypothesis.

Definition of reasoning A process of thought that yields a conclusion from percepts, thoughts, or assertions.

Dual-process theories The hypothesis that there are two reasoning systems. System 1 is automatic, fast, and contextualized. System 2 is controlled, slow, and abstract.

Eliminative strategy The attempt to falsify your hypotheses, and thus eliminate incorrect beliefs.

Emergent consequences One of three principles of Johnson-Laird's mental models theory, which states that you can get more out of a mental model than you put into it.

Fundamental computational bias Reasoners tend to be influenced by the context within which reasoning takes place.

Generative problem (Wason) Participants are told that the three numbers 2, 4, 6 conform to a simple relational rule that the experimenter has in mind, and that their task is to discover the rule by generating sequences of three numbers. The experimenter tells them each time whether the rule has been followed.

Iconic One of three principles of Johnson-Laird's mental models theory, which claims that the relations between the parts of the model correspond to the relations between the parts of the situation it represents.

Intuitive errors Errors made in reasoning problems where the obvious 'solution' is incorrect.

Logicism The belief that logical reasoning is an essential part of human nature.

Matching bias A process whereby people will see two things as similar to the extent that they share features.

Mental models (Johnson-Laird) The theory that people construct a mental model of the situation to which a set of premises refers, on the basis of which they draw conclusions.

Natural deduction system (Rips) A reasoning system made up of propositions and deduction rules to draw conclusions from these propositions.

Parsimony One of three principles of Johnson-Laird's mental models theory, which states that people tend to construct only one mental model if possible, and the simplest one at that.

Practical syllogism The conclusion drawn from two premises becomes an action.

Relational reasoning Reasoning involving premises that express the relations between items, such as *A is taller than B*.

Selection task (Wason) A four-card problem based on **conditional reasoning**, which requires the use of premises of an *IF . . . THEN . . .* form.

Social contract theory (Cosmides) The theory that inference procedures have evolved to deal with social contracts in which people give something up in order to gain something else.

Syllogistic reasoning A syllogism consists of two premises and a conclusion. Each of the premises specifies a relationship between two categories.

THOG problem A problem based on the relation of exclusive disjunction.

Three-term series problem Linear syllogisms consisting of two comparative sentences from which a conclusion must be drawn.

Truth tables A way of presenting the various combinations of the constituents of logical statements.

■ Links to Other Chapters

Mental models
    Chapter 6 (cognitive maps and mental models)

Emergent properties
    Chapter 2 (Sperry)
    Chapter 6 (imagery and ambiguous figures)

Confirmation bias
    Chapter 11 (heuristics and biases)

Dual-process theories
    Chapter 11 (overview)

■ Further Reading

Consider this problem. Suppose that the following assertions apply to a specific hand of cards:

> If there is a king in the hand then there is an ace in the hand,
> or else if there is a queen in the hand then there is an ace in the hand.
> There is a king in the hand.
> What, if anything, follows?

If you think that there *must* be an ace in the hand, then you should read Johnson-Laird, P.N., & Savary, F. (1999). Illusory inferences: A novel class of erroneous deductions. *Cognition, 71*, 191–229.

If you find paradoxes interesting, read Sainsbury, R.M. (1988). *Paradoxes*. Cambridge: Cambridge University Press.

A novel approach to the study of reasoning based on the centrality of linguistic processes is Polk, T.A., & Newell, A. (1995). Deduction as verbal reasoning. *Psychological Review, 102*, 533–566.

There has been intense research interest in the selection task. As a consequence, there are too many alternative explanations to fully cover in this text. For example, an account of the selection task based on relevance theory is in Sperber, D., & Girotto, V. (2002). Use or misuse of the selection task? Rejoinder to Fiddick, Cosmides, and Tooby. *Cognition, 85*, 277–290. A connectionist approach to the selection task may be found in Leighton, J.P., & Dawson, M.R.W. (2001). A parallel distributed processing model of Wason's selection task. *Journal of Cognitive Systems Research, 2*, 207–231.

Atran, S. (2001). A cheater detection module? Dubious interpretations of the Wason selection task and logic. *Evolution and Cognition, 7*, 1–7, argues that the selection task does not require a domain-specific interpretation.

Useful reviews of Stanovich's theories are given by Thompson, V. (2001). Intelligence, cognitive style, and rationality: Is being rational smart? Review of Keith E. Stanovich, 'Who is rational: Studies of individual differences in reasoning'. *Canadian Journal of Experimental Psychology, 54*, 77–79; and Evans, J. St B.T. (2004). Dual processes, evolution and rationality. *Thinking & Reasoning, 10*, 405–410.

Judgement
and Choice

Judgement and choice are two sides of the same coin. Good judgement is a prerequisite for being able to make good decisions. If one is able to make good judgements, then one will be able to appropriately choose between alternative courses of action. The circumstances under which we make good or bad judgements have been extensively explored. A parallel line of investigation concerns the nature of good judgement itself. A recurrent issue throughout this chapter will be the following question: How can we tell whether or not a particular judgement is a good one?

The study of judgement and choice has been strongly influenced by the collaborative research program of Amos Tversky (1937–96) and Daniel Kahneman, the latter of whom won the Nobel Prize in 2002. (You can watch Kahneman deliver his Nobel Prize lecture at http://nobelprize.org/economics/laureates/2002/kahneman-lecture.html.) Kahneman (2002, 2003; Kahneman & Frederick, 2002) adopted a version of the dual-process theory we considered at the end of the last chapter. He used the word **intuition** as a label for System 1, and **reason** as a label for System 2. Intuition is an involuntary process much like perception. Reason monitors the output of intuition, but not in a very vigilant manner. This relaxed form of supervision 'allows many intuitive judgements to be expressed, including some that are erroneous' (Kahneman, 2002, p. 451).

The similarity between perception and intuition, and why they both are prone to error, is commonly illustrated by means of visual illusions (e.g., Titchener, 1910/1966; Tversky & Kahneman, 1986/2000). Consider the Müller-Lyer illusion shown in Figure 11.1. People typically judge the horizontal line on the left to be longer than the one on the right. However, the horizontal line on the left is actually the same length as the

Figure 11.1 The Muller-Lyer Illusion.

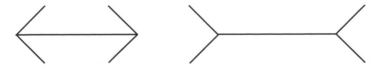

horizontal line on the right. The context in which the lines are presented determines the judgement that is made. However, if you were to take the trouble to measure the two lines, then you would reach a different judgement. Our intuitive judgement may lead us astray and require adjustment in the light of further investigation.

■ Heuristics and Biases

The research program initiated by Kahneman and Tversky is called the **heuristics and biases** program (Gilovich & Griffin, 2002). People often use heuristics, or rules of thumb, which may work in some situations, but which mislead them in others. When we reviewed Wason's work in the last chapter, we noted that people are prone to making errors in reasoning tasks due to such processes as *confirmation bias* and *matching bias*. Biases are ways in which we are predisposed to make judgements. Tversky and Kahneman along with other psychologists have uncovered several biases associated with particular heuristics. In what follows we examine some of the biases that arise in situations in which people must make judgements and/or decisions.

■ Intuitive Statistics

What happens when people try to estimate the relative frequency or proportion of times an event will occur? For example, suppose you are asked to predict how often an unbiased coin will come up heads in a series of four tosses? Obviously, the best guess is two out of four. Because the coin is unbiased, you would expect it to be heads 50 per cent of the time. However, it should not amaze you if there are no heads in a series of four tosses of an unbiased coin. In general, any particular sample of events may not mirror the proportions in the total population. That is because an unbiased coin will come up heads 50 per cent of the time in the long run, but may come up heads in other proportions in the short run. This fact is called the **law of large numbers**.

One of the misconceptions surrounding the law of large numbers is its relation to what is commonly called the **law of averages** (Newman, 1956, pp. 1450ff.). The law of large numbers allows us to believe that a particular proportion will obtain in the long run. Thus, we expect that an unbiased coin will have come up heads very close to 50 per cent of the time after a large number of tosses. Suppose that after 10 tosses a coin has never come up heads once. The common belief in the so-called law of averages often leads us to believe that in this situation it is more likely that the coin will come up tails than that it will come up heads. People appear to believe that because there will be an equal number of heads and tails in the long run, there must be more tails to compensate for the heads that have already come up.

That this conclusion is incorrect can be seen from the following hypothetical example, adapted from Schuh (1968, pp. 211ff.). It could be that after an initial run of 10 heads there are even numbers of heads and tails over the next 1,000 tosses. This would mean that there were 510 heads and 500 tails after 1,000 tosses of the coin. This is pretty close to a 50–50 split; in fact, it is a 50–50 split to two decimal places. All the law of large numbers requires is that the proportion of heads or tails increasingly approximate 0.50 after a sufficiently large number of tosses. The law of large numbers does not require that this proportion actually be 0.50 after some arbitrary number of tosses, such as 1,000. At no point in the sequence of tosses, regardless of how many there are, do the odds of throwing a head or a tail differ from 50–50. The odds on any particular coin toss are independent of any other coin toss. Believing otherwise is called the **gambler's fallacy**. Thus, it is a fallacy to believe that the odds of throwing a tail are better after a sequence of heads than after some other sequence.

■ Representativeness and the Belief in the Law of Small Numbers

It was pointed out above that a particular sample of events may not reflect the proportions that are in the entire population. Suppose that half the population of a university are men, the other half women. That does not mean that a small, random sample of 10 people at the university will contain five men and five women. However, people often seem to believe in what A. Tversky and Kahneman (1971) called the **law of small numbers**. This is the belief that a small sample should be representative of the population from which it is drawn. Belief in the law of small numbers leads to the use of the **representativeness heuristic**, which involves making inferences on the assumption that small samples resemble one another and the population from which they are drawn. An example of the use of the representativeness heuristic is as follows:

> There are two programs in a high school. Boys are a majority (65 per cent) in program A, and a minority (45 per cent) in program B. There are equal numbers of classes in each of the two programs.
>
> You enter a class at random, and observe that 55 per cent of the students are boys. What is your best guess—does the class belong to program A or program B? (Kahneman & Tversky, 1972, p. 431)

People will tend to guess that the class belongs to program A, because it has a majority of boys. The class is more *representative* of program A than it is of program B.

The same kind of representativeness heuristic operates when people judge sequences of events in terms of whether or not they were produced by a random process. Tversky and Kahneman discussed research showing that a sequence of coin tosses such as T T H H T T H H does not strike people as being truly random. This is because it has a pattern, and patterns are intuitively unlikely if a process is producing events randomly, and not according to some rule.

Lopes (1982) pointed out that even very sophisticated thinkers with a lot of mathematical training have difficulty clearly specifying what distinguishes a random from a non-random process. She noted that there is a difference between a random process and a random product. A random process, such as tossing an unbiased coin, may generate sequences that do not appear to be random. The product of a random process may itself strike us as non-random. Thus, it is perfectly possible for an unbiased coin to generate the sequence T T H H T T H H, but most of us will feel that this sequence is not one we would choose to represent random products.

Is There a Hot Hand in Basketball?

A controversial example of the way that the representativeness heuristic works was presented by Gilovich, Vallone, and Tversky (1985). They studied the so-called 'hot hand' in men's professional basketball. Fans sometimes perceive a player as having a hot hand, that is, as having a run of baskets, or streak shooting. Having a hot hand means that the player shoots a series of baskets (hits) that are very unlikely to have been produced by a random process. Gilovich et al. (1985) presented data showing that 91 per cent of fans believe that a player has 'a better chance of making a shot after having just made his last two or three shots than he does after having just missed his last two or three shots' (p. 297).

Gilovich et al. analyzed 48 home games of the Philadelphia 76ers. The games were played in the 1980–1 season. They could find no evidence that players were more likely to shoot a basket after making one, two, or three baskets than they were after missing one, two, or three baskets. That is, the chance of a player hitting a shot is not greater after a sequence of hits than it is after a sequence of misses. Thus, for example, if a player makes 50 per cent of his shots, then the probability of his hitting a shot is not greater than 50 per cent after a hit, nor is it lower than 50 per cent after a miss. There was no evidence that shooters' hits and/or misses are clustered. That is, sequences of hits and misses occurred no more frequently than would be expected on a purely chance basis.

An interesting additional fact is that the members of the basketball team themselves appear to have the same beliefs as do their fans. Gilovich et al. found that most of the Philadelphia 76ers players they interviewed endorsed the hot-hand beliefs of their fans. The players also tended to believe that hits were more likely following hits than following misses. Both fans and players apparently tend to perceive sequences of shots as streak shooting, even though these sequences do not in fact differ from sequences that would be produced by a random process in which the probability of a basket is independent of the outcome of preceding shots.

What sort of process might produce the illusion that basketball players are streak shooters? One possibility suggested by Gilovich et al. is that a belief in streak shooting is the result of misperceiving sequences of events generated by a random process. Occasionally, a shooter may hit a few baskets in a row, just as an unbiased coin may come up heads a few times in a row. A short sequence of heads may be the outcome of a random process, just as a short sequence of baskets may be the outcome of a random process. However, people expect all outcomes of a random process to contain frequent alternations between alternatives. As we saw earlier, people typically regard a short sequence of events that does not contain many alternations to be unrepresentative of a random process. As Gilovich et al. pointed out, the value of perceiving order where there is only randomness is difficult to understand. In the case of basketball, for example, believing that a player has a hot hand might lead players to pass the ball to their teammate with the 'hot hand' more than to other players.

Many people disputed Gilovich et al.'s conclusion, and the hot-hand belief may in fact be true for some sports (e.g., Gilden & Wilson, 1995). However, at least in the case of basketball, it is now generally accepted by statistically sophisticated observers that the hot-hand belief is false. However, even if the hot-hand belief is false, it may still be useful to behave as if it is true. Burns (2004) distinguished between the **hot-hand belief** and the **hot-hand behaviour**. The latter is a bias for a basketball player to take the next shot after previously scoring a basket. Players in the NBA reliably differ from one another in terms of the percentage of their shots that are baskets (i.e., shooting percentage). Burns showed that shooting percentages are correlated with streaks, such that players with higher shooting percentages tend also to be the players who have the most streaks of two or three baskets in a row. Moreover, players with higher shooting percentages tend also to be the players who have the *fewest* streaks of two or three *misses* in a row. Concretely, a player who makes 52 per cent of his shots will tend to have more streaks of two and three hits and fewer streaks of two or three misses than will a player who makes 38 per cent of his shots. Streakiness is a reliable predictor of shooting percentage. Thus, if a player hits two baskets in a row, it is reasonable to give that player the next shot. This is because players who hit two baskets in a row tend to be those with a better shooting percentage. The players themselves may believe that they give the ball to the person who has scored two baskets in a row because that player has a hot hand. However, the reality is that they are giving the ball to a player with a better shooting percentage. Belief in the hot hand may be false, but hot-hand behaviour is useful, in that it leads to better shooters getting the ball more often.

'The hot hand belief may be the way players explain to themselves why they follow the hot hand behavior' (Burns, 2004, p. 319). Professional basketball players are very experienced, and so the link between the hot-hand belief and hot-hand behaviour cannot be due to naïveté. Burns tested the hypothesis that the more experience one has as a basketball player then the more likely one is to say 'Yes' to both of the questions below. The first is the *hot-hand belief question*, and the second is the *hot-hand behaviour question*.

> Does a college/professional basketball player have a better chance of making a shot after having just made his/her last two or three shots than he/she does after having missed his/her last two or three shots?
>
> In college/professional basketball is it important to pass the ball to someone who has just made several (two, three, or four) shots in a row?

The participants were over 1,000 undergraduates who were classified according to their self-reported basketball experience, ranging from playing on a college team through playing pickup games to never having played basketball. Figure 11.2 gives the percentage of 'Yes' answers to the two questions as a function of skill level. You can see that 'Yes' answers to both questions increase with skill level. The more skilled participants are more likely to correctly endorse the hot-hand behaviour, but incorrectly to

Figure 11.2 Percentage of Participants Who Answered 'Yes' to the Hot-hand Belief and the Hot-hand Behaviour Questions as a Function of Skill Level.

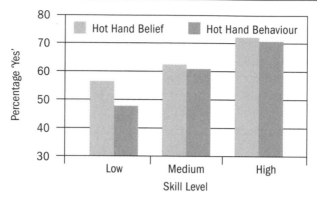

Data from Burns, B.D. (2004). Heuristics as beliefs and behaviors: The adaptiveness of the 'hot hand'. *Cognitive Psychology, 48*, p. 322.

endorse the hot-hand belief. This suggests that a fallacious belief may sometimes lead to useful behaviour. As Burns (2004) concludes, it is not necessarily the case that true beliefs and adaptive behaviour will always go together. Later in this chapter we will explore further the conditions under which we can do the right thing for the wrong reasons (and vice versa).

Streakiness and the Brain

The degree to which people perceive streaks of hits and misses is truly remarkable. It is almost as if they cannot help themselves, and that may indeed be true. In a functional Magnetic Resonance Imaging (fMRI) study, Huettel, Mack, and McCarthy (2002) presented participants with a series of 1,800 trials. On each trial participants saw either a circle or a square, and pressed one button for a square and another for a circle. The order in which the stimuli were presented was random. As you know, even in a random sequence there may be streaks of varying lengths. For example, a circle may occur six or more times in a row, and likewise for a square. Huettel et al. (2002, p. 488) informed their participants that 'the stimuli were presented in a random sequence, that there was no need to make explicit predictions, and that there was no benefit in doing so.' Nevertheless, the time participants took to respond increased when a streak came to an end (e.g., a circle occurred after six consecutive squares). In fact, the increase varied with the length of the preceding streak. This relationship is shown in Figure 11.3.

These behavioural data by themselves are evidence that people keep track of streaks. Otherwise their response times would not vary with streak length. The fMRI data also showed activation in the prefrontal cortex when a streak came to an end. Like response times, this activation also increased with streak length. In the chapter on attention we reviewed evidence of prefrontal cortex involvement in task switching. Now we see its involvement in 'moment to moment updating of mental models for

Figure 11.3 Time to Respond When a Streak Ends as a Function of Streak Length.

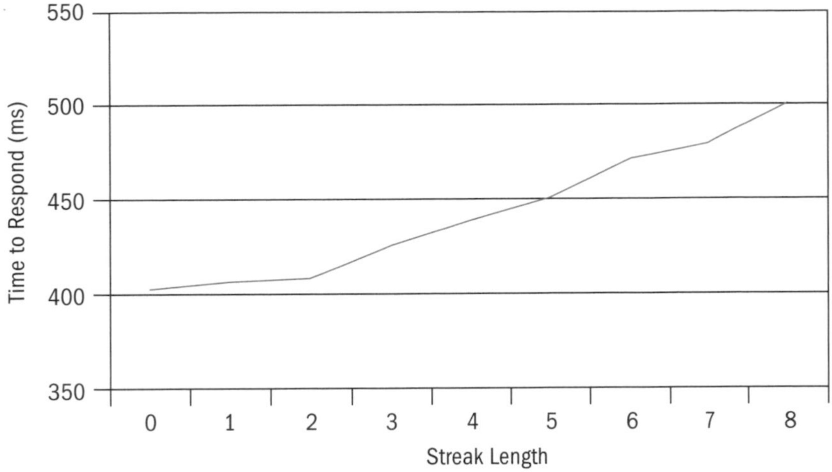

Data from Huettel, S.A., Mack, P.B., & McCarthy, G. (2002). Perceiving patterns in random series: Dynamic processing of sequence in prefrontal cortex. *Nature Neuroscience, 5*, p. 486.

pattern' (Huettel et al., 2002, p. 488). Although they knew that the sequences were random, participants nonetheless reported that they still noticed streaks. All of this suggests that the perception of streaks is involuntary. People do not need to be looking for them in order to notice them.

Ivry and Knight (2002) drew out some of the implications of the Huettel et al. study. The fact that people's response times increased when a streak comes to an end might mean that they expected the streak to continue. Knowledge that it was a random sequence did not matter. Perhaps the gambler's fallacy comes about at least partly in this way. Even though they may know better, people may find streaks compelling and make decisions based on their perception of them. As we saw in the case of the hot-hand belief, this may be a useful thing to do. However, in the case of games of chance, such as roulette, it may have unfortunate consequences.

■ Adjustment and Anchoring

Which of the following results in the larger number?

$8 \times 7 \times 6 \times 5 \times 4 \times 3 \times 2 \times 1$

$1 \times 2 \times 3 \times 4 \times 5 \times 6 \times 7 \times 8$

Because people typically do not actually multiply these numbers out, they rely on a heuristic to estimate the required number. Participants usually judge the second sequence to yield a smaller product than the first (A. Tversky & Kahneman, 1974). On average, the first sequence is believed to result in a product of 2,250, whereas the second sequence is believed to yield a product of 512. In fact, both sequences yield 40,320. (If you are in doubt, you should multiply the numbers yourself to verify this.) This discrepancy arises because people adjust their estimates depending on the starting value of the sequence. Because the first sequence starts with a larger number than the second, it appears to yield a larger outcome than the second. We can say that the sequences are each anchored by different values, and these anchors create the illusion that the sequences yield different outcomes.

In general, when people make judgements of the magnitude of something, the initial value to which they are exposed will bias their judgement (Chapman & Johnson, 2002, p. 121). Kahneman and Tversky (1974) presented evidence showing such effects on judgements of a variety of sequences. For example, suppose that participants are asked to estimate the number of African countries in the United Nations. To start with, they are given a random number, and are asked whether the number is higher or lower than their estimate of the required number. Those participants initially given a low number (e.g., 10) subsequently estimate the number of African countries in the United Nations to be lower than do participants initially given a higher number (e.g., 65). Thus, persons' judgement is not simply a function of what they know or think they know. Rather, judgement can be biased by aspects of the situation in which the judgement is made.

■ Availability

Some experiences are more easily recalled than others. We could say that the more easily recallable an item is, the more *available* it is (Asch & Ebenholtz, 1962). In general, **availability** refers to the ease with which an item can be brought to mind as a label for experience (Horowitz, Norman, & Day, 1966; Tversky & Kahneman, 1974; Schwartz & Vaughn, 2002). Obviously, availability plays a central role in the way we recall previous experiences. There may be many things we have experienced that do not come readily to mind. Tversky and Kahneman have shown how availability influences our judgement. Here is an example.

Suppose that you were asked to judge how frequently events of a particular class occur. For example, suppose you were asked to judge the relative frequency with which different letters occur in different positions in words. For example, the letter R could occur as the first letter in a word, or as the third letter in a word. Which occurs more frequently, R as the first letter in a word, or R as the third letter in a word? Tversky and Kahneman (1973a) reported that approximately 69 per cent of participants estimate that R occurs more frequently in the first position. However, the opposite is in fact the case.

Why do so many people believe that R occurs more frequently in the first position than in the third position? In order to judge the frequency of the two classes of words, participants may try to recall words of each type. R is a better cue for words beginning with R than for words with R in the third position. The letter R is more likely to elicit words such as *runner* than it is to elicit words such as *carpet*. In this situation, words beginning with R are more available. Because they are more easily recalled, we believe that there are more of them. We confuse the frequency with which we can remember something with how frequently it actually occurs.

Meaningful Coincidences

People often report the experience of **meaningful coincidence**, a phenomenon extolled by the analytical psychologist, C.G. Jung (1950, 1960/1973). Such a coincidence occurs when events appear to be meaningfully connected, even though they occur together by chance (i.e., are not causally related). Jung (1960/1973) gave the following example from his own experience:

> A young woman I was treating has, at a critical moment, a dream in which she was given a golden scarab. While she was telling me this dream I sat with my back to the closed window. Suddenly I heard a noise behind me, like a gentle tapping. I turned round and saw a flying insect knocking against the window-pane from outside. I opened the window and caught the creature in the air as it flew in. It was the nearest analogy to a golden scarab that one finds in our latitudes, a scarabaeid beetle the common rose-chafer (*Cetonia aurata*) which contrary to its usual habits had evidently felt an urge to get into a dark room at this particular moment. I must admit that nothing like it ever happened to me before or since, and that the dream of the patient has remained unique in my experience. (p. 22)

Jung went on to note that, when we have such experiences, they tend to make a vivid impression on us. He pointed out further that we find it difficult to believe that such coincidences are merely due to chance. Meaningful coincidences like the one Jung described may occur to people when they read their horoscopes, or have their fortunes told.

Falk (1989) showed that people judge their own coincidences differently from the way they judge other people's coincidences. In one experiment, participants were assigned to groups. Participants wrote a story containing an account of a coincidence that had occurred to them. Participants in the group then rated their own and each other participant's story for surprisingness. In general, participants rated their own coincidences as being more surprising than those of the other participants. Falk suggested that a coincidence strikes people as meaningful to the extent that it is personal. People tend to regard coincidences that happen to them as important and worth remembering. Falk called this an **egocentric bias**.

Falk noted that these results lend themselves to an interpretation in terms of the availability heuristic. We do not compare our experiences of personally meaningful coincidences with our other experiences that do not contain such coincidences. Consequently, it does not strike us that a personally meaningful coincidence could have arisen purely by chance, and thus not be particularly surprising. Our personally meaningful coincidence is the most available experience, and thus we overestimate its significance. When we consider other people's coincidences, however, we do compare them with the various alternatives that could have occurred to them. We are more objective about other people's experience, and do not regard their coincidences as remarkable. Falk pointed out that this account of meaningful coincidences is consistent with Kahneman and Miller's (1986) account of the way we evaluate the significance of events after they have occurred. We tend to overestimate the significance of something that actually happens without realizing that it is just one of many things that *could* have occurred.

■ Illusory Correlation

Availability may also be responsible for the phenomenon called **illusory correlation** (Chapman & Chapman, 1969). Sometimes people believe that events go together when in fact they do not. Tversky and Kahneman (1974) suggested that judgements of how frequently two events occur together depend on availability. If thinking of one kind of event makes you remember the other kind of event, then you may infer that both events tend to occur together in the real world.

Shweder (1977) provided an extensive review of this kind of thinking. As he pointed out, correlation is not an intuitive concept. **Intuitive concepts** are relatively easily acquired, and are used by almost all adults. Examples given by Shweder include the belief in the existence of an external world, that one thing can be a part of something else, that one word can be synonymous with another word, and so on. Such concepts do not require formal education for their acquisition. However, many statistical concepts appear to be non-intuitive. That is, they are the product of formal education, and thus are not acquired without deliberate instruction and a willingness to learn. Often the proper use of such concepts requires fairly detailed calculations. Consider the following problem: 'A piece of paper is folded in half. It is folded in half again, and again . . . . After 100 folds, how thick will it be?' (Shweder, 1977, p. 638). When I first heard this problem, I estimated a thickness of about 3 or 4 inches. In fact, the thickness is over 200,000 *miles*. Intuitively, the required thickness is about that of a large book. However, if you actually work out what happens when you fold the paper, then you will see why the thickness becomes so great.

The concept of correlation is a very good example of a non-intuitive concept. The reason why the concept of correlation is so difficult to acquire can be understood by means of an example used by Shweder and taken from Smedslund (1963). Consider the data in Table 11.1.

Smedslund found that his participants, who were nurses, generally inferred from these data that there was a connection between having the symptom and having the disease. The reason most often given for concluding that the symptom and the disease are correlated is that the largest number of cases occurs in the cell labelling the presence of both the disease and the symptom. That is, these participants focused on instances that are consistent with the hypothesis that the disease and the symptom are correlated. In part, this experiment is important because it is another illustration of confirmation bias, a phenomenon we considered in detail in the chapter on reasoning. However, it also shows how the tendency to pay attention to confirming instances, and ignore disconfirming instances, facilitates the occurrence of an illusory correlation.

Table 11.1 Relationship between a Symptom and a Disease in a Sample of 100 Cases

Symptom	Disease		
	Present	Absent	Total
Present	37	33	70
Absent	17	13	30
Total	54	46	100

From Shweder, R.A. (1977). Likeness and likelihood in everyday thought. *Current Anthropology*, *18*, pp. 637–658. Copyright 1977 by the University of Chicago. Reprinted by permission.

In order to properly determine whether or not the data in Table 11.1 demonstrate a correlation between the symptom and the disease, you must also consider those cases in which the symptom is absent but the disease is present. In fact, in these data, of those people who have the symptom (70), only 53 per cent (37) have the disease, whereas of those who do not have the symptom (30), 57 per cent have the disease. Thus, you can see that the symptom is not a very good predictor of who has the disease and who does not. You should not say that the symptom and the disease are correlated. On the contrary, on the basis of these data, you should conclude that these two events—symptom and disease—are unrelated.

Redelmeier and Tversky (1996) provided a good example of a common, real-world illusory correlation. The belief that arthritis pain is correlated with changes in the weather goes back thousands of years. Many doctors and patients alike still believe in this relationship. However, the research on this relationship has failed to find good evidence for it. Redelmeier and Tversky obtained data for 18 arthritis patients twice a month for 15 months. Sixteen of these patients believed in the weather/arthritis pain correlation. Patients' assessments of their pain on particular days were correlated with the local weather as measured by barometric pressure, temperature, or humidity. The average of these correlations was .01. Since correlations can vary from -1 to +1, with .00 denoting a complete absence of correlation, this result means that there is no evidence whatsoever that arthritis pain and the weather are related. Some patients believed that there might be a lag between the weather and their symptoms, so correlations were also computed between arthritis pain and the weather on two days before and two days after the day on which pain data was recorded. The average of these correlations was .00.

Given that it is extremely unlikely that weather and arthritis pain actually have anything to do with one another, what is it that prompts so many people to believe in a causal relation? Redelmeier and Tversky suggest that people may focus on days when they experience extreme pain and look for changes in the weather at that time. They thus ignore days in which the weather changes, but their pain remains the same. This explanation is similar to that for meaningful coincidences. 'A single day of severe pain and extreme weather might sustain a lifetime of belief in a relation between them' (Redelmeier & Tversky, 1996, p. 2896).

Thus far in this chapter we have considered many situations in which people believe there is order when there is really randomness. However it is also true that, on occasion, people may believe there is randomness where there really is order. An example of this is given in Box 11.1.

■ Regression Towards the Mean

Another way in which the concept of correlation is sometimes misused concerns the phenomenon of regression towards the mean. To illustrate how this works, consider two variables that are, in fact, correlated, such as the average height of parents and the average height of their children. There is a tendency for the height of parents to be related to the height of their children, so these variables are correlated. However, the correlation is not perfect. For purely mathematical reasons, whenever two variables are not perfectly correlated, extreme values on one variable tend to yield less extreme val-

Box 11.1 Let's Make a Deal!

Marilyn vos Savant writes the *Ask Marilyn* column in *Parade* magazine (www.parade.com/current/columns/askmarilyn.html). In a series of columns, vos Savant (1990a, 1990b, 1991) discussed what is called the **Monty Hall problem**. This is a decision-making problem derived from a television program called *Let's Make a Deal*, for which Hall was the master of ceremonies. If you were a contestant, you would be faced with three curtains. Let us call them A, B, and C. Behind two of the curtains is nothing of value, but behind the third curtain is the grand prize, usually a car. Monty knows which curtain conceals the car. Suppose you pick curtain C. At this stage you can infer that, while one of the two remaining curtains may have a car behind it, at least one of the remaining curtains has nothing of value behind it. Monty then opens one of the two remaining curtains, always revealing nothing of value. Monty knows whether A, or B, or neither one has a car behind it, and always opens a curtain without a car. Let us say he opens curtain A. That would leave two curtains, B and C. You would then be offered a choice: you can stick with curtain C, or switch to curtain B. Which choice would you make? Why?

Most contestants reasoned as follows. The odds are fifty–fifty that the car is behind curtain B or curtain C. Consequently, I do not increase my chances of getting the car by switching. So, I will stay with my original choice. Vos Savant told her readers that switching is in fact the better choice. The reasoning in favour of switching goes as follows (Nickerson, 1996, pp. 418–421). Each curtain has a one-third chance of having a car behind it. Once you pick curtain C, then there is a two-thirds chance that the car is behind curtains A or B. That remains true even after Monty has opened curtain A. Now that you know that the car is not behind curtain A, then you also know that there is a two-thirds chance the car is behind curtain B. Since there is still only a one-third chance that the car is behind curtain C, you are better off switching.

After vos Savant presented her analysis of the Monty Hall problem, she was deluged with mail from readers, many of them with Ph.D.s in mathematics, telling her that she was wrong. Overwhelmingly, her critics told her that the odds were fifty–fifty that the car was behind B or C. So who is right?

It can be shown empirically that vos Savant is right. Below is a table laying out all the possibilities when the contestant chooses door C, and Monty always chooses to open one of the other doors with nothing behind it (Krauss & Wang, 2003, p. 5; Johnson-Laird, Legrenzi, Girotto, Legrenzi, & Caverni, 1999, p. 82). The table below gives the possible outcomes under these circumstances.

| | Curtain | | | | | Outcome | |
Possibilities	A	B	C	Curtain Chosen by Contestant	Curtain Monty Opens	Switch	Don't Switch
1st	Nothing	Nothing	**Prize**	C	A or B	Lose	**Win**
2nd	Nothing	**Prize**	Nothing	C	A	**Win**	Lose
3rd	**Prize**	Nothing	Nothing	C	B	**Win**	Lose

You can see that the contestant who does not switch will win one-third of the time, while the contestant who does switch will win two-thirds of the time. If you work out the possibilities if the contestant initially chooses curtain A or B, then you will see that the result is the same. As we have seen so often in the last three chapters, once you take the time and trouble to represent the problem space correctly, then the solution follows. Of course, contestants on *Let's Make a Deal* had neither the time nor the inclination to figure it out.

The Monty Hall problem spawned an enormous amount of research into the reasons why participants find it so hard (e.g., Burns & Weith, 2004; Gilovich, Mevec, & Chen, 1995; Kraus & Wang, 2003). Perhaps we should give the last word to Monty Hall himself, who was the master of ceremonies of *Let's Make a Deal* from 1963 to 1986. Why did so many people, including mathematicians, insist that the probability is one-half that the door they have chosen has a car behind it?

> That's the same assumption contestants would make on the show after I showed them there was nothing behind one door. . . . They'd think the odds on their door had now gone up to 1 in 2, so they hated to give up the door. . . . By opening the door we were applying pressure. We called it the Henry James treatment. It was 'The Turn of the Screw.' (Tierney, 1991, p. 1)

ues on the other variable. Thus, very tall parents tend to have somewhat shorter off-spring, and very short parents tend to have somewhat taller offspring. The relationship between these two variables in a sample gathered by Galton (1886) is shown in Figure 11.4. The average, or mean, values of both parents and children are about the same (roughly 68 inches). The figure can be used to predict the height of children given the height of their parents. Notice how, for any value of parents' height, the predicted value of children's height is closer to the average, or mean, than is that of their parents. Thus, parents who are, on average, less than 65 inches tall tend to have children who are almost 66 inches tall, whereas parents who average about 72 inches tall tend to have children who are less than 71 inches tall. This phenomenon is called **regression to the mean**. Regression means returning, and in these data you can see that parents tend to have children who regress, or return, to the mean.

In general, for two variables that are not perfectly correlated, high values on the first variable are related to lower values on the second, and low values on the first are related to higher values on the second. This means that when you predict the values of one variable given the values of the other variable you will find that the predicted values of the second variable are somewhat closer to the mean, or average, of the second variable. Keep in mind that this occurs for purely mathematical reasons. Galton (1889, as cited by Walker, 1943, and Senders, 1958), who first discovered regression to the mean, put it this way:

> The law of Regression tells heavily against the full hereditary transmission of any gift. Only a few out of many children would be likely to differ as widely as the more exceptional of the two parents. The more bountifully the Parent is gifted by nature, the more rare will be his good fortune if he begets a son who is endowed yet more largely. But the law is even-handed: it levies an equal succession-tax on the trans-

Figure 11.4 Relation between the Height of Parents and Their Children.

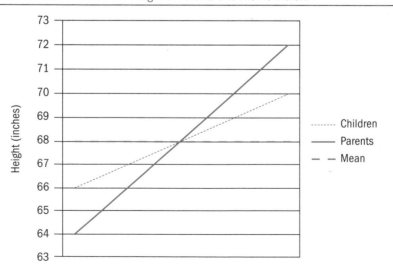

mission of badness as of goodness. If it discourages the extravagant hopes of a gifted parent that his children will inherit all his powers, it no less discountenances extravagant fears that they will inherit all his weakness and disease. (p. 106)

Regression to the mean occurs in a great many situations, in addition to the one that intrigued Galton. Tversky and Kahneman (1974) gave several examples. Suppose that some students do particularly well on an examination. That is, they obtain marks that are higher than what they would normally expect to obtain. What would you predict for their next examination? If you follow the logic of regression towards the mean, you would predict that their next examination would be closer to their average level of performance. Similarly, a dismal score on an examination should lead to the prediction of a better outcome next time.

There is no need for causal explanations of this variability. However, it is always tempting to try to give precisely such a causal explanation. After a poor performance is succeeded by a better one, we may say that we worked harder the second time, or that the exam was easier. Such explanations may account for some of the variability in our performance, but some variability will remain unexplained. It is just this uncertainty that people find hard to accept. Because we are anxious to understand the sources of our successes and failures, we sometimes impose unwarranted interpretations.

Tversky and Kahneman pointed out the relevance of regression to the mean for an understanding of the role that reward and punishment may, or may not, play in changing behaviour. If a child, for example, performs in an outstanding way on some task, then it is tempting for parents to offer praise. The parents might be disappointed when, on a subsequent occasion, the performance of the child declined. However, punishing a child for poor performance is likely to be followed by better results on the next occasion. Notice that these results may come about purely as a consequence of regression to the mean and have nothing to do with the fact that behaviour is being rewarded or punished. As Tversky and Kahneman (1973b) observed, 'the human condition is such that, by chance alone, one is most often rewarded for punishing others and most often punished for rewarding them' (p. 251).

■ Training in Statistical Reasoning

The Importance of the Problem Space

In the chapter on problem-solving, we considered the concept of a problem space within which reasoning takes place. As we noted then, the problem space consists of the way the problem is represented, including the goal to be reached and the various ways of transforming the given situation into the solution (Newell & Simon, 1972, p. 59). Keren (1984) has analyzed the ways in which different problem spaces affect the use of different heuristics. Consider the following problem:

> Three coins are to be given to two children (Dan and Mike) using the following rule. An ordinary deck of cards is shuffled and cut. If the top card is red, Dan gets a coin, but if it is black, Mike gets a coin. The deck is shuffled again, and the next

coin is assigned using the same procedure. Finally, the third coin is allocated, again following the same method. What is more likely to occur:

    a. One child will get three coins; the other will get none.

    b. One child will get two coins; the other one.

    c. Both possibilities (a) and (b) are equally likely.

The right answer is (b), but over 40 per cent of participants chose the incorrect alternative (c). In order to see why (b) is correct, examine Figure 11.5. It is a tree diagram of the various possible outcomes. Notice that there are eight possibilities, and that, in six of these, one child gets two coins and the other child gets one coin. Thus, alternative (b) is the most likely outcome. If participants think through the problem in this way, then they will get the right answer.

However, there is at least one other way of thinking about the problem, which leads to the wrong answer. Participants might imagine only the possible ways in which the coins could be divided, without thinking about how these divisions come about. When the problem is so construed, then there appear to be only four possible outcomes. Mike could get 3, and Dan 0; Mike could get 2 and Dan 1; Mike could get 1 and Dan 2; and Mike could get 0 and Dan 3. If the participant assumes that these alternatives are equally likely, then it appears as if alternative (c) is correct. Half the time one child gets 3 coins and the other 0; and the other half of the time one child gets 2 coins and the other gets 1.

By considering the different ways in which participants can represent a problem, we can understand why some answers seem more reasonable to people than do others. Different problem spaces provide different **frames** within which a problem can be understood or misunderstood (Kahneman & Tversky, 1984). As Tversky and Kahneman (1983) have noted, 'because we normally do not have adequate formal models for com-

Figure 11.5 Problem Space for the Keren Coin Problem.

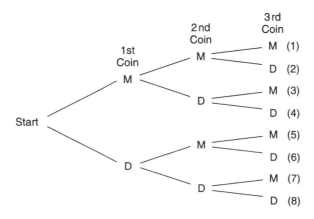

puting the probabilities of such events, intuitive judgement is often the only practical method for assessing uncertainty' (p. 293). In the Keren coin problem above, people may not think through the problem in the way required to get the right answer. Rather, they may rely on the second, more intuitive, solution procedure, and end up making an incorrect inference. However, as Nisbett, Krantz, Jepson, and Kunda (1983) have observed, people may be trained to think more appropriately about problems like these.

Nisbett et al. suggested that while the cognitive biases we have considered thus far may, in fact, regulate the way people make judgements in many situations, there are also other situations in which people use procedures that give rise to the correct conclusions. Nisbett et al. proposed that there are three factors that determine when people will use the appropriate reasoning procedures.

1. Clarity of the problem space. In the Keren problem described above, it is important that people be aware of all the alternatives. This is true for any problem that requires statistical reasoning. Some problem spaces are easier to grasp than others. When the problem space is poorly understood, errors may result.
2. Recognition of the operation of chance. It is easier to see chance at work in some situations rather than in others. In sports, the operation of chance factors, such as weather, injuries, and so on, is relatively obvious. The effect that these factors have on the outcome of games is clear. However, as we saw when we considered streakiness, people may perceive chance phenomena as orderly even when they know better. Nevertheless, when people are aware that chance influences a process, they may be more able to use sound reasoning procedures.
3. Cultural prescription. People may reason in a statistically sound manner if the culture to which they belong values such reasoning and has provided the appropriate training.

In one of their studies, Nisbett et al. (1983) gave participants two different problems. In one problem, participants were told about a football coach who typically finds two or three exciting prospects at the beginning of each season. The coach then discovers that these promising novices seldom go on to perform at the exceptional level they demonstrated at the outset. Participants are asked to explain why the coach has to revise downward his opinion of players that he originally thought were brilliant.

The second problem had a similar form, but was about a director of an acting company who was initially enthused by the stage presence of novice actors, and subsequently disappointed by their performances. Participants in this problem had to explain why the director found herself having to revise downward her opinion of actors who initially showed such promise.

Notice that both problems can be seen as requiring that participants have at least an intuitive understanding of regression to the mean. Thus, the explanation should be that the initial performance of the football tryouts, as well as that of the acting tryouts, was not typical of their usual ability. The tryouts simply behaved in a way that was above their average level of performance. Participants should not give causal explanations, such as 'The boys who did well at tryout may find that their teammates are jealous. They may slack off so as not to arouse jealousy.'

The results of the study showed that the participants who had experience that was relevant to the activity described in the problem were more likely to reason appropriately about it. Thus, participants who had played team sports in high school or college were more likely to recognize a regression effect in the first problem than were those who did not have such experience. Similarly, participants with acting experience were more likely to recognize a regression effect in the second problem.

Nisbett et al. interpreted these results as suggesting that expertise in an area may lead to an increased usage of appropriate statistical reasoning procedures. They also pointed out that becoming an expert in an area also involves becoming a member of a particular subculture (e.g., football players, actors). The process of enculturation may involve the acquisition of appropriate reasoning procedures in a particular domain. For this reason, the heuristics people use may be *domain-specific*. People may use the correct inference procedures in areas in which they have expertise, but not in areas in which such expertise does not exist. This means that people can be trained to use statistical reasoning in almost any context. Nisbett et al. believed that such training is increasingly becoming the norm in our culture, and that we may, with time, see a rise in the ability to reason statistically.

It is important to remember, however, that individuals who are trained in one discipline may be unaware of appropriate reasoning procedures in other fields. To be trained in the methods of one discipline does not mean that you are automatically an expert in the methods of another field. Lehman, Lempert, and Nisbett (1988) reviewed the training procedures in several different disciplines. Graduate students in psychology who had been trained in statistical reasoning were able to generalize their training to problems in everyday life. However, training in chemistry did not provide that kind of benefit. '[C]hemistry provides no improvement in statistical or methodological reasoning. . . . [T]here is little need to differentiate among the various types of causal relations because chemistry deals primarily with necessary-and-sufficient causes. . . . [T]he luxury of not being confronted with messy problems that contain a substantial uncertainty and a tangled web of causes means that chemistry does not teach some rules that are relevant to everyday life' (Lehman, Lempert, & Nisbett, 1988, p. 441). Thus, graduate training in some disciplines, such as psychology, may allow a student to cope more successfully with problems in everyday life, while graduate training in other disciplines such as chemistry will make the student a better chemist, but may not involve the acquisition of inferential procedures that are broadly useful.

Mill, Gray, and Mandel (1994, p. 247) further explored Lehman and Nisbett's (1990) claim that 'undergraduate training in the social sciences, particularly psychology, does lead students to apply statistical and methodological reasoning skills to a range of everyday situations.' Mill, Gray, and Mandel (1994) recruited participants from undergraduate research methods and statistics courses in psychology. These participants were given tests of their ability to apply what they were taught to situations in everyday life. For example, they were asked to evaluate the claims of a pharmaceutical company that their new drug led to recovery from illness in 75 per cent of patients who received it. Of course, such a claim is meaningless unless you know what percentage of people who do not receive the drug also recover. The methods and statistics courses did not by themselves lead to an improvement on 'critical thinking' items when compared with other students who did not take such courses. Only students who had additional tutorials in critical thinking showed improvement. Thus, undergraduate training in research methods may not automatically lead students to successfully apply what they have been taught. Recall Kahneman's (2002, p. 451) observation that reason is not very vigilant, and 'allows many intuitive judgements to be expressed, including some that are erroneous.' It is hard work to apply what one has learned about statistical reasoning to problems in everyday life. Sometimes people may prefer to forgo the effort.

■ Are Economists Rational?

People trained in economics play a crucial role in making decisions about monetary matters. The decisions economists make in their roles in government, banking, and finance have an enormous influence on the quality of the daily lives of ordinary people throughout the world. Consequently, it is of great importance to examine the processes whereby economists make decisions. Can the decision-making processes of economists be called 'rational'?

It is, of course, an oversimplification to say that there is one, and only one, model of rationality in economics. Nevertheless, it is true that one model of rationality is preeminent in economics. Students of economics are invariably exposed to the belief that it is rational to always act self-interestedly. To always act in one's own interest means that the interests of others are not taken into account when one makes a decision. The underlying belief, derived from the work of Adam Smith (1723–90), is that if everyone acted in his/her own interest in a free market, then the outcome would be the best one possible for society as a whole. 'Intervention of communal interests into the free market, as in government regulation, is thought simply to introduce distortions that lead to inefficiencies and corruption' (Sears, 1991, p. 12).

Because economics students are taught that self-interest is the only rational motive, it seems reasonable to hypothesize that economics students will act in a self-interested manner to a greater extent than will students in other disciplines. Carter and Irons (1991) tested this hypothesis by comparing the behaviour of economics and non-economics undergraduates in a **simple ultimatum bargaining game**. This is a two-person game in which the task is to divide $10 between two participants. One participant (the Proposer) offers a division of $10 between him/herself and a second person (the Responder). The Proposer can offer as little or as much to the Responder as he or she wishes, and keep the remainder, provided the two amounts are multiples of 50 cents. There is no negotiation, so it is take it or leave it as far as the Responder is concerned. If the Responder accepts the Proposer's offer, then they both split the money in the amounts proposed. If the Responder decides to reject the Proposer's offer, then both Proposer and Responder get nothing. Suppose you were the Proposer. What division would you propose? Suppose you were the Responder. What division would you accept? From a rational/self-interest point of view, the Proposer should offer the responder 50 cents, and keep $9.50. This is because from a rational/self-interest point of view, the Responder should take the 50 cents rather than refuse it and get nothing. If you were in the Responder's role in this game, would you take 50 cents? If so, why? If not, why not?

The results of the Carter and Irons experiment are given in Figure 11.6. The participants were economics undergraduates and undergraduates who had never taken a course in economics. Notice that the economics students are prepared to accept less, and keep more, than are non-economics students. However, it is also true that non-economics students keep more and accept less than the $5.00 that would be a 50–50 split. Thus, while economics students fit the rational/self-interest model better than do the others, it would still appear that self-interest is a very widespread motive for making decisions (Miller, 1999).

Frank, Gilovich, and Regan (1993, 1996) followed up on the Carter and Irons study by having participants play what is usually called a **prisoner's dilemma game**, which, as we shall see, need not be about prisoners. The game is illustrated on the next page, and works like this. There are two players, X and Y. If both player X and Player Y decide to co-operate, then both get $2.00. If player X decides to co-operate, but player Y does not, then player X gets nothing and player Y gets $3.00. Similarly, if player Y decides to co-operate, but player X does not, then player Y gets nothing and player X gets $3.00. Finally, if neither decides to co-operate, then they both get $1.00. It is often argued that, from a rational/self-interest point of view, a player should always defect (i.e., never co-operate). This is because the player will then get at least $1.00 and possibly $3.00. If one player co-operates and the other does not, then the former will get nothing. Something is always better than nothing.

Participants were either economics majors or majors in another discipline. In general, the economics majors only co-operated 39.6 per cent of the time, while the majors

Figure 11.6 Results of Ultimatum Bargaining Game.

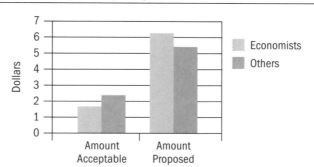

Data from Carter, J.R., & Irons, M.D. (1991). Are economists different, and if so, why? *Journal of Economic Perspectives*, 5, p. 173.

		Player X	
		Co-operate	Defect
Player Y	Defect	2 for X 2 for Y	3 for X 0 for Y
	Co-operate	0 for X 3 for Y	1 for X 1 for Y

in other disciplines co-operated 61.2 per cent of the time. Economics majors followed the rational/self interest model to a greater extent than did the others. It might be that economists learn to be self-interested or it might be that particularly self-interested people become economists. Whatever the reason, economists appear to be less willing to co-operate than others.

Self-interested behaviour is to be contrasted with *pro-social behaviour* (DeDreu & Boles, 1998). **Social value orientation** is a dimension anchored by those who have an extremely competitive, winner-take-all, individualistic orientation as opposed to those who have an extremely co-operative, share-and-share-alike, pro-social orientation. The former endorse statements such as 'your loss is my gain', while the latter endorse statements such as 'do unto others as you would have them do unto you.' Disciplines such as psychology may attract people with a pro-social orientation to a greater extent than does economics (James, Soroka, & Benjafield, 2001). Are pro-social people behaving irrationally when they engage in co-operative behaviour? Colman (2003) argued that the economists' definition of rationality works only when decision-making is understood as a purely individual matter. However, once one views decision-making as extended in time and involving other participants, then a co-operative strategy may begin to look better. For example, participants who can negotiate with each other prior to making a decision in the prisoner's dilemma game may not only promise to co-operate, but actually do so (Frank, Gilovich, & Regan, 1993, p. 166). By adopting **team reasoning** (Colman, 2003, p. 150), these players increase the payoff for both of them. In general, *team reasoning* involves individuals' acting together to determine the best solution for the group as a whole, and then choosing that alternative. Team reasoning violates the fundamental assumption of the self-interest model of rationality. Is team reasoning rational or irrational? What do you think?

■ Magical Thinking

Even though there is evidence that people can be trained to overcome biases, it is obvious that these biases are extremely common in everyday life. Some everyday biases are the result of a process called **magical thinking**. The classic investigation of magical thinking was undertaken by the British anthropologist Sir James Frazer (1911/1959). Frazer provided a detailed and fascinating description of the ways that so-called 'primitive' cultures used magical rituals designed to influence events.

As Rozin (Rozin & Fallon, 1987; Rozin, Fallon, & Augustoni-Ziskind, 1985; Rozin, Markwith, & Ross, 1990; Rozin, Millman, & Nemeroff, 1986) pointed out, Frazer believed that magical practices were regulated by two laws. The first was the **law of similarity**. This law maintains that *like produces like*. Causes and effects are similar to one another. Frazer called magical practices based on the law of similarity *homeopathic magic*. He gave many examples of homeopathic magic, such as the ritual used by Nootka (Nuu'chah'nulth) in British Columbia when the fish do not arrive at the time that they should. 'A Nootka wizard will make an image of a swimming fish and put it into the water in the direction from which the fish generally appear. This ceremony, accompanied by a prayer to the fish to come, will cause them to arrive at once' (Frazer, 1911/1959, p. 9). Because like effects like, one can influence events by manipulating something that is similar to the thing one wishes to control. The law of similarity leads 'the magician to infer that he can produce any effect he desires merely by imitating it in advance' (Frazer, 1911/1959, p. 5).

Frazer's second law is the **law of contagion**, which holds that things that have once been in contact continue ever afterward to act on each other (Frazer, 1959, p. 5). Practices based on the law of contagion are called *contagious magic*. An example of contagious magic, again from the Nootka of British Columbia, is the belief that 'an arrow, or any other weapon that has wounded a man, must be hidden by his friends, who have to be careful not to bring it near the fire until the wound is healed. If a knife or an arrow which is still covered with a man's blood were thrown into the fire, the wounded man would suffer very much' (Frazer, 1959, p. 19).

Of course there are cases in which these laws have a superficial credibility. Real cases of contagion exist. For example, contact with a virus can certainly have a long-term effect on an individual. As Rozin and Nemeroff (2002, p. 203) observed, the laws of similarity and contagion are heuristics 'that may be adaptive and function well in a variety of situations'. However, there are many examples of magical thinking that we, as adults in a technologically advanced twenty-first-century society, might regard as just childish superstitions. Nevertheless, as we shall see, we are still susceptible to this form of thought.

Good illustrations of magical thinking in people like us come from a series of experiments by Rozin and his colleagues. Consider the following procedure. You are given the choice of drinking apple juice from an ordinary glass or from one with a dead, but sterile cockroach in it. Which would you prefer? Would the glass with the cockroach in it seem neutral or somewhat disgusting? How about choosing between two pieces of fudge, one shaped like a muffin and the other just like a piece of dog feces? What about putting a rubber sink stopper between your lips, or putting a piece of rubber imitation vomit between your lips? Most people find even imagining the second of the two alternatives to be disgusting. The choices are obvious, and simply describing this procedure elicits quite strong reactions from people, and did so from the participants in Rozin's experiment, even when they knew that the disgusting choices were really quite harmless. The disgusting alternatives were perceived as contaminated because they had either been in contact with something disgusting or were similar to something disgusting.

Hejmadi, Rozin, and Siegal (2004) examined the development of magical thinking in American and Hindu children. In each case, children were divided into two groups, four- and five-year-olds and eight-year-olds. The children were shown a picture story that was narrated by an experimenter. The story described some form of contamination of a glass of juice. The participants made a judgement concerning whether or not the juice was drinkable following the contamination. For example, one especially powerful form of contamination occurred when the story involved a stranger sipping from the glass. This rendered the juice undrinkable for 87 per cent of the four- and five-year-old Hindu children and 68 per cent of the corresponding group of American children. In general, Hindu children were more sensitive to contamination than were their American counterparts. For the eight-year-olds, 98 per cent of the Hindu children rejected the contaminated juice, compared with 77 per cent of the American children. In general, the older children were more sensitive to contamination than were the younger ones. In the subsequent phase of the experiment, the juice was decontaminated by a variety of procedures. For example, a mother would drink from the glass herself, which might indicate that the juice was safe. The older children in both cultures tended to reject the juice even after decontamination to a greater extent than did the younger children.

The Hejmadi, Rozin, and Siegal (2004) study shows that sensitivity to contamination is present in both cultures, but more so among the Hindu. This may be because Hindu children, for health reasons, must be more careful about what they ingest. Alternatively it could be because the Hindu caste system has more stringent rules concerning who can accept food from whom. The other interesting finding is that sensitivity to contamination is already present in four- and five-year-olds and increases with age. Various decontamination procedures are still not regarded as effective by older children. For example, the majority of eight-year-olds in both cultures still reject the juice after it has had a sterile cockroach removed from it and the juice has been boiled. For many of these children, once a cockroach has come in contact with the juice, its essence remains therein.

Rozin's research has shown that it is easier for something to create a negative magical influence than a positive one. Contact by a negatively valued object yields contamination much more easily than contact with a positively valued object yields enhancement. Thus, a toothbrush used by someone to whom you are sexually attracted is not a better toothbrush than a brand-new one, but a toothbrush used by someone you dislike is a worse toothbrush than a brand-new one. Rozin and Royzman (2001) observed that such an asymmetry is consistent with the existence of a *negativity bias*, meaning that people are more affected by negative than by positive events. This is a topic to which we now turn.

■ Negativity Bias

I would like you to do the following task, which is adapted from Deese and Hamilton (1974). Take a sheet of paper and make two columns, one headed 'positive' and the other headed 'negative'. Write the numbers 1 to 20 down the left-hand side. Read the following list of words, and as you read each word, decide whether it makes you think of something good or positive or of something bad or negative. Make your decision on the basis of your immediate impression of the word. If your first reaction to the word is positive, write it in the positive column. Here are the words: (1) clean; (2) safe; (3) weak; (4) stingy; (5) wrong; (6) agile; (7) narrow; (8) true; (9) strong; (10) stale; (11) bright; (12) generous; (13) solid; (14) low; (15) clumsy; (16) honest; (17) faithful; (18) sour; (19) harsh; (20) coarse. The order of your choices is probably as follows: (1) +; (2) +; (3) −; (4) −; (5) −; (6) +; (7) −; (8) +; (9) +; (10) −; (11) +; (12) +; (13) +; (14) −; (15) −; (16) +; (17) +; (18) −; (19) −; (20) − . We may not agree on all of them, but most people do agree on about 80–90 per cent of them.

This correspondence may not strike you as remarkable, but it should. The point is that we all seem to be able to see some very different qualities as somehow belonging to the same class. Thus, *clean, safe, agile, true, strong, bright, generous, solid, honest*, and *faithful* are all seen as positive qualities, whereas *weak, stingy, wrong, narrow, stale, low, clumsy, sour, harsh*, and *coarse* are, in general, seen as negative qualities. Notice that the way we ordinarily classify words as either positive or negative does not appear to be on the basis of the things to which the words refer—that is, to their denotation. What observable characteristics do the events to which *clumsy* and *sour* refer have in common? There would seem to be no observable properties shared by such things as a *clumsy ox* and a *sour lemon* that allow us to see them as belonging to the same class. Rather, we judge events as either positive or negative because of our subjective reaction to them. The concepts we use to make these judgements are normally labelled by adjectives such as *happy, sad, strong, weak, active*, and *passive*. Thus, the study of the ways in which we express our subjective reactions to events is bound up with the study of how we use adjectives. Because our positive and negative reactions to things are very central in our lives, it is obviously important for us to understand how this type of judgement is made.

The first thing to notice about adjectives is that they usually, although not always, come in pairs of opposites, a point we mentioned briefly in the chapter on reasoning. For many of the positive adjectives you can think of, there are other adjectives that are their negative opposite. This appears to be a general feature not only of English but of other languages as well. The positive member of a pair of adjectival opposites is usually called an *unmarked adjective*, whereas the negative member is a *marked adjective* (Greenberg, 1966; D. Gross, Fisher, & Miller, 1989; Huttenlocher & Higgins, 1971; Witkowski & Brown, 1983). The basis of the marked-unmarked distinction is that, in certain contexts, an unmarked adjective is neutralizable, but a marked adjective is not. The neutral (or nominal) sense of an unmarked adjective is clearest when we ask questions such as 'How wide is the river?' 'How deep is the water?' and 'How good a swimmer is he?' Questions like these are requests for an evaluation of the position of something on a bipolar scale, like that given in Figure 11.7. When we ask for such a judgement, we specify the name of the scale involved by naming its positive pole. Thus, the name of the *good–bad* scale is *goodness*. The name of the *wide–narrow* scale is *width*. The name of the *deep–shallow* scale is *depth*. This means that a positive adjective not only names a pole on the scale, but is also the name of the scale. That is, positive adjectives have both a contrastive and a nominal sense.

Negative adjectives, however, have only a contrastive sense. They refer only to a pole on the scale and are not used to name the scale. When we ask questions such as 'How bad is the weather?' or 'How shallow is he?' we are not asking for an evaluation using the complete scale from *good* to *bad*, or from *deep* to *shallow*. Rather, we are pronouncing the weather *bad* and the person *shallow*, and we are only interested in just how *bad* or how *shallow* they are (H.H. Clark, 1969).

It also turns out that positive adjectives are typically used more often than their negative opposites (Boucher & Osgood, 1969). This tendency to make positive judgements more frequently than negative judgements has been called the **Pollyanna hypothesis**, named for a fictional character who tried always to look for the bright side of difficult situations. Because positive adjectives are used more frequently than negative ones, it seems reasonable to suppose that they are applied to events that are regarded as normal, and that negative adjectives are applied to events that we judge to be deviant (Zajonc, 1968).

Much research has been devoted to the Pollyanna phenomenon (e.g., Peeters & Czapinski, 1990). For example, Benjafield and Adams-Webber (1976) asked participants to divide a set of their acquaintances into positive and negative categories. Suppose we let P = the number of positive acquaintances, and N = the number of negative acquaintances. Then P/(P + N) is a measure of the proportion of positive judgements. Benjafield and Adams Webber (1976) found that this proportion was approximately .62. This result has been replicated and extended in numerous studies (e.g., Benjafield & Green, 1978; Gross & Miller, 1997; Lefebvre, 1985; Lefebvre, Lefebvre, & Adams-Webber, 1986; Messick, 1987; Rigdon & Epting, 1982; Ronan & Kendall, 1997; Schwartz, 1997; Schwartz & Garamoni, 1986; Schwartz & Michelson, 1987; Shalit, 1980). Across a wide range of different situations, people judge events positively about 62 per cent or

Figure 11.7 Scales for Evaluating Concepts.

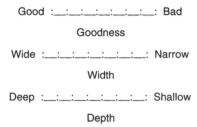

Good :__:__:__:__:__:__: Bad

Goodness

Wide :__:__:__:__:__:__: Narrow

Width

Deep :__:__:__:__:__:__: Shallow

Depth

63 per cent of the time, and negatively about 37 per cent or 38 per cent of the time. A possible explanation for these results is suggested by Frank (1959, 1964) and Berlyne (1971). They hypothesize that an arrangement in which one part occupies about 37 per cent of the total will allow the smaller part 'to occupy a proportion of the whole that makes it maximally striking' (p. 232). In general, the larger part acts as a background against which the smaller part stands out as figure. This means that the more infrequently occurring category will be the one to which attention tends to be directed (Baumeister, Bratslavsky, Finkenhauer, & Vohs, 2001, p. 356).

Although not intended as a test of the hypothesis that the less frequently occurring category attracts the most attention, a study by Klauer, Mierke, and Musch (2003) provides support for it. Klauer et al. did a masked priming study of the sort we considered in Chapter 3. In studies of this sort a masked prime is presented before another stimulus to which participants must make a response. Some of the primes in this study were positive words and some were negative words. Following a prime, participants were presented with a target word and had to judge it as either positive or negative. There were always 48 trials, but the proportion of positive target words varied. Sometimes there were 13 positive and 35 negative words, and other times there were 35 positive words and 13 negative words. As in a Stroop task, primes belonging to the same class as the target word facilitate a response, while primes belonging to the opposite class inhibit a response. It turned out that negative primes had a greater effect when negative stimulus words were in the minority, and positive primes had a greater effect when positive stimulus words were in the minority. In other words, 'primes from the less frequently presented category exerted a larger priming effect than did primes from the more frequently presented category' (Klauer et al., 2003, p. 963). One explanation considered by Klauer et al. is that repetition causes the members of the more frequently occurring category to become 'satiated', or neutralized, allowing the members of the more infrequent category to become more salient. Because the infrequently occurring category is more salient, it will be more susceptible to priming.

An interesting implication of the Klauer et al. study is that if people construed most events as negative, rather than positive, then positive events would stand out as figure against a negative background. However, the evidence is overwhelming that people generally categorize most events positively. Consequently, people will tend to pay more attention to negative events (e.g., Kanouse & Hanson, 1971; Peeters & Csapinski, 1990). As Tuohy and Stradling (1992, p. 484) observed, there is considerable evidence in favour of what might be called a **negativity bias**, such that people assign greater 'weight or importance to negative aspects of a stimulus'. For example, Kahneman and Tversky (1979) note that when people are making decisions they take potential negative outcomes more seriously than potential positive outcomes. Positive events, almost by definition, do not pose serious problems for people. Negative events, by contrast, are precisely those to which the person must attend (Tuohy, 1987, p. 44; Tuohy & Stradling, 1987). Negativity bias 'may confer a significant adaptive advantage for individuals, such that those who mobilized their attention and resources toward the bad would be more likely to survive and reproduce' (Baumeister et al., 2001, p. 358).

Cacioppo and his colleagues have provided concrete evidence that negative events attract our attention to a greater extent than do positive ones. For example, Crawford and Cacioppo (2002) hypothesized that people are more ready to learn the location of negative stimuli than they are to learn the location of positive stimuli. Participants were exposed either to a series of positive pictures or a series of negative pictures. Positive pictures included 'images of food, nature scenes, sport scenes', and so on, while negative pictures included 'images of snakes, spiders, and weapons' (Crawford & Cacioppo, 2003, p. 450). Within each series the degree to which the pictures were positive or negative varied, as did the location of the pictures on the screen on which they were exposed. There was a relationship between how positive (or negative) a picture was and its horizontal location on the screen. After participants were shown an initial series of pictures, they were then shown an additional series and asked to judge where on the screen that picture should go. They were able to make this judgement correctly for negative pictures far more reliably than for positive pictures. The participants were better at learning the locations of negative stimuli than the locations of positive stimuli. There is an obvious adaptive significance to being able to learn where negative things are. 'One cannot escape a threatening predator unless one knows the location of the predator relative to oneself' (Crawford & Cacioppo, 2003, p. 449).

Smith, Cacioppo, Larsen, and Chartrand (2003) showed that people pick up negative information extremely rapidly. In an event related potential (ERP) study, participants were presented with 20 positive and 20 negative pictures, similar to the ones used in the Crawford and Cacioppo study. The participants' task was to indicate whether they judged the pictures to be either positive or negative. The ERP data indicated that negative stimuli were receiving more attention than positive ones. Moreover, the distinction between positive and negative stimuli was being made within 100 milliseconds of exposure to an image. 'Clearly, the faster we can separate negative from positive stimuli, the faster we can engage in an appropriate response strategy' (Smith et al., 2003, p. 180).

◼ Ecological Rationality

A challenge to the heuristics and biases research program of Tversky and Kahneman has been mounted by Gigerenzer and his colleagues. For example, Gigerenzer and Goldstein (1996, p. 651) claimed that the heuristics and biases program presented an image of people as 'hopelessly lost in the face of real-world complexity, given their supposed inability to reason according to the canon of classical rationality, even in simple laboratory experiments.' By contrast, Gigerenzer and Goldstein proposed that people usually make good decisions by using simple heuristics that rely on ecologically valid cues. For example, consider the **recognition heuristic** (Goldstein & Gigerenzer, 2002).

When choosing between two objects (according to some criterion), if one is recognized and the other is not, then select the former. For instance, if deciding at mealtime between Dr. Seuss's famous menu choices of green eggs and ham (using the criterion of being good to eat), this heuristic would lead one to choose the recognized ham over the unrecognized odd-colored eggs. (Todd & Gigerenzer, 2000, p. 732)

The recognition heuristic relies on the fact than people are very good at telling the difference between events they have previously experienced and those they have not. The classic demonstration of this is an experiment by Shepard (1969), who allowed participants as long as they liked to examine 612 photographs. They were then given 68 pairs of photographs. One member of each pair was from the previous set and one was novel. Participants were able to tell which was which about 99 per cent of the time. The recognition heuristic will only work when two conditions are met. First, the person must recognize some, but not all, of the alternatives between which choices must be made. Second, the alternatives recognized by the person must also be the correct choices. Under those conditions, the recognition heuristic is ecologically valid, and using it is **ecologically rational**. A heuristic is ecologically rational if it 'produces useful inferences by exploiting the structure of information in the environment' (Todd, Fiddick, & Krauss, 2000, p. 375).

Gigerenzer and his colleagues have shown how the recognition heuristic works in a series of demonstrations. One demonstration requires participants to decide which of two cities is larger. For example, which is larger, San Diego or San Antonio? Both are American cities, and American students correctly choose San Diego two-thirds of the time. However, German students correctly choose San Diego 100 per cent of the time. This result is counter-intuitive because American students know more about American cities than do German students. The explanation is that American students recognize both San Antonio and San Diego as American cities, and so the recognition heuristic cannot discriminate between them. Rather, an American student will know which city is larger only if that knowledge is in her or his memory so that it can be recalled. However, the German students do not need to know which city is larger in order to make the correct choice. Rather, they pick San Diego because they recognize it and reject San Antonio because they do not recognize it. Recognition is ecologically valid in this instance because one is more likely to hear of large cities than small ones. Consequently, the recognition heuristic is *ecologically rational* in this case.

This example illustrates the difference between the recognition heuristic and the *availability heuristic*, which we considered earlier in this chapter. The availability heuristic inclines the participant to decide in favour of the most easily recallable alternative. By contrast, the recognition heuristic does not require participants to recall anything. They do not need to *recall* the population of San Diego or San Antonio. All they need to rely on is whether or not they *recognize* one of the two choices.

One of the implications of the recognition heuristic is that people who know less may sometimes be able to make better judgements than people who know more. Here is an example similar to one used by Goldstein and Gigerenzer (2002, p. 79). Consider three American sisters, each of whom must take a test on the relative size of Canadian cities. One of the Americans is housebound and knows nothing about Canada. The second only knows what she has read in the press and seen on television. The third has been studying Canadian geography and history. Who will do better on the test? One would predict that the second sister would do better than the others, because 'she is the only one who can use the recognition heuristic' (Goldstein & Gigerenzer, 2002, p. 79). The third sister knows *too much* to be able to use it, and the first sister knows *too little*. This outcome is called the **less-is-more effect**.

The Adaptive Significance of the Recognition Heuristic

'For any given species, an *adaptive problem* is defined as a problem (e.g., finding food, avoiding predators) that recurred over many generations in which the species evolved, and whose solution tended to promote the reproduction of an organism or its kin *in those environments*' (Brase, Cosmides, & Tooby, 1998, p. 5). What adaptive problem does the recognition heuristic solve? One would be that it allows the person to select potentially helpful people and objects, and avoid potentially dangerous ones. In prehistoric times, one can see the possible advantage in trusting people one recognized as opposed to strangers. Moreover, it would be safer to eat foods you recognized and avoid ones you did not. However, how might such a strategy confer additional benefits in a complex society like ours? Evidence that it might comes from a study by Borges, Goldstein, Ortmann, and Gigerenzer (1999). They asked a sample of Americans which of 298 German companies they recognized and a sample of Germans which of 500 American companies they recognized. The top 10 most recognized companies from each group were used to create stock portfolios that outperformed those managed by experts during the year 1996–7. This shows that 'heuristics designed to be fast and use as little information as possible can perform well even in a complex environment' (Todd & Gigerenzer, 2003, p. 156).

Criticisms of the Ecological Rationality Approach

Gigerenzer and his colleagues have proposed the existence of an *adaptive toolbox* containing other heuristics, of which the recognition heuristic is usually a component. Some have suggested that the recognition heuristic is much more limited in its generality than has been implied by Gigerenzer and his group (e.g., Oppenheimer, 2003; Newell, 2005). Others have suggested that simple heuristics might work well for some relatively unimportant decisions, but that they do not really apply to truly important decisions such as choosing a mate or raising a child.

> Mate selection does not just involve the self and the partner. It usually also involves the interests of parents, friends, members of reference groups, and so forth. A career decision, too, often involves many different parties, as do union–management negotiations, international negotiations, and the like. . . . I suspect that many others seeking decision rules for the high stakes decisions they encounter in their lives will not find that [these] rules . . . make their decisions all that easy. (Sternberg, 2000a, p. 764)

Kahneman and Tversky (1996) argued that Gigerenzer had exaggerated the difference between his work and theirs. There is no reason why the recognition heuristic could not be studied within the framework of the heuristic and biases program (Kahneman & Frederick, 2002, pp. 58–59). It is possible that, over time, these two approaches will become more complementary than antagonistic.

■ Questions for Study and Discussion

1. Define and give examples of each of the following: representativeness; adjustment and anchoring; availability. In each case, briefly describe a relevant experiment.

2. Do you believe in the hot hand? Give reasons for your belief. In what other situations might the hot hand be a true or a false belief?

3. Define and give examples of illusory correlation and regression to the mean. In your answer, include a discussion of the effect of statistical training on these phenomena.

4. Define and give examples of magical thinking. In your answer, discuss Rozin's experimental work.

5. What is negativity bias? Give examples of its occurrence, paying special attention to its adaptive significance.

6. What is rational about the recognition heuristic? Can you think of any other situations in which it might work in addition to those identified in the text?

■ Key Concepts

Adjustment and anchoring People's judgements of magnitude are biased by the initial value to which they are exposed.

Availability The ease with which an item can be brought to mind as a label for experience.

Ecologically rational A heuristic is ecologically rational if it produces useful inferences by exploiting the structure of information in the environment.

Egocentric bias The tendency to find an experience to be meaningful only if it is yours and not someone else's.

Gambler's fallacy The mistaken belief that an event that has not occurred for a number of independent trials (e.g., a head in coin-tossing) is more likely to happen on future trials.

Heuristics and biases (Tversky & Kahneman) People often use heuristics, or rules of thumb, which may work in some situations, but may bias or mislead them in others

Hot-hand belief and hot-hand behaviour The former is the belief in streak shooting by basketball players. The latter is a bias for a basketball player to take the next shot after previously scoring a basket.

Illusory correlation The mistaken belief that events go together when in fact they do not.

Intuition (Kahneman) System 1 judgement and decision-making processes.

Intuitive concept A concept that is easily acquired and used by almost all adults.

Law of averages A fallacy based on the assumption that events of one kind (e.g., tails in coin-tossing) are always balanced by events of another kind (e.g., heads in coin-tossing).

Law of large numbers The larger the sample, the more nearly a statistic (e.g., proportion of heads in coin-tossing) will be to the true value (e.g., 50 per cent).

Law of small numbers The mistaken belief that a small sample should be representative of the population from which it is drawn.

Less-is-more effect Sometimes the person who knows less can make a better judgement than the person who knows more.

Magical thinking Making decisions based on the **law of similarity**, which is the belief that like produces like, and the **law of contagion**, which is the belief that things once in contact continue afterward to act on each other.

Meaningful coincidence (Jung) Such a coincidence occurs when events appear to be meaningfully connected, even though they occur together by chance (i.e., are not causally related).

Monty Hall problem There are three curtains, behind one of which is a prize. You pick one curtain and Monty Hall then always opens another curtain behind which is nothing. What should you do next? Why?

Negativity bias People assign greater weight or importance to negative aspects of a stimulus.

Pollyanna hypothesis The tendency to make positive judgements more frequently than negative judgements.

Prisoner's dilemma game A two-person game in which different outcomes are contingent on whether each player chooses to co-operate or to defect.

Reason (Kahneman) System 2 judgement and decision-making processes.

Recognition heuristic (Gigerenzer) When choosing between two objects (according to some criterion), if one is recognized and the other is not, then select the former.

Regression to the mean (Galton) For purely mathematical reasons, whenever two variables are not perfectly correlated, extreme values on one variable tend to be related to less extreme values on the other variable.

Representativeness heuristic Making inferences on the assumption that small samples resemble one another and the population from which they are drawn.

Simple ultimatum bargaining game A two-person game in which the task is to divide a sum of money between two participants.

Social value orientation A dimension anchored by those who have an extremely competitive, winner take all, individualistic orientation as opposed to those who have an extremely co-operative, share-and-share-alike, pro-social orientation.

Team reasoning Individuals act together to determine the best solution for the group as a whole, and then choose that alternative.

■ Links to Other Chapters

Heuristics
Chapter 7 (commitment heuristic)
Chapter 13 (warm-glow heuristic)
Streakiness and the brain
Chapter 3 (task switching)
Availability
Chapter 13 (warm-glow heuristic)

Egocentric bias
Chapter 6 (egocentric perspective transformations)
Chapter 8 (social context of language)
Team reasoning
Chapter 9 (distributed reasoning)
Negativity bias
Chapter 13 (mere exposure and cognition)

■ Further Reading

A heuristic called the *quantity principle* was proposed in Josephs, R.A., Giesler, R.B., & Silvera, D.H. (1994). Judgement by quantity. *Journal of Experimental Psychology: General, 123*, 21–32. In one experiment, participants were asked to write an essay that they believed would earn them a very high grade. Participants who typed essays in a small font tended to write longer essays than participants who typed in a larger font, even though no restrictions were placed on the length of the essay. Of course, a small font requires more words to produce the same number of pages as a larger font. It appeared that the number of pages written was the important variable influencing participants' judgement of the quality of their essay. The saying 'more is better' describes the principle that is consistent with the *quantity principle*, a heuristic that tends to make us confuse quality with quantity. In your experience, do your professors also seem to believe that good essays have more pages than poor ones?

Some marvellous illustrations of how meaningful coincidences can mislead us are in Eco, U. (1989). *Foucault's pendulum*. New York: Knopf.

A good, brief critique of the ecological rationality issue is given by Over, D.E. (2000). Ecological issues: A reply to Todd, Fiddick, & Krauss. *Thinking and Reasoning, 6*, 385–388.

Chapter 12

Intelligence
and Creativity

■ The Concept of Intelligence: Historical Background

Perhaps no concept has been more central to the development of psychology as a discipline than the concept of intelligence. The measurement of intelligence has typically been accomplished by means of intelligence tests (Anastasi, 1965). The makers of intelligence tests patterned their work on the example set by Binet in France (Fraisse & Piaget, 1963, pp. 40–43).

The Binet-Simon Test

One of the best known of contemporary researchers on intelligence, Robert J. Sternberg (1992, p. 134), noted that 'the intelligence test of today is quite similar to that of Alfred Binet.' That is, in spite of variations in form and content, intelligence tests tend to be similar to the one originally invented by Binet in collaboration with Theophile Simon (Binet & Simon, 1905a/1965). The French educational authorities wanted to develop a test to measure the extent to which a child could benefit from schooling. The creation of such a test was left to Binet, who together with Simon created a test designed to discriminate between normally and subnormally intelligent children. Binet and Simon (1905b/1965) defined **intelligence** as:

> a fundamental faculty the alteration or lack of which is of the utmost importance for practical life. This faculty is judgment, otherwise called good sense, practical sense, initiative, the faculty of adapting oneself to circumstances. To judge well, to comprehend well, to reason well, these are the essential activities of intelligence. (p. 38)

Notice the *practical* nature of the definition—intelligence is 'practical sense', 'the faculty of adapting oneself to circumstances', and consists of 'activities' such as reasoning and comprehension. Some items from the Binet and Simon (1911/1915) test are given in Table 12.1. Binet and Simon were careful to base their scale on a substantial body of empirical research. Their items are 'arranged in a real order of increasing difficulty' (Binet & Simon, 1908/1965), in the sense that children tend not to fail items at a lower level and then pass items at a higher level. Moreover, of '203 children studied individually . . . 103 pupils . . . have exactly the mental level that we attribute to their age; 44 are advanced; 56 are' below their age level (Binet & Simon, 1908/1965, p. 44). The Binet-Simon scale allows children to be compared in terms of their *mental age*, which is determined by the age level of the items a child can pass.

The Binet-Simon scale seemed to many people in the United States to be just the sort of thing they were looking for. Lewis M. Terman (1877–1956) developed the most successful adaptation of the scale for the American context. Terman did this work at Stanford University, and so this version of the Binet test was called the *Stanford-Binet*. One of Terman's (1916/1948) most durable innovations was the intelligence quotient or IQ. The IQ was itself an adaptation of a suggestion by the German psychologist William Stern (1871–1938) that a useful measure of intelligence could be obtained by dividing the person's mental age (MA) by his/her chronological age (CA). Terman made use of Stern's (1912/1967, p. 453) idea in his equation for IQ:

$$IQ = \frac{MA}{CA} \times 100$$

The formula means that 'normal' children will have IQs of 100. Terman (1916/1948, p. 489) obtained Stanford-Binet IQ scores for 905 children between the ages of 9 and 14, and reported that they were approximately normally distributed. Moreover, there was a significant relationship between IQ and such variables as teachers' estimates of chil-

Table 12.1 Example of Binet and Simon's Items

Age	Item
3	Give family name
4	Repeat three numbers
5	Compare two weights
6	Distinguish morning and afternoon
7	Describe a picture
8	Give a day and date
9	Name months of the year in order
10	Criticize absurd statements
12	Describe abstract words
15	Give three rhymes for a word in one minute
Adult	Give three differences between a president and a king

dren's intelligence, suggesting that the test had some validity. Partly because of these properties, the Stanford-Binet became a very widely accepted test of intelligence.

Charles Spearman

It is not easy to decide whether the word 'intelligence' should be taken to refer to one ability or to many different abilities. If it is taken to mean many different abilities, then it is not easy to determine precisely how these abilities are related to one another. We can begin to appreciate some of these problems by considering the work of Charles Spearman (1863–1945), who laid the groundwork for what became **factor analysis** (Lovie & Lovie, 1993). Factor analysis begins with a set of correlations between several measures, such as different mental tests. One then applies statistical procedures to derive a number of underlying factors describing the structure of the set of correlations. As a result of his analysis of the pattern of correlations between different tests of mental abilities, Spearman (1904, 1927/1965) proposed what came to be called a *two-factor theory of intelligence*. This theory held that:

> every individual measurement of every ability . . . can be divided into two independent parts. . . . The one part has been called the 'general factor' and denoted by the letter *g*; it is so named because, although varying freely from individual to individual, it remains the same for any one individual. . . . The second part has been called the 'specific factor' and denoted by the letter *s*. It not only varies from individual to individual, but even for any one individual from each ability to another. (Spearman, 1932/1970, p. 75)

The two-factor theory is illustrated in Figure 12.1. As you can see, it is a hierarchical model, in which **general intelligence**, or *g*, underlies a set of specific abilities. In Figure 12.1, the specific factors are represented by the abilities to do well in different school subjects, such as French, English, mathematics, and music. Spearman found that these specific abilities all were correlated with each other, such that people who tend to do well in one specific ability tend to do well in the others, and vice versa. However, the inter-correlation between specific abilities is not perfect. Each specific ability was seen as determined in part by *g* and in part by circumstances specific to that ability. Thus, someone could have a high level of *g*, but varying specific abilities. This formulation is controversial, but still widely accepted (e.g., Johnson, Bouchard, Krueger, McGue, & Gottesman, 2004). Spearman was able to formulate a statistical criterion that enabled him to estimate the amount of *g* that contributed to each specific ability. However, it is far from easy to interpret the correlations between scales purporting to measure different abilities. Such interpretations must be made with great caution (Loehlin, 1989, 1992, pp. 18–23; Neisser et al., 1996, p. 81).

Spearman believed that *g* represented the amount of *mental energy* available to an individual. This was a general, non-specific energy that could be directed towards the specific abilities. The specific abilities were regarded as engines that were driven by *g*.

Figure 12.1 Spearman's Two-factor Theory of Intelligence.

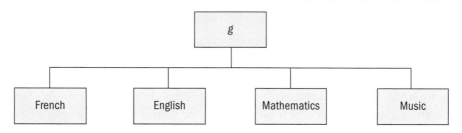

Spearman exercised considerable influence on the way succeeding generations of psychologists regarded intelligence. Although still a controversial opinion, many subsequent commentators argued that 'when the term intelligence is used it should refer to g, the factor common to all tests of complex problem solving' (Jensen, 1972, p. 77). When it came to estimating the effects of education on intelligence, Spearman concluded that heredity was more important than education in determining g, but that the specific factors could be shaped by schooling.

■ General Intelligence (g)

In a review of research done over the 100 years since Spearman (1904), Lubinski (2004) argued that, if anything, general intelligence is more important in the twenty-first century than it has ever been. General intelligence predicts academic achievement and work performance. However, general intelligence accounts for only approximately half of the variability in performance. As Lubinski points out, it is still essential for even highly intelligent people to be prepared to work hard if they are to fulfill their goals, and even harder if they are to become an outstanding in their field. On this point Lubinski cites Simonton (1994), whose work we will consider later in the chapter. Ambitious students would do well to heed the following quote.

> Making it big [becoming a star] is a career. People who wish to do so must organize their whole lives around a single enterprise. They must be monomaniacs, even megalomaniacs, about their pursuits. They must start early, labor continuously, and never give up the cause. Success is not for the lazy, procrastinating or mercurial. (p. 181)

All the same, general intelligence provides the foundation on which hard work can build. Moreover, contemporary environments in technological societies are increasingly complex, requiring 'abilities for "coping with change", "dealing with novelty", "quickly grasping" the relevance of innovative ideas for staying "ahead of the curve" and "anticipating change"' (Lubinsky, 2004, p. 107). These abilities tend to be regarded as characteristic of general intelligence, which may be central to the ability to adapt to a constantly changing environment.

Fluid Intelligence and g

A distinction that is often used in relation to general intelligence is that between fluid and crystallized intelligence (Cattell, 1963). **Crystallized intelligence** consists of things you have learned, and may increase throughout your lifetime. By contrast, **fluid intelligence** is the ability to think flexibly, and may increase when you are young, but levels off as you mature. Fluid intelligence and general intelligence are often thought to be highly similar if not identical (Lubinsky, 2004, p. 98). Thus, general intelligence is typically assessed using tests of the ability to grasp unfamiliar relationships, rather than tests of the content of your knowledge. Spearman's word for the ability that underlies *g* was **eduction**, meaning *to draw out*. Thus, general intelligence may be measured by the ability to draw out the relationships that obtain in a novel situation. One test designed to measure just this ability is the **Raven Progressive Matrices** (Carpenter, Just, & Shell, 1990; J.C. Raven, Styles, & J. Raven, 1998), which was explicitly developed to measure a central aspect of what Spearman meant by general intelligence (J. Raven, 2000).

Examples of items similar to those in the Raven test are given in Figure 12.2. Items consist of a matrix of nine configurations, the last of which is blank. You must decide which of the eight alternatives given beneath the matrix is the correct one to fill the blank. You should try to decide which is the correct answer to each of the three matrix problems in the figure before you read the answers at the end of the chapter. You will see that the reasoning required by Raven items can be quite subtle and varied. Spearman called this sort of reasoning *eduction of relations and correlates*: the ability to grasp how things are related to one another and what goes with what.

Working Memory and g

It has been suggested that **working memory capacity** may not only be an important aspect of intelligence, but also may even be synonymous with *g* (Conway, Kane, & Engle, 2003; Engle, Tuholski, Laughlin, & Conway, 1999). One reason for thinking that these two might be closely related is that Spearman's concept of *mental energy* and the *central executive function* of working memory are intuitively similar (Ackerman, Beier, & Boyle, 2005). At this point you should examine Figure 5.8 once again. As you may recall from Chapter 5, the central executive selects and integrates information, constituting a workspace within which solutions to problems are formulated (Baars, 2002). Recall the distinction in Figure 5.8 between *fluid* systems and *crystallized* systems. As we have just seen, this difference is between processes that manipulate information but are 'themselves unchanged by learning' and 'cognitive systems capable of accumulating long-term knowledge' (Baddeley, 2000b, p. 421). Thus, the central executive appears to perform a function similar to that ascribed to fluid intelligence, and, by extension, to *g*.

While there would appear to be an intuitive relationship between general intelligence and the central executive function of working memory, this does not mean there is an empirical one. If there were an empirical relationship then scores on a test of individual differences in working memory capacity would be correlated with

Figure 12.2 Items Similar to those on the Raven Progressive Matrices Test.

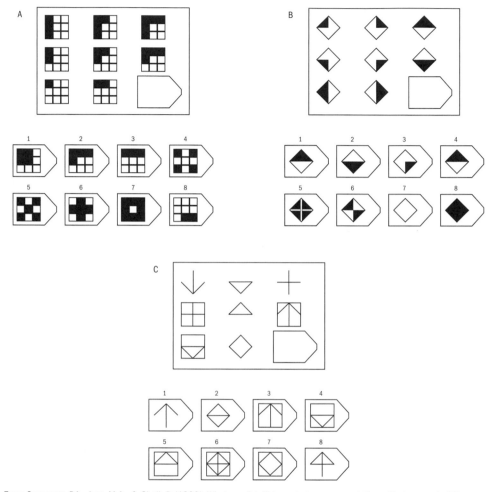

From Carpenter, P.A., Just, M.A., & Shell, P. (1990). What one intelligence text measures: A theoretical account of the processing in the Raven Progressive Matrices Test. *Psychological Review*, 97, p. 409. Copyright 1990 by the American Psychological Association. Reprinted with permission.

scores on a test of *g*. It has been suggested that a suitable test of working memory capacity would require a person to continue to work on a task in the face of distraction (Conway, Kane, & Engle, 2003, p. 551). Such a test would measure the person's ability to remain goal-oriented and not allow extraneous information to interfere with the problem at hand. One such task is the *operation span task* (Engle, Tuholski, Laughlin, & Conway, 1999, p. 315). In this task participants are shown an arithmetic problem on a screen. The problem requires a yes/no answer. For example: Is $(8/4) - 1 = 1$? Once the participant responds, a word, such as *tree*, appears on the screen, which the participant reads aloud. There then follows another arithmetic problem, followed by another word. This sequence may be repeated as many as six times. During the testing phase, the participant is shown the list of arithmetic problems, and must pair each one with the word that followed it. Thus, the person is not only doing arithmetic problems, but must also keep track of the relationship between each problem and the corresponding word. The participant's score is the number of words correctly recalled in the correct order.

Tests of working memory capacity do correlate positively with tests such as the Raven. However, this correlation is far from perfect. After a review of dozens of studies, Ackerman et al. (2005, p. 51) concluded that working memory capacity and g are not the same. In fact, measures of working memory capacity appear to correlate somewhat with many different measures of intellectual ability, and not simply with g. Barrett, Tugade, and Engle (2004) argued that working memory capacity should be conceptualized in terms of the ability to regulate attention. As such, it would play an important role in bringing cognitive processes under voluntary control.

Neural Plasticity and g

Garlick (2002, 2003) pointed out that Spearman's concept of *mental energy* is no longer a useful explanatory concept within the context of current neuroscientific theories. Rather, he advanced the hypothesis that **neural plasticity** underlies g. *Plasticity* is the ability of an organism to adapt to changes in the environment. *Neural* plasticity:

> is an experience dependent change in neuronal circuitry that occurs throughout life, though on a larger scale during infancy, childhood, and adolescence. . . . During this early part of life, long-term changes that may occur include the rewiring of existing networks and the establishment of new sets of connections, the results of which include increased capacity and improved efficiency. (Petrill, Lipton, Hewitt, Plomin, Cherny, Corley, & Defries, 2004, p. 811)

Good examples of neural plasticity are some of the phantom limb phenomena discussed in Chapter 4. Recall Ramachandran's (2004, p. 10) discussion of a man who had his arm amputated above the left elbow. He developed a phantom limb, but when stimulated with a Q-tip on the surface of his face felt as if parts of his missing hand were being stimulated. 'When an arm is amputated, no signals are received by the part of the brain's cortex corresponding to the hand. It becomes hungry for sensory input and the sensory input from the facial skin now invades the adjacent vacated territory corresponding to the missing hand' (Ramachandran, 2004, p. 13). The body schema is not fixed, but shows considerable plasticity (i.e., flexibility).

Individual differences in neural plasticity reflect the degree to which people can adapt to a changing environment by forming and/or altering connections between neurons. Individual differences in neural plasticity are likely due to genetic variation (Petrill et al., 2004, p. 811). However, the precise mechanisms whereby genes determine plasticity are as yet unknown.

Garlick's (2002, p. 121) hypothesis is that people vary in the extent to which their brains are 'able to adapt their neural circuitry to environmental stimulation during childhood'. The hallmark of neural plasticity is the ability to adapt to any circumstances with which the person is confronted, although there are obvious limits to this.

> This would mean that children would be able to learn to read and write, even though their early ancestors did not possess these skills, and such skills were not even required. In fact such a mechanism would allow the person to adapt and function intelligently no matter what the environmental requirements. (Garlick, 2002, p. 120)

Children low in neural plasticity would be less able to adapt to environmental change. Even children who are high in neural plasticity would develop intellectually only to the extent that they are exposed to appropriate environmental stimulation.

The Evolution of g

A theory of the evolution of g has been advanced by Kanazawa (2004). Central to this theory is a distinction made by Cosmides and Tooby (2002) between **dedicated intelligence** and **improvisational intelligence**. The former are domain-specific modules that have evolved to solve recurring problems. Examples we have considered in previous chapters are the *cheater detection module*, which we considered in the chapter on reasoning, and the *language acquisition device*, which we considered in the chapter on language. By contrast, improvisational intelligence has evolved to deal with relatively unique problems that are unpredictable. The ability to deal with such surprises (e.g., a bush fire, a flash flood) may have enabled survival, and thus been selected for. As Kanazawa pointed out, by definition unexpected problems cannot be solved by dedicated, preprogrammed mechanisms. Rather, what is required is the flexibility that general intelligence affords. Thus, Kanazawa argues, g and improvisational intelligence are the same.

As we have seen, our current circumstances are radically more complex and novel than those faced by prehistoric people. Kanazawa (2004, p. 515) pointed out that very few things in the environment of a technologically advanced society 'existed 10,000 years ago, at the end of the Pleistocene . . . virtually everything you see around you today in your natural environment (books, computers, telephones, televisions, automobiles, etc.) is evolutionarily novel.' Dedicated mechanisms are of limited use in such an environment. General intelligence is what is required (Gottfredson, 1997). This discussion may remind you of the distinction between System 1 and System 2, discussed in Chapter 11.

One implication of Kanazawa's theory is that general intelligence is valuable only in evolutionarily novel situations. For example, mating is certainly not an evolutionarily novel situation, and so we would not expect high g to be advantageous in that context. Indeed, people high in general intelligence do not have more children, for example, than do those low in g. In fact, g is *negatively* correlated with number of offspring (Kanazawa, 2004, p. 517). A possible explanation for this may be that the use of contraceptive methods varies with g. The use of contraceptives may help to solve the evolutionarily novel problem of no longer being able to rely on infant mortality to control the number of one's dependants (Kanazawa, 2004, p. 521).

■ The Flynn Effect

J.R. Flynn (1984, 1987, 1999, 2003) created a firestorm of controversy when he discovered that IQ scores had been increasing over time in every industrialized country he examined. These increases were not trivial. For example, Americans had gained 14 IQ points between 1932 and 1978. Samples of members of the military of the Netherlands, Israel, Norway, and Belgium show an average gain of six IQ points per decade between 1952 and 1982 (Flynn, 1999, p. 6). This last result is particularly noteworthy because it is based on Raven scores. Since the Raven is acknowledged to be the best measure of g (Neisser, 1997, p. 441), it would appear that g has been increasing over time. A few decades comprise far too short a time for evolution to have worked its magic. Consequently, the rapid rise in g must be due to environmental factors. Notice that this does not mean that g is completely determined by environmental factors, for the following reason. Suppose that g depends on neural plasticity. Variations in neural plasticity may be inherited. However, as we observed earlier, neural plasticity requires environmental stimulation in order to actualize its potential. One's actual level of g will depend on an interaction of neural plasticity and environmental conditions (Garlick, 2003, p. 188). Thus, the **Flynn effect** could be due to an enriched environment enabling potential g to become actual g (cf. Dickens & Flynn, 2001).

A great deal of attention has been devoted to trying to figure out which environmental changes have produced the Flynn effect (e.g., Neisser, 1998). Below is a list of possible candidates.

Nutrition and Health

Lynn (1998) presented a summary of evidence that nutrition has improved in industrialized countries since the 1930s. 'Improvements in nutrition have increased the growth of the brain, and probably also its neurological development, and this has increased intelligence' (p. 211). Daley, Whaley, Sigman, Espinosa, and Neumann (2003) have shown that the Flynn effect can also occur in a developing country. They examined children's IQ in 1984 and 1998 in a rural Kenyan sample. They also measured nutritional levels at both times. On the Raven, IQ scores were 26.3 points higher in 1998 than in 1984. Correspondingly, children's caloric intake had improved substantially. Moreover, fewer children in 1998 were infested with hookworm, which can cause anemia. Thus, nutrition and health gains may have contributed to the IQ gains.

Parasitic infections can have deleterious cognitive effects. Although such infections are rare in industrialized countries, they are extremely common in developing countries. Sternberg, Powell, McGrane, and Grantham-McGregor (1997) studied schoolchildren in Jamaica who were infected with whipworm, which has been associated with deficient cognitive functioning. After treatment for their infection, the previously infected children did not improve as much as was expected. Sternberg et al.

observed that the infected children tended to come from families with poorer socio-economic status than did the non-infected children. They suggested that simply removing the infection is insufficient to produce significant gains in cognitive abilities. One also needs to give such children 'academic remediation and enrichment to enable them to attain the level of acculturation achieved by other individuals' (p. 74).

Education

Williams (1998) pointed out that on average people in the United States in the 1930s attained eight–nine years of schooling, which had increased to 14 years by the 1990s. Blair, Gamson, Thorne, and Baker (2005) have presented evidence that people have not only had more access to education over the last century, but that the mathematics curricula to which they were exposed became more demanding after the mid-twentieth century. Almost all children in the United States were enrolled in primary schools by the 1950s. However, IQ gains subsequent to that time must have a source other than mere exposure to school. That is where mathematics comes in. By analyzing the curriculum in early primary grades from the 1890s to the 1990s, Blair et al. showed that there was almost no mathematics education in the early 1900s, but that mathematics then became increasing prevalent until it existed in all grades by the 1960s. Mathematics education may be expected to heighten fluid intelligence. Indeed, many of the tasks given primary school children are similar to the sort of reasoning tasks embodied in tests like the Raven.

Environmental Complexity

Coincident with changes in nutrition, health, and education, the environment in which children are raised has become increasingly complex over the last 100 years, especially in industrialized countries (Schooler, 1998). Neisser (1997) pointed out that the twentieth century witnessed a phenomenal growth in the degree to which people are exposed to visual media. A short list includes photographs, movies, computers, and television. Neisser hypothesized that:

> Exposure to complex visual media has produced genuine increases in a significant form of intelligence. This hypothetical form of intelligence might be called 'visual analysis'. Tests such as Raven's may show the largest Flynn gains because they measure visual analysis rather directly . . . . (p. 447)

Green and Bavelier (2003) studied the effects of video-game playing in a group of 18–23-year-olds who had played video games (e.g., *Grand Theft Auto, Halo*) for at least one hour per day for the previous six months. This group showed superior performance on a number of standard attention tasks when compared with a group that had no previous video game experience. Moreover, training naive participants for as little as 10 days on video games led to gains on standard attention tasks such as the flanker task and the attentional blink task, both of which we reviewed in Chapter 3. Although this study did not investigate the possibility that intelligence increases as a result of complex visual experience, it does show that such experience may enhance basic cognitive processes.

It is impossible to say whether any or all of these variables are crucial to the Flynn effect. As Williams (1998) pointed out, there may also be several other variables that have played a role in the rise in IQ. What do you think some of these might be?

■ Sternberg's Theory of Successful Intelligence

There are other approaches to intelligence that de-emphasize the importance of *g* in order to bring out alternative aspects of intelligence. Two of the most influential of these approaches are those of Robert J. Sternberg and Howard Gardner. We will consider Sternberg's theory first.

Instead of analyzing intelligence in terms of factors, Sternberg proposed to analyze intelligence in terms of **components**. Whereas factors define the *structure* of intelligence, components describe the *processes* of intelligence. A component is 'an elementary information process that operates upon internal representations of objects or symbols' (Sternberg, 1980, p. 574). We represent events to ourselves by means of such cognitive processes as perception and memory. We then manipulate these representations in a variety of ways. We can think about things, imagine them from different perspectives, remember similar things, and so on. The different ways in which we transform cognitive representations are the components of intelligence. Thus, for example, you can represent the object in which you are now sitting as a chair and then think of the super-ordinate category for that concept (*chair* is a member of the class *furniture*). People vary in the speed and accuracy with which they can carry out such operations. These differences are a part of what constitutes individual differences in intelligence.

Sternberg (1984b) identified three kinds of components. These are *metacomponents*, *performance components*, and *knowledge acquisition components*. These components may be found in all aspects of intelligence, and so may be said to be universal (Sternberg, 1998, 1999a, 1999b).

Metacomponents

Metacomponents are 'executive processes used in planning, monitoring, and decision making in task performance' (Sternberg, 1984c, p. 282). These components control the execution of other components. Before you attempt to solve a problem, you must make some decisions about the kind of problem with which you are faced and precisely how you will go about tackling it. The use of metacomponents means that the intelligent approach to solving a particular problem may not be the fastest approach. As Sternberg (1984c, p. 282) pointed out, many intelligence test items are timed, and a speedy response is often taken to signify intelligence more than does a slow, considered response. And yet, in many situations, careful consideration of the nature of the problem, thorough planning of the solution procedure, and monitoring the solution process as it proceeds lead to better results than does 'shooting from the hip'. Sternberg suggested that the distinction between reflective and impulsive approaches to problems is an important one. He reported evidence that people who tended to spend more time trying to understand what the problem was before tackling it were also judged to be more intelligent. This is a point we will develop further in the section below on creativity.

Performance Components

Having decided how you will attack a problem, it is necessary to engage **performance components**, which are 'the processes that are used in the execution of a task' (Sternberg, 1984a, p. 166). Performance components are used at every stage of the solution process. These stages include encoding the various aspects of the problem situation, comparing the different parts of the problem, and generating the appropriate response. The running example used by Sternberg (e.g., 1980, p. 576) in several places is the procedure for solving analogies. When asked to solve the analogy *fish is to water as worm is to: (a) earth or (b) hook*, one first must encode each term to determine its meaning. Then you can compare the parts of the analogy to find similarities (e.g., *fish* and *worm* are both living creatures). Mapping is a very important process whereby past knowledge is related to (mapped onto) the present situation. You already know the relation between *fish* and *water*: fish live in the water. You can then map this relation onto the pairs *worm, earth* and *worm, hook*. The relation of 'lives in' certainly fits the first pair better than the second. Worms live in the earth, but they die on hooks. After finding the solution you can then make the appropriate response (*earth*).

Knowledge Acquisition Components

As the name suggests, **knowledge acquisition components** are concerned with 'learning new information and storing it in memory' (Sternberg, 1983, p. 5). The key aspect of these components is selectivity. It is impossible to learn everything; the person must be able to filter out the irrelevant and pick up the relevant information. Information so acquired must be retained in a meaningful form so that it can be used later. An expert has acquired and is able to use information specific to a particular class of tasks.

The Triarchic Theory

The components just described are universal in that they enter into all intelligent behaviour. However, intelligent behaviour has three different content areas. These are **analytical intelligence**, **creative intelligence**, and **practical intelligence**. These three all make use of the same components, but vary with respect to the 'mental contents and representations' they use (Sternberg, Castejón, Prieto, Hautamäki, & Grigerenko, 2001, p. 2). As discussed in Box 12.1, Sternberg's triarchic theory has a surprising parallel with another, much older theory of intelligence.

Analytical Intelligence

Sternberg argued that analytical intelligence was the closest to what conventional intelligence tests measure. To the extent that g is important, it is with respect to analytical intelligence. Tests such as the Raven are good measures of analytical intelligence.

Box 12.1 An Ancient Parallel to Sternberg's Theory of Intelligence

---

The similarity of Sternberg's theory to Aristotle's classical theory of intelligence has been pointed out by Tigner and Tigner (2000). They observed that Aristotle (384–323 BC) also recognized three kinds of intelligence. The first is *theoretical intelligence*, which corresponds to what most people now think of as 'intelligence'. It is the ability to understand subjects such as mathematics and science. Aristotle's second kind of intelligence is *practical intelligence*. Here the focus is on being able to choose a wise course of action. Finally, there is *productive intelligence*, which is concerned with being able to make things. It is perhaps best exemplified in the arts.

As Tigner and Tigner (2000) point out, Aristotle's system has strong similarities to the *triarchic theory of intelligence* proposed by the Sternberg (1988). Although Sternberg uses different labels for them (*analytical*, *practical*, and *creative*), his three kinds of intelligence are essentially the same as Aristotle's. Sternberg did not copy Aristotle's system, but arrived at it using the empirical methods of contemporary psychology. Thus, one reason for believing that Aristotle's system has merit is that it has been independently verified by another investigator using different methods and in a very different era.

Sternberg (2000b) makes the sage observation that the similarity between his theory and Aristotle's illustrates the importance of revisiting historically important approaches to psychology. 'If both philosophical and psychological analysis support an idea, the idea gains credibility by virtue of the overlap in substantive findings across methods of analysis. . . . Tigner and Tigner's (2000) analysis shows how important it is to study the history and philosophy of psychology. There are many alternative paths to knowledge and understanding about the human mind' (Sternberg, 2000b, p. 178).

Creative Intelligence

Sternberg (e.g., 1999a, p. 304) argued that intelligence also involves the ability to reason using novel concepts. A familiar situation allows people to use what Sternberg (1982) called **entrenched concepts**. An entrenched concept strikes us as natural, and is easy to reason with. By contrast, unfamiliar, or novel, situations may involve the use of **nonentrenched concepts** that strike us as unnatural and are difficult to reason with. Here are examples of these two types of concept, which Sternberg adapted from Goodman (1955). Colour concepts *blue* and *green* are natural concepts. Robins' eggs have been blue ever since we can remember, and we expect that they will remain that colour forever. Emeralds are always green, and we expect them to be green in the future. However, we do not ordinarily possess colour concepts that refer to objects that change colour over time. For example, a freshly picked banana may be green and later turn to yellow as it ripens. We could invent a concept called *grellow* that describes objects that are green now, but later turn yellow. There could also be a novel concept *bleen* that describes objects that are blue now, but that turn green later. Another possibility is the concept *grue* that describes objects that are green now, but that will turn blue in the future. Reasoning with concepts such as *grellow, bleen*, and *grue* involves being able to reason in a novel conceptual system.

Sternberg invented several problems to measure people's ability to think with these kinds of novel concepts. Here is one such problem. Can there be an object to which the concept *blue* is applied in the year 2000, but to which the concept *green* properly applies in 2005? It is tempting to quickly answer 'Yes', but what do you think? The proper answer, given the possibility of *bleen*, is 'No'. If an object changes colour from green to blue, then it must be a *bleen* object in the year 2005. Conceptualizing it as *blue* in 2000 turns out to have been a mistake. When the object turned green in the year 2005, it became clear that it was really a *bleen* object.

The ability to reason with novel concepts enables the person to explore problem spaces that otherwise would remain closed to them. This increases the range of problems they can approach successfully.

Practical Intelligence

Sternberg (1999a, p. 305; Sternberg & Wagner, 1986, 1994) saw practical intelligence as important in familiar situations of a non-academic sort. He stressed the necessity of studying intelligence in the real-world settings in which it ordinarily occurs. To illustrate the difference between practical intelligence and IQ, Sternberg (1998, p. 494) cited the work of Silvia Scribner (1986, 1993; Herman, 1993). Scribner used the *ethnographic method* in her investigations. This method approaches the study of practical cognition in the same way that an anthropologist would approach the study of a particular culture or subculture. This method relies on naturalistic observation in the field, and should be seen as a part of the ecological approach to psychology (Scribner, 1993). A good example of the ethnographic method in action is Scribner's (1986) study of dairy workers.

A common stereotype of work in highly mechanized contexts such as assembly lines is that it does not engage the worker's cognitive processes at a very high level. There may be some truth to this, but perhaps not as much as is commonly believed. Scribner (1986, p. 15) defined practical thinking as 'mind in action . . . thinking that is embedded in the larger purposive activities of daily life and that functions to achieve the goals of these activities.' One of the contexts she investigated was a modern dairy. 'The dairy is a prototypical industrial system in which many occupational activities involve standardized and repetitive duties performed under highly constrained conditions' (Scribner, 1986, p. 21).

Scribner observed workers performing a variety of functions. For example, delivery truck drivers developed their own ways of working out the cost of a delivery. Scribner reported that experienced drivers made virtually no computational errors in on-the-job calculations. However, in pencil and paper tests of arithmetic they made many errors. It may be concluded that the pencil and paper test, which was similar to the sort of test that might be given in school, did not predict their on-the-job behaviour very well.

Sternberg and Kaufman (1998, p. 495) argued that Scribner's study shows the independence of practical intelligence from 'measures of academic skills, including intelligence test scores, arithmetic test scores, and grades'.

The Sternberg Triarchic Abilities Test

Sternberg, Castejón, Prieto, Hautamäki, and Grigerenko (2001) collected data from three international samples to validate the Sternberg Triarchic Abilities Test (STAT). This test contains items intended to measure the three content areas of intelligence according to the triarchic theory. Sternberg et al. argued that the data supported the hypothesis that the three content areas were distinct factors. However, the results were not unambiguous, and lend themselves to alternative interpretations, as we shall see below.

Successful Intelligence

For Sternberg (1999a, 1999b; Sternberg & Kaufman, 1998, pp. 493–496), all three aspects of intelligence are important in their own way. An individual is seldom going to be strong in all three. In order to be successful in life people need to make the most of their individual strengths while at the same time recognizing their weaknesses. Someone strong in analytical intelligence may find the most success in an academic career. Someone high in creative intelligence may be a successful entrepreneur, sniffing out novel opportunities before others. Practical intelligence may enable a person to 'work effectively in an environment' without being 'explicitly taught' what is required (Sternberg, 1999a, p. 305). To the extent that one is strong in all these intelligences, then one will perform well in a greater variety of contexts.

Criticisms of Sternberg's Theory

Although Sternberg's approach to the study of intelligence has been extremely influential, it is not without its critics. For example, Brody (2003a, 2003b) observed that the STAT measures of analytical, practical, and creative intelligences are all intercorrelated. Brody concluded that these three abilities are all 'substantially related to one another' (p. 341). In a similar vein, Gottfredson (2003a, 2003b) argued that there was no evidence unequivocally supporting the independent existence of a practical intelligence. Indeed, Gottfredson suggested that Sternberg underplayed the importance of g in practical affairs. The thrust of these criticisms is that the STAT adds nothing to existing measures of g, and that the triarchic theory is superfluous when compared to the wealth of evidence for g theory. In replies to his critics, Sternberg (2003a, 2003b) observed that investigations of the triarchic theory are relatively recent compared to g theory, and expressed the hope that future research will fulfill the promise of the triarchic theory.

■ Howard Gardner and the Theory of Multiple Intelligences

For Gardner (1983, 1993a), intelligence is not one thing, but many things. Rather than claim that there is an underlying ability common to all intelligent activity, Gardner

(1983) argued that there are **multiple intelligences**, or 'relatively autonomous human intellectual competences' (p. 8). He played down the importance of general intelligence (*g*), claiming that it emerges only as a result of sampling too narrow a range of abilities (Walters & Gardner, 1986, p. 177).

Gardner saw his approach as descended in part from the nineteenth-century phrenology of Gall and Spurzheim, which we discussed in Chapter 1. The basic idea behind phrenology was that particular areas of the brain have unique functions, similar to the faculties we considered in Chapter 1. The phrenologists argued that basic differences between people in abilities arose because the areas of the brain that were responsible for controlling these functions were differentially developed. If we translate the basic phrenological insight about brain organization into a statement about intelligence, then we could say, with Gardner (1983, p. 55), that there are a number of distinctive intelligences each of which is supported by its own parts of the brain. Although there may be several different parts of the brain involved in the execution of a complex task, such as playing the violin, it is not the case that all parts of the brain are equally involved in all forms of intelligence. In fact, this is one of Gardner's criteria for the existence of a separate intelligence. 'To the extent that a particular faculty can be destroyed, or spared in isolation, as a result of brain damage, its relative autonomy from other human faculties seems likely' (Gardner, 1983, p. 63). Research with neuroimaging techniques has lent some support to Gardner's 'distinction among domains in terms of the separable anatomical networks they activate' (Posner, 2004, p. 25). However, these networks do not operate in complete isolation, but interact with one another.

Gardner (1983, p. 63) had several other criteria for defining an intelligence. Here are three of his most distinctive criteria of 'an intelligence'.

First, a separate intelligence requires some sort of **symbol system**. A human intelligence finds expression in a symbol system that allows us to represent what we know about the world. Of course, there are several different ways of representing what we know. Usually we think of knowledge as being represented by means of some sort of language. Thus, this textbook is written in English and represents some of what we know and think about cognition. If this were a physics course, then there would be a physics text that contains what we know about physics.

If I ask you to describe the route to your residence, you could do it, and what you would be doing is describing the contents of your cognitive map. However, there are also a great many other ways of representing our information in our cognitive maps. You could draw the route to your residence, or a map of your campus, as well as describe it in words. To take a somewhat different example, if I ask you how you are feeling, you could tell me in words, or you could say what sort of song describes how you feel. Music can represent states of mind. We often listen to music precisely because it echoes our own state of mind. So here we have, in drawing and music, at least two different **symbolic forms** (Cassirer, 1953–1959), or ways of representing events. Things like language, making pictures, music, and mathematics are examples of symbol systems that are important all over the world, and that are, in different contexts, important for adaptation and survival. One hypothesis that Gardner investigated is the possibility that each of these different symbolic forms is the expression of a separate intelligence.

Second, a separate intelligence is likely to exist where there are exceptional individuals, such as *prodigies*. The existence of prodigies (people with truly outstanding ability in some area of endeavour) cannot be easily explained by a general theory of intelligence. How is it that an individual can show an advanced level of performance in one aspect of his or her activities, but not in other aspects? Furthermore, there can be prodigies in disciplines such as mathematics and music, but not in other disciplines, such as history (Gardner, 1983, p. 28). The symbolic forms in which prodigies specialize may be the separate intelligences that underlie competence in other areas. Competence in a discipline such as history may not reflect the operation of a specific symbolic form, but may be built on a variety of specific intelligences, as well as long-term study.

Third, a separate intelligence has a distinctive *developmental history* (Gardner, 1983, p. 64). There should be a characteristic way in which expertise develops, with everyone beginning in the same way. Some, but not all, practitioners will reach very high levels of competence. Describing an intelligence in this way presumes that it is possible to objectively define what constitutes the expert use of a particular symbolic form. The study of the development of expertise is a significant part of the study of specific intelligences.

Here is Gardner's original list of intelligences, together with one or two examples of an outstanding practitioner of each intelligence: musical intelligence (Mozart, Louis Armstrong), bodily-kinesthetic intelligence (Babe Ruth, Wayne Gretzky), linguistic intelligence (William Shakespeare, T.S. Eliot), logico-mathematical intelligence (Isaac Newton, Albert Einstein), spatial intelligence (Polynesian sailors have extremely complex cognitive maps that enable them to navigate for thousands of miles), personal intelligence (Anne Sullivan, Helen Keller's teacher). Gardner (2004) did not consider this list to be final, and other candidates are always being considered. Gardner's unique contribution has been to focus our attention on symbol systems that are not always seen as central to the concept of intelligence.

In what follows, we will consider two symbol systems. Gardner's (1980, 1982) work has had the salutary influence of drawing attention to neglected but extremely important aspects of intelligence. For example, our ability to make pictures is one facet of what Gardner (1983) called *spatial intelligence*. After considering drawing, we examine music. Musical ability appears to be an intelligence of its own. We begin by talking about the development of these symbolic forms as they take place normally. Then we consider the way in which these symbolic forms express themselves in exceptional cases, such as prodigies.

Drawing—The Typical Developmental Pattern

The course of the development of artistic skill is not linear. It is not as if the preschool child is a bad artist, the school-age child a better artist, and the trained adult a superior artist. Rather, Gardner and Winner (1982; Winner, 1982, p. 175) suggest that the development of this skill, and perhaps many others, follows a **U-shaped** pattern. This pattern is illustrated in Figure 12.3. As Siegler (2004) observed, U-shaped development is particularly interesting because it contradicts the widespread assumption that per-formance always improves with age. U-shaped patterns are cases in which 'perform-ance is initially relatively good, . . . subsequently becomes worse, and . . . eventually improves' (p. 3).

A child's early productions are relatively high in what might be called *aesthetic pleasingness*. Preschool children's artistic performance is aesthetically pleasing because they draw with a lot of vitality, indicating that their drawings are very important to them. Parents often take these drawings with both pleasure and respect, as shown by the existence of the *refrigerator art gallery* in many homes (L. Gross, 1983; for examples of refrigerator art, see www.artcontest.com/refrigerator/Hall_Of_Fame.html).

Preschoolers' work is called *preconventional* for several reasons. The colours are unrealistic: there is only a passing attempt to match colour with real-world colour. Moreover, in the preschooler's drawing, there is only a passing attempt to organize the objects in the drawing in the way they are actually organized in space. Objects appear to float on top the page (Winner, 1982, p. 152): there is no consistent perspective, or even the attempt at perspective. However, what makes a drawing like this valuable, in many art critics' eyes, is its vitality (Gardner, 1980, pp. 94ff.). Winner (1982, p. 169) lists these characteristics of this *golden age of children's drawing*: the use of bright colours, freedom from the constraint of trying to be realistic, an absence of stereotyped forms, and a willingness to explore and experiment.

When children go to school, their art enters the *conventional period*. Gardner and Winner argued that the dip in the U is not so much because the child has lost a freedom of self-expression, but because the child is preoccupied with learning the conventions that are a part of expertise in drawing. If individuals ever master the rules of this sym-bolic form, then they will be able to make the rules work for them in a creative way. No longer entirely bound by attempts to be conventional, their work can become *postcon-*

Figure 12.3 U-shaped Development.

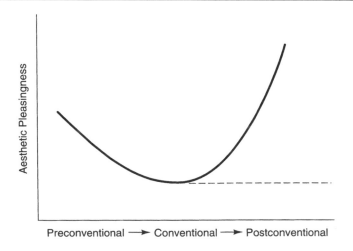

ventional and can be admired for its vitality as well as its mastery. A well-known example is the work of Picasso (e.g., www.moma.org/collection/conservation/demoiselles/ and www.pbs.org/treasuresoftheworld/guernica/gmain.html).

Many professional artists have admired preschoolers' art because of the qualities that it embodies. Mature artists' work often has the lack of constraint by conventional norms that characterizes young children's art. However, mature artists are not doing what the preschooler is doing. They are doing something very difficult: they are achieving what the child achieves, but in a different and more skilful way. The mature artist knows every inch of the canvas and how to exploit it to achieve the representation desired. The mature artist achieves intentionally what the child achieves without thinking (Winner, 1982, p. 175).

> However, it is important to see that very few people in our culture ever make it very far along in this developmental progression. Although we prize some forms of intelligence, it is perfectly alright to be artistically incompetent in our culture. Thus, the most accurate developmental curve for most people in our culture may be the one represented by the dotted line [see Figure 12.3]. Very often, we descend to the conventional stage, and stay there.

Music

The development of musical intelligence is similar in some respects to the development of drawing. During the first few years of life, children spontaneously do a number of musical things. 'Toddlers commonly invent songs before they can reproduce conventional songs' (Trehub, 2003, p. 669). They sing tunes, invent tunes, and beat rhythmic patterns. Dowling and Harwood (1986, pp. 144ff.) have reviewed some of the musical phenomena of the preschool years. The emergence of early musical activity, such as singing, may depend on having older models, such as parents and siblings, to imitate. In any case, when children reach the second year, they begin to produce what adults will accept as something at least vaguely resembling singing.

Some theorists, notably Bernstein (1976, p. 16), argued that young children typically produce a particular melodic pattern spontaneously, and have argued that this pattern is due to innate musical knowledge. He argued that sound patterns, such as those used by children to tease each other (when they go Nya-Nya-Nya-Nya-Nya) or call each other by name (A-lice, Tom-my) reflect this innate musical knowledge.

Gardner (1982, pp. 144ff.) examined the possible existence of such a basic melody, which he called the **ur-song**. *Ur* refers to something that is original; the earliest. Thus, the ur-song, if it existed, would be the first song that children spontaneously sing. Gardner noted that there is actually not much evidence for such a spontaneous innate pattern, but it is an intriguing speculation all the same (see also Dowling & Harwood, 1986, p. 147).

By the end of the third year, children begin reproducing culturally provided song models. Here they begin to get coherent, conventional songs, like the 'Alphabet Song', 'Twinkle, Twinkle Little Star', or 'Old MacDonald Had a Farm'. Like drawing, music does not typically develop during the school years the way that linguistic skills do. The latter are, of course, honed through schooling. Gardner (1983, p. 111) observed that there are wide cross-cultural variations in this respect. In other cultures that value musical competence more highly, such as some European or African countries, musical intelligence typically progresses much further. Here again we can see the role of culture in determining the profile of the intelligences that are encouraged to develop.

There has been widespread speculation concerning the possibility that music lessons enhance IQ. One of the most persuasive studies was done by Schellenberg (2004). Four different groups of six-year-olds were exposed to keyboard lessons, voice lessons, drama lessons, or no lessons. The IQ scores of all groups improved, probably due to the onset of schooling in general. However, the two groups exposed to music lessons showed additional IQ gains compared to the other two groups. This suggests that music in the school curricula of particular kinds might have beneficial effects on IQ. In addition to music, Shellenberg speculates that chess lessons or science lessons may also have a beneficial effect. Such activities may provide instruction in a wide range of abilities (e.g., spatial, mathematical) that may transfer to other contexts.

Bamberger's (1982, 1986) studies of the development of musical knowledge indicate that it varies along the tacit–explicit dimension, which we considered in the chapter on concepts. Remember when we reviewed Reber's work we noted that some knowledge can be tacit. It can exist without the person's being able to say what it is that he or she knows. Bamberger's observations of musically gifted children suggest that their knowledge is at first of this tacit kind. For example, the ability of a child to imitate an older, well-known performer appears to be the result of the child having a feeling for the task as a whole, rather than being brought about through a reflective analysis of the situation.

About the tacit nature of young people's musical ability, Bamberger (1986) said, 'Indeed, exposing it to scrutiny is almost to be feared: . . . "it won't work if you think about it"' (p. 393). However, as these students become adolescents, they inevitably become more reflective about their music, as they do about other aspects of their life. They feel an inconsistency between a more explicit understanding of music and the earlier, spontaneous, non-reflective understanding (and love) of music. Bamberger referred to this phase as the **mid-life crisis of the musician** because gifted musicians typically begin studying music very early in their lives (e.g., before five years of age), and so are well into their musical career by adolescence. Winner (2000) observed that gifted children may feel that they are learning music more for their parents or teachers than for themselves. She noted that many music students give up studying music at this point.

Bamberger's analysis may hold true for more than just the musically gifted student. (How may people do you know who stopped taking music lessons at about age 14? How many of them loved the music, but hated the lessons?) The integration of the tacit and explicit aspects of music is a difficult task, but necessary if the person is to achieve adult mastery of this symbolic form (Gardner, 1982, p. 111).

Prodigies

As was mentioned earlier, one of Gardner's criteria for an intelligence is the existence of prodigies in that area. **Prodigies** show an expert level of performance well before one would normally expect to observe it (Feldman, 1986, Gardner, 1993b). One type of prodigy about whom we know a good deal is the musical prodigy. How do you know when you have a prodigy, and not just a very clever kid? Consider the following example, given by Ruthsatz and Detterman (2003, p. 514):

> The subject was a 6-year-old musical prodigy. At the time of testing, the subject had played in numerous concerts, appeared several times on national television, and been in two movies. He had released two musical CD's in which he sings in two languages and plays several musical instruments. Unlike the mechanical flat performance often reported in the savant literature, his performance was expressive. He is able to entertain large paying audiences with his musical skill. He is capable of many instruments but prefers the piano and accordion. He is the only child of an intact family from the Southern United States. No one in his immediate family reported any knowledge of accelerated musical ability. However, his mother has played the piano. The young music prodigy, Derek, has not engaged in structured musical lessons but masters his music by listening to other performers and improvising his own musical pieces.

Derek (a pseudonym) was given the Stanford-Binet IQ test, which includes several subscales such as verbal reasoning, abstract/visual reasoning, quantitative reasoning, and short-term memory. Derek scored above average on all scales. However, his most striking score was on short-term memory, where he scored 158 (the average score is 100). 'Derek seems to compensate for an absence of formal training and deliberate practice by his enhanced ability to remember melodies and recreate them' (Ruthsatz & Detterman, 2003, p. 517).

Although Derek does not yet devote time to lessons and practice, most prodigies end up having to do so in order to fully develop their prodigious skills. Feldman (1986, Chap. 5) notes that a critical part of the cultural support that a prodigy requires is the nurturance provided by the family. In most of the cases that Feldman studied, the family played a dramatic role in fostering prodigious development. Although it may not be this way in other cultures, in North America the family must be prepared to shoulder the burden of having a child prodigy. The parents of prodigies soon become aware of the fact that they alone cannot do the job that is required. The family must decide how much control of their child's life they will give up to teachers and coaches, how much money they will spend on developing the child's abilities, how much familial dislocation they will tolerate for the sake of developing that talent. For example, a phenomenally good young hockey player may find himself being asked to move to another city to get the kind of coaching he cannot get in his home town. This might involve considerable strain for all members of the family, including the child.

Criticisms of Multiple Intelligence Theory

Walters and Gardner (1986) reviewed some of the early objections to the theory of multiple intelligences. One criticism was that this theory concentrates on what are more properly called talents or gifts than on what is usually called intelligence. However, Walters and Gardner saw no reason to reserve the word 'intelligence' for the kind of logical/mathematical or linguistic skills that are most valued by our culture. Certainly, Gardner's approach has had considerable influence on parents' and educators' beliefs that 'people differ in their abilities to solve problems and make contributions to society in diverse ways' (Cuban, 2004).

A persistent criticism of the theory is that it is not grounded in scientific data (Chen, 2004). This criticism has much truth to it. However, the theory of multiple intelligences does have support from case studies (e.g., Gardner, 1993b). Gardner (1999, 2004) has persistently argued that the study of intelligence is interdisciplinary and benefits from a variety of approaches ranging from the humanities and the arts to the sciences.

■ Expertise

Recall that one of Gardner's criteria for an intelligence was that it is possible to define what constitutes expertise in that area. Independent of Gardner's theory, there has been a great deal of interest in understanding what goes into making a person an expert. The classic study of expertise was undertaken by Chase and Simon (1973), who extended earlier work by de Groot (1965). They compared the ability of chess masters and chess novices to remember the positions of chess pieces they had been shown arranged on a chessboard. Memory was tested by having participants reproduce the positions they had seen. Masters could remember the piece positions better than novices particularly if the pieces they had been shown represented an arrangement that had been reached as a result of a game. The relations between the pieces in such an arrangement are meaningful to **chess experts** when contrasted with a random placement of pieces on the chessboard, which is relatively meaningless to both experts and novices. For a random arrangement of chess pieces, experts are only slightly superior to novices in their ability to remember the way the pieces had been arranged (Gobet & Simon, 1996). Chess experts respond differently to game position arrangements from random arrangements.

Chase and Simon suggested that experts perceive the game position arrangements in larger units, or chunks. However, for the novice, game position and random arrangements amount to the same thing. They do not know enough to be able to see the meaning in game position arrangements. The novice is not able to 'chunk' the pieces, and must remember the position of each piece separately. This constraint causes a memory decrement relative to the expert, particularly when the situation to be remembered resembles one that could occur in a game. Gobet and Simon (1996, p. 31) observed that 'chess players have seen thousands of positions, and for expert players, most positions they see readily remind them of positions or types of positions they have seen before.'

Ericsson and Charness (1994) reviewed the literature on expert performance and concluded that *practice* is its most important determinant. They downplay the importance of innate talent and emphasize the degree to which 'extended intense training' (p. 730) is necessary for someone to become a world-class expert in some domain. Whether it is becoming a chess master or an Olympic medallist, at least 10 years of full-time practice is required. This is called the **10-year rule** (Rossano, 2003, p. 210). This works out to roughly 10,000 hours of practice in order to reach the top-level of performance. Not just any practice will do. In music, for example, morning practice appears to be best, and it is important not to practise so much that the performer 'burns out' (Ericsson & Charness, 1994, p. 742).

There is no evidence for anatomical differences between the brains of novices and experts, at least in the case of expert memorizers. Maguire, Valentine, Wilding, and Kapur (2003) studied participants who were of the first rank at the World Memory Championships, held in London each year. They were compared with a group of participants matched for age and intelligence. MRI images revealed no structural differences in the brains of the two groups. However, the expert memorizers reported using the *method of loci* when given memorization tasks, such as remembering strings of digits. You should recall from Chapter 6 that the method of loci involves taking a mental walk through a series of images. Functional magnetic resonance imaging scans revealed that the expert memorizers showed greater activity in parts of the brain associated with navigation, such as the hippocampus. That is, while there is no *anatomical* difference between novice and expert memorizers, there is a *functional* difference in the parts of the expert brain that are active. This result should be compared with that for London taxi drivers, which we also discussed in Chapter 6. Recall that their knowledge of London streets is vastly greater than normal, and it is accompanied by an *anatomical* difference, namely an enlarged part of the hippocampus. This difference between expert memorizers and taxi drivers is probably due to the fact that the memorizers have learned to employ the same strategy—the method of loci—for different materials, while the taxi drivers have had to acquire their knowledge of streets by sheer repetition. Ericsson (2003) noted that the Maguire et al. study supports the view that there needs to be nothing innately different about the brains of experts. Rather, years of practice make true expertise possible.

■ Creativity

It is no easier to find a consensus concerning the meaning of **creativity** than it is to find a consensus for the meaning of *intelligence*. However, one definition that has received wide acceptance is that creativity involves 'the production of novel, socially valued products' (Mumford & Gustafson, 1988, p. 28). Such a definition acknowledges the fact that creativity cannot sensibly be defined only in terms of the ability to behave in novel or original ways. The meaning of the term also includes some criterion of appropriateness (Vinacke, 1974, p. 354). Behaving in an original way would not qualify as creative unless the product also provides some 'solution to a significant social problem'

(Mumford & Gustafson, 1988, p. 28). This definition is quite broad, and admits of several different approaches to understanding creativity. Some research has focused on the processes responsible for original behaviours, without considering very thoroughly the criterion of appropriateness. Other research has more thoroughly explored the social context within which creative behaviour is evaluated.

Creativity and Problem-Finding

Psychologists exploring creativity and original thinking have been especially interested in **problem-finding** (Runco, 2004, p. 675). The best-known researcher associated with the topic of problem-finding is Getzels (1975). He observed that problem-finding may strike some people as a luxury because there are already enough problems to go around. Why do we need more people finding problems? The answer is that the quality of a solution often depends on the way a problem is formulated. To make this point Getzels (1975) quoted Einstein:

> The formulation of a problem is often more essential than its solution, which may be merely a matter of mathematical or experimental skill. To raise new questions, new possibilities, to regard old questions from a new angle, requires creative imagination and marks real advance in science. (p. 12)

However, problem-finding is not an activity that is valuable only in science. Getzels (1975, p. 15) gives the following example of problem-finding in the real world. Suppose you have a flat tire on a deserted country road. Your car lacks a jack, and you define the problem as getting a jack. One solution would be to walk back to town to get a jack to raise the car. Someone else might define the problem as raising the car. This is a more productive way of putting the matter because it allows you to see the potential relevance of things other than jacks to the solution of your problem. In Getzels's example, the person who defines the problem as raising the car notices that there is a pulley attached to the hay loft of a nearby barn. By pushing the car underneath the pulley, the car can be raised and the tire changed. The creative solution is made possible by the way the problem is formulated.

Getzels (1975) contrasted problem-finding with other forms of cognition in terms of three dimensions: the way the problem is stated, the method used to solve the problem, and the solution itself. In many of the cognitive processes in which we engage, all three of these aspects are already known and simply given to us. For example, students can be asked to multiply 1,232 by 54,762. In this case (a) the problem is provided by the teacher to the students; (b) the solution procedure is known by the teacher (and, we hope, by the students); and (c) the students simply generate a solution, which can be evaluated by the teacher as either right or wrong. In the course of solving the problem the students do not discover anything; they simply apply rules that are already known. Of course, problems can be provided to the students in a way that allows them to discover something in the course of problem-solving. Sometimes the teacher knows the correct method for approaching a problem, but allows the students to discover the method on their own. Many of the so-called insight problems (e.g., the nine-dot problem) that we considered in Chapter 9 are problems of this sort. The person to whom the problem is given does not know how to solve it initially, but discovers the correct method in the course of attempting a solution.

However, even in problems such as these, the problem itself is still given to the person and not one that he or she discovers alone. True problem-finding does not occur until all three aspects are generated by the person, who formulates the problem, devises the method, and provides the solution, all of which are unknown to anyone else. Such problem-finding occurs in all areas of endeavour. Getzels's

> most generative idea has been the concept of 'problem finding'—the notion that whereas most approaches to understanding creativity focus on its problem-solving aspects, what really differentiates a creative thought from a less original one is that it deals with an issue no one had seen as problematic before. Thus, it is the formulation of a hitherto unperceived problem, rather than its solution, that is the hallmark of creativity. (Csikszentmihalyi, 2002, p. 290)

What turns one from being a solver of provided problems to being a problem-*finder* may be a vague sense that a problem exists without knowing exactly what it is. In order to see how people discover a problem, Getzels and Csikszentmihalyi (1972, 1976) observed the behaviour of art students before they actually drew anything. They provided undergraduate fine art students with an experimental studio in which to work. In this studio were 27 objects that could be arranged to provide a still life subject. The objects included such things as a velvet hat, a horn, a book, and a bunch of grapes. The student was asked to choose some of the objects, arrange them, and then draw the arrangement. The students' behaviour during the pre-drawing phase was coded using such variables as the number of objects examined, the way objects were explored (e.g., was the shape of any object changed?), and the way the objects were arranged. The resulting drawings were evaluated by five well-known artist-critics in terms of such dimensions as overall aesthetic value, originality, and craftsmanship.

The art students are engaged in problem-finding during the pre-drawing phase of the experiment. They are not provided with an arrangement of objects to draw, but have to set their own problem by arranging the objects themselves. The issue addressed by this experiment is whether or not the students' problem-finding behaviour during the pre-drawing phase is related in any way to the artist-critics' evaluation of their work. It turned out that, in fact, there were relationships between some aspects of pre-drawing behaviour and the final product. There was wide variation in terms of the number of objects examined and the way these objects were examined. Some participants examined only a few objects and did not feel their texture or change their shape; other participants interacted in a more direct way with more objects (e.g., feeling the texture of objects and not just looking at them).

There was also wide variation in the originality of the arrangement of the objects. Some objects were chosen by many participants, whereas others were chosen less often. Participants who scored high on these problem-finding variables also tended to be judged as having produced the most aesthetically pleasing and original work. However, there was no relation between pre-drawing behaviour and judgements of craftsmanship or technical skill.

Getzels and Csikszentmihalyi interpreted their results as meaning that problem-finding behaviour is closely related to the artistic value and originality of the finished product. Only technical skill is not a function of problem-finding behaviour. An artist can execute a drawing with great skill, and yet it will not be as highly valued as another drawing done with similar skill but displaying a more creative approach. Creativity and problem-finding are intimately linked from this point of view. The more the person actively explores the problem space prior to attempting to produce a solution, the more creative will be the result.

Csikszentmihalyi and Beattie (1979) showed how personal problem-finding could lead to solutions of value to people other than oneself. For example, suppose you find a problem in your own life that needs resolution. This does not need to be a big problem; it just needs to be a problem that to your knowledge no one has faced before. Thus, for you it is a discovered problem. In the course of defining and ultimately solving your problem, it may occur to you that other people could use a solution to this problem as well, although they may not realize it yet. Some entrepreneurs may be especially good at making the transition from a personally defined problem to a solution for general consumption. Here are two examples. One person enjoyed camping, but found that sleeping on the ground aggravated his allergies (Alaimo, 1996a). His solution was to rig a tent in the back of his pickup. However, he did not stop there. Together with a designer he put together a prototype for a two-person tent that is easily erected in the back of a pickup. It took several years of development, but the tent eventually ended up on the market. Another person 'had become fed up using twist ties or elastic bands to keep his own fishing rod together while trekking to his favorite fishing holes' (Alaimo, 1996b). He invented soft plastic snap-on devices that keep fishing tackle in order. After doing research to determine that nothing like his invention was on the market, he spent years getting financial backing and ended up selling his creation in mass-market stores across the country.

Both of the preceding examples are deliberately quite prosaic to show that you do not need to be a Thomas Edison in order to create something that other people will find useful. However, you do need to be able to see that a solution to your problem might also be a solution to someone else's problem. Furthermore, in keeping with a point we made at the beginning of the chapter, you also need to be prepared to put considerable time and resources into developing your idea.

(The examples of problem-finding given above come from my local newspaper. It would be a good exercise for you to ask a librarian to help you search the archives of your local paper for similar examples. Successful problem-finding on a small scale can and does occur in communities everywhere.)

Creativity as Evolution in Miniature

An influential theory of the creative process was advanced by Campbell (1960), who applied Darwinian evolutionary theory to the process of knowledge acquisition. As Campbell saw it, there are two key aspects to the evolutionary process. One of these aspects is **blind variation**, which refers to a process whereby alternatives are explored without knowing in advance which alternative will have the desired consequences. An example of blind variation is pure trial and error, of the sort that was perhaps first described by the comparative psychologist C. Lloyd Morgan (1894). Morgan noted that his dog learned how to escape from the fenced-in back yard by lifting the latch on the gate. This was not the result of any insight on Tony's part but of a process whereby the animal explored his environment, finally by chance hitting on a response that would free him.

Some forms of blind variation involve the organism's actively moving in the environment, but other forms of blind variation allow the organism to pick up information from the environment without actually moving around in it. Campbell mentioned the process of *echolocation* as an example of this type of blind variation. Some species such as bats will emit a sound that bounces off objects in the environment. The returning echo is a cue to the location of objects. The animal can behave appropriately on the basis of the feedback it gets from the sound it emits. People can also learn to echolocate, and many blind people appear to do so.

As it happens, I was once a participant in an echolocation experiment (Taylor, 1966). The layout of the experiment is given below (Figure 12.4). As one of the participants, I sat blindfolded at the table, and a rectangular metal target was placed at one of the positions on the table. My task was to move my head from left to right and back again, all the while saying 'Where is it? Where is it?' and to reach for the target when I thought that I might know where it was. I would continue reaching for it until I hit it. The target would then be placed at another randomly determined position. While the target was moved, a white noise generator would be turned on. White noise contains all audible frequencies, and it masked the sound of the target as it was

Figure 12.4 Apparatus for an Echolocation Experiment.

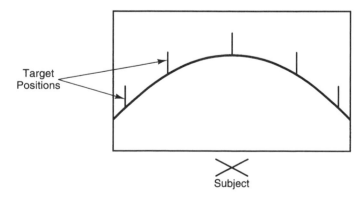

moved, so that I could not hear it being moved. Although it is impossible not to feel foolish at first, after numerous trials on several subsequent days, I could begin to vaguely sense where the target was, even though I could not see it. Coincident with this vague sense of the target's position was an increase in the ability to hit the metal target the first time I reached for it, although being aware of the target's position is not necessary in order to hit it. The words 'Where is it?' were apparently enough to produce an echo from the target, and the echo was a cue that I could learn to use to determine the target's position.

Campbell's point about echolocation was that it is a *blind* process, both literally and figuratively: the sound that is emitted is not emitted in any particular direction. In order for echolocation to work properly, it is necessary that all locations have an equal chance of being sampled. It is the feedback from the environment that tells you which direction is the correct one. The environment provides the selection criterion for a correct action. Without such blind variation, you will not get any information from the environment, and you will not learn anything new.

Creative thinking, from Campbell's viewpoint, involves blind variation on a symbolic level. The person can imagine various alternative courses of action, as well as the selection criterion for an appropriate action. The person may have a fairly clear idea of the sort of solution a problem requires, and may then vary his or her thinking until an idea occurs that fits the requirements. The variation is *blind* in that the person has no idea what the answer will be, and any idea is a possible candidate. There is no restriction on the ideas this process may generate. Of course, most of the ideas generated will be of little or no value (Campbell, 1960, p. 393). However, eventually the process of generating alternative ideas may result in a hit. The key mechanism of creative thinking is *serendipity*—accidental discovery. Alternatives that turn out to meet the selection criteria, whatever they happen to be, are then retained for future use in similar contexts.

As an example of the process of **blind variation and selective retention**, Campbell cited the famous case of the great French mathematician Poincaré (1924/1960). Poincaré recounted the way in which he discovered a theorem concerned with Fuchsian functions. As Poincaré observed, psychologists do not need to concern themselves with the precise meaning of Fuchsian functions, but only with the process through which Poincaré came to discover his theorem. He described this process as follows:

> For a fortnight I had been attempting to prove that there could not be any function analogous to what I have since called Fuchsian functions. I was at that time very ignorant. Every day I sat down at my table, and spent an hour or two trying a great number of combinations, and I arrived at no result. One night I took some black coffee, contrary to my custom, and was unable to sleep. A host of ideas kept surging in my head; I could almost feel them jostling one another, until two of them coalesced, so to speak, to form a stable combination. When morning came, I had established the existence of one class of Fuchsian functions, those that are derived from the hypergeometric series. I had only to verify the results, which only took a few hours. (Poincaré, 1960, p. 53)

Poincaré believed that on this occasion he was able to experience the process of variation that normally proceeds outside of awareness. After initially formulating a problem, or, in Campbell's terms, establishing the selection criterion, the problem is given over to a period of unconscious work:

> What is the part to be played by the preliminary conscious work? Clearly it is evidently to liberate some of these atoms, to detach them from the wall and set them in motion. We think we have accomplished nothing, when we have stirred these elements in a thousand different ways to try to arrange them, and have not succeeded in finding a satisfactory arrangement. But after this agitation imparted to them by our will, they do not return to their original repose, but continue to circulate freely. (Poincaré, 1960, p. 61)

Poincaré's description of the process of creative thought has influenced many people in addition to Campbell. It was one of the sources of Wallas's (1926) stage theory of the creative process, a theory that still informs research in creativity (Lubart, 2001, p. 297). Wallas suggested that creative thought progressed from a stage of preparation, during which the problem was formulated, to a stage of incubation, during which the problem was not consciously thought about, but unconsciously worked on, leading to illumination, at which point a useful alternative emerges, followed by verification, during which the soundness of the proposed alternative is evaluated. Subsequent studies have not yielded very great support for the existence of discrete **stages in the creative process** (Vinacke, 1974). Nor is it necessary for a period of unconscious work to occur in order for a number of alternative solutions to be generated. Procedures exist that allow the thinker to deliberately vary the possibilities considered (Crovitz, 1970). The important thing is not how blind variation is achieved, but only that it must occur.

All of the foregoing can be summarized in terms of Simonton's (1984, 1988, 1993, 1994, 2003) version of Campbell's theory. Simonton stated three 'core propositions':

1. Creative solutions to problems require some process of variation. These variations are **chance permutations** of mental elements. Permutations are different combinations of cognitive units such as ideas and concepts.
2. Variations are selected on the basis of a set of criteria.
3. Variations that meet the criteria are retained.

Some combinations of mental elements are more stable and better organized than others. These are called *configurations*. Some configurations will meet the requirements of a particular problem situation. These requirements may be of a variety of sorts. Criteria may be conventional. For example, a novel should at least be grammatical, and a symphony should meet conventional criteria for music. Other criteria may involve the satisfaction that comes from putting together simpler configurations into higher order units. Simonton argued that people attempt to create stable, well-organized, inclusive mental structures.

If a configuration is to become culturally relevant, it is obviously necessary that it be communicated to others. The process of communication may lead to further alterations in the configuration as it is put in a format others can assimilate. As you may have noticed when you have written your own essays, having a good idea is one thing; being able to write a paper about it is quite another. Ensuring your paper will be well received is something else again. Communication of a configuration shifts the selection criteria from the personal to the social realm. In order to survive, the configuration must be seen to be useful by other people. If it meets whatever social criteria are in force at the time, then it may eventually become a part of cultural norms. Today's successful innovation is tomorrow's tradition.

Not all workers contribute equally to creativity in a particular discipline. Rather, most of the important contributions to an area are made by relatively few people. **Price's law** (Price, 1963) is an approximate description of the way that productivity is distributed. This law holds that half of all contributions in a field will be produced by the square root of the total number of workers in the field. Thus, if there are 100 workers in an area, then 10 of them will produce half the contributions. If there are 10,000 workers, then half the work will be done by 100, and so on. Simonton presented evidence suggesting that this law is approximately true not only for scientific disciplines, but also holds for productivity in such fields as classical music, literature, and legislation.

Simonton interpreted the way that productivity is distributed in terms of the chance permutation process. He argued that productive people have available to them a greater number of mental elements. The more mental elements available to the person, the more combinations of these elements are possible. It turns out that, as the number of mental elements increases, the number of permutations of these elements increases at a much faster rate. A few people with a large number of mental elements to work with can generate vastly more permutations of these elements than can the great majority of people who have fewer elements. These few people make the greatest contribution simply because they are much more likely to generate a useful configuration. We could say that it is only a few people who have the greatest **creative potential**.

It would be nice to know what the determinants of creative potential are. Simonton (1988) noted the importance of a 'diversified, enriching environment' (p. 107). This general statement can be broken down into several developmental antecedents of creative potential. We will discuss only a few of these, to give you the flavour of the sort of variable that is important. Among the antecedents of creative potential, family background is an obviously important variable. Simonton reviewed research suggesting that parental loss is associated positively with creative potential, perhaps because it heightens the individual's sense of independence. Independence might be associated with a willingness to try out new combinations of ideas. Of course, it is not necessary to be orphaned in order to be creative.

In particular cases, other variables, such as the cultural stimulation provided by the household into which the person is born, can also be important. Interestingly, level of formal education is not related to creative potential in a simple way. Simonton presented evidence that people acknowledged to be creative in their fields have neither too much nor too little education. In general, these people had achieved an undergraduate level of education, but did not have doctorates. Some training is an obvious necessity in order to instill a sufficient quantity of mental elements. Apparently, however, too much formal education inhibits the chance permutation process. Of course, the optimal level of education will vary with different disciplines. For example, the optimal level in the sciences may be higher than that in the humanities. In any case, you would be well advised not to quit school simply to avoid constraining your creative potential.

Remote Associations and Creativity

The ability to generate **remote associations** was something that Simonton (2003, p. 483) believed was characteristic of the creative individual. Remote associations are uncommon associations. Most adults provide common associations in a word association task. For example, when asked to name the first word they think of when they hear 'chair',' people tend to say 'table'; when they hear 'body', adults most often say 'mind', although they can also think of other things as well (Deese, 1965). We may think of words and objects as having a hierarchy of responses associated with them. These responses are things we see as possible to do with the objects. An example of such a hierarchy is given in Figure 12.5. This kind of structure is sometimes called a *divergent hierarchy* because it consists of a set of associations that diverge from a single object (Berlyne, 1965, p. 88). Responses that are low in the hierarchy are less obvious and less available to most of us as responses. The availability of responses is related to their frequency of usage in the past experience of the person, with the most frequently used being at the top of the hierarchy.

As we saw in Chapter 9, one of the difficulties that may arise when we try to solve problems is that the response we need is low in the hierarchy of associations we have to the objects we can use to solve the problem. If I want to build a bookcase and have a supply of bricks at hand, but do not think of bricks as a possible component in a bookcase, then I will miss one possible way of solving the problem. As we saw in Chapter 9, it is easy to be functionally fixed, that is, to be unable to see anything but the familiar or obvious uses for things. Functional fixedness is the opposite of originality. In fact, a widely used test of original thinking is the **alternate uses test** (Barron, 1963; Vartanian, Martindale, & Kwiatkowski, 2003), which requires the person to list as many uses as they can for common objects. The more unusual the uses chosen, the higher the person's score.

Figure 12.5 A Hierarchy of Responses to a Brick.

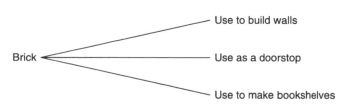

Mednick (1962) suggested that people who are creative are people with **flat hierarchies**. Most of us see only the best obvious uses for things, but a creative person sees unusual uses for things as easily as the obvious uses for things. As Simonton (2003, p. 483) observed, 'a flat associative hierarchy means that for any given stimulus, the creative person has many associations available, all with roughly equal probabilities of retrieval.' This means that the associations of creative people will be relatively unpredictable (cf. Mohr, Graves, Gianotti, Pizzagalli, & Brugger, 2001). This variability will lead the creative person to generate a greater variety of ideas that can be subjected to selection criteria.

Mednick (1967) invented a widely used test of originality called the **remote associations test** (RAT). It requires the person to come up with a single association to link three apparently unrelated words. Consider these three words: *soda, buffalo, fall*. Can you think of one word that is an association of all three words? How about *water*? *Water* can be used in association with all three words, as in *soda water, water buffalo,* and *water fall*. Here are a number of other items that are similar to RAT items, although they are not taken from the RAT. Some are much easier than others, depending on how strongly associated the answer is to one or more of the three words. However, these should give you an idea of what taking the RAT is like. (Answers are at the end of the chapter.)

> *worm juice blossom*
> *fish gun up*
> *head sick port*
> *blood grass eyes*
> *guard blow some*
> *log ship boy*
> *sugar man hard*
> *foot rat course*
> *time end fare*
> *new good leap*
> *craft broom hunt*
> *pin top rack*
> *man air black*
> *chase work news*
> *name poison pig*

The ability apparently being measured by this test is the degree to which a person can produce associations that will provide a link between words that at first do not appear to be strongly related. The RAT has been criticized on the grounds that it does not really measure what it claims to measure. Independent measures of the ability to give remote associations do not correlate well with the RAT (Perkins, 1981, p. 252). The role of remote associations in creative thinking remains unclear. This is especially true if one defines creativity in terms of the production of not only novel, but of socially valued material. Remote associations may play a part in the production of novel ideas, but their role in the production of socially relevant ideas is less obvious.

■ Questions for Study and Discussion

1. Discuss the nature and evolution of general intelligence.
2. What is the Flynn effect? Which explanation of it do you find most plausible? Why?
3. After discussing the triarchic theory of intelligence, briefly criticize Sternberg's approach to the study of intelligence.
4. Discuss Gardner's criteria for an intelligence. Then outline his approach to the study of a particular symbol system, such as drawing or music. Briefly state a criticism of this approach.
5. Do you prefer Sternberg's or Gardner's approach? Why?
6. What makes someone an expert? Answer this question by considering some of the properties of expertise as these are outlined in your text.
7. What is problem-finding? Why is it important in the creative process?
8. Discuss the role of associations in the creative process. In your answer, review at least two measures of creativity.

■ Key Concepts

Alternate uses test (Barron) A test that requires the person to list six uses for common objects.

Blind variation and selective retention (Campbell) The generation of alternative problem solutions without foresight, and the retention of those that work in a particular context.

Chance permutations Different combinations of mental elements produced according to no set rule.

Chess experts (Chase and Simon) Chess players who perceive game position arrangements in larger units, or chunks, than do novices.

Creative potential The ability to generate useful configurations of ideas.

Creativity The production of novel, socially valued products.

Crystallized intelligence Consists of things you have learned, and may increase throughout your lifetime.

Dedicated intelligence Domain-specific modules that have evolved to solve recurring problems.

Education (Spearman) Literally means *to draw out*. General intelligence may be the ability to draw out the relationships that obtain in a novel situation.

Entrenched and non-entrenched concepts An entrenched concept strikes us as natural and is easy to reason with, while non-entrenched concepts strike us as unnatural and are difficult to reason with.

Factor analysis A statistical procedure that derives a number of underlying factors that may explain the structure of a set of correlations.

Flat hierarchies The hypothesis that creative people have associative hierarchies in which the alternatives are equally likely to occur.

Fluid intelligence The ability to think flexibly, which may increase when you are young but levels off as you mature.

Flynn effect An increase in IQ scores over historical time.

General intelligence (g) The part of intelligence that is common to all abilities.

Improvisational intelligence Deals with relatively unique problems that are unpredictable.

Intellectual components (Sternberg) An elementary information process that operates on internal representations of objects or symbols.

Intelligence (Binet and Simon) A fundamental faculty, the alteration or lack of which is of the utmost importance for practical life.

Knowledge acquisition components (Sternberg) Processes concerned with learning new information and storing it in memory.

Metacomponents (Sternberg) Executive processes used in planning, monitoring, and decision-making in task performance.

Mid-life crisis of musicians (Bamberger) As music students become adolescents, they may feel a conflict between a more explicit understanding of music and their earlier, spontaneous love of music.

Multiple intelligences (Gardner) The hypothesis that intelligence does not consist of one underlying ability but many different abilities.

Neural plasticity *Plasticity* is the ability of an organism to adapt to changes in the environment. *Neural* plasticity changes in neuronal circuitry as a function of experience.

Performance components (Sternberg) The processes that are used in the execution of a task.

Price's law The hypothesis that half of all contributions in a field will be produced by the square root of the total number of workers in the field.

Problem-finding (Getzels) The ability to discover new problems, their methods and solutions.

Prodigies Children who show an expert level of performance well before one would normally expect to observe it.

Raven Progressive Matrices The most widely accepted test of *g*.

Remote associations test—RAT (Mednick) A test that requires the person to come up with a single association to link three apparently unrelated words.

Stages in the creative process (Wallas) Preparation, incubation, illumination, and verification.

Symbol systems Different forms of representation, such as drawing, music, and mathematics, which are the expressions of different forms of intelligence.

10-year rule The hypothesis that roughly 10 years of intense practice is necessary in order to become an expert in a domain.

Triarchic theory of intelligence Sternberg's three-part theory of intelligence consisting of analytic, practical, and creative intelligence.

Ur-song The hypothesis that there is a first song that all children spontaneously sing.

U-shaped development The hypothesis that the development of many symbolic forms is initially delightfully pre-conventional, then descends to the merely conventional, but may ultimately achieve the integration of the post-conventional.

Working memory capacity The theory that working memory capacity and *g* are closely related.

■ Links to Other Chapters

Fluid and crystallized intelligence
  Chapter 5 (working memory)
Working memory capacity
  Chapter 5 (working memory)
Neural plasticity
  Chapter 4 (phantom limbs and the body schema)

Blind variation and selective retention
  Chapter 5 (evolution of memory systems)
Remote associations test
  Chapter 13 (cognition and emotion)

■ Further Reading

A website with a wealth of material associated with the study of intelligence is at: www. indiana.edu/~intell/.

There is not enough room in a cognition text to discuss the problems associated with attempting to study group differences in intelligence. If you wish to investigate this topic in the context of American culture, you could begin by reading Chapter 5 of Ciancialo, A.T., & Sternberg, R.J. (2004). *Intelligence: A brief history.* Oxford: Blackwell. A contentious approach to the topic is Herrnstein, R.J., & Murray, C. (1994). *The bell curve: Intelligence and class structure in American life.* Glencoe, Ill.: Free Press. This book touched off a fierce controversy, as you will see if you read Jacoby, R., & Glauberman, N. (1995). *The bell curve debate.* New York: Times Books. An alternative to Herrnstein and Murray's viewpoint is Gould, S.J. (1996). *The mismeasure of man* (2nd ed.). New York: Norton.

The relation between problem-finding and risk-taking has been explored in Sternberg, R.J., & Lubart, T.I. (1992). Buy low and sell high: An investment approach to creativity. *Current Directions in Psychological Science, 1,* 1–5.

You can hear Leonard Bernstein not only talking about the ur-song, but singing it, in the DVD version of his book: Bernstein, L. (2001). *The unanswered question* (DVD).Available from www. kultur.com/page/kultur/PROD/dvd_classical_music/D1570.

Both Gardner and Winner belong to Project Zero, www.pz.harvard.edu/, the mission of which 'is to understand and enhance learning, thinking, and creativity in the arts, as well as humanistic and scientific disciplines, at the individual and institutional levels.'

A useful overview of multiple intelligences theory is Shearer, B. (2004). Multiple intelligences theory after 20 years. *Teacher's College Record, 106,* 2–16.

More on the psychology of music is in Lewis, P.A. (2002). Musical minds. *Trends in Cognitive Sciences, 6,* 364–366; and Moore, D.G., Burland, K., & Davidson, J.W. (2003). The social context of musical success: A developmental account. *British Journal of Psychology, 94,* 529–549.

The evolution of intelligence is further explored by Roth, G., & Dicke, U. (2005). Evolution of the brain and intelligence. *Trends in Cognitive Sciences, 9,* 250–257.

■ Answers to Problems in Chapter 12

Raven Progressive Matrices problems. Problem a: The number of black squares in the top of each row increases by one from the first to the second and the second to the third column. The number of black squares along the left stays the same within a row but changes between rows from 3 to 2 to 1. Answer: 3. Problem b: The figures in the first two columns (or rows) combine to form the figure third column (or row). Answer: 8. Problem c: In each row, look for three elements—for example, horizontal line, vertical line, and V, each of which occurs only twice in a row. Answer: 5.

Answers to the remote association items: *apple, blow, air, blue, body, cabin, candy, race, zone, year, witch, hat, mail, paper, pen.*

Chapter 13

Personal
Cognition

In this chapter we will deal in more detail with the more personal forms of cognition that we have only touched on in previous chapters. In particular, we will focus on studies of personal cognition that relate to aspects of cognitive processes that we have already reviewed. Such topics as memory, implicit learning, and concepts all are relevant to understanding personal aspects of cognition. Three areas of personal cognition that have been extensively explored are the relation between emotion and cognition, autobiographical memory, and the nature of the self.

As William James (1890/1983, pp. 220–221) observed, 'every thought is part of a personal consciousness . . . . My thought belongs with my other thoughts, and your thoughts with your other thoughts.' What makes our thoughts personal is that they are accompanied by feelings of 'warmth and intimacy and immediacy' (p. 232). Our feelings and our thoughts are intimately bound up with one another as complementary aspects of our selves. Thus, it makes sense to begin a discussion of personal cognition with the relation between cognition and emotion.

■ Cognition and Emotion

Cognitive psychologists have long understood that emotion influences our cognitive processes in important ways. 'Emotional experience is an essential aspect of the process of cognition and must be considered in any adequate description of it' (Blumenthal, 1977, p. 101). We will not deal with general theories of emotion, but only with those approaches that focus on the process of emotion as it relates to cognition. In what follows we consider some of the ways that cognition and emotion interact. We begin by examining studies that demonstrate a connection between emotion and the kind of creative behaviour we reviewed in the previous chapter.

Positive Affect and Cognition

Isen, Daubman, and Nowicki (1987) presented evidence that people's performance on a test of creative thinking is influenced by how they feel when they take the test. In one study, the experimenters gave one group of participants a bag of candy before the participants took a version of the Remote Associations Test (RAT), which is one of the creativity tests we examined in the last chapter. These participants performed better on the RAT than did participants who were not given anything before they took the test. In another experiment, participants who saw an amusing film performed better on a version of the RAT than did participants who did not see a funny film, or who exercised prior to taking the test. Other experiments conducted by Isen and her co-workers indicated that inducing negative feelings (e.g., by watching a sad movie) did not heighten creative responding in a problem-solving situation, but that inducing positive feelings did improve creative problem-solving. Overall, there is impressive evidence that feeling good is good for creative responding. Isen (1984) argued that cognitive processes generally vary with affect (i.e., moods and feelings). Mildly positive affect appears to enable people to think more flexibly.

Ashby, Isen, and Turken (1999; Ashby & Casale, 2003) have hypothesized that positive affect influences cognition through the action of the neurotransmitter **dopamine**. Neurotransmitters are chemicals that modify communication between neurons (LeDoux, 2003, pp. 45–49). The process whereby affect results in greater cognitive flexibility has three parts. First, positive affect is associated with heightened dopamine levels. Second, heightened dopamine levels influence the anterior cingulate cortex, which we discussed in Chapter 3. The anterior cingulate cortex is involved in switching from one set to another, and heightened dopamine levels facilitate this process. 'It is possible that much of the improvement in' a variety of cognitive tasks 'that is observed under conditions of positive affect . . . is due to . . . increased dopamine release into the anterior cingulate, which increases the flexibility of the executive-attention system' (Ashby et al., 1999, p. 540).

As evidence for their hypothesis, Ashby et al. observed that patients with Parkinson's disease not only suffer from reduced dopamine levels, but also show impaired performance on tasks requiring a change in set. Nevertheless, it should be emphasized that the effects of dopamine are complex and not fully understood (LeDoux, 2003, p. 246). Dreisbach and Goschke (2004) agree with Ashby et al. that positive affect acts through dopamine to heighten flexibility in cognitive tasks. However, they also present evidence that positive affect also makes people more easily distracted by irrelevant information. That is, positive affect tips the balance between stability and flexibility in favour of the latter. 'Adaptive action requires a dynamic, context dependent balance between maintenance and switching of goals, cognitive sets and behavioral dispositions' (Dreisbach & Goschke, 2004, p. 352). The presence of positive affect may be a signal that all is well, and that the person can afford to let attention wander while considering novel ideas.

Uncertainty and Cognition

Berlyne (1965, Chap. 9; 1971, pp. 68ff.) believed that there is one kind of stimulus variable that is particularly important as a determinant of cognitive activity. He called this kind of stimulus variable *collative properties of stimuli*. Collative means comparative.

Collative stimulus variables include properties of stimuli that arise through comparison with other stimuli. For example, determining how novel or how surprising a stimulus is requires comparison between that stimulus and other stimuli. Novelty and complexity are examples of collative stimulus properties. One of Berlyne's most important contributions was to begin investigating this kind of stimulus (Cupchik, 1988; Loewenstein, 1994, p. 85).

Collative stimulus variables can be related to uncertainty. For example, the more novel a stimulus is, the more uncertain the person will be about how to respond to it. The same can be said for surprising or complex stimuli. When confronting novel, complex, or surprising situations, the person experiences what Berlyne (1965, p. 256) called **conceptual conflict** due to incompatible thoughts. By contrast, being in a highly familiar, very simple, or totally expected situation means that the person will not experience conflict about what to do in that situation.

When people experience conceptual conflict, they engage in what Berlyne called **specific exploration** that is designed to reduce uncertainty. Thus, having a problem of some kind usually means that you are uncertain about what to do in a particular situation. Problem-solving is the kind of cognitive activity that involves exploring the situation to find an alternative to solve the problem (i.e., eliminate conflict). Whereas specific exploration reduces conflict, **diversive exploration** is undertaken in order to increase it. Highly predictable situations may be experienced as boring, for example. Diversive exploration involves increasing the uncertainty the person experiences. Daydreaming and various forms of entertainment are examples of diversive exploration.

In order to represent the relationship between conflict and pleasantness, Berlyne (1971) revived an idea originally proposed by Wundt in the nineteenth century. This idea is best described in terms of the graph in Figure 13.1. The curve in that figure is called the **Wundt curve**.

This curve can be used to summarize the relationships between uncertainty and how positively or negatively a person feels. On the vertical axis is plotted the degree to which a person feels positively or negatively in a particular situation, or the *hedonic value* of the situation. How positively or negatively you feel is a function that rises and

Figure 13.1 The Wundt-Berlyne Curve.

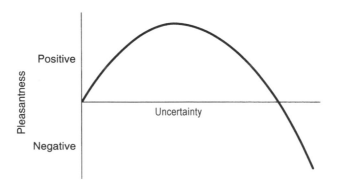

then falls as conflict increases (i.e., as an inverted U). Thus, for example, highly familiar events are not conflicting, and give rise to a neutral emotional state (i.e., neither positive nor negative). At the other end of the continuum, totally unfamiliar events are highly conflicting, and may even be experienced negatively. Moderately conflicting events yield the greatest pleasure. One implication of the theory is that up to a certain point familiarity breeds liking, but after that it begins to breed boredom, if not contempt.

The Wundt curve implies that we will get the most pleasure from situations eliciting a moderate degree of conceptual conflict. Does this mean that once we have understood something, we will no longer be interested in it? The point has often been made (e.g., Kreitler & Kreitler, 1972) that what makes something enduringly interesting is that it has multiple levels that always encourage further exploration. Something deeply interesting is, in a sense, inexhaustible: there are always new levels of meaning to explore. For truly interesting things, as you become more familiar with them, new ways of thinking about them open up. Complex works of art, such as Shakespeare's plays, may, for certain people, tend to remain at the midpoint of the Wundt curve, no matter how familiar they become. Repeated exposure does not diminish the gratification that can be obtained from them. The more complex something is, the more possibilities it affords and the greater the potential it has to engage your attention and give you pleasure for a long time.

Even though something complex may have the potential to give you pleasure, there may need to be an initial period during which you must become somewhat familiar with it, and that period may be fairly unpleasant. The period of initially becoming familiar with something is described by the far-right portion of the Wundt curve, which dips down below the horizontal axis into the region of unpleasant feelings. Any number of examples could be given to illustrate this state. The initial stages of acquiring a complex skill or subject matter (such as playing the piano or learning mathematics) may be full of false starts, which may be experienced so negatively that the person never keeps working at them long enough to begin to experience the pleasure that comes from moving to the left on the Wundt curve.

Wickelgren (1979) speculated about the relation between the complexity of a stimulus and our willingness to learn about it. Wickelgren noted that stimuli, such as music, are the most pleasing when they are of moderate complexity. Wickelgren (1979) suggested that this aesthetic pleasure is a guide to learning:

> We dislike subjects that are too elementary for us (and so boringly familiar) and subjects that are too far over our heads. . . . Human beings choose what they will learn on the basis of this aesthetic pleasure principle to an enormous extent. . . . It is highly speculative but rather fun to imagine that the primary purpose of our aesthetic sense is to guide learning in fruitful directions. (pp. 119–120)

Another application of the Wundt curve is to try to understand some of the ways in which styles wax and wane in a culture like ours (Bianchi, 2002; Sluckin, Colman, & Hargreaves, 1980). Although the rate at which styles come in and go out of favour differs for different types of stimulus pattern—for example, slowly in the case of classical music, quickly in the case of popular music—one might still be able to detect a cycle that can be described by the Wundt curve. An initially novel way of doing things at first attracts no favour, and may even be experienced as noxious, then gradually becomes accepted as a legitimate form of expression, and finally is increasingly ignored as old-fashioned or irrelevant. After a suitable interval, a style that was previously thought to be outdated may reappear as something refreshingly novel. As a boring style falls out of fashion, it moves to the right on the curve in Figure 13.1 and consequently is able to elicit greater pleasure.

Although Berlyne cited several experimental studies that supported the inverted-U-shaped theory of the relation between complexity and pleasantness, there are other studies that contradict it. One such is by Heinrichs (1984), who had participants rate 36 human figure paintings on a series of scales, including collative stimulus properties (e.g., simple vs complex; familiar vs unfamiliar), and hedonic value (e.g., pleasing vs displeasing). There was no evidence of an inverted-U relationship between collative stimulus properties and pleasantness. Rather, it appeared that simple, familiar paintings were rated as more pleasant than complex, unfamiliar ones. Thus, it is unlikely that the Wundt curve accurately describes the relation between familiarity and liking (Konečni, 1996; Martindale, Moore, & Borkum, 1988). Nevertheless, collative stimulus properties continue to be the focus of research interest (Silvia, 2005, p. 99). We now turn to another approach that presents a very different view of the relationship between familiarity and pleasantness.

Mere Exposure and Cognition

In the section on negativity bias in the chapter on judgement, we referred to work by Zajonc (1968) suggesting that positive adjectives are used more frequently than negative ones because positive adjectives are applied to events that are common, or normal, whereas negative adjectives are applied to events that are uncommon, or deviant. Zajonc has presented much evidence that the more often people are exposed to an event, the more they like it. The slogan 'familiarity breeds liking' is a good summary of this finding, which is also called the **mere exposure effect**.

A very influential series of experiments dealing with the effects of mere exposure was conducted by Moreland and Zajonc (1977, 1979). In one of their experiments, they showed 25 pairs of American participants a series of slides made up of 10 Japanese characters (ideographs) on slides. Presumably, these ideographs were unfamiliar to these participants. Some of the ideographs were repeated more than once, up to 27 times for the most frequently presented ideograph. At the end of the series of slides, one member of each pair of participants rated the ideographs for recognizability (new vs old), whereas the other participant rated the ideographs for likability (like vs dislike). This is called a *yoked participants design*: two participants at a time receive the identical series of stimuli, but respond to them on different scales.

The recognizability scale gives a measure of subjective familiarity, the extent to which the participant felt that the stimulus was one that had been seen before. The results showed that ideographs rated as more familiar were also rated as more likable. However, it was also the case that ideographs presented more often were rated as more likable. It is possible that repeated exposure increases subjective familiarity, which in turn heightens liking. However, repeated exposure and subjective familiarity were not perfectly correlated. Some frequently exposed slides were not rated as highly recognizable. Moreland and Zajonc's analysis of their data suggested that both subjective familiarity and repeated exposure had separate effects on liking. Even for stimuli rated as unfamiliar, those exposed often were liked more than those exposed fewer times (Zajonc, 1980, p. 161). This implies that mere exposure has an effect on liking that is not due to subjective familiarity.

The importance of Moreland and Zajonc's analysis, and others like it (e.g., Tuohy, 1987), concerns the model of the relation between affect and cognition that it implies. Liking is a measure of the affective reaction to a stimulus. Familiarity is a measure of the cognitive response to a stimulus because it depends on being able to recognize the stimulus as one that has been seen before. The Moreland and Zajonc results seem to be consistent with a model such as that shown in Figure 13.2, which is based on the model presented by Zajonc (1980).

In this model emotion and cognition are separate systems. The arrow between cognition and emotion is meant to indicate that these two systems interact. However, stimuli can have a direct effect on the emotional system without first going through the cognitive system (Zajonc, 1984, p. 117). Feelings can be influenced by events in ways that are independent of people's cognition of them. Zajonc (1980, p. 172) observed that this view of the cognition–emotion relationship implies emotional processes can take place unconsciously, without being regulated by cognition.

Many psychologists took issue with Zajonc's theory of the emotion–cognition relationship (e.g., J.O. Brooks & Watkins, 1989). Some, such as Birnbaum and Mellers (1979), argued that a simpler model of the affect–cognition interface is consistent with the data. Such a model holds that stimulus exposure has a cognitive effect before it has an emotional one. This would mean, for example, that some form of cognitive appraisal of a situation occurs before it has an emotional impact (Lazarus, 1984). From this latter viewpoint, what a situation *means* to a person determines how he or she will feel about it. However, in a review of 208 experiments bearing on this issue, Bornstein (1989) found generally strong support for the mere

Figure 13.2 The Relation of Stimulus Exposure, Emotion, and Cognition.

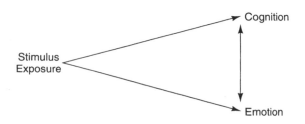

exposure effect. In this connection, an interesting result was obtained by Bornstein and D'Agostino (1992), who varied the exposure duration of stimuli between 5 milliseconds and 500 milliseconds. Repetition of the briefly exposed stimuli caused a greater increase in liking ratings than did repetition of stimuli exposed for a longer duration. Since it is likely that participants were not aware of the briefly exposed stimuli, this finding is consistent with the view that 'subliminal stimuli produce significantly larger mere exposure effects than stimuli that are clearly recognized' (p. 549).The vast majority of studies have tended to confirm Zajonc's (2001, p. 224) position that 'no cognitive mediation, rational or otherwise' is necessary in order for mere exposure to produce liking.

What adaptive advantage does the mere exposure effect confer? Zajonc (2001, p. 227) argued that it provides 'a flexible means of forming selective attachments'. Events that occur frequently in one's immediate environment are likely to be ones that will do no harm. Becoming attached to frequently occurring events will tend to promote 'social organization and cohesion—the basic sources of psychological and social stability' (pp. 227–228).

The Warm Glow Heuristic

Not only does familiarity breed liking, but liking breeds a sense of familiarity (Monin, 2003). These are not two sides of the same coin. The mere exposure effect occurs when people are repetitively exposed to a stimulus. However, it also turns out that if a stimulus elicits a feeling of liking, then you will tend to conclude that you have seen it before, whether you have or not. Monin (2003, p. 1037) calls this the **warm glow heuristic**, and defines it as the tendency for liking to be 'taken as an indicator of mere exposure'. The warm glow heuristic may lead you to falsely conclude that you have seen someone or something before. 'Haven't I seen you somewhere before?' may be the expression of a genuine, if mistaken, sense of familiarity towards others.

Monin demonstrated the existence of the warm glow heuristic in a series of experiments in which people judged the attractiveness and familiarity of faces. The stimuli were 80 pictures of men's and women's faces that had previously been ranked for attractiveness. Participants were initially shown 40 of the pictures, which sampled the entire range of attractiveness. The participants' task was to indicate the gender of each face. The 40 pictures were then mixed in with 40 new pictures, and participants were unexpectedly asked to judge which of the pictures they had seen before. There was a tendency for attractive faces to be judged as having been seen before, and this tendency was present for both old and new pictures. The recognition threshold for attractive faces appeared to be lower than that for unattractive faces.

The function of the warm glow heuristic may be to simplify the task of recognizing people. We meet a great many people in the course of daily life and often are called on to recognize them after meeting them only once or twice. We may not be sure if we have met someone before, and it may be socially awkward to ask 'Have we met before?' People may instead rely on the warm glow heuristic to make a quick judgement. Monin compares the warm glow heuristic to the availability heuristic we considered in Chapter 11 on judgement and choice. The only information available in some situations may be a warm glow, and people may use that information as a substitute for actual recognition. The warm glow heuristic would be an example of System 1 reasoning, in terms of the theory we considered in Chapter 10 on reasoning. As such, it would be a fast, automatic way of making decisions that may work in some situations but would be prone to error in others.

Mere Exposure and Implicit Learning

Gordon and Holyoak (1983) have related the mere exposure effect to implicit learning. We considered research on implicit learning in Chapter 7 on concepts. You may wish to go back and review Reber's work suggesting that simply showing participants strings of letters was sufficient to enable them to learn the grammar underlying the strings. Moreover, Reber argued that learning the grammar did not require that the participant be aware that learning had taken place. Thus, implicit learning may take place unintentionally, as a consequence of mere exposure only.

Gordon and Holyoak repeated Reber's implicit learning procedure. After exposing participants to a series of strings of letters, participants were shown a new set of letter strings, some of which followed the grammar underlying the first set and some of which did not. Participants rated these new strings for grammatical correctness and for liking. Participants gave higher ratings to grammatically correct strings, indicating that they had learned something about grammar in the first phase of the experiment. Participants also *liked* grammatical strings more than ungrammatical ones. Mere exposure to a set of grammatical strings in the first part of the experiment had led to a liking for novel strings that exemplified correct grammar. The experiment demonstrated both cognitive and affective consequences of mere exposure. Gordon and Holyoak interpreted this result to mean that 'affective consequences of mere exposure were dependent on the cognitive process of implicit learning' (Gordon & Holyoak, 1983, p. 498).

Zizak and Reber (2004) not only replicated Gordon and Holyoak's findings but also extended them in important ways. In one experiment they used strings of unfamiliar Japanese Kana characters. Participants learned the underlying grammar, but did not increase their liking for grammatical strings. However, when familiar letters were used to make up the strings, then a mere exposure effect was found for grammatical strings. Zizak and Reber call this a **structural mere exposure effect**. Learning to like an underlying structure can occur through mere exposure, but it depends on the elements of the structure themselves being familiar. This process may explain the way in which new styles in art and literature can become appreciated. In avant-garde work, familiar objects may be represented in novel relations to one another. Only repeated exposure will make people begin to like such structures. Moreover, the mere exposure effect will work especially well to the extent that people are unaware of its occurrence.

■ Emotion and Memory

Mood and Memory

The study of the relation between emotion and memory has extensively employed network models of memory (Blaney, 1986, p. 229; Levine & Pizarro, 2004, p. 537). Network models of memory include those by such theorists as Anderson, Collins and Quillian, and Collins and Loftus, which we examined in the chapter on memory systems. Figure 5.1 gives a typical network model of memory.

According to Bower's (1981; Gilligan & Bower, 1984) theory, emotions are units, or nodes, in a network. Although emotion units are largely innate, over time they become connected to other units in the network, which represent non-emotional events. An emotion node, when activated, is capable of activating other units in the network to a greater extent than are non-emotional units. When an emotion occurs, it can colour subsequent thoughts (Gilligan & Bower, 1984, p. 572). Emotional activation can spread throughout a network and be a part of what the person retains from an experience.

Such a view of emotion predicts a phenomenon called **mood-dependent recall**. Mood-dependent recall is best understood in relation to a related phenomenon called *context-dependent recall* (Baddeley, 1987b). Many studies have shown that memory is better when the context within which recall takes place is more similar to the context within which learning took place. A classic study in this vein is one by Godden and Baddeley (1975). They had divers learn a list of words either above or below the water. The divers then recalled the words in the same context in which they learned them or in the other context. When there was a match between the learning and recall contexts (i.e., learn and recall above water or learn and recall below water), more words were remembered than when the two contexts were incongruent (i.e., learn above water, recall below water or learn below water and recall above water).

Mood can be seen as an aspect of the context in which something is learned. For example, if a person is in a sad mood and learns a list of words, will memory for the words be better if the person is sad at the time of recall? If mood is a part of the network within which the list is stored, then mood congruence between learning and recall session should facilitate recall. This would be because of a greater similarity between the recall context and the way the information is encoded in memory. Although there are several studies suggesting that recall is best when undertaken in the same mood in which learning took place, the effect is not always found (Blaney, 1986; Eich & Forgas, 2003, pp. 70–72).

Another phenomenon that has been extensively studied is **mood congruence**, which refers to the possibility that 'mood might cause selective learning of affective material' (Gilligan & Bower, 1984, p. 557). For example, if a participant is in a sad mood and listens to a story containing both happy and sad episodes, will that participant later remember more sad episodes than a participant who was happy when listening to the story? Gilligan and Bower reported that, in fact, mood does appear to affect the kind of material that is learned. Blaney (1986, p. 236) summarized the results of 29 studies that generally support the reality of mood congruence.

Mood Dependence for Internally Generated Events

Eich and Metcalfe (1989) examined mood-dependent memory as a function of internal versus external events. This distinction was made initially by Johnson (e.g., Johnson, 1985, 1988; Johnson & Raye, 1981), and we considered some of its implications in Chapter 4, on memory traces and memory schemas. External events are ones we actually perceive, whereas internal events are ones we generate ourselves. For example, the word *north* as it is written on this page is an external event that you perceive. Imagining a word beginning with *n*, having five letters, and meaning a direction on the compass is an internal event because you generate the word *north* yourself rather than perceive it. One of the criteria of emotion words is that they refer to internal conditions. It seems intuitively plausible that emotions would be more easily associated with internal than with external events. The hypothesis that Eich and Metcalfe investigated was that memory for internal events would be more dependent on mood than would memory for external events.

In order to investigate memory for internal versus external events, Eich and Metcalfe made use of a procedure invented by Slamecka and Graf (1978). This procedure allows the comparison of memory for items that are presented to participants (external items) with memory for the same items when they are generated by participants (internal items). For example, the word *gold* is an external item when it is presented in the following context: *precious metals: silver, gold*. In one of Eich and Metcalfe's experiments, participants were presented with 32 items, half of which were external and half internal. They were subsequently given a test of free recall for those items. The ability to remember the external items can be compared with the ability to remember items when participants must first generate them, as in the following example: *precious metals: silver, g——*. It is very unlikely that the participant will generate anything other than the desired item, *gold*.

Participants received the set of 32 items under different mood conditions. Mood was manipulated by having participants listen either to music that sounded happy or to music that sounded sad. For the test of memory, which took place two days after the first session, half the participants who had been induced to have a happy mood in the acquisition session were now induced to have a sad mood, whereas the other half were again induced to have a happy mood. Similarly, half the participants who had previously been induced to have a sad mood were now induced to have a happy mood, with the remainder again being induced to have a sad mood. At each stage of the experiment, participants were asked to rate their moods along the happy versus sad dimension.

The memory test had several parts to it, but the most interesting measure was a free recall test. Participants were asked to recall the 32 items that they had either received or generated. One of the results was that, across all conditions, internal items were recalled with greater success than external items. It was also true that recall for both types of items was better when the recall mood matched the acquisition mood (i.e., happy/happy or sad/sad) than when it did not (i.e., happy/sad or sad/happy). However, internal items benefited more from being recalled under matching mood conditions than did external items. This implies that memory for **internal events** is more mood dependent than is memory for external events.

In an overview of research on mood dependent memory, Eich (1995) provided further evidence that substantiated the conclusions reached by Eich and Metcalfe (1989). Eich (1995) reinforced the hypothesis that internally generated events are susceptible to the mood dependent memory effect. In one study, by Eich, Macaulay, and Ryan (1994), participants were asked to generate eight positive and eight negative autobiographical events in the first experimental session. In a second experimental session that took place two or three days later, participants were asked to recall the events that they had generated in the first session. The participants' mood was manipulated in both sessions, using the music technique described above. Participants who experienced the same mood in both sessions were able to recall more of the autobiographical experiences they had generated in the first session than were participants whose moods were mismatched across the two sessions. This result is consistent with the conclusion that 'the prospects of finding evidence of mood dependent memory are enhanced by having people generate the target events through internal mental processes, such as reasoning, imagination, and thought' (Eich, 1995, p. 70). The effect of mood dependent memory is particularly evident when the internally generated events are autobiographical experiences (Eich & Forgas, 2003, p. 720). It is also obviously important that the moods experienced by the participants be genuinely felt, authentic moods (Eich & Macaulay, 2000).

Depression and Memory

The study of how mood affects memory is important because of the relevance of such research to an understanding of phenomena such as depression (Ellis, 1990). A series of experiments by Hertel and Hardin (1990) investigated the relation between depressed mood and memory using an experimental procedure similar to those we discussed in Chapter 5 on memory systems. Briefly, it involves presenting participants with homophones. A homophone is a word that sounds like another word with a different meaning (e.g., *pear* and *pair*). In the Hertel and Hardin studies, participants heard homophones embedded in questions (e.g., *What colour is a pear?*). The context in which the homophone was presented always favoured the least common spelling of the homophone (e.g., *pear* instead of *pair*). Then participants were asked to spell a series of words, which included some of the homophones they had heard in the previous phase of the experiment, as well as some homophones they had not heard before and some non-homophones. Finally, they were given a recognition test, in which they were read all the homophones used in the questions, mixed with other words, including some that were in the spelling test but had not been in the original set used in the questions. Participants were asked to indicate for each word whether or not it had been heard in the questions asked in the first phase of the experiment.

In all their experiments, Hertel and Hardin used a mood-induction procedure. A depressed mood was induced by having participants read a set of depressive statements (e.g., *I am feeling sad today*). Other participants read a set of neutral statements (e.g., *There are 26 breeds of cats*). Hertel and Hardin found an effect of the initial exposure to homophones in questions on subsequent spelling. Such exposure caused participants to adopt the least frequently used spelling on the spelling test, regardless of mood. This means that the questions did lead all participants to learn something about the homophones used in the questions. There was also an effect of the mood-induction procedure on the number of words recognized. Participants in a depressive mood recognized fewer words than participants in a neutral mood.

The deficit shown by participants in a depressive mood could be eliminated by giving participants explicit strategies for recognizing the homophones. For example, telling participants to try to remember if the word was on the spelling test can provide participants with another source of information about whether or not a word was in a question in the first phase of the experiment. Hertel and Hardin suggested that nondepressed participants spontaneously use a strategy for remembering that depressed participants must explicitly be given. This implies that the memory deficits associated with depression may be due to a lack of **initiative**. Depression may result in people failing to use strategies that they are in principle fully capable of employing.

Hertel and Hardin (1990) suggested that depressives be given well-organized tasks that require little initiative to complete successfully. Successful completion of tasks may act to reduce depression and aid in the recovery of normal levels of initiative. In one study, Hertel and Rude (1991) showed both depressed and non-depressed participants a word (e.g., *artist*) followed by a sentence frame (e.g., *The young man's portrait was painted by the* ———). Participants had to decide whether or not the word fit into the sentence frame. Sometimes the participants had to pay close attention to the word because it disappeared from the computer screen before the sentence frame appeared. Other times the word and the frame were present together, so that participants did not have to focus as much on the word. Then participants were given an unexpected test of memory for the words. The depressed participants recalled words better if they had been forced to pay attention to them, an effect that was not as pronounced for nondepressed participants. This shows that unless depressed people are required to focus on a task, their attention may wander and their learning may suffer. Depressed people may be *competent* to learn and remember new material, but fail to *perform* at a level consistent with this competence unless their attention is properly focused.

Depression and Forgetting

Hertel and Gerstle (2003, p. 573) observe that 'anyone who has experienced heartbreak, remorse, or failure can imagine the benefits of forgetting.' However, depressed people seem to ruminate about their troubles, which only serves to keep the depression going. Depressed people may not only learn new material less well than non-depressed people, but they may also be less able to forget material they have already learned.

To investigate the relation between depression and forgetting, Hertel and Gerstle had participants fill out scales that measure depression and the tendency to ruminate about sad events. People who score high on both these measures are said to be *dysphoric*, meaning ill at ease. Participants then learned a set of 40 adjective-noun pairs. Some pairs were relatively positive, such as *wedding dress* or *cozy chair*, compared to others that were relatively negative, such *funeral dress* or *electric chair.* After learning the adjective-noun pairs, participants were then shown 15 of the adjectives and asked to try to 'avoid saying or thinking anything' about the noun that had been paired with it. That is, participants were to suppress the response for these items. Participants were then given a final memory test in which they were given all 40 adjectives and asked to recall the corresponding nouns.

The interesting result was that the more dysphoric participants recalled more items for the set they been told to suppress than did the other participants. This result could also be explained as due to faulty attentional control. Whether it be learning or forgetting, depression appears to lead to an inability to focus on the task at hand.

■ Cognition and the Self

Neisser (1988, 1993) suggested that it is wrong to think of cognition as a process that is solely a function of events in the nervous system. Rather, cognitive processes are a function of 'the whole person who perceives, acts, and is responsible' (p. 3). Thus, 'a self is not a special part of a person (or of a brain); it is a whole person considered from a particular point of view' (p. 4). Depending on the point of view, different selves, or aspects of the person, become important. (This holistic view of the self does not appeal to everyone. For a more hard-nosed approach to the self, see Box 13.1.)

Neisser (1993) drew attention to two fundamental selves: the **ecological self** and the **interpersonal self**. The ecological self, as Gibson (1979) and Neisser (1976, p. 115) observed, is the self that one perceives as a result of moving around in the environment. As a result of the person's movement, what is experienced in the environment changes. Walking down a corridor, for example, provides a continually changing pattern of stimulation. This continually changing pattern not only provides information

---

Box 13.1   Are We Losing Our Selves?

People have routinely believed themselves capable of regulating their own behaviour. Willpower and self-control have been seen as ways of helping oneself lead a better life. But can we actually choose to eat and drink less, for example, or is our conscious will an illusion (e.g., Wegner, 2003)? Farah (2005a, 2005b; Gillihan & Farah, 2005) suggested that people increasingly believe that our behaviour is determined by the brain, rather than by a conscious self. She argued that neuroscience is rapidly replacing traditional methods for controlling and changing behaviour. People are increasingly using substances and techniques that modify brain processes in order to modify their behaviour.

A striking example of Farah's point is the use of Ritalin and Adderall as treatments for people diagnosed with attention deficit hyperactivity disorder (ADHD). This diagnosis may be applied to children who are extremely inattentive, hyperactive, and impulsive. Between 1987 and 1997 the number of doses of Ritalin administered per day in the United States went from a little over 50 million to over 350 million. Farah also observed that drugs such as Ritalin are being consumed by people who have not been diagnosed with any disorder as a way of boosting their memory and executive function performance. There are two ethical questions raised by examples such as this. One is whether or not children's parents should be coerced by authorities in the schools and other institutions to give medication to their children diagnosed with ADHD. Second, is it fair for some people to boost their performance in competitive situations to the detriment of those who do not take a drug? What do you think?

Whatever the outcome of the ethical debate, Farah observed that the advances in neuroscience and related fields may undermine a belief in the distinction between things and persons. 'With brain images adorning our websites and magazine articles on everything from children's learning to compulsive gambling, neuroscience is gradually being incorporated into people's understanding of human behavior' (Farah, 2005a, p. 39). If purely neuroscientific explanations of behaviour become universally accepted, as Farah argued that they inevitably will, then the concept of a person who is morally responsible for his or her behaviour may disappear.

In a comment on Farah (2005a), Jedliça (2005) argued that the belief that 'we are *nothing else but* a pack of neurons' leaves out the reality of conscious experience. This is a point that Farah (2005b, p. 173) acknowledged by saying that 'no matter how good neurioscience gets at reducing functional psychological mechanisms to neural mechanisms . . . it will not necessarily ever explain or dispense with' consciousness.

The problem that consciousness poses for a purely materialistic view of mind has been brilliantly discussed by Montero (1999). The issue may be framed as follows. 'Are mental properties, such as the property of *being in pain* or *thinking about the higher orders of infinity* actually physical properties' (p. 183)? More generally, what does it mean when we say that something is physical? For example, we think of the body as physical. What kind of physical entity would the body need to be in order to have conscious experiences? Montero calls this question the **body problem**. As Farah conceded, our current understanding of what the body is like has no place for conscious experience. Therefore, one might conclude, our current conception of what it means for something to be a physical entity is incomplete. Science may be able to develop a more inclusive conception of the physical in which 'concepts such as consciousness and free will could end up being part of physics proper' (Farah, 2005b, p. 173).

It is far too early to conclude that we are witnessing the demise of the self. Unforeseen developments in science may lead to the eventual unification of what may now seem to be irreconcilable phenomena (Jedliça, 2005, p. 172).

about the environment, but also information about oneself in relation to that environment. Moving towards something, such as a car, makes that object an increasingly large part of what you perceive. This not only gives you information about the car, but also about your location relative to it. You do not need to make inferences about where your ecological self is located, because the ecological self is perceived directly. The ecological self 'includes an awareness of where we are, what we are doing, and what we have done' (Neisser, 1993, p. 9).

The interpersonal self arises whenever one is active as a member of a social interaction. Human beings are intrinsically social, and the perception of other people is as fundamental as the perception of physical events. 'Without the special contribution of interpersonal experience, normal human forms of knowing could not exist' (Neisser, 1993, p. 12). Neisser (1993, p. 10) realized that what he means by the interpersonal self is similar to what William James (1890) meant by the *social self*. 'No more fiendish punishment could be devised, were such a thing physically possible, than that one should be turned loose in society and remain absolutely unnoticed by all the members thereof' (James, 1890, p. 293). James made a shrewd observation when he noted that 'we have as many social selves as there are people who know us' (p. 294), implying that each of us shows different sides of ourselves depending on the company we keep. That is, one facet of the social self is to be concerned with presenting ourselves in as good a light as possible to those whose opinions we value. The process of self-presentation has been extensively researched, and we will now examine one aspect of it.

The Presentation of Self

The way in which a person wants to be represented may be shown when the person poses for a portrait. Humphrey and McManus (1973) discovered that Rembrandt showed the left side of the sitter's face more frequently if it was that of a female and/or non-kin, while the right side of the face was shown more frequently if it was Rembrandt himself, or male and/or kin. They argued that the side of the face shown by Rembrandt in a portrait was determined by how socially similar the sitter was to him (www.rijksmuseum.nl/aria/aria_artists/00016943?lang=en). The more similar the sitter was to Rembrandt the more likely the right side of the sitter's face was shown. Gordon (1974) examined portraits by Goya (en.wikipedia.org/wiki/Francisco_Goya). He found that the left side of the sitter's face was shown more often if it was female, with the opposite being true for male sitters. However, there was no effect of the kin/non-kin distinction. Benjafield and Segalowitz (1993) asked participants to rate a sample of Leonardo da Vinci's drawings of faces (en.wikipedia.org/wiki/Leonardo_da_Vinci). Drawings portraying the right side of the face were rated as stronger and as more active than were drawings of the left side of the face. All this evidence suggests that there are at least two **sides of the self**, one presented by the left side of the face and one presented by the right side of the face.

Nicholls, Clode, Wood, and Wood (1999) hypothesized that people show the left side of the face when expressing emotion, but the right side of the face when expressing the ability to control emotion. They tested this hypothesis by asking participants to pose under two conditions. In the first condition, each participant was asked to imagine that 'you are a warm-hearted and affectionate person' who is having their portrait done as a gift to a loving family. In the second condition, each participant was asked to imagine that 'you are a cool-headed, calm and reasonable' person who wants to give an impression of being intelligent as you pose for a portrait for the Royal Society, a prestigious group of scientists. All participants were seated in front of a video camera and were asked not to look directly into it. The experimenter, who was unaware into which condition the participant fell, recorded which side of the face was turned towards the camera.

The results are shown in Figure 13.3. The 'emotional' instructions elicited a bias for the left cheek, while the 'impassive' instructions elicited a bias for the right cheek. This was true for both men and women. Nicholls et al. concluded that people show the left side of their face when they want to *display* emotion and show the right side in order to *conceal* emotion. This interpretation was reinforced in another study by Nicholls, Wolfgang, Clode, and Lindell (2002). They had participants rate pictures of faces that featured the right cheek, left cheek, or looked directly into the camera (thus showing both cheeks). Participants rated the faces on scales such as 'displays their emotions to other people'. Faces displaying the left cheek and both cheeks were rated as more emotionally expressive than faces displaying the right cheek. Thus, only when the left cheek is concealed are faces perceived as lacking emotional expressiveness.

Nichols et al. (1999, 2002) pointed out that there is no evidence that people have learned to use the left side of the face to portray emotion. They suggest that this tendency may be a universal form of facial expression (cf. Ekman, 1999). In any case, 'if you want to make an emotional impact on the person you are talking to, try turning your left cheek towards them' (Ogilvie, 2002, p. 234).

Autobiographical Memory

Not only do we present ourselves to other people, but we also construct our own life stories for ourselves (Fivush & Hayden, 2003). The story of one's life contains memories

Figure 13.3 Tendency to Expose the Left or Right Cheek as a Function of Emotion Expressed.

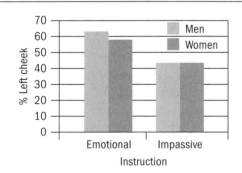

Data from Nicholls, M.E.R., Clode, D., Wood, S.J., & Wood, A.G. (1999). Laterality of expression in portraiture: Putting your best cheek forward. *Proceedings of the Royal Society of London, Series B, 266*, p. 1521.

of the events of which one has been a part. **Autobiographical memories** are episodic memories, with each event recalled in terms of the time of its occurrence in our lives. Research in autobiographical memory benefited from the technique invented by Crovitz and Schiffman (1974), which was introduced in Chapter 5. They gave participants a list of 20 words and asked them to generate a personal memory for each word. The participants then dated these memories in terms of how long ago they occurred. The words were common nouns. For example, *hall* and *oven* are words occurring frequently in English, and easily elicit a mental image in most people. The units the participants in the Crovitz and Schiffman experiment used to date their memories were the usual categories of minutes, hours, days, weeks, months, and years. This procedure is similar to one invented by Galton (1879a, 1879b), who used to attend to each object he came across during the course of a walk. He would take note of the personal memory that was cued by each object. (This is a very simple task, and I would encourage you to try it. If you make a list of these memories as you experience them on your walk, you can later date their occurrence in your own life.)

Crovitz and Schiffman found that, in general, there was a regular decline in the frequency of episodic memories as a function of how long ago the event occurred. Crovitz, Schiffman, and Apter (1991) attempted to determine the number of autobiographical memories to which people will typically have access. Their data suggests that people usually should be able to recall about 220 autobiographical episodes from the last 20 years. They called this **Galton's number**. However, Crovitz and Schiffman noted that it was difficult to generalize from their findings to all persons. As we shall see, autobiographical memory has a different form for different people.

Childhood Amnesia

One process that may have an effect on autobiographical memory is **childhood amnesia** (Freud, 1916/1977). There appear to be fewer memories from the first few years of life than would be expected if memory decayed smoothly as a function of time. Wetzler and Sweeney (1986) examined a series of studies of early memories and concluded that childhood amnesia sets in sometime before age five. Trying to be more precise than that has proven difficult. Rubin (2000) reviewed 10 studies that used four different methods to sample early childhood memories. In addition to the Crovitz and Schiffman technique, there is the *exhaustive search technique*, in which participants spend several hours trying to remember childhood memories; the *focused method*, in which people are asked to recall events from a particular period of childhood; and the *intensive personal interview method*. Combining data from all these methods, Rubin (2000) found that the first three years accounted for only 1.1 per cent of all memories during the first 10 years of life. After age three, the percentage of childhood memories in each year begins to increase rapidly. Rubin noted that these data were for Americans, and that children in other cultures may well show a different pattern (cf. Fivush & Nelson, 2004).

The fact that *some* memories occur before age three has been observed in studies by Usher and Neisser (1993) and Eacott and Crawley (1998). The accuracy of such memories (e.g., remembering being told that your mother was going to have a baby) was often confirmed by the mothers of the participants. This led Neisser (2004) to conclude that there may be no definite age before which there are no autobiographical memories.

In spite of the uncertainty surrounding childhood amnesia, it is still true that the way in which children experience and later remember events will change as they develop. As children begin to use different means for representing events in memory, they may lose contact with early memories (Schactel, 1947). Very young children experience events in a way that differs radically from how they experience events after they are able to describe them using language (Neisser, 1962; Fivush & Nelson, 2004). Neisser (1962) suggested that any discontinuity in development will tend to produce an amnesia for events prior to the change. The rapid onset of language is certainly one of the more profound discontinuities in development, and memories represented with or without language can be expected to be very different. A similar discontinuity would occur for bilinguals who learned one language as a child and then another after moving to another country. For example, Marian and Neisser (2000) investigated cases of Cornell students who had immigrated to the United States from Russia when they were 14, on average. Two sets of English cue words (e.g., *summer, neighbours*) were constructed. Half the participants were given the first list followed by a Russian translation of the second list. The other half were given a Russian translation of the second list, followed by the first list. The participants produced autobiographical memories to each cue word. Russian cue words elicited more 'Russian memories', meaning that everyone in the event recalled spoke only Russian. English cue words tended to elicit 'English memories', meaning that everyone in the event recalled spoke only English. That is, each language tends to elicit autobiographical memories originally experienced in the context of that language. As Shrauf and Rubin (2003, p. 141) put it, 'insofar as memory is language specific, it makes sense to think of the bilingual immigrant as inhabiting different worlds and having the experience of language-specific selves.'

The Bump

Rubin, Wetzler, and Nebes (1986) combined data from several studies that employed the Crovitz and Schiffman technique with a wide range of age groups. They summarized the data concerning autobiographical memory as follows. There are three processes determining whether or not an event will be remembered. One process is childhood amnesia, which acts to make very early memories relatively inaccessible. Another process is simply the tendency for memories to become increasingly unavailable as time passes, a process we discussed in Chapter 4. Thus, something that happened many years ago will in general be less recallable than something that happened just a short time ago. This general tendency for memories to decay with time is complicated by the fact that, for people over the age of about 50, there is a heightened tendency to recall events that occurred between 10 and 30 years of age (Rubin, 2000). These three processes combine to produce the curve shown in Figure 13.4. **The bump** shows up as an increase in the number of memories between 10 and 30 years of age over and above what would be expected if memories decayed smoothly over time.

Figure 13.4 Percentage of Autobiographical Memories in Different Decades.

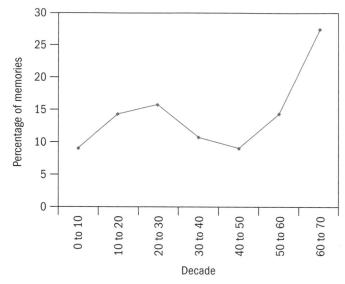

Data from Chu, S., & Downs, J.J. (2000). Long live Proust: The odour-cued autobiographical memory bump. *Cognition, 75*, p. B43.

Although the bump is a reliable phenomenon, it depends to a certain extent on the way in which autobiographical memories are elicited. Usually such cues are verbal. However, Chu and Downs (2000) showed that using odours as cues produces a different pattern of recall. The novelist Marcel Proust (en.wikipedia.org/wiki/Marcel_Proust) is famous for describing the power of odours as autobiographical memory cues, so this could be called a **Proust effect**. Chu and Downs demonstrated it by using as cues a variety of spices (e.g., cloves, mint), beverages (e.g., coffee, whisky), and assorted other common materials (e.g., paint, baby powder). Participants ranged from 65 to 83 years of age. Some participants were given each substance in a bottle and asked to sniff it, and report any autobiographical events that occurred to them. These participants had their eyes closed and were not told the name of the substance. Other participants were given the verbal label of the odour as a cue and did not sniff the substance. The verbal cue condition produced the bump in autobiographical memories. However, the odour cue produced more memories between ages 6 and 10 than did the verbal cue. Thus, odours may bypass verbally coded memories and make contact with relatively early, non-verbally coded memories.

Theories of the Bump

Even though the occurrence of the bump depends to some extent on the method whereby autobiographical memories are elicited, it is still a robust enough phenomenon to require an explanation. One explanation has been based on Erik Erikson's (1959; Erikson, Erikson, & Kivnick, 1986) theory of the role of identity in the life cycle. The generation of people who are now over 50 probably made their most important choices (e.g., marriage, career) in late adolescence and young adulthood. This group might be expected to demonstrate the phenomenon of **reminiscence**, a process whereby an older person increasingly tends to recall events from the earlier part of their life. When one reflects on one's life, it is likely that the focus will be on episodes from periods in which particularly formative decisions were made (Boylin, Gordon, & Nehrke, 1976; Mackavey, Malley, & Stewart, 1991, p. 52). Consequently, it is natural for the process of reminiscence to dwell on this period, as aging persons come to judge what they have done with their lives.

As a test of this theory, Mackavey, Malley, and Stewart (1991) did a content analysis of the autobiographies of 49 well-known psychologists (31 men and 18 women). These autobiographies were written when the psychologists were an average of 72 years of age, with a range of 54 to 86 years. By counting and dating **autobiographically consequential experiences** (ACEs) in the autobiographies, Mackavey, Malley, and Stewart (1991) found that about 80 per cent of the ACEs occurred between the ages of 18 and 35. This result is consistent with the hypothesis that it is their importance in the formation of a person's identity that makes experiences occurring between 10 and 30 particularly memorable (Conway & Pleydell-Pearce, 2000, p. 280)

Erikson's theory is far from being the only theory of the bump (Rubin, Rahhal, & Poon, 1998). Another alternative emphasizes the importance of **life scripts** as culturally provided narratives that guide autobiographical memories (Berntsen & Rubin, 2002, 2004; Rubin & Berntsen, 2003). We briefly considered this hypothesis in Chapter 4. To refresh your memory, life scripts prescribe the age norms for important events in an individual's life. Life scripts are 'handed down from older generations, from stories, and from observations of the behavior of other, typically older, people within the same culture' (Berntsen & Rubin, 2004, p. 429).

One reason for thinking that life scripts may be important is that the bump occurs when older people are asked for their most positive and important memories but not for their most negative or saddest memories (Berntsen & Rubin, 2002). The latter tend to be much more recent, as one would expect as the death of loved ones occurs and one's own death approaches. By contrast, life scripts tend to be structured around positive events, such as falling in love and getting a job. The life script is a schema that biases the recall of life events in the direction of positive events that tend to occur during the period of the bump. The net result is that people will tend to recall a life story that is a relatively happy one, but that may not include some of the more difficult times in one's life (Rubin & Berntsen, 2003, p. 12).

Finally, there is a theory of the bump that is based on the action of basic cognitive processes (Rubin, 2005). In this regard, recall our discussion of *distinctiveness* in Chapter 4 on memory traces and schemas and Chapter 6 on imagery. We observed that a relatively novel event will tend to be remembered better than events similar to one another. The period between 10 and 30 years of age is a period when the person is likely to experience a number of distinctive events (Rubin, 2000, p. 173), such as falling in love for the first time, having the first child, and so on. The first time an event occurs, it should be more distinctive both because of its novelty and because more attention is paid to details that the person will learn to ignore in later occurrences (Rubin, Rahhal, & Poon, 1998, p. 14).

Of course, all of these explanations are compatible with one another. Autobiographically consequential experiences and those prescribed by life scripts are distinctive, almost by definition. Each explanation highlights different aspects of what very well may be the same underlying process of development during a particularly important period of the lifespan.

Self-Deception?

People often overestimate their performance in a wide variety of situations (Metcalfe, 1998). A good example is Bahrick, Hall, and Berger's (1996) study of the accuracy of recall for grades achieved in school. University students were asked to recall their grades in high school, and these were then checked against their high school transcripts. Recall accuracy declined from 89 per cent correct for A grades to 29 per cent correct for D grades. This is consistent with the hypothesis that we tend to remember pleasant events better than unpleasant ones. Moreover, it is consistent with the existence of a bias for reconstructing past events as more positive than they actually were.

Metcalfe (1998) has provided an inventory of situations that illustrate the **overconfidence effect**. For example, Metcalfe cites a study by Metcalfe and Wiebe (1987) that we considered in Chapter 9 on problem-solving. Not only were people unable to predict when they *will* solve an insight problem, but when they thought that they were on the verge of achieving a solution they were most often about to produce an error. The tip-of-the-tongue effect, which we considered in Chapter 5, provides another example. Suppose people are asked a question such as 'What is the last name of the only woman who signed the Declaration of Independence?' Of course, no woman signed the Declaration of Independence, but people still can experience a tip-of-the-tongue state. In this case they feel as if they know something that they cannot possibly know. The Moses illusion, which we also considered in Chapter 5, illustrates a similar phenomenon. When people answer *two* to the question *How many animals did Moses take on the Ark?* they are assuming that they know something that cannot be known.

Perhaps we might make errors of this sort as a result of self-deception. This would be true if we persuaded ourselves that we knew something that we did not know. However, Metcalfe argued that self-deception was not at the root of these difficulties. People are not trying to make themselves look better in their own or others' eyes. Rather, Metcalfe suggested, people retrieve whatever information is easiest to retrieve in the current situation, and 'everything retrieved is assumed to be correct' (p. 106). There will be a tendency to assume that whatever you can remember is the information that you need.

As Metcalfe observed, there is a similarity between the overconfidence effect and the various heuristics and biases we discussed in Chapter 11 on judgement and choice. Like them, the overconfidence effect happens more or less automatically. One can try to overcome the overconfidence effect by not responding quickly, but rather by taking one's time and thinking things through carefully.

■ Thinking about Persons

In this section we will not attempt to review the huge literature on social cognition. Rather, we focus on the implications of some of the work of Solomon Asch (www. psych.upenn.edu/sacsec/about/solomon.htm), a pioneering cognitive psychologist who did seminal work in social cognition (Leyens & Corneille, 1999; Rock, 1990). We have already come across some of Asch's work in our discussion of concepts in Chapter 7. There we discussed his observation that words such as *warm* and *cold* are used first to describe physical states, and later used metaphorically to describe personal characteristics.

Asch used the gestalt concept as a guide in his research. You should remember from Chapter 2 that *gestalt* means *form* or *configuration*. Asch's (1946; Asch & Zukier, 1984) studies of social cognition are consistent with a basic premise of Gestalt psychology, which is that we tend to experience events as coherent and related to one another. In the social sphere, the corresponding premise is that we experience people as psychological units. Concretely, this means that the individual attributes of people are treated as parts of an overall gestalt. We do not perceive others as being merely the sum of their pieces. To illustrate this point, consider one of Asch's (1946) experiments. Participants were presented with one of two lists of traits. One group of participants heard a person described as 'intelligent, skilful, industrious, *warm*, determined, practical and cautious', while another group of participants heard a person described as described as 'intelligent, skilful, industrious, *cold*, determined, practical and cautious'. Notice that the difference between the two lists lies in only one word, *warm* in the first list, and *cold* in the second list. Although the two lists differed by only one feature the impressions formed by the two groups of participants were strikingly different. The group given the *warm* list formed an impression of the target person as someone who was 'wise, humorous, popular, and imaginative', while the participants given the *cold* list formed an impression of the target person as not possessing these qualities. Thus, 'a change in one quality produces a fundamental change in the entire impression' (Asch, 1952, p. 210). People do not form an impression by simply adding up pieces of information about others. If that was the way we form impressions, then changing only one attribute would have only a small effect, and not alter the entire impression. Rather, we appear to relate personal qualities to each other as parts to a whole. In general, people tend to experience aspects of another person as coherent and related to one another.

Asch and Zukier (1984) pointed out that some attributes seem to go together more easily than others. An example that they gave is that *warm* and *humorous* seem to go together better than *generous* and *vindictive*. The first pair fit together, whereas the second pair seem to clash. Asch and Zukier examined the process whereby we think about people using attributes that vary in fitness, which is the degree to which attributes seem to be concordant or harmonious. In their experiment, Asch and Zukier asked the question, 'How do we integrate attributes which lack fitness and still preserve a unitary impression of a person?'

Participants were given two words labelling attributes of a person. For example, the two words might be *sociable* and *lonely*. Groups of participants evaluated the attribute pairs for fitness. The criteria for discordant pairs were that they were rated as incongruent, did not imply each other, and neither term brought the other term to mind. Fitting pairs were ones that met the opposites of these criteria (i.e., were rated as congruent, implied each other, and each term brought the other to mind). The result of this exercise was an estimate of the extent to which different attribute pairs were discordant, and which fit together nicely. For each attribute pair, participants were asked to describe what such a person might be like, and how the two attributes might be related.

One interesting result was that participants were usually able to form a **unitary impression** based on incongruent pairs as easily as they were able to form an impression based on fitting pairs. Thus, for example, participants had little difficulty saying what a person who was sociable and lonely might be like. Participants adopted a variety of strategies for harmonizing discordant attributes. For example, sometimes they would regard one attribute as reflecting a deeper aspect of the person, whereas the other attribute was more superficial. Thus, one participant said that a person might appear sociable on the surface, 'but is unable to form deep relations, so that he feels lonely' (Asch & Zukier, 1984, p. 1234).

Asch and Zukier concluded that thinking about persons takes place in a coherent way. We seem to assume that 'a person is a psychological unit' (Asch & Zukier, 1984). The relations between attributes are understood as following from this basic assumption. If people are understood as psychological units, then the interactions between attributes must reflect this underlying organization. The views of Asch and Zukier are representative of a well-established tradition in the study of social cognition, going back at least as far as F. Heider (1958). This tradition maintains that interpersonal cognition tends towards states of affairs that are internally consistent. However, as Asch and Zukier pointed out, even though people create impressions of other people that are internally consistent, it does not follow that these impressions are simple. As the example above illustrates, very often people manage to create a coherent impression that allows the other person to retain a measure of complexity.

Hampson (1998; Casselden & Hampson, 1990) replicated and extended Asch and Zukier's findings by using Peabody's (1990) distinction between the *evaluative* and *descriptive* aspects of personal descriptors. To illustrate this distinction consider the four terms in the table below, adapted from Peabody (1990, p. 59). Both *generous* and *thrifty* are evaluatively positive, but *generous* describes behaviour that differs from *thrifty*. Similarly, *extravagant* and *stingy* are evaluatively negative, but describe behaviours that are opposite in kind.

	Evaluative Distinction	
Descriptive Distinction	generous	extravagant
	thrifty	stingy

Saying that someone is *generous but thrifty* would be behaviourally inconsistent. However, saying that someone is *generous but extravagant* would be evaluatively inconsistent. Which type of inconsistency is the most difficult for participants to resolve? In one experiment participants were asked to judge traits as accurate or inaccurate descriptions either of acquaintances or of themselves. Descriptive inconsistencies (e.g., *generous but thrifty*) were judged as accurate more often than evaluative inconsistencies (e.g., *generous but extravagant*). Participants explained the descriptive inconsistencies in terms of behaviours that were appropriate in different situations. For example, the participant may argue that in some specific situations it is good to be generous, but in general, one must be thrifty. However, the evaluative dimension is conserved across situations (e.g., both generous and thrifty are evaluatively positive).

Hampson concluded that people can easily explain behavioural inconsistency, but are much more concerned to maintain a consistent evaluation of themselves and others. 'Thus, the use of descriptive inconsistencies is an excellent strategy for maintaining overall evaluative coherence (*Jane is a nice person*), while allowing for situationally limited behavioral weaknesses (*Jane is extravagant as well as generous*)' (Hampson, 1998, p. 116).

■ **Questions for Study and Discussion**

1. Consider the theories of the relation between emotion and cognition advanced by Berlyne and Zajonc. First, discuss the ways in which they are similar. Then, discuss the ways in which they are different. Which approach do you prefer? Why?

2. Discuss the relation between mere exposure and cognition. Include in your answer a discussion of the warm glow heuristic.

4. Discuss some of the possible relations between emotion and memory. Cite relevant experiments where appropriate.

5. Are we losing our selves?

6. Why does the bump in autobiographical memory occur? How does it relate to other processes responsible for the curve in Figure 13.4?

7. How do we resolve conflicting information about persons? Which kind of conflicts are the easiest to resolve?

■ **Key Concepts**

Autobiographically consequential experiences Tend to occur between the ages of 18 and 35.

Autobiographical memories Episodic memories, with each event recalled in terms of the time of its occurrence in our lives.

Body problem What kind of physical entity would the body need to be in order to have such things as conscious experiences?

Childhood amnesia There appear to be fewer memories from the first few years of life

than would be expected if memory decayed smoothly as a function of time.

Collative stimulus variables (Berlyne) Properties of stimuli that arise through comparison with other stimuli.

Conceptual conflict Confronting novel, complex, or surprising situations tends to elicit incompatible thoughts.

Depression and initiative The hypothesis that depressed persons lack the initiative to learn and remember information.

Dopamine   A neurotransmitter associated with positive affect.

Ecological self (Neisser)   An awareness of where we are, what we are doing, and what we have done.

Galton's number   People should be able to recall about 220 autobiographical episodes from the last 20 years.

Inconsistencies   People can easily explain behavioural inconsistency, but are much more concerned to maintain a consistent evaluation of themselves and others.

Internal items   Items generated by the person show a greater effect of mood dependence than do items presented to the person.

Interpersonal self   The self that arises whenever we are active as a member of a social interaction.

Life scripts   Culturally provided narratives that guide autobiographical memories and prescribe the age norms for important events in an individual's life.

Mere exposure effect (Zajonc)   The more often people are exposed to an event, the more they like it.

Mood congruence   The possibility that mood might cause selective learning of affective material.

Mood-dependent recall (Bower)   The hypothesis that mood congruence between learning and recall session should facilitate recall.

Overconfidence effect   People tend to overestimate their performance in a wide range of situations.

Proust effect   The power of odours as autobiographical memory cues.

Reminiscence   A process whereby an older person increasingly tends to recall events from the earlier part of his or her life.

Specific and diversive exploration   Whereas specific exploration reduces uncertainty, diversive exploration is undertaken to increase uncertainty.

Structural mere exposure effect   Learning to like an underlying structure (e.g., a particular music or art form) can occur through mere exposure, but it depends on the elements of the structure themselves being familiar.

The bump   An increase in the number of memories between 10 and 30 years of age over and above what would be expected if memories decayed smoothly over time.

Two sides of the self   People show the left side of the face when expressing emotion, but the right side of the face when expressing the ability to control emotion.

Unitary impression   We tend to perceive other people as coherent wholes.

Warm glow heuristic   The tendency for liking something or someone to be taken (or mistaken) as an indicator of previous exposure to that thing or person.

Wundt curve   A graph of the curvilinear relationship between arousal and how positively or negatively a person feels.

■ Links to Other Chapters

Berlyne
  Chapter 11 (negativity bias)
  Chapter 12 (remote associations and
    creativity)
  Chapter 14 (successful versus unsuccessful
    metacognition)
Internally generated items
  Chapter 4 (source monitoring)

Autobiographical memories
  Chapter 5 (episodic memory)
Life scripts
  Chapter 4 (scripts)
Overconfidence effect
  Chapter 14 (illusions of competence)

■ Further Reading

The interaction of cognition and emotion is further discussed in Ochsner, K.N., & Gross, J.J. (2005). The cognitive control of emotion. *Trends in Cognitive Science, 9,* 242–249.

A good overview of some of the relevant literature on mood and memory is Walter, H., Kiefer, M., & Erk, S. (2002). Content, context and cognitive style in mood-memory interactions. *Trends in Cognitive Sciences, 7,* 433–434; and Lewis, P.A., & Critchley, H.D. (2003). Mood-dependent memory. *Trends in Cognitive Sciences, 7,* 431–433.

The importance of reading fiction as a way of simulating the interaction of cognition and emotion is discussed in Oatley, K. (1999). Why fiction may be twice as true as fact: Fiction as cognitive and emotional simulation. *Review of General Psychology, 3,* 101–117.

More on the philosophical implications of the self is in Gallagher, S. (2000). Philosophical conceptions of the self: Implications for cognitive science. *Trends in Cognitive Sciences, 4,* 14–21.

Scientists tend to present their right cheek, as shown by ten Cate, C. (2002). Posing as professor: Laterality in posing orientation for portraits of scientists. *Journal of Nonverbal Behavior, 26,* 175–192.

Neisser, U. (1981). John Dean's memory: A case study. *Cognition, 9,* 1–22, pioneered the detailed analysis of a single case of autobiographical memory with his study of John Dean, who had been one of President Nixon's lawyers prior to the Watergate scandal in 1974.

The question of the accuracy of autobiographical memories was suggested as being beside the point in Edwards, D., & Potter, J. (1992). The Chancellor's memory: Rhetoric and truth in discursive remembering. *Applied Cognitive Psychology, 6,* 187–215. When people remember the events of their lives, they are not trying to be accurate. Rather, autobiographical memories are shaped by the goals we are trying to achieve. It is not that we deliberately lie; it is simply that 'truth' is irrelevant.

In addition to personal memories, our autobiographies contain memories of the important historical events that influenced and gave meaning to the episodes of our lives. This was called *historical memory* by N.R. Brown. He found that for Americans a historical period corresponds to the term of a US president. Perhaps in the UK or Canada the meaningful unit of a historical period is the reign of a sovereign or the term of a prime minister. What do you think? See Brown, N.R. (1990). Organization of public events in long-term memory. *Journal of Experimental Psychology: General, 119,* 297–314.

Chapter 14

Applied Cognitive Psychology

Cognitive psychology has developed to the point where it is able to make recommendations concerning the solution of real-world problems. The *Journal of Applied Cognitive Psychology* has as its mission to publish 'the best of contemporary applications of cognitive theory to phenomena and events of the real world' (Hoffman & Deffenbacher, 1992, p. 2). We have already covered several examples of applied cognitive psychology. For example, mnemonics and eyewitness testimony demonstrate cognitive psychologists applying their expertise to the solution of real-world problems.

Mnemonics. In the chapter on imagery, we dealt with the results of the work that has been done by many psychologists on ways to facilitate remembering and to prevent forgetting. Such work has been a very widely applied part of cognitive psychology.

Eyewitness testimony. In the chapter on memory traces and memory schemas, we examined work, particularly by Loftus, which has clear implications about the conditions under which we should take eyewitness testimony seriously and the conditions under which we should be skeptical. Such work has put psychologists in the position of being advisers to the legal process.

Of course, an emphasis on *ecologically valid* investigations has contributed to turning the attention of some cognitive psychologists towards applied problems (Hoc, 2001). However, many of the most important applications of cognitive psychology have come from those working in the information-processing tradition, as well as other orientations. A book bearing the same title as this chapter (Barber, 1988) highlighted several sources of applied cognitive psychology, of which we will mention two. One is a paper by Broadbent (1980) pointing out that when psychologists examine applied settings, such as the workplace, they quickly discover important aspects of behaviour that may be overlooked in other forms of investigation. Thus, working in applied settings may not only lead to the solution of practical problems, but also provide information about basic psychological processes that may not be obtainable in any other way.

Another important issue is **problem-centred versus method-centred** approaches in psychology, a distinction that was made popular many years ago by Maslow (1946). Cognitive psychology can be so concerned with doing methodologically correct studies that it loses sight of the practical problems that need to be addressed. However, a problem-centred cognitive psychology runs the risk of methodological sloppiness. Great care needs to be taken to ensure that applied cognitive psychology is done in as methodologically sound a way as possible. Applied cognitive psychology requires a delicate balance between being problem-centred and being method-centred.

◼ Human Error

One of the central concerns of applied cognitive psychology has always been the discovery of ways to reduce the tendency we all have to make errors in a variety of situations. For example, consider those occasions in which you plan a sequence of action but fail to carry it out as you intended. Some of you may have had the experience of intending to do one thing, only to discover that you have done quite another thing. William James once described how 'some absent-minded persons, in going to their bedroom to dress for dinner, took off one garment after another and finally got into bed, merely because that was the habitual issue of the first few movements when performed at a later hour' (1890, p. 115). Of course, over a century later most of us need not worry about this particular example of absent-mindedness because the formality of dressing up to come to the dinner table is no longer common.

Both D.A. Norman (1981) and Reason (1984, 1990) put forward influential explanations of such lapses of attention. Norman proposed to explain this and other errors of attention by means of an **activation-trigger-schema theory** (ATS). Remember that the word *schema* refers to the way in which people organize their past experience and use it to plan for action. There can be several different schemas for different kinds of action, and more than one schema can be activated at any one time. One example given by Norman is that when you are engaged in an extended sequence of actions, as in driving home from work, there will be a number of specific actions that are cued at different times in the sequence. You need to pay attention to what you are doing at certain critical points, such as stopping at a red light, but much of what is done does not require much attention. If you intend to vary your routine, then problems may result. For example, if your roommate asks you to buy a loaf of bread on your way home, then your usual driving-home schema must be modified. You must keep the intention to buy a loaf of bread active in working memory or you will end up at home having forgotten to pick up the loaf of bread. The habitual sequence of action continues to operate without much attention, and the newer action sequence never gets activated. Betsch, Haberstroh, Molter, and Glöckner (2004) call this the **oops, I did it again** effect.

To test the fragility of intentions, Einstein, McDaniel, Williford, Pagan, and Dismukes (2003) asked participants to postpone doing one task until they had finished another. They found that participants were very poor at remembering to do the postponed task, and concluded that 'when busily engaged in activities, it is difficult for the cognitive system to maintain delayed intentions in focal awareness even for 5 s' (p. 161).

We can begin to understand errors by attempting to classify them in terms of the possible sources of different kinds of error. The first type of error Norman describes is a lapse that occurs because we have inadequately formulated what it is we actually want to do. These errors due to faulty formulation of intentions fall into two subclasses. **Mode errors** occur when we carry out an action that would be fine for one situation (or mode), but not for the situation in which we happen to find ourselves. Examples given by Norman and Reason include a person trying to take off his or her eyeglasses when not actually wearing them, or picking up the telephone and saying 'Come in!' Errors of intention can also occur because we do not have a detailed enough understanding of our situation. These are called **description errors**. Two examples Norman has given are: a person intends to pour orange juice into a glass, but instead pours it into a coffee cup next to it; a person intends to stop the car and unbuckle his or her seatbelt, but unbuckles his or her watchband instead.

The second type of error may be due to faulty activation of a schema. In this category are **capture errors**. As the name indicates, such errors result when a familiar schema captures behaviour in the place of an unfamiliar one. Particularly when you are trying to do something instead of an overlearned sequence it is likely that the overlearned sequence will run itself off instead. The Stroop task is a good example of this sort of thing. Norman recounted the case of a person standing at the photocopying machine counting the copies as they were made. Thus, the person said '1, 2, 3, 4, 5, 6, 7, 8, 9, 10' and then 'Jack, Queen, King, Ace'. Reason (1990, p. 70) gives the example of a person intending to get the car out of the garage, 'but as I passed through the back porch on the way to the garage, I stopped to put on my . . . boots and gardening jacket as if to work in the garden.'

Faulty activation also reveals itself in errors due to loss of activation of the appropriate schema. A good example of this is walking into a room in your house for some reason and then not being sure why you are there. The remedy for this may be returning to the place where you started, at which point you may remember what it was that you were seeking. Other examples given by Norman and Reason include pouring water into the kettle a second time without realizing that it had already been done; or not being sure whether or not you have shaved this morning.

The third type of error occurs because, although the proper schema has been activated, it is triggered inappropriately. In this class are **anticipation errors**, in which a response may occur earlier in a sequence than it should if it is only being elicited by the immediately preceding stimulus. Thus, people who are expert at using keyboards may still occasionally make anticipatory errors, such as typing 'wrapid writing' rather than 'rapid writing', as if the *w* in *writing* had been *primed,* or activated, before the phrase had been typed.

A famous type of error of this sort is the *spoonerism*, named after a British academic who was reputed to have a propensity for making anticipatory errors. For example, suppose Spooner wanted to rebuke a student for poor performance. He should have said, 'You have wasted two terms.' Instead, he is reputed to have said, 'You have tasted two worms' (*Oxford Dictionary of Quotations*, 1959). The *t* in *term* was not elicited by the word *two*. Rather, the *t* was *primed* before the sentence was uttered and intruded earlier in the sequence. It is as if the entire sequence of words is selected before the sentence is uttered. Spoonerisms can be elicited experimentally and are a useful tool for studying speech errors (Baars, 1992).

Norman noted that the existence of errors such as these points out the importance of monitoring one's own behaviour. Often people will notice that they have made a slip. However, to catch themselves making a mistake, they must be paying attention to what they are doing at the right level. Intending to drive home is a very molar piece of behaviour. Such an intention will not lead to monitoring your behaviour at a molecular level, and it is at such unmonitored levels of behaviour that slips are most likely to occur. It is unrealistic to expect to eliminate slips. As Wagenaar, Hudson, and Reason (1990, p. 277) observed, 'it does not help to tell people not to make slips, because it is beyond their control.'

Most of the slips we have considered thus far are relatively harmless, and even amusing. However, Panji and Chariker (2004) observed that similar errors occur in professional settings where their consequences are much more serious. In line with the hypothesis that continuous monitoring of activity is necessary to avoid error, they pointed out that:

> there is insufficient appreciation within the medical community that errors find fertile ground where there is confidence that they will not happen. It needs to be made clearer to surgeons that the one who confidently breezes in to conduct a tour de force in the middle of a busy day may be the one who carries out a procedure on the wrong person. (p. 140)

A traditional way of attempting to avoid human errors in the future is to attempt to understand how human errors came about in the past. For example, after an airplane crash there is an intensive effort made to reconstruct what went wrong. The hope is that by understanding what made accidents happen, we can better predict, and thus avoid, their occurrence in the future. Whether or not this hope is justified is the subject of Box 14.1.

■ Ergonomics

Traditionally, the applied issues to which cognitive psychologists have made the biggest contribution belong to an area of inquiry called ergonomics. **Ergonomics** began as the study of people in relation to their working environment. Ergonomists help to design objects and machines so that people can interact with them not only efficiently but also with the maximum possible amount of satisfaction. For example, ergonomists have studied such things as how to arrange keyboards, chairs, and desks so as to make office work both productive and enjoyable (e.g., Pheasant, 1986). Ergonomics takes the potential user into account when something is being designed, and so is sometimes also called *human factors research*. Over the years, the scope of ergonomics has broadened, and it now encompasses the study of the entire range of situations in which people interact with manufactured objects (e.g., D.A. Norman, 1988/2002).

Box 14.1 Does Understanding Improve Prediction?

Dawes (1988, 1993, 1994) argued that there is an asymmetry between under-standing and prediction. By this he meant that prediction does not necessarily fol-low from understanding. One can understand something extremely well and yet not be able to predict its future occurrence. Conversely, one can predict some-thing reasonably well without having a very good understanding of why the pre-diction works. What follows are some examples illustrating why this is true.

Let us call the event we want to understand the *consequence* and the events that lead up to it the *antecedents*. Let us use plane crashes as an example of a con-sequence. Plane crashes are the sort of consequence we want very much to under-stand, in the hope that we can forestall their future occurrence. There is usually an inquiry into major plane crashes, with a view to determining their antecedents. Here is one of Dawes's (1993, pp. 14ff.; 1999, pp. 36ff.) examples illustrating how we can understand a particular plane crash without being able to predict future occurrences of plane crashes.

An airplane crashed at Mexico City airport in 1979. It crashed at night under conditions of poor visibility into a truck left on a runway. The runway was under construction and closed to traffic. Unfortunately, the radar guidance system led pilots to the runway under construction, at which time they were supposed to switch to another runway. The pilots on this particular flight were very tired, hav-ing had three–four hours of sleep in the previous 24 hours. Just before landing, the control tower issued imprecise instructions about which runway to use. Then the pilots' radio malfunctioned. The antecedents for this catastrophe are fatigue, poor visibility, misleading communications, and breakdown of the radio. All of these antecedents contributed jointly to the crash.

It is important to realize that the antecedents identified in this case are not very useful as predictors of future accidents. All of them can precede successful landings as well. Pilots are often tired, communication is often poor, poor visibility is a com-mon problem, equipment failures are not rare, and yet the overwhelming major-ity of landings are successful. Dawes (1993) recalled a flight into Chicago during which he overheard the flight controller yelling at the pilot, 'I said runway 5, dammit, runway 5, 5, not 6, oh s**t!' (p. 16). He landed successfully anyway.

When we attempt to understand unusual events, we tend to assume that they must be the result of unusual antecedents. However, it is more often the case that the antecedents are ordinary events that have combined in a singular way to yield an undesirable outcome. When we reach an understanding of a particular disaster, we are able to create a narrative that makes sense of it. Remember our discussion of Bartlett in Chapter 3, and how easily we are able to reconstruct the past in line with our prior beliefs and attitudes. It is very unlikely that our story will generalize to any future occurrence (Dawes, 1999).

In order to attempt to generalize to future occurrences, we would at a minimum need to systematically compare the antecedents of successful flights with the antecedents of crashes. However, the flight recorder data of successful flights are routinely erased, eliminating precisely the data we need for comparison with flight recorder data from crashes (Dawes, 1999, p. 36).

The work of Dawes and other psychologists has important implications for the legislative process. Following inquiries into disastrous events, new laws are often promulgated in the hope of preventing future occurrences. Mitchell (2004) has analyzed this process in the case of Enron (en.wikipedia.org/wiki/Enron), a huge company that went bankrupt in 2001. This resulted in the loss of billions of dollars and thousands of jobs. A congressional investigation followed, as did legislation designed to prevent future Enrons. Drawing on the work of Dawes and others, Mitchell shows that the stories created to explain Enron have the same flaws as do the stories created to explain other disasters. The assumption is made that if the antecedents of the bankruptcy had been different, then it would not have occurred. This is sometimes called the **Cleopatra's nose problem** (Mitchell, 2004, p. 1562). If Cleopatra had an ugly nose, then would Antony still have fallen in love with her? If Enron had used proper accounting practices, then would it have survived? One can invent any number of hypothetical events that *might* have changed the course of history without any certainty of being able to predict any future occurrences. Designing legislation based on such thought experiments is unlikely to improve future prospects.

If storytelling based on prior disasters will not allow us to predict the future, what will? Dawes (1988, 1993, p. 2) described several studies in which a simple model based on a few empirically derived antecedents will outperform even the most sophisticated observers. For example, we would all like to know which offenders will successfully stay out of jail for a year after being released. Three variables—seriousness of crime, number of past convictions, and number of prison violations—yielded a better prediction than did the judgement of experienced parole interviewers. One variable alone—past heroin use—will outperform the judgement of parole officers. I can make up a story about why heroin use predicts recidivism, but such a story does not improve my predictions. One does not need to understand individual criminals in order to make predictions about their future behaviour. It must be admitted that even empirical research into the antecedents of destructive behaviour does not yield very good predictions. However, such research is still the best alternative.

A concept that gained enormous popularity is the idea that objects should be made *user friendly*. According to *The Oxford English Dictionary, user friendliness* is a phrase that emerged in the 1970s to describe the ease with which a person could interact with a computer. The concept has since been more widely applied to describe a desirable feature of virtually any interaction between a person and any device. A widely cited definition is that something is user friendly if it 'helps a person to perform a task in a natural way, which is easy to understand and use' (Stevens, 1983).

There have been many comparisons of user-friendly objects with what might be called user-unfriendly objects. One of the examples of the former is the flexible straw, which can be adjusted to suit the sipper's position relative to a drink. This illustrates the fact that simple changes in an object can sometimes have a big effect on its ease of use. One of the examples of a user-unfriendly object is the so-called child-proof medicine bottle. Adults also sometimes find the caps to these bottles impossible to open, illustrating the point that changing an object to solve one problem may occasionally create another problem. Ergonomics can sometimes be a tricky business.

The User Interface

A work situation can be analyzed in terms of three different interfaces (Giroux & Larochelle, 1988; Sime & Coombs, 1983). The organizational interface concerns the relation between the organization, such as a manufacturing company, and the types of tasks the organization requires. In a large corporation, such as General Motors, there will be many different tasks related to the organization in a variety of complex ways. In a small business, such as a corner store, there may be only a few tasks required to maintain the business. In any case, the organization, however large or small, must make decisions about which tasks are important. This brings us to the task interface, which refers to the relation between a job and the devices required to perform the job. Obviously, different tasks require different devices, and it is important that the right device ends up being used. Within an organization, a lot of debate can go on concerning which devices can best perform the tasks required.

As T. Winograd and Flores (1986, chap. 12) showed, such decisions are often made without anyone being sufficiently clear about precisely what problems the introduction of new technology is meant to solve. Someone may decide that the business could benefit from the introduction of a new computer system but have only a vague idea about what tasks the new system will actually be used to perform. Winograd and Flores gave the example of an owner of a small store who expands her operation to a chain of stores. Although lacking any computer experience, the owner believes that introducing computers may have a beneficial effect on accounting procedures and customer relations. Such a person may not be able to specify in advance any details of the task interface. The definition of the task interface may be a process that evolves over a long period of using the system, rather than being anything that can be precisely stated at the outset.

However, in addition to defining the task interface, the **user interface** is also crucial. The user interface refers to the relationship between the person and the device being used to perform a task. The organizational and task interfaces are of concern to such people as device manufacturers, administrators, and industrial/organizational psychologists. However, the interface to which cognitive psychology is most applicable is the user interface (e.g., Edmonds & Green, 1984). The goal is to design interfaces that take the user's point of view into account (Norman, 1992, p. 171).

Cognitive Ergonomics

The phenomenal growth in the use of computers focused attention on person/computer interactions (Broadbent, 1990). Cognitive psychology was found to be very useful for analyzing such interactions. **Cognitive ergonomics** refers to the combination of cognitive psychology and ergonomics used to understand the user interface (Giroux & Larochelle, 1988, p. 14; T.R.G. Green, Payne, & van der Veer, 1983; D.A. Norman & Draper, 1986).

There are several different aspects of the user interface. One aspect is the machine itself, with which the user interacts. This hardware includes such things as a keyboard or other device for inputting information; a screen for displays; other peripheral devices such as printers; and so on. The structure of the hardware has a significant impact on the efficiency with which the user interacts with the computer.

The software that runs on the computer determines to a large extent precisely what operations the user is required to perform. Word-processing programs require different responses from the user than do computer games. Another important aspect of the user interface is the way that the user thinks about the computer. It is desirable for the user interface to be designed to make use of the user's existing knowledge, in order to minimize the amount of learning required to interact with the computer (Maas, 1983). The design of computer keyboards is a good example of the interaction between all of these aspects of the user interface.

Keyboards

Keyboards have been the subject of a great deal of research over the past several decades (Greenstein & Arnaut, 1987; Lemmons, 1982; D.A. Norman, 1988, pp. 145ff.; Pheasant, 1986, pp. 241ff.; Shneiderman, 1998, pp. 306ff.). In the latter part of the nineteenth century, there were a great many different styles of keyboard in use (en.wikipedia.org/wiki/QWERTY). One obvious arrangement for the keys represent-ing individual letters is alphabetical, as shown below. However, this pattern of keys did not last. One reason appears to be that it was too easy to use! The early mechanical typewriters jammed if the operator typed too fast (D.A. Norman, 1988, p. 150). The orderly, alphabetical arrangement of keys allowed the operator to do the task too efficiently for the state of the technology. It was necessary to slow the typist down. The alternative keyboard arrangement that took precedence over its competitors is the so-called QWERTY keyboard, named after the order of the first six keys on the left in the top row. The QWERTY arrangement is shown below the alphabetical one.

Alphabetic Keyboard

```
A    B    C    D    E    F    G    H    I    J
  K    L    M    N    O    P    Q    R    S
    T    U    V    W    X    Y    Z
```

QWERTY Keyboard

Q	W	E	R	T	Y	U	I	O	P
	A	S	D	F	G	H	J	K	L
		Z	X	C	V	B	N	M	

It seems intuitively obvious that the alphabetic arrangement should be easier to use as long as the machine can keep up with the speed of the operator. Thus, you would think that contemporary keyboards would benefit from an alphabetic design. However, the issue is more complex than it appears to be at first. D.A. Norman and Fisher (1982) studied the task of continuously typing words using different keyboard arrangements. Their participants were not expert typists, and their task was to type some prose from a popular magazine. Norman and Fisher reported that typing speed on the alphabetic keyboard was not as good as typing speed on the QWERTY keyboard. D.A. Norman (1988/2002, p. 147) has explained results like these in terms of the ease with which the operator can use the knowledge he or she brings to the situation. Many people have at least casual experience with the QWERTY keyboard, and that knowledge may be quite useful. Moreover, skilled typists, who have learned the QWERTY system, will not be able to transfer what they have learned to the alphabetical keyboard. As Norman noted, once a system such as QWERTY becomes entrenched, it is very difficult to change it.

There have been several attempts to reintroduce the alphabetic keyboard (e.g., Nicolson & Gardner, 1985). However, Shneiderman (1998, pp. 308ff.) observed that people resent having to use it when there are so many more keyboards that have the QWERTY arrangement. Learning the QWERTY keyboard is perceived as a more valuable investment of time. There is some controversy over why QWERTY has persisted. One view holds that the QWERTY keyboard is an example of the way in which 'an accidental series of events may lock technology into a particular irreversible path' (Zhai, Kristensson, & Smith, 2005, p. 233). The other view holds that, counterintuitively, it may be the case that other keyboards are not actually easier to use (Liebowitz & Margolis, 1996).

On computer keyboards there are a number of keys in addition to those found on typewriters. The placement of these keys is more idiosyncratic. Numeric keypads have been a source of considerable variation (Greenstein & Arnaut, 1987, p. 1459; Lemmons, 1982; D.A. Norman, 1988/2002, pp. 17ff.; Pheasant, 1986, p. 242). Many of the numeric keypads used in calculators and computer keyboards have their keys laid out like this:

7	8	9
4	5	6
1	2	3
	0	

This would seem to be a perfectly good arrangement because it conforms to our knowledge about numbers. It proceeds from 0 at the bottom to 9 at the top, in a perfectly straightforward way. However, not all numeric keypads are like this. For example, the keypad on your phone is likely to have this layout:

$$
\begin{array}{ccc}
1 & 2 & 3 \\
4 & 5 & 6 \\
7 & 8 & 9 \\
 & 0 &
\end{array}
$$

Notice that this arrangement has a certain logic as well. It goes from top to bottom, and left to right, which is also the way we read (Lemmons, 1982). For dialing telephone numbers, this format appears to work well and seems to allow faster input (Shneiderman, 1998). However, neither arrangement appears to interfere with the other, in that people do not make mistakes entering numbers on a computer by unthinkingly using the telephone pattern. Thus, to make an important point, different contexts may allow for different solutions.

Text Messaging

Mobile phones have had a profound effect on behaviour throughout the world. In 2002, 'the number of mobile subscribers overtook the number of fixed-line subscribers on a global scale' (Srivastava, 2005, p. 111). This device satisfies an extraordinary range of social and business needs. Although the keypad on a mobile phone is small and unsuited for typing text, an increasingly ubiquitous use of mobile phones is *text messaging*. Phone companies initially believed that text messaging would be only a tiny aspect of mobile telephone use (Faulkner & Culwin, 2005). However, beginning in Finland, the volume of text messaging spread rapidly throughout Europe and other parts of the world. There were 20.5 *billion* text messages sent in Britain alone in 2003. Text messages 'fill an ever-narrowing gap in modern communication tools, combining the immediacy of a phone call with the convenience of an answering machine message and the premeditation of e-mail' (Barron, 2005).

Because the interface is so difficult to use for typing text, text messages are often written in a special code called **textish**. Thus, 'd8ing' is used instead of 'dating', and 'CU' instead of 'see you'. The tendency to use textish increases with the intimacy of the relationship between sender and receiver (Faulkner & Culwin, 2005, p. 182). In this respect, textish resembles inner speech, which we considered in Chapter 8 on language. The less the social distance between oneself and another, the more communication will approximate speech for oneself. One of the advantages of textish is that it makes communication more private. This is one of the more desirable features of text messages for adolescents, who constitute a very large subset of the most devoted users (Srivastava, 2005, p. 121).

The popularity of text messaging illustrates the fact that if a device can satisfy a need, then people will use it, no matter how labour-intensive it is (Faulkner & Culwin,

2005, p. 168). Modifications in a device to make it more user friendly are likely to come about only after the device has demonstrated its utility. There is no point in designing a friendly user interface for a device that no one cares to use.

Pointing Devices

Fitts's law is one of the most robust relationships in all of psychology. As stated by Fitts (1954/1992), it specified the difficulty of moving a stylus to a target. Obviously, this difficulty will vary as the distance to the target varies. The further the stylus has to be moved, the more difficult the task. It will also vary as the size of the target varies. The narrower the target the more difficult it will be to hit it. Although Fitts's law can be stated with considerable precision, for our purposes it can be put like this (Guiard & Beaudouin-Lafon, 2004, p. 748).

$$\text{ID} = f(D/W)$$

ID is an index of difficulty and is a function of the target distance (D) divided by the width of the target (W). Thus, ID will increase with target distance and decrease with target width. Typically, as ID increases, so will the time taken to hit the target.

There is a demonstration of Fitts's law at www.tele-actor.net/fitts/. It mimics one of the original conditions in Fitts's experiments, and will give you a good idea of what being a participant would have been like.

Card, English, and Burr (1978) discussed Fitts's law in relation to computer displays. When the user moves a mouse, for example, the pointer also moves from one part of the screen to another. This movement is intended to reach a target, which may be anything from a location in a document to a clickable icon. Fitts's law appears to hold for such pointing devices as the computer mouse. The time taken to hit a target, such as an entry in a drop-down menu, depends on the distance the pointer must be moved and the width of the target. Fitts's law leads to two principles (Soukoreff & Mackenzie, 2004, p. 752). First, the more frequently used a target is, the closer it should be to the pointer. This can be accomplished by means of pop-up targets that are displayed by right-clicking the mouse, for example. Second, if the user must make the pointer travel a longer distance, then the target should be made as large as possible. These principles are seldom instantiated very well in most interfaces.

■ Affordances

The concept of **affordances** is highly relevant for understanding the user interface (D.A. Norman (1988/2002; 1993; Greeno, 1994). We discussed affordances, a notion introduced by J.J. Gibson, in Chapter 2. 'The affordances of an object refers to its possible functions' (Norman, 1993, p. 105). Objects afford particular actions. For example, a piano affords playing in a particular way that is different from what a guitar affords. 'The set of possible actions is called the affordances of the object. An affordance is not a property; it is a *relationship* that holds between the object and the organism that is acting on the object' (D.A. Norman, 1998, p. 123)

Sometimes you can tell what actions an object supports or even requires just by looking at it. As Norman pointed out, when an object affords a particular action, then no instructions to the user may be necessary. People do not mistake the use of such things as hammers, coffee cups, and pens in part because the actions appropriate to them are given by their properties. An important aspect of designing an object is to try to create an object that will afford those actions that are appropriate, and not afford those actions that are inappropriate. Ideally, the correct action will be directly perceptible.

Instructions

Of course, it is difficult to design something so that the user knows how to use it simply by looking at it. In practice, many of the products of technology cannot be used without instructions. The instructions are usually in the form of text that accompanies the device. Green and Payne (1982) reviewed some of the properties that such texts should have. Some of these properties are quite straightforward. For example, the text should be organized in a way that reflects the actions the user must perform. This is not a serious problem so long as the operations to be performed follow one another in a linear order. Many instructions can be laid out in a straightforward way, if the user makes only one action at a time. The sequence of instructions in the text can then correspond to the proper sequence of the user's actions.

However, many processes require the user to perform actions concurrently (Townsend, 1990). Instructions for the use of an object requiring concurrent processing present special problems. An example of an object requiring a **concurrent process** is the digital watch (D.A. Norman, 1988/2002, pp. 30–31). Notice that ordinary watches, the ones with hands instead of digital displays, are easy to use. A stem in the side can be rotated to set the time. Here we have a good example of an object affording its use. Turning the stem by a fixed amount corresponds to changing the time by a fixed amount. Digital watches, however, often require the user to interact with them in complex ways. There are often four buttons, two on either side of the watch. Looking at the buttons provides no information about what to do with them. The instructions that come with the watch are often hard to follow. Functions of the watch may be controlled in a complicated way, requiring not only a sequence of actions, but that two actions be performed simultaneously (e.g., hold this button while pressing that button). It is unlikely that the user will remember these operations, and even less likely that the user will discover them on his or her own. Of course, ideally digital watches would have a more user-friendly structure, but in the meantime, as D.A. Norman (1988/2002, p. 31) pointed out, many objects will continue to have a structure that is arbitrary, unnatural, and complicated. Unfortunately, the instructions that accompany such devices may also have the same properties as the object they describe.

Green and Payne observed that, ironically, a very old notation may serve as a model for the sort of notation required to represent complex processes for users. Consider the way music is presented. Figure 14.1 shows a schematic example of a series of notes to be played on a piano keyboard. The piano player must play both left and right hands concurrently. The parallel actions of the hands are clearly presented by this notation. The sequence of the left hand is visually matched to the sequence of the right hand. As Sloboda (1981) noted, the cues to action are directly perceptible; the notation affords the proper action.

Figure 14.1 suggests that pictures might be useful instructional devices. Pictures, like images, can represent concurrent information successfully. Recall our discussion in the chapter on imagery of the way in which images present information synchronously, meaning that the parts they contain are simultaneously available for inspection. The relations between these simultaneously available parts can convey information to the user about appropriate actions. Pictures, in the form of *graphical user interfaces*, are standard aspects of person/computer interactions (Guastello, Traut, & Korienek, 1989).

Presenting Information

Presenting statistical information in graphical form is an art as well as a science. **Statistical graphics** is concerned with presenting data in a visual form that is not only readily understood but that also enables the user to draw the correct inferences (Wainer & Velleman, 2001). Examine Michael Friendly's page on statistical graphics (www.math.yorku.ca/SCS/Gallery/). It presents the best and worst of statistical graphics in an informative as well as entertaining way. Make sure you inspect the entries on Charles Minard's graph of Napoleon's Russian campaign of 1812. This graph is often said to be a model of excellence in statistical graphics (e.g., Wainer & Velleman, 2001, p. 316).

Some ways of representing data may unintentionally mislead the consumer. Here is an example from Rosnow and Rosenthal (1989). It comes from a study of the role of aspirin in reducing the risk of heart attack, or myocardial infarction (Steering Committee of the Physicians' Health Study Research Group, 1988). This study has an extremely

Figure 14.1 Music for the Right (top) and Left (bottom) Hands.

From Robert Schumann, *Album for the young*, Op. 68.

large sample size: a total of over 22,000 participants, divided into two groups of roughly 11,000 each. One group got aspirin every other day, while the other group got no aspirin. During the period of the study, 104 participants in the aspirin group had heart attacks, while 189 participants in the no aspirin group had heart attacks. In media accounts of this study, these data were interpreted to mean that the participants not taking aspirin were about twice as likely as the aspirin participants to get a heart attack. That interpretation is sort of correct, in that dividing the no-aspirin heart attack participants (189) by the no-aspirin heart attack participants (104) gives a value of 1.82. However, notice that when one uses the actual frequencies of participants who had heart attacks, the size of the effect appears less impressive than when one uses phrases such as 'twice as likely'. The latter phrase is harder for the average consumer to interpret. The relative size of each of the groups of participants is shown in Figure 14.2. We are talking about 85 more people getting heart attacks in the no-aspirin group out of a sample of over 11,000. This translates into a correlation of about .03 (Rosnow & Rosenthal, 1989, p. 1279) between taking aspirin vs no aspirin and presence vs absence of a heart attack. This is an example of a small effect being detected in a very large sample. If the sample had been smaller, it is unlikely that such a small effect would have been detected. Obviously, aspirin has an effect, however small. However, you would be unwise to rely on aspirin alone to prevent heart attacks.

Figure 14.2 Graphical Display of Data from Rosnow and Rosenthal.

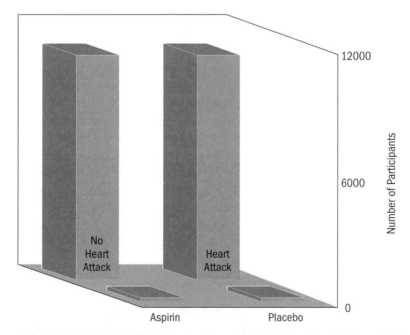

Gigerenzer and Edwards (2005) pointed out that presenting data in the form of frequencies 'is a simple and effective mind tool to reduce the confusion resulting from' presenting data in other ways. For example, women over 50 are often told that mammography screening will reduce the risk of dying from breast cancer by 25 per cent. In a way this is true. However, if one casts the data in terms of frequencies, it turns out that of 1,000 people who do not get a mammogram, about four will die from breast cancer within 10 years. Of 1,000 people who do get a mammogram, three will die of breast cancer within 10 years. The difference is one person in 1,000. When the matter is presented in that way, it seems less risky to not have a mammogram. Gigerenzer and Edwards note a disturbing trend for health authorities to present data in ways that may exaggerate the risks of refusing a medical procedure. The result may be that health authorities tend to fund treatments that state their outcomes in ways that 'make the numbers look larger', rather than presenting a '**population impact number** (the number of people in the population among whom one event will be prevented by an intervention)' (p. 743). In the case of mammography, the population impact number is one in 1,000.

Gigerenzer and Edwards claimed that people are good intuitive statisticians if the data are presented in a way that is 'natural' for them. 'Natural frequencies correspond to the way humans have encountered statistical information during most of their history' (p. 744). The moral of the story is that frequencies will be the best way in which to present data for statistically naïve consumers.

We cannot leave this topic without observing that information is sometimes presented in a deliberately misleading way, and that consumers of information need to be wary of such attempts to take advantage of them. For example, there has been an explosion in on-line gambling, which is a largely unregulated activity. Typically, once consumers log onto a gambling site, they can enjoy a trial period before committing themselves to play for real money. Sévigny, Cloutier, Pelletier, and Ladouceur (2005) tested the hypothesis that the trial period provided the user with a higher payout than actually existed when the consumer was playing for real.

Using Google and the search term 'slot machines', the researchers obtained a sample of 117 gambling sites. Since gambling sites cannot survive by paying out more than they take in, a demonstration period in which potential customers made more 'play money' than they spent would be indicative of a misleading site. Sévigny et al. found that 39 per cent of sites had an inflated payout rate during the demo period. The authors then played for real money at five randomly selected sites in which the demo period had been inflated. They lost in four out of five and were not allowed to cash in at the one site where they made money. Although not conclusive, the study suggests that, in this as in so many things, *caveat emptor.*

Searching for Information

Throughout this book we have documented the activities of human beings as '**infor-mavores**: a species that hungers for information in order to gather it and store it as a means for adapting to the world' (Pirolli, 2005, p. 344). It is a commonplace to observe that there is much more information in the environment than we can possibly use. As Herbert Simon put it (as quoted by Pirolli & Card, 1999; p. 643):

> What information consumes is rather obvious: it consumes the attention of its recipients. Hence a wealth of information creates a poverty of attention, and a need to allocate that attention efficiently among the overabundance of information sources that might consume it.

Attention is a precious resource that can be depleted by the indiscriminate consumption of information. How do we understand the processes whereby people allocate their attention in order to acquire useful information? Pirolli and Card (1999) suggested that it is useful to think of **information foraging** as a process analogous to that engaged in by animals when they forage for food. A successful foraging strategy will return the most task-relevant information with a minimum of effort. Effort might be measured in terms of the number of articles read, or Web pages visited, for example. A successful forager acquires a lot of task-relevant information with a little effort. An unsuccessful forager acquires a little relevant information with a lot of effort.

Most task environments are *patchy*. The information sources that might be relevant may exist 'in piles of documents, file drawers, office bookshelves, libraries, or in various on-line collections' (Pirolli & Card, 1999, p. 645). In order to forage between and within patches, the forager must follow **information scents**, just as predators follow the scents of their prey. Such scents are imperfect clues to the information being sought. For example, search for 'information foraging' in your favourite search engine. You will likely get over 20,000 hits. You are unlikely to want to look at them all! Find one that strikes you as having a particularly strong scent with respect to elaborating your knowledge of this topic so that you could better write an essay on it. What properties does your selection have? The accuracy of users' assessment of information scent will determine how successful their foraging strategy will be. Once a site has been selected for viewing, then it should also have a strong scent that leads you to other sites. However, the scent may diminish rapidly. There is evidence that users want to pick up a scent in no more than three clicks of the mouse, or they will leave the site for another patch (Olson & Olson, 2003, p. 500).

Pirolli and Card presented two case studies of information foraging. One involved an analyst who wrote a newsletter and the other involved a group of MBA students. The former needed to collect information relevant to writing a newsletter on new developments in technology. He had a workstation in a larger organization that produced a number of publications. The organization subscribed to a variety of magazines that are circulated to individuals such as the newsletter writer. This is the first opportunity for him to pick up a scent. If any article strikes him as promising, he will copy it and put it in a pile. He then skims the articles in the pile, looking for those with a particularly strong scent. These go into another, smaller pile. This process continues until he has a pile about one inch high, which he uses to produce his newsletter.

Two groups of two to three MBA students each were given the task on a Saturday of producing a report by Monday on a well-known food and beverage company. They began by searching a database for relevant articles. From about 300 possibilities, about 50 were selected for their scent and the relevant database citations printed out. The students then had a meeting, in which these materials were reduced to about 25. These articles were then chased down in the library. Some were not found, yielding a final total of 18. On the basis of reading these articles, the groups produced a report by Monday. You may recognize this process as similar to one you may use when producing essays or projects.

Both examples show how the information scent is enriched by filtering information so that only a fraction of the available articles are actually read. It would take too much time to read everything and then decide what is relevant. Instead, an **information diet** is created by initially examining a large number of possible sources of information in a cursory manner and rejecting those that do not look promising. Pirolli and Card (1999, p. 646) point out this process is similar to initially scanning your e-mail for potential junk, which you then discard. Junk mail is like junk food. By eliminating it you improve your information diet.

The newsletter writer and the MBA students displayed different forms of information foraging. The former stayed in one place and let the information come to him. The latter moved about in the environment to find what they needed. A similar distinction occurs between animals foraging for food (Pirolli & Card, 1995, p. 670). Some, such as spiders, weave their web and wait for prey. Others, like sharks, are constantly on the move searching for prey. Depending on the context, either strategy may be a legitimate way of foraging for information.

■ Designing the User Interface

An enormous amount of work has been done by psychologists in collaboration with others to try to determine the properties that should be incorporated in any user interface (e.g., Carroll, 1997; Chalmers, 2003; Green, 1982; Olson & Olson, 2003; Shneiderman, 1998, pp. 74ff.). Below is a list of some of the properties that are most often mentioned.

Recognition

Recognition means that it should be obvious to the user precisely what is being represented. As an example of the way in which a picture can be worth considerably less than 1,000 words, consider the following example from Adobe Acrobat Reader (version 7), an indispensable program for reading documents posted on the Web. Like every other program, this one makes extensive use of icons to represent alternative actions that the program is capable of executing. Alternatives can be chosen by pointing at the appropriate icon and pressing a button on the mouse. This system works fine as long as the icon has an obvious meaning. One of the icons on the screen is a pair of binoculars. Do you have any intuitions about what action such a symbol might produce? Many users initially think that it zooms in on the document. However, that is wrong.

This symbol enables searches for specified text. In retrospect, that seems like a reasonable meaning for this symbol, but it is unlikely that the meaning of the icon can always be recognized simply by looking at it.

It is easy to find other examples of cases in which a symbol that is supposed to be instructive does not always convey the intended meaning to the user. (It would be a useful exercise for you to try to find such symbols in the programs you use.) Guastello et al. (1989) did an experiment in which they examined users' preferences when information was presented pictorially, verbally, or both. Users preferred to interact with a mixture of verbal and pictorial symbols. Presenting information in both forms may make contact easier with information the user already possesses. This in turn may make the user's responses more reliable.

Modularity

Modularity means that the representation should indicate the chunks into which the process can be decomposed. This is a feature that was extensively documented by Herbert Simon (1969), some of whose work we have already considered in Chapter 9. Simon illustrated the evolution of complex systems by means of what has since become the well-known *parable of the watchmakers*.

Two watchmakers, Hora and Tempus, each made high-quality watches. However, each built his watches using a different procedure. Tempus's procedure meant that if he was interrupted while he was working on a watch and had to put the watch down, then the watch would fall apart. He then had to start all over again because he built the watch as a single unit.

Hora, by contrast, had designed his watches so that they could be built in parts, or modules. He would complete each of 10 modules separately and then put the modules together to make a watch. This meant that if Hora was interrupted while he was working, he would not lose the entire watch but only the module on which he was working at the time.

The moral is that if a task is designed so that parts of it can first be completed and then the whole put together at the end, it will be much easier to complete the task than if the task requires completion in an all-or-none fashion. If a task cannot be decomposed into modules, then users may find themselves having always to keep in mind all the information relevant to the task, which may not be practical. In a task that can be decomposed into modules, the user can complete each part before moving on to the next. Of course, it is not enough for the task itself to be modular. In addition, the user interface should be constructed so that the user knows into what modules the task can be decomposed.

Consistency

Consistency is one of the most frequently cited properties of a good user interface (e.g., Carroll, 1997, p. 505; Green & Payne; 1984; Payne & Green, 1989; Shneiderman, 1998). Although difficult to define precisely, consistency is attractive because it appears to allow the user to be able to work out the correct responses in the absence of complete knowledge of the interface. With a consistent interface, the user need only understand a part of the interface in order to generate the whole range of possible interactions with the system. An inconsistent interface would be one in which actions had to be learned separately because there was no easily understood set of rules regulating the interface.

Here is a simple example. In Microsoft Word (2003), characters can be formatted by highlighting them and then pressing a key while holding down another key marked Ctrl (control). Thus, Ctrl + I makes italics, Ctrl + B makes bold. Based on these two examples, it looks like there might be a simple rule here: press Ctrl plus the first letter of the format name. Thus, what would you press to turn text into all capitals? Ctrl + C, right? Wrong. It turns out that Ctrl + C copies text. As Norman (1998, pp. 80–81) observed, in 1992 Microsoft Word had 311 commands, which at the time seemed like a lot. By 1997, the same program had 1,033 commands. Norman called this sort of progression **rampant featurism**. Not only will most users never need the majority of these commands, but it will be impossible to deduce what they are by learning a simple, consistent subset. The user will need to learn the majority of commands by sheer effort.

Although consistency would appear to be an obvious virtue for a user interface, there are also arguments in favour of introducing at least some **inconsistency** into the user interface. Grudin (1989) gave several examples in which consistency may be harmful. One example comes from the history of keyboards. As we saw earlier, there is no evidence that a consistent pattern of keys will be equally easy to learn and/or to use across all contexts and types of user. Grudin (1989, p. 1171) suggested that an interface may start out with a consistent design, but that inconsistency will need to be introduced as the user's task becomes better understood by designers. As a consistent system is used across different contexts, the requirements of the specific work situation will make it necessary to make modifications in a consistent system to suit the needs of individual users.

Grudin gave a simple, non-technical example to make this point. At first, it might seem reasonable to keep all of your knives in one drawer. There would be a single, consistent rule for knives that allowed you to find them. However, the things you do with knives are often very far removed from that drawer. You may have several different kinds of knives, such as a carving knife, a Swiss Army knife, a carpet knife, a bread knife, and you may find yourself storing each knife near the location in which it will be used. (I keep my Swiss Army knife in my jacket pocket, for example. I usually wear a jacket, and I never know when I will find the Swiss Army knife useful. If it is in my jacket pocket, then I am more likely to have it when I need it than if it is stored with all the other knives in a drawer in my house.) Storing knives in different places introduces inconsistency. But, as Grudin (1989) observed, 'we have made the knives easier to use by placing them according to how they are used, according to the tasks in which they are involved' (p. 1165).

The evolution of person–machine interface designs towards increasing inconsistency may very well take place as psychologists become more aware of the context in which the user works. As Carroll, Kellogg, and Rosson (1991) put it, 'Analyses of human activity [should] emphasize possibilities for self-regulation, and therein for greater engagement, satisfaction, growth, freedom, and dignity' (p. 83). There may be no single 'best' design, but a design may have to change according to the demands of individual users.

Books or Computers?

We have been hearing for years now about the inroads that computers have made into how people acquire information. One common belief has been that we were witnessing the end of the book as a source of information and pleasure. However, Noyes and Garland (2005) presented evidence that rumours of the death of the book may be premature. They compared attitudes towards books and computers in a large sample of British undergraduates. Their measuring instrument was adapted from an 'attitudes towards computers' questionnaire designed and validated by Kay (1989, 1993). Among the results was that the participants had positive attitudes towards both books and computers, but evaluated books more positively. One question was 'Which do you prefer to learn from?' Over half preferred books, under 5 per cent preferred computers, with the rest preferring to use both or neither. Another question was 'What level of learning from material presented on computers do you think you achieve?' Over 60 per cent said that the level of learning is less than that from books. Only 11 per cent thought it would be more, with the rest expecting it to be the same. Thus books are viewed more positively, are preferred for learning, and students believe that they learn more from them.

These participants were highly computer literate, so their preferences are not due to ignorance. Noyes and Garland considered and rejected the hypothesis that familiarity with books makes students view them more positively. You will recall from the last chapter that there is overwhelming evidence that familiarity breeds liking. Noyes and Garland believed that their participants were thoroughly familiar with computers and books, and used both frequently. However, it seems likely that these participants may still have experienced books *before* they experienced computers, either when they were being read to or learning to read. Therefore, there may be a primacy effect that is a source of a preference for books.

Whatever may be the ultimate source of the preference, Noyes and Garland point out that there are objective reasons for valuing books above computers. One is that books are still more portable than computers (e.g., they are easier to read on the subway). Documents are still easier to read on paper than on a screen. Furthermore, one can compare pages in a printed document much more easily than on a screen. Moreover, all one needs to do in order to use a book is know how to read. One must know more, sometimes much more, to use a computer successfully. It may be some time before people abandon books for computers, if, indeed, they ever do.

■ Learning by Design

As we discussed in the previous chapter, the role of *context* in determining our ability to recall what we have learned has been extensively documented. Memory is better if it takes place in a context similar to the one in which learning took place. Here is a practical example of such a context effect, adapted from Bjork and Richardson-Klavehn

(1989). Some people find that they excel in a course that taught them a skill that was valuable to their profession, but that they never attain the same level of performance on the job. Given the importance of context, how should we design training that would enable people to use their education in a practical setting?

It is important to realize that the effects of context can sometimes be adaptive and sometimes be disruptive. (Depending on the context!) They are adaptive to the extent that they lead us to recall information relevant to the current context (Bjork & Richardson-Klavehn, 1989, p. 314). Having learned something in one context we tend not to recall it in inappropriate contexts, but only in the context in which it is needed. Thus, context effects often serve to focus our recall in useful directions. However, context effects are not always benign. As Schmidt and Bjork (1992) observe, sometimes factors that facilitate learning can have a detrimental effect on subsequent performance, while factors that retard learning can enhance subsequent performance. This means, for example, that students who are quickest to acquire a skill may not be the ones who perform best on the job. Several studies have explored learning procedures that make a difference in performance over the long haul.

Massed versus Distributed Practice

One of the oldest and most reliable findings in psychology is that distributing your learning over several different sessions leads to better results than does cramming all your learning into a single session. This is called the **spacing effect**. Although there have been over 300 studies of this phenomenon since 1885 (Bruce & Bahrick, 1992), little is known about the optimal lengths between practice sessions. Bahrick and Hall (2005) attempted to remedy this state of affairs by having three groups of participants learn Swahili–English word pairs (e.g., *cloud–winghu*), with each group given different lengths of time between sessions. All participants were told that such pairs can be learned by repetition, by verbal elaboration, or by visual elaboration. All groups had four training sessions. One group had massed practice, with all sessions on the same day. Another group had each of their sessions spaced by one day. The third group had sessions 14 days apart. After each training session there was a test, and a final test was given 14 days after the last training session.

After one training session, all groups performed alike. The massed and one-day groups performed better than the 14-day group on tests 2–4. However, the performance of the first two groups declined on the final test, while the performance of the 14-day group kept improving. The performance of the massed practice group declined the most. The best long-term results came from the two groups receiving distributed practice.

Why does distributed practice work? Bahrick and Hall suggested that it is because spacing your practice gives you a better opportunity to discover what you do not know. Remember that the massed practice group did better during test 2–4 than did the 14-day group. The 14-day group experienced more failures to recall items during these tests. These failures are informative and allow learners to adjust the strategy they are using. The 14-day group reported more use of verbal and visual elaboration in the latter training sessions. This is evidence for a *metacognitive advantage* for spaced practice. Under conditions of distributed practice, learners are better able to discover what they will not be able to recall in the long term and can take appropriate steps to remedy this deficiency. Bahrick and Hall concluded that 'spaced retrieval failures preceding successful retrievals are more beneficial to long-term retention of difficult targets than are an equal number of massed, successful retrievals' (p. 576). Students must weigh the advantages of spaced practice against the fact that it requires more planning, but the long-term advantages are obvious.

Rereading as a Study Strategy

One of the simplest methods of studying is reading something over and over again. However, little was known about the effects of massed versus spaced rereading. This deficiency was remedied by Rawson and Kintsch (2005), who had participants read a *Scientific American* article. Some participants reread the article immediately after reading it for the first time (massed practice). Other participants reread the article seven days after reading it for the first time (distributed practice). Participants were tested for recall of the article either immediately after study or two days after study.

Massed practice led to better performance immediately after study, but distributed practice led to better results when testing was delayed. 'Given . . . that students are most likely to face delayed testing conditions in real educational settings, we would still recommend distributed study as the most effective rereading schedule for students' (Rawson & Kintsch, 2005, p. 79).

Random versus Systematic Practice

Intuitively, one thinks the best way to learn is to practise systematically. That is, break down a task into its parts, and then practise each part in turn. Once one part has been learned, then you would move on to another. Alternatively, one could practise each component in a random order. You would work on one part selected at random, then another part, again selected at random, never knowing from trial to trial what you would be working on next. Counterintuitively, it turns out that a skill can be acquired faster when learned systematically, but performance in the long run is better if the skill is acquired through random practice. This may be because the real world does not present itself in a nicely systematic fashion. **Random practice** leads to the ability to remember things in a way that real-world situations will require. Among the skills Schmidt and Bjork (1992) list as benefiting from random practice are keyboarding, arithmetic, and spelling.

Immediate versus Periodic Feedback

Intuitively, it would seem that receiving feedback immediately after every trial is the best way to learn. However, giving feedback only after several trials (e.g., Lavery, 1962) leads to better subsequent performance. Here again, the learning situation should teach the skills that the real-world situation will require, and people seldom receive continuous feedback on the job. Rather, they receive feedback periodically, and so a skill learned through **periodic feedback** will be better suited to real-world conditions.

Schmidt and Bjork (1992) mentioned that difficult tasks, such as learning a computer language, may particularly benefit from such a regime.

Successful versus Unsuccessful Metacognition

We saw in the last chapter that people often have **illusions of competence** in that they believe they will perform better than in fact they do. Benjamin, Bjork, and Schwartz (1998) suggested that one culprit is *retrieval fluency*, which is the ease with which information can be recalled. They pointed out that students are often certain that they are well prepared for an exam, only to later find out otherwise. This can be seen as a failure of metacognition, which, as we have seen, is the knowledge we have of the way that our cognitive processes work.

'Imagine a student preparing for an upcoming psychology exam by preparing flash cards that have an experiment name, authors, and year, on one side and the details of the appropriate research on the other. Further suppose that the student's gauge of learning is how quickly and easily she responds to the referential information of authors, and so forth, in recalling the details of the experiment' (Benjamin, Bjork, & Schwartz, 1998, p. 65). The student will experience retrieval fluency of the studied material, but will be unprepared for the exam if it requires the integration of information into an essay. The experience of retrieval fluency will be a misleading index of preparedness.

In a clever study, Koriat and Bjork (2005) investigated illusions of competence in the context of **judgements of learning**. They observed that there are different ways in which pairs of words can be seen as meaningfully related. Sometimes previously learned associations render word pairs meaningful. For example, the word *lamp* will elicit the word *light* as an association. If asked to learn the word pair *lamp–light*, participants will correctly predict that *light* will be easy to recall given *lamp* as the cue. Other word pairs are not associatively linked, but can be seen as meaningfully related anyway. For example, the word *find* does not elicit the word *seek* as an association. Nevertheless, participants asked to learn the word pair *find–seek* will incorrectly predict that it will be easy to recall *seek* given the word *find*. That is because *find* and *seek* can be meaningfully related when seen together. However, at the time of test, the word *find* is much more likely to elicit the word *lose*, with which it is more strongly associated.

Thus, sometimes judgements of learning lead to correct predictions, but other times they do not. Koriat and Bjork argued that there is a **foresight bias** that leads one to predict that one will be able to recall an answer when that answer is present. Thus, when shown *find–seek*, participants show a foresight bias in predicting that they will be able to recall *seek* given *find*, when in fact they are more likely to recall *lose*. Participants would have to monitor their learning in a more sophisticated way to avoid a foresight bias. They would have to realize that previous learning can sometimes interfere with what is currently being learned.

Although our metacognition is often flawed, there are cases in which it works reasonably well. Metcalfe and Kornell (2003, 2005) pointed out that our metacognition should enable us to allocate our study time appropriately, in such a way that we will be able to perform well in future situations. One possibility is that we should spend our time studying the material with which we have the most difficulty. Another possibility derives from the work of theorists such as Berlyne (who we considered in Chapter 13) and Vygotsky (who we considered in Chapter 8 on language). Berlyne believed that material of moderate difficulty attracted the most interest. In a similar vein, Vygotsky's concept of the *zone of proximal development* suggested that learning is optimal when we work on material that is just challenging enough, but not too challenging. The **region of proximal learning** model suggests that people will choose to work on material of moderate difficulty.

Metcalfe and Kornell (2003) reported a study in which participants were asked to learn English–Spanish word pairs (Metcalfe, 2002). Some pairs were easy in that the English word was similar to its Spanish equivalent (e.g., *fantastico–fantastic*). Some were moderately difficult, in that other words in English might give you a clue (e.g., *brillantez–brightness*). Others were obviously difficult (e.g., *arandano–cranberry*). Participants were allowed to allocate their study time to whichever items they wished. It turned out that more study time was allocated to items of intermediate difficulty. However, as the experiment progressed participants began to increasingly study more difficult items. Thus, the region of proximal learning is dynamic and not fixed. Once people are comfortable with items of intermediate difficulty, they can graduate to studying more difficult items.

The region of proximal learning model describes the way in which people's learning progresses. Of course, people may make erroneous judgements of learning, and as a result stop studying items that they should continue to work on. Thus, the model appears successful in explaining what people actually do when they study, but that does not mean that this process is what they should do (Metcalfe & Kornell, 2005, p. 476). It could be that there are better strategies awaiting discovery, or it could even be that a strategy focused on region of proximal learning is indeed optimal. If so, then this would be an instance in which people's metacognition is working well.

■ Questions for Study and Discussion

1. Discuss some common sources of human error. Are errors completely preventable? Why or why not?

2. What is cognitive ergonomics? Discuss its limitations with respect to keyboards and mobile phones.

3. What is Fitts's law? Discuss its importance for the use of pointing devices.

4. Why do we need instructions for some devices? What features should instructions have?

5. How should we present information so as to make it less misleading than it often is?

6. Discuss the process of searching for information in terms of information foraging theory.

7. Review the important issues involved in designing a user interface. Pay particular attention to the role that *consistency* may play in the design process.

8. What is the role of metacognition in a successful study strategy? What errors should we try to avoid?

■ Key Concepts

Activation-trigger-schema theory There can be several different schemas for different kinds of action, and more than one schema can be activated at any one time. Schemas may be inappropriately activated, resulting in attentional errors.

Affordances The potential functions of an object.

Asymmetry between understanding and prediction One can understand something extremely well and yet not be able to predict its future occurrence. Conversely, one can predict something reasonably well, without having a very good understanding of why those predictions work.

Capture errors Errors that occur when a familiar schema captures behaviour in the place of an unfamiliar one.

Cleopatra's nose problem One can invent any number of hypothetical events that *might* have changed the course of history without any certainty of being able to predict any future occurrences.

Cognitive ergonomics The combination of cognitive psychology and ergonomics used to understand the person/machine interface.

Concurrent processes Many different processes going on at the same time but that terminate at different times.

Consistency The degree to which a user need only understand a part of the interface in order to generate the whole range of possible interactions with the system.

Description errors Errors that occur because we do not have a detailed enough understanding of our situation.

Ergonomics The study of people in relation to their working environment.

Fitts's law Specifies the difficulty of moving a stylus to a target. Obviously, this difficulty will vary as the distance to the target varies. The further the stylus has to be moved, the more difficult the task. It will also vary as the

size of the target varies. The narrower the target the more difficult it will be to hit it.

Foresight bias The tendency to believe that you will be able to recall something later if it is present now.

Illusions of competence People often believe that they will perform better than in fact they do.

Importance of inconsistency The requirements of the specific work situation that make it necessary to make modifications in a consistent system to suit the needs of individual users.

Information diet Created by initially examining a large number of possible sources of information in a cursory manner and rejecting those that do not look promising.

Information foraging A process analogous to that engaged in by animals when they forage for food. A successful foraging strategy will return the most task-relevant information with a minimum of effort.

Information scents Just as predators follow the scents of their prey, people follow imperfect clues to the information they seek.

Informavore A species that hungers for information in order to gather it and store it as a means for adapting to the world.

Judgements of learning The judgement, often wrong, that you have learned something and will be able to recall it later.

Mode errors Carrying out an action that would be appropriate for one situation, but not for the situation in which we happen to find ourselves.

Modularity The degree to which a representation indicates the chunks into which the process can be decomposed.

Oops, I did it again effect A habitual sequence of action continues to operate without much attention, and a newer, intended action sequence never gets activated.

Periodic feedback A skill learned through

periodic feedback will be better suited to real-world conditions.

Population impact number The number of people in the population among whom one event will be prevented by an intervention within that entire population, e.g., the ratio of mammography preventing death from breast cancer is 1:1,000.

Problem-centred versus method-centred Cognitive psychology can be so concerned with doing methodologically correct studies that it loses sight of the practical problems that need to be addressed. However, a problem-centred cognitive psychology runs the risk of methodological sloppiness. Applied cognitive psychology requires a delicate balance between being problem-centred and being method-centred.

Rampant featurism The tendency for the features of interfaces to expand beyond necessity.

Random practice A skill can be acquired faster when learned systematically, but performance in the long run is better if the skill is acquired through random practice.

Recognition The degree to which a user can recognize what process is occurring.

Region of proximal learning The theory that people will choose to work on material of moderate difficulty.

Spacing effect The distribution of learning over several different sessions, which leads to better results than does cramming all learning into a single session.

Statistical graphics Presenting data in a visual form that is not only readily understood but also enables the user to draw the correct inferences.

Textish Because the keypad on a mobile phone is so difficult to use for typing text, text messages are often written in a special code.

User interface The relationship between the person and the machine being used to perform a task.

■ Links to Other Chapters

Activation-trigger-schema theory
Chapter 4 (schema theories of memory)
Textish
Chapter 8 (social context of language)
Affordances
Chapter 2 (ecological validity)
Modularity
Chapter 1 (cognition as a faculty)

Chapter 7 (folk biology)
Chapter 10 (domain-specific reasoning)
Illusions of competence
Chapter 9 (insight is involuntary)
Chapter 13 (self-deception)
Region of proximal learning
Chapter 8 (social context of language)

■ Further Reading

Some of the risks attendant upon using phones while driving are considered in Spence, C., & Read, L. (2003). Speech shadowing while driving. *Psychological Science, 14*, 251–256.

A clever analysis of a common error in cognitive psychology is Bedford, F.L. (1997). False categories in cognition: The Not-The-Liver fallacy. *Cognition, 64*, 231–248.

The philosophical implications of the concept of affordances are considered in Scarantino, A. (2003). Affordances explained. *Philosophy of Science, 70*, 949–961.

An intriguing overview of the importance of graphs in psychology is Smith, L.D., Best, L.A., Stubbs, D.A., Archibald, A.B., & Roberson-Nay, R. (2002). Constructing knowledge: The role of graphs in hard and soft psychology. *American Psychologist, 57*, 749–761.

Some of the obstacles to creating transparent user interfaces are illustrated nicely in Condon, C., Perry, M., & O'Keefe, R. (2004). Denotation and connotation in the human computer interface: The 'Save as . . .' command. *Behavior and Information Technology, 23*, 21–31.

More on strategies for learning is in Simon, D.A., & Bjork, R.A. (2002). Models of performance in learning multisegment movement tasks: Consequences for acquisition, retention, and judgments of learning. *Journal of Experimental Psychology: Applied, 8*, 222–232; and Goodman, J.S., & Wood, R.L. (2004). Feedback specificity, learning opportunities, and learning. *Journal of Applied Psychology, 89*, 809–821. The role of feedback in learning is explored by Pashler, H., Cepeda, N.J., Wixted, J.T., & Rohrer, D. (2005). When does feedback facilitate learning of words? *Journal of Experimental Psychology: Learning, Memory, and Cognition, 31*, 3–8.

References

Abraham, C. (2004, Dec. 4). Marooned in the moment. *The Globe and Mail*, pp. F1, F4–F5.

Ackerman, P.L., Beier, M.E., & Boyle, M.O. (2005). Working memory and intelligence: The same or different constructs? *Psychological Bulletin, 31*, 30–60.

Adelson, R. (2005). Hues and views: A cross-cultural study reveals how language shapes color perception. *Monitor on Psychology, 36.* Retrieved March 23, 2005, from APA Online, at: www.apa.orgmonitor/feb05/hues.html

Alaimo, C. (1996a, December 2). No ordinary sales pitch. *St. Catharines Standard*, p. B1.

Alaimo, C. (1996b, November 4). A rags to fishes story. *St. Catharines Standard*, p. D1.

Alba, J.W., & Hasher, L. (1983). Is memory schematic? *Psychological Bulletin, 93*, 203–231.

Allen, R., & Reber, A.S. (1980). Very long term memory for tacit knowledge. *Cognition, 8*, 175–186.

Allis, L.V., van den Herik, H.J., & Huntjens, H.J. (1996). Go-Moku solved by new search techniques. *Computational Intelligence, 12*, 7–23.

Allport, D.A. (1980). Attention and performance. In G. Claxton (Ed.), *New directions in cognitive psychology* (pp. 26–64). London: Routledge & Kegan Paul.

Allport, D.A., Styles, E.A., & Hsieh, S. (1994). Shifting intentional set: Exploring the dynamic control of tasks. In C. Umiltà & M. Moscovitch (Eds.), *Attention and performance XV: Conscious and unconscious information processing* (pp. 421–452). Cambridge, Mass.: MIT Press.

Altmann, G.T.M. (2001). The language machine: psycholinguistics in review. *British Journal of Psychology, 92*, 129–170.

Anastasi, A. (1965). *Individual differences.* New York: Wiley.

Anderson, C.A., & Bushman, B.J. (1997). External validity of 'trivial' experiments: The case of laboratory aggression. *Journal of General Psychology, 1*, 19–41.

Anderson, J.R. (1976). *Language, memory and thought.* Hillsdale, NJ: Erlbaum.

Anderson, J.R. (1978). Arguments concerning representations for mental imagery. *Psychological Review, 85*, 249–277.

Anderson, J.R. (1983). *The architecture of cognition.* Cambridge, Mass.: Harvard University Press.

Anderson, J.R. (1984). Spreading activation. In J.R. Anderson & S.M. Kosslyn (Eds.), *Tutorials in learning and memory* (pp. 61–90). San Francisco: Freeman.

Anderson, J.R., Bothell, D., & Douglass, S. (2004). Eye movements do not reflect retrieval processes. *Psychological Science, 15*, 225–231.

Anderson, J.R., & Bower, G.H. (1973). *Human associative memory.* Washington: Hemisphere Press.

Anderson, J.R., & Reder, L.M. (1999). The fan effect: New results and new theories. *Journal of Experimental Psychology: General, 128*, 186–197.

Anderson, R.C., & Pichert, J.W. (1978). Recall of previously unrecallable information following a shift in perspective. *Journal of Verbal Learning and Verbal Behavior, 17*, 1–12.

Andrews, P.W., Gangestad, S.W., & Matthews, D. (2002). Adaptationism—how to carry out an exaptationist program. *Behavioral and Brain Sciences, 25*, 489–553.

Anzai, Y., & Simon, H.A. (1979). The theory of

learning by doing. *Psychological Review, 86,* 124–140.

Armstrong, S.L., Gleitman, L.R., & Gleitman, H. (1983). What some concepts might not be. *Cognition, 13,* 263–308.

Arrington, C.M., & Logan, G.D. (2004). The cost of a voluntary task switch. *Psychological Science, 15,* 610–615.

Asch, S.E. (1946). Forming impressions of personality. *Journal of Abnormal and Social Psychology, 41,* 258–290.

Asch, S.E. (1955). On the use of metaphor in the description of persons. In H. Werner (Ed.), *On expressive language* (pp. 29–38). Worcester, Mass.: Clark University Press.

Asch, S.E. (1958). The metaphor: A psychological inquiry. In R. Tagiuri & L. Petrillo (Eds.), *Person perception and interpersonal behavior* (pp. 86–94). Stanford, Calif.: Stanford University Press.

Asch, S.E. (1969). A reformulation of the problem of associations. *American Psychologist, 24,* 92–102.

Asch, S.E., & Ebenholtz, S.M. (1962). The principle of associative symmetry. *Proceedings of the American Philosophical Society, 106,* 135–163.

Asch, S.E., & Nerlove, H. (1960). The development of double function terms in children. In H. Wapner & B. Kaplan (Eds.), *Perspectives in psychological theory* (pp. 41–60). New York: International Universities Press.

Asch, S.E., & Zukier, H. (1984). Thinking about persons. *Journal of Personality and Social Psychology, 6,* 1230–1240.

Ashby, F.G., & Casale, M.B. (2003). A model of dopamine modulated cortical activation. *Neural Networks, 16,* 973–984.

Ashby, F.G., Isen, A.M., & Turken, A.U. (1999). A neuropsychological theory of positive affect and its influence on cognition. *Psychological Review, 106,* 529–550.

Atkinson, R.C., & Shiffrin, R.M. (1968). Human memory: A proposed system and its control processes. In K.W. Spence & J.T. Spence (Eds.), *The psychology of learning and motivation.* (Vol. 2, pp. 89–105). New York: Academic Press.

Atkinson, R.C., & Shiffrin, R.M. (1971). The control of short-term memory. *Scientific American, 225,* 82–90.

Atran, S. (1999). Folk biology. In R. Wison & F. Keil (Eds.), *The MIT encyclopedia of the cognitive sciences* (pp. 316–317). Cambridge, Mass.: MIT Press.

Atran, S. (2005). Adaptationism for human cognition: Strong, spurious or weak? *Mind and Language, 20,* 39–67.

Atran, S., Medin, D., & Ross, N. (2004). Evolution and evolution of knowledge: A tale of two biologies. *Journal of the Royal Anthropological Institute, 10,* 395–420.

Attance, C.M., & O'Neill, D.K. (2001). Episodic future thinking. *Trends in Cognitive Sciences, 5,* 533–539.

Baars, B.J. (1986). *The cognitive revolution in psychology.* New York: Guilford Press.

Baars, B.J. (1992). *Experimental slips and human error: Exploring the architecture of volition.* New York: Plenum Press.

Baars, B.J. (2002). The conscious access hypothesis: origins and recent evidence. *Trends in Cognitive Sciences, 6,* 47–52.

Baddeley, A.D. (1978). The trouble with levels: A re-examination of Craik and Lockhart's framework for memory research. *Psychological Review, 85,* 139–152.

Baddeley, A.D. (1986). *Working memory.* Oxford: Oxford University Press.

Baddeley, A.D. (1987a). Amnesia. In R.L. Gregory (Ed.), *The Oxford companion to the mind* (pp. 20–22). Oxford: Oxford University Press.

Baddeley, A.D. (1987b). Memory and context. In R.L. Gregory (Ed.), *The Oxford companion to the mind* (pp. 463–464). Oxford: Oxford University Press.

Baddeley, A.D. (1989). The psychology of remembering and forgetting. In T. Butler (Ed.), *Memory: History, culture and mind* (pp. 36–60). Oxford: Blackwell.

Baddeley, A.D. (2000a). Short-term and working memory. In E. Tulving & F.I.M. Craik (Eds.), *The Oxford handbook of memory* (pp. 77–92). New York: Oxford University Press.

Baddeley, A.D. (2000b). The episodic buffer: A

new component of working memory? *Trends in Cognitive Sciences, 11*, 417–423.

Baddeley, A.D. (2001). The concept of episodic memory. *Philosophical Transactions of the Royal Society (Series B), 356*, 1345–1350.

Baddeley, A.D. (2002a). Fractionating the central executive. In D.T. Stuss and R.T. Knight (Eds.), *Principles of frontal lobe function* (pp. 246–260). New York: Oxford University Press.

Baddeley, A.D. (2002b). Is working memory still working? *European Psychologist, 7*, 85–97.

Baddeley, A.D. (2003a). Working memory and language: An overview. *Journal of Communication Disorders, 36*, 189–203.

Baddeley, A.D. (2003b). Working memory: Looking back and looking forward. *Nature Reviews Neuroscience, 4*, 829–839.

Baddeley, A.D., & Hitch, G.J. (1974). Working memory. In G. Bower (Ed.), *Recent advances in learning and motivation* (Vol. 8, pp. 47–89). New York: Academic Press.

Bahrick, H.P. (1984). Semantic memory in permastore: Fifty years of memory for Spanish learned in school. *Journal of Experimental Psychology: General, 113*, 1–31.

Bahrick, H.P. (2000). Long-term maintenance of knowledge. In E. Tulving & F.I.M. Craik (Eds.). *The Oxford handbook of memory* (pp. 347–362). New York: Oxford University Press.

Bahrick, H.P., & Hall, L.K. (1991). Lifetime maintenance of high school mathematics content. *Journal of Experimental Psychology: General, 120*, 20–33.

Bahrick, H.P., & Hall, L.K. (2005). The importance of retrieval failures to long-term retention: A metacognitive explanation of the spacing effect. *Journal of Memory and Language, 52*, 566–577.

Bahrick, H.P., Hall, L.K., & Berger, S.A. (1996). Accuracy and distortion in memory for high school grades. *Psychological Science, 5*, 265–271.

Bailey, M.E.S., & Johnson, K.J. (1997). Synaesthesia: Is genetic analysis feasible? In S. Baron-Cohen & J.E. Harrison (Eds.), *Synaes-thesia: Classic and contemporary readings* (pp. 182–207). Oxford: Blackwell.

Baker, M.C. (2003). Linguistic differences and language design. *Trends in Cognitive Sciences, 7*, 349–353.

Baldwin, J.M. (1897). *Mental development of the child and the race* (2nd ed.). New York: Macmillan.

Ballard, P.B. (1913). Oblivescence and reminiscence. *British Journal of Psychology Monograph Supplements, 1*, 1–82.

Bamberger, J. (1982). Growing up prodigies: The mid-life crisis. In D.H. Feldman (Ed.), *Developmental approaches to giftedness* (pp. 61–77). San Francisco: Jossey-Bass.

Bamberger, J. (1986). Cognitive issues in the development of musically gifted children. In R.J. Sternberg & J. Davidson (Eds.), *Conceptions of giftedness* (pp. 388–413). New York: Cambridge University Press.

Banaji, M.R., & Crowder, R.G. (1989). The bankruptcy of everyday memory. *American Psychologist, 44*, 1185–1193.

Bar, M. (2004). Visual objects in context. *Nature Reviews Neuroscience, 5*, 617–629.

Barber, P. (1988). *Applied cognitive psychology.* New York: Methuen.

Barnard, P.J., Scott, S., Taylor, J., May, J., & Knightley, W. (2004). Paying attention to meaning. *Psychological Science, 15*, 179–186.

Barrett, L.F., Tugade, M.M., & Engle, R.W. (2004). Individual differences in working memory capacity and dual-process theories of mind. *Psychological Review, 130*, 553–573.

Barron, F. (1963). The disposition toward originality. In C.W. Taylor & F. Barron (Eds.), *Scientific creativity: Its recognition and development* (pp. 139–152). New York: Wiley.

Barron, S. (2005, July 24). R we D8ting? *New York Times*. Accessed July 24, 2005.

Barsalou, L.W. (1983). Ad hoc categories. *Memory & Cognition, 11*, 211–227.

Barsalou, L.W. (1987). The instability of graded structure: Implications for the nature of concepts. In U. Neisser (Ed.), *Concepts and conceptual development* (pp. 101–140). Cambridge: Cambridge University Press.

Barsalou, L.W. (1999). Perceptual symbol systems. *Behavioral and Brain Sciences, 22,* 577–660.

Barsalou, L.W. (2003). Abstraction in perceptual symbol systems. *Philosophical Transactions of the Royal Society of London (Series B), 358,* 1177–1187.

Barsalou, L.W., Simmons, W.K., Barbey, A.K., & Wilson, C.D. (2003). Grounding conceptual knowledge in modality-specific systems. *Trends in Cognitive Sciences, 7,* 84–91.

Barsalou, L.W., Solomon, K.O., & Wu, L.L. (1999). Perceptual simulation in conceptual tasks. In M.K. Hiraga, C. Sinha, & S. Wilcox (Eds.), *Cultural, typological, and psychological perspectives in cognitive linguistics: The proceedings of the 4th conference of the International Cognitive Linguistics Association: Vol. 3* (pp. 209–228). Amsterdam: John Benjamins.

Bartlett, F.C. (1932). *Remembering.* Cambridge: Cambridge University Press.

Bartlett, F.C. (1958). *Thinking: An experimental and social study.* New York: Basic Books.

Baumeister, R.F. (1984). Choking under pressure: Self-consciousness and paradoxical effects of incentives on skillful performance. *Journal of Personality and Social Psychology, 46,* 610–620.

Baumeister, R.F., Bratslavsky, E., Finkenhauer, C., & Vohs, K.D. (2001). Bad is stronger than good. *Review of General Psychology, 5,* 323–370.

Bavalier, D., Corina, D., Jezzard, P., Padmanabhan, S., Clark, V.P., Karni, A., Prinster, A., Braun, A., Lalwani, A., Rauschecker, J.P., Turner, R., & Neville, H. (1997). Sentence reading: A functional MRI study at 4 Tesla. *Journal of Cognitive Neuroscience. 9,* 664–686.

Beck, J. (Ed.). (1982). *Organization and representation in perception.* Hillsdale, NJ: Erlbaum.

Begg, I. (1982). Imagery, organization and discriminative processes. *Canadian Journal of Psychology, 36,* 273–290.

Begg, I. (1987). Some. *Canadian Journal of Psychology, 41,* 62–73.

Begg, I., & Denny, J.P. (1969). Empirical reconciliation of atmosphere and conversion interpretations of syllogistic reasoning errors. *Journal of Experimental Psychology, 81,* 351–354.

Begg, I., & Harris, G. (1982). On the interpretation of syllogisms. *Journal of Verbal Learning and Verbal Behavior, 21,* 595–620.

Benjafield, J. (1969a). Evidence that 'thinking aloud' constitutes an externalization of inner speech. *Psychonomic Science, 15,* 83–84.

Benjafield, J. (1969b). Logical and empirical thinking in a problem-solving task. *Psychonomic Science, 14,* 285–286.

Benjafield, J. (1983). Some psychological hypotheses concerning the evolution of constructs. *British Journal of Psychology, 74,* 47–59.

Benjafield, J. (1987). An historical, social analysis of imagery and concreteness. *British Journal of Social Psychology, 26,* 155–164.

Benjafield, J., & Adams-Webber, J. (1976). The Golden Section hypothesis. *British Journal of Psychology, 67,* 11–15.

Benjafield, J., & Giesbrecht, L. (1973). Context effects and the recall of comparative sentences. *Memory & Cognition, 1,* 133–136.

Benjafield, J., & Green, T.R.G. (1978). Golden Section relations in interpersonal judgement. *British Journal of Psychology, 69,* 25–35.

Benjafield, J., & Segalowitz, S. (1993). Left and right in Leonardo's drawings of faces. *Empirical Studies of the Arts, 11,* 25–32.

Benjamin, A.S., Bjork, R.A., & Schwartz, B.L. (1998). The mismeasure of memory: When retrieval fluency is misleading as a metamnemonic index. *Journal of Experimental Psychology: General, 127,* 55–68.

Bergman, E.T., & Roediger, H.L. (1997). Can Bartlett's repeated reproduction experiments be replicated? *Memory & Cognition, 27,* 937–947.

Berk, L.E. (1994, November). Why children talk to themselves. *Scientific American, 271,* 78–83.

Berlin, B., Breedlove, D.E., & Raven, P.H. (1973). General principles of classification and nomenclature in folk biology. *American Anthropologist, 89,* 914–920.

Berlin, B., & Kay, P. (1969). *Basic color terms: Their universality and evolution.* Berkeley: University of California Press.

Berlyne, D.E. (1965). *Structure and direction in thinking*. New York: Wiley.

Berlyne, D.E. (1971). *Aesthetics and psychobiology*. New York: Appleton-Century-Crofts.

Bernstein, L. (1976). *The unanswered question*. Cambridge, Mass.: Harvard University Press.

Berntsen, D., & Rubin, D.C. (2002). Emotionally charged autobiographical memories across the life span: The recall of happy, sad, traumatic, and involuntary memories. *Psychology and Aging, 17*, 636–652.

Berntsen, D., & Rubin, D.C. (2004). Cultural life scripts structure recall from autobiographical memory. *Memory & Cognition, 32*, 427–442.

Berry, D.C., & Dienes, Z. (1991). The relationship between implicit memory and implicit learning. *British Journal of Psychology, 82*, 359–373.

Best, J.B. (2001). Conditional reasoning processes in a logical deduction game. *Thinking and Reasoning, 7*, 235–254

Betsch, T., Haberstroh, S., Molter, B., & Glöckner, A. (2004). Oops, I did it again—relapse errors in routinized decision-making. *Organizational Behavior and Human Decision Processes, 93*, 62–74.

Bianchi, M. (2002). Novelty, preferences, and fashion: When goods are unsettling. *Journal of Economic Behavior & Organization, 47*, 1–18.

Bielock, S.L., Carr, T.H., MacMahon, C., & Starkes, J.L. (2002). When paying attention becomes counterproductive: Impact of divided versus skill-focused attention on novice and experienced performance of sensorimotor skills. *Journal of Experimental Psychology: Applied, 8*, 6–16

Bigelow, P. (1986). The indeterminability of time in 'Sein und Zeit'. *Philosophy and Phenomenological Research, 46*, 357–379.

Binet, A., & Simon, T. (1965). New methods for the diagnosis of the intellectual level of subnormals. In A. Anastasi (Ed.), *Individual differences* (pp. 35–41). New York: Wiley. (Original work published 1905b).

Binet, A., & Simon, T. (1965). The development of intelligence in the child. In A. Anastasi (Ed.), *Individual differences* (pp. 41–44). New York: Wiley. (Original work published 1908).

Binet, A., & Simon, T. (1965). Upon the necessity of establishing a scientific diagnosis of inferior states of intelligence. In A. Anastasi (Ed.), *Individual differences* (pp. 30–34). New York: Wiley. (Original work published 1905a).

Binet, A., & Simon, T. (1915). *A method of measuring the development of the intelligence of young children* (C.H. Town, trans.). Chicago: Chicago Medical Books. (Original work published 1911).

Binkofski, F., Amunts, K., Stephan, K.M., Posse, S., Schormann, T., Freund, H.J., Zilles, K., & Seitz, R.J. (2000). Broca's region subserves imagery of motion: A combined cytoarchitectonic and fMRI study. *Human Brain Mapping, 11*, 273–285.

Birnbaum, M.H., & Mellers, B.A. (1979). Stimulus recognition may mediate exposure effects. *Journal of Personality and Social Psychology, 37*, 391–394.

Birnboim, S. (2003). The automatic and controlled information-processing dissociation: Is it still relevant? *Neuropsychology Review, 13*, 19–31.

Bjork, R.A., & Richardson-Klavehn, A. (1989). On the puzzling relationship between environmental context and memory. In C. Izawa (Ed.), *Current issues in cognitive processes* (pp. 313–344). Hillsdale, NJ: Erlbaum.

Black, M. (1962). Linguistic relativity: The views of Benjamin Lee Whorf. In M. Black (Ed.), *Models and metaphors* (pp. 244–257). Ithaca, NY: Cornell University Press.

Blair, C., Gamson, D., Thorne, S., & Baker, D. (2005). Rising mean IQ: Cognitive demand of mathematics education for young children, population exposure to formal schooling, and the neurobiology of the prefrontal cortex. *Intelligence, 33*, 96–106.

Blaney, P.H. (1986). Affect and memory: A review. *Psychological Bulletin, 99*, 229–246.

Bloom, A. (1981). *The linguistic shaping of thought*. Hillsdale, NJ: Erlbaum.

Bloom, P., & Keil, F.C. (2001). Thinking through language. *Mind & Language, 16*, 351–367.

Blumenthal, A.L. (1970). *Language and psychology*. New York: Wiley.

Blumenthal, A.L. (1977). *The process of cognition.* Englewood Cliffs, NJ: Prentice-Hall.

Bodner, G.E., & Masson, M.E.J. (2003). Beyond spreading activation: An influence of relatedness proportion on masked semantic priming. *Psychonomic Bulletin & Review, 10,* 645–652.

Bohannon, J.N. (1988). Flashbulb memories for the space shuttle disaster: A tale of two theories. *Cognition, 29,* 179–196.

Borges, B., Goldstein, D.G., Ortmann, A., & Gigerenzer, G. (1999). Can ignorance beat the stock market? In G. Gigerenzer, P.M. Todd, & the ABC Research Group (Eds.), *Simple heuristics that make us smart* (pp. 59–72). New York: Oxford University Press.

Borges, J. (1966). *Other inquisitions.* New York: Washington Square Press.

Bornstein, R.F. (1989). Exposure and affect: Overview and meta-analysis of research, 1968–1987. *Psychological Bulletin, 106,* 265–289.

Bornstein, R.F., & D'Agostino, P.R. (1992). Stimulus recognition and the mere exposure effect. *Journal of Personality and Social Psychology, 63,* 545–552.

Boucher, J., & Osgood, C.E. (1969). The Pollyanna hypothesis. *Journal of Verbal Learning and Verbal Behavior, 8,* 1–8.

Bourne, L.E. (1966). *Human conceptual behavior.* Boston: Allyn & Bacon.

Bower, G.H. (1970a). Analysis of a mnemonic device. *American Scientist, 58,* 496–510.

Bower, G.H. (1970b). Imagery as a relational organizer in paired-associate learning. *Journal of Verbal Learning and Verbal Behavior, 9,* 529–533.

Bower, G.H. (1981). Mood and memory. *American Psychologist, 26,* 129–148.

Bower, G.H., & Morrow, D.G. (1990). Mental models in narrative comprehension. *Science, 247,* 44–48.

Boylin, W., Gordon, S.K., & Nehrke, M.F. (1976). Reminiscing and ego integrity in institutionalized elderly males. *Gerontologist, 16,* 118–124.

Bradley, D.R., & Petry, H.M. (1977). Organizational determinants of subjective contour: The subjective Necker cube. *American Journal of Psychology, 90,* 253–262.

Braine, M.D.S. (1978). On the relation between the natural logic of reasoning and standard logic. *Psychological Review, 85,* 1–21.

Brandimonte, M.A., & Gerbino, W. (1993). Mental reversal and verbal recoding: When ducks become rabbits. *Memory & Cognition, 21,* 23–33.

Bransford, J.D., & Franks, J. (1971). The abstraction of linguistic ideas. *Cognitive Psychology, 2,* 331–350.

Brefczynski, J.A., & Yoe, E.A. (1999). A physiological correlate of the 'spotlight' of visual attention. *Nature Neuroscience, 2,* 370–374.

Bregman, A.S. (1977). Perception and behavior as compositions of ideals. *Cognitive Psychology, 9,* 250–292.

Brentano, F.C. (1874). *Psychologie von dem Empirischen Standpunkt* [Psychology from an empirical standpoint]. Leipzig: Duncker & Humblot.

Broadbent, D.E. (1980). The minimization of models. In A.J. Chapman & D.M. Jones (Eds.), *Models of man* (pp. 113–128). Leicester: British Psychological Society.

Broadbent, D.E. (1984). The Maltese cross: A new simplistic model for memory. *Behavioral and Brain Sciences, 7,* 55–94.

Broadbent, D.E. (1990). A problem looking for solutions. *Psychological Science, 1,* 240–246.

Broadbent, D.E. (1992). Listening to one of two synchronous messages. *Journal of Experimental Psychology, General, 121,* 51–55. (Original work published 1952).

Broca, P. (1966). Paul Broca on the speech center. In R. Herrnstein & E. Boring (Eds.), *A source book in the history of psychology* (pp. 223–229). Cambridge, Mass.: Harvard University Press. (Original work published 1861).

Brockmole, J.R., Wang, R.F., & Irwin, D.E. (2002). Temporal integration between visual images and visual percepts. *Journal of Experimental Psychology: Human Perception and Performance, 28,* 315–334.

Brody, N. (2003a). Construct validation of the

Sternberg Triarchic Abilities Test: Comment and reanalysis. *Intelligence, 31,* 319–324.

Brody, N. (2003b). What Sternberg should have concluded. *Intelligence, 31,* 339–342.

Brokate, B., Hildebrandt, H., Eling, P., Fichtner, H., Runge, K., & Timm, C. (2003). Frontal lobe dysfunctions in Korsakoff's syndrome and chronic alcoholism: Continuity or discontinuity? *Neuropsychology, 17,* 420–428.

Brooks, J.O., & Watkins, M.J. (1989). Recognition memory and the mere exposure effect. *Journal of Experimental Psychology: Learning, Memory, and Cognition, 15,* 968–976.

Brooks, L.R. (1968). Spatial and verbal components of the act of recall. *Canadian Journal of Psychology, 22,* 349–368.

Brown, A.S. (1991). A review of the tip-of-the-tongue experience. *Psychological Bulletin, 109,* 204–223.

Brown, A.S. (2003). A review of the déjà vu experience. *Psychological Bulletin, 129,* 394–413.

Brown, A.S., Bracken, E., Zoccoli, S., Douglas, K. (2004). Generating and remembering passwords. *Applied Cognitive Psychology, 18,* 641–651.

Brown, J. (1958). Some tests of the decay theory of immediate memory. *Quarterly Journal of Experimental Psychology, 10,* 12–21.

Brown, R. (1968). *Words and things.* New York: Free Press.

Brown, R. (1973). *A first language.* Cambridge, Mass.: Harvard University Press.

Brown, R., & Hanlon, C. (1970). Derivational complexity and the order of acquisition in child speech. In J.R. Hayes (Ed.), *Cognition and the development of language* (pp. 11–53). New York: Wiley.

Brown, R., & Kulik, J. (1977). Flashbulb memories. *Cognition, 5,* 73–99.

Brown, R., & Lenneberg, E. (1956). A study in language and cognition. *Journal of Abnormal and Social Psychology, 49,* 454–462.

Brown, R., & McNeill, D. (1966). The 'tip of the tongue phenomenon'. *Journal of Verbal Learning and Verbal Behavior, 5,* 325–337.

Brown, S.C., & Craik, F.I.M. (2000). Encoding and retrieval of information. In E. Tulving &

F.I.M. Craik (Eds.), *The Oxford handbook of memory* (pp. 93–107). New York: Oxford University Press.

Bruce, D. (1985). The how and why of ecological memory. *Journal of Experimental Psychology: General, 114,* 78–90.

Bruce, D. (1986). Lashley's shift from bacteriology to neuropsychology, 1910–1917, and the influence of Jennings, Watson, and Franz. *Journal of the History of the Behavioral Sciences, 22,* 27–43.

Bruce, D., & Bahrick, H.P. (1992). Perceptions of past research. *American Psychologist, 47,* 319–328.

Bruner, J.S. (1983). *Child's talk.* New York: Norton.

Bruner, J.S. (1985). Vygotsky: A historical and conceptual perspective. In J. Wertsch (Ed.), *Culture, communication and cognition* (pp. 21–34). Cambridge: Cambridge University Press.

Bruner, J.S., Goodnow, J.J., & Austin, G.A. (1956). *A study of thinking.* New York: Wiley.

Brunswik, E. (1956). *Perception and the representative design of experiments.* Berkeley: University of California Press.

Bryant, D.J., Tversky, B., & Franklin, N. (1992). Internal and external spatial frameworks for representing described scenes. *Journal of Memory and Language, 31,* 74–98.

Burke, D.M., MacKay, D.G., Worthley, J.S., & Wade, E. (1991). On the tip of the tongue: What causes word finding failures in young and older adults? *Journal of Memory and Language, 30,* 542–579.

Burns, B.D. (2004). Heuristics as beliefs and behaviors: The adaptiveness of the 'hot hand'. *Cognitive Psychology, 48,* 295–331.

Burns, B.D., & Weith, M. (2004). The collider principle in causal reasoning: Why the Monty Hall dilemma is so hard. *Journal of Experimental Psychology: General, 133,* 414–449.

Cabeza, R., & Nyberg, L. (2003). Special issue on functional neuroimaging of memory. *Neuropsychologia, 41,* 241–244.

Cacioppo, J.T., Berntson, G.G., Lorig, T.S., Norris, C.J., Rickett, E., & Nusbaum, H. (2003). Just because you're imaging the brain doesn't mean you can stop using your head: A primer and set of first principles. *Journal of Personality and Social Psychology, 85*, 650–661.

Campbell, D.T. (1960). Blind variation and selective retention in creative thought as in other knowledge processes. *Psychological Bulletin, 67*, 380–400.

Campbell, M., Hoane, A.J., & Hsu, F. (2002). Deep Blue. *Artificial Intelligence, 134*, 57–83.

Caplan, D., Alpert, N., Waters, G., & Olivieri, A. (2000). Activation in Broca's area by syntactic processing under conditions of concurrent articulation. *Human Brain Mapping, 9*, 65–71.

Card, S.K., English, W.K., Burr, B.J. (1978). Evaluation of mouse, rate controlled isometric joystick, step-keys, and text keys for selection on a CRT. *Ergonomics, 21*, 601–613.

Carpenter, P.A., Just, M.A., & Shell, P. (1990). What one intelligence test measures: A theoretical account of the processing in the Raven Progressive Matrices Test. *Psychological Review, 97*, 404–431.

Carroll, J.B. (1953). *The study of language*. Cambridge, Mass.: Harvard University Press.

Carroll, J.M. (1997). Human-computer interaction: Psychology as a science of design. *International Journal of Human-Computer Studies, 46*, 501–522.

Carroll, J.M., Bever, T.G., & Pollack, C.R. (1981). The non-uniqueness of linguistic intuitions. *Language, 57*, 368–383.

Carroll, J.M., Kellogg, W.A., & Rosson, M.B. (1991). The task-artifact cycle. In J.M. Carroll (Ed.), *Designing interaction: Psychology at the human-computer interface* (pp. 74–102). New York: Cambridge University Press.

Carter, J.R., & Irons, M.D. (1991). Are economists different, and if so, why? *Journal of Economic Perspectives, 5*, 171–177.

Casselden, P.A., & Hampson, S.E. (1990). Forming impressions from incongruent traits. *Journal of Personality and Social Psychology, 59*, 353–362.

Cassirer, E. (1953–1959). *The philosophy of symbolic forms* (3 vols.). New Haven: Yale University Press.

Cattell, J. McK. (1903). Statistics of American psychologists. *American Journal of Psychology, 14*, 310–328.

Cattell, R.B. (1963). Theory of fluid and crystallized intelligence: A critical experiment. *Journal of Educational Psychology, 54*, 1–22.

Cazden, C.B. (1976). Play with language and metalinguistic awareness. In J.S. Bruner, A. Jolly, & K. Sylva (Eds.), *Play: Its role in development and evolution* (pp. 603–608). London: Penguin.

Ceraso, J., & Provitera, A. (1971). Sources of error in syllogistic reasoning. *Cognitive Psychology, 2*, 400–410.

Chalmers, P.A. (2003). The role of cognitive theory in human computer interface. *Computers in Human Behavior, 19*, 593–607.

Chambers, D., & Reisberg, D. (1985). Can mental images be ambiguous? *Journal of Experimental Psychology: Human Perception and Performance, 11*, 317–328.

Chambers, D., & Reisberg, D. (1992). What an image depicts depends on what an image means. *Cognitive Psychology, 24*, 145–174.

Chang, T.M. (1986). Semantic memory: Facts and models. *Psychological Bulletin, 99*, 199–220.

Chapman, G.B., & Johnson, E.J. (2002). Incorporating the irrelevant: Anchors in judgments of belief and value. In T. Gilovich, D. Griffin, & D. Kahneman (Eds.), *Heuristics and biases: The psychology of intuitive judgment* (pp. 120–138). Cambridge: Cambridge University Press.

Chapman, L.J., & Chapman, J.P. (1959). Atmosphere effect re-examined. *Journal of Experimental Psychology, 55*, 220–226.

Chapman, L.J., & Chapman, J.P. (1969). Illusory correlation as an obstacle to the use of valid psychodiagnostic signs. *Journal of Abnormal Psychology, 74*, 271–280.

Chase, W.G., & Simon, H.A. (1973). Perception in chess. *Cognitive Psychology, 4*, 55–81.

Chaytor, N., & Schmitter-Edgecomb, M. (2003). The ecological validity of neuropsychological tests: A review of the literature on everyday cognitive skills. *Neuropsychological Review, 13*, 181–197.

Cheesman, J., & Merikle, P.M. (1986). Distinguishing conscious from unconscious perceptual processing. *Canadian Journal of Psychology, 40,* 343–367.

Chen, J.-Q. (2004). Theory of multiple intelligences: Is it a scientific theory? *Teacher's College Record, 106,* 17–23.

Cherniak, C. (1984). Prototypicality and deductive reasoning. *Journal of Verbal Learning and Verbal Behavior, 23,* 625–642.

Cherry, E.C. (1953). Some experiments on the recognition of speech with one and with two ears. *Journal of the Acoustical Society of America, 25,* 975–979.

Chomsky, N. (1957). *Syntactic structures.* The Hague: Mouton.

Chomsky, N. (1959). Review of Skinner's verbal behavior. *Language, 35,* 26–58.

Chomsky, N. (1965). *Aspects of the theory of syntax.* The Hague: Mouton.

Chomsky, N. (1966). *Cartesian linguistics.* New York: Harper & Row.

Chomsky, N. (1967). The formal nature of language. In E. Lenneberg, *Biological foundations of language* (pp. 397–442). New York: Wiley.

Chomsky, N. (1968). *Language and mind.* New York: Harcourt, Brace & World.

Chomsky, N. (1972). *Language and mind* (Enlarged ed.). New York: Harcourt Brace Jovanovich.

Chomsky, N. (1980a). *Rules and representations.* New York: Columbia University Press.

Chomsky, N. (1980b). Rules and representations. *Behavioral and Brain Sciences, 3,* 1–61.

Chomsky, N. (1981). *Lectures on government and binding.* Dordrecht, the Netherlands: Fortis.

Chomsky, N. (1995). Language and nature. *Mind, 104,* 1–61.

Chomsky, N. (2005). Three factors in language design. *Linguistic Inquiry, 36,* 1–22.

Chouinard, M.M., & Clark, E.V. (2003). Adult reformulations of child errors as negative evidence. *Journal of Child Language, 30,* 637–669.

Christian, J., Bickley, W., Tarka, M., & Clayton, K. (1978). Measures of free recall of 900 English nouns. *Memory & Cognition, 6,* 379–390.

Chronicle, E.P., Ormerod, T.C., & MacGregor, J.N. (2004). What makes an insight problem? The roles of heuristics, goal conception, and solution recoding in knowledge-lean problems. *Journal of Experimental Psychology: Learning, Memory, and Cognition, 30,* 14–27.

Chu, S., & Downs, J.J. (2000). Long live Proust: The odour-cued autobiographical memory bump. *Cognition, 75,* B41–B50.

Chwilla, D.J., & Kolk, H.H.J. (2002). Three-step priming in lexical decision. *Memory & Cognition, 30,* 217–225.

Claparède, E. (1951). Recognition and 'meness'. In D. Rapaport (Ed.), *Organization and pathology of thought* (pp. 58–75). New York: Columbia University Press. (Original work published 1911).

Clark, E.V. (2004). How language acquisition builds on cognitive development. *Trends in Cognitive Sciences, 8,* 472–478.

Clark, H.H. (1969). Linguistic processes in deductive reasoning. *Psychological Review, 76,* 387–404.

Clark, H.H. & Card, S.K. (1969). The role of semantics in remembering comparative sentences. *Journal of Experimental Psychology, 82,* 545–553.

Clark, H.H., & Clark, E. (1977). *The psychology of language.* New York: Harcourt Brace Jovanovich.

Clark, H.H., & Fox Tree, J.E. (2002). Using *uh* and *um* in spontaneous speaking. *Cognition, 84,* 73–111.

Clark, H.H., & Gerrig, R. (1984). On the pretense theory of irony. *Journal of Experimental Psychology: General, 113,* 121–126.

Clark, H.H., & Haviland, S.E. (1977). Comprehension and the given-new contract. In R.O. Freedle (Ed.), *Discourse production and comprehension* (pp. 1–40). Norwood, NJ: Ablex.

Clark, J.M., & Paivio, A. (1989). Observational and theoretical terms in psychology: A cognitive perspective on scientific language. *American Psychologist, 44,* 500–512.

Clayton, N.S., & Dickinson, A. (1998). Episodic-like memory during cache recovery by scrub jays. *Nature, 395,* 272–278.

Cleeremans, A., Destrebecqz, A., & Boyer, M.

(1998). Implicit learning: News from the front. *Trends in Cognitive Sciences, 2*, 406–416.

Clifford, B.R. (2004). Celebrating levels of processing. *Applied Cognitive Psychology, 18*, 486–489.

Cofer, C. (1973). Constructive processes in memory. *American Scientist, 61*, 537–543.

Cole, W.G., & Loftus, E.F. (1979). Incorporating new information into memory. *American Journal of Psychology, 92*, 413–425.

Collins, A.M., & Loftus, E.F. (1975). A spreading-activation theory of semantic processing. *Psychological Review, 82*, 407–428.

Collins, A.M., & Quillian, M.R. (1972). Experiments on semantic memory and language comprehension. In L.W. Gregg (Ed.), *Cognition in learning and memory* (pp. 117–137). New York: Wiley.

Colman, A.M. (2003). Cooperation, psychological game theory, and limitations of rationality in social interaction. *Behavioral and Brain Sciences, 26*, 139–198.

Colvin, M.K., Dunbar, K., & Grafman, J. (2000). The effects of frontal lobe lesions on goal achievement in the water jug task. *Journal of Cognitive Neuroscience, 13*, 1129–1147.

Conway, A.R.A., Kane, M.J., & Engle, R.W. (2003). Working memory capacity and its relation to general intelligence. *Trends in Cognitive Sciences, 7*, 547–552.

Conway, M.A., & Pleydell-Pearce, C.W. (2000). The construction of autobiographical memories in the self-memory system. *Psychological Review, 107*, 261–288.

Corballis, M.C. (1997). Mental rotation and the right hemisphere. *Brain and Language, 57*, 100–121.

Corballis, M.C. (2003). From mouth to hand: Gesture, speech and the evolution of right handedness. *Behavioral and Brain Sciences, 26*, 199–260.

Corballis, M.C. (2004a). The origin of modernity: Was autonomous speech the critical factor? *Psychological Review, 111*, 543–552.

Corballis, M.C. (2004b). FOXP2 and the mirror system. *Trends in Cognitive Sciences, 8*, 95–96.

Coren, S., & Girgus, J.S. (1980). Principles of perceptual organization and spatial distortion: The Gestalt illusions. *Journal of Experimental Psychology: Human Perception and Performance, 6*, 404–412.

Cosmides, L. (1989). The logic of social exchange: Has natural selection shaped how humans reason? Studies with the Wason selection task. *Cognition, 31*, 187–276.

Cosmides, L., & Tooby, J. (1994). Origins of domain specificity: The evolution of functional organization. In L.A. Hirschfeld & S.A. Gelman (Eds.), *Mapping the mind: Domain specificity in cognition and culture* (pp. 85–116). New York: Cambridge University Press.

Cosmides, L., & Tooby, J. (2002). Unraveling the enigma of human intelligence: Evolutionary psychology and the multimodular mind. In R.J. Sternberg & J.C. Kaufman (Eds.), *The evolution of intelligence* (pp. 145–198). Mahwah, NJ: Erlbaum.

Cowan, N. (1988). Evolving conceptions of memory storage, selective attention, and their mutual constraints within the human information-processing system. *Psychological Review, 104*, 163–191.

Craik, F.I.M. (1980). *Cognitive views of human memory* (Cassette Recording). Washington: American Psychological Association.

Craik, F.I.M. (2002). Levels of processing: Past, present . . . and future? *Memory, 10*, 305–318.

Craik, F.I.M., & Grady, C.L. (2002). Aging, memory, and frontal lobe functioning. In D.T. Stuss and R.T. Knight (Eds.), *Principles of frontal lobe function* (pp. 528–540). New York: Oxford University Press.

Craik, F.I.M., & Lockhart, R.S. (1972). Levels of processing: A framework for memory research. *Journal of Verbal Learning and Verbal Behavior, 11*, 671–684.

Crawford, L.E., & Cacioppo, J.T. (2002). Learning where to look for danger: Integrating affective and spatial information. *Psychological Science, 13*, 449–453.

Cree, G.S., & McRae, K. (2003). Analyzing factors underlying the structure and computation of the meaning of *Chipmunk, Cherry, Chisel, Cheese,* and *Cello* (and many other such concrete nouns). *Journal of Experimental Psychology: General, 132*, 163–201.

Crovitz, H.F. (1970). *Galton's walk*. New York: Harper & Row.

Crovitz, H.F., & Schiffman, H. (1974). Frequency of episodic memories as a function of their age. *Bulletin of the Psychonomic Society, 4*, 517–518.

Crovitz, H.F., Schiffman, H., & Apter, A. (1991). Galton's number. *Bulletin of the Psychonomic Society, 29*, 331–332.

Csikszentmihalyi, M. (1990). *Flow: The psychology of optimal experience*. New York: Harper & Row.

Csikszentmihalyi, M. (2002). Jacob Warren Getzels (1912–2001). *American Psychologist, 57*, 290–291.

Csikszentmihalyi, M., & Beattie, O.V. (1979). Life themes: A theoretical and empirical exploration of their origins and effects. *Journal of Humanistic Psychology, 19*, 46–63.

Csikszentmihalyi, M., & Getzels, J. (1973). The personality of young artists: An empirical and theoretical exploration. *British Journal of Psychology, 64*, 91–104.

Cuban, L. (2004). Assessing the 20-year impact of multiple intelligences on schooling. *Teacher's College Record, 106*, 140–146.

Cupchik, G.C. (1988). The legacy of Daniel E. Berlyne. *Empirical Studies of the Arts, 6*, 171–186.

Curran, T. (2001). Implicit learning revealed by the method of opposition. *Trends in Cognitive Sciences, 5*, 503–504.

Curtis, C.E., & D'Esposito, M. (2003). Persistent activity in the prefrontal cortex during working memory. *Trends in Cognitive Sciences, 7*, 415–423.

Cytowic, R.E. (2002). *Synaesthesia: A union of the senses* (2nd ed.). Cambridge, Mass.: MIT Press.

Daley, T.C., Whaley, S.E., Sigman, M.D., Espinosa, M.P., & Neumann, C. (2003). IQ on the rise: The Flynn effect in rural Kenyan children. *Psychological Science, 14*, 215–219.

D'Andrade, R. (1987). A folk model of the mind. In D. Holland & N. Quinn (Eds.), *Cultural models in language and thought* (pp. 112–148). Cambridge: Cambridge University Press.

Darwin, C. (1859). *On the origins of species by means of natural selection*. London: Murray.

Davidoff, J. (2001). Language and perceptual categorization. *Trends in Cognitive Sciences, 5*, 382–387.

Davidoff, J., Davies, I., & Roberson, D. (1999). Colour categories in a stone-age tribe. *Nature, 398*, 203–204.

Dawes, R.M. (1988). *Rational choice in an uncertain world*. San Diego: Harcourt Brace Jovanovich.

Dawes, R.M. (1993). Prediction of the future versus understanding of the past: A basic asymmetry. *American Journal of Psychology, 106*, 1–24.

Dawes, R.M. (1994). *House of cards: Psychology and psychotherapy built on myth*. New York: Free Press.

Dawes, R.M. (1999). A message from psychologists to economists: Mere predictability doesn't matter like it should (without a good story appended to it). *Journal of Economic Behavior & Organization, 39*, 29–40.

Dawkins, R. (1976). *The selfish gene*. Oxford: Oxford University Press.

Dawkins, R. (1988). *The blind watchmaker*. London: Penguin.

Dawson, M.R.W. (2005). *Connectionism: A hands-on approach*. Malden, Mass.: Blackwell.

Debner, J.A., & Jacoby, L.L. (1994). Unconscious perception: Attention awareness, and control. *Journal of Experimental Psychology: Human Learning and Memory, 20*, 304–317.

DeDreu, C.K.W., & Boles, T.L. (1998). Share and share alike or winner take all? The influence of social value orientation upon the choice and recall of negotiation heuristics. *Organization Behavior and Human Decision Processes, 76*, 253–276.

Deese, J. (1965). *The structure of associations in language and thought*. Baltimore: Johns Hopkins University Press.

Deese, J. (1970). *Psycholinguistics*. Boston: Allyn & Bacon.

Deese, J. (1984). *Thought into speech: The psychology of a language.* New York: Prentice-Hall.

Deese, J., & Hamilton, H.W. (1974). Marking and propositional effects in associations to compounds. *American Journal of Psychology, 87*, 1–15.

Defeyter, M.A., & German, T.P. (2003). Acquiring an understanding of design: Evidence from children's insight problem-solving. *Cognition, 89*, 133–155.

de Groot, A.D. (1965). *Thought and choice in chess.* The Hague: Mouton.

Dehaene, S. (2003). The neural basis of the Weber-Fechner law: A logarithmic mental number line. *Trends in Cognitive Science, 7*, 145–147.

Denis, M., & Kosslyn, S.M. (1999). Scanning visual mental images: A window on the mind. *Current Psychology of Cognition, 18*, 409–465.

Dennett, D. (1991). *Consciousness explained.* Boston: Little, Brown.

Dennett, D. (1995). *Darwin's dangerous idea.* New York: Simon & Schuster.

Dennett, D. (2003). The Baldwin effect: A crane, not a skyhook. In B.H. Weber & D.J. Depew, *Evolution and learning: The Baldwin effect reconsidered* (pp. 69–80). Cambridge, Mass.: MIT Press.

Depew, D.J. (2003). Baldwin and his many effects. In B.H. Weber & D.J. Depew, *Evolution and learning: The Baldwin effect reconsidered* (pp. 3–31). Cambridge, Mass.: MIT Press.

de Saussure, F. (1916). *Cours de linguistique generale* [Course in general linguistics]. Paris: Bally & Sechehaye.

DeSoto, C.B., London, M., & Handel, S. (1965). Social reasoning and spatial paralogic. *Journal of Personality and Social Psychology, 2*, 513–521.

Di Carlo, A., Baldereschi, M., Amaducci, L., Lepore, V., Bracco, L., Maggi, S., Bonaiuto, S., Perissinotto, E., Scarlato, G., Farchi, G., & Inzitari, D. (2002). Incidence of dementia, Alzheimer's disease, and vascular dementia in Italy. The ILSA Study. *Journal of the American Geriatric Society, 50*, 41–48.

Dickens, W.T., & Flynn, J.R. (2001). Heritability estimates versus large environmental effects: The IQ paradox resolved. *Psychological Bulletin, 108*, 346–369.

Dietrich, E. (1999). Algorithm. In R.A. Wilson, & F.C. Keil, (Eds.), *The MIT encyclopedia of the cognitive sciences* (pp. 11–12). Cambridge, Mass.: MIT Press.

DiLiilo, V., Kawahara, J.-I., Zuvic, S.M., & Visser, T.A.W. (2001). The preattentive emperor has no clothes: A dynamic redressing. *Journal of Experimental Psychology: General, 130*, 479–492.

DiSessa, A. (1983). Phenomenology and the evolution of intuition. In D. Gentner & A.L. Stevens, (Eds.), *Mental models* (pp. 15–33). Hillsdale, NJ: Erlbaum.

Dixon, M.J., Smilek, D., Cudahy, C., & Merikle, P.M. (2000). Five plus two equals yellow. *Nature, 406*, 365.

Dixon, N.F. (1971). *Subliminal perception: The nature of a controversy.* London: McGraw-Hill.

Dixon, R.M.W. (1982). *Where have all the adjectives gone?* Berlin: Walter de Gruyter.

Dominowski, R.L. (1981). Comment on 'An examination of the alleged role of "fixation" in the solution of several "insight" problems' by Weisberg and Alba. *Journal of Experimental Psychology: General, 110*, 199–203.

Dowling, W.J., & Harwood, D.L. (1986). *Music cognition.* New York: Academic Press.

Downing, P.E., Bray, D., Rogers, J., & Childs, C. (2004). Bodies capture attention when nothing is expected. *Cognition, 93*, B27–B38.

Downs, R.M., & Stea, D. (1977). *Maps in minds: Some reflections on cognitive mapping.* New York: Harper & Row.

Dreisbach, G., & Goschke, T. (2004). How positive affect modulates cognitive control: Reduced perseveration at the cost of increased distractibility. *Journal of Experimental Psychology: Learning, Memory, and Cognition, 30*, 343–353

Dudai, Y. (2004). The neurobiology of consolidations, or, how stable is the engram? *Annual Review of Psychology, 55*, 51–86.

Dulany, D., Carlson, R., & Dewey, G. (1984). A case of syntactical learning and judgment.

Journal of Experimental Psychology: General, 113, 541–555.

Dulany, D., Carlson, R., & Dewey, G. (1985). On consciousness in syntactic learning and judgment: A reply to Reber, Allen and Regan. *Journal of Experimental Psychology: General, 114*, 25–32.

Dunbar, K. (2000). How scientists think in the real world: Implications for science education. *Journal of Applied Developmental Psychology, 21*, 49–58.

Dunbar, K. (2001). What scientific thinking reveals about the nature of cognition. In K. Crowley & C.D. Schunn (Eds.), *Designing for science: Implications from everyday, classroom, and professional settings* (pp. 115–140). Mahwah, NJ: Erlbaum.

Dunbar, K., & Blanchette, I. (2001). The *in vivo/in vitro* approach to cognition: The case of analogy. *Trends in Cognitive Sciences, 5*, 334–339.

Duncker, K. (1945). On problem-solving. *Psychological Monographs, 58* (5, Whole No. 270).

Dupré, J. (1987). *The latest on the best: Essays on evolution and optimality.* Cambridge, Mass.: MIT Press.

Eacott, M.J., & Crawley, R.A. (1998). The offset of childhood amnesia: Memory for events that occurred before age 3. *Journal of Experimental Psychology: General, 127*, 22–33.

Eagle, M., Wolitzky, D.L., & Klein, G.S. (1966). Imagery: The effect of a concealed figure in a stimulus. *Science, 151*, 837–839.

Ebbinghaus, H. (1964). *Memory: A contribution to experimental psychology*. New York: Dover. (Original work published 1885).

Eco, U. (1989). *Foucault's pendulum*. New York: Knopf.

Edgerton, S. (1975). *The Renaissance rediscovery of linear perspective*. New York: Basic Books.

Edmonds, E.A., & Green, T.R.G. (Eds.). (1984). Ergonomics of the user interface (Special Issue). *Behaviour and Information Technology, 3*(2).

Edwards, D., & Potter, J. (1992). The Chancellor's memory: Rhetoric and truth in discursive remembering. *Applied Cognitive Psychology, 6*, 187–215.

Eich, E. (1984). Memory for unattended events: Remembering with and without awareness. *Memory & Cognition, 12*, 105–111.

Eich, E. (1995). Searching for mood dependent memory. *Psychological Science, 6*, 67–75.

Eich, E., & Forgas, J.P. (2003). Mood, cognition, and memory. In A.F. Healy & R.W. Proctor (Eds.), *Handbook of psychology: Vol 4. Experimental psychology* (pp. 61–83). Hoboken, NJ: Wiley.

Eich, E., & Macaulay, D. (2000). Are real moods required to reveal mood-congruent and mood-dependent memory? *Psychological Science, 11*, 244–248.

Eich, E., Macaulay, D., & Ryan, L. (1994). Mood-dependent memory for events of the personal past. *Journal of Experimental Psychology: General, 123*, 201–215.

Eich, E., & Metcalfe, J. (1989). Mood-dependent memory for internal versus external events. *Journal of Experimental Psychology: Learning, Memory, and Cognition, 15*, 443–455.

Einstein, G.O., & McDaniel, M.A. (1987). Distinctiveness and the mnemonic benefits of bizarre imagery. In M.A. McDaniel & M. Pressley (Eds.), *Imagery and related mnemonic processes: Theories, individual differences and applications* (pp. 78–102). New York: Springer-Verlag.

Einstein, G.O., McDaniel, M.A., & Lackey, S. (1989). Bizarre imagery, interference, and distinctiveness. *Journal of Experimental Psychology: Learning, Memory, and Cognition, 15*, 137–146.

Einstein, G.O., McDaniel, M. A., Smith, R.E., & Shaw, P. (1998). Habitual prospective memory and aging: Remembering intentions and forgetting actions. *Psychological Science, 9*, 284–288.

Einstein, G.O., McDaniel, M.A., Williford, C.L., Pagan, J.L., & Dismukes, R.K. (2003). Forgetting of intentions in demanding situations is rapid. *Journal of Experimental Psychology: Applied, 9*, 147–162.

Eisenstadt, M., & Kareev, Y. (1977). Perception in game playing. In P.N. Johnson-Laird & P.C. Wason (Eds.), *Thinking* (pp. 548–564). Cambridge: Cambridge University Press.

Eisenstadt, S.A., & Simon, H.A. (1997). Logic and thought. *Minds and Machines, 7*, 365–385.

Ekman, P.D. Facial expressions. (1999). In T. Dalgleish & M. Power (Eds.), *Handbook of cognition and emotion* (pp. 45–60). New York: Wiley.

Ellen, P. (1982). Direction, past experience, and hints in creative problem-solving. *Journal of Experimental Psychology: General, 111*, 316–325.

Ellis, H.C. (1990). Depressive deficits in memory: Processing initiative and resource allocation. *Journal of Experimental Psychology: General, 119*, 60–62.

Emerson, M.J., & Miyake, A. (2003). The role of inner speech in task switching: A dual-task investigation. *Journal of Memory and Language, 48*, 148–168.

Engle, R.W., Tuholski, S.W., Laughlin, J.E., & Conway, A.R.A. (1999). Working memory, short-term memory, and general fluid intelligence: A latent variable approach. *Journal of Experimental Psychology: General, 128*, 309–331.

Erdelyi, M.H. (1970). Recovery of unavailable perceptual input. *Cognitive Psychology, 1*, 99–113.

Erdelyi, M.H. (1985). *Psychoanalysis: Freud's cognitive psychology*. New York: Freeman.

Erdelyi, M.H. (2004). Subliminal perception and its cognates: theory, indeterminacy, and time. *Consciousness and Cognition, 13*, 73–91.

Erdelyi, M.H., & Becker, J. (1974). Hypermnesia for pictures: Incremental memory for pictures but not for words in multiple recall trials. *Cognitive Psychology, 6*, 159–171.

Erdelyi, M.H., & Kleinbard, J. (1978). Has Ebbinghaus decayed with time? The growth of recall (hypermnesia) over days. *Journal of Experimental Psychology: Human Learning and Memory, 4*, 275–289.

Erdmann, E., & Stover, D. (2000). *Beyond a world divided: Human values in the brain-mind science of Roger Sperry*. San Jose, Calif.: Authors Choice Press. (Originally published 1991).

Erickson, T.D., & Mattson, M.E. (1981). From words to meaning: A semantic illusion. *Journal of Verbal Learning and Verbal Behavior, 20*, 540–551.

Ericsson, K.A. (2003). Exceptional memorizers: Made, not born. *Trends in Cognitive Sciences, 7*, 233–235.

Ericsson, K.A., & Charness, N. (1994). Expert performance: Its structure and acquisition. *American Psychologist, 49*, 725–747.

Ericsson, K.A., & Simon, H.A. (1980). Verbal reports as data. *Psychological Review, 87*, 215–251.

Ericsson, K.A, & Simon, H.A. (1993). *Protocol analysis*. Cambridge, Mass.: MIT Press.

Eriksen, C.W., Azuma, H., & Hicks, R. (1959). Verbal discrimination of pleasant and unpleasant stimulus prior to specific identification. *Journal of Abnormal and Social Psychology, 59*, 114–119.

Erikson, E.H. (1959). Identity and the life cycle. *Psychological Issues, 1*, 50–100.

Erikson, E.H., Erikson, J., & Kivnick, H.Q. (1986). *Vital involvement in old age*. New York: Norton.

Evans, G.W. (1980). Environmental cognition. *Psychological Bulletin, 88*, 259–287.

Evans, J. St B.T. (1980). Current issues in the psychology of reasoning. *British Journal of Psychology, 71*, 227–239.

Evans, J. St B.T. (1982). *The psychology of deductive reasoning*. London: Routledge & Kegan Paul.

Evans, J. St B.T. (2002). Logic and human reasoning: An assessment of the deduction paradigm. *Psychological Bulletin, 128*, 978–996.

Evans, J. St B.T. (2003). In two minds: Dual process accounts of reasoning. *Trends in Cognitive Sciences, 7*, 454–459.

Evans, J. St B.T., & Johnson-Laird, P.N. (2003). Editorial obituary: Peter Wason (1924–2003). *Thinking and Reasoning, 9*, 177–184.

Evans, J. St B.T., Handley, S.J., & Harper, C.N.J. (2001). Necessity, possibility and belief: A study of syllogistic reasoning. *Quarterly Journal of Experimental Psychology, 54*, 935–958.

Falk, R. (1989). Judgment of coincidences: Mine versus yours. *American Journal of Psychology, 102*, 477–493.

Farah, M.J. (1989). Mechanisms of imagery-perception interaction. *Journal of Experimental Psychology: Human Perception and Performance, 15,* 203–211.

Farah, M.J. (1996). Is face recognition 'special'? Evidence from neuropsychology. *Behavioural Brain Research, 76,* 181–189.

Farah, M.J. (2005a). Neuroethics: The practical and the philosophical. *Trends in Cognitive Sciences, 9,* 34–40.

Farah, M.J. (2005b). Reply to Jedliça: Neuroethics, reductionism and dualism. *Trends in Cognitive Sciences, 9,* 173.

Farah, M.J., & McClelland, J.L. (1991). A computational model of semantic impairment: Modality specificity and emergent category specificity. *Journal of Experimental Psychology: General, 120,* 339–357.

Farah, M.J., & Rabinowitz, C. (2003). Genetic and environmental influences on the organization of semantic memory in the brain: Is 'living things' an innate category? *Cognitive Neuropsychology, 20,* 401–408.

Faulkner, X., & Culwin, F. (2005). When fingers do the talking: A study of text messaging. *Interacting with Computers, 17,* 167–185.

Fechner, G.T. (1876). *Vorschule der Aesthetik.* Leipzig: Breitkopf und Hartel.

Feeney, A., Scrafton, S., Duckworth, A., & Handley, S.J. (2004). The story of *some*: Everyday pragmatic inference by children and adults. *Canadian Journal of Experimental Psychology, 58,* 121–132

Feldman, D.H. (1986). *Nature's gambit.* New York: Basic Books.

Feldman, J. (2003). The simplicity principle in human concept learning. *Current Directions in Psychological Science, 12,* 227–232.

Fellbaum, C., & Miller, G.A. (1990). Folk psychology or semantic entailment? *Psychological Review, 97,* 565–570.

Fernandez-Duque, D., & Johnson, M.L. (2002). Cause and effect theories of attention: The role of conceptual metaphors. *Review of General Psychology, 6,* 153–165.

Fiddick, L., Cosmides, L., & Tooby, J. (2000). No interpretation without representation: The role of domain-specific representations and inferences in the Wason selection task. *Cognition, 77,* 1–79.

Fiebach, C.J., & Friederici, A.D. (2003). Processing concrete words: fMRI evidence against a specific right hemisphere involvement. *Neuropsychologia, 42,* 62–70.

Findlay, C.S., & Lumsden, C.J. (1988). Thinking creatively about creative thinking. *Journal of Social and Biological Structures, 11,* 165–175.

Finger, S. (1994). *Origins of neuroscience : A history of explorations into brain function.* New York : Oxford University Press.

Finger, S. (2000). *Minds behind the brain: A history of the pioneers and their discoveries.* New York: Oxford University Press.

Finke, R.A. (1996). Imagery, creativity, and emergent structure. *Consciousness and Cognition, 5,* 381–393.

Finke, R.A., Pinker, S., & Farah, M.J. (1989). Reinterpreting visual patterns in mental imagery. *Cognitive Science, 13,* 51–78.

Fitts, P.M. (1992). The information capacity of the human motor system in controlling the amplitude of movement. *Journal of Experimental Psychology: General, 121,* 262–269. (Original work published 1954).

Fivush, R., & Hayden, C.A. (Eds.). (2003). *Autobiographical memory and the construction of a narrative self.* Mahwah, NJ: Erlbaum.

Fivush, R., & Nelson, K. (2004). Culture and language in the emergence of autobiographical memories. *Psychological Science, 15,* 573–577.

Flavell, J. (1979). Metacognition and cognitive monitoring. *American Psychologist, 34,* 906–911.

Fleck, J., & Weisberg, R.W. (2004). The use of verbal protocols as data: An analysis of insight in the candle problem. *Memory & Cognition, 32,* 990–1006.

Flynn, J.R. (1984). The mean IQ of Americans: Massive gains 1932 to 1978. *Psychological Bulletin, 95,* 29–51.

Flynn, J.R. (1987). Massive IQ gains in 14 nations: What IQ tests really measure. *Psychological Bulletin, 101,* 171–191.

Flynn, J.R. (1999). Searching for justice: The

discovery of IQ gains over time. *American Psychologist, 54,* 5–20.

Flynn, J.R. (2003). Movies about intelligence: The limitations of *g. Current Directions in Psychological Science, 12,* 95–99.

Fodor, J.A. (1983). *The modularity of mind: An essay in faculty psychology.* Cambridge, Mass.: MIT Press.

Fodor, J.A. (2000). *The mind doesn't work that way.* Cambridge, Mass.: MIT Press.

Fowler, H.W. (1965). *A dictionary of modern English usage* (2nd ed.). Oxford: Oxford University Press.

Fraisse, P., & Piaget, J. (1963). *Experimental psychology: History and method.* New York: Basic Books.

Frank, H. (1959). *Grundlagenprobleme der Informations-sthetik und erste Anwendung auf die mime pure.* Schnelle: Quickborn.

Frank, H. (1964). *Kybernetische Analysen Subjektiver Sachverhalte.* Schnelle: Quickborn.

Frank, R.H., Gilovich, T., & Regan, D.T. (1993). Does studying economics inhibit cooperation? *Journal of Economic Perspectives, 7,* 159–171.

Frank, R.H., Gilovich, T., & Regan, D.T. (1996). Do economists make bad citizens? *Journal of Economic Perspectives, 10,* 187–192.

Franklin, N., & Tversky, B. (1991). Searching imagined environments. *Journal of Experimental Psychology: General, 119,* 63–76.

Franz, S.I. (1912). New phrenology. *Science, 35,* 321–328.

Frase, L.T., & Kamman, R. (1974). Effects of search criterion upon unanticipated free recall of categorically related words. *Memory & Cognition, 2,* 181–184.

Frazer, J.G. (1959). *The golden bough* (abridged). New York: Doubleday (Ed. T.H. Gaster, 1922). (Original work published 1911).

Freeman, W., & Watts, J.W. (1968). Prefrontal lobotomy. In W.S. Sahakian (Ed.), *History of psychology: A source book in systematic psychology* (pp. 377–379). Itaska, Ill.: Peacock. (Originally published 1950).

French, C.C., & Richards, A. (1993). Clock* this! An everyday example of a schema-driven error in memory. *British Journal of Psychology, 84,* 249–253.

French, R.M. (2000). The Turing test: The first 50 years. *Trends in Cognitive Sciences, 4,* 115–122.

Frenkel, K.A. (1989). The next generation of interactive technologies. *Communications of the ACM, 32,* 872–881.

Freud, S. (1961). A note upon the mystic writing pad. In J. Strachey (Ed. & Trans.), *The standard edition of the complete psychological works of Sigmund Freud* (Vol. 19). London: Hogarth Press. (Original work published 1925).

Freud, S. (1977). *Introductory lectures on psychoanalysis* (J. Strachey, Trans.). New York: Norton. (Original work published 1916).

Fugelsang, J.A., Stein, C.B., Green, A.E., & Dunbar, K.N. (2004). Theory and data interactions of the scientific mind: Evidence from the molecular and the cognitive laboratory. *Canadian Journal of Experimental Psychology, 58,* 86–95.

Gallistel, C.R. (2002a). Language and spatial frames of reference in mind and brain. *Trends in Cognitive Sciences, 6,* 321–322.

Gallistel, C.R. (2002b). Conception, perception and the control of action. *Trends in Cognitive Sciences, 6,* 504.

Gallotti, K.M. (1989). Approaches to studying formal and everyday reasoning. *Psychological Bulletin, 105,* 331–351.

Gallotti, K.M., Baron, J., & Sabini, J. (1986). Individual differences in syllogistic reasoning: Deduction rules or mental models? *Journal of Experimental Psychology: General, 115,* 16–25.

Galton, F. (1879a). Psychometric experiments. *Brain, 2,* 148–160.

Galton, F. (1879b). Psychometric facts. *The Nineteenth Century,* 425–433.

Galton, F. (1886). Regression toward mediocrity in hereditary stature. *Journal of the Anthropological Institute, 15,* 246–263.

Gardiner, J.M. (2001). Episodic memory and autonoetic consciousness: A first-person approach. *Philosophical Transactions of the Royal Society (Series B), 356,* 1351–1361.

Gardiner, J.M., & Richardson-Klavehn, A. (2000). Remembering and knowing. In E.

Tulving & F.I.M.Craik, (Eds.), *The Oxford handbook of memory* (pp. 229–244). New York: Oxford University Press.

Gardner, H. (1980). *Artful scribbles*. New York: Harper & Row.

Gardner, H. (1982). *Art, mind and brain*. New York: Basic Books.

Gardner, H. (1983). *Frames of mind*. New York: Basic Books.

Gardner, H. (1985). *The mind's new science*. New York: Basic Books.

Gardner, H. (1993a). *Multiple intelligences: The theory in practice*. New York: Basic Books.

Gardner, H. (1993b). *Creating minds*. New York: Basic Books.

Gardner, H. (1999) *The disciplined mind: What all students should understand*. New York: Simon & Schuster.

Gardner, H. (2004). Audiences for the theory of multiple intelligences. *Teacher's College Record*, 212–220.

Gardner, H., & Winner, E. (1982). First intimations of artistry. In S. Straus (Ed.), *U-shaped behavioral growth* (pp. 147–168). New York: Academic Press.

Garlick, D. (2002). Understanding the nature of the general factor of intelligence: The role of individual differences in neural plasticity as an explanatory mechanism. *Psychological Review, 109*, 116–136.

Garlick, D. (2003). Integrating brain science research with intelligence research. *Current Directions in Psychological Science, 12*, 185–192.

Garner, W.R. (1962). *Uncertainty and structure as psychological concepts*. New York: Wiley.

Gauthier, I., Curran, T., Curby, K.M., & Collins, D. (2003). Perceptual interference supports a non-modular account of face processing. *Nature Neuroscience, 6*, 428–432.

Gauthier, I., Skudlarski, P., Gore, J.C., & Anderson, A.W. (2000). Expertise for cars and birds recruits brain areas involved in face recognition. *Nature Neuroscience, 3*, 191–197.

Gelman, S.A. (2004). Psychological essentialism in children. *Trends in Cognitive Sciences, 8*, 404–409.

Gelman, S.A., & Welman, H.M. (1991). Insides and essences: Early understandings of the non-obvious. *Cognition, 38*, 213–244.

Gentner, D. (1983). Structure-mapping: A theoretical framework for analogy. *Cognitive Science, 7*, 155–170.

Gentner, D. (2002). Mental models. In N.J. Smelser & P.B. Bates (Eds.), *International Encyclopedia of the Social and Behavioral Sciences* (pp. 9683–9687). Amsterdam: Elsevier Science.

Gentner, D., & Gentner, D.R. (1983). Flowing waters or teeming crowds: Mental models of electricity. In D. Gentner & A.L. Stevens (Eds.), *Mental models* (pp. 99–129). Hillsdale, NJ: Erlbaum.

Gentzen, G. (1964). Investigations into logical deduction. *American Philosophical Quarterly, 1*, 288–306.

German, T.P., & Barrett, H.C. (2005). Functional fixedness in a technologically sparse culture. *Psychological Science, 16*, 1–5.

German, T.P., & Defeyter, M.A. (2000). Immunity to functional fixedness in young children. *Psychonomic Bulletin & Review, 7*, 707–712.

Getzels, J.W. (1975). Problem finding and the inventiveness of solutions. *Journal of Creative Behavior, 9*, 12–18.

Getzels, J.W., & Csikszentmihalyi, M. (1972). Concern for discovery in the creative process. In A. Rothenberg & C. Hausman (Eds.), *The creativity question* (pp. 161–165). Durham, NC: Duke University Press.

Getzels, J.W., & Csikszentmihalyi, M. (1976). *The creative vision: A longitudinal study of problem finding in art*. New York: Wiley.

Ghiselin, M.T. (1981). Categories, life and thinking. *Behavioral and Brain Sciences, 4*, 269–313.

Gibbs, R.W. (1986). On the psycholinguistics of sarcasm. *Journal of Experimental Psychology: General, 115*, 3–15.

Gibbs, R.W. (1996). Why many concepts are metaphorical. *Cognition, 61*, 309–319.

Gibbs, R.W. (2004). Metaphor is grounded in embodied experience. *Journal of Pragmatics, 36*, 1189–1210.

Gibson, J.J. (1941). A critical review of the concept of set in contemporary experimental psychology. *Psychological Bulletin, 38*, 781–817.

Gibson, J.J. (1950). *The perception of the visual world.* Boston: Houghton Mifflin.

Gibson, J.J. (1966). *The senses considered as perceptual systems.* Boston: Houghton Mifflin.

Gibson, J.J. (1969). Outline of a theory of direct visual perception. Paper presented at the Conference on the Psychology of Knowing, Edmonton, Alberta.

Gibson, J.J. (1977). The theory of affordances. In R. Shaw & J. Bransford (Eds.), *Perceiving, acting and knowing* (pp. 67–82). Hillsdale, NJ: Erlbaum.

Gibson, J.J. (1979). *The ecological approach to visual perception.* Boston: Houghton Mifflin.

Gigerenzer, G., & Edwards, A. (2005). Simple tools for understanding risks: From innumeracy to insight. *British Medical Journal, 327*, 741–744.

Gigerenzer, G., & Goldstein, D.G. (1996). Reasoning the fast and frugal way: Models of bounded rationality. *Psychological Review, 103*, 650–669.

Gigerenzer, G., & Hug, K. (1992). Domain-specific reasoning: Social contracts, cheating, and perspective change. *Cognition, 43*, 127–171.

Gilden, G.L., & Wilson, S.G. (1995). Streaks in skilled performance. *Psychonomic Bulletin & Review, 2*, 260–265.

Giles, G.M., & Clark-Wilson, J. (1988). Functional skills training in severe brain injury. In I. Fussey & G.M. Giles (Eds.), *Rehabilitation of the severely brain-injured adult* (pp. 69–101). London: Croom Helm.

Gilhooly, K. (2003). Problems in problem-solving. *Trends in Cognitive Science, 7*, 477–478.

Gilligan, S.G., & Bower, G.H. (1984). Cognitive consequences of emotional arousal. In C. Izard, J. Kagan, & R. Zajonc (Eds.), *Emotions, cognition and behavior* (pp. 547–588). New York: Cambridge University Press.

Gillihan, S.J., & Farah, M.J. (2005). Is self special? A critical review of evidence from experimental psychology and cognitive neuroscience. *Psychological Bulletin, 131*, 76–97.

Gilovich, T., & Griffin, D. (2002). Introduction-heuristics and biases: Then and now. In T. Gilovich, D. Griffin, & D. Kahneman (Eds.), *Heuristics and biases: The psychology of intuitive judgment* (pp. 1–19). Cambridge: Cambridge University Press.

Gilovich, T., Mevec, V.H., & Chen, S. (1995). Commission, omission, and dissonance reduction: Coping with regret in the 'Monty Hall' problem. *Personality and Social Psychology Review, 21*, 182–190.

Gilovich, T., Vallone, R., & Tversky, A. (1985). The hot hand in basketball: On the misperception of random sequences. *Cognitive Psychology, 17*, 295–314.

Gil-White, F. (2001). Are ethnic groups biological 'species' to the human brain? *Current Anthropology, 42*, 515–554.

Giroux, L., & Larochelle, S. (1988). *The cognitive ergonomics of computer systems.* Laval, Que.: Canadian Automation Research Centre.

Glenberg, A. (1997). What memory is for. *Behavioral and Brain Sciences, 20*, 1–55.

Glenberg, A., Smith, S.M., & Green, C. (1977). Type I rehearsal: Maintenance and more. *Journal of Verbal Learning and Verbal Behavior, 16*, 339–352.

Glicksohn, J., Steinbach, I., & Elimalac-Malmilyan, S. (1999). Cognitive dedifferentiation in eidetics and synaesthesia: Hunting for the ghost once more. *Perception, 28*, 109–120.

Glisky, E.L., & Schacter, D.L. (1989). Extending the limits of complex learning in organic amnesia: Computer training in a vocational domain. *Neuropsychologia, 27*, 107–120.

Glosser, G., & Friedman, R.B. (1991). Lexical but not semantic priming in Alzheimer's disease. *Psychology and Aging, 6*, 522–527.

Glucksberg, S (2003). The psycholinguistics of metaphor. *Trends in Cognitive Sciences, 7*, 92–96.

Godden, D., & Baddeley, A.D. (1975). Context-dependent memory in two natural environments: On land and underwater. *British Journal of Psychology, 66*, 325–331.

Goffman, E. (1978). Response cries. *Language, 54*, 787–815.

Gold, I., & Stoljar, D. (1999). A neuron doctrine in the philosophy of neuroscience. *Behavioral and Brain Sciences, 22*, 809–869

Goldinger, S.D. (1998). Echoes of echoes: An episodic theory of lexical access. *Psychological Review, 105*, 251–279.

Goldman-Eisler, F. (1968). *Psycholinguistics: Experiments in spontaneous speech*. London: Academic Press.

Goldstein, D.G., & Gigerenzer, G. (2002). Models of ecological rationality: The recognition heuristic. *Psychological Review, 109*, 75–90.

Gonsalves, B., Reber, P.J., Gitelman, D.R., Parrish, T.B., Mesulam, M.-M., & Paller, K.A. (2004). Neural evidence that vivid imagining can lead to false remembering. *Psychological Science, 15*, 655–660.

Goodman, N. (1955). *Fact, fiction and forecast*. Cambridge, Mass.: Harvard University Press.

Goodwin, G.P., & Johnson-Laird, P.N. (2005). Reasoning about relations. *Psychological Review, 112*, 468–493.

Gordon, I.E. (1974). Left and right in Goya's portraits. *Nature, 249*, 197–198.

Gordon, P.C., & Holyoak, K.J. (1983). Implicit learning and the 'mere exposure' effect. *Journal of Personality and Social Psychology, 45*, 492–500.

Gorfein, D.S., & Hoffman, R.R. (1987). *Memory and learning: The Ebbinghaus centennial conference*. Hillsdale, NJ: Erlbaum.

Gorman, M.E. (1986). How the possibility of error affects falsification on a task that models scientific problem-solving. *British Journal of Psychology, 77*, 85–96.

Gorman, M.E. (1989). Error, falsification and scientific evidence. *Quarterly Journal of Experimental Psychology, 41 A*, 385–412.

Gottfredson, L.S. (1997). Why *g* matters: The complexity of everyday life. *Intelligence, 24*, 79–132.

Gottfredson, L.S. (2003a). Dissecting practical intelligence theory: Its claims and evidence. *Intelligence, 31*, 343–397.

Gottfredson, L.S. (2003b). On Sternberg's 'Reply to Gottfredson'. *Intelligence, 31*, 415–424.

Gottschaldt, K. (1967). Gestalt factors and repetition. In W.D. Ellis (Ed.), *A source book of Gestalt psychology* (pp. 109–135). New York: Humanities Press. (Original work published 1926).

Gould, S.J. (1985). *The flamingo's smile*. New York: Norton.

Gould, S.J., & Lewontin, R.C. (1979). The spandrels of San Marco and the Panglossian paradigm: A critique of the adaptationist programme. *Proceedings of the Royal Society of London (Series B), 205*, 581–98.

Gould, S.J., & Vrba, E.S. (1982). Exaptation: A missing term in the science of form. *Paleobiology, 8*, 4–15.

Graf, P., & Schacter, D.L. (1985). Implicit and explicit memory for new associations in normal and amnesic subjects. *Journal of Experimental Psychology: Learning, Memory, and Cognition, 11*, 501–518.

Grainger, J., & Whitney, C. (2004). Does the human mind raed wrods as a wlohe? *Trends in Cognitive Sciences, 8*, 58–59.

Grant, E.R., & Spivey, M.J. (2003). Eye movements and problem-solving. *Psychological Science, 14*, 462–466.

Gray, R. (2004). Attending to the execution of a complex sensorimotor skill: Expertise differences, choking, and slumps. *Journal of Experimental Psychology: Applied, 10*, 42–54.

Green, C.S., & Bavelier, D. (2003). Action video game modifies visual selective attention. *Nature, 423*, 534–537.

Green, T.R.G. (1982). Pictures of programs and other processes, or how to do things with lines. *Behaviour and Information Technology, 1*, 3–36.

Green, T.R.G., & Payne, S. (1982). The wooly jumper: Typographic problems of concurrency in information display. *Visible Language, 16*, 391–403.

Green, T.R.G., & Payne, S.J. (1984). Organization and learnability in computer languages. *International Journal of Man-Machine Studies, 21*, 7–18.

Green, T.R.G., Payne, S.J., & van der Veer, G.C. (Eds.). (1983). *The psychology of computer use*. London: Academic Press.

Greenberg, D.L. (2004). President Bush's false

'flashbulb' memory of 9/11/01. *Applied Cognitive Psychology, 18*, 363–370.

Greenberg, J.H. (1966*). Language universals.* The Hague: Mouton.

Greene, J. (1972). *Psycholinguistics: Chomsky and psychology.* Baltimore: Penguin.

Greene, R.L. (1987). Effects of maintenance rehearsal on human memory. *Psychological Bulletin, 102*, 403–413.

Greeno, J.G. (1994). Gibson's affordances. *Psychological Review, 101*, 336–342.

Greenstein, J.S., & Arnaut, L.Y. (1987). Human factors aspects of manual computer input devices. In G. Salvendy (Ed.), *Handbook of human factors* (pp. 1450–1489). New York: Wiley.

Grice, H.P. (1971). Meaning. In D. Steinberg & L. Jakobovits (Eds.), *Semantics: An interdisciplinary reader* (pp. 53–59). Cambridge: Cambridge University Press. (Original work published 1957).

Grice, H.P. (1975). Logic and conversation. In P. Cole & J.P. Morgan (Eds.), *Syntax and semantics: Vol. 3. Speech acts* (pp. 41–58). New York: Academic Press.

Grice, H.P. (1978). Further notes on logic and conversation. In P. Cole (Ed.), *Syntax and semantics: Vol. 9. Pragmatics.* New York: Academic Press.

Griggs, R.A., & Cox, J.R. (1982). The elusive thematic materials effect in Wason's selection task. *British Journal of Psychology, 73*, 407–420.

Griggs, R.A., & Newstead, S.E. (1983). The source of intuitive errors in Wason's THOG problem. *British Journal of Psychology, 74*, 451–459.

Groen, G.J., & Parkman, J.M. (1972). A chronometric analysis of simple addition. *Psychological Review, 79*, 329–342.

Gross, L. (1983, March). Why Johnny can't draw. *Arts Education*, 74–77.

Gross, S.R., & Miller, N. (1997). The 'golden section' and bias in perceptions of social consensus. *Personality and Social Psychology Bulletin, 1*, 241–271.

Grossenbacher, P.G., & Lovelace, C.T. (2001).

Mechanisms of synesthesia: Cognitive and physiological constraints. *Trends in Cognitive Sciences, 5*, 36–41.

Gruber, H.E. (1981). *Darwin on man: A psychological study of scientific creativity* (2nd ed.). Chicago: University of Chicago Press. (Original work published 1974).

Gruber, H.E., & Wallace, D.B. (2001). Creative work: The case of Charles Darwin. *American Psychologist, 56*, 346–349.

Grudin, J. (1989). The case against user interface consistency. *Communications of the ACM, 32*, 1164–1173.

Guastello, S.J., Traut, M., & Korienek, G. (1989). Verbal versus pictorial representations of objects in a human-computer interface. *International Journal of Man-Machine Studies, 31*, 99–120.

Guiard, Y., & Beaudoin-Lafon, M. (2004). Fitts' law 50 years later: Applications and contributions from human-computer interaction. *International Journal of Human-Computer Studies, 61*, 747–750.

Guilford, J. (1967). *The nature of human intelligence.* New York: McGraw-Hill.

Haber, R.N. (1979). Twenty years of haunting eidetic imagery: Where's the ghost? *Behavioral and Brain Sciences, 2*, 583–629.

Haber, R.N. (1983). The impending demise of the icon: A critique of the concept of iconic storage in visual information processing. *Behavioral and Brain Sciences, 6*, 1–13.

Halper, F. (1997). The illusion of *The Future. Perception, 26*, 1321–1322.

Halpern, S. (2002, Aug. 15). Heart of darkness. *New York Review of Books, 49*, 16–22.

Hamilton, H.W., & Deese, J. (1971). Does linguistic marking have a psychological correlate? *Journal of Verbal Learning and Verbal Behaviour, 10*, 707–714.

Hampson, S.E. (1998). When is an inconsistency not an inconsistency? Trait reconciliation in personality description and impression formation. *Journal of Personality and Social Psychology, 74*, 102–117.

Hampton, R.R., & Schwartz, B.L. (2004). Episodic memory in nonhumans: What, and where, is when? *Current Opinion in Neurobiology, 14,* 192–197.

Hanson, N.R. (1969). *Patterns of discovery.* Cambridge: Cambridge University Press.

Harris, J. (1984). Methods of improving memory. In B.A. Wilson & N. Moffat (Eds.), *Clinical management of memory problems* (pp. 46–62). Rockville, Md: Aspen Publications.

Harris, R.J. (1973). Answering questions containing marked and unmarked adjectives and adverbs. *Journal of Experimental Psychology, 97,* 399–401.

Harrison, J. (2001). *Synaesthesia: The strangest thing.* Oxford: Oxford University Press.

Harshman, R.A., & Paivio, A. (1987). 'Paradoxical' sex differences in self-reported imagery. *Canadian Journal of Psychology, 41,* 287–302.

Hatfield, G. (1992). Empirical, rational, and transcendental psychology: Psychology as science and as philosophy. In P. Guyer (Ed.), *The Cambridge companion to Kant* (pp. 200–227). Cambridge: Cambridge University Press.

Hatfield, G. (1998). Kant and empirical psychology in the 18th century. *Psychological Science, 9,* 423–428.

Hatfield, G., & Epstein, W. (1987). The status of the minimum principle in the theoretical analysis of visual perception. *Psychological Bulletin, 97,* 155–186.

Hauser, M.D., Chomsky, N., & Fitch, W.T. (2002). The faculty of language: What is it, who has it, and how did it evolve? *Science, 298,* 1569–1579.

Hayman, C.A., & Tulving, E. (1989). Contingent dissociation between recognition and fragment completion: The method of triangulation. *Journal of Experimental Psychology: Learning, Memory, and Cognition, 15,* 228–240.

Hazeltine, E., Teague, D., & Ivry, R.B. (2002). Simultaneous dual-task performance reveals parallel response selection after practice. *Journal of Experimental Psychology: Human Perception and Performance, 28,* 527–545.

Heath, S.B. (1986). The functions and uses of literacy. In S. de Castell, A. Luke, & K. Egan (Eds.), *Literacy, society and schooling* (pp. 15–26). Cambridge: Cambridge University Press.

Heath, S.B. (1989). Oral and literate traditions among black Americans living in poverty. *American Psychologist, 44,* 367–373.

Hebb, D.O. (1949). *The organization of behavior.* New York: Wiley.

Heckhausen, H., & Beckmann, J. (1990). Intentional action and action slips. *Psychological Review, 97,* 36–48.

Heider, E.R. [Eleanor Rosch]. (1971a). Focal color area and the development of color names. *Developmental Psychology, 4,* 447–455.

Heider, E.R. [Eleanor Rosch]. (1971b). On the internal structure of perceptual and semantic categories. Paper presented at the Conference on Developmental Psycholinguistics, Buffalo, NY.

Heider, E.R. [Eleanor Rosch], & Olivier, D. (1972). The structure of the color space in naming and memory for two languages. *Cognitive Psychology, 3,* 337–354.

Heider, F. (1958). *The psychology of interpersonal relations.* New York: Wiley.

Heim, S., Opitz, B., Friederici, A.D. (2003). Distributed cortical networks for syntax processing: Broca's area as the common denominator. *Brain and Language, 85,* 402–408.

Heinrichs, R.W. (1984). Verbal responses to human figure paintings: A test of the uncertainty hypothesis. *Canadian Journal of Psychology, 38,* 512–518.

Hejmadi, A.H., Rozin, P., & Siegal, M. (2004). Once in contact, always in contact: Contagious essence and conceptions of purification in American and Hindu Indian children. *Developmental Psychology, 40,* 467–476.

Henle, M. (1968). Deductive reasoning. In P.C. Wason & P.N. Johnson-Laird (Eds.), *Deductive reasoning* (pp. 93–107). Baltimore: Penguin. (Original work published 1962).

Henle, M. (1987). Koffka's principles after fifty years. *Journal of the History of the Behavioral Sciences, 25,* 14–21.

Hering, E. (1961). Principles of a new theory of the color sense. In R.C. Teevan & R.C. Birney

(Eds.), *Color vision* (pp. 28–31). New York: Van Nostrand. (Original work published 1878).

Herrmann, D.J. (1993). The ethnographic method and the investigation of memory. *Applied Cognitive Psychology, 7*, 184.

Herrmann, D.J., & Neisser, U. (1979). An inventory of everyday memory experiences. In M.M. Gruneberg & P.E. Morris (Eds.), *Applied problems in memory*. London: Academic Press.

Hertel, P.T., & Gerstle, M. (2003). Depressive deficits in forgetting. *Psychological Science, 14*, 573–578.

Hertel, P.T., & Hardin, T.S. (1990). Remembering without awareness in a depressed mood: Evidence of deficits in initiative. *Journal of Experimental Psychology: General, 119*, 45–59.

Hertel, P.T., & Rude, S.S. (1991). Depressive deficits in memory: Focusing attention improves subsequent recall. *Journal of Experimental Psychology: General, 120*, 301–309.

Heyes, C. (2003). Four routes of cognitive evolution. *Psychological Review, 110*, 713–727.

Hilgard, E.R. (1980). The trilogy of mind: Cognition, affection and conation. *Journal of the History of the Behavioral Sciences, 16*, 107–117.

Hilgard, E.R. (1987). *Psychology in America: An historical survey*. New York: Harcourt Brace Jovanovich.

Hintzman, D.L. (1986). 'Schema abstraction' in a multiple-trace memory model. *Psychological Review, 93*, 411–428.

Hintzman, D.L., Curran, T., & Oppy, B. (1992). Effects of similarity and repetition on memory: Registration without learning? *Journal of Experimental Psychology: Learning, Memory, and Cognition, 18*, 667–680.

Hirschfeld, L.A., & Gelman, S.A. (1994). *Mapping the mind: Domain specificity in cognition and culture*. Cambridge: Cambridge University Press.

Hirschfeld, L.A., & Gelman, S.A. (1997). What young children think about the relationship between language variation and social difference. *Cognitive Development, 12*, 213–238.

Hirst, W. (1986). The psychology of attention. In J. LeDoux and W. Hirst (Eds.), *Mind and brain: Dialogues in cognitive neuroscience* (pp. 105–141). New York: Cambridge University Press.

Hirst, W., & Kalmar, K. (1987). Characterizing attentional resources. *Journal of Experimental Psychology: General, 116*, 68–81.

Hirst, W., & Levine, E. (1985). Ecological memory reconsidered: A comment on Bruce's 'The how and why of ecological memory'. *Journal of Experimental Psychology: General, 114*, 269–271.

Hirst, W., Neisser, U., & Spelke, E. (1978). Divided attention. *Human Nature, 1*, 54–61.

Hirst, W., Spelke, E.S., Reaves, C.C., Caharack, G., & Neisser, U. (1980). Dividing attention without alteration or automaticity. *Journal of Experimental Psychology: General, 109*, 98–117.

Hoc, J.M. (2001). Towards ecological validity of research in cognitive ergonomics. *Theoretical Issues in Ergonomic Science, 2*, 278–288.

Hodges, J.R. (2000). Memory in the dementias. In E. Tulving & F.I.M. Craik (Eds.), *The Oxford handbook of memory* (pp. 645–648). New York: Oxford University Press.

Hodges, J.R., Salmon, D.P., & Butters, N. (1992). Semantic memory impairment in Alzheimer's disease: Failure of access or degraded knowledge? *Neuropsychologia, 30*, 301–314.

Hoff, E. (2004). Progress, but not a full solution to the logical problem of language acquisition. *Journal of Child Language, 31*, 923–926.

Hoffman, R.R., & Deffenbacher, K.A. (1992). A brief history of applied cognitive psychology. *Applied Cognitive Psychology, 6*, 1–48.

Hofstadter, D. (1979). *Godel, Escher, Bach: An eternal golden braid*. New York: Basic Books.

Hofstadter, D. (1982). Meta-font, metamathematics, and metaphysics: Comments on Donald Knuth's 'The concept of a meta-font'. *Visible Language, 16*, 309–338.

Hollins, M. (1985). Styles of mental imagery in blind adults. *Neuropsychologia, 23*, 561–566.

Holloway, C. (1978). *Cognitive psychology: Units 22–23*. Milton Keynes, UK: Open University.

Hoptman, M.J., & Davidson, R.J. (1994). How and why do the two cerebral hemispheres interact? *Psychological Review, 116*, 195–219.

Horowitz, L.M., Norman, S.A., & Day, R.S. (1966). Availability and associative symmetry. *Psychological Review, 73*, 1–15.

Horstmann, G. (2002). Evidence for attentional capture by a surprising color singleton in visual search. *Psychological Science, 13*, 499–505.

Howard, D.V., Fry, A., & Brune, C. (1991). Aging and memory for new associations: Direct versus indirect measures. *Journal of Experimental Psychology: Learning, Memory, and Cognition, 17*, 779–792.

Howe, M.L., & Courage, M.L. (1993). On resolving the enigma of infantile amnesia. *Psychological Bulletin, 113*, 305–326.

Huettel, S.A., Mack, P.B., & McCarthy, G. (2002). Perceiving patterns in random series: Dynamic processing of sequence in prefrontal cortex. *Nature Neuroscience, 5*, 485–490.

Hughes, G. (1988). *Words in time*. Oxford: Blackwell.

Hughes, P., & Brecht, G. (1975). *Vicious circles and infinity*. New York: Penguin.

Humphrey, G. (1963). *Thinking: An introduction to its experimental psychology*. New York: Wiley. (Original work published 1951).

Humphrey, N.K., & McManus, C. (1973). Status and the left cheek, *New Scientist, 59*, 437–439.

Hunt, E.B., & Agnoli, F. (1991). The Whorfian hypothesis: A cognitive psychology perspective. *Psychological Review, 98*, 377–389.

Hunt, E.B., & Hovland, C.I. (1960). Order of consideration of different types of concept. *Journal of Experimental Psychology, 59*, 220–225.

Hunt, R.R. (1995). The subtlety of distinctiveness: What von Restorff really did. *Psychonomic Bulletin and Review, 2*, 105–112.

Hunt, R.R., & Lamb, C.A. (2001). What causes the isolation effect? *Journal of Experimental Psychology: Learning, Memory, and Cognition, 27*, 1359–1366.

Hunter, I.M.L. (1977). An exceptional memory. *British Journal of Psychology, 68*, 155–164.

Hunter, I.M.L. (1979). Memory in everyday life. In M.M. Gruneberg & P.E. Morris (Eds.), *Applied problems in memory*. London: Academic Press.

Hurvich, L., & Jameson, D. (1957). An opponent-process theory of color vision. *Psychological Review, 64*, 384–390.

Hutchins, E. (1983). Understanding Micronesian navigation. In D. Gentner & A.L. Stevens (Eds.), *Mental models*. Hillsdale, NJ: Erlbaum.

Huttenlocher, J., & Higgins, E.T. (1971). Adjectives, comparatives and syllogisms. *Psychological Review, 78*, 487–504.

Huttenlocher, J., Vasilyeva, M., Cymerman, E., & Levine, S. (2002). Language input and child syntax. *Cognitive Psychology, 45*, 337–374.

Hyams, N.M. (1986). *Language acquisition and the theory of parameters*. Dordrecht, the Netherlands: Reidel.

Hyman, I.E., & Neisser, U. (1991). *Reconstructing mental images: Problems of method* (Emory Cognition Project Tech. Rep. No. 19). Atlanta: Emory University.

Indian and Northern Affairs Canada (2000). *Nunavut, Canada's third territory 'North of 60'.* Retrieved March 21, 2005, from Indian and Northern Affairs Canada. website: www.ainc-inac.gc.ca/ks/pdf/nunavu_e.pdf

Isen, A.M. (1984). Toward understanding the role of affect in cognition. In R.S. Wyer & T.K. Srull (Eds.), *Handbook of social cognition* (pp. 174–236). Hillsdale, NJ: Erlbaum.

Isen, A.M., Daubman, K.A., & Nowicki, G.P. (1987). Positive affect facilitates creative problem-solving. *Journal of Personality and Social Psychology, 52*, 1122–1131.

Ivry, R., & Knight, R.T. (2002). Making order from chaos: The misguided frontal lobe. *Nature Neuroscience, 5*, 394–396.

Jack, A.I., & Shallice, T. (2001). Introspective physicalism as an approach to the science of consciousness. *Cognition, 79*, 161–196.

Jack, A.I., & Roepstorff, A. (2002). Introspection and cognitive brain mapping: From stimulus-response to script report. *Trends in Cognitive Sciences, 6*, 333–339.

Jackson, M.A., & Simpson, K.H. (2004). Pain after amputation. *Continuing Education in Anaesthesia, Critical Care & Pain, 4*, 20–23.

Jacoby, L.L. (1999). Ironic effects of repetition: Measuring age-related differences in memory. *Journal of Experimental Psychology: Learning, Memory, and Cognition, 25*, 3–22.

Jacoby, L.L., & Dallas, M. (1981). On the relationship between autobiographical memory and perceptual learning. *Journal of Experimental Psychology: General, 110*, 306–340.

Jacoby, L.L., & Hollingshead, A. (1990). Reading student essays may be hazardous to your health. *Canadian Journal of Psychology, 44*, 345–358.

Jacoby, L.L., & Kelley, C.M. (1994). A process-dissociation framework for investigating unconscious influences: Freudian slips, projective tests, subliminal perception, and signal detection theory. *Current Directions in Psychological Science, 1*, 174–179.

Jacoby, L.L., & Witherspoon, D. (1982). Remembering without awareness. *Canadian Journal of Psychology, 36*, 300–324.

James, T., Soroka, L., & Benjafield, J. (2001). Are economists rational, or just different? *Social Behavior and Personality, 29*, 359–364.

James, W. (1983). *Principles of psychology*. Cambridge, Mass.: Harvard University Press. (Original work published 1890).

Jaynes, J. (1977). *The origins of consciousness in the breakdown of the bicameral mind*. Boston: Houghton Mifflin.

Jaynes, J. (1979). Paleolithic cave paintings as eidetic images. *Behavioral and Brain Sciences, 2*, 605–607.

Jedliça, P. (2005). Neuroethics: Reductionism and dualism. *Trends in Cognitive Sciences, 9*, 172.

Jenkins, J.G., & Dallenbach, K.M. 1924. Oblivicence during sleep and waking. *American Journal of Psychology, 35*, 605–612.

Jenkins, J.J. (1974). Remember that old theory of memory? Well, forget it! *American Psychologist, 29*, 785–795.

Jensen, A.R. (1972). *Genetics and education*. New York: Harper & Row.

Jersild, A. (1927). Mental set and shift. *Archives of Psychology, 14* (Whole No. 89), 5–82.

Johnson, C.J., Paivio, A., & Clark, J.M. (1996). Cognitive components of picture naming. *Psychological Bulletin, 120*, 113–139.

Johnson, M., & Lakoff, G. (2002). Why cognitive linguistics requires embodied realism. *Cognitive Linguistics, 13*, 245–263.

Johnson, M.K. (1985). The origin of memories. In P.C. Kendall (Ed.), *Advances in cognitive-behavioral research and therapy* (Vol. 4, pp. 1–27). New York: Academic Press.

Johnson, M.K. (1988). Reality monitoring: An experimental phenomenological approach. *Journal of Experimental Psychology: General, 117*, 390–394.

Johnson, M.K., Hashtroudi, S., & Lindsay, D.S. (1993). Source monitoring. *Psychological Review, 114*, 3–28.

Johnson, M.K., & Raye, C.L. (1981). Reality monitoring. *Psychological Review, 88*, 67–85.

Johnson, M.K., & Raye, C.L. (1998). False memories and confabulation. *Trends in Cognitive Sciences, 2*, 137–145.

Johnson, W., Bouchard, T.J., Krueger, R.F., McGue, M., & Gottesman, I.J. (2004). Just one *g*: Consistent results from three test batteries. *Intelligence, 32*, 95–107.

Johnson-Laird, P.N. (1972). The three-term series problem. *Cognition, 1*, 57–82.

Johnson-Laird, P.N. (1983). *Mental models*. Cambridge, Mass.: Harvard University Press.

Johnson-Laird, P.N. (1988). *The computer and the mind*. Cambridge, Mass.: Harvard University Press.

Johnson-Laird, P.N. (1997a). Rules and illusions: A critical study of Rips's *The psychology of proof*. *Minds and Machines, 7*, 387–407.

Johnson-Laird, P.N. (1997b). An end to the controversy: A reply to Rips. *Minds and Machines, 7*, 425–432.

Johnson-Laird, P.N. (1999). Deductive reasoning. *Annual Review of Psychology, 50*, 109–135.

Johnson-Laird, P.N. (2001). Mental models and deduction. *Trends in Cognitive Sciences, 5*, 434–442.

Johnson-Laird, P.N., & Byrne, R.M.J. (1990). Meta-logical problems: Knights, knaves, and Rips. *Cognition, 36*, 69–84.

Johnson-Laird, P.N., & Byrne, R.M.J. (1993). Precis of 'deduction'. *Behavioral and Brain Sciences, 16*, 323–380.

Johnson-Laird, P.N., Herrmann, D.J., & Chafin, R. (1984). Only connections: A critique of semantic networks. *Psychological Bulletin, 96*, 292–315.

Johnson-Laird, P.N., Legrenzi, P., Girotto, V., Legrenzi, M.S., & Caverni, J.P. (1999). Naïve probability: A mental model theory of extensional reasoning. *Psychological Review, 106*, 62–88.

Johnson-Laird, P.N., & Steedman, M. (1978). The psychology of syllogisms. *Cognitive Psychology, 10*, 64–99.

Johnson-Laird, P.N., & Wason, P.C. (1970). A theoretical analysis of insight into a reasoning task. *Cognitive Psychology, 1*, 134–148.

Johnston, E.B. (2001). The repeated reproduction of Bartlett's 'Remembering'. *History of Psychology, 4*, 341–366.

Johnston, W.A., & Dark, V.J. (1986). Selective attention. In M. Rosenzweig & L. Porter (Eds.), *Annual Review of Psychology* (pp. 43–75). Palo Alto, Calif.: Annual Reviews.

Jones, G. (2003). Testing two cognitive theories of insight. *Journal of Experimental Psychology: Learning, Memory, and Cognition, 29*, 1017–1027.

Jones, W.P., & Hoskins, J. (1987, October). Back propagation: A generalized delta learning rule. *Byte Magazine*, pp. 155–162.

Jonides, J., Badre, D., Curtis, C., Thompson-Schill, S.L., & Smith, E.E. (2002). Mechanisms of conflict resolution in prefrontal cortex. In D.T. Stuss & R.T. Knight (Eds.), *Principles of frontal lobe function* (pp. 233–245). New York: Oxford University Press.

Jorgenson, J., Miller, G.A., & Sperber, D. (1984). Test of the mention theory of irony. *Journal of Experimental Psychology: General, 113*, 112–120.

Judson, H.F. (1984). Century of the sciences. *Science 84*, 41–43.

Jung, C.G. (1950). Foreword. In *The I Ching or book of changes* (C.F. Baynes, Trans.). Princeton, NJ: Princeton University Press.

Jung, C.G. (1973). *Synchronicity: An acausal connecting principle*. Princeton, NJ: Princeton University Press.

Kahneman, D. (1973). *Attention and effort*. Englewood Cliffs, NJ: Prentice-Hall.

Kahneman, D. (2002). Maps of bounded rationality: A perspective on intuitive judgment and choice. In Tore Frängsmyr (Ed.), *Les Prix Nobel/The Nobel Prizes 2002*. Stockholm: Nobel Foundation. Retrieved May 2, 2005, from http://nobelprize.org/economics/laureates/2002/kahnemann-lecture.pdf

Kahneman, D. (2003). A perspective on judgment and choice: Mapping bounded rationality. *American Psychologist, 58*, 697–720.

Kahneman, D., & Frederick, S. (2002). Representativeness revisited: Attribute substitution in intuitive judgement. In T. Gilovich, D. Griffin, & D. Kahneman (Eds.), *Heuristics and biases: The psychology of intuitive judgment* (pp. 49–81). Cambridge: Cambridge University Press.

Kahneman, D., & Miller, D.T. (1986). Norm theory: Comparing reality to its alternatives. *Psychological Review, 93*, 136–153.

Kahneman, D., & Treisman, A. (1984). Changing views of attention and automaticity. In R. Parasuraman & D.R. Davies (Eds.), *Varieties of attention* (pp. 29–61). Orlando, Fla: Academic Press.

Kahneman, D., & Tversky, A. (1972). Subjective probability: A judgment of representativeness. *Cognitive Psychology, 3*, 430–454.

Kahneman, D., & Tversky, A. (1979). Prospect theory: An analysis of decision under risk. *Econometrica, 47*, 263–271.

Kahneman, D., & Tversky, A. (1984). Choices, values, and frames. *American Psychologist, 39*, 341–350.

Kahneman, D., & Tversky, A. (1996). On the reality of cognitive illusions. *Psychological Review, 103*, 582–591.

Kanazawa, S. (2004). General intelligence as a domain-specific adaptation. *Psychological Review, 111*, 512–523.

Kanisza, G. (1979). *Organization in vision*. New York: Praeger.

Kanouse, D.E., & Hanson, L.R. (1971). Negativity in evaluations. In E.E. Jones (Ed.), *Attribution: Perceiving the causes of behavior.* Morristown, NJ: General Learning Press.

Kant, I. (1929). *Critique of pure reason* (N.K. Smith, Trans.). New York: St Martin's Press. (Original work published 1781).

Kanwisher, N., McDermott, J., & Chun, M. (1997). The fusiform face area: A module in human extrastriate cortex specialized for face perception. *Journal of Neuroscience, 17,* 4302–4311.

Kaplan, C.A., & Simon, H.A. (1990). In search of insight. *Cognitive Psychology, 22,* 374–419.

Kapur, N., Glisky, E.L., & Wilson, B.A. (2002). External memory aids and computers in memory rehabilitation. In A.D. Baddeley, M.D. Kopelman, & B.A. Wilson (Eds.), *The handbook of memory disorders* (pp. 757–783). New York: Wiley.

Katz, A.N., Blasko, D.G., & Kazmerski, V.A. (2004). Saying what you don't mean: Social influences on sarcastic language processing. *Current Directions in Psychological Science, 13,* 186–189.

Katz, A.N., Paivio, A., Marschark, M., & Clark, J.M. (1988). Norms for 204 literary and 260 non-literary metaphors on 10 psychological dimensions. *Metaphor and Symbolic Activity, 3,* 191–214.

Katz, J. (1993). Phantom limb experience in children and adults: Cognitive and affective contributions. *Canadian Journal of Behavioural Science, 25,* 335–354.

Kay, P., & McDaniel, C.K. (1978). The linguistic significance of the meanings of basic color terms. *Language, 54,* 610–646.

Kay, P., & Regier, T. (2003). Resolving the question of color naming universals. *Proceedings of the National Academy of Sciences, 100,* 9085–9089.

Kay, R.H. (1989). A practical and theoretical approach to assessing computer attitudes: The Computer Attitude Measure (CAM). *Journal of Research on Computing Education, 21,* 456–463.

Kay. R.H. (1993). An exploration of theoretical and practical foundations for assessing atti-

tudes towards computers: The Computer Attitude Measure (CAM). *Computers in Human Behavior, 9,* 371–386.

Kelley, C.M., & Jacoby, L.L. (2000). Recognition and familiarity; process dissociation. In E. Tulving & F.I.M. Craik (Eds.), *The Oxford handbook of memory* (pp. 215–228). New York: Oxford University Press.

Kennedy, H., Batardiere, A., Dehay, C., & Barone, P. (1997). Synaesthesia: Implications for developmental neurobiology. In S. Baron-Cohen & J.E. Harrison (Eds.), *Synaesthesia: Classic and contemporary readings* (pp. 243–256). Oxford: Blackwell.

Keren, G. (1984). On the importance of identifying the correct 'problem space'. *Cognition, 16,* 121–128.

Kihlstrom, J.F. (1987). The cognitive unconscious. *Science, 237,* 1335–1552.

Kihlstrom, J.F. (1995). Memory and consciousness: An appreciation of Claparède and 'Recognition et Moité'. *Consciousness and Cognition, 4,* 379–386.

Kihlstrom, J.F. (2004). Availability, accessibility, and subliminal perception. *Consciousness and Cognition, 13,* 92–100.

Kinder, A., Shanks, D.R., Cock, J., & Timney, R.J. (2003). Recollection, fluency, and the explicit/implicit distinction in artificial grammar learning. *Journal of Experimental Psychology: General, 132,* 551–565.

Kingstone, A., Smilek, D., Ristic, J., Friesen, C.K., & Eastwood, J.D. (2003). Attention researchers! It's time to take a look at the real world. *Current Directions in Psychological Science, 12,* 176–180.

Kinsbourne, M., & Wood, F. (1975). Short-term memory processes and the amnesic syndrome. In D. Deutsch & J.A. Deutsch (Eds.), *Short-term memory.* New York: Academic Press.

Kirasic, K. (1991). Spatial cognition and behavior in young and elderly adults: Implications for learning new environments. *Psychology and Aging, 6,* 10–18.

Klahr, D., & Simon, H.A. (1999). Studies of scientific discovery: Complementary approaches and convergent findings. *Psychological Bulletin, 125,* 524–543.

Klahr, D., & Simon, H.A. (2001). What have psychologists (and others) discovered about the process of scientific discovery? *Current Directions in Psychological Science, 10,* 75–79.

Klatzky, R.L., Clark, E.V., & Macken, M. (1971). Asymmetries in the acquisition of polar adjectives. *Journal of Experimental Child Psychology, 16,* 32–46.

Klauer, K.C., Mierke, J., & Musch, J. (2003). The positivity proportion effect: A list context effect in masked affective priming. *Memory & Cognition, 31,* 953–967.

Klein, S.B., Cosmides, L., Tooby, J., & Chance, S. (2002). Decisions and the evolution of memory: Multiple systems, multiple functions. *Psychological Review, 109,* 306–329.

Klein, S.B., Loftus, J., & Kihlstrom, J.F. (1996). Self-knowledge of an amnesic patient: Toward a neuropsychology of personality and social psychology. *Journal of Experimental Psychology: General, 125,* 250–260.

Knoblich, G., Ohlsson, S., Haider, H., & Rhenius, D. (1999). Constraint relaxation and chunk decomposition in insight problem-solving. *Journal of Experimental Psychology: Learning, Memory, and Cognition, 25,* 1534–1555.

Knoblich, G., Ohlsson, S., & Raney, G.E. (2001). An eye movement study of insight problem solving. *Memory & Cognition, 29,* 1000–1009.

Koenig, C.S., & Griggs, R.A. (2001). Elementary my dear Wason: The role of problem representation in the THOG task. *Psychological Research, 65,* 289–293.

Koenig, C.S., & Griggs, R.A. (2004a). Analogical transfer in the THOG task. *Quarterly Journal of Experimental Psychology, 57A,* 557–570.

Koenig, C.S., & Griggs, R.A. (2004b). Facilitation and analogical transfer in the THOG task. *Thinking and Reasoning, 10,* 355–370.

Koffka, K. (1935). *Principles of Gestalt psychology.* New York: Harcourt, Brace.

Köhler, W. (1925). *The mentality of apes.* London: Routledge & Kegan Paul.

Köhler, W. (1940). *Dynamics in psychology.* New York: Liveright.

Köhler, W. (1956). *The mentality of apes.* New York: Vintage. (Original work published 1925).

Köhler, W. (1969). *The task of Gestalt psychology.* Princeton, NJ: Princeton University Press.

Komatsu, L.K. (1992). Recent views of conceptual structure. *Psychological Bulletin, 112,* 500–526.

Konečni, V.J. (1996). Daniel E. Berlyne (1924–1976): Two decades later. *Empirical Studies of the Arts, 14,* 129–142.

Korf, R. (1999). Heuristic search. In R.A. Wilson & F.C. Keil (Eds.), *The MIT encyclopedia of the cognitive sciences* (pp. 372–373). Cambridge, Mass.: MIT Press.

Koriat, A. (2000). Control processes in remembering. In E. Tulving & F.I.M. Craik (Eds.), *The Oxford handbook of memory* (pp. 333–346). New York: Oxford University Press.

Koriat, A., & Bjork, R.A. (2005). Illusions of competence in monitoring one's knowledge during study. *Journal of Experimental Psychology: Learning, Memory, and Cognition, 31,* 187–194.

Koriat, A., & Goldsmith, M. (1996). Memory metaphors and the real life/laboratory controversy: Correspondence versus storehouse conceptions of memory. *Behavioral and Brain Sciences, 19,* 167–228.

Koriat, A., Goldsmith, M., & Pansky, A. (2000). Toward a psychology of memory accuracy. *Annual Review of Psychology, 51,* 481–537.

Kornmeier, J., & Bach, M. (2004). Early neural activity in Necker-cube reversal: Evidence for low-level processing of a gestalt phenomenon, *Psychophysiology, 41,* 1–8.

Korsakoff, S.S. (1899). Étude médico-psychologique sur une forme des malades de la mémoire [Medical-psychological study of a form of diseases of memory]. *Revue Philosophique, 28,* 501–530.

Kosslyn, S.M. (1980). *Image and mind.* Cambridge, Mass.: Harvard University Press.

Kosslyn, S.M. (1983). *Ghosts in the mind's machine.* New York: Norton.

Kosslyn, S.M., Ball, T.M., & Reiser, B.J. (1978). Visual images preserve metric spatial information: Evidence from studies of image scanning. *Journal of Experimental Psychology: Human Perception and Performance, 4,* 47–60.

Kosslyn, S.M., Ganis, G., & Thompson, W.L. (2003). Mental imagery: Against the null hypothesis. *Trends in Cognitive Sciences, 7,* 109–111.

Kosslyn, S.M., Ganis, G., & Thompson, W.L. (2001). Neural foundations of imagery. *Nature Reviews Neuroscience, 2,* 635–642.

Kosslyn, S.M., Thompson, W.L., & Ganis, G. (2002). Mental imagery doesn't work like that. *Behavioral and Brain Sciences, 25,* 198–201.

Kraus, S., & Wang, X.T. (2003). The psychology of the Monty Hall problem: Discovering psychological mechanisms for solving a tenacious brain teaser. *Journal of Experimental Psychology: General, 132,* 3–22.

Krech, D. (1962). Cortical localization of function. In L. Postman (Ed.), *Psychology in the making.* New York: Wiley.

Krech, D., & Crutchfield, R.S. (1958). *Elements of psychology.* New York: Knopf.

Kreitler, H., & Kreitler, S. (1972). *The psychology of the arts.* Durham, NC: Duke University Press.

Kreuz, R.J., & Glucksberg, S. (1989). How to be sarcastic: The echoic reminder theory of verbal irony. *Journal of Experimental Psychology: General, 118,* 374–386.

Kristol, A. (1980). Color systems in southern Italy: A case of regression. *Language, 56,* 137–145.

Kuhn, D. (1989). Children and adults as intuitive scientists. *Psychological Review, 96,* 674–689.

Kuhn, D. (1991). Thinking as argument. *Harvard Educational Review, 62,* 155–178.

Kuhn, T.S. (1970). *The structure of scientific revolutions* (2nd ed.). Chicago: University of Chicago Press.

Kunda, Z., & Nisbett, R.E. (1986). The psychometrics of everyday life. *Cognitive Psychology, 18,* 195–224.

Kvavilashvili, L., & Mandler, G. (2004). Out of one's mind: A study of involuntary semantic memories. *Cognitive Psychology, 48,* 47–94.

LaBerge, D.L. (1990). Attention. *Psychological Science, 1,* 156–162.

Lachter, J., & Bever, T.G. (1988). The relationship between linguistic structure and associative theories of language learning: A constructive critique of some connectionist learning models. *Cognition, 28,* 195–247.

Lagnado, D.A., & Shanks, D.R. (2003). The influence of hierarchy on probability judgement. *Cognition, 89,* 157–178.

Lakatos, I. (1970). Falsification and the methodology of scientific research programmes. In I. Lakatos & A. Musgrave (Eds.), *Criticism and the growth of knowledge* (pp. 91–195). Cambridge: Cambridge University Press.

Lakoff, G. (1987). *Women, fire and dangerous things.* Chicago: University of Chicago Press.

Lakoff, G., & Johnson, M. (1980). *Metaphors we live by.* Chicago: University of Chicago Press.

Lakoff, G., & Johnson, M. (1999). *Philosophy in the flesh.* New York: Basic Books.

Langer, E.J. (1989). *Mindlessness/mindfulness.* Reading, Mass.: Addison-Wesley.

Langer, E.J. (2000). Mindful learning. *Current Directions in Psychological Science, 9,* 220–223.

Langer, E.J., & Piper, A.I. (1987). The prevention of mindlessness. *Journal of Personality and Social Psychology, 53,* 280–287.

Langley, P., Simon, H.A., Bradshaw, G.L., & Zytkow, J.M. (1987). *Scientific discovery: Computational explorations of the creative process.* Cambridge, Mass.: MIT Press.

Lashley, K.S. (1929). *Brain mechanisms and intelligence.* Chicago: University of Chicago Press.

Lashley, K.S. (1978). Basic neural mechanisms in behavior. In E.R. Hilgard (Ed.), *American psychology in historical perspective* (pp. 265–283). Washington: American Psychological Association. (Original work published 1930).

Lasnik, H. (2002). The minimalist program. *Trends in Cognitive Sciences, 6,* 432–437.

Laughlin, P., Lange, R., & Adamopoulos, J. (1982). Selection strategies for 'Master-mind' problems. *Journal of Experimental Psychology: Learning, Memory, and Cognition, 8,* 475–483.

Lavery, J.J. (1962). Retention of simple motor skills as a function of type of knowledge of results. *Canadian Journal of Psychology, 16,* 300–311.

Lavie, N., Hirst, A., Fockert, J.W. de, & Viding, E. (2004). Load theory of selective attention and cognitive control. *Journal of Experimental Psychology: General, 133*, 339–354.

Lavie, N., Ro, T., & Russell, C. (2003). The role of perceptual load in processing distractor faces. *Psychological Science, 14*, 510–515.

Lazarus, R.S. (1984). On the primacy of cognition. *American Psychologist, 39*, 124–129.

Lazarus, R.S., & McCleary, R. (1951). Autonomic discrimination without awareness: A study of subception. *Psychological Review, 58*, 113–122.

LeDoux, J. (2003). *Synaptic self.* New York: Penguin.

Lefebvre, V.A. (1985). The Golden Section and an algebraic model of ethical cognition. *Journal of Mathematical Psychology, 29*, 289–310.

Lefebvre, V.A., Lefebvre, V.D., & Adams-Webber, J. (1986). Modeling an experiment on construing self and others. *Journal of Mathematical Psychology, 30*, 317–330.

Lehar, S. (2003). Gestalt isomorphism and the primacy of subjective conscious experience: A gestalt bubble model. *Behavioral and Brain Sciences, 26*, 375–444.

Lehman, D.R., & Nisbett, R.E. (1990). A longitudinal study of the effects of undergraduate training on reasoning. *Developmental Psychology, 26*, 952–960.

Lehman, D.R., Lempert, R.O., & Nisbett, R.E. (1988). The effects of graduate training on reasoning. *American Psychologist, 43*, 431–442.

Lemmons, P. (1982, November). A short history of the keyboard. *Byte Magazine*, pp. 386–387.

Levine, L.J., & Pizarro, D.A. (2004). Emotion and memory research: A grumpy overview. *Social Cognition, 22*, 530–554.

Levinson, S.C. (1996). Language and space. *Annual Review of Anthropology, 25*, 353–382.

Levinson, S.C., Kita, S., Haun, D.B.M., & Rasch, B.H. (2002). Returning the tables: Language affects spatial reasoning. *Cognition, 84*, 155–188.

Levy, D.A., Stark, C.E.L., & Squire, L.R. (2004). Intact conceptual priming in the absence of declarative memory. *Psychological Science, 15*, 680–686.

Leyens, J.-P., & Corneille, O. (1999). Asch's social psychology: Not as social as you may think. *Personality and Social Psychology Review, 3*, 345–357.

Liebowitz, S., & Margolis, S.E. (1996). Typing errors. *Reason, 28*, 28–36.

Lightfoot, D. (1982). *The language lottery: Toward a biology of grammars.* Cambridge, Mass.: MIT Press.

Lindsay, D.S. (1993). Eyewitness suggestibility. *Current Directions in Psychological Science, 2*, 86–88.

Lindsay, D.S., & Johnson, M.K. (1989). The eyewitness suggestibility effect and memory for source. *Memory & Cognition, 17*, 349–358.

Lindsay, D.S., & Johnson, M.K. (2001). False memories and the source monitoring framework: Reply to Reyna and Lloyd (1997). *Learning and Individual Differences, 12*, 145–161.

Lindsay, D.S., Hagen, L., Read, J.D., Wade, K.A., & Garry, M. (2004). True photographs and false memories. *Psychological Science, 15*, 149–154.

Link, S. (1994). Rediscovering the past: Gustav Fechner and signal detection theory. *Psychological Science, 5*, 335–340.

Livingston, R. (1967). Reinforcement. In G. Quarton, T. Melenchuk, & F. Schmidt (Eds.), *The neurosciences: A study program* (pp. 499–514). New York: Rockefeller University Press.

Lockhart, R.S., & Craik, F.I.M. (1990). Levels of processing: A retrospective commentary on a framework for memory research. *Canadian Journal of Psychology, 44*, 87–112.

Loehlin, J.C. (1989). Partitioning environmental and genetic contributions to behavioral development. *American Psychologist, 44*, 1285–1292.

Loehlin, J.C. (1992). *Latent variable models: An introduction to factor, path and structural analysis* (2nd ed.). Hillsdale, NJ: Erlbaum.

Loftus, E.F. (1991). The glitter of everyday memory . . . and the gold. *American psychologist, 46*, 16–18.

Loftus, E.F. (1992). When a lie becomes memory's truth: Memory distortion after exposure to misinformation. *Current Directions in Psychological Science, 1*, 121–123.

Loftus, E.F. (2003). Make-believe memories. *American Psychologist, 58*, 867–873.

Loftus, E.F. (2004). Memories of things unseen. *Current Directions in Psychological Science, 13*, 145–147.

Loftus, E.F., & Hoffman, H.G. (1989). Misinformation and memory: The creation of new memories. *Journal of Experimental Psychology: General, 118*, 100–104.

Loftus, E.F., & Loftus, G.R. (1980). On the permanence of stored information in the human brain. *American Psychologist, 35*, 409–420.

Loftus, E.F., & Palmer, J.C. (1974). Reconstruction of automobile destruction: An example of the interaction between language and memory. *Journal of Verbal Learning and Verbal Behavior, 13*, 585–589.

Loftus, E.F., & Yuille, J.C. (1984). Departures from reality in human perception and memory. In H. Weingartner & E.S. Parker (Eds.), *Memory consolidation: Psychobiology of cognition* (pp. 163–184). Mahwah, NJ: Erlbaum.

Lopes, L.L. (1982). Doing the impossible: A note on induction and the experience of randomness. *Journal of Experimental Psychology: Learning, Memory, and Cognition, 8*, 626–636.

Lorayne, H., & Lucas, J. (1976). *The memory book*. London: Allen.

Lovie, A.D., & Lovie, P. (1993). Charles Spearman, Cyril Burt, and the origins of factor analysis. *Journal of the History of the Behavioral Sciences, 29*, 308–321.

Lowenstein, G. (1994). The psychology of curiosity: A review and reinterpretation. *Psychological Bulletin, 116*, 75–98.

Lubart, T.I. (2001). Models of the creative process: Past, present and future. *Creativity Research Journal, 13*, 295–308.

Lubinski, D. (2004). Introduction to the special section on cognitive abilities: 100 years after Spearman's (1904) '"General intelligence" objectively determined and measured'. *Journal of Personality and Social Psychology, 86*, 96–111.

Luce, R.D. (2003). Whatever happened to information theory in psychology? *Journal of General Psychology, 7*, 183–188.

Luchins, A.S. (1942). Mechanization in problem-solving. *Psychological Monographs, 54*, Whole No. 248.

Luchins, A.S., & Luchins, E.H. (1950). New experimental attempts at preventing mechanization in problem-solving. *Journal of General Psychology, 42*, 279–297.

Luchins, A.S., & Luchins, E.H. (1994a). The water jar experiments and einstellung effects. Part I: Early history and surveys of textbook citations. *Gestalt Theory, 16*, 101–121.

Luchins, A.S., & Luchins, E.H. (1994b). The water jar experiments and einstellung effects. Part II: Gestalt psychology and past experience. *Gestalt Theory, 16*, 205–270.

Luncageli, D., Tressoldi, P.E., Bendotti, M., Bonaomi, M., & Siegel, L.S. (2003). Effective strategies for mental and written arithmetic calculation from the third to the fifth grade. *Educational Psychology, 23*, 507–520.

Luo, J., & Niki, K. (2003). Function of hippocampus in 'insight' of problem-solving. *Hippocampus, 13*, 316–323.

Luo, J., Niki, K., & Philips, S. (2004). Neural correlates of the 'Aha!' reaction. *Neuroreport, 15*, 2013–2017.

Luria, A.R. (1961). *The role of speech in the regulation of normal and abnormal behavior*. New York: Liveright.

Luria, A.R. (1976). *Cognitive development: Its cultural and social foundations*. Cambridge, Mass.: Harvard University Press.

Lyddy, F. (2002). Interpreting visual images, individually. *Trends in Cognitive Sciences, 6*, 500.

Lynch, K. (1960). *The image of the city*. Cambridge, Mass.: MIT Press.

Lynn, R. (1998). In support of the nutrition theory. In U. Neisser (Ed.), *The rising curve* (pp. 207–218). Washington: American Psychological Association.

Maas, S. (1983). Why systems transparency? In T.R.G. Green, S.J. Payne, & G.C. van der

Veer (Eds.), *The psychology of computer use.* London: Academic Press.

McClelland, J.L. (1979). On the time relations of mental processes: An examination of systems of processes in a cascade. *Psychological Review, 86,* 287–330.

McClelland, J.L. (1981). Retrieving general and specific knowledge from stored knowledge of specifics. Proceedings of the Third Annual Conference of the Cognitive Science Society, Berkeley, Calif.

McClelland, J.L. (2000). Connectionist models of memory. In E. Tulving & F.I.M. Craik (Eds.), *The Oxford handbook of memory* (pp. 583–596). New York: Oxford University Press.

McClelland, J.L., & Rumelhart, D.E. (1981). An interactive activation model of context effects in letter perception. Part I. An account of basic findings. *Psychological Review, 88,* 380.

McClelland, J.L., & Rumelhart, D.E. (1986a). A distributed model of memory. In J.L. McClelland & D.E. Rumelhart (Eds.), *Parallel distributed processing* (Vol. 2, pp. 170–215). Cambridge, Mass.: MIT Press.

McClelland, J.L., & Rumelhart, D.E. (Eds.). (1986b). *Parallel distributed processing: Explorations in the microstructure of cognition: Vol. 2. Psychological and biological models.* Cambridge, Mass.: MIT Press.

McClelland, J.L., & Rumelhart, D.E. (1988). *Explorations in parallel distributed processing: A handbook of models, programs and exercises.* Cambridge Mass.: MIT Press.

McClelland, J.L., Rumelhart, D.E., & Hinton, G.E. (1986). The appeal of PDP. In D.E. Rumelhart & J.L. McClelland (Eds.), *Parallel distributed processing* (Vol. 1, pp. 33–44). Cambridge, Mass.: MIT Press.

McCloskey, M., Wible, C.G., & Cohen, N.J. (1988). Is there a special flashbulb-memory mechanism? *Journal of Experimental Psychology: General, 117,* 171–181.

McDaniel, M.A., DeLosh, E.L., & Merritt, P. (2000). Order information and retrieval distinctiveness: Recall of common versus bizarre material. *Journal of Experimental Psychology: Learning, Memory, and Cognition, 26,* 1045–1056.

McDaniel, M.A., Einstein, G.O., DeLosh, E.L., May, C.P., & Brady, P. (1995). The bizarreness effect: It's not surprising, it's complex. *Journal of Experimental Psychology: Learning, Memory, and Cognition, 21,* 422–435.

Mack, A. (2003). Inattentional blindness: Looking without seeing. *Current Directions in Psychological Science, 12,* 180–184.

Mack, A., Pappas, Z., Silverman, M., & Gay, R. (2002). What we see: Inattention and the capture of attention by meaning. *Consciousness and Cognition, 11,* 488–506.

Mack, A., & Rock, I. (1998). *Inattentional blindness.* Cambridge, Mass.: MIT Press.

Mackavey, W.R., Malley, J.E. & Stewart, A.J. (1991). Remembering autobiographically consequential experiences: Content analysis of psychologists' accounts of their lives. *Psychology and Aging, 6,* 50–59.

McKelvie, S.J. (1995). *Vividness of visual imagery: Measurement, nature, function and dynamics.* New York: Brandon House.

Mackworth, N. (1965). Originality. *American Psychologist, 20,* 51–66.

MacLeod, C.M. (1991). Half a century of research on the Stroop effect: An integrative review. *Psychological Bulletin, 109,* 163–203.

MacLeod, C.M. (1992). The Stroop task: The 'gold standard' of attentional measures. *Journal of Experimental Psychology: General, 121,* 12–15.

MacLeod, C.M., & MacDonald, P.A. (2000). Interdimensional interference in the Stroop effect: Uncovering the cognitive and neural anatomy of attention. *Trends in Cognitive Sciences, 4,* 382–391.

MacLeod, C.M., & Sheehan, P.W. (2003). Hypnotic control of attention in the Stroop task: A historical footnote. *Consciousness and Cognition, 12,* 347–353.

McManus, I.C. (1983). Basic colour terms in literature. *Language and Speech, 26,* 247–252.

McNamara, T.P. (1992). Priming and constraints it places on theories of memory and retrieval. *Psychological Review, 99,* 650–662.

McNamara, T.P., Rump, B., & Werner, S. (2003). Egocentric and geocentric frames of reference in memory of large-scale space. *Psychonomic Bulletin & Review, 10,* 589–595.

McNeill, D. (1970). *The acquisition of language.* New York: Harper & Row.

McNeill, D. (1980). *Conceptual basis of language activity* (cassette recording). Washington: American Psychological Association.

McNeill, D. (1985a). Language viewed as action. In J. Wertsch (Ed.), *Culture, communication and cognition* (pp. 258–270). Cambridge: Cambridge University Press.

McNeill, D. (1985b). So you think gestures are nonverbal? *Psychological Review, 92,* 350–371.

McNeill, D. (1989). A straight path—to where? Reply to Butterworth and Hadar. *Psychological Review, 96,* 175–179.

McRae, K., & Boisvert, S. (1998). Automatic semantic similarity priming. *Journal of Experimental Psychology: Learning, Memory, and Cognition, 24,* 558–572.

MacWhinney, B. (2000). *The CHILDES project: Tools for analyzing talk.* Mahwah, NJ: Erlbaum.

MacWhinney, B. (2004). A multiple process solution to the logical problem of language acquisition. *Journal of Child Language, 31,* 883–914.

Maess, B., Ko'lsch, S., Gunter, T.C., & Friederici, A.D. 2001. Musical syntax is processed in Broca's area: An MEG study. *Nature Neuroscience, 4,* 540–545.

Maguire, E.A., Gadian, D.G., Johnsrude, I.S., Good, C.D., Ashburner, J., Frackowiak, R.S.J., & Frith, C.D. (2000). Navigation-related structural change in the hippocampi of taxi drivers. *Proceedings of the National Academy of Science, 2000,* 4398–4403.

Maguire, E.A., Valentine, E.R., Wilding, J.M., & Kapur, N. (2003). Routes to remembering: The brains behind superior memory. *Nature Neuroscience, 6,* 90–95.

Mai, X.-Q., Luo, J., Wu, J.-H., & Luo, Y.-J. (2004). 'Aha!' effects in a guessing riddle task: An event-related potential study. *Human Brain Mapping, 22,* 261–270.

Maier, N.R.F. (1968). Reasoning in humans: II. The solution of a problem and its appearance in consciousness. In P.C. Wason & P.N. Johnson-Laird (Eds.), *Thinking and reasoning* (pp. 17–27). (Original work published 1931).

Maier, N.R.F. (1970). *Problem-solving and creativity in individuals and groups.* Belmont, Calif.: Wadsworth.

Majid, A., Bowerman, M., Kita, S., Haun, D.B.M., & Levinson, S.C. (2004). Can language restructure cognition? The case for space. *Trends in Cognitive Sciences, 8,* 108–114.

Mandler, G. (2002). Organization: What levels of processing are levels of. *Memory, 10,* 333–338.

Marcel, A.J. (1983a). Conscious and unconscious perception: Experiments on visual masking and word recognition. *Cognitive Psychology, 15,* 197–237.

Marcel, A.J. (1983b). Conscious and unconscious perception: An approach to the relations between phenomenal experience and perceptual processes. *Cognitive Psychology, 15,* 238–300.

Marcel, A.J., Katz, L., & Smith, M. (1974). Laterality and reading proficiency. *Neuropsychologia, 12,* 131–139.

Marian, V., & Neisser, U. (2000). Language-dependent recall of autobiographical memories. *Journal of Experimental Psychology: General, 129,* 361–368.

Marks, D.F. (1972). Individual differences in the vividness of visual imagery and their effect on function. In P.W. Sheehan (Ed.), *The function and nature of imagery* (pp. 83–108). New York: Academic Press.

Marks, D.F. (1999). Consciousness, mental imagery and action. *British Journal of Psychology, 90,* 567–585.

Marks, L.E. (1978). *The unity of the senses: Interrelations among the modalities.* New York: Academic Press.

Marks, L.E. (1982). Bright sneezes and dark coughs, loud sunlight and soft moonlight. *Journal of Experimental Psychology: Human Perception and Performance, 8,* 177–193.

Marschark, M., Richman, C.L., Yuille, J.C., & Hunt, R.R. (1987). The role of imagery in memory: On shared and distinctive information. *Psychological Bulletin, 102,* 28–41.

Marshall, J.C., & Fink, G.R. (2003). Cerebral localization, then and now. *NeuroImage, 20,* S2–S7.

Martin, A., & Caramazza, A. (2003). Neuropsychological and neuroimaging perspectives on conceptual knowledge: An introduction. *Cognitive Neuropsychology, 20,* 195–212.

Martin, L. (1986). Eskimo words for snow: A case study in the genesis and decay of an anthropological example. *American Anthropologist, 88,* 418–423.

Martindale, C. (1981). *Cognition and consciousness.* Homewood, Ill.: Dorsey Press.

Martindale, C. (1984). The pleasures of thought: A theory of cognitive hedonics. *Journal of Mind and Behavior, 5,* 49–80.

Martindale, C., Moore, K., & West, A. (1988). Relationship of preference judgments to typicality, novelty, and mere exposure. *Empirical Studies of the Arts, 6,* 79–96.

Martino, G., & Marks, L.E. (2001). Synesthesia: Strong and weak. *Current Directions in Psychological Science, 10,* 61–65.

Maslow, A.H. (1946). Problem-centering versus means-centering in science. *Philosophy of Science, 13,* 326–331.

Mast, F.W., and Kosslyn, S.M. (2002) Visual mental images can be ambiguous: Insights from individual differences in spatial transformation abilities. *Cognition, 86,* 57–70.

Maurer, D. (1997). Neonatal synaesthesia: Implications for the processing of speech and faces. In S. Baron-Cohen & J.E. Harrison (Eds.), *Synaesthesia: Classic and contemporary readings* (pp. 224–242). Oxford: Blackwell.

Mayer, E. (1991). The ideological resistance to Darwin's theory of natural selection. *Proceedings of the American Philosophical Society, 135,* 123–139.

Mayer, R.E. (2004). Teaching of subject matter. *Annual Review of Psychology, 55,* 715–744.

Mayer, U. (2004). Conflict, consciousness and control. *Trends in Cognitive Sciences, 8,* 145–148.

Medin, D.L. (1989). Concepts and conceptual structure. *American Psychologist, 44,* 1469–1481.

Medin, D.L., & Atran, S. (2004). The native mind: Biological categorization and reasoning in development and across cultures. *Psychological Review, 111,* 960–983.

Mednick, S.A. (1962). The associative basis of the creative process. *Psychological Review, 69,* 220–227.

Mednick, S.A. (1967). *The remote associations test.* Boston: Houghton Mifflin.

Mehler, J. (1963). Some effects of grammatical transformations: On the recall of English sentences. *Journal of Verbal Learning and Verbal Behavior, 2,* 560–566.

Meiran, N., Hommel, B., Bibi, U., & Lev, I. (2001). Consciousness and control in task switching. *Consciousness and Cognition, 11,* 10–33.

Merikle, P.M. (1992). Perception without awareness: Critical issues. *American Psychologist, 47,* 792–795.

Merikle, P.M., & Daneman, M. (2000). Conscious vs. unconscious perception. In M.S. Gazzaniga (Ed.), *The new cognitive neurosciences* (2nd ed.) (pp. 1295–1303). Cambridge, Mass.: MIT Press.

Merikle, P.M., & Joordens, S. (1997). Measuring unconscious influences. In J.D. Cohen & J.W. Schooler (Eds.), *Approaches to consciousness* (pp. 109–123). Hillsdale, NJ: Erlbaum.

Merikle, P.M., & Reingold, E.M. (1998). On demonstrating unconscious perception: Comment on Draine and Greenwald. *Journal of Experimental Psychology: General, 3,* 304–310.

Merikle, P.M., Smilek, D., & Eastwood, J.D. (2001). Perception without awareness: Perspectives from cognitive psychology. *Cognition, 79,* 115–134.

Messick, D.M. (1987). Egocentric biases and the golden section. *Journal of Social and Biological Structures, 10,* 241–247.

Metcalfe, J. (1998). Cognitive optimism: Self-deception or memory-based heuristics? *Personality and Social Psychology Review, 2,* 100–110.

Metcalfe, J. (2002). Is study time allocated selectively to a region of proximal learning? *Journal of Experimental Psychology: General, 131,* 349–363.

Metcalfe, J., & Kornell, N. (2003). The dynamics

of learning and allocation of study time to a region of proximal learning. *Journal of Experimental Psychology: General, 132,* 530–542.

Metcalfe, J., & Kornell, N. (2005). A region of proximal learning model of study time allocation. *Journal of Memory and Language, 52,* 463–477.

Metcalfe, J., & Wiebe, D. (1987). Intuition in insight and non-insight problem-solving. *Memory & Cognition, 15,* 238–246.

Meyer, D.E., & Schvaneveldt, R.W. (1976). Meaning, memory structure, and mental processes. In C. Cofer (Ed.), *The structure of human memory* (pp. 54–89). San Francisco: Freeman.

Meyer, G.E. & Hilterbrand, K. (1984). Does it pay to be 'Bashful'? The seven dwarfs and long-term memory. *American Journal of Psychology, 97,* 47–55.

Milgram, R.M., & Rabkin, L. (1980). Developmental test of Mednick's associative hierarchies of original thinking. *Developmental Psychology, 16,* 157–158.

Milham, M.P., Banich, M.T., & Barad, V. (2003). Competition for processing increases prefrontal cortex's involvement in top-down control: An event-related fMRI study of the Stroop task. *Cognitive Brain Research, 17,* 212–222.

Milivojevic, B., Johnson, B.W., Hamm, J.P., & Corballis, M.C. (2003). Non-identical neural mechanisms for two types of mental transformation: Event-related potentials during mental rotation and mental paper folding. *Neuropsychologia, 41,* 1345–1356.

Mill, D., Gray, T., & Mandel, D.R. (1994). Influence of research methods and statistics courses on everyday reasoning, critical abilities, and belief in unsubstantiated phenomena. *Canadian Journal of Behavioural Science, 26,* 246–258.

Miller, D.R. (1999). The norm of self-interest. *American Psychologist, 54,* 1053–1060.

Miller, G.A. (1953). What is information measurement? *American Psychologist, 8,* 3–11.

Miller, G.A. (1956). The magical number seven, plus or minus two. *Psychological Review, 63,* 81–97.

Miller, G.A. (1986). Dictionaries in the mind. *Language and Cognitive Processes, 1,* 171–185.

Miller, G.A., Galanter, E., & Pribram, K. (1960). *Plans and the structure of behavior.* New York: Holt, Rinehart & Winston.

Milner, P. (2003). A brief history of the Hebbian learning rule. *Canadian Psychology, 44,* 5–9.

Minsky, M., & Papert, S. (1969). *Perceptrons.* Cambridge, Mass.: MIT Press.

Mischel, T. (1967). Kant and the possibility of a science of psychology. *The Monist, 51,* 599–622.

Mischel, T. (1969). Scientific and philosophical psychology: An historical introduction. In T. Mischel (Ed.), *Human action* (pp. 1–40). New York: Academic Press.

Mitchell, D.B. (1989). How many memory systems are there? Evidence from aging. *Journal of Experimental Psychology: Human Learning and Memory, 15,* 31–49.

Mitchell, D.B., & Bruss, P.J. (2003). Age differences in implicit memory: Conceptual, perceptual or methodological? *Psychology and Aging, 18,* 807–822.

Mitchell, G. (2004). Case studies, counterfactuals, and causal explanations. *University of Pennsylvania Law Review, 152,* 1517–1608.

Mitchell, K.J., & Johnson, M.K. (2000). Source monitoring: Attributing mental experiences. In E. Tulving & F.I.M. Craik (Eds.). *The Oxford handbook of memory* (pp. 179–195). New York: Oxford University Press.

Moeser, S.D. (1982). Memory integration and memory interference. *Canadian Journal of Psychology, 36,* 165–188.

Mohr, C., Graves, R.E., Gianotti, L.R.R., Pizzagalli, D., & Brugger, P. (2001). Loose but normal: A semantic association study. *Journal of Psycholinguistic Research, 30,* 475–483.

Monin, B. (2003). The warm glow heuristic: When liking leads to familiarity. *Journal of Personality and Social Psychology, 85,* 1035–1048.

Moniz, E. (1968). Prefrontal leucotomy. In W.S. Sahakian (Ed.), *History of psychology: A source book in systematic psychology* (pp. 372–377). Itaska, Ill.: Peacock. (Original work published 1954).

Monsell, S. (2003). Task switching. *Trends in Cognitive Sciences, 7*, 134–140.

Montero, B. (1999). The body problem. *Noûs, 33*, 183–200.

Moray, N. (1959). Attention and dichotic listening: Affective cues and the influence of instructions. *Quarterly Journal of Experimental Psychology, 11*, 56–60.

Moreland, R.L., & Zajonc, R.B. (1977). Is stimulus recognition a necessary condition for the occurrence of exposure effects? *Journal of Personality and Social Psychology, 35*, 191–199.

Moreland, R.L., & Zajonc, R.B. (1979). Exposure effects may not depend on stimulus recognition. *Journal of Personality and Social Psychology, 37*, 1085–1089.

Morgan, C.L. (1894). *Introduction to comparative psychology.* London: Walter Scott.

Morris, N., & Jones, D.M. (1990). Memory updating in working memory: The role of the central executive. *British Journal of Psychology, 81*, 111–121.

Morris, P.E., Jones, S., & Hampson, P. (1978). An imagery mnemonic for the learning of people's names. *British Journal of Psychology, 69*, 335–336.

Morton, J. (1969). Interaction of information in word recognition. *Psychological Review, 76*, 165–176.

Morton, J. (1976). On recursive reference. *Cognition, 4*, 309.

Muller, M. (2001). Global and local tree game searches. *Information Sciences, 135*, 187–206.

Mullin, P., & Egeth, H.E. (1989). Capacity limitations in visual word processing. *Journal of Experimental Psychology: Human Perception and Performance, 15*, 111–123.

Mumford, M.D., & Gustafson, S.B. (1988). Creativity syndrome: Integration, application and innovation. *Psychological Bulletin, 103*, 27–43.

Murphy, G.L. (2003). The downside of categories. *Trends in Cognitive Sciences, 7*, 513–514.

Murray, D.J. (1993). A perspective for viewing the history of psychophysics. *Behavioral and Brain Sciences, 16*, 115–186.

Nader, K. (2003). Memory traces unbound. *Trends in Neurosciences, 26*, 65–72.

Nappe, G.W., & Wollen, K.A. (1973). Effects of instructions to form common and bizarre mental images on retention. *Journal of Experimental Psychology, 100*, 6–8.

Natsoulas, T. (1978). Consciousness. *American Psychologist, 33*, 906–914.

Naveh-Benjamin, M. (2000). Adult age differences in memory performance: Tests of an associative deficit hypothesis. *Journal of Experimental Psychology: Learning, Memory, and Cognition, 26*, 1170–1187.

Naveh-Benjamin, M., Guez, J., Kilb, A., & Reedy, S. (2004). The associative memory deficit of older adults: Further support using face-name associations. *Psychology and Aging, 19*, 541–546.

Naveh-Benjamin, M., Hussain, Z., Guez, J., & Bar-On, M. (2003). Adult age differences in episodic memory: Further support for an associative deficit hypothesis. *Journal of Experimental Psychology: Learning, Memory, and Cognition, 29*, 826–837.

Necker, L.A. (1964). On an apparent change of position in a drawing or engraved figure of a crystal. In W. Dember (Ed.), *Visual perception: The nineteenth century* (pp. 78–83). New York: Wiley. (Original work published 1832).

Neisser, U. (1962). Cultural and cognitive discontinuity. In T.E. Gladwin & W. Sturtevant (Eds.), *Anthropology and human behavior.* Washington: Anthropological Society of America.

Neisser, U. (1967). *Cognitive psychology.* New York: Appleton-Century-Crofts.

Neisser, U. (1970). Visual imagery. In J. Antrobus (Ed.), *Cognition and affect* (pp. 159–178). Boston: Little, Brown.

Neisser, U. (1976). *Cognition and reality.* San Francisco: Freeman.

Neisser, U. (1978a). Anticipations, images, and introspection. *Cognition, 6*, 169–174.

Neisser, U. (1978b). Memory: What are the important questions? In M.M. Gruneberg, P.M. Morris, & R.N. Sykes (Eds.), *Practical aspects of memory* (pp. 3–24). London: Academic Press.

Neisser, U. (1979). Tracing eidetic imagery. *Behavioral and Brain Sciences, 2,* 612–613.

Neisser, U. (1980). *Toward a realistic cognitive psychology* (cassette recording). Washington: American Psychological Association.

Neisser, U. (1981). John Dean's memory: A case study. *Cognition, 9,* 1–22.

Neisser, U. (1982a). Snapshots or benchmarks? In U. Neisser (Ed.). *Memory observed: Remembering in natural contexts* (pp. 43–48). San Francisco: Freeman.

Neisser, U. (Ed.). (1982b). *Memory observed: Remembering in natural contexts.* San Francisco: Freeman.

Neisser, U. (1983). Components of intelligence or steps in routine procedures? *Cognition, 15,* 189–197.

Neisser, U. (1985). The role of theory in the ecological study of memory: Comment on Bruce. *Journal of Experimental Psychology: General, 114,* 272–276.

Neisser, U. (Ed.). (1986). *The school achievement of minority children.* Hillsdale, NJ: Erlbaum.

Neisser, U. (1988). Five kinds of self-knowledge. *Philosophical Psychology, 1,* 35–59.

Neisser, U. (1988). What is ordinary memory the memory of? In U. Neisser & E. Winograd (Eds.), *Remembering reconsidered: Ecological and traditional approaches to the study of memory* (pp. 356–373). New York: Cambridge University Press.

Neisser, U. (1991). A case of misplaced nostalgia. *American Psychologist, 46,* 34–36.

Neisser, U. (1993). The self perceived. In U. Neisser (Ed.), *The perceived self* (pp. 3–21). New York: Cambridge University Press.

Neisser, U. (1997). Rising scores on intelligence tests. *American Scientist, 85,* 440–447.

Neisser, U. (1997). The ecological study of memory. *Proceedings of the Royal Society of London (Series B), 352,* 1697–1701.

Neisser, U. (Ed.). (1998). *The rising curve.* Washington: American Psychological Association.

Neisser, U. (2003). New directions for flashbulb memories: Comments on the Applied Cognitive Psychology special issue. *Applied Cognitive Psychology, 17,* 1149–1155.

Neisser, U. (2004). Memory development: New questions and old. *Developmental Review, 24,* 154–158.

Neisser, U., & Becklen, R. (1975). Selective looking: Attending to visually specified events. *Cognitive Psychology, 7,* 480–494.

Neisser, U., Boodoo, G., Bouchard, T.J., Boykin, A.W., Brody, N., Ceci, S.J., et al. (1996). Intelligence: Knowns and unknowns. *American Psychologist, 51,* 77–101.

Neisser, U., & Weene, P. (1962). Hierarchies in concept attainment. *Journal of Experimental Psychology, 64,* 640–45.

Nelson, K., & Gruendel, J. (1981). Generalized event representations: Basic building blocks of cognitive development. In M.E. Lamb & A.L. Brown (Eds.), *Advances in developmental psychology* (pp. 131–158). Hillsdale, NJ: Erlbaum.

Nersessian, N.J. (1995). Opening the black box: Cognitive science and the history of science. *Osiris, 10,* 194–211.

Newell, A. (1977). On the analysis of human problem-solving protocols. In P.N. Johnson-Laird & P. Wason (Eds.), *Thinking: Readings in cognitive science* (pp. 46–61). Cambridge: Cambridge University Press.

Newell, A. (1983). The heuristic of George Polya and its relation to artifical intelligence. In R. Groner & M. Groner (Eds.), *Methods of heuristics* (pp. 195–243). Hillsdale, NJ: Erlbaum.

Newell, A. (1985). Duncker on thinking: An inquiry into progress in cognition. In S. Koch & D. Leary (Eds.), *A century of psychology as science: Retrospections and assessments* (pp. 392–419). New York: McGraw-Hill.

Newell, A., & Simon, H.A. (1972). *Human problem-solving.* Englewood Cliffs, NJ: Prentice-Hall.

Newell, A., Shaw, J.C., & Simon, H.A. (1958). Chess-playing programs and the problem of complexity. *IBM Journal of Research and Development, 2,* 320–335.

Newell, A., Simon, H., & Shaw, J.C. (1962). The processes of creative thinking. In H.E. Gruber, G. Terrell, & M. Wertheimer (Eds.), *Con-*

temporary approaches to creative thinking (pp. 63–119). New York: Atherton.

Newell, B.R. (2005). Re-visions of rationality? *Trends in Cognitive Sciences, 9*, 11–15.

Newman, J.R. (1956). *The world of mathematics.* New York: Simon & Schuster.

Newstead, S.E., Pollard, P., Evans, J. St B.T., & Allen, J.L. (1992). The source of belief bias effects in syllogistic reasoning. *Cognition, 45*, 257–284.

Nicholls, M.E.R., Clode, D., Wood, S.J., & Wood, A.G. (1999). Laterality of expression in portraiture: Putting your best cheek forward. *Proceedings of the Royal Society of London (Series B), 266*, 1517–1522.

Nicholls, M.E.R., Wolfgang, B.J., Clode, D., & Lindell, A.K. (2002). The effect of left and right poses on the expression of facial emotion. *Neuropsychologia, 40*, 1662–1665.

Nichols, S. (2004). Folk concepts and intuitions: From philosophy to cognitive science. *Trends in Cognitive Science, 8*, 514–518.

Nickerson, R.S. (1996). Ambiguities and unstated assumptions in probabilistic reasoning. *Psychological Review, 120*, 410–433.

Nicolson, R.I., & Gardner, P.H. (1985). The QWERTY keyboard hampers school-children. *British Journal of Psychology, 76*, 525–531.

Nisbett, R.E., Krantz, D.H., Jepson, C., & Kunda, Z. (1983). The use of statistical heuristics in everyday inductive reasoning. *Psychological Review, 90*, 339–363.

Noble, C.E. (1952). An analysis of meaning. *Psychological Review, 59*, 421–430.

Noë, A., & Thompson, E. (2004). Are there neural correlates of consciousness? *Journal of Consciousness Studies, 11*, 3–28

Noice, H. (1991). The role of explanations and plan recognition in the learning of theatrical scripts. *Cognitive Science, 15*, 425–460.

Noice, H. (1992). Elaborative memory strategies of professional actors. *Applied Cognitive Psychology, 6*, 417–427.

Noice, H. (1993). Effects of rote versus gist strategy on the verbatim retention of theatrical scripts. *Applied Cognitive Psychology, 7*, 75–84.

Norman, D.A. (1981). Categorization of action slips. *Psychological Review, 88*, 1–15.

Norman, D.A. (1983). Some observations on mental models. In D. Gentner & A.L. Stevens (Eds.), *Mental models* (pp. 7–14). Hillsdale, NJ: Erlbaum.

Norman, D.A. (1992). *Turn signals are the facial expressions of automobiles.* Reading, Mass.: Addison-Wesley.

Norman, D.A. (1993). *Things that make us smart.* Reading, Mass.: Addison-Wesley.

Norman, D.A. (1998). *The invisible computer.* Cambridge, Mass.: MIT Press.

Norman, D.A. (2002). *The psychology of everyday things.* New York: Basic Books. (Original work published 1988).

Norman, D.A., & Bobrow, D.G. (1976). Active memory processes in perception and cognition. In C. Cofer (Ed.), *The structure of human memory* (pp. 114–132). San Francisco: Freeman.

Norman, D.A., & Draper, S.W. (1986). *User-centered system design.* Hillsdale, NJ: Erlbaum.

Norman, D.A., & Fisher, D. (1982). Why alphabetic keyboards are not easy to use: Keyboard layout doesn't much matter. *Human Factors, 24*, 509–519.

Noveck, I.A. (2001). When children are more logical than adults: Experimental investigations of scalar implications. *Cognition, 78*, 165–188.

Noyes, J., & Garland, K. (2005). Students' attitudes toward books and computers. *Computers and Human Behavior, 21*, 233–241.

Nyberg, L. (2002). Levels of processing: A view from functional brain imaging. *Memory, 10*, 345–348.

O'Brien, D.P., Noveck, I.A., Davidson, G.M., Fusch, S.M., Lea, R.B., & Freitag, J. (1990). Sources of difficulty in deductive reasoning: The THOG task. *Quarterly Journal of Experimental Psychology, 42A*, 329–351.

Oakhill, J.V., & Johnson-Laird, P.N. (1985). Rationality, memory and the search for counterexamples. *Cognition, 20*, 79–94.

Oakhill, J.V., Johnson-Laird, P.N., & Garnham, A. (1989). Believability and syllogistic reasoning. *Cognition, 31*, 117–140.

O'Brien, E.J., & Wolford, C.R. (1982). Effect of delay of testing on retention of plausible versus bizarre mental images. *Journal of Experimental Psychology: Learning, Memory, and Cognition, 8*, 148–152.

Ogilvie, J. (2002). Turn the other cheek. *Trends in Cognitive Sciences, 6*, 234.

Ohlsson, S. (1984). Restructuring revisited. *Scandinavian Journal of Psychology, 25*, 65–78.

Olson, D.R. (1977). From utterance to text: The bias of language in speech and writing. *Harvard Educational Review, 47*, 257–281.

Olson, D.R. (Ed.). (1985). *Literacy, language and learning: The nature of reading and writing*. New York: Cambridge University Press.

Olson, D.R. (1986). The cognitive consequences of literacy. *Canadian Psychology, 27*, 109–121.

Olson, D.R. (1996). Towards a psychology of literacy: On the relations between speech and writing. *Cognition, 60*, 83–104.

Olson, D.R., & Astington, J.W. (1986a). Children's acquisition of metalinguistic and metacognitive verbs. In W. Demopoulos & A. Marras (Eds.), *Language learning and concept acquisition* (pp. 184–199). Norwood, NJ: Ablex.

Olson, D.R., & Astington, J. (1986b). Talking about text: How literacy contributes to thought. Paper presented to the Boston University Conference on Language Development, Boston.

Olson, G.M., & Olson, J.S. (2003). Human-computer interaction: Psychological aspects of the human use of computing. *Annual Review of Psychology, 54*, 491–516.

Oppenheimer, D.M. (2003). Not so fast! (and not so frugal!): Rethinking the recognition heuristic. *Cognition, 90*, B1–B9.

Ormerod, T.C., MacGregor, J.N., & Chronicle, E.P. (2002). Dynamics and constraints in insight problem-solving. *Journal of Experimental Psychology: Learning, Memory, and Cognition, 28*, 791–799

Osgood, C.E. (1979). From Yang and Yin in cross-cultural perspective. *International Journal of Psychology, 14*, 1–35.

Osgood, C.E., & Richards, M.M. (1973). From Yang and Yin to 'and' or 'but'. *Language, 49*, 380–412.

Ost, J., & Costall, A. (2002). Misremembering Bartlett: A study in serial reproduction. *British Journal of Psychology, 93*, 243–255.

Paige, J.M., & Simon, H.A. (1966). Cognitive processes in solving algebra word problems. In B. Kleinmuntz (Ed.), *Problem-solving* (pp. 51–119). New York: Wiley.

Paivio, A. (1965). Abstractness, imagery and meaningfulness in paired-associate learning. *Journal of Verbal Learning and Verbal Behavior, 4*, 32–38.

Paivio, A. (1969). Mental imagery in associative learning and memory. *Psychological Review, 76*, 241–263.

Paivio, A. (1971). *Imagery and verbal processes*. New York: Holt, Rinehart & Winston.

Paivio, A. (1983). The empirical case for dual coding. In J. Yuille (Ed.), *Imagery, memory and cognition: Essays in honor of Allan Paivio* (pp. 307–332). Hillsdale, NJ: Erlbaum.

Paivio, A. (1986). *Mental representations*. Oxford: Oxford University Press.

Paivio, A. (1991). Dual coding theory: Retrospect and current status. *Canadian Journal of Psychology, 45*, 255–287.

Paivio, A., & Begg, I. (1981). *The psychology of language*. Englewood Cliffs, NJ: Prentice-Hall.

Paivio, A., Khan, M., & Begg, I. (2000). Concreteness and relational effects on recall of adjective-noun pairs. *Canadian Journal of Experimental Psychology, 54*, 149–159.

Paivio, A., Walsh, M., & Bons, T. (1994). Concreteness effects on memory: When and why? *Journal of Experimental Psychology: Learning, Memory, and Cognition. 20*, 1196–1204.

Paivio, A., Yuille, J., & Madigan, S. (1968). Concreteness, imagery and meaningfulness values for 925 nouns. *Journal of Experimental Psychology Monograph Supplement, 76*(1), Pt. 2.

Palmer, C.F., Jones, R.K., Hennessy, B.L., Unze, M.G., & Pick, A.D. (1989). How is a trumpet known? The 'basic object level' concept and the perception of musical instruments. *American Journal of Psychology, 102*, 17–37.

Palmer, S.E. (1992). Common region: A new

principle of perceptual grouping. *Cognitive Psychology, 24*, 436–447.

Pani, J.F., & Chariker, J.H. (2004). The psychology of error in relation to medical practice. *Journal of Surgical Oncology, 88*, 130–142.

Papanicolauo, A.C. (1998). *Fundamentals of functional brain imaging*. Lisse: Swets & Zeitlinger.

Paprotte, W., & Sinha, C. (1987). A functional perspective on early language development. In M. Hickmann (Ed.), *Social and functional approaches to language and thought* (pp. 203–222). New York: Academic Press.

Parker, A.J., Krug, K., & Cumming, B.G. (2003). Neuronal activity and its links with the perception of multistable figures. In A. Parker, A. Derrington, & C. Blakemore (Eds.), *The physiology of cognitive processes* (pp. 139–156). Oxford: Oxford University Press.

Parkin, A.J., & Hunkin, N.M. (2001). British memory research: A journey through the 20th century. *British Journal of Psychology, 92*, 37–52.

Pashler, H.E. (1998). *The psychology of attention*. Cambridge, Mass.: MIT Press.

Pashler, H., Johnston, J.C., & Ruthruff, E. (2001). Attention and performance. *Annual Review of Psychology, 52*, 629–651.

Paul, I.H. (1967). The concept of schema in memory theory. In R.R. Holt (Ed.), *Motives and thought: Psychoanalytic essays in honor of David Rapaport* (pp. 215–258). New York: International Universities Press.

Payne, S.J., & Green, T.R.G. (1989). The structure of command languages: An experiment on task-action grammar. *International Journal of Man-Machine Studies, 30*, 213–234.

Peabody, D. (1990). The role of evaluation in impressions of persons. In I. Rock (Ed.), *The legacy of Solomon Asch* (pp. 57–75). Hillsdale, NJ: Erlbaum.

Pederson, E., Danziger, E., Wilkins, D., Levinson, S., Kita, S., & Senft, G. (1998). Semantic typology and spatial conceptualization. *Language, 74*, 557–589.

Peeters, G., & Czapinski, J. (1990). Positive-negative asymmetry in evaluations: The distinction between affective and informational negativity effects. In W. Stroebe & M. Hewstone (Eds.), *European Review of Social Psychology* (Vol. 1). Chichester: Wiley.

Pelli, D.G., Farell, B., & Moore, D.C. (2003). The remarkable inefficiency of word recognition. *Nature, 423*, 752–756.

Perkins, D.N. (1981). *The mind's best work*. Cambridge, Mass.: Harvard University Press.

Perner, J. (2000). Memory and theory of mind. In E. Tulving & F.I.M. Craik (Eds.), *The Oxford handbook of memory* (pp. 297–312). New York: Oxford University Press.

Pessoa, L., Kastner, S., & Ungerleider, L.G. (2003). Neuroimaging studies of attention: From modulation of sensory processing to top-down control. *Journal of Neuroscience, 23*, 3990–3998.

Peterson, L.R., & Peterson, M.J. (1959). Short-term retention of individual verbal items. *Journal of Experimental Psychology, 58*, 193–198.

Peterson, M.A., Kihlstrom, J.F., Rose, P.M., & Glisky, M.L. (1992). Mental images can be ambiguous: Reconstruals and reference-frame reversals. *Memory & Cognition, 20*, 107–123.

Petrill, S.A., Lipton, P.A., Hewitt, J.K., Plomin, R., Cherny, S.S., Corley, R., & Defries, J.C. (2004). Genetic and environmental contributions to general cognitive ability through the first 16 years of life. *Developmental Psychology, 40*, 805–812.

Petry, S., & Meyer, G. (1987). *The perception of illusory contours*. New York: Springer.

Pheasant, S. (1986). *Bodyspace: Anthropometry, ergonomics and design*. London: Taylor & Francis.

Piatelli-Palmarini, M. (1989). Evolution, selection and cognition: From 'learning' to parameter setting in biology and in the study of language. *Cognition, 31*, 1–44.

Pikas, A. (1966). *Abstraction and concept formation*. Cambridge, Mass.: Harvard University Press.

Pillemer, D.B. (1990). Clarifying the flashbulb memory concept. *Journal of Experimental Psychology: General, 119*, 92–96.

Pinker, S. (1988). Learnability theory and the acquisition of a first language. In F. Kessel

(Ed.), *The development of language and language researchers: Essays in honor of Roger Brown* (pp. 97–119). Hillsdale, NJ: Erlbaum.

Pinker, S. (1994). *The language instinct.* London: Penguin.

Pinker, S. (1997). *How the mind works.* New York: Norton.

Pinker, S. (1999). *Words and rules.* New York: HarperCollins.

Pinker, S., & Finke, R.A. (1980). Emergent two-dimensional patterns in images rotated in depth. *Journal of Experimental Psychology: Human Perception and Performance, 6,* 244–264.

Pinker, S., & Jackendoff, R. (2005). The faculty of language: What's special about it? *Cognition, 95,* 201–236.

Pirolli, P. (2005). Rational analyses of information foraging on the web. *Cognitive Science, 29,* 343–373.

Pirolli, P., & Card, S. (1999). Information foraging. *Psychological Review, 106,* 643–675.

Podgorny, P., & Shepard, R.N. (1978). Functional representations common to visual perception and imagination. *Journal of Experimental Psychology: Human Perception and Performance, 4,* 21–35.

Poeppel, D., & Hickock, G. (2004). Introduction: Towards a new functional anatomy of language. *Cognition, 92,* 1–12.

Poincaré, H. (1960). *Science and method.* New York: Dover. (Original work published 1924).

Polanyi, M. (1958). *Personal knowledge.* Chicago: University of Chicago Press.

Pollio, H.R., Barlow, J.M., Fine, H.J., & Pollio, M.R. (1972). *Psychology and the poetics of growth.* Hillsdale, NJ: Erlbaum.

Pollio, H.R., Smith, M.K., & Pollio, M.R. (1990). Figurative language and cognitive psychology. *Language and Cognitive Processes, 5,* 141–167.

Polya, G. (1957). *How to solve it.* New York: Anchor. (Original work published 1945).

Popper, K.R. (1959). *The logic of scientific discovery.* New York: Basic Books.

Posner, M.I. (1969). Abstraction and the process of recognition. In G.H. Bower & J.T. Spence (Eds.), *The psychology of learning and motivation* (Vol. 3, pp. 44–100). New York: Academic Press.

Posner, M.I. (1973). *Cognition: An introduction.* Glenview, Ill.: Scott, Foresman.

Posner, M.I. (1986). *Chronometric explorations of mind.* Oxford: Oxford University Press.

Posner, M.I. (2004). Neural systems and individual differences. *Teacher's College Record,* 24–30.

Posner, M.I., & Keele, S.W. (1968). On the genesis of abstract ideas. *Journal of Experimental Psychology, 77,* 353–363.

Posner, M.I., Goldsmith, R., & Welton, K.E. (1967). Perceived distance and the classification of distorted patterns. *Journal of Experimental Psychology, 73,* 28–38.

Posner, M.I., & Keele, S.W. (1970). Retention of abstract ideas. *Journal of Experimental Psychology, 83,* 304–308.

Postman, L., Bruner, J., & McGinnis, E. (1948). Personal values as selective factors in perception. *Journal of Abnormal and Social Psychology, 43,* 142–154.

Price, D. (1963). *Little science, big science.* New York: Columbia University Press.

Puente, A.E. (1995). Roger Wolcott Sperry (1913–1994). *American Psychologist, 50,* 940–941.

Pullum, G.K. (1991). *The great Eskimo vocabulary hoax, and other irreverent essays on the study of language.* Chicago: University of Chicago Press.

Pullum, G.K., & Scholz, B.C. (2002). Empirical assessment of stimulus poverty arguments. *Linguistic Review, 19,* 9–50.

Pylyshyn, Z.W. (1973). What the mind's eye tells the mind's brain: A critique of mental imagery. *Psychological Bulletin, 80,* 1–24.

Pylyshyn, Z.W. (2002). Mental imagery: In search of a theory. *Behavioral and Brain Sciences, 25,* 157–238.

Pylyshyn, Z.W. (2003a). Explaining mental imagery: Now you see it, now you don't. *Trends in Cognitive Sciences, 7,* 111–112.

Pylyshyn, Z.W. (2003b). Return of the mental image: Are there really pictures in the brain? *Trends in Cognitive Sciences, 7,* 113–118.

Qin, Y., & Simon, H.A. (1990). Laboratory replication of scientific discovery processes. *Cognitive Science, 14,* 281–312.

Quillian, R. (1969). The teachable language comprehender: A simulation program and theory of language. *Communications of the ACM, 12,* 459–476.

Quinlan, P.T. (2003). Visual feature integration theory: Past, present, and future. *Psychological Bulletin, 129,* 643–673.

Rabbitt, P. (1990). Applied cognitive gerontology: Some problems, methodologies and data. *Applied Cognitive Psychology, 4,* 225–246.

Raichle, M.E. (2003). Functional brain imaging and human brain function. *Journal of Neuroscience, 23,* 3959–3962.

Ramachandran, V.S. (1993). Filling in gaps in perception: Part II: Scotomas and phantom limbs. *Current Directions in Psychological Science, 2,* 56–65.

Ramachandran, V.S. (2004). *A brief tour of consciousness.* New York: Pi Press.

Ramachandran, V.S., & Hirstein, W. (1998). The perception of phantom limbs: The D.O. Hebb lecture. *Brain, 121,* 1603–1630.

Ramachandran, V.S., & Rogers-Ramachandran, D. (2005). *Scientific American: Mind, 14(5),* 99–100.

Ramachandran, V.S., Rodgers-Ramachandran, D., & Cobb, S. (1995). Touching the phantom limb. *Nature, 377,* 489–490.

Rastle, K.G., & Burke, D.M. (1996). Priming the tip of the tongue: Effects of prior processing on word retrieval in young and older adults. *Journal of Memory and Language, 25,* 586–605.

Ratliff, F. (1976). On the psychophysiological bases of universal color terms. *Proceedings of the American Philosophical Society, 120,* 311–330.

Ratneshwar, S., Barsalou, L.W., Pechmann, C., & Moore, M. (2001). Goal-derived categories: The role of personal and situational goals in category representations. *Journal of Consumer Psychology, 10,* 147–157.

Raven, J. (2000). The Raven's progressive matrices: Change and stability over culture and time. *Cognitive Psychology 41,* 1–48.

Raven, J.C., Styles, I., & Raven, M.A. (1998). *Raven's progressive matrices: SPM plus test booklet.* Oxford: Oxford Psychologists Press/San Antonio, Tex.: Psychological Corporation.

Rawson, K.A., & Kintsch, W. (2005). Rereading effects depend on time of test. *Journal of Educational Psychology, 97,* 70–80.

Raz, A., Landzberg, K.S., Schweizer, H.R., Zephrani, Z.R., Shapiro, T., Fan, J., & Posner, M.I. (2003). Posthypnotic suggestion and the modulation of Stroop interference under cycloplegia. *Consciousness and Cognition, 12,* 332–346.

Reason, J.T. (1984). Lapses of attention in everyday life. In R. Parasuraman & D.R. Davies (Eds.), *Varieties of attention* (pp. 515–549). Orlando, Fla: Academic Press.

Reason, J.T. (1990). *Human error.* New York: Cambridge University Press.

Reber, A.S. (1967). Implicit learning of artificial grammars. *Journal of Verbal Learning and Verbal Behavior, 5,* 855–863.

Reber, A.S. (1985). *The Penguin dictionary of psychology.* London: Penguin.

Reber, A.S. (1989). Implicit learning and tacit knowledge. *Journal of Experimental Psychology: General, 118,* 219–235.

Reber, A.S. (1990). On the primacy of the implicit: Comment on Perruchet and Pacteau. *Journal of Experimental Psychology: General, 119,* 340–342.

Reber, A.S. (1997). Implicit ruminations. *Psychonomic Bulletin & Review, 4,* 49–55.

Reber, A.S., & Allen, R. (1978). Analogy and abstraction strategies in synthetic grammar learning: A functionalist interpretation. *Cognition, 6,* 189–221.

Reber, A.S., Allen, R., & Regan, S. (1985). Syntactical learning and judgment, still unconscious and still abstract: Comment on Dulany, Carlson and Dewey. *Journal of Experimental Psychology: General, 114,* 17, 24.

Reber, A.S., Kassin, S.M., Lewis, S., & Cantor, G. (1980). On the relationship between implicit and explicit modes in the learning of a complex rule structure. *Journal of Experimental Psychology: Human Learning and Memory, 8,* 492–502.

Reber, A.S., & Lewis, S. (1977). Implicit learning: An analysis of the form and structure of a body of tacit knowledge. *Cognition, 5,* 333–362.

Reber, A.S., Walkenfeld, F.F., & Hernstadt, R. (1991). Implicit and explicit learning: Individual differences and IQ. *Journal of Experimental Psychology: Human Learning and Memory, 17,* 888–896.

Rebok, G.W. (1987). *Life-span cognitive development.* New York: Holt, Rinehart & Winston.

Redelmeier, D.A., & Tversky, A. (1996). On the belief that arthritis pain is related to the weather. *Proceedings of the National Academy of Sciences, 93,* 2895–2896.

Reder, L. (1980). The role of elaboration in the comprehension and retention of prose. *Review of Educational Research, 50,* 5–53.

Reder, L.M., & Kusbit, G.W. (1991). Locus of the Moses illusion: Imperfect encoding, retrieval or match? *Journal of Memory and Language, 30,* 385–406.

Regier, T., & Kay, P. (2004). Color naming and sunlight. *Psychological Science, 15,* 289–290.

Reicher, G.M. (1969). Perceptual recognition as a function of meaningfulness of stimulus material. *Journal of Experimental Psychology, 81,* 275–280.

Reisberg, D., Pearson, D.G., & Kosslyn, S.M. (2003). Intuitions and introspections about imagery: The role of imagery experience in shaping an investigator's theoretical views. *Applied Cognitive Psychology, 17,* 147–160.

Rhodes, G., Byatt, G., Michie, P.T., & Puce, A. (2004). Is the fusiform face area speciized for faces, individuation, of expert individuation? *Journal of Cognitive Neuroscience, 16,* 189–203.

Rice, M.L. (1989). Children's language acquisition. *American Psychologist, 44,* 149–156.

Richman, C.L. (1994). The bizarreness effect with complex sentences: Temporal effects. *Canadian Journal of Experimental Psychology, 48,* 444–450.

Rigdon, M.A., & Epting, F. (1982). A test of the Golden Section hypothesis with elicited constructs. *Journal of Personality and Social Psychology, 43,* 1080–1087.

Rinck, M., & Denis, M. (2004). The metrics of spatial distance traversed during mental imagery. *Journal of Experimental Psychology: Learning, Memory, and Cognition, 30,* 1211–1218.

Rips, L.J. (1983). Cognitive processes in propositional reasoning. *Psychological Review, 90,* 38–71.

Rips, L.J. (1988). Deduction. In R.J. Sternberg & E.E. Smith (Eds.), *The psychology of human thought* (pp. 116–152). Cambridge: Cambridge University Press.

Rips, L.J. (1989). The psychology of knights and knaves. *Cognition, 31,* 85–116.

Rips, L.J. (1990). Paralogical reasoning: Evans, Johnson-Laird, and Byrne on liar and truth-teller puzzles. *Cognition, 36,* 291–314.

Rips, L.J. (1994). *The psychology of proof: Deductive reasoning in human thinking.* Cambridge, Mass.: MIT Press.

Rips, L.J. (1997). Goals for a theory of deduction: Reply to Johnson-Laird. *Minds and Machines, 7,* 409–424.

Rips, L.J., & Conrad, F.G. (1989). Folk psychology of mental activities. *Psychological Review, 96,* 187–207.

Rips, L.J., & Conrad, F.G. (1990). Parts of activities: Reply to Fellbaum and Miller. *Psychological Review, 97,* 571–575.

Ro, T., Russell, C., & Lavie, N. (2001). Changing faces: A detection advantage in the flicker paradigm. *Psychological Science, 12,* 94–99.

Roberson, D., Davidoff, J., Davies, I.R.L., & Shapiro, L.R. (2004). The development of color categories in two languages: A longitudinal study. *Journal of Experimental Psychology: General, 133,* 554–571.

Roberson, D., Davies, I., & Davidoff, J. (2000). Color categories are not universal: Replications and new evidence from a stone-age culture. *Journal of Experimental Psychology: General, 129,* 369–398.

Roberts, R.M., & Kreuz, R.J. (1994). Why do people use figurative language? *Psychological Science, 5,* 159–163.

Rock, I. (1983). *The logic of perception.* Cambridge, Mass.: MIT Press.

Rock, I. (1984). *Perception*. New York: Freeman.

Rock, I. (Ed.). (1990). *Legacy of Solomon Asch: Essays in cognition and social psychology*. Hillsdale, NJ: Erlbaum.

Rock, I., & Ceraso, J. (1964). A cognitive theory of associative learning. In C. Scheerer (Ed.), *Cognition* (pp. 110–146). New York: Harper & Row.

Rock, I., Wheeler, D., & Tudor, L. (1989). Can we imagine how objects look from other viewpoints? *Cognitive Psychology, 21*, 185–210.

Roediger, H.L. (1997). Remembering. *Contemporary Psychology, 42*, 488–492.

Roediger, H.L., III, & Blaxton, T.A. (1987). Effects of varying modality, surface features, and retention interval on priming in word fragment completion. *Memory & Cognition, 15*, 379–388.

Roediger, H.L., Gallo, D.A., & Geraci, L. (2002). Processing approaches to cognition: The impetus from the levels-of-processing framework. *Memory, 10*, 319–332.

Roediger, H.L., & McDermott, K.B. (1993). Implicit memory in normal human subjects. In F. Boller & J. Grafman (Eds.), *Handbook of neuropsychology* (Vol. 8, pp. 63–131). Amsterdam: Elsevier.

Ronan, K.R., & Kendall, P.C. (1997). Self-talk in distressed youth: States of mind and content specificity. *Journal of Clinical Child Psychology, 26*, 330–337.

Rosch, E.H. (1975). Cognitive representations of semantic categories. *Journal of Experimental Psychology: General, 104*, 192–233.

Rosch, E.H. (1978). Principles of categorization. In E. Rosch & B. Lloyd (Eds.), *Cognition and categorization* (pp. 27–48). Hillsdale, NJ: Erlbaum.

Rosch, E.H. (1988). Coherences and categorization: A historical view. In F. Kessel (Ed.), *The development of language and language researchers: Essays in honor of Roger Brown* (pp. 373–392). Hillsdale, NJ: Erlbaum.

Rosch, E.H., & Mervis, C.B. (1975). Family resemblances: Studies in the internal structure of categories. *Cognitive Psychology, 7*, 573–605.

Rosch, E.H., Mervis, C.B., Gray, W.D., Johnson, D.M., & Boyes-Braem, P. (1976). Basic objects in natural categories. *Cognitive Psychology, 8*, 382–439.

Rosnow, R.L., & Rosenthal, R. (1989). Statistical procedures and the justification of knowledge in psychological science. *American Psychologist, 44*, 1276–1284.

Rossano, M.J. (2003). Expertise and the evolution of consciousness. *Cognition, 89*, 207–236.

Rouse, W.B., & Morris, N.M. (1986). On looking into the black box: Prospect and limits in the search for mental models. *Psychological Bulletin, 100*, 349–363.

Rozin, P., & Fallon, A.E. (1987). A perspective on disgust. *Psychological Review, 94*, 23–41.

Rozin, P., Fallon, A., & Augustoni-Ziskind, M. (1985). The child's conception of food: The development of contamination sensitivity to 'disgusting' substances. *Developmental Psychology, 21*, 1075–1079.

Rozin, P., Markwith, M., & Ross, B. (1990). The sympathetic magical law of similarity, nominal realism and neglect of negatives in response to negative labels. *Psychological Science, 1*, 383–384.

Rozin, P., Millman, L., & Nemeroff, C. (1986). Operation of the laws of sympathetic magic in disgust and other domains. *Journal of Personality and Social Psychology, 50*, 703–712.

Rozin, P., & Nemeroff, C. (2002). Sympathetic magical thinking: The contagion and similarity 'heuristics'. In T. Gilovich, D. Griffin, & D. Kahneman (Eds.), *Heuristics and biases: The psychology of intuitive judgment* (pp. 201–216). Cambridge: Cambridge University Press.

Rozin, P., & Royzman, E.B. (2001). Negativity bias, negativity dominance, and contagion. *Personality and Social Psychology Review, 5*, 296–320.

Rubin, D.C. (1975). Within word structure in the tip-of-the-tongue phenomenon. *Journal of Verbal Learning and Verbal Behavior, 14*, 392–397.

Rubin, D.C. (2000). The distribution of early childhood memories. *Memory*, 265–269.

Rubin, D.C. (2002). Autobiographical memory across the lifespan. In P. Graf & N. Ohta

(Eds.), *Lifespan development of human memory* (pp. 159–184). Cambridge, Mass.: MIT Press.

Rubin, D.C. (2005). A basic-systems approach to autobiographical memory. *Current Directions in Psychological Science, 11*, 79–83.

Rubin, D.C., & Berntsen, D. (2003). Life scripts help to maintain autobiographical memories of highly positive, but not highly negative, events. *Memory & Cognition, 31*, 1–14.

Rubin, D.C., & Friendly, M. (1986). Predicting which words get recalled: Measures of free recall, availability, goodness, emotionality, and pronounceability for 925 nouns. *Memory & Cognition, 14*, 79–94.

Rubin, D.C., Rahhal, T.A., & Poon, L.W. (1998). Things learned early in adulthood are remembered best. *Memory & Cognition, 26*, 3–19.

Rubin, D.C., Wetzler, S.E., & Nebes, R.D. (1986). Autobiographical memory across the lifespan. In D.C. Rubin (Ed.), *Autobiographical memory* (pp. 202–221). Cambridge: Cambridge University Press.

Ruby, L. (1960). *Logic: An introduction*. New York: Lippincott.

Rugg, M.D. (1995). Event-related potential studies of memory. In M.D. Rugg & M.G.H. Coles (Eds.), *Electrophysiology of mind* (pp. 132–170). New York: Oxford University Press.

Rugg, M.D. (2002). Functional neuroimaging of memory. In A.D. Baddeley, M.D. Kopelman, & B.A. Wilson (Eds.), *The handbook of memory disorders* (pp. 57–80). Chichester: Wiley.

Rugg, M.D., Otten, L.J., & Henson, R.N.A. (2003). The neural basis of episodic memory: Evidence from functional neuroimaging. In A. Parker, A. Derrington, & C. Blakemore (Eds.), *The physiology of cognitive processes* (pp. 211–233). Oxford: Oxford University Press.

Rumelhart, D.E., & McClelland, J.L. (Eds.). (1986). *Parallel distributed processing: Explorations in the microstructure of cognition: Vol. I Foundations*. Cambridge, Mass.: MIT Press.

Runco, M.A. (2004). Creativity. *Annual Review of Psychology, 55*, 657–687.

Rundus, D. (1977). Maintenance rehearsal and single-level processing. *Journal of Verbal Learning and Verbal Behavior, 16*, 665–681.

Ruthruff, E., Johnston, J.C., Van Selst, M., Whitsell, S., & Remington, R. (2003). Vanishing dual-task interference after practice: Has the bottleneck been eliminated or is it merely latent? *Journal of Experimental Psychology: Human Perception and Performance, 29*, 280–289.

Ruthsatz, J., & Detterman, D.K. (2003). An extraordinary memory: The case of a musical prodigy. *Intelligence, 31*, 509–518.

Ryle, G. (1949). *The concept of mind*. London: Hutchison.

Sachs, J. (1967). Recognition memory for syntactic and semantic aspects of connected discourse. *Perception and Psychophysics, 2*, 437–442.

Sadoski, M., & Paivio, A. (2001). *Imagery and text: A dual-coding theory of reading and writing*. Mahwah, NJ: Erlbaum.

Sainsbury, R.M. (1988). *Paradoxes*. Cambridge: Cambridge University Press.

Salmon, D.P., Butters, N., & Chan, A.S. (1999). The deterioration of semantic memory in Alzheimer's disease. *Canadian Journal of Experimental Psychology, 53*, 108–116.

Samson, D., & Pilon, A. (2003). A case of impaired knowledge for fruit and vegetables. *Cognitive Neuropsychology, 20*, 373–400.

Sapir, E. (1949). *Selected writings of Edward Sapir*. Berkeley: University of California Press.

Sarter, M., Berntson, G.G., & Cacioppo, J.T. (1996). Brian imaging and cognitive neuroscience. *American Psychologist, 51*, 13–21.

Saunders, B.A.C., & van Brakel, J. (1997). Are there nontrivial constraints on colour categorization? *Behavioral and Brain Sciences, 20*, 167–228.

Schachter, S.S., Christenfeld, N., Ravina, B., & Bilous, F. (1991). Speech disfluency and the structure of knowledge. *Journal of Personality and Social Psychology, 60*, 362–367.

Schachter, S.S., Rauscher, F., Christenfeld, N., & Crone, K.T. (1994). The vocabularies of academia. *Psychological Science, 5*, 37–41.

Schactel, E. (1947). On memory and childhood amnesia. *Psychiatry, 10*, 1–26.

Schacter, D.L. (1987). Implicit memory: History

and current status. *Journal of Experimental Psychology: Learning, Memory, and Cognition, 13,* 501–518.

Schacter, D.L. (1992). Understanding implicit memory. *American Psychologist, 47,* 559–569.

Schacter, D.L. (1999). The seven sins of memory: Insights from psychology and cognitive neuroscience. *American Psychologist, 54,* 182–203.

Schacter, D.L., & Dodson, C.S. (2001). Misattribution, false recognition and the sins of memory. *Philosophical Transactions of the Royal Society (Series B), 356,* 1385–1393.

Schacter, D.L., & Graf, P. (1986). Effects of elaborative processing on implicit and explicit memory for new associations. *Journal of Experimental Psychology: Learning, Memory, and Cognition, 12,* 432–444.

Schacter, D.L., & Tulving, E. (1994). What are the memory systems of 1994? In D.L. Schacter & E. Tulving (Eds.), *Memory systems 1994* (pp. 1–38). Cambridge, Mass.: MIT Press.

Schacter, D.L., Wagner, A.D., & Buckner, R.L. (2000). Memory systems of 1999. In E. Tulving & F.I.M. Craik (Eds.). *The Oxford handbook of memory* (pp. 627–643). New York: Oxford University Press.

Schaeffer, J., & van den Herik, H.J. (2002). Games, computers, and artificial intelligence. *Artificial Intelligence, 134,* 1–7.

Schank, R.C. (1982a). Depths of knowledge. In B. de Gelder (Ed.), *Knowledge and representation* (pp. 170–216). London: Routledge & Kegan Paul.

Schank, R.C. (1982b). *Dynamic memory.* New York: Cambridge University Press.

Schank, R.C., & Abelson, R.P. (1975). *Scripts, plans and knowledge.* Proceedings of the Fourth International Joint Conference on Artificial Intelligence. Tbilisi, USSR.

Schank, R.C., & Abelson, R.P. (1977). *Scripts, plans, goals and understanding.* Hillsdale, NJ: Erlbaum.

Schellenberg, E.G. (2004). Music lessons enhance IQ. *Psychological Science, 15,* 511–514.

Schlenker, B.R., & Leary, M.R. (1982). Social anxiety and self-presentation: A conceptualization and model. *Psychological Bulletin, 92,* 641–669.

Schmidt, R.A., & Bjork, R.A. (1992). New conceptualizations of practice: Common principles in three paradigms suggest new concepts for training. *Psychological Science, 3,* 207–217.

Schmidt, S.R. (2002). The humour effect: Differential processing and privileged retrieval. *Memory, 10,* 127–138.

Schmidt, S.R., & Williams, A.R. (2001). Memory for humorous cartoons. *Memory & Cognition, 29,* 305–311.

Schmuckler, M.A. (2001). What is ecological validity: A dimensional analysis. *Infancy, 2,* 419–436.

Schneider, W. (1987). Connectionism: Is it a paradigm shift for psychology? *Behavior Research Methods, Instruments, & Computers, 19,* 73–83.

Schneider, W., & Chein, J.M. (2003). Controlled and automatic processing: Behavior, theory, and biological mechanisms. *Cognitive Science, 27,* 525–559.

Scholz, B.C., & Pullum, G.K. (2002). Searching for arguments to support linguistic nativism. *Linguistic Review, 19,* 185–223.

Schooler, C. (1998). Environmental complexity and the Flynn effect. In U. Neisser (Ed.), *The rising curve* (pp. 67–79). Washington: American Psychological Association.

Schubotz, R.I., & von Cramon, D.Y. 2001. Interval and ordinal properties of sequences are associated with distinct premotor areas. *Cerebral Cortex, 11,* 210–222.

Schuh, F.C. (1968). *The masterbook of mathematical recreations.* New York: Dover.

Schwartz, N., & Vaughn, L.A. (2002). The availability heuristic revisited: Ease of recall and content of recall as distinct sources of information. In T. Gilovich, D. Griffin, & D. Kahneman (Eds.), *Heuristics and biases: The psychology of intuitive judgment* (pp. 103–119). Cambridge: Cambridge University Press.

Schwartz, R.M. (1997). Consider the simple screw: Cognitive science, quality improvement, and psychotherapy. *Journal of Consulting and Clinical Psychology, 65,* 970–983.

Schwartz, R.M., & Garamoni, G.L. (1986). A structural model of positive and negative states of mind: Asymmetry in the internal dialogue. In P.C. Kendall (Ed.), *Advances in cognitive-behavioral research and therapy* (Vol. 5, pp. 1–62). New York: Academic Press.

Schwartz, R.M., & Michelson, L. (1987). States of mind model: Cognitive balance in the treatment of agoraphobia. *Journal of Consulting and Clinical Psychology, 55*, 557–565.

Schweich, M., van der Linden, M., Bredart, S., Bruyer, R., Nelles, B., & Schils, J.-P. (1992). Daily life difficulties reported by young and elderly subjects. *Applied Cognitive Psychology, 6*, 161–172.

Scott, S.K. (2004). The neural representation of concrete nouns: What's right and what's left? *Trends in Cognitive Sciences, 8*, 151–153.

Scribner, S. (1986). Thinking in action: Some characteristics of practical thought. In R.J. Sternberg & R.K. Wagner (Eds.), *Practical intelligence* (pp. 13–30). New York: Cambridge University Press.

Scribner, S. (1993). An activity theory approach to memory. *Applied Cognitive Psychology, 7*, 185–190.

Searle, J. (2000). Consciousness. *Annual Review of Neuroscience, 23*, 557–578.

Sedgwick, H.A. (1980). The geometry of spatial layout in pictorial representation. In M.A. Hagen (Ed.), *The perception of pictures* (pp. 33–90). New York: Academic Press.

Selfridge, O. (1959). Pandemonium: A paradigm for learning. In *The mechanization of thought processes*. London: Her Majesty's Stationery Office.

Semon, R. (1923). *Mnemic psychology* (B. Duffy, Trans.). London: George Allen & Unwin. (Original work published 1909).

Senders, V.L. (1958). *Measurement and statistics*. New York: Oxford University Press.

Sévigny, S., Cloutier, M., Pelletier, M.-F., & Ladouceur, R. (2005). Internet gambling: Misleading payout rates during the 'demo' period. *Computers in Human Behavior, 21*, 153–158.

Shafto, M., & MacKay, D.G. (2000). The Moses, mega-Moses, and Armstrong illusions: Integrating language comprehension and semantic memory. *Psychological Science, 11*, 372–378.

Shalit, B. (1980). The Golden Section relation in the evaluation of environmental relations. *British Journal of Psychology, 71*, 39–42.

Shanks, D.R. (2004). Implicit learning. In K. Lamberts & R. Goldstone (Eds.), *Handbook of cognition* (pp. 202–220). London: Sage.

Shannon, C.E., & Weaver, W. (1949). *The mathematical theory of communication*. Urbana: University of Illinois Press.

Shapiro, K.L., Arnell, K.M., & Raymond, J.E. (1997). The attentional blink. *Trends in Cognitive Sciences, 1*, 291–296.

Shepard, R.N. (1966). Learning and recall as organization and search. *Journal of Verbal Learning and Verbal Behavior, 5*, 201–204.

Shepard, R.N. (1967). Recognition memory for words, sentences, and pictures. *Journal of Verbal Learning and Verbal Behavior, 6*, 156–163.

Shepard, R.N. (1978). The mental image. *American Psychologist, 33*, 125–137.

Shepard, R.N. (1984). Ecological constraints on internal representation: Resonant kinematics of perceiving, imagining, thinking, and dreaming. *Psychological Review, 91*, 417–447.

Shepard, R.N., & Cooper, L.A. (1982). *Mental images and their transformations*. Cambridge, Mass.: MIT Press.

Shepard, R.N., & Metzler, J. (1971). Mental rotation of three-dimensional objects. *Science, 171*, 701–703.

Shettleworth, S.J. (2004). Review of B.H. Weber & D.J. Depew, 'Evolution and learning: The Baldwin effect reconsidered'. *Evolutionary Psychology, 2*, 105–107.

Shiffrin, R.M., & Atkinson, R.C. (1969). Storage and retrieval processes in long-term memory. *Psychological Review, 76*, 179–193.

Shiffrin, R.M., & Schneider, W. (1977). Controlled and automatic human information processing: II. Perceptual learning, automatic attending, and a general theory. *Psychological Review, 84*, 155–171.

Shipp, S. (2004). The brain circuitry of attention. *Trends in Cognitive Sciences, 8*, 223–230.

Shneiderman, B. (1998). *Designing the user interface* (3rd ed.). Reading, Mass.: Addison-Wesley.

Sholl, M.J. (1987). Cognitive maps as orienting schemata. *Journal of Experimental Psychology: Learning, Memory, and Cognition, 13*, 615–628.

Shrauf, R.W., & Rubin, D.C. (2003). On the bilingual's two sets of memories. In R. Fivush & C.A. Hayden (Eds.), *Autobiographical memory and the construction of a narrative self* (pp. 121–146). Mahwah, NJ: Erlbaum.

Shweder, R.A. (1977). Likeness and likelihood in everyday thought. *Current Anthropology, 18*, 637–658.

Siegler, R.S. (2004). U-shaped interest in U-shaped development—and what it means. *Journal of Cognition and Development, 5*, 1–10.

Silvia, P.J. (2005). What is interesting? Exploring the appraisal structure of interest. *Emotion, 5*, 89–102.

Sime, M.E., & Coombs, M.J. (Eds.). (1983). *Designing for human computer communication.* London: Academic Press.

Simmel, M.L. (1953). The coin problem: A study in thinking. *American Journal of Psychology, 66*, 229–241.

Simmel, M.L. (1956). Phantoms in patients with leprosy and in elderly digital amputees. *American Journal of Psychology, 69*, 529–545.

Simmons, W.K., & Barsalou, L.W. (2003). The similarity in topography principle: Reconciling theories of conceptual deficits. *Cognitive Neuropsychology, 20*, 451–486.

Simon, H.A. (1969). *The sciences of the artificial.* Cambridge, Mass.: MIT Press.

Simon, H.A. (1975). The functional equivalence of problem-solving skills. *Cognitive Psychology, 7*, 268–288.

Simon, H.A. (1979). *Models of thought.* New Haven: Yale University Press.

Simon, H.A. (1981). *The sciences of the artificial* (2nd ed.). Cambridge, Mass.: MIT Press.

Simon, H.A. (1986). The information-processing explanation of Gestalt phenomena. *Computers in Human Behaviour, 2*, 241–255.

Simon, H.A. (1992). What is an 'explanation' of behavior? *Psychological Science*, 150–161.

Simon, H.A. (1995). Explaining the ineffable: AI on the topics of intuition, insight and inspiration. *Proceedings of the Fourteenth International Joint Conference on Artificial Intelligence*, 939–948.

Simon, H.A. (1995). The information-processing theory of mind. *American Psychologist, 50*, 507–508.

Simon, H.A. (2000). Artificial intelligence. In A.E. Kazlin (Ed.), *American Psychological Association encyclopedia of psychology* (vol. 1, pp. 248–255). New York: Oxford University Press.

Simon, H.A., Valdéz-Pérez, R.E., & Sleeman, D.H. (1997). Scientific discovery and simplicity of method. *Artificial Intelligence, 91*, 177–181.

Simons, D.J. (2000). Attentional capture and inattentional blindness. *Trends in Cognitive Sciences, 4*, 147–155.

Simons, D.J., & Chabris, C.F. (1999). Gorillas in our midst: Sustained inattentional blindness for dynamic events. *Perception, 28*, 1059–1074.

Simonton, D.K. (1984). *Genius, creativity and leadership.* Cambridge, Mass.: Harvard University Press.

Simonton, D.K. (1988). *Scientific genius.* New York: Cambridge University Press.

Simonton, D.K. (1993). Genius and chance: A Darwinian perspective. In J. Brockman (Ed.), *Creativity* (pp. 176–201). New York: Simon & Schuster.

Simonton, D.K. (1994). *Greatness: Who makes history and why.* New York: Guilford.

Simonton, D.K. (2003). Scientific creativity as constrained stochastic behavior: The integration of product, person, and process perspectives. *Psychological Bulletin, 129*, 475–494.

Sinha, P. (2002). Recognizing complex patterns. *Nature Neuroscience Supplement, 5*, 1093–1097.

Skinner, B.F. (1957). *Verbal behavior.* New York: Appleton-Century-Crofts.

Skinner, B.F. (1964). Behaviorism at fifty. In T.W. Wann (Ed.), *Behaviorism and phenomenology* (pp. 79–97). Chicago: University of Chicago Press.

Skinner, B.F. (1989). The origins of cognitive thought. *American Psychologist, 44*, 13–18.

Slamecka, N. (1985). Ebbinghaus: Some associations. *Journal of Experimental Psychology, 11,* 414–435.

Slamecka, N., & Graf, P. (1978). The generation effect: Delineation of a phenomenon. *Journal of Experimental Psychology: Human Learning and Memory, 4,* 592–604.

Sloboda, J. (1981). Space in musical notation. *Visible Language, 15,* 86–110.

Sloman, S.A. (1996). The empirical case for two systems of reasoning. *Psychological Bulletin, 119,* 3–22.

Sluckin, W., Colman, A.M., & Hargreaves, D.J. (1980). Liking words as a function of the experienced frequency of their occurrence. *British Journal of Psychology, 71,* 163–169.

Smedslund, J. (1963). The concept of correlation in adults. *Scandinavian Journal of Psychology, 4,* 165–173.

Smilek, D., Dixon, M.J., Cudahy, C., & Merikle, P.M. (2002). Synesthetic color experiences influence memory. *Psychological Science, 13,* 548–552.

Smith, N.K., Cacioppo, J.T., Larsen, J.T., & Chartrand, T.L. (2003). May I have your attention, please: Electrocortical responses to positive and negative stimuli. *Neuropsychologia, 41,* 171–183.

Smith, V.L., & Clark, H.H. (1993). On the course of answering questions. *Journal of Memory and Language, 32,* 25–38.

Smullyan, R.M. (1978). *What is the name of this book? The riddle of Dracula and other logical puzzles.* Englewood Cliffs, NJ: Prentice-Hall.

Smyth, M.M., & Clark, S.E. (1986). My half-sister is a THOG: Strategic processes in a reasoning task. *British Journal of Psychology, 77,* 275–287.

Sohn, M., Anderson, J.R., Reder, L.M., & Goode, A. (2004). Differential fan effect and attentional focus. *Psychonomic Bulletin and Review, 11,* 729–734.

Sokal, M. (2001). Practical phrenology as psychological counseling in the 19th-century United States. In C. Green, M. Shore, & T. Teo (Eds.), *The transformation of psychology: The influences of 19th-century natural science, technology, and philosophy* (pp. 21–44). Washington: American Psychological Association.

Soukoreff, R.W., & Mackenzie, I.S. (2004). Toward a standard for pointing device evaluation, perspectives on 27 years of Fitts' law research in HCI. *International Journal of Human-Computer Studies, 61,* 751–789.

Spearman, C. (1904). 'General intelligence' objectively determined and measured. *American Journal of Psychology, 15,* 201–292.

Spearman, C. (1965). The abilities of man: Their nature and measurement. In A. Anastasi (Ed.), *Individual differences* (pp. 51–57). New York: Wiley. (Original work published 1927).

Spearman, C. (1970). *The abilities of man: Their nature and measurement.* New York: AMS Press. (Original work published 1932).

Spelke, E., Hirst, W., & Neisser, U. (1976). Skills of divided attention. *Cognition, 4,* 215–230.

Spence, D.P. (1973). Analog and digital descriptions of behavior. *American Psychologist, 28,* 479–497.

Sperber, D. (2002). In defense of massive modularity. In E. Dupoux (Ed.), *Language, brain and cognitive development: Essays in honor of Jacques Mehler* (pp. 47–57). Cambridge, Mass.: MIT Press.

Sperber, D., & Hirschfeld, L.A. (2004). The cognitive foundations of cultural stability and diversity. *Trends in Cognitive Sciences, 8,* 40–48.

Sperber, D., & Wilson, D. (1995). *Relevance: Communication and cognition* (2nd ed.). Oxford: Blackwell.

Sperber, D., & Wilson, D. (2002). Pragmatics modularity and mind-reading. *Mind & Language, 17,* 3–23.

Sperling, G. (1960). The information available in brief visual presentations. *Psychological Monographs, 74,* No. 11.

Sperry, R. (1987). Consciousness and causality. In R.L. Gregory (Ed.), *The Oxford companion to the mind* (pp. 164–166). Oxford: Oxford University Press.

Sperry, R. (1988). Psychology's mentalist paradigm and the religion/science tension. *American Psychologist, 43,* 607–613.

Sperry, R.W. (1964, January). The great cerebral commissure. *Scientific American, 210*, 42–52.

Squire, L.R. (2004). Memory systems of the brain: A brief history and current perspective. *Neurobiology of Learning and Memory, 82*, 171–177.

Squire, L.R., & McKee, R. (1992). Influence of prior events on cognitive judgments in amnesia. *Journal of Experimental Psychology: Learning, Memory, and Cognition, 18*, 106–115.

Srivastava, I. (2005). Mobile phones and the evolution of social behavior. *Behavior and Information Technology, 24*, 111–129.

Stanovich, K.E. (2004). *The robot's rebellion: Finding meaning in the age of Darwin.* Chicago: University of Chicago Press.

Stanovich, K.E., & Cunningham, A.E. (1992). Studying the consequences of literacy within a literate society: The cognitive correlates of print exposure. *Memory & Cognition, 20*, 51–68.

Stanovich, K.E., & West, R.F. (1998). Individual differences in rational thought. *Journal of Experimental Psychology: General, 127*, 161–188.

Stanovich, K.E., & West, R.F. (2000). Individual differences in reasoning: Implications for the rationality debate? *Behavioral and Brain Sciences, 23*, 645–726.

Stanovich, K.E., & West, R.F. (2003a). The rationality debate as a progressive research program. *Behavioral and Brain Sciences, 26*, 531–534.

Stanovich, K.E., & West, R.F. (2003b). Evolutionary versus instrumental goals: How evolutionary psychology misconceives human rationality. In D.E. Over (Ed.), *Evolution and the psychology of thinking: The debate.* Hove, UK: Psychology Press.

Steering Committee of the Physicians' Health Study Research Group. (1988). Preliminary report: Findings from the aspirin component of the ongoing physicians' health study. *New England Journal of Medicine, 318*, 262–264.

Stein, B., Bransford, J., Franks, J., Owings, R., Vye, N., & McGraw, W. (1982). Differences in the precision of self-generated elaborations. *Journal of Experimental Psychology: General, 111*, 399–405.

Stern, W. (1966). On the mental quotient. In R.J. Herrnstein & E. Boring (Eds.), *A source book in the history of psychology* (pp. 450–453). Cambridge, Mass.: Harvard University Press. (Original work published 1912).

Sternberg, R.J. (1980). Sketch of a componential subtheory of intelligence. *Behavioral and Brain Sciences, 3*, 573–614.

Sternberg, R.J. (1982). Natural, unnatural, and supernatural concepts. *Cognitive Psychology, 14*, 451–488.

Sternberg, R.J. (1983). Components of human intelligence. *Cognition, 15*, 1–48.

Sternberg, R.J. (1984a). Mechanisms of cognitive development: A componential approach. In R.J. Sternberg (Ed.), *Mechanisms of cognitive development* (pp. 163–209). San Francisco: Freeman.

Sternberg, R.J. (1984b). Toward a triarchic theory of human intelligence. *Behavioral and Brain Sciences, 7*, 269–316.

Sternberg, R.J. (1988). *The triarchic mind: A new theory of human intelligence.* New York: Viking.

Sternberg, R.J. (1992). Ability tests, measurements, and markets. *Journal of Educational Psychology, 84*, 134–140.

Sternberg, R.J. (1999a). The theory of successful intelligence. *Review of General Psychology, 3*, 292–316.

Sternberg, R.J. (1999b). Successful intelligence: Finding a balance. *Trends in Cognitive Sciences, 3*, 436–442.

Sternberg, R.J. (2000a). Damn it, I still don't know what to do! *Behavioral and Brain Sciences, 23*, 764.

Sternberg, R.J. (2000b). Cross-disciplinary verification of theories: The case of the triarchic theory. *History of Psychology, 3*, 177–179.

Sternberg, R.J. (2003a). Issues in the theory and measurement of successful intelligence: A reply to Brody. *Intelligence, 31*, 331–337.

Sternberg, R.J. (2003b). Our research program validating the triarchic theory of successful intelligence: Reply to Gottfredson. *Intelligence, 31*, 399–413.

Sternberg, R.J., Castejón, J.L., Prieto, M.D., Hautamäki, J., & Grigerenko, E.L. (2001). Confirmatory factor analysis of the Sternberg tri-archic abilities test in three international samples. *European Journal of Psychological Assessment, 17*, 1–16.

Sternberg, R.J., & Kaufman, J.C. (1998). Human abilities. *Annual Review of Psychology, 49*, 479–502.

Sternberg, R.J., Powell, C., McGrane, P., & Grantham-McGregor, S. (1997). Effects of a parasitic infection on cognitive functioning. *Journal of Experimental Psychology: Applied, 3*, 67–76.

Sternberg, R.J., & Wagner, R.K. (1986). *Practical intelligence.* New York: Cambridge University Press.

Sternberg, R.J., & Wagner, R.K. (1994*). Mind in context: Interactionist perspectives on human intelligence.* New York: Cambridge University Press.

Stevens, A., & Coupe, P. (1978). Distortions in judged spatial distances. *Cognitive Psychology, 10*, 422–437.

Stevens, G.C. (1983). User-friendly computer systems? A critical examination of the concept. *Behaviour and Information Technology, 2*, 3–16.

Stich, S. (1983). *From folk psychology to cognitive science: The case against belief.* Cambridge, Mass.: MIT Press.

Stickgold, R., & Walker, M. (2004). To sleep, perchance to gain creative insight? *Trends in Cognitive Sciences, 8*, 191–192.

Stover, D., & Erdmann, E. (2000). *A mind for tomorrow: Facts, values, and the future.* Westport, Conn.: Praeger.

Strawson, P.F. (1952). *Introduction to logical theory.* London: Methuen.

Strohmeyer, C.F. (1982). An adult eidetiker. In U. Neisser (Ed.), *Memory observed: Remembering in natural contexts* (pp. 399–404). San Francisco: Freeman. (Original work published 1970).

Stroop, J.R. (1992). Studies of interference in serial verbal reactions. *Journal of Experimental Psychology: General, 121*, 15–23. (Original work published 1935).

Suddendorf, T., & Busby, J. (2003). Mental time travel in animals? *Trends in Cognitive Sciences, 7*, 391–396.

Sugiyama, L.S., Tooby, J., & Cosmides, L. (2002). Cross-cultural evidence of cognitive adaptations for social exchange among the Shiwiar of Ecuadorian Amazonia. *Proceedings of the National Academy of Sciences, 99*, 11537–11542.

Suzuki, R., & Arita, T. (2004). Interactions between learning and evolution: The outstanding strategy generated by the Baldwin effect. *BioSystems, 77*, 57–71.

Swanson, L.W. (2003). *Brain architecture: Understanding the basic plan.* New York: Oxford University Press.

Talarico, J.M., & Rubin, D.C. (2003). Confidence, not consistency, characterizes flashbulb memories. *Psychological Science, 14*, 455–461.

Talland, G.A. (1968). *Disorders of memory and learning.* Baltimore: Penguin.

Taylor, H.A., & Tversky, B. (1992). Descriptions and depictions of environments. *Memory & Cognition, 20*, 483–496.

Taylor, J.G. (1966). Perception generated by training echolocation. *Canadian Journal of Psychology, 20*, 64–81.

Terman, L.M. (1948).The measurement of intelligence. In W. Dennis (Ed.), *Readings in the history of psychology* (pp. 485–496). New York: Appleton-Century-Crofts. (Original work published 1916).

Terrace, H.S. (1985). In the beginning was the 'Name'. *American Psychologist, 40*, 1011–1028.

The Oxford English Dictionary [compact disk] (1992). Oxford: Oxford University Press.

The Right Stuff. (1983, December), *Psychology Today, 17(12)*, 58–63.

Thompson, C.P. (1997). Schematic and social influences on memory. *Contemporary Psychology, 42*, 492–493.

Thorndike, E.L. (1898). Animal intelligence: An experimental study of the associative processes in animals. *Psychological Review Monograph Supplement, 2(8)*.

Thornton, M.T. (1982). Aristotelian practical reason. *Mind, 91*, 57–76.

Tibbetts, P.E. (2001). The anterior cingulate cortex, akinetic mutism, and human volition. *Brain and Mind, 2*, 323–341.

Tierney, J. (1991, July 21). Behind Monty Hall's doors: Puzzle, debate and answer? *New York Times*, pp. 1, 20.

Tigner, R.B., & Tigner, S.S. (2000). Triarchic theories of intelligence: Aristotle and Sternberg. *History of Psychology, 3*, 168–176.

Titchener, E.B. (1966). From 'A text-book of psychology'. In R.J. Herrnstein & E. Boring (Eds.), *A source book in the history of psychology* (pp. 599–605). Cambridge, Mass.: Harvard University Press. (Original work published 1910).

Todd, P.M., Fiddick, L., & Krauss, S. (2000). Ecological rationality and its contents. *Thinking and Reasoning, 6*, 375–384.

Todd, P.M., & Gigerenzer, G. (2000). Précis of 'Simple heuristics that make us smart'. *Behavioral and Brain Sciences, 23*, 737–780.

Todd, P.M., & Gigerenzer, G. (2003). Bounding rationality to the world. *Journal of Economic Psychology, 24*, 143–165.

Toglia, M., & Battig, W. (1978). *Handbook of semantic word norms*. Hillsdale, NJ: Erlbaum.

Tolman, E.C. (1948). Cognitive maps in rats and men. *Psychological Review, 55*, 189–208.

Tolman, E.C. (1959). Principles of purposive behavior. In S. Koch (Ed.), *Psychology: A study of a science* (pp. 92–157). New York: McGraw-Hill.

Toppino, T.C. (2003). Reversible-figure perception: Mechanisms of intentional control. *Perception & Psychophysics, 65*, 1285–1295

Toth, J.P. (2000). Nonconscious forms of human memory. In E. Tulving & F.I.M. Craik (Eds.), *The Oxford handbook of memory* (pp. 245–261). New York: Oxford University Press.

Townsend, J.T. (1990). Serial vs. parallel processing: Sometimes they look like Tweedledum and Tweedledee but they can and should be distinguished. *Psychological Science, 1*, 46–54.

Trachtenberg, L., Streumer, J., & van Zolingen, S. (2002). Career counseling in the emerging post-industrial society. *International Journal for Educational and Vocational Guidance, 2*, 85–99.

Trehub, S.E. (2003). The developmental origins of musicality. *Nature Neuroscience, 6*, 669–673.

Treisman, A. (1969). Strategies and models of selective attention. *Psychological Review, 76*, 282–299.

Treisman, A. (1986). Features and objects and visual processing. *Scientific American, 255*, 114–125.

Treisman, A. (1996). The binding problem. *Current Opinion in Neurobiology, 6*, 171–178.

Treisman, A., & Gelade, G. (1980). A feature-integration theory of attention. *Cognitive Psychology, 12*, 97–136.

Treisman, A., & Gormican, S. (1988). Feature analysis in early vision: Evidence from search asymmetries. *Psychological Review, 95*, 15–48.

Tulving, E. (1972). Episodic and semantic memory. In E. Tulving & W. Donaldson (Eds.), *Organization of memory* (pp. 382–403). New York: Academic Press.

Tulving, E. (1983). *Elements of episodic memory*. Oxford: Clarendon Press.

Tulving, E. (1984). Relations among components and processes of memory. *Behavioral and Brain Sciences, 7*, 257–268.

Tulving, E. (1985). Memory and consciousness. *Canadian Psychology, 26*, 1–12.

Tulving, E. (1986). What kind of a hypothesis is the distinction between episodic and semantic memory? *Journal of Experimental Psychology: Learning, Memory, and Cognition, 12*, 307–311.

Tulving, E. (2000). Concepts of memory. In E. Tulving & F.I.M. Craik (Eds.), *The Oxford handbook of memory* (pp. 33–43). New York: Oxford University Press.

Tulving, E. (2001a). The origin of autonoesis in episodic memory. In H.L. Roediger, J.S. Nairne, I. Neath, & A.I. Surprénant (Eds.), *The nature of remembering* (pp. 17–34). Washington: American Psychological Association.

Tulving, E. (2001b). Episodic memory and common sense: How far apart? *Philosophical Transactions of the Royal Society (Series B), 356*, 1505–1515.

Tulving, E. (2002a). Episodic memory: From mind to brain. *Annual Review of Psychology, 53*, 1–25.

Tulving, E. (2002b). Chronesthesia: Conscious awareness of subjective time. In D.T. Stuss and R.T. Knight (Eds.), *Principles of frontal lobe function* (pp. 311–325). New York: Oxford University Press.

Tulving, E., & Donaldson, W. (Eds.). (1972). *Organization of memory*. New York: Academic Press.

Tulving, E., & Schacter, D. (1990). Priming and human memory systems. *Science, 247*, 301–306.

Tulving, E., & Thomson, D.M. (1973). Encoding specificity and retrieval processes in episodic memory. *Psychological Review, 80*, 352–373.

Tulving, E., & Wiseman, S. (1975). Relation between recognition and recognition failure of recallable words. *Bulletin of the Psychonomic Society, 6*, 79–82.

Tunney, R.J., & Shanks, D.R. (2003). Subjective measures of awareness and implicit cognition. *Memory & Cognition, 31*, 1060–1071.

Tuohy, A.P. (1987). Affective asymmetry in social perception. *British Journal of Psychology, 78*, 41–51.

Tuohy, A.P., & Stradling, S.G. (1987). Maximum salience vs golden section proportions in judgemental asymmetry. *British Journal of Psychology, 78*, 457–464.

Tuohy, A.P., & Stradling, S.G. (1992). Positive-negative asymmetry in normative data. *European Journal of Social Psychology, 22*, 483–496.

Turing, A. (1950). Computing machinery and intelligence. *Mind, 59*, 433–450.

Tversky, A., & Kahneman, D. (1971). Belief in the law of small numbers. *Psychological Bulletin, 76*, 105–110.

Tversky, A., & Kahneman, D. (1973a). Availability: A heuristic for judging frequency and probability. *Cognitive Psychology, 5*, 207–232.

Tversky, A., & Kahneman, D. (1973b). On the psychology of prediction. *Psychological Review, 80*, 237–251.

Tversky, A., & Kahneman, D. (1974). Judgement under uncertainty: Heuristics and biases. *Science, 185*, 1124–1131.

Tversky, A., & Kahneman, D. (1983). Extensional versus intuitive reasoning: The conjunctive fallacy in probability judgement. *Psychological Review, 90*, 293–314.

Tversky, A., & Kahneman, D. (2000). Rational choice and the framing of decisions. In D. Kahneman & A. Tversky (Eds.), *Choices, values, and frames* (pp. 209–223). Cambridge: Cambridge University Press.

Tversky, B. (2003). Structures of mental spaces: How people think about space. *Environment and Behavior, 35*, 66–80.

Tweney, R.D. (1991). Faraday's notebooks: The active organization of creative science. *Physics Education, 26*, 301–306.

Tweney, R.D. (1999). Toward a cognitive psychology of science: Recent research and its implications. *Current Directions in Psychological Science, 7*, 150–154.

Uhr, L. (1966). Pattern recognition. In L. Uhr (Ed.), *Pattern recognition* (pp. 365–381). New York: Wiley.

Ullmann, S. (1957). *The principles of semantics: A linguistic approach to meaning* (2nd ed.). Cambridge, Mass.: MIT Press.

Uriagereka, J. (1998). *Rhyme and reason: An introduction to minimalist syntax*. Cambridge, Mass.: MIT Press.

Usher, J.A., & Neisser, U. (1993). Childhood amnesia and the beginnings of memory for four early life events. *Journal of Experimental Psychology: General, 122*, 155–165.

Uttal, W.R. (2001). *The new phrenology: The limits of localizing cognitive processes in the brain*. Cambridge, Mass.: MIT Press.

Van der Henst, J.B., Carles, L., & Sperber, D. (2002). Truthfulness and relevance in telling the time. *Mind and Language, 17*, 457–466.

Vartanian, O., Martindale, C., & Kwiatkowski, J. (2003). Creativity and inductive reasoning: The relationship between divergent thinking and performance on Wason's 2–4–6 task. *Quarterly Journal of Experimental Psychology, 56*, 1–15.

Vendler, Z. (1972). *Res cogitans: An essay in rational psychology*. Ithaca, NY: Cornell University Press.

Vicente, K.J., & Brewer, W.F. (1993). Reconstructive remembering of the scientific literature. *Cognition, 46,* 101–128.

Vinacke, W.E. (1974). *The psychology of thinking.* New York: McGraw-Hill.

von Restorff, H. (1933). Über die Wirkung von Bereichsbildungen im Spurenfeld. *Psychologische Forschung, 18,* 299–342.

Vos Savant, M. (1990a, September 9). Ask Marilyn. *Parade Magazine,* p. 15.

Vos Savant, M. (1990b, December 2). Ask Marilyn. *Parade Magazine,* p. 25.

Vos Savant, M. (1991, February 17). Ask Marilyn. *Parade Magazine,* p. 12.

Vygotsky, L.S. (1986). *Thought and language* (A. Kozulin, Trans.). Cambridge, Mass.: MIT Press. (Original work published 1934).

Vygotsky, L.S. (1978). *Mind in society.* Cambridge, Mass.: Harvard University Press. (Original work published 1935).

Wagenaar, W.A., Hudson, P.T.W., & Reason, J.T. (1990). Cognitive failures and accidents. *Applied Cognitive Psychology, 4,* 273–294.

Wagner, U., Gais, S., Haider, H., Verleger, R., & Born, J. (2004). Sleep inspires insight. *Nature, 427,* 352–355.

Wainer, H., & Velleman, P.F. (2001). Statistical graphics: Mapping the pathways of science. *Annual Review of Psychology, 52,* 305–335.

Walker, H.M. (1943). *Elementary statistical methods.* New York: Holt.

Wallas, G. (1926). *The art of thought.* London: Cape.

Walters, J.M., & Gardner, H. (1986). The theory of multiple intelligences: Some issues and answers. In R.J. Sternberg (Ed.), *Practical intelligence* (pp. 163–182). New York: Cambridge University Press.

Wang, R.F., & Spelke, E.S. (2000). Updating egocentric representations in human navigation. *Cognition, 77,* 215–250.

Wang, R.F., & Spelke, E.S. (2002). Human spatial representation: Insights from animals. *Trends in Cognitive Sciences, 6,* 375–382.

Ward, J., & Simner, J. (2003). Lexical gustatory synaesthesia: Linguistic and conceptual factors. *Cognition, 89,* 237–261.

Warrington, E., & Weiskrantz, L. (1982). Amnesia: A disconnection syndrome? *Neuropsychologia, 20,* 233–248.

Warrington, E.K., & Shallice, T. (1984). Category specific semantic impairments. *Brain, 107,* 829–854.

Wason, P.C. (1960). On the failure to eliminate hypotheses in a conceptual task. *Quarterly Journal of Experimental Psychology, 12,* 129–140.

Wason, P.C. (1966). Reasoning. In B.M. Foss (Ed.), *New horizons in psychology* (pp. 135–151). Harmondsworth, UK: Penguin.

Wason, P.C. (1977a). 'On the failure to eliminate hypotheses . . .': A second look. In P.N. Johnson-Laird & P.C. Wason (Eds.), *Thinking: Readings in cognitive science* (pp. 307–314). Cambridge: Cambridge University Press.

Wason, P.C. (1977b). Self-contradictions. In P.N. Johnson-Laird & P.C. Wason (Eds.), *Thinking: Readings in cognitive science* (pp. 114–128). Cambridge: Cambridge University Press.

Wason, P.C. (1978). Hypothesis testing and reasoning. In *Cognitive Psychology* (Block 4, Unit 25, pp. 17–56). Milton Keynes, UK: Open University Press.

Wason, P.C., & Brooks, P.G. (1979). THOG: The anatomy of a problem. *Psychological Research, 41,* 79–90.

Wason, P.C., & Evans, J. St B.T. (1975). Dual processes in reasoning? *Cognition, 3/2,* 141–154.

Wason, P.C., & Johnson-Laird, P.N. (1972). *Psychology of reasoning: Structure and content.* London: Batsford.

Wason, P.C., & Shapiro, D. (1971). Natural and contrived experience in a reasoning problem. *Quarterly Journal of Experimental Psychology, 23,* 63–71.

Waugh, N.C., & Norman, D.A. (1965). Primary memory. *Psychological Review, 72,* 89–104.

Weaver, C.A. III. (1993). Do you need a flash to form a flashbulb memory? *Journal of Experimental Psychology: General, 122,* 39–46.

Wegner, D.M. (2003). The mind's best trick: How we experience conscious will. *Trends in Cognitive Sciences, 7,* 65–69.

Weidman, N. (1994). Mental testing and

machine intelligence: The Lashley-Hull debate. *Journal of the History of the Behavioral Sciences, 30*, 162–180.

Weisberg, R.W. (1986). *Genius, creativity and other myths*. New York: Freeman.

Weisberg, R.W. (1994). Genius and madness? A quasi-experimental test of the hypothesis that manic-depression increases creativity. *Psychological Science, 5*, 361–367.

Weisberg, R.W. (1995). Prolegomena to theories of insight in problem-solving: A taxonomy of problems. In R.J. Sternberg & J. Davidson (Eds.) *The nature of insight*. Cambridge, Mass.: MIT Press.

Weisberg, R.W., & Alba, J.W. (1981). An examination of the role of fixation in the solution of several insight problems. *Journal of Experimental Psychology: General, 110*, 169–192.

Weiskrantz, L. (2000). Epilogue: The story of memory and the memory of a story. In E. Tulving & F.I.M. Craik (Eds.), *The Oxford handbook of memory* (pp. 645–648). New York: Oxford University Press.

Weitzenhooffer, A.M., & Hilgard, E.R. (1962). *Stanford Hypnotizability Scale Form C.* (Revised by J. Kihlstrom). Retrieved October 5, 2004, from http://ist-socrates.berkeley.edu/~kihlstrm/PDFfiles/Hypnotizability/SHSSC%20Script.pdf.

Werner, H. (1961). *Comparative psychology of mental development*. New York: Science editions. (Original work published 1948).

Werner, H., & Kaplan, B. (1963). *Symbol formation*. New York: Wiley.

Wertheimer, M. (1959). *Productive thinking*. New York: Harper.

Wertheimer, M. (1967a). Laws of organization in perceptual forms. In W.D. Ellis (Ed.), *A source book of Gestalt psychology* (pp. 71–88). New York: Humanities Press. (Original work published 1923).

Wertheimer, M. (1967b). The syllogism and productive thinking. In W.D. Ellis (Ed.), *A source book of Gestalt psychology* (pp. 274–282). New York: Humanities. (Original work published 1925).

Wertheimer, Michael (1985). A Gestalt perspective on computer simulations of cognitive processes. *Computers in Human Behaviour, 1*, 19–33.

Wertsch, J.V. (Ed.). (1985). *Vygotsky and the social function of mind*. Cambridge, Mass.: Harvard University Press.

Wertsch, J.V., & Stone, C. (1985). The concept of internalization in Vygotsky's account of the genesis of higher mental functions. In J.V. Wertsch (Ed.), *Culture, communication and cognition* (pp. 162–179). Cambridge: Cambridge University Press.

Wetzler, S.E., & Sweeney, J.A. (1986). Childhood amnesia: An empirical demonstration. In D.C. Rubin (Ed.), *Autobiographical memory* (pp. 191–201). Cambridge: Cambridge University Press.

Wheeler. M.A. (2000). Episodic memory and autonoetic awareness. In E. Tulving & F.I.M. Craik (Eds.), *The Oxford handbook of memory* (pp. 597–608). New York: Oxford University Press.

Wheeler, M.A., Stuss, D.T., & Tulving, E. (1997). Toward a theory of episodic memory: The frontal lobes and autonoetic consciousness. *Psychological Bulletin, 121*, 331–354.

Whitehead, D. (2003). Review of Sadoski & Paivio, 'Imagery and text: A dual coding theory of reading and writing'. *Reading and Writing: An Interdisciplinary Journal, 16*, 159–262.

Whorf, B.L. (1956). *Language, thought and reality*. Cambridge, Mass.: MIT Press.

Wickelgren, W.A. (1979). *Cognitive psychology*. Englewood Cliffs, NJ: Prentice-Hall.

Wickens, C.D. (1984). Processing resources in attention. In R. Parasuraman & D.R. Davies (Eds.), *Varieties of attention* (pp. 63–102). Orlando, Fla: Academic Press.

Wickens, D.D. (1970). Encoding categories of words: An empirical approach to meaning. *Psychological Review, 77*, 1–15.

Williams, L.P. (1991). Michael Faraday's chemical notebook: Portrait of the scientist as a young man. *Physics Education, 26*, 278–283.

Williams, R. (1976). *Keywords: A vocabulary of culture and society*. New York: Oxford University Press.

Williams, W.M. (1998). Are we raising smarter children today? School and home-related influences on IQ. In U. Neisser (Ed.), *The rising curve* (pp. 125–154). Washington: American Psychological Association.

Wilson, B.A. (2002). Management of remediation of memory problems in brain-injured adults. In A.D. Baddeley, M.D. Kopelman, & B.A. Wilson (Eds.), *The handbook of memory disorders* (pp. 655–682). New York: Wiley.

Wilson, B.A., & Moffat, N. (1984). *Clinical management of memory problems*. Rockville, Md: Aspen Publications.

Wilson, B.A., & Patterson, K. (1990). Rehabilitation for cognitive impairment: Does cognitive psychology apply? *Applied Cognitive Psychology, 4*, 247–260.

Wilson, M. (2002). Six views of embodied cognition. *Psychonomic Bulletin & Review, 9*, 625–636.

Winner, E. (1982). *Invented worlds*. Cambridge, Mass.: Harvard University Press.

Winner, E. (2000). The origins and ends of giftedness. *American Psychologist, 55*, 159–169.

Winograd, E., & Soloway, R. (1986). On forgetting the locations of things stored in special places. *Journal of Experimental Psychology: General, 115*, 366–372.

Winograd, T., & Flores, F. (1986). *Understanding computers and cognition: A new foundation for design*. Norwood, NJ: Ablex.

Witkowski, S.R., & Brown, C.H. (1983). Marking reversals and cultural importance. *Language, 59*, 569–582.

Wittgenstein, L. (1953). *Philosophical investigations*. Oxford: Blackwell.

Wittgenstein, L. (1974). *Tractatus logico-philosophicus*. London: Routledge & Kegan Paul. (Original work published 1921).

Wixted, J.T. (2004a). The psychology and neuroscience of forgetting. *Annual Review of Psychology, 55*, 235–269.

Wixted, J.T. (2004b). On common ground: Jost's (1897) law of forgetting and Ribot's (1881) law of retrograde amnesia. *Psychological Review, 111*, 864–879.

Wolfe, J.M. (2003). Moving towards solution to some enduring controversies in visual search. *Trends in Cognitive Sciences, 7*, 70–76.

Wolff, P., Medin, D.L., & Pankratz, C. (1999). Evolution and devolution of folk biological knowledge. *Cognition, 73*, 177–204.

Woltz, D.J., Gardner, M.K., & Bell, B.G. (2000). Negative transfer errors in sequential cognitive skills: Strong-but-wrong sequence application. *Journal of Experimental Psychology: Learning, Memory, and Cognition, 26*, 601–625.

Wood, N., & Cowan, N. (1995). The cocktail party phenomenon revisited: Attention and memory in the classic selective listening procedure of Cherry (1953). *Journal of Experimental Psychology: General, 124*, 243–262.

Woodworth, R.S. (1940). *Psychology* (4th ed.). New York: Holt.

Wright, E. (1992). Gestalt switching: Hanson, Aronson, and Harre. *Philosophy of Science, 59*, 480–486.

Wundt, W. (1970). The psychology of the sentence. In A.L. Blumenthal (Ed.), *Language and psychology* (pp. 9–33). New York: Wiley. (Original work published 1890).

Yaden, D.B., & Templeton, S. (Eds.). (1986). *Metalinguistic awareness and beginning literacy: Conceptualizing what it means to read and write*. Portsmouth, NH: Heinemann.

Yang, C.D. (2004). Universal grammar, statistics or both? *Trends in Cognitive Sciences, 8*, 451–456.

Yates, F.A. (1966). *The art of memory*. Chicago: University of Chicago Press.

Yeung, N., & Monsell, S. (2003). The effects of recent practice on task switching. *Journal of Experimental Psychology: Human Perception and Performance, 29*, 919–936.

Yoshida, H., & Smith, L.B. (2005). Linguistic cues enhance the learning of perceptual cues. *Psychological Science, 16*, 90–95.

Yovel, G., & Paller, K.A. (2004). The neural basis of the butcher-on-the-bus phenomenon: When a face seems familiar but is not remembered. *NeuroImage, 21*, 789–800.

Yuille, J. (1968). Concreteness without imagery in PA learning. *Psychonomic Science, 11*, 55–56.

Zacks, J.M., Mires, J., Tversky, B., & Hazeltine,

E. (2000). Mental spatial transformations of objects and perspective. *Spatial Cognition and Computation, 2*, 315–332.

Zajonc, R.B. (1968). Attitudinal effects of mere exposure. *Journal of Personality and Social Psychology Monograph, 9* (2, Pt. 2), 1–28.

Zajonc, R.B. (1980). Feeling and thinking: Preferences need no inferences. *American Psychologist, 35*, 151–175.

Zajonc, R.B. (1984). On the primacy of affect. *American Psychologist, 39*, 117–123.

Zajonc, R.B. (2001). Mere exposure: A gateway to the subliminal. *Current Directions in Psychological Science, 10*, 224–228.

Zangwill, O.L. (1972). Remembering revisited. *Quarterly Journal of Experimental Psychology, 24*, 123–138.

Zeigarnik, B. (1967). On finished and unfinished tasks. In W.D. Ellis (Ed.), *A source book of Gestalt psychology* (pp. 300–315). New York: Humanities Press. (Original work published 1927).

Zhai, S., Kristensson, P.O., & Smith, B.A. (2005). In search of effective text input interfaces for off the desktop computing. *Interacting with Computers, 17*, 229–250.

Zimler, J., & Keenan, J. (1983). Imagery in the congenitally blind: How visual are visual images? *Journal of Experimental Psychology: Learning, Memory, and Cognition, 9*, 269–282.

Zizak, D.M., & Reber, A.S. (2004). Implicit preferences: The role(s) of familiarity in the structural mere exposure effect. *Consciousness and Cognition, 13*, 336–362.

Index